The Formula: Simplifying your path to Success | Nir Kunik

D0839788

Producer & International Distributor
eBookPro Publishing
www.ebook-pro.com

The Formula: Simplifying your path to Success
Nir Kunik
Copyright © 2022 Nir Kunik

Contact: nir.kunik@myformulabook.com

ISBN 9798361253739

There are only two days in the year that nothing can be done. One is called Yesterday, and the other is called Tomorrow. Today is the right day to love, believe, do, and mostly live.

– Dalai Lama XIV

Contents

I. KEEPING IT SIMPLE

Simplicity is the ultimate sophistication
– Leonardo Da Vinci

Life is simple. We complicate it.

Everything in life can be simplified, even the most complicated tasks and problems. Einstein inspired the most sophisticated weapon on earth by simplifying the complexity of the universe into a short formula: $E=MC^2$. Sending a spaceship to the moon is a complicated task. But, in essence, it is achieved by the combination of a million simple things.

If I accomplish my mission, "The Formula" will improve the quality of your life – not by making it more complicated, but by showing you how to simplify it.

By simplifying the apparent complexities of life, it will equip you with the tools you need to improve your physical and mental health, gain financial freedom, build better relationships, become a happier person, and bring about the ultimate success you wish for.

> **Breaking down complex issues into smaller, simpler chunks, will enable you to gain control over the steering wheel of your life.**

The universe operates according to clear, simple, and defined laws. By studying these laws, observing nature, and following my intuition, I have had enormous success in all areas of my life. While these laws apply equally, without discrimination, to us all, they can work for, or against, us. From our beating hearts and breath to the financial markets, the universe is in constant motion, expanding and shrinking. Nothing goes up without coming down and then going up again. Everything is in a spiral movement, either in growth or contraction. Nothing stays in the same place.

> **Change is an integral necessity of reality.**

We're all in one big funnel, drawn in by the forces of creation. Any deviation from the course causes resistance in an attempt to force us to get back "on track." Like swimming against the tide, opposition to the natural laws is a waste of energy that causes discomfort and suffering. We all have, within us, the ability to connect to the forces of creation. Like nature, our potential is infinite. As children, we are connected, and we know how to exploit this potential. We make progress at a dizzying pace, learning to walk, talk, read and become our best selves. And, at the same time, we are also learning to be jealous, angry, and insulted. Our souls are "soft," and we are easily offended. We begin to shut down and disconnect. We mature, with our infinite potential untapped, the shining diamond that is our essence becomes covered by the layers of life's dust and grime.

The day I recognized my infinite potential was the day I decided to shake off the dust and uncover the diamond. It took work and discipline; layer by layer, the diamond began to reveal itself. The toughest layer, the one that I had built over many years, was my ego – the imaginary "I" in the real world. It had protected me when

I was small and vulnerable; it had also helped me on my climb to the top, while trampling on others to get there.

I arrived at the summit burnt out and injured, lonely and detached. The air there is thin, and breathing is difficult. After years of climbing and racing, I stopped to rest for a while. Out of the deafening silence, I heard voices coming from within; they were soft and pleasant. I heard a child laugh; it was the child I used to be many years ago. The child was loving, curious, innocent, happy, effortless, natural, free of barriers and defenses. The child who was connected to his soul. I began a journey to dis-cover my soul and set the child free.

***

Although each of us is a unique individual with a unique fingerprint, we have many things in common. We all have dreams and hopes and a need for connection, certainty, variety, significance, growth, and contribution. As unique as you are, the challenges and the difficulties you face, are not. "The Formula" addresses the common challenges we all face. It has worked for me, making me successful and satisfied beyond anything I could have imagined. Today, I understand that life offers us infinite possibilities. Similarly, our mind and spirit, when engaged, offer us unlimited resources. Life is not a zero-sum game; if I can enjoy the wealth of a successful life, so can others. We can all be happy, healthy, and wealthy, simultaneously. Nothing has to come at the expense of others.

I am passionate about helping others to find what I have found, to become happier, better people, and to have more love and compassion for others.

> **My dream is that, by using the tools in this book, at least one parent, exhausted from a long day at work, will come home and, rather than seeing the mess, they will see their children's souls, and rather than raising their voice, they will open their hearts and give them a hug.**

Big changes start with the little things. Love at home will translate into love and respect for others and expand into the universe in which we live. When that happens, "reality" will change and create a world that is worth bequeathing to future generations.

It is in this spirit that I share "The Formula" with you.

There is a catch, however. The book will only assist you if you are ready and willing to assist yourself. Again, it is a very simple concept. You need to say, "I'm ready."

If you are ready, let's begin.

II. NO ONE WILL KILL MY DREAMS

The only source of knowledge is experience.
– Albert Einstein

Both of my parents were born to Holocaust survivors who had horrific first-hand experiences of the Nazis during World War II. All four of my grandparents witnessed thousands of people being murdered in the gas chambers, and others being abused and humiliated under conditions that no human soul should have to bear.

When World War II started, my maternal grandmother, Mira Baum, was 19 years old. She was imprisoned, by the Nazis, with her family, in the Warsaw ghetto, in 1940. In 1942, she was forcefully separated from them and transported, in a freight train, to the Majdanek concentration camp, before being transferred to Auschwitz. At the gates of Auschwitz, in a process known as "selection," SS officers decided, at a glance, who would be taken to work, and who would be doomed to die. My grandmother was chosen to work in a "warehouse" in which the prisoners' belongings were stored, just before they were forced to walk consciously, into the gas chambers, to their deaths.

She risked her life every day by hiding gold and diamonds that she found inside the pockets of the clothes and in the soles of the dead people's shoes. She then found creative ways to exchange these valuables with the Nazis, for a piece of bread or potato peels, to ensure her survival for another day.

During the war, for a period of six years, my grandparents, starving, freezing, and ill, swung between life and death. They were among the few who survived. In 1946, at the end of the war, they immigrated to Israel to start a new life, after the Nazis had wiped out their respective families. But the scars remained on their souls, and the mental illness, trauma, and fears were passed down to my parents and influenced my childhood in innumerable ways.

I was born in 1972 to an average Israeli family, with an average income, and average dreams. I, on the other hand, could best be described as below average. I hated studying, never did my homework, and my results reflected this. "If you can become ten percent of what your Uncle Joseph is, I will be so happy." These words uttered by my mother, throughout my childhood, about my uncle who worked as a doctor of aeronautics at NASA, have continued to echo through my life. My frustrated mom implored me, "Read books, read the Yellow Pages, just read something... If you don't start learning, you will become a garbage truck driver."

The odds were stacked against me from the start. I was born with a black birthmark, the size of a ping pong ball, on my left cheek. My older sister would walk around the school with me, hiding the birthmark with her hand, to protect her little brother from being humiliated and getting hurt. I was not a "popular" kid and always felt weird and different. To make matters worse, when I was ten, I was diagnosed with scoliosis and kyphosis, which are spinal curvature disorders. I was locked in a brace, which covered my back and neck, for three years. I looked like a character from a sci-fi movie. In summer, my entire torso would sweat and itch, giving the kids even more ammunition to make fun of me. It was a physically and mentally painful, nightmarish experience.

***

My father was a bus driver. He worked day and night to support his family. To supplement his income, my father sold paintings, meat, and other goods, door to door. He had natural sales skills that, as we will see later, were passed down to me.

My mother worked as a medical secretary for 40 years. She has always been very smart and intelligent, displaying a natural curiosity that has made her a lifelong learner. Her potential to succeed was enormous but her fears and doubts held her back. Her parents' attitudes, which kept them alive during the war, became her attitude. "Never give up, there is always a way," were words I heard throughout my childhood. Everything relating to her children was treated that way.

> **My mother planted in me the knowledge that anything was possible for me.**

By observing her life experiences, I realized that the only limitations she had were the boundaries she set for herself.

Despite my mother's can-do attitude when it came to her children, both my parents were deeply affected by the suffering, fear, and scarcity beliefs of their parents. No matter how hard they worked, my parents regularly started the month with an overdraft and continuously struggled to get ahead.

My father had great ideas and always wanted to run his own business. But, leaving the safety of a regular and guaranteed paycheck, at the bus company, simply felt too risky for both parents. During my childhood, my father considered investing in land and property, but again, fear held him back from taking action. He would consult with my mom, but she merely instilled more fear and doubt in him, often before even seriously considering the opportunity. The result was one rejected opportunity after another. Every missed opportunity could have changed their economic situation and brought them financial independence. But they chose security and scarcity over risk and reward.

Every time I left my room, I remember my father shouting, "Switch off the light. I don't work for the electric company!" Their financial situation caused a lot of strain and was the source of many fights between my parents. This saddened me, even as a child. I wanted to see my parents acting and taking risks. They just talked (or fought) about it, but never really acted. Nothing changed and my father's hands always seemed tied.

In a strange, almost counterintuitive way, the feeling of scarcity I had at home, and my parents' fears of taking risks, paved my way to success. My instincts told me what to adopt and what to ignore. I knew from an early age that I had to seek a different route for my life.

> **I wanted a life of infinite abundance, and I was willing to dare!**

As a child, when all my friends went to play soccer, I spent my time building model airplanes and playing the trumpet. I never voluntarily participated in sports activities. At school, during gym classes, I did the minimum required, if I even bothered to show up at all. My friends would invite me to play soccer with them, but I was a lousy player. I figured out that the safest position would be goalkeeper. Once, after a few easily blocked goals, I had to jump high to catch the ball with my hand. Not only did I not save the goal, but I also broke my hand!

* * *

Luckily, I seemed to have been born a hopeless optimist. I grew and developed out of my difficulties both at home and at school.

I never pitied myself, always listened to my intuition, and took myself in directions that suited me, no matter what others around me said or felt.

My childhood ignited in me the desire to do things differently. I was determined to be the master of my future.

> **One thought became engraved in my head: No one will kill my dreams!**

I was a passionate entrepreneur long before I even knew the word. When I was seven years old, during the summer vacation, I opened my first sandwich business. I woke up every morning at 5 am to buy fresh rolls and chocolate milk. I made the sandwiches and went out to the nearby main street. I passed shop after shop, proudly displaying my wares. People loved to buy from the cute kid with his lovely smile. I always found ways to convince them to buy. If they had just eaten, I would sell them my drinks. Each "deal" brought me great joy. Don't get me wrong, it was neither smooth nor easy. One day I was robbed by a group of delinquent children who took all the money I had earned that day. I got hundreds of rejections, and some days I would walk for miles with my sandwiches in a huge bag that weighed more than me! But I never returned home before had I sold all my merchandise. I would come home with great pride, and one candy bar, as a reward. I saved the rest of my money for the next day and my next business. Sales, cash, and a sense of independence made me feel so wonderful. When I was ten years old, I imported shirts from China and sold them shop by shop. At age fifteen, I sold flowerpots door to door, while, at age seventeen, I ran model airplane workshops for the children of hotel guests.

Being entrepreneurial gave me unlimited possibilities to express myself, as well as the freedom that I desired.

Selling is truly my God-given gift. I developed skills and spent the proverbial 10,000 hours as a child without even knowing that I was doing it.

> **With less fear, I dared to take risks. Each failure taught me and changed me. With each success, my faith became stronger.**

I learned that my potential is unlimited. There is always someone more resourceful and successful, faster, stronger, happier, wealthier, you name it. So, if my potential is unlimited, the only thing holding me back is my faith. I learned to expand my faith and to dream bigger. I dared to make bigger plans for my life.

***

My other passion is technology and innovation. In 1982, when I was ten years old, my parents finally managed to leave Israel for the first time and flew to the big world of Europe. It had taken them more than twenty years of saving, but finally, they made it. Even though I did not go, their vacation would change my life forever.

Upon their return, my parents brought me an expensive gift, one of the first personal computers available for home use, the Sinclair Spectrum. It ran on 16KB RAM; not even enough to store a single picture today! The only way to do something with it was to learn a programming language called BASIC (which people, of a certain age, will remember). Once I switched the computer on, I couldn't turn it off. It looked like a magic box to me, and I felt addicted, entering a zone I couldn't leave for months. I ran my first programs, calculated numbers, played with different colors on the screen (colored TV had just been launched in Israel), and created music out of different frequencies.

I was fascinated by the endless possibilities the "magic box" offered. Programming allowed me to express my creativity and desire for innovation. The gift, which marked the beginning of my love affair with technology, sparked a passion that has never left me. As a child, I spent my days and nights programming, building electric circuits and model airplanes, and creating innovative robots to entertain myself. My mother's original family name was Baum which means "tree" in German. My grandfather was a carpenter, and I am descended from a long line of carpenters. Perhaps my creativity and love for innovation are rooted in my genes.

My passion for technology led me to study electronics in high school. At age 18, I joined the Israeli Air Force in one of the technology units. I did not like the military structure. During my military service, I realized that I wanted to be the one who decides what to do, how to do it, and when. I disliked the routines and repetitive jobs and hated taking orders from my commanders. I found myself ducking out at every opportunity to the nearest bank to buy and sell stocks and bonds (in the days when mobile trading was only a dream). I was confined to base myriad times, as punishment for this, during my three years of service. Military discipline simply did not suit my character. I had a desire for freedom and creativity; I wanted to be the master of my future. I counted down the hours and days to freedom and the start of my career.

Right after the army, I met Talia, who had just finished high school. She was gorgeous, sweet, smart, and funny, and we fell in love. We got married six years later when I was 28 and she was 24, but that was still a way off. At age 22, with my military service behind me, and a girl by my side, all I knew is that I wanted a job that would somehow allow me to combine my love for sales and technology.

I applied for many jobs, had many interviews, and just as many rejections. Unfortunately, I was stuck in the classic first-time job seeker's dilemma: tons of enthusiasm, very little experience. And then I spotted an advert in a newspaper that seemed perfect for me – a sales job at Motorola. The job required a minimum of five years' experience in high-tech sales, a degree in electronic engineering, and a track record in networking and communication. I met none of the requirements.

My mom's question which, unfortunately, she has been unable to apply to her own life, prompted me to submit my CV: "Is there anything to lose by trying?" A VP at Motorola, Mr. Kobi Paz, saw my CV and decided that he had to meet this 22-year-old guy who had the guts to apply for this role.

Fortunately, talented people have a natural curiosity, which, in Kobi's case, worked in my favor. I was invited to an interview, which Kobi began by asking about my sales experience. Without hesitation, I told him about selling sandwiches, T-shirts from China, and the countless other things I had peddled in my youth, proudly boasting that I was "the best in my field." I had no idea if Kobi thought that this experience applied to selling for Motorola. But he did ask me why I thought I was such a good salesperson. Again, I didn't hesitate. "My way of selling is authentic; people like me, and they feel good buying from me. The value I give them is my cheerful attitude, positive outlook, and my smile."

"What about an engineering diploma?" he asked. "I know how to program," I replied, "And I am a very fast learner. But, most importantly, I am passionate about technology."

Against all odds, I got the job. I was fully aware that the chances were slim, but I decided to dare, and it had paid off! This was a defining moment for me. My self–confidence soared, my faith grew stronger, and I was determined to accomplish every task that would be presented to me.

Many years later, I asked Kobi why he hired a kid with no experience. He told me, "You didn't meet any criteria, but your belief, courage, and enthusiasm got you the job. When you choose people, use your brain to evaluate them professionally, but, more importantly, use your intuition to make the right decision."[1] It is a lesson that has served me well throughout my life, in general, and, specifically, when hiring new staff.

And so, my rock star career began. 1995 was a wonderful time to be selling technology. Cisco had just started, and Nortel Networks were pioneering some of the most innovative technologies. Communication and networking were booming, and Motorola was in the middle of it all. All my colleagues were relatively older than me; they used to call me "the kid." I looked up to them, all of whom had made a lot of money in their high-tech careers and were planning, or already constructing, their dream homes.

Observing them, I realized that I was merely in my takeoff stage. I sold. I learned. I succeeded. I felt deep inside that I could do so much more.

After three years at Motorola, I decided to enroll for an electronic engineering degree. I found a program at Tel Aviv University that would allow me to work and study. I asked Motorola management to grant me two days off a week to study. They declined. I kept pushing though, asking what I needed to do to get a positive answer. After two weeks, they came back to me with an offer: Work on commission only. Translation: Give up your company car, your base salary (that was very high for those days), your pension, and

---

1 Kobi died of cancer in 2020, at age 57. He was undoubtedly the smartest person I have ever met.

all other benefits. They were sure that, with these terms, I would give up my plan.

I didn't hesitate. I immediately accepted their offer.

Many people thought I was insane. I, however, did not see the offer as a setback. For me, it was a challenge – albeit not a blind one. I knew how to do my job. I was confident that I would be able to earn both my degree and my salary if I focused five working days into three. That was the challenge I set myself, and that is what I did.

For three focused working days each week, I sold like crazy. But now I was working on commission only, so I earned more per sale than if I had remained on salary. I did so well that, after two years, management realized that my take-home salary had more than tripled. They tried to convince me to go back to base salary, to my convenient company car, and all the other "perks." Of course, I said no. I had fallen in love with the concept of "what I sow is what I reap." My earnings were in direct correlation to my performance. This was the true beginning for me, a good lesson, and the springboard on the way to my "freedom." The seeds of running my own business, and becoming an entrepreneur, were being sowed.

***

In 2001, I was offered a position at a new company called "NetApp." The salary was higher but, more importantly to me, the product was innovative. The new field of network storage had just launched, and it excited me. Of course, my parents and friends advised me to stay – "Who leaves a company like Motorola?"

I took the offer.

After the first year, the company gave me new territories – Turkey, Greece, and Cyprus. I improved my English, which was very poor at the time. I became the top performer – a feat I managed to achieve for five years in a row.

I did a good job developing the new territories, and, in 2002, I was asked to develop the African continent. At the time, "Africa" to me, was jungles, civil wars, and disease. The offer frightened me.

The company did not have business in Africa at that time, and no one wanted to go there. The number of vaccinations I had to receive before leaving wasn't a great pleasure either. Getting visas for African countries was a nightmare and leaving home, for months at a time, was tough for me and my wife. There were a million reasons to reject the offer. Obviously, I asked Talia for her opinion. Her response was immediate: "You always do the right thing; I fully trust whatever decision you make." I felt a great sense of achievement; Talia was exactly the supportive and enabling partner I wanted beside me. I accepted the challenge. I decided to dare.

And what a challenge it proved to be! The welcome I received, in Nigeria, gave me a hint about the place. I was held in a small room for four hours before being cleared to leave the airport. The traffic to the Lagos city center was unlike anything I had ever experienced. It took six hours to travel 20 km (about 13 miles), and I had a lot of time to stare out the window of the taxi.

When we hit the road, it was still daylight, but gradually, the night began to take over the entire place. The drive to the city was scary – and fascinating. Millions of cars were stuck in one big traffic jam, hooting with all their might, trying to squeeze into through traffic that was moving to nowhere. The noise was deafening. Thousands of people appeared to be fighting, shouting, and arguing with each other. Motorcycles, which I learned later were called Okada and served as the local taxis, carried entire families – a mom, dad, and six children on a tiny seat! It was unlike anything I had seen before. Broken trucks, moving on three wheels, emitted thick black smoke everywhere. And then there were the very old oil trucks with holes in their tank from which the oil flowed like water from a tap. I was sure that the whole place would explode before I even got to my hotel! The fact that fires were being lit on the side of the roads, to illuminate the absolute darkness, did not make me feel any better, while children played in sewer ditches, very close to the fires, as if they were municipal swimming pools. Everything was strange. I felt like thousands of eyes were staring at me. A white guy with a suit and tie sitting alone in the back of a taxi. I felt like a man who had accidentally entered a rodeo stadium during a bull riding event.

As we, once again, stood still, for what seemed like a journey to nowhere, I saw piles of burning tires covering something. When I looked closer, my stomach turned.

"Are those bodies?" I asked the taxi driver.

"Those are thieves!" he replied. "They were caught stealing, but they're lucky. They got the easy punishment."

"Easy?" I asked. "What's worse?"

"They deserve the cement."

"The cement?" I replied.

"When the crowd catches someone stealing, there are two ways to deal with them. The easy one is to put tires on their body and burn them alive. The other is to force them to drink cement. This guy on the road is a thief, he deserves the cement! I don't know why the crowd didn't punish him as he deserves," the taxi driver said.

Eventually, I arrived at the ECO hotel, the only suitable "business" hotel in Nigeria at that time. It was a long journey from Tel Aviv, and, when I got into my room, I immediately went to the bathroom. When I flushed, the water got darker. Did I flush? I flushed it again, nothing changed, and the color remained the same. I began to realize the magnitude of what I had gotten myself into.

I wanted a shower. I opened the tap and the same dark brown

water poured out. I waited, assuming that the color would eventually change, and clean water would flow from the tap. It didn't. I ordered six bottles of mineral water and used this to wash. I did this for the entire week that I was there.

The environment was tough; the opportunities were endless.

I fell in love with Africa immediately. The people, the opportunities, the challenges, everything was fascinating. It is the least boring place that exists on earth. I experience Africans as gentle, fair, and kind people. I have made many friends, special people who opened their homes and their hearts to me. I taught them advanced technologies and they taught me simplicity. None of this is said patronizingly. I am fully aware that Africa has many problems. But my experiences in Africa have been positive and Africa has blessed me both financially and spiritually. My connection with the local people has been the key to this success. A friend brought a friend, who brought a friend. Within a few years, we had expanded our activities, recruited local teams, and opened offices in Ghana and Angola. Without noticing, I was building an extensive infrastructure of business partners and clients that would become the next springboard to my future.

My dare paid off. The business boomed as we closed one deal after another. We built a $30 million business, from scratch, in less than four years.

> **During this time, I learned many lessons: always look for the potential, dare to take calculated risks, and never surrender to your internal fears.**

After four years, I was ready for new challenges. I knew that I would be leaving the company just as I was peaking. But I also knew that I was in a comfort zone. The comfort zone made me feel relaxed, satiated, and sleepy. At the same time, I felt less alive and knew that I was stagnating. The comfort zone began to feel uncomfortable. I needed excitement; I was too young not to feel strongly alive.

The fear of getting stuck was greater than the fear of making a change. It was the right time to dare again. As always, everyone around me, especially my parents, tried to convince me to stay. In answer to the refrain, "Who leaves a job like this?" my answer was clear: "Me!"

Ironically, this was where my winning streak ended.

***

In 2006, I joined Storwize, an Israeli start-up, as the worldwide VP of Sales. I started sales operations in California, Houston, New York, Germany, the UK, Japan, and Australia. The concept was great. However, like most start–ups, the product had many bugs when it was launched.

The worst thing, for a salesperson, is to sell a product that does not work properly. I felt terrible. I had customers who trusted me, and who had bought the product based on my recommendation. Now, the bugs were damaging their reputations within their respective companies. I had even persuaded people, who trusted me, to join the company. They were looking to me for solutions and I was lost. I understood that I could not sell this product anymore. I learned my lesson. A start-up is like a newborn baby. There are no mature babies, no matter how smart they are, nor how fast they learn. You can teach a baby to walk and talk, but it will not graduate from university when it is three years old. It is just a baby. It is the same with start-ups. They need time to mature, and the process cannot be hurried or short-circuited.

I realized that I had no control over what was happening. I could not fix the problem and I felt helpless. A sense of disappointment and fear gripped me. But I didn't fall into melancholy. I analyzed the situation rationally and decided to cut my losses and move on. I went back to the drawing board to plan my next steps.

Naturally, I had a lot of people tell me, "We told you so. You always complicate things; you're restless. Why didn't you just stay in your previous job? You were very successful there."

Many voices echoed inside my head. I chose to listen to the voices that lifted me up, and my mom's voice was the strongest: "There is always a way." I knew for sure that I would find it. The only question that occupied my mind was: What next?

I believe that the brain builds new neural pathways and comes up with brilliant ideas when it has no alternatives, and all bridges seem burnt.

> **When it looks like there is no way, a new pathway is found.**

My brain worked non-stop looking for an alternative. It took a while, but when the answer came, it was like the proverbial lightning strike, and it felt so simple: Go back to Africa.

So, I did.

***

My plan was simple: to build a successful business as I did with NetApp. If I could do it for them, I assumed, I could do it again with multiple suppliers. But this time I would be doing it for myself. In my mind, the plan was clear.

I had met Gbade Alabi, in 2002, soon after I arrived in Lagos for the first time.

He was running what was then the largest IT company in Nigeria. He liked the products I was representing, but, more than that, he liked me. And I liked him too, very much. We hit it off immediately and there seemed to be a special chemistry between us. Gbade clearly saw the potential, and our first meeting ended with his saying, "We will do great things together in the future." Gbade would prove to be not only a business partner, but also a friend and, as we shall see later, my spiritual mentor too.

This future had finally arrived.

On the night that I decided to go back to Africa, I called Gbade: "We have to establish a distribution business together. We will be the gateway to Africa for leading technologies from all over the world."

Gbade loved the idea.

At that moment, in July 2007, DatagroupIT was born. We contacted a few suppliers to offer our services. They all liked it. It was a win-win solution for all parties. We had access to the markets, the customers liked the technology, and Gbade and I felt like the conductors in an orchestra. All went well, at first. We focused on Nigeria and Angola and signed exclusive agreements with three suppliers. About 90 percent of the business was being generated from one supplier in one country.

By 2012, the company had generated sales of over $200M. I felt blessed and successful. All I wanted was to put up my legs, relax and enjoy life.

And then the crisis hit. Our primary supplier decided to change direction and leave Africa. I had a company, with over thirty employees, and almost nothing to sell.

Trouble tends to come in big packages. At the same time, the global oil price dropped, and the countries in which we operated fell into recession. Almost all our clients halted their purchases.

It was a tough time and as usual, many people came to console the bereaved. Giving up, however, was not an option. Once again, I replayed my mom's lesson in my mind: "There is always a way." I had to come up with a recovery plan.

The company shifted its focus from IT infrastructure to cybersecurity. We signed ten new suppliers. We brought the world's leading cybersecurity vendors to the continent. We opened branches in countries whose economies did not depend on oil. The recovery was instant. The new countries made up for the decline of business in the oil and gas territories, and the new suppliers covered the revenue we had lost from our previous single supplier. We ended 2013 with a positive bottom line and have had double-digit growth every year since.

***

In building my career, and chasing success, I had felt invincible and paid little attention to my health. Despite my sedentary childhood, my body functioned very well until my mid-thirties. And then I turned 39. In the years leading up to that age, however, my physical neglect had begun to take a toll. I just didn't want to admit it. I was riddled with headaches and allergies and had put on 20 kg (45 pounds). At that year's annual physical, my doctor told me that I needed to have my arteries tested. Indeed, they had become narrow and stiff, and I was diagnosed with early-stage atherosclerosis[2]. I was in the high-risk category for a heart attack or stroke, and certainly not invincible.

I was so busy running on autopilot mode that I had had little time for self-observation. Although I was very successful, and I had achieved my financial goals, I felt unhappy and unsatisfied. While I

---

2 Atherosclerosis is the build-up of fats, cholesterol and other substances in and on your artery walls. This build-up is called plaque. The plaque can cause your arteries to narrow, blocking blood flow. The plaque can also burst, leading to a blood clot.

had maintained good relationships with my clients and business partners, I had neglected my relationships with my loved ones. I had made no time for my family, friends, hobbies, exercise, or spiritual rituals. I was spending endless days and nights abroad, far away from home, and there were too many lonely nights when my wife and I slept apart. I had missed my four daughters' birthdays, holidays, kindergarten, and school events. Luckily, I did not miss any of their births, as I believe that this would have caused irreversible damage.

During these years, Talia tried to share with me what she was going through. She expressed her feelings, from sadness to happiness, anger, and enthusiasm, but I had become hard-hearted. She was talking from her heart, but I was listening with my head. She wanted empathy; I offered practical solutions. At that time, I, mistakenly, believed that every problem could be solved with the right amount of money.

I was disconnected physically and mentally, and my emotional system had switched off. This was not an overnight crisis; it was the culmination of years of neglect. The physical damage was visible, a round face and a flabby stomach are hard to hide. But the significant damage was occurring below the surface. I had become a tourist in my own home. I no longer even figured in the day-to-day planning of my household. When I finally "woke up," the ruins had piled up around me.

Like a physical disease, where the pus appears on the skin, my physical deterioration and the breakdown of my relationships were just symptoms of a problem that had started long before the "pus" appeared.

And then, I had my epiphany – success in work is just that: success in one thing. I had no clue how to be successful in the other areas of my life. I'd never thought about these areas. I had always figured that if I made a lot of money, and had stature in the business community, the rest would just fall into place. I was so wrong. Instead of falling into place, things start falling apart. I realized that I still had a lot of work to do. I had wasted enough time and there was an urgency to my mission. I decided to allocate serious time and energy to investigating how I could improve the quality of my life. I would tackle the other areas of my life with the same commitment and dedication that I had given to my financial and business affairs.

I began by asking myself many questions:
- Where do I find happiness?
- How do I strengthen my relationships with my wife and children?
- How do I improve my health?
- Why do some people, at 40, look and feel like 60, while others, at 60, look and feel like 40?
- Can I succeed, as I have succeeded in my business life, in the other fields of my life?
- Is there a formula I can use to achieve these goals?

In asking these questions, and contemplating my next move, Einstein's famous quote came to mind: "The definition of insanity is doing the same thing over and over again but expecting different results."

I was determined to find the ingredients for happiness, for a healthy life, for financial independence, strong relationships, and a life of faith without worries and fear.

> **I realized that, first, I had to change.**

I embarked on a fascinating journey in search of answers to the most profound questions. I read many books, from biblical stories to modern technological journals. I learned from experts, emulated them, and applied the knowledge to my own life.

I analyzed the various fields of life, including health, fitness, relationships, and wealth, and discovered formulae for all of them.

I observed that the formulae had many similarities and that there was a clear path to follow. The first step required me to change both my attitude and my behavior. This was the key to improving my life's results.

The formulae were simple. Overwhelmingly, they required a return to basics, to the natural laws of the universe.

> **The overarching similarity between all of them was the understanding that my life's results were completely up to me.**

All of the resources which I required for my success were abundantly available. In fact, they were inside me! Once I learned to access them within, they "miraculously" appeared in the external world.

I learned how to manage my thoughts, my emotions, and my actions.

> **I became the creator of my reality.**

Most people do not take responsibility for their lives. They see life as a series of coincidences, influenced randomly by luck or by the mercy of external forces that are beyond their control. When they get negative results, they blame everyone besides themselves, with no ability to understand why they are failing to succeed. Little do they realize, as I will demonstrate throughout this book, that they are acting in contradiction to the laws of nature.

***

The Talmud[3] tells a story of Joseph, the son of a learned sage, who became very ill and died (in what would, today, be called a "clinical death"). Then he suddenly regained consciousness. It was as if he had returned from a faraway place. As he regained consciousness, his father said to him, "What did you see?" Joseph said, "I saw a world turned upside down. What is above was below and what is below was above...." His father said to him, "My son, you have seen a clear world, you have seen the world clearly...."[4]

In the earthly world, reality is deceptive. When you look at a tree you can only see the outer part, the part that is "revealed" to your eyes. The source of the tree's life, the part that is invisible to us, is hidden deep beneath the surface.

The tree feeds through its roots. The larger and stronger the tree, the deeper and healthier are the roots. When the tree is sick, the only effective treatment is to deal with the roots. We must take care of the environment which nourishes the roots – be it by adding minerals, water, or whatever else may be required.

Cosmetic treatment, for the leaves or the fruit, will only deal with the symptoms. It will not lead to a real resolution.

As it is with the tree, so too is it with us.

Most people treat the symptoms rather than deal with the root causes of the problem. While the root causes of the problem may be hidden, the only way to get the desired results is to identify and deal with them.

We do indeed live in a world that is upside down! What is important is invisible to the eye. We place value on expensive items, such as diamonds and gold, that add little value to our lives. Nature provides a limited quantity of them because they are not essential!

---

3 The Talmud is the central text of Rabbinic Judaism and the primary source of Jewish religious law.
4 Talmud Bagli, Pesachim 50a

Nature doesn't make mistakes. That which is important, nature provides freely and in abundance. Yet we place little value on air, the thing we need most. We pollute it and take it for granted. It is the same with our bodies, our relationships, and our spiritual well-being. Managing the contradictions between what we see or have been taught – and what is 'real' or 'natural' – is difficult but, the more I investigated, the clearer it became. If you want to build a tall building, you need to dig deep. The deeper you go beneath the surface, the taller is the building you can build.

Intuitively, we think that the permanent things in our life are physical. But, in reality, they are always temporary. The things that last, such as feelings of joy and happy memories, are intangible. Our intuition fools us in so many ways. True happiness is created by what we give, not by what we get. Yet, intuitively, we feel the opposite – pursuing and accumulating "stuff," while happiness remains elusive.

"Reality" also fools us. Life is a bit like having an itch in a wound. We are inclined to scratch the itch, hoping for a sense of relief, but that just makes the situation worse. In practice, any scratching just deepens the wound and worsens the condition. The right thing to do is to conquer our instincts, and just not scratch.

***

It's easy to talk about all these concepts in theory, but what do they mean for us, in practice?

Our brain is a supercomputer, of whose capacity we utilize only a small percentage at most. By raising our consciousness level, we shift our automatically driven behavior, stemming from our sub-conscious, into conscious behavior which is powered by our brain. Conscious behavior allows us to take responsibility. In practice, it shifts our focus from the ancient mind, the amygdala, which is responsible for our primitive instincts, to the prefrontal cortex, the more advanced part of our brain. This allows us to begin utilizing the power of our supercomputer.

When I understood that I could not flip the world, I decided to flip my point of view. I changed my perspective on almost everything. I released my old habits, flexed the way I think, strengthened my faith, and stopped fighting reality. I stopped scratching and wounding myself. By liberating my mind, the insights began to appear.

Like Joseph, I saw an inverted world.

The formulae, and their factors, when applied repetitively, will bring clarity, and success. If you find the formula to earn $1 per transaction, all you have to do is multiply the transaction. A million transactions will make you a millionaire. It is the same with all the other aspects of your life. Health, happiness, and successful relationships all have common formulae which generate consistent results.

I invite you to explore with me the wonders of our creation, its secrets, and its formulae.

III. THE PATTERNS OF LIFE

What we call chaos is just patterns we haven't recognized. What we call random is just patterns we can't decipher.

– Chuck Palahniuk

Terry Laughlin was a swimming coach who developed a method of swimming instruction known as total immersion. While observing swimmers in the pool, he noticed that those with the fastest times usually completed their laps with the fewest strokes, slipping through the water with ease instead of struggling against it. Laughlin observed that elite swimmers move through the water in a highly efficient way, rather than trying to beat the water into submission. Rather than moving the water, and moving around it, they move through the water.[5]

Fish leave barely a ripple when they swim. Humans churn up the water, struggle for breath, and exhaust themselves by pushing against the water. Fish, at whatever speed, give no impression of "trying," they just go! In a similar vein, the primary cause of drowning in the ocean is that, when caught in a riptide, people try to swim against the flow. But it is the flow that takes them out of the riptide!

---

5 hhttps://www.nytimes.com/2017/10/27/obituaries/terry-laughlin-dead-taught-swimmers-not-to-struggle-with-total-immersion-method.html

Understanding the forces of nature can literally save your life.

Whether swimming, running, dancing, or even working, nature is my teacher. When I learned to use the laws of the universe, and flow with nature's forces, rather than resisting them, my life became smoother and easier. Our body, mind, and soul need this flow to live a healthy and successful life.

Nature is unbeatable. Resistance to it consumes endless energy, leading to frustration, failure, misery, and even disease. Nature consists of patterns, cycles, and formulae. The natural world may seem complex, even chaotic. But, when looked at from a distance, everything is in a very precise order – with natural roles, as well as accurate cycles and patterns.

Most of us are not aware of the rhythmic cycles which synchronize the activities of our universe. From the smallest atom to the largest solar system, everything – including human beings – is mysteriously regulated by these patterns, cycles, and formulae. The moon takes 29½ days to orbit the Earth. The Earth orbits the Sun every 365 days. There are four seasons in an annual cycle. Our solar system orbits the center of the Milky Way every 250 million years. It takes nine months for a child to be born. There are no shortcuts in the cycles. You cannot hurry, or shorten, the gestation period. Circumventing nature's rhythms is a recipe for disaster.

The easiest way to create success is to place your actions into a repetitive pattern, system, or... a formula. If a baker bakes her bread with a recipe, the results will always be delicious, no matter how many loaves she bakes. It is the same for playing a melody or splitting atoms. There are recipes and formulae for almost everything that we need to be successful. There is a formula to become rich or healthy, and there is a formula to become poor or sick.

> **The repetitive actions we take determine the results we get.**

On our planet, some forces constantly exist, such as the laws of gravity, momentum, and action and reaction. The law of gravity did not come into existence when the proverbial apple fell on Isaac Newton's head. The law has always been there and will always be. If you jumped from twenty floors – praying for gravity not to pull you down – you would not be reading this book right now!

We do not pay much attention to these laws. However, if we forget, or go against, the laws of nature, we get harmed. The harm does not come from the law itself. We harm ourselves by not obeying the law. When we touch fire, we get burnt by our actions, not by the fire. The fire has no intention to harm us.

The universe contains everything: good and bad; darkness and light; love and hate. For everything that exists, its opposite exists as well. Everything is connected and, for every action, there is a reaction. The universe also contains a wide range of frequencies. Like with a radio, you can choose the station you wish, to tune into. But, be warned: tune into the wrong wave and you'll hear something you don't like. It is up to you to choose a station that will fill your life with love, hope, positivity, and peace of mind.

***

A story is told about a university professor who entered his classroom and informed his students that they were about to have a surprise test. They all waited anxiously at their desks for it to begin. The professor handed out the test with the text facing down, as usual. He then asked the students to turn over their papers.

To everyone's surprise, there were no questions – just a black dot in the center of the paper. The professor, seeing the expression on everyone's faces, told them, "I want you to write about what you see there." The students, confused, got started on the inexplicable task.

At the end of the class, the professor took all the tests and started reading each one of them out loud in front of all the students. All of them, without exception, defined the black dot, trying to explain its position in the center of the sheet.After all their answers had been read, the classroom was silent. Each student was wondering who was the closest to what the professor was expecting. Who would get the best grade? The professor kept them wondering for a few moments and then he explained the purpose of the test.

"I'm not going to grade you on this, I just wanted to give you something to think about. No one wrote about the white part of the paper, everyone focused on the black dot. The same thing happens in our lives. We insist on focusing only on the black dot – the health issues that bother us, the lack of money, the complicated relationship with a family member, the disappointment with a friend. The dark spots are tiny when compared to everything we have in our lives, but they are the ones that pollute our minds. Take your eyes away from the black dots in your lives. Enjoy each one of your blessings, each moment that life gives you. Be happy and live a life filled with love!" [6]

Just like the university students, I used to be a "black dot" person. I would get home from work, open the front door, and see a big mess; shoes all over the floor, dirty dishes, and noisy children. Immediately, I was in a bad mood. I did not realize that I was the cause of my suffering.

Years later, I decided consciously to begin changing my focus. Now, when I open the same door, I open my arms and ask, "Who's coming to daddy?" Now, I see a home full of life. I notice the love which surrounds me. My house is not a museum; it is a place where

---

6 https://purposefocuscommitment.com/story-about-happiness-meaning-black-dot-white-paper

my precious family feels safe. I ignore the mess and embrace the noise as a sign of life. I see the "white space," not the "black dot."

We all have the power to choose what to see and what to have.

> **We always have the power to change our focus.**

Picture a window: When you want light to be part of your life, you open the window, and the light fills you with warmth, love, joy, and happiness. Darkness cannot exist in the presence of light.

Many people keep their windows closed. Faithlessness, fear, and a fixation on darkness and superstitions prevent them from seeing the light. The light is always there. It was there yesterday, it is here now, and it will be there tomorrow. But you must take the action and open the window.

***

When the sun goes down in the evening, we expect it to rise in the morning.

When children are born, we expect them to grow, and when we plant a vegetable garden, we expect to harvest it after a certain amount of time. When it comes to the natural world, humans have no problem seeing patterns and cycles. We understand cause and effect perfectly.

> **For some reason, however, when it comes to our own lives, we struggle to see, or we easily dismiss, the connections between our actions and our results.**

If I eat unhealthy food and do not exercise regularly, over time, I will get sick. If I do not care for the people around me, over time I will not have healthy relationships.

It is the same with our thoughts. If my thoughts are negative, how can I manifest positive results? We are a part of the natural world. Its laws apply equally to us.

A thought creates and plants a seed in your mind. When you speak about it, the seed begins to grow. When you give it an emotion, whether happiness or sadness, you feed the thought. When you act upon it, you water it. There is no stopping now. The cycle is in motion. Just as the growth period for each plant is different, the amount of time required for each thought to manifest, or become tangible, is different. The more you engage in positive acts, the more water, and sunshine you add. Keep on watering your thoughts and don't stop until you harvest the crop.

***

Human beings are one entity with many layers. We have a physical body, mental capabilities, emotional responses, as well as a divine soul.

Ultimately, everything is made of energy, and like attracts like. Therefore, things that vibrate at the same frequency will be attracted to each other. Negative attracts negative and positive attracts positive. I have seen this play out in so many ways in my life, and that of others.

When you understand this principle, you begin to understand your "operating system," which has five stages, and works in a very simple way:

The results you get have a direct correlation to your actions; your actions, in turn, are influenced by your emotions, which spring from your thoughts and imagination. Motivation is the fuel that fires up the whole system. The conclusion is clear: The results we get in our lives do not happen by accident. We control our lives by the seeds we choose to plant in our heads.

The ability to manage our thoughts starts with self–awareness, with our ability to do deep observation, to be silent, to look inside, and to listen to our true inner voice. The more you dream and imagine, the clearer the pictures and focused destinations are in your mind, the greater will be the results that appear in your life.

We are the heroes, the creators, of our life stories. How do you want your life to look? If your thoughts are negative, what results can you expect to receive? What kind of movie do you think you will see?

Plant a winning picture in your mind and your supercomputer, your brain, will help to take you there.

In the following chapters, we will look at each aspect of our lives using these principles. We will see that, whether it is physical health or spirituality, nature always points the way. I'll show you what I learned and how to apply the formulae in your own life. Since I discovered the secrets of "The Formula," my life has changed completely.

Welcome to the journey of "The Formula."

IV. THE FORMULA FOR HAPPINESS

Happiness =
1. Positive Attitude
2. Growth
3. Relationships
4. Generosity
5. Gratitude

Why do we not have what we want?
Because we don't want what we have.
If we wanted what we have, We would have what.
Is missing

– Rabbi David Mnobhrdok

For years, I had dreamed of retiring by the age of 40. When I turned 38, I was ready to do that. My life looked perfect. I was married, had three beautiful daughters, had created assets, and bought properties. I had also established several companies that were generating cash, and mostly operating without me. I could finally relax.

So, I did.

I gave myself a few weeks to throttle back, something I had never done before. To be honest, I was not sure how to handle it. The phone stopped ringing; the emails stopped flowing. I had plenty of spare time. Rather than feeling relaxed, however, I was bored. My magic touch was not necessary anymore.

After a short while, I began to feel uncomfortable and restless. I thought I would enjoy relaxing. But the exact opposite happened. I felt an awful sense of desperation. Suddenly, I was in the middle of the worst year of my life. First, I was unhappy. And then I was depressed. My depression shocked me. "You should be happy," I told myself. "You've earned it, you have everything you want, you should feel like the happiest person on earth. What's going wrong here?" My mind-talk was endless.

> **The more I forced myself to be happy, the unhappier I became.**

I could not find my happiness anywhere. And so, I gave myself a research project. I decided to investigate the mystery of my disappearing happiness.

Like any good detective, I began by asking myself some questions:
- Why are some people happy and others not?
- What makes us truly happy?
- Can happiness be "switched on"?
- Is there a way to make other people happy?
- Can money buy happiness? If yes, how much would it cost?
- Is there any way to "synthesize" happiness?

Ultimately, all the questions led to another question: What do we really want?

In winter, we want summer. In summer, we want winter. Children want to be adults. Adults want to recapture their childhood. Students want to graduate, and workers want to be students. Single people want to be married. Married people want to be single. Workers want to retire. Retirees want to work.

Human beings simply struggle to stay in the present. We focus on what is missing; we miss what is right in front of us.

> **When I'm here, I want to be there.**
> **When I'm there, I want to be here.**
> **We want the things we do not have.**
> **We have the things we do not want.**

As my research deepened, it dawned on me, that the first step to finding my happiness and turning my negativity upside down, was to appreciate my now.

I had to shift my focus by learning to embrace reality.

I needed to focus less on myself and my material wealth, and more on others and my relationships. Most importantly, I had to learn to focus less on external factors beyond my control and begin to look inward, focusing on how I was responding to my experiences.

What I learned, on my detective hunt, is that happiness comes from within. Any attempt to generate happiness from an external reality – delicious meals, luxury vacations, or recognition from others – will be temporary and is destined for failure.

Happiness is generated by the power of our brain. It comes from your personal perceptions and thoughts. If I perceive an event as being good for me, I become happy. But if my perception about the same event is bad, that it is not good enough, or that I need more, I will feel unhappy and suffer.

In the same way that paralysis affects the body, so too does sadness paralyze the soul.

> **Sadness comes from a deficit. It is the result of the gap**
> **between our desires and our reality.**

Let me demonstrate this with a simple example:

John, who works as a teller in the bank, earns $10,000 per month, but thinks he deserves to earn $12,000. John's deficit is $2,000.

His manager, Debbie, who earns $100,000 per month, thinks she deserves to earn $120,000. Debbie's deficit is $20,000.

Debbie's deficit is much higher than John's. Her perception causes her much more misery than John!

Mary, who works as a secretary in the same bank, earns $2,000 and is fairly satisfied with a salary that meets her expectations. She gets to work, every morning, with a smile on her face.

So, who is poor and who is rich?

The Talmud says, "The wealthy man is the one who is happy with his lot."[7]

For the most part, scarcity is imaginary. People imagine they have a lack of money, lack of respect, lack of attention, or lack of love. These shortages are not physical, they are interpretations of our thoughts. Obviously, if you have no food, or you are homeless and freezing, then scarcity is not imaginary. If, however, your basic needs have been met, and yet you still live with a distressing sense of scarcity, then you need to look towards your thoughts, and not your external circumstances or imagined lack, to find the cause.

My research convinced me that happiness is an art. Unfortunately, even though life is driven by our desire to gain happiness and avoid pain, it would appear to be an art in which we are not very skilled.

> **The art of happiness lies in understanding with our brain and feeling in our heart, that what we currently have is the absolute best.**

---

7 Ethics of the Fathers, 4.1

Happiness comes from a feeling of wholeness. So many of us are professional goal-setters, skilled at setting higher and higher expectations. But we have lost our ability to enjoy what we currently have. We keep wanting more – a bigger house, a better car, a partner who performs better. As soon as we achieve our targets, we automatically increase our need for more and better. We are never complete, never whole.

So, how do we achieve this feeling of wholeness? The answer to this question lies in the factors that make up the formula for happiness.

Factor #1: Positive attitude

Happiness is a choice, not a result. Nothing will make you happy, until you choose to be happy. No person will make you happy unless you decide to be happy. Your happiness will not come to you. It can only come from you.

– Ralph Marston

In August 1995, during the Lebanon war, my friend, Gadi Yarkoni, was injured. Gadi was serving as a sniper in the Israeli Defense Force, when, one night, he spotted three Hizballah terrorists walking four meters in front of the troop. The soldiers immediately opened fire. Gadi hit the first terrorist in front of him, and his friend hit the second one. Just before the third terrorist was killed, he managed to shoot in the direction of the Israelis. The bullet, which hit the body of the rifle of Gadi's friend who was standing beside him, changed direction and hit Gadi's head. The bullet split into two, one part entered his mouth, and the other part penetrated his brain. Gadi was immediately evacuated and underwent multiple surgeries. The doctors fought to keep him alive and, after hours of his hanging between life and death, they succeeded in saving Gadi's life. A few weeks later, he was released from the hospital. Not only was his head scarred from the shrapnel, but he had also lost his sight. My friend was completely blind.

Gadi did not ask for war. He certainly did not ask for the shrapnel. Gadi had a choice. He could have wallowed in despair and made his family and friends miserable. But he chose not to. Instead, he became a successful physiotherapist. In the absence of sight, his sense of touch was heightened, giving him a marked advantage as a physiotherapist. Today, he has a fantastic reputation, and his clinic, where he treats patients with sports injuries, is always full. But it gets better! He trains daily and, twice a year, he runs marathons. He also cycles on a tandem mountain bike, skis, climbs mountains and he recently told me that he is learning kite surfing! He is also happily married with three lovely children.

What is Gadi's take on his experience? "For me, my life before and after the injury is the same. My quality of life has not been affected at all. If anything, it has improved dramatically. I now see and appreciate life more than ever before. I'm grateful. I found my destiny. I thank God every day that I'm alive. I'm happier than I ever been."

It is easy to dismiss Gadi as a rare case. But you would be wrong. I run marathons with people who have lost their legs, who have had (or have) cancer, and other diseases that have impacted their lives drastically.

The world is replete with stories of people whose attitude has allowed them to rise above their circumstances. I keep Viktor Frankl's book, *Man's Search for Meaning,* within arms' reach of my desk. Frankl, who lost his entire family and survived the Holocaust, emerged with the following belief:

Everything can be taken from a man but one thing: the last of the human freedoms — to choose one's attitude in any given set of circumstances, to choose one's own way.

> **When the circumstances of your life change, the impact of the occurrence depends completely on your attitude towards it.**

Look around you. It's not complicated. People with a positive attitude enjoy life more, and are generally happier, than negative people who walk around grumpy and pessimistic. A positive attitude simply helps you to cope more easily with the affairs of life. It brings optimism, and optimism, in turn, makes it easier to avoid worrying and negative thinking. If you adopt optimism as an outlook, constructive changes become possible. You, and your life, become happier and more successful. We have little, if any, control over our life's events, but we have 100% control over how we respond to them.

> **Self—control is the fuel that runs the happiness engine.**

When you feel a sense of control over yourself, your thoughts, and your responses, you are happy. When you lose control, your happiness is at risk. Rather than focusing on things you cannot control, for example past events or other people's behavior, shift your focus toward things that you can control, for example changing your own attitude or behavior.

> **The door to happiness opens from the inside!**

Ask yourself an honest question, and take some time to think about the answer: Are you controlling your thoughts, or are your thoughts controlling you? Who is the master and who is the slave? Realizing what the problem is, i.e., that your thoughts are controlling you, is the beginning of the solution. When you learn to master your thoughts, you start to wake up.

By consciously choosing our thoughts, we give ourselves the power to decide whether we want to be happy. Life is ten percent of what happens to us and ninety percent of how we respond to it. You are in charge of your attitude.[8]

Consciously decide to replace thoughts about negative events with positive ones:

- When you get a parking ticket, be grateful for having a car. Think of it as an expensive and luxurious parking spot.
- When you are stressed about work, be grateful for having a job.
- When your kids are shouting and running wild, be grateful that they are healthy enough to create the noise. You are blessed to have children.

The list of possibilities is endless. A positive attitude will completely change your life. It is the key to your happiness.

---

8 I find Albert Ellis's "ABCDE" model extremely helpful for keeping my attitude in check. The things we believe, and the stories we tell ourselves, affect the way we respond to difficult events. By changing our beliefs, and embracing positivity as a way of being, we can begin to respond differently.

Factor #2: Growth

Life is like riding a bike; when it's too easy, you are going downhill.
– Nir Kunik

The depression, that prompted my research into happiness, taught me a valuable lesson. I realized, with almost startling clarity, that I had a different, much more important need, than financial success and "retirement": I had the need to grow.

All biological organisms on earth are in constant motion. Be it a cell, bacteria, plant, animal, or human being – nothing remains constant.

> **There are only two directions – growth or contraction.**

A negative, or fixed, mindset is all about contraction and retreat: "Nothing will ever change for the better, I tried that, it didn't work, etc., etc."

A growth mindset is all about expansion, discovery, and seeing opportunity even when bad things happen: "I failed, but I can learn from it, grow past it, and I can turn the negative into a positive."

When you stop growing, you wilt and die. I keep it very simple:

> **"Future Me" > "Me in the Now" = Happiness**
> **"Future Me" < "Me in the Now" = Unhappy**

The secret is to keep growing. And, while we all grow older, this is not the growth to which I am referring.

"Future Me" grows:

- physically, through healthy eating and exercise;
- mentally, by reading, studying, and goal setting;
- emotionally, by practicing gratitude, forgiveness, love, and deepening your connections; and
- spiritually, by silence, meditation, retreats, and prayers.

Growth, as a factor of happiness, is quite simple: Invest time and effort into growing at any given point in time. Start now – and don't stop till you die. Become a better version of yourself, every single day.

Grow in as many directions as possible; the more variety you have, the better will be your quality of life.

Embrace curiosity: Enrich your knowledge; read books; read your bible; listen to audiobooks and music; play a musical instrument; seek mentors; attend workshops; ask questions. Information is infinite. Grow yourself in all these directions and get your free boost of happiness!

Grow in your relationships: Develop intimate and deep relationships with your spouse, children, friends, colleagues, and neighbors. Every time you get closer to someone, and the relationship grows, you get another free boost of happiness. Happiness does not come only from your own growth, but also from the growth of people around you. When they are constantly progressing, you get satisfaction and happiness too. When your children, employees, and partners emulate you, they imbibe the passion to acquire more knowledge, skills, patience and even love. When they become better versions of themselves, your own happiness increases.

Grow yourself professionally: Invest time and effort in developing your career. When you invest in your career, you receive more attention, more love, more money, and more prestige. And here is a little secret: People like working with happy people.

Stretch yourself physically: Physical activity is essential for happiness.[9] There are simple things you can do to be more active every day. Climb the stairs instead of using the elevator or walk rather than driving your car. Being active will instantly improve your mood and can even alleviate depression. This doesn't mean that we all need to run marathons. Start small, get moving!

Grow everything: Your mind, your assets, your expertise, your love, your willingness to give to others, your passion, your fitness, your spirit, and whatever else you can grow. Pick one. Work on it. Then pick another. There is an unlimited amount of money, love, knowledge, and resources in the world. Endless happiness awaits you. You will get happiness in both directions – when you achieve it for yourself and when you give it to others.

Setting goals for growth

Goals are the best way for us to turn our desires and dreams into reality. Happiness doesn't just happen – it comes from thinking, planning, and pursuing things that are important to us.

Goals can be long–term, short–term, or even day–to–day. A long–term goal might be a big career or life goal, for example learning a new language, climbing Mount Everest, or writing a book. A short–term goal might be a plan for the coming weeks or months – for example, to write a new chapter every month. A day–to–day goal might be thirty minutes of daily writing.

---

9 In fact, I believe that physical fitness is such a crucial component of life, that I have devoted an entire chapter to it (Chapter VII).

Smaller goals may seem unimportant. However, having personal projects that matter to us – and are manageable – can boost happiness, especially when they're supported by others. It's even better if we can link our smaller goals to our bigger desires and priorities. Achieving smaller goals builds our confidence, brings us a sense of accomplishment, and makes us feel more optimistic about the future.

We all need goals to motivate us, and these need not only be challenging enough to excite us, but also achievable. Choosing ambitious, yet realistic, goals gives our life direction and brings a sense of accomplishment and satisfaction.

Feeling good about the future also increases the levels of the "feel-good" hormone, serotonin. Happiness, like most other emotions, is a result of chemicals being released into our brains.

Four chemicals are instrumental in aiding our happiness – Dopamine, Serotonin, Endorphins, and Oxytocin. Each of these chemicals is released in response to different emotional states.

Dopamine and endorphins are the chemicals that specifically aid "growth."

Dopamine is released in the brain when we receive a reward, achieve a long-sought goal, or even simply take a step towards a goal. It is extremely easy to increase your dopamine levels. Getting eight hours of sleep a day and regular exercise helps keep dopamine levels in balance. It is also important to remember that the brain releases a little dopamine whenever you achieve something or succeed. One way to get a "hit" of dopamine regularly is to break down bigger goals into smaller goals, more easily achievable chunks so that you can keep getting "runs on the board" and feel good about making progress. You should always celebrate the "little" wins. No matter how small they may seem, they are worthy of acknowledgment and will help to boost your happiness chemicals.

Factor #3: Relationships

People are lonely because they build walls instead of bridges.

– Joseph F. Newton

Studies have shown that the quality and quantity of our social connections both have an impact on our health, happiness, and longevity.[10]

Close relationships with family and friends provide love, meaning, support, and increase our feelings of self-worth. Broader networks, like community, bring a sense of belonging. Thus, taking action to strengthen our relationships and build connections is essential for happiness.

Just as relationships are a two-way thing, it seems the connection between happiness and relationships is, too. Not only do relationships help to make us happier, but happy people tend to have more, and better quality, relationships. Without healthy relationships, happiness is a near impossibility.[11]

When it comes to relationships, our body produces a special chemical, Oxytocin, which is also known as the "love hormone." Oxytocin creates intimacy, trust, and helps build strong, healthy relationships. It is essential for creating powerful bonds and improving social interactions. A very simple way to keep oxytocin flowing is to give someone a hug and not a handshake. Research has shown that hugging someone for 20 seconds a day releases oxytocin.[12]

---

10 https://www.ncbi.nlm.nih.gov/pmc/articles/PMC3150158/

11 Relationships are not just about happiness. They are integral to "The Formula" and so I have devoted an entire chapter to the topic (Chapter IX).

12 https://www.thetimes.co.uk/article

Factor #4: Generosity

The only thing in life that no one can take from you is what you have given to others.

– Nir Kunik

An apocryphal story is told of a man who spends his days with a fishing rod immersed in the Dead Sea. For those who may not know, the Dead Sea, located on the eastern side of Israel, lies 400 meters (1300 feet) below sea level and is known as being the lowest body of water on the surface of Earth. Nothing can flourish in it; there is no life, only desolation and death.

Tourists, who walk by the fisherman, wonder if there is something wrong with him. How can he be fishing in a place that has nothing alive in it? One day, a tourist, unable to resist, asked him, "What are you doing?" Without hesitation, the man replied, "I'm catching fish."

Of course, the tourist responded by suggesting that the man must be joking,

"Are you serious? There are no fish in the Dead Sea!"

The fisherman smiled and replied, "Of course there are fish here. You just need to be patient and the fish will come. In fact, I'm willing to bet you 50 bucks that there are fish here."

The tourist, knowing he was right, thought to himself, "Let's make some easy money." Placing his hand in his pocket, he handed the man $50.

The fisherman, taking the money, was quick off the draw: "You see, you are the third fish I have caught today!"

The Dead Sea, which is actually a lake, gets its water from rain, the Jordan River, the Sea of Galilee, and the perennial springs that surround it. It gets from others but gives nothing in return. It is a fitting metaphor for this factor: Taking from others – without giving back – will take you to the lowest point, to a desolate place where nothing grows inside – physically, mentally, or spiritually.

In my experience, giving is the ultimate source of happiness.

You cannot, of course, give away what you do not have. You can't give money, love, or knowledge if you don't have them. You also can't give time if you never have any to spare. The more you have, the more you can give. And you have more than you think.

There are so many ways of giving; most of them are free and easy to give away. You can pay attention to your loved ones, for example. You can offer someone a "well done" or a sincere smile. You can simply say "thank you." These acts of giving often mean more than material gifts.

Helping others boosts happiness, provides a sense of meaning, increases feelings of competence, improves our mood, and reduces stress. Giving to others also meets one of our basic human needs – the need for community. Winston Churchill expressed this sentiment perfectly when he said, "We make a living by what we get, but we make a life by what we give."

What about giving to myself? Is that good or bad? If your motivation is selfish, and for personal gain only, then the amount of joy will be limited and will not last long. But, if the same act of giving to myself is in order to give to others too, the outcome will be true happiness that will, in all probability, last for a substantial period.

For example, studying for seven years to become a doctor will give you knowledge, a decent job, and, hopefully, joy and satisfaction. But using this knowledge later to save people's lives will boost your satisfaction and take your happiness to a different level. Doctors without patients, clowns without an audience, or a teacher without students, all have high potential but no way to fulfill their purpose.

> **Our life goal is to become a channel for the abundance that the universe has to offer us.**[13]

Our major task is to expand the channel. It is the work of a lifetime. Expanding your knowledge, capabilities, love, and patience, will enlarge the channel. The more you give, the more happiness you get.

The feeling of giving produces serotonin, a chemical that flows when you feel satisfied, accomplished, and significant. Conversely, a lack of serotonin can make you feel lonely, bleak, and unhappy.

---

13 I will speak more about this in the chapter on spirituality (Chapter X).

Factor #5: Gratitude

The more grateful I am, the more beauty I see.

– Mary Davis

Every morning, when I wake up, I thank God for granting me another day of life. If I'm healthy and those around me are safe, I feel blessed and fortunate. There are so many reasons to be grateful. Many prayers, in almost all religions, are made up of immense gratitude. It is difficult to be grateful and angry at the same time. Feeling and expressing gratitude directs our focus to the positive, which compensates for our brain's natural tendency to focus on threats, worries, and the negative aspects of life. Gratitude essentially leads to the positive emotions of happiness, love, and joy.

Happiness, like physical health, is daily work. If I want to keep in shape, I need to wake up every morning and exercise. So too, if I want to stay happy, I need to keep practicing.

> **The human brain is a few million years old. It was not designed to make you happy; it is there to help you survive. Happiness is your job!**

Scientists find that being thankful for three things every day, when you wake up in the morning and before going to sleep, dramatically boosts your happiness in life.[14] Write them down. Daily gratitude exercises create new neural pathways in your brain. Try

14 https://www.apa.org/monitor/oct06/key

it for 40 days and you will begin to witness amazing changes in your life. Thank God, Jesus, Allah, Buddha, or even yourself. Say thanks for the health of your children, for the lovely evening you had yesterday with your friends, for the food you eat and the family you eat it with, for the lights you switch on, the water that flows from the tap, and for your ability to see, hear, smell, and feel.

For every problem you find within and around you, there are a myriad other things that are working properly. Where is your focus?

V. THE FORMULA FOR SUCCESS

Success =
1. Attitude
2. Courage
3. Discipline
4. Focus

Don't let the fear of losing be greater than the excitement of winning.
— Robert Kiyosaki

Who doesn't want to be successful? When you succeed, people like you, and want to get closer to you. Your children are proud of you, your colleagues want to learn from and emulate you, your partner admires you, and life smiles at you.

Success is a magnet.

There are many kinds of success. You can become famous, rich, a top athlete, or an expert in your field of interest. Success is not just about money or material results. Ultimately, you define what success means to you.

While there is usually an element of luck associated with success, in my experience, becoming successful is a matter of choice.[15] Are you willing to say, "This is what I want and I'm going to get it!"? And will you continue saying that when things don't go your way? If it takes years? That's what I mean by success being a choice. Are you willing to be patient? Are you resilient enough to take the knocks on the way to success? Learning to manage your thoughts, feelings, and actions is the key to becoming successful.

> **Success is a state of mind and a decision. Ultimately, your attitude will determine whether you are successful or not.**

Success is a skill that can be learned. Mastery of the skill is in your hands. As with most things in life, you must invest in advance; the rewards come later. First, you sow, then you reap. Unfortunately, a lot of people try to reverse the order.

Successful people have certain traits in common. You can't wake up one day and be successful. It's not like winning a jackpot. The achievement of success requires hard work and determination.

When it comes to success, I have found that there are four types of people: cowards, hesitators, average, and winners.

---

15 There are, of course, factors beyond our control that can impede our success. Inequity is real and we are not all born equal. But we all know privileged people who are not successful and people, who seemingly have all the odds stacked against them, who have achieved success.

The Cowards	The Average
They look at the mountain (the challenge) and say, "It would be nice to achieve that, but... it's too dangerous. I can't do it." Believing that the challenge is beyond their scope, they talk about wanting success but never do anything about it. They may be afraid, lazy, or both. Their lack of action is a combination of negative emotions and attitudes. But the bottom line is that they never really attempt to climb the mountain.	These folks see the mountain, get enthusiastic, start climbing, and when it starts to get "too difficult," they give up. These people are the "normal," the majority. They have a good job, a decent salary, a house with a 20-year mortgage, and a car. They save for retirement, have a pension fund or two, and pray that they will die before their money does!
The Hesitators	**The Winners**
They look at the mountain and say, "It's amazing, one day I will do it, I know exactly how to do it, I have a good plan and it'll work." But the day never comes. Procrastination is their way of life.	Winners see the mountain and set clear goals, with a timeline, to reach its summit. They start climbing and, should something go wrong, they make a new plan and adjust their path and pace. Most importantly, they keep climbing. They have a clear picture of themselves at the summit. They sweat, they never give up, and they make sacrifices. They're serious but, along the way, they allow themselves to enjoy the journey. They celebrate victories and cherish their team. Despite the difficulties, they reach their destination.

So, what is the major difference between the four types of people? Is it their IQ? Wisdom? Skills? Luck? Were they born with a golden spoon? Absolutely not. It is their attitude, the first factor in the formula for success. The good news is that anyone can learn how to become successful.

Factor #1: Attitude

Our attitude toward life determines life's attitude towards us.

– Earl Nightingale

I remember, as a child, hearing my grandmother telling me of her joy when she found rotten, uncooked potatoes in the concentration camp. She had food! I cannot imagine one of my daughters getting excited about a potato, let alone a rotten one.

I was ten years old when Grandma Mira told me, "The only way I survived the Nazis was to be mentally strong. If I hadn't planted positive stories in my mind, if I had lost my hope, and my attitude had become negative, my chances of survival would have been zero."

A positive attitude will uplift you; a negative attitude will pull you down. Changing your attitude will change your life. A new attitude may save your life or elevate you to the ranks of a "winner."

> **Your attitude brought you to where you are now; maintaining the same attitude will keep you in the same place.**

Time will pass and life will go on whether you like it or not. The question is whether you choose to participate in life, or simply to be a spectator.

Look back over your life, and consider the following questions:

- Do I feel generally satisfied with my life?
- What achievements am I most proud of?
- Have I spent my time in a truly meaningful way?
- What impact, values, and legacy am I leaving my children? Family? Friends? Community? The universe?
- What will people say about me at my funeral? What would I like them to say?

> **How you will be remembered is up to you. Start now.**
> **Become the type of person you want people to remember.**

Many people plan to start living when they retire. When it arrives, they realize that it's too late. They are not as fit or healthy as they used to be, and no longer have the passion or the energy of their youth. They realize that they have missed the train.

The journey of your life is made up of the actions you take every single day, what you achieve, the people you touch and influence, the love you give, the places you see, the experiences you collect, the assets you possess, and the amount of joy and happiness you accumulate along the way. To live fully, to lead a meaningful and successful life, you must choose to be a "winner" – to utilize your full potential. It does not come for free. You must be willing to pay the price of becoming successful.

> **Success means that you utilize your full potential.**

If you want to become successful, then your goal needs to be to transform yourself from the person you are now to becoming a "winner." It is a sure-fire way to reap the fruits that life is ready to give you. The only person who controls your destiny, your future, your success, or your failure, is you. Blaming others – the economy, the government, your business partner, your spouse, your children, or even your own luck – for your circumstances, is the root of the problem.

> **Change occurs when you begin to take full responsibility for the results of your life.**

When you blame external forces, you basically give up. You want others to fix your problems, but they can't. Change needs to come from within. You are the answer to your challenges, and the only thing over which you have absolute control is yourself. When you understand this, you can make changes, do things differently, and begin to get different results.

When the economy is bad, stop blaming, adjust your business, change the target market, change the product line, change the team. The economy will not change for you. If another company in your field has succeeded during this "difficult" period, then find ways to be this kind of company.

When your relationships are not working, stop blaming, take responsibility, change your behavior, try a different approach, love unconditionally, accept them as they are, find compassion within you, and share it with them. Don't try to change them; they are who they are.

The loudest and most influential voice we hear is our own inner voice. We can choose an inner voice of self-encouragement and self-motivation, or we can choose one of self-defeat and self-pity. It is a choice we all have. Which voice are you tuning into?

Today's thoughts and attitudes will determine your future. You must learn how to manage your thoughts and take charge of your attitude if you are to be successful. Train your mind to think positively, make that your focus, and success will become a part of your life.

Successful people say "yes" to life. They believe they can accomplish their mission and say "yes" to every opportunity. When you say, "I can't do it" or when you say "no," you fail in advance. When you say, "Yes, I can do it," you will often succeed or, worst-case scenario, you will not. But you will never fail. You will only fail when you give up and say, "no." This is why successful people succeed. They choose to persevere, while the unsuccessful choose to quit before trying or give up too soon. Keep going. Believe that you will succeed.

A positive, can-do attitude will eliminate procrastination and fear. When your default is, "Yes, I can do it here and now" and "no" is not a part of your vocabulary, things will get done. Saying "yes" prevents things from being postponed. Trying and succeeding – more often than failing – will strengthen your self-confidence and diminish your fears

I work constantly on improving my attitude. It's a never-ending process. I have drifted away from the negative people who surrounded me in the past, and now I seek out and stay close to people with positive attitudes. I preach to, and teach, my family and my friends about the power of a positive attitude.

According to Jim, "You are the average of the five people you spend the most time with." Who are the people who surround you? And what effect are they having on your attitude?

Factor #2: Courage

I learned that courage was not the absence of fear, but the triumph over it. The brave man is not he who does not feel afraid, but he who conquers that fear.

– Nelson Mandela

As children, we have the passion and creativity to dream. Most importantly, we have courage. Unfortunately, many adults, usually parents or teachers, cut our wings, pull us to the ground, force us to "land" by repeatedly saying, "Don't touch," "It's too dangerous," "Don't even try, you will not succeed," "You're too small," "It's not for you," "Let's do it tomorrow," "Not now," "Stop talking nonsense," "Don't ask so many questions!" and my favorite, "You're dreaming..." Unintentionally, they kill our dreams and instill fear within us.

When we were children, we had big dreams even though the possibilities were limited. We depended on our parents, but we dared to dream big. As a child, you dream of becoming an astronaut, reaching the moon, and exploring other planets. Children can save the world in their imaginations. Our imaginations have no boundaries.

No other creatures on earth can imagine. It's a unique gift that we humans should use endlessly. And it's free!

Almost every invention is preceded by "a big dream." The wheel was invented 5000 years ago. The electronic light in 1879 by Thomas

Edison. In 1903, the Wright brothers invented the first aircraft. The telephone in 1876 by Alexander Graham Bell. Henry Ford, Bill Gates, Steve Jobs, Elon Musk ... Imagine the world today without these dreamers. They dared to dream big, followed their dreams, and made them a reality. They succeeded in changing the world in ways that even their own imaginations could not have conceived!

We underestimate the power of imagination. But imagination is the engine that creates reality. Everything "out there" starts within; it is born from imagination. Richard Bach expressed it perfectly when he said, "to bring anything into your life, imagine that it's already there."

Of course, imagination is just the starting point; in itself, it's not sufficient for success.

You must have the courage to realize your dreams.

That is why risk is essential to success.

How does the word "risk" make you feel? Does it fill you with excitement, or does it frighten you?

Successful people take big risks to achieve extraordinary results.

No risk, no rewards **No guts, no glory!**

The equation is linear: the more risks you take, the more rewards you get. If you wish to become successful, you need to start taking risks!

My greatest successes came when I risked entering the African market. It was scary, but it was also exciting. However, I knew instinctively that when you take risks, there are only two options:

you either succeed or you fail. And, of course, you always have the option to try again! If you persist, you will learn from your mistakes, improve, attempt different things, and, eventually, you will succeed. My risk paid off. And, if it hadn't, I would have taken another risk. Napoleon Hill said that "most great people attained their greatest success just one step beyond their greatest failure." Giving up is not an option if success is your desired destination.

Michael Jordan is widely considered to be one of the greatest basketball players of all time. And yet, he was cut from his high-school basketball team because his coach didn't think he had enough skills. Warren Buffet, one of the world's richest and most successful businessmen, was rejected by Harvard University. Similarly, Richard Branson, the founder of the Virgin empire, is a high-school dropout. "Failure" is part of the journey to success.

We all have fears. Many of us are afraid of failing, at least some of the time. But fear of failure stops us from doing the things that move us closer towards achieving our goals.

It is natural to fear the unknown.

Fear is an essential survival function; it was meant to protect us. Without fear, the human species would be extinct. Darwin concluded that our fear response is an ancient instinct. Millions of years ago, Homo sapiens managed to survive in the wild savanna by developing fight or flight instincts to eliminate the risk of being hunted by wild animals or killed by enemies and natural disasters. These fears are hardwired into our ancient brain, the amygdala, which acts as a radar system, constantly scanning for danger. When a threat is perceived by the amygdala, stress hormones are released, and the entire body turns into fight or flight mode. The body shifts maximum energy to the muscles, senses, and the heart, while dramatically reducing the less relevant systems, such as the digestive system, and the "new brain" that is responsible for rational thinking, planning, judgment, as well as our values, personalities, and social skills.

Those days are gone. Most of us are no longer in the savanna, and the survival threats are mostly gone. We need our "new brain" to take back control if we want to avoid irrational fears. Over millions of years of evolution, the amygdala has improved and now works speedily and automatically, way faster than our "new brain," the cerebral cortex. As a result, we first freeze in the face of perceived danger. Only afterward, does the cerebral cortex analyze the event and make rational decisions about whether the danger was real or a false alert.

Millions of years of evolution have hardwired us so tightly that even a cockroach can scare us to death. It's irrational! When last did you hear of a cockroach attacking a human being? But our fears still manage us, we are not in control. It would seem to be true that "you can take the person out of the Stone Age, but not the Stone Age out of the person."[16]

Experience has taught me that almost all my fears were overblown and self-created.

The way to manage your fears is to act – jump into the water and start swimming. Another way is to take the big "risk" and break it down into smaller pieces. It's easier to push through smaller fears, achieve smaller milestones, and then build your confidence – with every achievement – until you've executed the entire mission.

> **When you act again and again – and find that the fear was pointless – you learn to diminish the fear and to feed your courage.**

---

16 https://www.speakingtree.in

Factor #3: Establish routines

Self–discipline is the ability to make yourself do what you should do, when you should do it, whether you like it or not.

– Elbert Hubbard

Self-discipline is the key to achieving success. At the heart of almost every success lies a person practicing some form of self-discipline. Whether you want success in your personal or professional life, you must cultivate the habit of self – discipline. But how is discipline created? What allows one person to be in control of their life, wake up every day at 5 a.m., and run 10 kilometers while another fails to lose 5 kilograms, no matter what they do? The answer lies in our ability to develop habits.

Our brain is a lazy machine that needs to be programmed. Self-discipline is like writing a program. It takes some time and effort, but when the program is ready, the CPU runs it in the core without any latency.[17] It's fast and efficient. It behaves "automatically."

More than 40% of our behaviors are habit-driven.[18] So, the best way to build self-discipline is by developing habits and routines. You have no chance of forcing yourself to brush your teeth twice a day by practicing self-discipline. The only way to do it is by developing a habit and, from that point onwards, your brain is no longer

---

17 Latency is the delay between a user's action and a web application's response to that action, often referred to, in networking terms, as the total round trip time it takes for a data packet to travel.
18 https://www.theworldcounts.com/happiness/psychology-of-habits

occupied with the task. It becomes automatic. Perhaps that is what Aristotle meant when he said that "good habits formed at youth make all the difference."

A habit is a behavior that, having been repeated often enough, becomes automatic. The formula, the secret that is not common knowledge, is that building almost any new habit takes 40 days. That's it! Not years, not randomness, not luck. 40 days is all we need to build habits! Almost all religions mark 40 days as a spiritually significant period. As Rick Warren puts it, "Whenever God wanted to prepare someone for his purposes, he took 40 days." In fact, the number 40 appears 146 times in the Bible. Moses spent "40 days and nights" on Mount Sinai receiving his instructions from God, while Jesus appeared to his disciples 40 days after being resurrected. Numerologists see the number 40 as signifying "trials, testing and a period that comes before results."

One day, you wake up in the morning and say, "I must start exercising. I'm strong. I'm not postponing it anymore, it's important for my health and my self– esteem, I'm starting." You set your alarm for 5:00 a.m., you wake up, brush your teeth(!), and put on your running shoes. They look brand new. You bought them two years ago and have hardly used them since then. You say to yourself, "This time I will not quit. I'm taking it seriously." You manage to run for 30 minutes. You get home feeling alive, take a shower, and go to work. You did it. You feel great and understand the importance of exercise to your quality of life. You make the decision: "From now on I'm exercising three times a week!" You're motivated, and your self–discipline is strong now. In the first week, you run three times, as planned. And then life turns against you, there's pressure at work, you go to sleep late, and suddenly you can't find the time. The shoes go back into the closet, and you get on with your daily challenges. Sound familiar? The same thing happened to you with your diet, saving money, reading, and learning to play the guitar... You're not the only one...

So, what went wrong? You simply drifted back into the old, well-rooted, habit of not doing your new activity.

Adding a new habit sometimes means breaking very old ones.

You can develop habits for every important aspect of life, just like brushing your teeth: habits for daily exercise, healthy eating, or even making money. With self – discipline, whether at home or work, we can build habits to do tasks that we don't like but which are important for our long-term results. Self-discipline, like the muscles in your body, gets tired when used frequently and intensely. This is the main reason we fail to make changes in our life. Self-discipline can last a week or two, but to make it a habit, you need 40 days in a row.

This window of three to four weeks is the gap between success and failure. I call it the "habit gap." Once you're aware of it, you need to push yourself for another three to four weeks. That's it! You need to "fool" your inner motivation system. You can also use external support, such as a coach, or be part of a team that will assist you to close the habit gap.

You need to cross the extra mile by building a bridge to close the gap.

Once you complete another three to four weeks in a row, you have programmed your brain to make it a routine. You have created a new habit. When the new habit is established, you are in autopilot mode. You no longer have to think about doing it. From now on it will be difficult for you to live without the new habit. Maintaining an activity as a daily routine is ten times easier when it becomes a habit. You can and should build new habits! I do this exercise even for small habits that I want to form. I have trained my "habits generator" with small changes, for example drinking coffee with two sugars to no sugar. At first, when you don't put sugar in, the coffee will taste awful. After a few days, it will not taste so bad. After a week, it will be okay. But after 40 days? Now, I can't drink coffee with sugar.

My next challenge was to stop drinking diet soda and switch to water. In the beginning, I didn't like drinking water at all. I forced myself to start drinking water every time I wanted my soft drink. After 40 days, and subsequently, I only drink water. Now I can't drink diet or regular soda. I changed my bad habit into a healthy one.

Our lives are filled with hundreds of habits. Some habits lift you up and some habits pull you down. Healthy people have healthy habits while unhealthy people have unhealthy habits. Successful people have successful habits, while unsuccessful people don't! The earlier you start working on creating habits, the larger will be the success you achieve in life.

The main reason that people do not achieve success is quite simply that they procrastinate. People say, "I must keep in shape, I'll start practicing tomorrow," "I must lose some weight, I'll start a diet tomorrow," "I must stop drinking... ," "I must quit smoking... ," "I must change my career..." "I must stop shouting at my children..." We all understand that taking a certain action is a must, but we keep postponing it. When postponing things to a later stage is your habit, the result you get is procrastination as a way of life. It is as simple as that. Start now.

For every moment of procrastination, you pay a big price – you waste your life and miss the opportunity to benefit from the wonders that life is willing to offer you when you're successful. When you say, "I'll start tomorrow," you're throwing away an entire day that will never come back.

> **We have a limited time on earth. When you change the habit of procrastinating, and make a new habit of doing things now, you change your life results.**

Don't lose hope. Self–discipline and habits are behaviors that can be learned.

Setting goals for success

The first step in breaking old habits and creating new ones lies in setting goals. As Napoleon Hill, one of my heroes, said, "A goal is a dream with a deadline." A Harvard MBA Business School study on goal setting found that the 3% of the students, that had both written goals and a plan, were making ten times as much as the 97% that did not![19]

Set goals for the important aspects of your life, the ones where success is most important, your family, children, relationships, lifestyle, finances, and career.

The importance of goal–setting is expressed, a little more humorously, but no less accurately, in this piece from Alice in Wonderland, by Lewis Carroll:

Alice: Would you tell me, please, which way I ought to go from here?

The Cheshire Cat: That depends a good deal on where you want to get to.

---

19 https://www.wanderlustworker.com/the-harvard-mba-business-school-study-on-goal-setting/

Alice: I don't much care where–

The Cheshire Cat: Then it doesn't matter which way you go.

Even with the most accurate GPS, you will not find your way if you don't know your destination. Clear goals and targets are the keys to success. Once you have a clear vision of your big dream and a winning picture, goals are the milestones, the details, of the plan. It is important to have a detailed plan and to commit to a timeline. Your goals need specific details and execution dates. Not general ones. You can adjust and correct goals and timelines. As with a GPS, re-routing is a feature, not a bug. There are many different routes you can take to reach your "big dream." Once the destination is set and clear, your brain (your GPS) will hit the target. It doesn't matter if it takes you more time than you planned or if you choose alternative routes. If your GPS is configured, and your goals are set and clear, you will reach your destination.

It's very important to write down your goals on a piece of paper in your own handwriting. Then read and review them daily. Once you write your goals down and read them daily, you are committed, and they become a part of you.

An ambitious goal excites you and gives you energy and passion. At the same time, it needs to scare you and plant some doubt about your ability to achieve the challenge. If the goal does not look big and scary enough, it will not motivate you enough to wake up and chase it each day.

You can work hard to achieve your major goals only when the "why" and the "what" are crystal clear in your mind. Ask yourself:

• Why exactly do I need to achieve my big goal?

• Why is it important to me?

• What kind of a person will I become when I have attained it?

• What quality of life will I and my loved ones have when I have attained it?

When your "why" is strong and important enough, you will find your "how," and you will become unbeatable. When you encounter challenges along the way, you will not give up. You will persevere until you succeed.

I had a dream to complete an Ironman. The goal was to stand on the starting line in Frankfurt on July 8th, 2018, and then consecutively swim 3.8 km, cycle 180 km, and run a marathon of 42.2 km. It's one of the most difficult competitions in the world. The picture of myself "winning," by achieving this feat, was clear in my head. My arms extended into the sky, the smile spread over my face, I could feel the joy of making it happen, the mental strength of being invincible. I imagined myself exhausted and energized at the same time. I wanted to be a role model for my four daughters – to lead by example – not with empty words, but to show them that anything is possible if you really want it. My daughters saw me working hard, sweating, waking up every day at 5 a.m., and practicing through rain and cold. They saw me, in winter and summer, outside, training for hours. I got injured, I struggled, I failed, and I recovered. I never gave up.[20]

When I finally achieved my goal, I had become a different person. I had developed the strength that I had imagined. I succeeded by creating habits that got me out of bed every day at 5 a.m., whether I wanted to or not. I built brick after brick, and I broke wall after wall. Every day, I increased my distance. I improved, I built a stronger body, a stronger mentality, and a stronger spirit.

My first Ironman competition was tough. At the "breaking points," I imagined myself talking to my daughters, telling them that they could succeed at every challenge they have in their lives, that there are no boundaries and no limitations, they can become anything

---

20 I will speak more about this process in Chapter VIII, Physical Fitness.

they want if they just want it enough. These conversations inspired and encouraged me to continue, just don't stop, just do another step forward I told myself. It took me 13 hours and 40 minutes to cross the finish line.

On 8 July 2018, I became the Ironman I had seen myself becoming in my imagination.

Do you have written goals? If not, this is the right time. Now.

Start creating new habits today. Write a list of new habits you want to create and old habits you want to remove. Start small with an easier one, then move to the next one, and strengthen your confidence until you master it.

Factor #4: Focus

Wherever focus goes, energy flows.

– Tony Robbins

We live in a world with so many distractions. We're spending time with our children and getting emails from work; we're at work and are continuously distracted by WhatsApp messages from our families. Nowadays, people struggle to focus. There are too many parallel tasks and too much competition for our attention.

If you take a magnifying glass and focus the sunbeams, you can light a fire in 50 seconds. That's the kind of focus I am talking about here. Focus is power. Focus is taking all your attention and concentrating it through a magnifying glass. No matter what you're doing, give it 100%. That is what focus means. Do only that task. When you spend time with your children, be 100% present with them. Turn off your phone, give them all your attention. Do the same with work, with your partner, your friends, and your hobbies. Spending 30 minutes with 100% focus on your children is way better than being with them for an entire day that is full of distractions.

Picture the following scene: You are sitting on your comfortable sofa; your children are playing around you. Your mind is elsewhere. You're worried about the meeting tomorrow and how you're going to pay the bills at the end of the month. You tell yourself endless stories that make the future look even darker and more frightening. Your mind moves from the future to the past. You think about the opportunity you missed to buy real estate back in 2005. The prices were so low then. You feel regret and anger. You blame yourself and your spouse. You move to the past again, thinking that if you had just dared to buy it at that time, you would be in a completely different place now. You could have had a big house and a garage to park your luxury car. You fall asleep and wake up on the sofa at 6:30 a.m., disturbed by the garbage truck outside. The children left the lounge long ago. They've eaten their dinner, thanked God for the food they have, showered, and shared their excitement about school with their mother. During the time you were sitting on the sofa, moving between the future and the past, you have missed the only thing that really exists – the present, the moment of now.

The reason we find it so difficult to focus is that we simply struggle to stay in the present.

> **The past is history, the future is a myth. The present, now, is all we have.**

Life only happens in the here and now. Many people are not present most of the time. They are busy with everything except the most important thing, the only thing that is real – the present.

The past is history and can't be changed. It's a memory. It can be a good memory or a bad memory, and we can learn from it. But dwelling on it, complaining about what we missed, having regrets, and, of course, blaming others, will not change a thing. If you are holding too tightly to the past, do what you need to forgive and let it go. Carrying the past into the present, through resentment and regret, is a burden that impedes success.

The future is fiction. It doesn't exist. It's all in our head, stories about stories. Worrying about the future does not change it. Worry is a waste of energy and imagination! Taking action, and choosing trust and hope, has more impact on the "future" than worrying about fears and disasters that haven't happened and probably never will.

When you understand that life is only now and that there is nothing else, you start to live. You start connecting with others, having an impact on them, influencing them, and inspiring them. Your life becomes meaningful.

Do you have a real reason to postpone things to tomorrow? Tomorrow will be your "now" again. Is there a real difference between the now of the present moment and the now in one minute or one month or one year from now? So why would you postpone anything that you can do now to the same "now" later?

| **Procrastination is a misunderstanding of the power of now.** |

Be present in every single moment. Do what you want to do, now; execute, act, don't postpone. You will succeed in ways you cannot even begin to imagine.

Give your focus, time, and attention to what matters most. The "urgent" things will always try to steal time from the "important" things. Choose your priorities and act accordingly. Stay in focus!

Afterword: Balance is the key to success

Balance is not something you find, it's something you create.
– Jana Kingsford

When you fly in an airplane, the safety instruction guide tells you that when there is a lack of oxygen, and the mask is released, you should first use it for yourself and only then take care of your child. The reason is simple. If you use the oxygen first for your child, you will probably die from asphyxiation and your child will not be able to take care of him/herself. Neither of you will survive.

My family is the most important thing in my life. To be able to take care of them, I need to be in balance. That means I must take care of myself – my whole self. If I ignore my career, my financial situation will deteriorate, and my family will suffer. If I don't take care of my body, my energy levels will drop, disease and illness will follow, and I will become a burden to my family. If I don't invest in my personal growth, I will not be able to pass knowledge and wisdom on to my children. If my emotional intelligence is undeveloped, I will be unable to control my anger and my moods will suffer. That is why balance is essential for success. Hillary Clinton expressed it best when she said, "Don't confuse having a career with having a life." In my view, balance is about "having a life."

Imagine your life as a bicycle wheel. Each aspect of your life is represented as a spoke in the wheel, ranked from 1 to 10. To have a successful life, the wheel needs to spin smoothly. When the wheel is not balanced, for example, your financial status ranks at 9, your career is at 10, but your health or family relationships are at 1 or 2, you will not be balanced. The wheel will not spin properly or move at all.

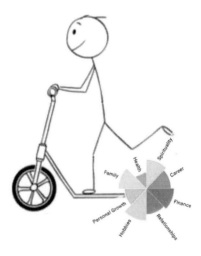

Your life is stuck! You are not in balance, and you will feel pain and stress. To be successful, your life needs to be balanced. When you have balance, you can manage the speed of your life. You can slow down when you want to relax, and you can accelerate when you want to grow and achieve more.

> **Balance ties everything in this chapter – and probably this book – together. There is no real success without balance.**

VI. THE FORMULA FOR HEALTH

Health =

1. Eat when hungry; drink when thirsty
2. Eat food without labels
3. Recharge your battery
4. Keep active
5. Keep your emotions in motion

When a flower doesn't bloom, you fix the environment in which it grows, not the flower.

– Alexander Den Heijer

During my early twenties, I, like most of my friends, was strong and healthy.

Twenty years later, as we began to hit our forties, the picture had changed. I felt like the member of a wrong club – a club of unhealthy people. One friend had diabetes, another had arthritis, the third had asthma and the fourth had cancer. The "lucky" ones were just overweight and overstressed, and I was no exception. I no longer wanted to be a member of this club.

The amount of illness seemed irrational and unnatural to me. I wanted to understand the phenomenon. Looking at international statistics, it seemed to be a worldwide club. I found a piece of research, called "The China Study," which found a direct correlation between the food we eat, as well as environmental conditions, and illness and mortality.[21] The number of diseases human beings were facing, and the amount of people afflicted by these diseases looked completely unrealistic to my amateur eye. There were literally billions of sick people in the world![22]

I was amazed by the magnitude of the problem. Medicine was seemingly advancing but there were almost no cures. Long before Covid−19, we faced a pandemic of diseases that the mainstream media did not seem to be making a lot of noise about.

I knew that I had to find ways to reclaim my health.

So, at age 40, I changed my lifestyle completely. I was determined to become healthier than I'd ever been. No more excuses or delays. I knew that the future status of my health would be a direct result of my actions from that day forward.

> **Today's lifestyle equals tomorrow's quality of life.**

Health is a funny thing. We understand its importance and pray for good health. When asked, most people say that it is the most important thing in life. But healthy behavior is often the first thing we neglect and look at what happens: The only time we appreciate health is when we're sick. When you have a headache, a cold, or a grain of sand in your eye, you suddenly understand how fragile life is. The smallest ailment can shift your life, disrupt your routine, and make you miserable. Suddenly, all your "big issues" become irrelevant. At that moment, all you want is your healthy life back, and you are willing to do anything to return to your "normal" state.

---

21 https://nutritionstudies.org/the-china-study/

22 All indicators point to a causal link between modernization in the last 100 years and morbidity. Research has shown a clear relationship between the number of fast food stores in a country and the prevalence of cancer, diabetes and heart disease.

What would you be willing to pay to recover from diabetes, cancer or a stroke? Is there any limit to the amount you would be willing to pay? Is there any action you would not take to reverse your illness?

> **Good health is like oxygen. You only realize its importance when you don't have it.**

Because our bodies can regenerate, maintaining a healthy lifestyle can postpone, or even eliminate, the risk of illness. Within the next seven years, almost all the cells in your body will die and be replaced. Each type of cell goes through this cycle at a different pace. The cells that make up your stomach lining, for instance, complete the cycle of renewal every five days. For your blood cells, the cycle takes four months. Your skin renews itself every year and the bones are renewed every seven years. These ongoing cycles of cellular replacement mean that, every day, your body is rebuilding itself to be potentially better, stronger, and more vital. That also means that no matter what condition you're currently in physically, mentally, and emotionally, you can start now to make meaningful changes!

From the age of 40, your body's metabolism gets slower, the regeneration of cells slows down, stem cells divide less quickly and efficiently, and eventually, the rate of dying cells outpaces the rate of new cells being born. Consequently, the aging process begins to accelerate.

Each one of us has a chronological age and a biological age. While we can't do anything about the growing number of candles on our birthday cakes, the good news is that we can directly influence our biological age. At the age of 40, your biological age can be 15 years more or less than your chronological age. We all know people in their 40's who look like, feel like, and have the energy of, a

25 – year-old, and we all know people at 50 who look like, feel like, and have the exhaustion of, a 70-year-old. Research has found that some form of daily physical activity can reduce your biological age by up to nine years.[23] Other parameters that influence our biological age are our environment, the food we eat, our stress levels, the quality and amount of sleep we get, and our attitude towards life. The bad news is that to slow down the aging process, we must work harder each year to get effective results.

> **We have the power to create our future. What price are you willing to pay to stay youthful?**

In my pursuit of health, I got lost in so many details. There are endless guidelines on what, when, and how much we should be eating. In a desperate attempt to keep up with the rapid pace at which health and nutritional information is thrown at us, we lose touch with something invaluable. We forget about simplicity – going back to the basics.

I was curious to know whether there is one "truth" that covers all aspects of life. It took me a long time to find it. I had to go almost 900 years back in time to find the answers.

Rabbi Moshe ben Maimon (Rambam), who was born in 1138 in Cordova, was one of the most illustrious Jewish figures in medicine and philosophy. His most famous declaration was:

Whoever conducts himself in the ways which we have drawn up, I will guarantee that he will not become ill throughout his life, until he reaches an advanced age and dies. He will not need a doctor.

His body will remain intact and healthy throughout his life.

When you study the Rambam manuscript, you begin to understand

---

23 https://www.sciencedaily.com/releases/2017/05/170510115211.htm

that this declaration is rock solid and deserves to be taken seriously.

This concept of "natural health" was taken up by others, most notably by Herbert M. Shelton (1895–1985), who was an American physician best known in circles of alternative healthcare. According to the Rambam, Shelton, and many other followers, the root of all disease comes from one source: an accumulation of toxins in the blood above the toleration point. And the crisis, the so-called disease—be it cold, flu, pneumonia, headache, or typhoid fever—is an attempt to eliminate the toxins.

> **Dis-ease is simply nature endeavoring to rid the body of toxins.**

Shelton stated it best when he said:

It is the law of life that the body resists and expels whatever it cannot use.

Disease is vital resistance to non-usable, therefore, injurious substances.[24]

Long before Shelton, in the first chapter of one of his most famous books, "Deo't," the Rambam wrote:

Since maintaining a healthy and sound body is among the ways of God – for one cannot understand or have any knowledge of the Creator, if he is ill – therefore, he must avoid that which harms the body and accustom himself to that which is healthful and helps the body become stronger. They are as follows: a person should never eat unless he is hungry, nor drink unless thirsty.

He should never put off relieving himself, even for an instant. Rather, whenever he [feels the] need to urinate or move his bowels, he should do so immediately.

---

24 Hygienic Review. Vol. XXXIV July 1978 No. 11, Disease Is Remedial Activity, by Herbert M. Shelton

> **The formula for a healthy life, free of illness, is simple.**
> **We need to keep the toxic levels in our bodies low. We need**
> **to stop poisoning ourselves to death.**

For optimal health, the toxins that enter our body minus the toxins we remove from our body should be zero or close to it. Put simply:

Toxins In minus Toxins Out = 0

Toxins enter our body through breath (inhalation), food, drink, skin, thoughts and emotions. We remove toxins from our body through breath (exhalation), urine, excrement, sweat (skin), and the power of our mind.

> **Every illness is the right reaction to the wrong stimulation!**

Nature does not make mistakes. It operates according to natural laws, in this case, the law of action-reaction. Every illness has a cause and is a response to our digression from natural laws. The laws are accurate and absolute. If we put our hands into a fire, we will get burnt. If we put our finger into a power socket, we will get electrocuted.

The purpose of every illness is self-correction. The pain that comes with it is a warning signal, a wake-up call, as it were. It may come as a gentle reminder, or it may present as an aggressive intrusion. It is nature's way of forcing us to change, of assisting us to fix what is broken, and to bring us back to health.

> **Nature always strives for perfection!**

We are responsible for both our health and its absence. External forces very rarely cause our health problems. We are the source of our problems, and we are the source of our own salvation. Advanced science clearly shows the connection between the disease and the place it is found in our bodies. Nothing happens randomly.

> **We get punished by our acts, not because of the acts!**

You are walking in the street when there is a gust of wind, and a grain of dust gets stuck in your throat. You start coughing. You go to the doctor and your doctor writes you a prescription to cure your illness, i.e., the cough. But the truth is that the cough is the cure and not the illness; it is your body's way of eliminating the grain of dust from your throat. The illness is the grain of dust.

The conventional health care system has confused illness and cure. It calls the cure illness and the illness cure.

Disturbing the body's ability to cure itself, through external medicine, often damages the natural process of health. The body is a very smart and strong machine. We abuse our bodies in so many ways. We smoke, drink alcohol, eat unhealthy food, do not sleep enough, and live with high-stress levels, anxiety, anger, and fear – yet our bodies continue to serve us. And while our bodies may continue to serve us, they are also accumulating toxins. The toxic levels increase until the body reaches a phase called the "healing crisis." Your body halts you; it shuts down the systems and forces you to rest. You lose your appetite so that your digestive system can shut down, and your fever goes up to accelerate your metabolism. All your internal forces begin shifting towards one mission: the elimination of toxins to shift your body back to its natural state of health. The toxins may emerge in the form of colds, sore throats, pneumonia, inflammation, dermatitis, or other smart ways that the body uses to cure itself.

The conventional healthcare system continues to fight the symptoms, trying to stop the runny nose, prescribing antibiotics against infection, and fighting the fever. Big Pharma peddles products that suppress our body's attempt to cure itself. And they do a great job! Just look at how many people are obese, or have high blood pressure, diabetes, and various cancers.

How can it be that there is so much illness in the modern world? Perhaps we are doing something wrong? The global pharmaceutical market is valued at over US$ 1.25 trillion. We spend so much on such poor results.

> **There are plenty of drugs for every disease, but almost no cure!**

Whenever possible, I avoid going to doctors.[25]

The modern healthcare system treats the symptoms rather than investigating their root causes. If you have a fever, the doctor will give you aspirin to reduce the fever. If you have an infection, you will be given antibiotics to fight it. If you suffer from anxiety or depression, a psychiatrist will give you antidepressants. If you have high blood pressure, you will get a lifetime prescription for beta – blocker pills, which block the effects of the hormone epinephrine. When you take beta-blockers, your heart beats more slowly and with less force, thereby reducing blood pressure. It is the equivalent of closing the tap in your garden when you are mistakenly standing on the hosepipe and water is splashing everywhere. The solution is not to close the tap, but to remove your foot.

The cause of high blood pressure is the constriction of the arteries. The cause of the constriction is fat that sticks to the inner shell of the arteries and blocks the flow of blood. Change your nutrition, the fat will disappear, and the flow will go back to its normal pressure.

---

25 Except for urgent life-saving medicine in which conventional medicine provides excellent solutions.

From cold to cancer

When your levels of toxicity rise, your body will look for alternative options to eliminate the toxins. When your body knows that you have enough vitality to be able to start and finish the cure, or cleansing process, the so-called "healing crisis" will begin.

It always starts small.

Your body cleans the toxins using a simple "cold." When your nose drips, the process of cleansing has started. Unfortunately, we are spoiled, and we do not understand our bodies' mechanisms. We would rather take a pill. We shoot the natural health process right in the foot (or some other part of our anatomy!). The leaking stops and the toxins have no way out. They stay in our bodies and look for alternative ways to exit. Your body waits for the second round while you continue to accumulate toxins. Your body gains energy, waiting to have enough vitality to win the second round. The symptoms now appear as stronger, for example, pneumonia. Your body tries to take the infected fluid out. It's a hard job; expelling the fluid from the lungs can be painful. We don't want to suffer, mainly because we think that our body is "confused," almost seeing it as "bad luck." This pneumonia is a disease that we must fight and kill. We return to the doctor who gives us antibiotics to kill the infection. Unfortunately, it works. We suppress the infection and hold the toxins inside. The toxicity levels continue to rise. The body waits for the next round. The ways of mother nature are wonderful. She does not give up so quickly. The next cycle kicks off. Your body now tries to expel the toxins through the skin, eyes, or ears. Medicine calls it by many names – dermatitis, if it is through the skin, ophthalmic, if it is through the eyes, or otitis, if it is through the ears. The list of conditions is endless and modern healthcare has a problem for every natural solution!

The "system" knows how to suppress every attempt by the body to cure itself.

And when your body has no vitality left to fight, the last phase appears. The toxic levels reach a stage when the cells are too toxic to rebuild correctly. Cancer appears.

Genetic defects are the weakest link in the chain. Each one of us comes with certain genetic predispositions, a family legacy. That is where the cancer will creep in. Some get brain cancer, while others get liver cancer. The cause of the cancer is not our defective genes, it is the accumulated toxins!

> **You need to keep your body clean of toxins, to let it do its job. Believe in your internal healing powers. Put simply, "Do not disturb."**

Except for rare and unfortunate cases, our bodies are naturally healthy. We cannot generate health. No external force, super food, or magic pill can create health. We look for shortcuts and buy fairytales. We want the pill that will bring us health without effort. A pill for longevity. A pill to stay young. We look for medicinal herbs that will reverse our illness. Whatever is quick and easy. But it does not exist. It is all wishful thinking. It is like dreaming of becoming a millionaire but not buying a lottery ticket. Huge industries exist solely to sell us magic potions that address these fake dreams.

Natural health

Fire's food is oxygen. Seeds need water, sun, and soil to grow. Ovules need offspring to generate new life. Babies need warmth and love to grow. Chickens need to incubate an egg for 20 days to spawn a healthy chick; disobey this law of nature and you end up with an omelet on your plate!

Nature is accurate and it works according to laws. We call it science. Health exists when we are in harmony with the laws of nature. Illness is a violation of the laws of nature. Knowing the laws – and acting accordingly – is the secret to a healthy life. Every creature knows instinctively, which food is best for it to consume. Lions are born to be carnivorous. They have the hunting senses, the physical structure, as well as the intestines, to digest raw meat. This is the type of food that lions need, to prosper. Cows are born to be vegetarian. Their entire anatomy, from their teeth to their digestive system, makes them fit to eat grass. They are too slow and clumsy to run after food. If cows had to hunt, they would starve to death! If the lion and the cow were to lose their instincts, resulting in the cow eating meat and the lion eating grass, they would both become extinct.

Imagine you are outside walking in the fields, enjoying nature, surrounded by oranges, apples, bananas, and mangos. The colors of the fruit shine and bring you joy. A few cows and chickens are running around you, enjoying eating the grass and seeds. After a few hours, you start feeling hungry. Nature offers you many options. You listen to your instincts. What are they telling you? "Go for the chicken, let's catch it, break its neck, cut the wings and eat a chicken snack? Or would you prefer bananas, mangos, or apples?"

Essentially, our cells require 16 main building blocks to function optimally. Carbon and nitrogen which we breathe, hydrogen and oxygen in the water that we drink, and another 11 elements (including magnesium, copper, calcium, sulfur, selenium, phosphorus, potassium, chlorine, iron, fluorine, zinc, and sodium).

> **Fruit and vegetables, which all contain these elements, provide the fuel that the human tank needs to function optimally.**

Like all creatures, humans need specific and accurate food compositions to grow and prosper. We do not have a natural appetite for raw meat. We were not born, and we are not anatomically fit, to be carnivorous. According to our instincts and our physical anatomy, we were born to eat mostly fruits and vegetables. The vitamins and minerals that we need are abundantly available from the earth. Our body cannot digest these elements directly. We need mediators. The roots of the tree collect the minerals and vitamins from the ground and package them into a "magic capsule" called fruit and vegetables. Our body has the mechanisms to decompose the fruit and vegetables and make the vitamins and the minerals available so that our cells can regenerate themselves.

We can, of course, also get these elements from meat or dairy. When we eat steak, we get these elements through the cow which ate these elements from the ground. But, as we get it second-hand, it is not the same quality as getting it from a piece of fruit.

Fooling our senses

All creatures are programmed to save energy and be efficient.

When a shark sees two fish, one which is 50m away and another which is 75m away, by instinct, it will always target the closer (or slower) fish. The shark will always try to expend minimum energy, on the one hand, while gaining maximum calories, on the other hand.

All creatures – including humans – operate according to the same principle. You are standing in the supermarket where you are faced with two choices:

- A 100-gram chocolate bar that contains 520 calories and can be eaten within 20 seconds.
- 100 grams of lettuce which contains 13 calories and takes 5 minutes to chew and swallow.

Your instincts want to gain maximum calories with minimum effort. So, the chocolate will clearly be your choice.

Unfortunately, modern food engineering has fooled our natural instincts. The industrial revolution, which began in the 18th century, shifted us away from our basic instincts. Today, when you eat schnitzel, your instincts do not recognize it as the same chicken you saw in the field. The chicken is covered with breadcrumbs and spices and deep-fried in oil. Add ketchup to it and you are as far away from a chicken as you could be!

Industrial food producers understand human behavior and have learned how to mislead our brains. Food engineering, which is now responsible for about 95% of the food we have in our supermarkets, has created unhealthy, concentrated foods that our natural instincts find almost impossible to resist. This "programming" starts early. Our children eat their Kinder Eggs, Doritos, Cheetos, Cheerios, fries with tomato sauce, and mayonnaise. So, we should not be surprised when they are not willing to eat fruit, vegetables, or salad. We damage our children's natural instincts from an early age. Most of the foods we buy are full of fats and sugars. Our children, and even we, cannot enjoy the sweet taste of a cucumber or an apple. We have covered our senses with layers of artificial substances. Everything we eat needs to be heavily salty or sweet to satisfy our faulty senses. We can hardly sense any natural tastes anymore.

Health comes from within.

All you must do is follow nature's rules. And do not disturb! Give your body the types of foods and liquids that it needs. Give it sleep, exercise, and peace of mind. Going back to the basics will have the most profound impact on your life. The formula for a healthy life is simple to deploy, follow me.

Factor #1: Eat when hungry; drink when thirsty

One should not eat until his stomach is full. Rather, [he should stop when] he has eaten to close to three-quarters of full satisfaction.

– Rambam, Deo't, Chapter 4

Fasting is practiced in many religions. While the specific reasons may differ, most fasting is associated with sacrifice and cleansing oneself.[26] There is a discipline, and self-sacrifice, associated with fasting that has positive effects on much more than just our physical bodies. The act of saying "no" to our desire for food creates an internal willpower that serves us beyond just fasting. It is a bit like playing "hard to get"; we become more attractive to positive forces and good energy when we resist the urge to give in to physical cravings.

I use fasting as a tool to balance my body and my soul. Fasting assists me to concentrate, and my brain becomes much sharper during the fasting period. Sometimes I drink water while fasting, while, at other times, I do not drink at all. My preferred fasting regime consists of restricting my eating to 8 hours and then not eating for 16 hours. The benefits of this practice, which is known as intermittent fasting, have been scientifically proven. I highly recommend it.

Nowadays, people eat for the wrong reasons. We have combined eating with our social lives. We eat by arrangement; nutrition is not really on the menu. We meet for "coffee," and we have business

26 www.culturalawareness.com

meetings at any given time of the day, including late dinners with alcohol. We eat because of stress, boredom, anxiety, depression, addiction, or just for the sake of temporary pleasure. The result is that we overeat, leading to our being overweight, obese, and ill.

Our stomach, which plays a major part in digestion, acts as both a mixer and a grinder of food. The stomach produces acids and powerful enzymes that break food down and change it into liquid. When we fill our stomachs, the acids and the liquids cannot enter the inner layers, meaning that only the food on the external level is digested. Our stomach is like a washing machine; if you fill it too much, the clothes come out dirty. Undigested food poisons our bodies. The conclusion is clear: never fill your stomach to its capacity. While the volume of our stomach, at around 50ml, is tiny, it can expand to four liters. When we eat to our full capacity, we drain our energy. Because the digestive system consumes huge amounts of our energy, all you want to do, after such a meal, is sleep. When we overeat, the other systems in our body also struggle to function.

We confuse hunger and starvation. Consequently, many of us have developed a fear of hunger. We may be living in an age of abundance, but the reality is that skipping a meal or two will not cause any harm. In fact, the opposite is true – the practice benefits and heals our bodies.

> **Connecting ourselves to a feeling of hunger is one of the keys to a healthy life.**

Hunger before meals boosts your growth hormones, which aids in regeneration and keeps you looking and feeling younger. It even promotes better digestion and improves your body's blood sugar regulation and insulin sensitivity which facilitate weight regulation.

When we're hungry, the levels of a hormone called ghrelin rise which boosts our mood and energizes us.

Now that you understand the importance of feeling hungry, don't fear it. Search for this feeling, stay there for a while, and enjoy the free benefits it provides!

While depriving your body temporarily of food may have advantages, keeping it hydrated is no less important. Staying hydrated by drinking enough fluids is one of the most important things you can do for the health of your body.

Here are the top three reasons that you should give water more of your attention:[27]

- **Dehydration impairs brain function:** On average, our body is made up of 60% water, and our brain is made up of 75% water. Research shows that a total body water loss of merely 2% can lead to poor concentration, impaired mental performance, low mood, and frequent headaches. This loss can happen easily during normal daily activities.

- **Water helps to prevent and relieve constipation:** Dehydration of the colon is one of the major reasons that people experience dry, pebbly, or no stool at all for one or more days in a row. Having one or two well-formed bowel movements each day is essential for detoxification. Therefore, drinking enough water helps rid the body of excess hormones, toxins, and many other substances that can pose a threat to our health.

- **Water helps keep the skin looking healthy:** Your skin is your largest organ and is made up of about 65% water. Dehydration can result in dry, flaky, and sometimes wrinkled–looking skin. Drink water; look younger!

---

27 https://www.healthline.com/nutrition

A river without a flow of water turns to mud. It is the same for our bodies. Without proper hydration, toxins and other body waste remain in the system, causing disease. Many people drink coffee, soft drinks, alcohol, and everything besides water. Patrick Holford, the author of "The Optimum Nutrition Bible," had an overweight patient with chronic headaches, high blood pressure, and low levels of energy. After a short interview, he found that she was totally dehydrated. For years, she had only drunk diet soda and coffee. Her cells were dehydrated, which affected her health badly. Just by changing the habit of drinking diet soda to eight glasses of water a day, the chronic headaches disappeared, and, after six weeks, she had lost weight and felt more energetic.

I quit drinking sweetened fizzy drinks and have moved completely to water and sparkling water. As I recounted earlier, I went from coffee and milk, with two spoons of sugar, to unsweetened black coffee. Now, my coffee tastes like coffee. I used to drink eight cups of coffee a day. I reduced it to once a day, and, after a while, to one cup of coffee per week. I drink at least eight glasses of water a day. Now, my body cleanses itself, flushing the toxins from my body.

Factor #2: Eat food without labels

Look deep, deep into nature, and then you will
understand everything better.

– Albert Einstein

You are what you eat! Healthy food will keep you healthy while unhealthy food will cause you to become unhealthy. Knowing this, I have simplified how I choose which foods to eat and which to avoid. I choose "food without labels," and I avoid the rest.

Foods contain different combinations of nutrients, minerals, and other healthy substances. No single food can supply all the nutrients in the quantity you need. For example, oranges provide vitamin C but not vitamin B12; carrots provide vitamin A but not vitamin C. To make sure you get all the nutrients and other substances needed for health, choose the recommended number of daily servings from each of the five major food groups – whole grains, vegetables, fruits, proteins, and fat.

While food is the key to health, nature also provides us with a great source of vitamins in the form of sunlight. The reason we feel better in summer is that exposure to sunlight increases our vitamin D which boosts our mood, mind, immunity, and bone health.

Although sunlight may be free, food is not. It is difficult to find healthy food in supermarkets, these days. Americans spend the majority of their food budget on processed foods.[28] Unlike whole

---

28 https://grist.org/food

foods, processed foods are treated in some ways after being harvested or butchered. Almost all these processed foods contain additives, substances intended to change the food in some way before they are sold to consumers. Industrial foods contain antibiotics, hormones, pesticides, and chemicals to keep them unspoiled for a long period, reduce the production cost, and add sweetness and color to market the products.

> **Manufacturers do everything to make the food cheap and tasty, and nothing to make it healthy for you.**

Once I became aware of this information, I went looking for healthy food at the supermarket for my family. I began studying the labels on the back of the products, and immediately knew that something was wrong. All the foods contained so many additives. The more I investigated foods and their ingredients, the more I began to understand the severity of the problem.

I decided to keep it simple: I eat food that is unprocessed and as close to its natural state as possible. 95% of what I now eat is natural food: fresh unprocessed food, free of labels, and preservatives, wherever possible. While my knowledge may have caused behavior that some would see as "extreme," I am not a fanatical person. However, knowing the truth – and ignoring it – is a crime.

I also brought these changes home. I asked Talia to avoid buying unhealthy food, sweets, and salty snacks. Twice a week, I go to the market and buy fresh vegetables, fruits, and eggs, from farms around my city. I begin my day by drinking water with lemon, mint and ginger as this keeps my blood pH level alkaline, thereby avoiding a build-up of acid in my system (which is called acidosis). I then do my daily exercise regime of running, cycling, or swimming.

One hour later, I have a fresh juice made of carrots, apples, celery, and ginger. If I feel hungry before lunch, I eat seasonal fruits. For lunch, I eat a salad with seasonal vegetables or a hot meal which may include steamed vegetables, and beans, peas, and, of course, Israel's staple – chickpeas. I try to finish my day with a light, fresh salad, and fruit such as watermelon, apples, or bananas. By 7 pm, I have finished eating for the day.

Antioxidants (for a longer life)

An optimal intake of antioxidant nutrients is the key to living a long and healthy life. Antioxidants "switch on" Sirtuin 1, nicknamed the survival gene, which promotes DNA repair. Further, it also favorably affects over a hundred genes that help to program longevity. So apart from its specific effects in slowing down various aspects of cellular aging, Sirtuin 1 also protects against heart disease, brain damage, and even cancer. It's one of the strongest anti-aging agents.

Fruit and vegetables have the highest antioxidant levels, so eating a variety of them daily will keep your antioxidants at a good level. Fruits that have strong natural colors – greens, yellows, reds, oranges, and blues, such as grapes, blueberries, blackberries, raspberries, Goji berries, prunes, and raisins – contain lots of antioxidants. Herbs and spices, such as cinnamon, turmeric, clove, oregano, cumin, ginger, basil, and mustard, are also high in antioxidants.

By eating these foods, your body is more able to fight bacteria or disease. High levels of antioxidants cure infections that the body needs to fight daily. You can see this easily from the color of your urine; once your body is not infected, your urine becomes light yellow.

Since changing my diet, my uninfected, un-poisoned body can function normally, replacing and repairing cells on a daily basis. The cycle of my body now functions smoothly. Defective cells are replaced by new and healthy cells, and my body continuously rebuilds itself to an ever-improving condition. My body is strong now. I am not afraid of microbes or viruses; I have the confidence that my body can defeat any flu or infections. In 2020, before vaccinations had been produced, I tested positive for Covid-19. After two days of symptoms, I recovered fully.

Try it yourself. Don't believe me blindly. Make the changes and, in 40 days, you will feel lighter, more energetic, and will have much more vitality than you have ever had.

Control your sugar

Not all sugars are born equal. Natural sugar from fruits, in the right quantity, is healthy while processed sugar can kill you. The USDA estimates that the average American consumes 42½ teaspoons (168 grams) of sugar per day. That is 61 kilograms of sugar a year! [29]

When your blood sugar is low, you feel tired and hungry. If you refuel with fast-energy-releasing, high-glycemic loaded carbohydrates (sweet or refined foods), you cause your blood sugar to rise rapidly, and your body dumps the excess into storage as fat. Then, your blood sugar level drops again. This cycle leads to weight gain and increases the likelihood of diabetes. To balance your blood sugar, eat more slow-release foods, such as fresh fruit and vegetables and whole-grain carbohydrates.

Moshe, an elderly relative of mine, turned 74 in 2020. At 35, he was diagnosed with Type II Diabetes. To control his sugar levels, he used to inject a few doses of insulin every day. Over the years, as a result of the injections, his pancreas weakened, and the quantity of insulin increased accordingly. By his late 60s, he was injecting about 60 units of short-acting insulin per day. He started to

29 https://www.dhhs.nh.gov/dphs/nhp/documents/sugar.pdf

havedifficulty walking, and amputation of his legs loomed large.

During my natural health studies, I had heard about many Type II diabetics who had fully weaned themselves off insulin by changing their lifestyles and diets. The theoretical explanations were clear to me, i.e., it was all about removing toxins from the body and controlling the diet to control the sugar. I was fully convinced that I could assist Moshe. I asked him to read and listen to the testimonies of people who had healed themselves. I spent days trying to convince him that there are natural alternatives to insulin. I gave him all the rational explanations of what he needed to do. Eventually, his only objection was: "If it's so simple to cure diabetes, why is this not well known? Why does the conventional health system use insulin as the default treatment?" I did not give up, however. Finally, something shifted inside him, and I got his attention: "I'm ready, please give me the menu and I will follow your instructions for a few months." He changed his diet completely and started exercising daily. The change was faster than I had expected. Within one month, Moshe had completely stopped needing his short-acting insulin at all! His nightly dose of long-acting insulin was sufficient. Two months later, his walking had improved and the risk of losing his legs had passed. He still "steals" chocolate and cakes, from time to time, and runs to inject some insulin. But at least he can run! It's very difficult to change a 70-year-old person's habits, but the alternative to not changing these habits is unbearable. Moshe developed his diabetes after very traumatic experiences during the Lebanon War. He believes that had he had the nutritional knowledge then, his pancreas would have been able to rejuvenate itself, and that he could have lived a life free of the insulin on which he had become dependent since his late 30s.

Food intolerances and allergies

I used to suffer from allergic rhinitis. My allergies used to hit every spring, like clockwork when the blossoms are in the air and the olive trees bloom. For a few weeks, my nose was blocked and bleeding, I could hardly breathe, and I suffered from persistent headaches. I was not alone. Millions of people have seasonal, environmental, and food allergies. Some food ingredients cause classic food allergies. This is when the immune system produces specific IgE antibodies. These antibodies cause an immediate allergic reaction. The symptoms appear within seconds or minutes: severe swelling, breathing difficulty, rash, itching skin, or even anaphylactic shock. People with these allergies usually know which foods, or which type of tree, flower, or animal is causing the problems because the symptoms appear right away, alerting us to avoid them. It's difficult to cure these types of allergies, but it's possible to minimize their effect on the quality of your life. Since I changed my diet and began to exercise daily, my allergy symptoms have almost completely disappeared.

When she was about two years old, my daughter, Yael, began displaying extreme mood swings, as well as developing skin problems (notably dermatitis) all over her body. Talia and I tried so many treatments, from skin cream to baobab tree oil and powders, Dead Sea mud, relaxation techniques, and, in general, walking around her on eggshells. Nothing seemed to help. The turning point came when she was seven years old. Following my success with eliminating my own allergies, Talia and I suspected that there was a high probability that our daughter's problems came from something she had been eating since she was a baby or was eating regularly now. I did further research on food allergies and sensitivities. The pieces of the puzzle suddenly came together. We had my daughter tested for food sensitivities at a lab in the UK and they came back to us with a list of eight potential foods (out of a possible 132) that she should avoid. These included wheat, dairy, and eggs. We started there.

Four weeks after we eliminated these foods, we began to notice major changes. Her eczema disappeared, as did her moods and anger. We had a new daughter. Looking back, it seemed so simple. We had found a direct correlation between the food she was eating and her body's reactions. We could have spent a lifetime treating her symptoms. It took one change of direction to address the underlying cause, and it worked.

This type of allergy (IgG), or food intolerance, while unknown to most people, is the hidden cause of many chronic illnesses. The symptoms caused by food intolerance are varied. They usually cause gastrointestinal symptoms, such as bloating, diarrhea, nausea, vomiting, irritable bowel, and can include skin rashes and sometimes fatigue, joint pains, dark circles under the eyes, night sweats, and other chronic conditions. Food intolerance, which is much more common than food allergies (IgE), is not caused by the immune system but by toxicity in the digestive tract. Enzymes are required to help with the breakdown of natural substances found in certain foods. If these enzymes are missing, or in short supply, then eating the food can cause the above symptoms because a part of the food content cannot be properly processed by the body. The major problem with food intolerance is that the symptoms can appear days or weeks after consuming the food. Hence, finding a correlation between the food and symptoms is not straightforward, making it difficult to eliminate the food that our body has rejected. Because we are not aware of what food caused the problem, we continue to regularly consume this food. After a while, the food intolerance, which has been left unattended, compromises the immune system. The consequences are infection and inflammation. When infection and inflammation remain unmanaged in our body, the infection becomes chronic. When I understood food intolerances, I was shocked. In some extreme cases, children with ADHD, and even mental deficiencies, which remain unmanaged for years, can be cured by changing the foods that are causing "infections" in their brain. The children continue to eat these foods without knowing that they are causing chronic infections and illnesses. Food intolerance (IgG) can, in many cases, be cured. Our bodies generate new enzymes at their own pace. For example, when we drink milk, there are specific lactase enzymes that digest the lactose (milk sugar). Drinking milk daily depletes the lactase enzyme and leaves the body with a shortage. When there are not enough enzymes to digest the lactose from the milk, we suffer from abdominal pains and other symptoms. The way to cure food intolerances is to eliminate the specific food for 40 days. During this period, the body generates sufficient enzymes to digest the specific food completely. If you maintain a sufficient level of enzymes in your body, the problem will be solved. Listen to your body; it will tell you the right quantity of food to consume to keep yourself in balance.

I highly recommend that you and your family get checked for food intolerances and change your diets accordingly. Waking up every morning with abdominal pain, constipation, and headaches simply isn't normal, it's not a part of you, it's not "the way my body is." These symptoms shouldn't be part of your life. Feeling good and pain-free should be your "standard."

Reduce your exposure to heavy metals
While not causally related to food, it is important to mention one more important factor in keeping your body free of toxins. We need

to keep our exposure to heavy metals, such as lead, mercury, arsenic, and cadmium, as low as possible as they have toxic effects.

Throughout our lives, our bodies accumulate heavy metals from sources such as seafood (mercury); dental fillings (mercury); tap water (lead); air pollution (zinc, copper, lead, mercury); cosmetics, deodorants, and shampoo (aluminum); and cigarettes (cadmium).

Technology now enables us to conduct simple tests to measure the level of heavy metal in our bodies. One single hair is all that's needed to determine your exposure level.[30]

The best foods for removing heavy metals from your body are wheatgrass, chlorella, spirulina, cilantro, and garlic.

There are many detoxification programs and recipes depending on your individual needs. Many programs follow a seven-day schedule, as that is the amount of time it takes the body to cleanse the blood. Most programs suggest fasting on liquids for two days, followed by a carefully planned five-day detox diet to allow the digestive system to rest by drinking only water and fresh fruit and vegetable juices.

---

30 It can also be tested through blood, feces, or urine.

Factor #3: Recharge your battery

Each night, when I go to sleep, I die. And the next morning, when I wake up, I'm reborn.

— *Gandhi*

When I chose to "remake" my lifestyle, one of the most powerful things I did for myself was to set aside time for good sleep – respectful sleep – and to stick to that routine. For me, the habit of going to sleep at a set time was just as important as the sleep itself. I go to bed at 10 p.m., aim to be asleep by 10.30 p.m. and I wake up at 5.30 a.m. My body has become accustomed to this routine and is ready for sleep, at this time, each night. Waking up early energizes me for the day, focuses me, and has created discipline in my life. Try it for 40 days and see how you feel.

In 1959, a radio presenter named Peter Tripp decided to broadcast his show from the middle of Times Square for 201 hours straight to raise money for a children's foundation. By the third day, Tripp had begun acting out, cursing at people around him, and hallucinating about spiders. Although he managed to finish the experiment and recover shortly after, his family members said he was never quite the same again.

Sleep is critical for good health, while a lack of it can drive you mad. On average, babies need ten hours of sleep a day to grow. Unfortunately, sleep is usually the first thing we skimp on when we're too busy, working too hard, or trying to fit everything into a long day.

If you're not getting at least seven quality hours of sleep, you're harming yourself. Just think about how you feel when you've had a full night's sleep. You are alert, energetic, and ready to take on the world. In other words, healthy.

Factor #4: Keep active

I don't ride a bike to add days to my life.
I ride a bike to add life to my days.

– Unknown

There are points in life when you feel that change must take place. My diagnosis of early-stage atherosclerosis, as recounted earlier, was that moment. I was eating unhealthy food at odd hours, sleeping for four hours a night, and was completely inactive. I knew that if I did not make a 180-degree change in my life, the price for my negligence would hit me with full force. I decided to act. My decision to change had been taken! I began looking for the right path to kick it off.

In the next chapter, I will describe my physical journey of going from a couch potato to an Ironman. For now, it is important to state a simple truism:

> **Daily physical activity of 30 to 60 minutes is vital for a healthy life.**

The skin is the largest organ in the body. During exercise, our body sweats, and toxins are released. In addition, physical activities contribute to muscle development, coordination, and cardiovascular health. They can prevent chronic diseases, including cardiovascular disease, diabetes, cancer, hypertension, obesity, mental illnesses including depression, and age-related degeneration from bone and muscle loss. Physical activity is associated with hormone regulation and the strengthening of the immune system. Having fitness goals, and acting upon them, leads to weight loss, muscle development, and fat reduction.

Our bodies aren't the only thing that benefits. Exercise contributes to mental health and reduces stress while increasing self-esteem and body image. More importantly, when we physically exert ourselves, the mental stress, and non – physical toxins (that our body accumulates from anger, anxiety, fear, and envy), find ways to be discharged.

So, what kind of exercise should you try? Each one of us has different passions and different talents – the things we do naturally without extraordinary effort, the places in which we feel the flow, and where time seems to fly.

If you like the water, try swimming or surfing. If you like nature, rock climb, hike, or bike. Cold weather is great for skiing, skating, or snowboarding. If you love being part of a group, local leagues exist for soccer, baseball, softball, basketball, or just about any team sport you can think of.

I admire my friend who is a passionate surfer, and it doesn't matter if the weather's warm or cold, rain or shine, rough surf, or calm, he's in that wetsuit at 5 a.m. waiting to catch the next available wave. He used to sneak out of school when we were young, and, as we have grown up, nothing has changed. You will never find him at work on a good day of waves. This is a passion for a sport in its full magnificence. Sporting activities are so diversified. Do the activity that you love. Follow your passion and natural talents; it will naturally make physical activity an integral part of your life.

As Nike's tagline says, "Just Do It." In the next chapter, I will tell you how. But before we go there, we cannot leave the subject of health without attending to a key factor: your mental health.

Factor #5: Keep your emotions in motion.

Life is like riding a bicycle. To keep your balance,
you must keep moving.

– Albert Einstein

Longevity and health depend on your body being in a state of homeostasis[31]. Blood tests can measure the indicators of the body. Every indicator needs to be in a specific range, and any deviation from the norm indicates a dysfunction or the presence of toxins. So far, we have discussed the physical factors that create toxicity and how to eliminate them. But they are not the only factors. Toxicity is also created in our bodies by uncontrolled emotions.

There is a direct brain-gut connection. When we are nervous, or when we receive bad news, we say that we have "butterflies in our stomach," and we describe extremely unpleasant or upsetting things as "gut-wrenching." Put simply, the gastrointestinal tract is sensitive to emotions. The brain has a direct effect on the stomach, intestines, and each cell of our body. Emotions such as anger, sadness,

---

31 Homeostasis is any self-regulating process by which an organism tends to maintain stability while adjusting to conditions that are best for its survival. (www.britannica.com)

and anxiety trigger physical reactions in our bodies, releasing stress hormones such as adrenaline and cortisol. Over time, uncontrolled emotions poison us. The emotional aspects of our lives have a large influence on the overall condition of our health.

When my emotions are out of control, and I am unbalanced, toxins accumulate and illness creeps in. To maintain our mental health, we need a healthy flow of emotions. When we learn not to get "stuck" in an emotion, we begin to take care of our mental wellbeing. Just as a lack of flow of water, and undigested food which gets stuck in the body, causes an accumulation of toxins, which leads to disease, so too does a lack of "flow of emotions" lead to illness.

> **Intangible emotions affect us physically and chemically.**

While driving, I used to hoot immediately as the traffic light turned green, impatient that the cars in front of me were not moving quickly enough. Every traffic jam and long queue would drive me crazy. Even though I am great at mathematics, my daughters didn't want me to tutor them. When I did, I'd get angry easily, and end up shouting: "I've said it for the third time now. Cutting a cake in four pieces instead of three pieces gives you smaller cake pieces. So, why is it so difficult to understand that a third is bigger than a quarter?" I would get home from work, see my house in a mess, shout at Talia, and not talk to my children. I was totally out of control. My emotional responses toward others had become toxic. If truth be told, I had become unbearable.

I used to find it difficult to express my love and appreciation. I didn't understand the meaning of compassion. The mask of the tough, unbreakable man was my disguise. I could not cry; every aspect of my life was affected. My self-awareness was low, and I truly believe that I was "emotionally disabled." Running so fast, locked in the rat race, I never stopped to introspect, and to observe myself. I was completely blind. I was operating on autopilot mode, disconnected from my feelings.

And then I began to explore my emotions, be attentive to them, and gain mastery over them. The process took time. It certainly did not happen overnight. The "crack" appeared when I was faced with the reality of my physical ill-health.

I began to spend many hours alone, in a meditative state of running, riding, and swimming. Through my physical activities, I learned to listen to my inner voice. The challenges and the difficult moments on the way to becoming a marathon runner and Iron Man stretched my limits to the extreme. At moments of unbearable pain, I "saw" my soul and had deep conversations with it. The energy – provided by my soul – gave me the strength to continue. When the energy of my physical body was exhausted, my soul carried my body, step after step, towards the finish line.

Increasingly, I began to hear my inner voice outside of exercise. I began to practice meditation, and my faith in the existence of a universal spiritual power got stronger. The more I focused on physical health, the more I felt my spirituality strengthen.[32] The darkness inside me began to be filled with a gentle light.

My level of consciousness increased, and I began the lifetime journey of learning to feel, taking control of my emotions, and getting closer to my soul. I found so many important aspects of my life that were left behind; primitive, untouched, undeveloped parts of myself began to surface. My heart started to open, I began to feel, and my love towards others flourished. I learned to see the good

---

32 I describe this journey in more detail in Chapter X (The Formula for Spirituality).

in things that had, previously, seemed irritating. I looked at nature and my soul exploded at the beauty of creation. In every person, I allowed myself to see a 3-year-old smiling child with a pure soul. It hurt me to see other creatures suffering. I developed compassion within myself. I even opened my house to our dog, Louis, after years of my daughters' pleading.

There are many ways to get closer to your soul and to find peace. We need to learn to listen to our inner voice. Daily meditation and breathing techniques are useful in this regard. Sadness and depression are often a sign of a "trapped" spirit, buried deep beneath layers of shields and ego. The more I uncovered these layers and freed my spirit, the more I felt happiness and joy filling every cell of my body.

I made the most progress when I strengthened my faith. Now, I believe that the universe is in perfect order. There is no chaos "out there." I believe in providence. Nothing happens to me without a reason. Whatever comes into my life is 100% accurate for me. It is meant to be. The good and the bad; it couldn't be different under any circumstances. Thinking this way, and knowing it in my heart, gives me peace of mind.

The most precious gift that I received was to learn to accept that people are different from me. I stopped needing to change others and learned to look for beauty in everyone.

I learned to control my responses. I stopped blaming others and took full responsibility for my life. I call it "hugging my reality." It's a life-changer. It brings you back to controlling the steering wheel of your emotions. You become the pilot of your life.

I learned to observe and recognize my emotions as being a separate entity inside me. There is me and there are my emotions. I was not my anger! Observe your emotions with empathy and compassion, without criticism and judgment. Forgiveness and love will melt them, and you will learn to let them go. Take responsibility for yourself, your thoughts, and your emotions.

> **Responsibility = "Response–ability."**
> **This is the true meaning of responsibility.**

Bottled-up feelings are like snakes and scorpions inside a well. The way to expel them is not by fighting the snakes and the scorpions – but by filling the well with water. When the well is full, the snakes and scorpions will no longer be there. Fill your life with positivity and generosity; love and compassion will drive out the negative emotions.

> **To banish total darkness, all you need is a little bit of light.**

Our emotions should be balanced. The general principle is that one should follow the midpoint quality of each temperament until all the traits are aligned at the midpoint. Even good things in the wrong proportion will cause damage. Too much food causes obesity; too little causes malnutrition. Too much water causes floods; too little causes droughts.

Everything should be in the right proportion. Our emotions work on the same principles. Every quality should be balanced, and in the right proportions:

• Generosity lies between extravagance and miserliness.
• Courage lies between adventurousness and cowardice.
• Procrastination will hold your life back while impulsiveness may ruin your results.
• Anger will cause pressure and destruction; indifference will keep you stuck.

Choosing the midpoint will give you a peaceful life. Envy, animosity, pessimism, and greed will take you down. Mastering your qualities and emotions shifts you from self-destruction to peace of mind.

Deep and honest self-observation is the starting point of the process. Using your brainpower and your wisdom will shift you from the extreme side to the midpoint. To change behavior, which is strongly rooted in you, you should move to the opposite side, and stay there for a while. This behavior will bring you to the middle. For example, a stingy person must force himself to act lavishly for 40 days. After this period, he will find himself closer to the midpoint.

Taking care of your mental health is your job. A coach or a therapist can guide you but, ultimately, no one can do it for you.

Looking for external solutions, such as drugs to fix you, will not work; you are not broken.

Afterword: Save your own life!

Can you really find a good reason not to make the changes that have the potential to save your life?

I'm not "selling" anything here; I have no hidden agenda. All I want is to spread the knowledge that has significantly improved the quality of my life. It hurts me to see so much suffering on this planet. People have gone blindly along the wrong path to health. Your healthy life without pain and misery, with renewed energy and vitality, is just around the corner.

Here are my "ten commandments" for a healthy life:

1. Eat only when hungry.
2. Drink eight glasses of water a day.
3. Avoid food with labels. Eat mainly fruit, vegetables, and grains.
4. Natural foods containing antioxidants should be your natural medicine.
5. Reduce your exposure to heavy metals and get rid of the existing metal in your body.
6. Expose yourself to adequate sunlight.
7. Check for food intolerances.
8. Sleep well and listen to your body.
9. Exercise daily.
10. Keep your emotions in motion.

Knowledge is power. You have the power to choose to be healthy and to decide not to poison yourself to illness and death.

The formula for a healthy life is not complicated. So, keep it simple, follow the basics, and your life will change instantly. Our body is an amazing vehicle; if you put in the right fuel, it will drive smoothly for a long distance.

VII. THE FORMULA FOR PHYSICAL FITNESS

What seems impossible today will one day become your warm-up.

– Unknown

Physical Fitness =
1. Put on your shoes
2. Set a goal and commit to it
3. Put a plan in place
4. Schedule your exercise
5. Be persistent

When I started exercising nine years ago, I couldn't even run for five minutes.

Fitness wasn't a part of my life. I was a 39-year-old couch potato.

Fortunately, my two close friends, Noy Hazan and David Dan, had done the Ironman competition. They looked like superhumans to me. While I talked about business all day long, my friends had different topics on their minds. Hawaii or Austria? Where would be a better place to have our next competition? What bike did Chris Froome use to win the Tour de France? Where can we import this model from? Where are we meeting tomorrow for our 5.30 a.m. run? What is the optimal nutrition for the race? The topics were endless; the details fascinating. The passion and enthusiasm, with which my friends spoke about their sports activities, lit a spark within me. When I decided to reclaim my life, I vowed to become an Ironman.

My first big goal, on the way to becoming an Ironman, was to complete an Olympic triathlon by age 40. And so, I set up smaller goals to propel me forward. As mentioned previously, a good way to achieve a "big" goal is to break it up into small achievable goals and then focus on each of them individually. Each goal must be challenging, yet doable.

Every goal I achieved took me to the next level, strengthened my self-confidence, and propelled me to the next milestone.

My business partner, and closest friend, Noy is a top athlete. Sport has been a part of his life since he was a child. It's easier to start something new and make life changes when you have a supportive environment. For a long while, I planned to start, but fear and doubt held me back. Like most people, I needed a little push to get into the cold water. Noy set up a meeting for me with Gal, a personal trainer. "Wednesday at the Tel Aviv University coffee shop, at noon. I will be there with you, don't be late!" Noy said. We had a one-hour sit-down at the coffee shop, and Gal explained the various options to me. We worked out a detailed plan, with milestones, based on the time I could invest every week. At the end of this meeting, I had a plan on how to achieve my goal. In 12 months, I would be a triathlete. I felt both terrified and excited. I couldn't run for more than five minutes, the only swimming technique I knew was breast-stroke (not suitable for triathlons), and the last time I had ridden a bike was when I was 15 years old!

Every journey starts with the first step...

And so, I started with a regime that combined walking and running. I built up my time and distance. I persevered, I focused, and I improved. There is no feeling like being on a run and suddenly feeling that you can go further than you did the previous week. Progress is exhilarating.

When I felt ready, I began racing. I did a 5km race and then a 10km one. Finally, I felt ready for a 15km race. But I just could not get there. Every time I got past 13km, I got injured and developed stress fractures (shin splints). Shin splints take a long time to heal. After a while, I wasn't sure if I could achieve my goal of a 21.1 km race. Perhaps my body just wasn't built for running. Maybe I was born to sit in front of the TV, drink beer, and eat junk food. After all, quite a few people have taken that life goal seriously – and achieve it nightly! I consulted with my trainer, sports doctors, and professional athletes. I discovered that the recovery time between activities is a science, all on its own, and that recovery was essential if I were going to get to a place where I would not be injuring myself. Good sleep, stretches and frequent massages became a part of my routine. They helped me to push past 13km. At age 40, I completed my first Olympic triathlon. I had realized my first big goal.

Two years later, at age 42, I finished my first marathon (42.2km) without any injuries. I then took it to the next level and did a half Ironman when I was 43. At age 45, I did the unbelievable. I crossed the finish line, in Frankfurt, as a full Ironman.

Factor #1: Put on your shoes

You don't have to be great to start,
but you have to start to be great.

– Joe Sabah

Close your eyes, imagine yourself standing at the starting line along with 30,000 other runners, the air full of energy and excitement. The gun goes off and you're running your first 10km race. You hear the music on the sidelines, and people are cheering you on, as a big smile spreads across your face. Fifty minutes pass like five, there is only one kilometer left. You accelerate. It's the final 500m, and then you spot the finish line as you empty your tank, and sprint to the end. You cross the finish line with your arms raised. You made it! Your first 10km goal has been achieved. That can be you!

Everyone, without exception, can do physical activities. Too many people have decided that exercise is not for them. My friend, who is a smoker, says he can't exercise until he stops smoking. I say, "Start running and you may stop smoking." I also have a friend who finishes an Ironman and lights a cigarette at the finish line (I kid you not!). Everyone, I repeat, everyone can exercise.

Most of the people I know have taken up exercise because of a crisis. In my case, it was my health and a strong desire to lose weight. For others, it may be a divorce, the loss of a loved one, or just a general dissatisfaction with life.

> **Any reason to start exercising is a good reason.**

In fact, why wait for the crisis? Fix the roof while it's sunny, as the old saying goes.

We all started from scratch. As babies, we struggle to crawl, to walk, to talk, but nothing holds us back. We all made it; we started, failed, but never gave up. Were you a baby too? Or did you skip the initial steps? Every journey starts with the first step. In the case of physical fitness, putting on your shoes is the only way to get started.

Research has found that physical activity not only increases your life expectancy but, more importantly, it improves the quality of your life well into old age. You build a stronger immune system, get sick less, and, should you get sick, your recovery time is faster. I have observed many people who have tested positive for the Covid-19 virus. In almost all cases, I also noticed a close correlation between the severity of the disease and the physical condition of their bodies. My athletic friends had very moderate, or no, symptoms, while my unfit friends suffered badly, were hospitalized, and needed artificial respiration.

One of my biggest life goals is to keep exercising and racing until age 80 (and hopefully beyond). To hit my target, a few elements need to be into place. First, exercise should be like brushing my teeth, something I do every day. Second, it should be varied and challenging. Boredom can kill continuity over a long period. The third challenge is not to get injured. That means conditioning my body to withstand training. Running by itself doesn't build supportive muscles. The peripheral muscles – which support the knee, pelvis, and other key areas of the body that get the heavy load of every step – need to be strong enough to support the activity.

I chose to be a triathlete, combining swimming, cycling, and running. This provides my body with diversity so that I don't over-train for one activity. Each sport is a whole world in itself.

Swimming, for example, is an extremely healthy activity. There are plenty of different swimming styles. Becoming skilled in each of them is a challenge that can take a lifetime. Cycling, be it off-roading on mountain bikes or riding on country roads, is my favorite sport. But it can be dangerous and needs to be done with extra care. A safe option is to cycle indoors at a spinning class or on a bike trainer. The advantage is that you get the optimal training without the risk of accidents. The disadvantage is that it can be boring to cycle 50 km and stay in the same place. Cycling is a very healthy sport. The load on your body is minimal, and it's an aerobic activity, meaning that your heart, blood vessels, and lungs all get a workout.

Running is the most accessible activity. No matter where you travel in the world, all you need to pack is shorts, a T-shirt, socks, and, of course, your running shoes. There is no need for special equipment or coordination with other people. There is no better way to experience a place than to run in it! Because it involves almost every muscle in our body, running is an extremely effective sport that makes you feel better physically, mentally, and emotionally. It is also among the best aerobic exercises for the physical condition-ing of your heart and lungs. The health benefits are enormous, and evidence suggests that running reduces the likelihood of illness, from the common cold to cancer. It is also great for alleviating stress and depression. Studies have found that healthy adults who exercise regularly are generally happier than those who don't. Run-ning is also effective for weight loss. The average calories burnt per hour of running is around 700 calories, as compared to 550 calories with cycling or swimming.

The beginning of my exercise journey was hard. I hated running. The stress fractures didn't help, but, even after that, I had to have hernia surgery during this practice period. Each time I accelerated my pace, something held me back. Every day I'd wonder whether I was meant to be a runner. "Maybe I was born with some kind of or physical shortcoming," I'd tell myself. But I kept going, and it got better. In fact, it got a lot better. Miles better.

Four years after I started, I registered for the Paris Marathon. In April 2015, as I stood at the starting line with enormous pride, I looked down at my feet. It had been a four-year journey that began when I dared to put on my running shoes.

Factor #2: Set a goal and commit to it

The trouble with not having a goal is that you can spend your life running up and down the field and never score.

– Bill Copeland

Setting well-defined targets motivates me to wake up and train every morning. It's hard, at first, and the distance you can run, swim or cycle is too short for it to be enjoyable. When you exercise, your body begins to release endorphins that give it a positive feeling, not unlike that of morphine. The trick is that it takes around 30 minutes of exercise before the endorphins kick in. Perseverance gives you a healthy – and free – drug!

Like many gifts in life, you need to want them enough and be willing to cross the "frustration gap," to enjoy the fruits. I highly recommend having a personal trainer or joining a running group to have something or someone that will pull you through the "frustration gap."

It is important to start small. I've seen so many people who start with a lot of enthusiasm, but, after a short while, without the right guidance, they get injured and quit. The day I started to exercise for real, I searched Google for a competition that was being held during the next 12 months. When I found a triathlon that was being held in Eilat, on December 12, 2012, I hesitated. It looked frightening, but I signed up. The commitment had been made. Now, for the first time, it was real. Not theoretical, not "I will start tomorrow," no more procrastinating. The date set, the ship left the port for its destination. To make it even more official, I announced my intention to Talia and close friends: "A year from now, you're invited to be with me at my first race. I will be a triathlete."

After this announcement, I was committed. There was not a chance in the world that I would not do it. My word is my reputation. I would not damage the reputation I had built up over the years. To make a promise to yourself and fail, is one thing. But to tell everyone around you, to commit and not to deliver, is an entirely different matter. Setting, and announcing, my goal worked perfectly for me. Every morning, when I had to wake up, thinking about the date of the race got me out of bed. "The clock is ticking, the deadline is getting closer, I don't feel ready, and each day counts," became my mantra and fueled my motivation. During the year, I faced obstacles and challenges. I got injured, I got flu, I had loads of work and many distractions. Without a clear goal, i.e., the competition date, and the pronouncements to my friends and family, there was a real chance that I would have quit.

Between 2012 and 2022, I completed 20 triathlons, a marathon, four half – Ironmen, and a full Ironman.

Determination and persistence are unbeatable. When I first started, I couldn't see myself running a 10km race. But the only way to finish the 10km race when you start, is to go kilometer by kilometer. So too, with a marathon; kilometer after kilometer, you count 42 times, and the target is achieved. It's impossible to describe in words how hard the Iron Man competition is. Again, the way to achieve such a difficult mission is to chunk it into small pieces. Swim 100 meters after 100 meters, cycle 10 kilometers after 10 kilometers, and run kilometer by kilometer.

Factor #3: Put a plan in place

A goal without a plan is just a wish.
– Antoine de Saint–Exupéry

Detailed plans are the building blocks of every big target. The best option is to have a coach who will help to set your weekly plans and define what exercise you have to do each day, for how long, and for what distance. The more detailed and accurate your training plan is, the easier it will be to execute.

If you don't have a coach, many apps, and websites offer personalized plans which are accessible to everyone. Low–cost technologies, such as Polar or Garmin watches, enable you to share your exercise data, measure speed, distance, heartbeat, cadence, and many other parameters that make running an exact science. A good coach can analyze the data and guide you towards achieving maximum results with minimum injuries.

The perfect plan to run 10km, from zero, is a combination of running and walking. This formula has worked for me and many friends who began running from scratch. You need to do each activity at least three to four times a week. Here is a good plan to follow:

Week	Activity	Frequency	Total
1	9-minute walk + 1-minute easy run	2 times	20 minutes
2	9-minute walk + 1-minute easy run	3 times	30 minutes
3	5-minute walk + 1-minute easy run	5 times	30 minutes
4	4-minute walk + 1-minute easy run	6 times	30 minutes
5	6-minute warmup walk (2-minute walk + 1-minute easy run)	8 times	30 minutes
6	5-minute warmup walk (1-minute walk + 1-minute easy run)	10 times	25 minutes
7	6-minute warmup walk (1-minute walk + 1-minute easy run)	12 times	30 minutes
8	5-minute warmup walk (2-minute easy run + 1-minute walk)	15 times	35 minutes
9	8-minute warmup walk (3-minutes' easy run + 1-minute walk)	8 times	40 minutes
10	10-minute warmup walk (5-minute easy run + 1-minute walk)	5 times	40 minutes
11	8-minute warmup walk (7-minute easy run + 1-minute walk)	4 times	40 minutes
12	10-minute warmup walk (9-minute easy run + 1-minute walk)	3 times	40 minutes
13	10-minute warmup walk (14-minute easy run + 1-minute walk)	2 times	40 minutes
14	10-minute warmup walk (19-minute easy run + 1-minute walk)	2 times	40 minutes
15	10-minute warmup walk (24-minute easy run + 1-minute walk)	2 times	60 minutes
16	5-minute warmup walk 60-minute easy run	Once	70 minutes

If you follow this plan, your 10km run target will be achieved within four months. If you feel that a few steps need to be repeated, take your time, no one is running after you! If you reach your goal in six months, where's the harm? Don't get confused. The goal is just a milestone. The journey, your growth, and your progress are what matter most. The important thing is to be active, constantly to build momentum, and to add a building block, each day, that propels you forward. If you fail and stop for a few days or a week, don't be discouraged. Don't give up. Continue. This is the power of momentum. Initially, it may be difficult. But, once the ball is moving, it's not easily stopped. No matter what activity you try, I also recommend adding 15 to 20 minutes of strength training two to three times per week. Start with basic bodyweight exercises, such as squats, lunges, planks and side planks, sit-ups, and push-ups. Adding strength will make everything you do easier and dramatically reduce the risk of injuries. After four months, you will have achieved your 10km run (or whatever else you have committed to) with pride and, hopefully, no injuries. You will be stronger, healthier, happier, and will have built a healthy habit.

Fitness is now a part of your life! Be proud. You have become "Me, version 2.0." Being fit will improve many aspects of your life. You'll lose weight, be more energetic and powerful, and you'll look and feel better. Your mood will also be calmer, and people will enjoy being around you more.

Your strengthened discipline will be reflected in your work too, and your professional goals will seem more attainable. You will have the self–confidence to set new goals, create detailed plans, and, most importantly, the ability to execute. Any challenge that excites and enthuses you is a worthwhile goal.

When I decided to run the Paris Marathon, I worked with Ariel, a professional long-distance running coach. I defined three goals. I wanted to learn to enjoy running, to finish the marathon without injury, and then to put the 42.2 km sticker on the back of my car! Ariel was attentive to my limitations and every potential problem. Each session was based on my feedback from the previous session. We slowed down when needed, added sleeping hours for recovery (during sleep, the body cures itself), and I replaced my shoes after every 500km.

The Paris Marathon was unforgettable. It was a city-wide festival; crowds cheered, and bands played music on every corner. By the 36th kilometer, I was exhausted, my quadricep muscles felt as if they were going to jump out of my legs. I didn't think that I could continue for another five meters, let alone kilometers. I pushed through. The crowd encouraged me and fueled my adrenaline. I crossed the finish line, without injury, with tears of happiness in my eyes. I had accomplished the three goals that I had set for myself, 12 months previously.

Besides the fitness and other obvious benefits, running afforded me time with myself and my thoughts. I use my running time to enrich myself by listening to podcasts and audiobooks. It takes about eight hours to listen to a book, and I run around four times a week for an hour, so I can finish a full book in two weeks, which is about 24 books a year. In a decade, that's 240 books. The vast knowledge you will accumulate from 240 books will completely transform you and your life.

Like many things in life, in which you succeed, they become a part of you, and you enjoy them. I learned to enjoy running. Today, it is a part of me and my life. I am proud to have entered the prestigious club of people who drive around with a 42.2 km sticker on the back of their car. What is your equivalent goal? Don't wait. Start now.

Factor #4: Schedule your exercise

Time is an illusion, timing is an art.

– Stefan Edmunds

I am frequently asked "When will I find time to exercise?"

After a long day at work, you are tired, have dealt with so many challenges, and your willpower is simply not as strong as it is in the morning. Willpower is like a muscle; you utilize this muscle, all day, for all sorts of tasks where discipline is required. By the end of the day, it is tired. This is one of the reasons that many people prefer to come home, eat unhealthy food, and watch a series. Now, the chances of going outside and exercising are negligible. Don't blame yourself; your willpower is not the problem. The solution is to schedule your exercise smartly.

In my experience, if you postpone the activity to the late afternoon, or even evening, the chance of success is low. I have always preferred the late hours of the night when distractions are limited, and relaxation is in the air. No one calls me, and I can focus on important tasks. For many years, I found myself working at 3 am. I would then, of course, wake up late which would affect my whole day. I would be late for work, late for meetings, and late to get home. Consequently, I would try to exercise at night. But I couldn't. I wanted to, but I just couldn't make it. I became frustrated, and the continuous attempts and failures destroyed my motivation.

I knew that I had no option; I either wake up early or I don't exercise. Any other option was lying to myself. I decided to give it a try. On the first morning, when my alarm went off at 5 a.m., I struggled to get up. For the first few weeks, I had a tough fight with my old habits. Slowly, despite the challenges, I began to feel the rewards. It did not take long (40 days, as you already know) for me to get used to going to sleep earlier which allowed me to begin my day at 5 a.m. I soon felt the advantages of an early start. With my energy boosted, my productivity increased tremendously. I suddenly had one to two extra hours a day to do things. Throughout an average lifetime, that is an additional four to eight years of wakefulness! An early start also lifted my mood and improved my attitude. There is a magical feeling in the early morning hours that is hard to describe. As I run, I imagine the birds, who are waking up, are cheering me on, while the flowers, whose petals are opening, are smiling at me. In the winter, the chill in the air and the sight of the dewdrops lift my spirit and make my day.

As the earth rotates on its axis, it switches between the sunlight side (day) and the dark side (night). Strong magnetic fields, surrounding our planet, influence all creatures, including humans. All of nature wakes up at dawn to enjoy the serene power of growth, re-creation, and regeneration. As the sun rises, the first rays of sunlight strike our bodies and minds with powerful magnetic fields which cause our bodies to release hormones such as melatonin, which boost our overall capabilities. At this time of day, activities and thoughts have the ability to render immense success. Waking up late disconnects us from the rhythm of nature's cycle and we miss the potential powers that the universe offers us. Don't get me wrong, I don't know many people who look at their clock at 5:00 a.m. without hating that moment. I dread those first few minutes, too. But, like many things in life, good things come to those who want them, and who are willing to pay a price. The feeling after daily exercise is total self−victory. You "win" over yourself time and time again when you defeat the internal voice that is saying, "I'm too tired, I'll start tomorrow."

Becoming an "early bird" initiates you into the 5:00 a.m. club.[33] You will have joined the top five percent of humanity −people who are enjoying happier, healthier and more successful lives.

Factor #5: Be persistent

A river cuts through rock, not because of its power,
but because of its persistence.

− Jim Watkins

Many of us are familiar with Aesop's fable, "The Tortoise and the Hare". Despite the potential of the hare to beat the tortoise, his arrogant behavior, and decision to take a nap midway through the race, caused his defeat. The hare's inconsistency resulted in the slow, and persistent, tortoise's victory.

We tend to underestimate the enormous power of persistence.

The things we can achieve in a lifetime are unbelievable. In an average lifetime, people sleep for about 25 years, eat 35 tons of food, and grow about 900 km of hair! The power of accumulative accomplishment is imperceptible. As Bill Gates says: "Most people

---

33 Robin Sharma, The 5am Club: Own your morning; Elevate your life.

overestimate what they can do in one year and underestimate what they can do in ten years."

Fifty years ago, running a marathon was only for super athletes. Today, we understand that almost everyone can do a marathon. We see records being broken repeatedly in every sport. Every time a record breaks, it looks like that's the limit. But there are no limits. Our capabilities are unlimited, and records will continue to be broken forever.

> **The only limitations we have are the limits we place on ourselves**

Following the formula for physical fitness will inaugurate you into a prestigious community. Disciplined people like you, with high standards, who appreciate life, take care of their health, and live with enhanced energy, passion, and enthusiasm.

VIII. THE FORMULA FOR WEALTH

The world is full of talented poor people.

– Robert T. Kiyosaki

Wealth =

1. Collect assets, not liabilities
2. No risks; no rewards
3. Utilize your talents
4. Two is better than one
5. Play it smart
6. Money makes more money
7. Diversify
8. Never quit!

For almost as long as I can remember, I have had a burning desire to be financially independent. I grasped the rules of the game early. As recounted earlier, I established my first business at age seven and have traded in the global markets since I was 15 years old. I have had ups and downs, faced successes and failures, and made – and lost – a lot of money several times.

I learned from top league businessmen, entrepreneurs, fund managers, millionaires, and billionaires. I found patterns and similarities which made them wealthy. They had all, consciously or unconsciously, connected to the channel of abundance to become successful. I analyzed their behavior and followed the paths that led them to their successful destinations. I summarized it all into a formula for wealth, which I have deployed throughout my life. It has worked for me, and I believe that if followed, it will work for you too.

Despite my humble beginnings, I am proud that I had achieved financial independence by the age of 34. And, while I can't say that money buys happiness, it certainly does make a lot of things easier. It afforded me the privilege to think and plan, without the daily pressures of worrying about how to pay my bills. It provided a high level of certainty and gave my family freedom of choice in many areas of our lives. With that state of mind, I was able to establish new businesses and invest without fear.

Being financially independent, undoubtedly, made it easier for me to expand my wealth. As I accumulated assets, I was able to afford a better lifestyle for my family and myself. I gained time not only for self–development, but also to be with my family. My assets pay for my lifestyle while the income from my businesses helps me to accumulate assets to keep raising my wealth.

In hindsight, I can say that I was quite"lucky." But what is luck, actually?

"Luck is what happens when preparation meets opportunity."

This quote, attributed to Roman philosopher Seneca, reminds us that luck does not fall from the sky. There are accurate natural laws, mostly unseen, which once followed, pave the way to great success.

Luck comes to you when you are prepared and ready for it. I was prepared for the opportunities when they presented themselves.

Wealth is largely a matter of know–how, planning, and execution.

I have educated friends who struggle to finish the month with any money in the bank, and I have uneducated friends who have made fortunes.

The first step is to understand what money is. Where does money pull its power from? What gives Dollars, Euros, Bitcoins, or any other currency, their weight?

Money is all about value and trust.

A $100 bill is a piece of paper that costs a few cents to produce. Its power is derived from its tradable value and people's trust in the American economy. Consequently, they trust, and are willing to trade with, this currency. When the world loses trust in the American economy, the value of the US Dollar depreciates (in comparison to other currencies). Similarly, when there were cyber threats on Bitcoin and a few thousand tokens were stolen, Bitcoin's value dropped dramatically. When people lost trust, the value declined. If I can trade one Bitcoin with a Tesla X or its equivalent, then that is the value of one Bitcoin. The value of any currency comes from its tradable power.

The formula for making money is the same – you need to know how to provide value and trust.

**Once trust is established,
the more value you provide, the more money you make.**

Focus on how you can generate more value for your clients, thereby assisting them to become more successful in their respective businesses. The more clients you assist, the more successful you will become.

A healthy relationship is based on two questions:

- Can I trust you? and
- Can I be trusted?

Trust is the glue that keeps everything together. Trust connects the client to you, your employees, and your suppliers. Without trust, everything falls apart. Trust builds over time and is based on the fundamentals of integrity, reliability, certainty, stability, and consistency.

Trust is about mutually beneficial relationships in which communication is open and transparent. You need to be able to put yourself in the other's shoes and see their point of view. If you are creating win-lose or lose-win situations, trust will not last. Always look for a win-win outcome, despite the obstacles and challenges.

You achieve this by:

- Being attentive, clear, and direct.
- Setting firm, yet flexible, boundaries and expectations.
- Doing what you say you will (keeping your word).
- Not over-promising and under-delivering.
- Taking responsibility for your mistakes.

Building trust is like building a house of cards: it is difficult to build and easy to destroy. As Warren Buffett says, "It takes 20 years to build a reputation and five minutes to ruin it."

***

As I believe I have demonstrated previously, your mind is the most powerful tool you have at your disposal. You can configure it to achieve whatever you want, and your mind will oblige.

> **If your goal is to be wealthy, then you need to have the mindset of a wealthy person.**

You need to adjust your "blueprint." If your mindset consists of thoughts such as, "rich people are thieves," or "money corrupts" or even "I have to earn enough money to pay my bills," then you will make just enough to pay your bills. That's it.

If your mindset is that of a wealthy person, and your thoughts about your future wealth status consist of statements such as, "I'm earning much more than I need, living in my dream home and driving a luxury car," you can begin to configure your mind and act accordingly.

Notice that all these statements are written in the present tense. This is intentional. To create future success, you need to think of it as already existing. Visualization is a tool that wealthy people employ on the road to success.

Ultimately, the aim is to become worry-free. You get there by becoming financially independent. But what does this mean? Financial independence does not mean becoming a millionaire or a billionaire. It simply means the following:

> **The monthly income from your assets must be higher than your monthly expenses.**

From that point, you work because you *want* to and not because you need to. Financial independence frees up your time. You have time to focus on what matters to you. Time to make everything you want to happen, happen. That's the first step to true wealth.

> **The level of your financial independence relies on two parameters: You can either raise the bridge or you can lower the water.**

Put simply:
- When you increase your income, you are raising the bridge; and
- When you decrease your expenses, you are lowering the water.

I have been in a positive cash flow state since the age of 18 when I was in the Air Force. Although my monthly salary was only $150, I managed to keep my expenses at $100 and then wisely invested the remaining $50 into the markets, to enrich my working capital. After I got married and started to have children, I adjusted my lifestyle to fit into an annual asset level of $100,000. My salary went to acquiring additional assets to keep my wealth growing. Over time, I have continued to grow the level of my assets. But the principle remains the same. I spend up to the level of the income from my assets. And every dollar I earn, above this amount, is used to acquire additional assets.

By keeping the level of water below the bridge, the income from my assets has kept me financially independent at every stage of my life. I have never exceeded the level. I never bought yachts and sports cars, or any other liabilities that would pull me down. I was in charge of my lifestyle. When I had very little, I spent accordingly. When I had more, I may have spent more – but never more than I had. Most people live way above their means, never saving enough to start accumulating assets.

> **If your needs are higher than the income from your assets, you will always live in shortage. But if your needs are lower, you will live a life of abundance.**

Ultimately, the level of your lifestyle will define your freedom point. Some people can have financial independence with an annual income of $10,000, while others need $10,000,000 just to maintain their lifestyle.

The best way to gain financial independence, and the freedom that comes with it, is to be in control of your desires. Put simply:

> **Don't want what you don't need!**

Do we really need to keep surrendering to our desires? Why do you need a new jeep? Whatever you're driving will get you where you need to get. You can use a bicycle, bus, train, or even an Uber. If the new car is just a status symbol, for your ego or added comfort, can you conquer your desire for it?

Once your basic needs are met, the root cause of most financial challenges is a feeling of internal deficiency, not one of real need. Thus, we must distinguish between what we need (existentially) and what we want (emotionally).

I heard a great tale about a man who wanted nothing in life. He sat on a hill, equipped with just a jug for drinking water. When Napoleon, who had conquered the world and accumulated fortunes, heard about this strange creature, he decided he wanted to meet him. Napoleon's bodyguards ran ahead to tell the man, who was sunning himself on the hill, to stand up and show respect as the emperor was arriving. The man casually looked up and said, "Leave me to enjoy the sunlight." Napoleon arrived and was greeted by the man, relaxing on his hill, taking in the sun. Surprised by the man's apparent lack of fear, he began engaging him in casual conversation and found himself quite enjoying the man's company. He said to the man, "I actually like you. Ask me for anything you need. I'll give it to you." The man said, "Look at you. You're the one running around, conquering, looting, and taking. You're the one who needs things. I don't need anything. I'm rich. You're the poor one."

Napoleon seemed to understand the man. "That's fine," he said. "But, still, you must need something. Ask me for anything."

Looking up, the man said, "Ok. Please can you move? You're blocking the sun."

The man was indeed rich as he wanted for nothing.

Thankfully, most people whom I know are blessed to have food clothes, water to drink, education for their children, and even some kind of vehicle. Their egos, however, push them to want things that they don't really need. They acquire too many things for the wrong reasons. The real fight for our financial freedom should start from within and not from outside. The solution, the salvation, is inside us.

> **For financial freedom, work as hard on your brain,**
> **as you do on your job.**

We are born whole. As we grow up, we begin to lose this feeling of wholeness, and we try to fill it in any possible way. Our basic needs for joy and happiness must be fulfilled one way or another. Trying to "fill" these needs from external sources, such as emotional eating, fancy restaurants, luxury vacations, extensive shopping, covering ourselves with brands, splashing out on luxuries, and seeking approval from others, does not work. They are all illusions. These illusions put us into physical overdrafts, in our bank accounts, as we try to fill the emptiness. They give us temporary satisfaction as we swipe the credit card and get a few minutes, hours, or even days, of joy. The minus in the bank is real, but the joy is fake, it's just an illusion. We remain empty. It's like filling a bucket with a hole in it. You can fill it until it is full. But when you reach your doorstep, it will be empty. Over time, the hole will expand, and the stimulus threshold will rise. In order to get another dose of pleasure, you will have to pay much more.

When you stop seeking external stimuli, you begin to resolve your financial challenges! Rather, invest time in building a meaningful life, enriching your wisdom, building true relationships, influencing others, spreading love, and strengthening your faith.

The wise King Solomon said: "He who has a hundred wants two hundred; he who has two hundred wants four hundred. And no man dies with half his lust in his hand." My translation of Solomon's wisdom is the following: "The punishment for greediness is more greediness." Please don't get me wrong. I am not saying you need to live an ascetic life. I'm certainly not "the monk who sold his Ferrari." I drive a beautiful car and I enjoy the comforts that wealth brings. But I reached this point by having control over my desires at every stage of my life. I controlled my desires; they did not control me. I have learned that true happiness is not located in the material world.

To become financially independent, you must play both sides of the coin:

> **Don't want what you don't need: Control your desires and your spending, and, at the same time, become an expert money-maker!**

In school, and even in university, no one teaches you about the "real" financial world, how to build a solid business, or how to invest intelligently. We are simply not taught how to play the Monopoly Game of Life. Terms such as revenue, operational cost, net profit, EBITDA, cash flow, dividends, bonds, equities, options, assets, liabilities, coupons, offshore, tax planning, leverage, commodities, and cryptocurrency all sound frightening. But they are not. These basic terms are a part of the vocabulary required to succeed financially, and they are not difficult to learn.

The road to financial independence looks complicated, if not impossible, for most people. The truth is that it is possible to live a financially independent life without debts and worries of existential livelihood. Once you make the decision to adjust your mindset and set the destination in your GPS, you must do whatever it takes to make things happen. You will have to plan, work hard, sacrifice, succeed, fail, and pick yourself up, until you reach your destination.

I worked for several international companies in my twenties. Until 2007, I – and many of my friends – earned decent salaries and large bonuses, the markets went up and the companies' stocks made us huge theoretical "paper profits."[34] By 2007, my friends had leveraged those paper profits to acquire liabilities: big houses with large mortgages and equally large monthly bills. Then the housing bubble burst. Their huge financial obligations became nightmares when the massive layoffs hit. I had many good friends – who were experienced and talented – who suddenly found themselves un-employed. It took some of them years to find new jobs. They lost their houses, their confidence, and they burned all their savings in an effort to survive. Scary!

On April 5th, 2007, I woke up and was zapped by a thought: I refuse to be part of the next layoff. Layoffs always hit when you aren't ready. When times are good, your employers treat you like a king, give you vacations, company cars, and other benefits, and you feel safe. The moment the economy shifts, they cut you off. You gave them your heart, your soul, your family time, your best years. And, one morning, you come to the office and a termination letter awaits you. They take away your laptop, your ID card, pack your personal belongings, and revoke your access. You are history.

The question is not *if*, it's only *when*.

This is the ratty part of the rat race. You run, run, and run until

---

34 Stock gains aren't profit until you sell.

the cat eats the rat. You can run, but you can't hide. I had seen it coming and decided it would not happen to me. There was only one way out: The only way I could control my destiny was to run my own company. I could fail, but, at least, no one could fire me. In 2007, in the month that I turned 34 years old, I established DatagroupIT. It succeeded. I made – and changed – my fortune before I turned 40.

We live in an abundant world, with endless opportunities. The opportunities were there in the past, they are here now, and they will continue to be here in the future.

In this chapter, I will share with you how to prepare yourself for endless opportunities. I always wondered why, if it's this simple, are most people not rich? I realized that there is a huge volume of know-how but little clarity. It created in me the desire to simplify the apparent complexity of creating financial independence and making the formula for wealth accessible.

Factor #1: Collect assets, not liabilities

Debt is one person's liability, but another person's asset.
– Paul Krugman

Three years after Talia and I were married, our first daughter, Roni, was born. I felt as though angels were accompanying us on the way home from the hospital. It was magical. Like many new couples, with a newborn baby, we began looking for a home in which to raise our family.

The perception of success had been set for me since childhood: Graduate university, find a job, get married, buy your own house, have children, wait for retirement, and pray to die before you run out of money.

Everybody, our parents, close friends, and colleagues, had done, or were doing, the same. Same route; same results.

The problem was that they had all bought liabilities rather than assets.

An asset is a resource that generates positive income for its owner. It is as simple as that.

> **Essentially, an asset wakes up every morning and works for its owners, while a liability forces its owners to wake up every morning to pay for it.**

Like the people around me, I had accumulated the initial capital to buy my dream home. It was a small, cute, three-bedroom apartment in a good neighborhood with lovely neighbors, and 25 years of a heavy mortgage. Just before I was about to sign on the dotted line, and dive into the deep water, I paused to ask myself a few basic questions:

- Is our dream home an asset or a liability?
- Is it financially better to buy or rent?
- Should I do what most people do or is it better to swim against the tide?
- Is it possible to have a 25-year mortgage and to be financially independent at the same time?

Ultimately, the big question I had to answer was this: Was I going to have to work for this home, for the next 25 years, or could I make it work for me? I decided to do my homework and began to study the subject in detail. I entered the data into a spreadsheet. The numbers were clear, and simple, to me.

To my amazement, twenty years ago, I found that most people, when buying a house, imagine that they are buying an asset, while, in reality, they are buying a liability! This liability is like a 100kg weight, tied to your leg, pulling you down, giving you no option to move forward. It keeps you in the rat race, working around the clock, taking loan after loan, dragging you deeper and deeper into the quicksand of debt.

My research showed me that I basically had two options. I could do what everyone else seemed to be doing and buy a house. Alternatively, I could buy a house as an investment, while renting another place in which to live.

I showed the numbers to my friends and colleagues. Unsurprisingly, most of them focused on the scary part, rather than the clear and simple part. They were skeptical and cynical. It was as if they all had a blind spot. Despite clear facts and calculated numbers, they still found reasons and excuses not to follow the data. "It sounds too risky. I'm sure you forgot to add many other costs in your calculations. What if no one rents from you and you must pay the mortgage from your own pocket? What if the tenants ruin your house? What if they don't pay the rent? You will have to maintain the property, it sounds too difficult and frightening, it's so much work..."

I did it anyway.

I chose to do it because I discovered a "secret," hidden between two numbers: The interest rate of the mortgage vs. the property yield (the annual rental income divided by the property value).

Let me demonstrate.

My dream house then cost $500,000 (I had 20% in cash, with support from both my and Talia's parents, so my initial capital was $100,000).

Option 1: Buy my own house.

At the time, I could rent this house out at $1,000 per month ($12,000 p.a.).

The total yield on the property, was 2.4% (1,000 x 12/500,000 x 100).

The interest rate for a mortgage at that time was 4.4%.

This meant a negative excess interest of 2%. Essentially, every year I would need to wake up, go to work, and pay the bank an annual interest of $8,000, with this amount growing year after year. After 25 years, including compound interest, the total interest (without the principal amount) came to $350,000 without including mortgage and other bank fees.

Option 2: Buy a house as an investment and rent elsewhere.

I searched and found four old apartments in Beer Sheva, which were close to the University and could serve as student accommodation. I could divide each apartment into two studio units of 40 sq/m each. The cost was $100,000 for such an apartment plus $25,000 for the cost of renovation. Each student would pay $500 per month and the apartment would generate a monthly income of $1,000.

The total property yield on four apartments was 9.6%. (4 x 1,000 x 12/ (4 x 125,000) x 100).

The choice was a no-brainer.

With the initial money I had, plus an 80% leveraged mortgage from the bank, I bought four apartments and set about converting them into eight studio units.

The apartments would generate a positive excess interest of 5.2%. This meant that the apartments would work for me 24 hours a day, 365 days a year. Every year, they would generate an annual income of $48,000.

After eight years, the excess annual income covered the cost of the mortgage, and the apartments became 100% mine. Since 2011, they have continued to work for me around the clock.

The apartments became my first fixed-income portfolio.

Every month I would get $4,000 (which has obviously increased with time). In my early 30s, I was generating an annual fixed income of $60,000.

I rented our dream home, for $1,000 a month ($12,000 annually) while my studio apartments were generating $4000 every month ($48,000 annually).

Every investment should also take into consideration the cost of taxes in each investment channel. If the $60,000 was coming from hard work, they would, in Israel at least, be 50% taxed. Taxation on rental, on the other hand, is about 10%. Over the years, the neighborhood in Beer Sheva has improved and the value of the apartments has tripled.

Talia and I didn't stop there. Over the years, whenever we have had "spare money" from working capital, we have bought another asset. These assets, which were all bought before we turned 40, using the banks' money, with rental income paying the mortgages, generated an annual income of more than $100,000 with little work. They are pure assets that we own and that we have had to pay virtually nothing to keep.

Understanding this factor worked for me. I simplified something that scares most people. I focused on this factor, and I achieved my positive outcome: Financial independence generated by real estate assets.

"Keep the math simple" is my mantra. When a property you buy generates less than what the mortgage costs, you have a liability. When the property generates more than what the mortgage costs, you have an asset. I call it "free money."

Think about it. If you get an annual income from a property, which is even one cent higher than the mortgage or the loan, then you have "free money." The more properties you have, the greater free money you will receive.

My friends and colleagues had doubts when I first shared with them what I intended to do. Admittedly, there have been a few months, in all the years, when some of the apartments were empty, and I had a few maintenance expenses along the way. And, yes, I must spend a few hours, every year, making this investment work for me. The funny (and sad) part is that my friends and colleagues are willing to work for others every day, from sunrise to sunset, 365 days a year. But working for themselves, for a few hours a year, sounds like a heavy burden to them!

Rich people use other people's money. It's called leverage (loans that cost you less than the income). Poor and middle-class people use their own money. By using leverage, you make money not only on your own money, but also on the bank's, or borrower's, money. Using leverage dramatically shortens the time it takes you to pay for the asset.

Life is short, and you want to be financially independent while you are still young, not when you are too old. If you want many years of prosperity, start young, leverage, and accumulate assets before you turn 40. It's better to start when you are young, but it's never too late to take the right action. Start now.

The opportunities are endless. We live in a global world, and there are always neighborhoods, cities, countries, and continents where the loan interest rates are lower than the income from the property. The opportunities may move frequently, but they are always available. You need to look for them.

The more you play in the field of finance and property, the more you learn, and the more confidence you get. When your eyes are open, you can spot opportunities. Today, I invest in a wide variety of projects in the USA, South America, Europe, and Asia. Does that sound scary? It's not. The formula, which never changes, is simple to adopt and deploy.

The financial aspect of life is like the board game Monopoly. The player with the greatest number of assets wins. You must start collecting assets early along your life's journey; the sooner you begin, the more assets you will possess.

Assets make you rich and lift you up; liabilities pull you down. Herein lies the difference between the rich – who work to build assets – and the rest of the world who are working to pay for their liabilities.

What are you waiting for? The monopoly board of life awaits you.

Factor #2: No risks; no rewards

A ship in harbor is safe, but that is not what ships are built for.
– William Shedd

Three percent of the world's population has more money than the remaining 97%! Interestingly, most of the three percent have made their fortune in the last 20 to 30 years. Almost all the "new" millionaires (and billionaires) made their fortune by having a vision and taking risks. They opened start-ups in their garages and chased "crazy" dreams that turned into successful businesses. Elon Musk, the world's wealthiest person (at the time of writing), with a net worth of around $200 billion, founded Tesla in 2003 and Space X in 2002. And then, of course, there is Bill Gates, the world's second wealthiest person, at the time of writing, who started Microsoft in 1975.[35]

We are all afraid of the unknown. Some of us let the fear paralyze us, while others let the fear energize us. I belong to the latter group. I believe that to be successful, you must learn to conquer your fears. You cannot become financially independent without embracing this simple factor:

> **You must seek out the unknown, search for risks,
> and welcome them into your life.**

Don't run away from risk, turn towards, and embrace it. It's a gift, wrapped in the form of risk. The higher the risk, the bigger the gift is likely to be. Most people say, "It's too risky, it's not for me, let's run from it as we would from a fire." Those who are truly seeking financial independence will look the risk in the eye, run towards it ... and the rest, as they say, is history.

In business, the equation is constant and linear:

> **The more risks you take, the more rewards you get.**

Most people try to hold the stick at both ends, but it's not possible. They want high gains with low risks.

A comparative analysis of historical data between a solid investment in federal funds (cash deposit) against an investment in the equity index, such as S&P, clearly shows the risk-rewards factor. An investment of $100,000, seventy years ago, would, today generate multiples of 30 times in the solid channel compared to 90 times in

---

35 At the time of writing, Elon Musk, a South African-born American entrepreneur and businessman, overtook Bezos as the world's wealthiest person. Musk founded X.com in 1999 (which later became PayPal), SpaceX in 2002 and Tesla Motors in 2003. Musk became a multimillionaire in his late 20s when he sold his start-up company, Zip2, to a division of Compaq Computers.

the equity channel.

Today, in the non-risky channel, you would have $3,000,000 while in the "risky" channel you would have $9,000,000.

Taking the principal amount, as a loan from the bank, and investing it into the S&P will make you a profit of $6,000,000. It is possible to make money out of nowhere. When you are willing to take risks, risk works like magic.

I have participated in the stock market for countless years and have taken many risks on the way to financial independence. I bought internet stocks long before the internet was popular, when only universities were using the internet to connect between themselves. I bought the cloud companies' stocks before they become trendy, I bought cybersecurity stocks when the first anti-virus software was launched and, of course, I bought Bitcoins when everyone said that they were too dangerous.

Ironically, it is playing "safe" that is dangerous. The risk-takers win the prize.

> **The major risk you take in life is not to take risks.**

Factor #3: Utilize your talents

Every artist was first an amateur.
— Ralph Waldo Emerson

My career has enabled me to combine my technological abilities with my talent for sales. We all have unique abilities and talents. To find your God-given gift talent, you must be attentive to your inner voice. What was your true childhood passion? What interested you? What were you doing while your friends were playing hide-and-seek outside? What is the gift with which God blessed you?

If you build your "vessel" around this passion, your chances of success increase dramatically. It does not matter whether you run your own business or work for someone else. On the top 100 richest people list in the world, during the last decade, there are founders of successful companies but there are also top executive employees. These include Steve Ballmer, the former CEO of Microsoft, who joined Microsoft in 1980 as employee no. 30 after dropping out of Stanford's MBA program, and Eric Schmidt, who was Google's CEO from 2001 to 2011. Before that Schmidt had stints as CEO of Novell and CTO of Sun Microsystems. They were both talented employees who had a passion for what they are doing.

Your talent is the foundation, or vehicle, for your success. However, other elements are essential too: Hard work, determination, learning, trials, and errors, dealing with challenges and crises, all the while improving constantly at each step of the way.

As Eddie Cantor put it, in one of my favorite sayings, "It takes 20 years of hard work to make an overnight success!"

Factor #4: Two is better than one

Individually, we are one drop. Together, we are an ocean.

– Ryūnosuke Santoro

I have been blessed to have two amazing partners, Noy and Gbade, with me on my journey. I consider each of them to be "soul mates." Outside of business, Noy has provided physical fitness inspiration, while Gbade has provided spiritual inspiration.

Noy is smart and has deep analytical insight. He is the operational guy who gets things done. Gbade is a visionary, who has given me the faith and ability to see beyond what is visible. Full of love and compassion, Gbade is connected to God, and God is truly a part of him.

Business success is, in my view, a function of trust, execution, and true partnership. Without my partners, I would never have succeeded in the way that I have. More than my business partners, they are also my friends for life. Not only have we made money together, but we have also had a fun and an unforgettable journey.

Whether you run your own business or are an employee, it's impossible to succeed by the separate power of each individual. Teamwork, collaboration, and harmony are essential for success. A successful business requires cooperation between sales, marketing, research & development, operations, finance, business development, and human resources. Organizations are big machines that need all the separate parts to operate simultaneously. If one gear is missing, and there are disconnections, the machine will not function well, and productivity will be damaged.

> **A successful business must include strong partnerships, teamwork, synergy, and collaboration.**

In Ecclesiastes 4:9–12, we read:

"Two are better than one, because they have a good return for their labor. If either of them falls down, one can help the other up. But pity anyone who falls and has no one to help them up. Also, if two lie down together, they will keep warm. But how can one keep warm alone? Though one may be overpowered, two can defend themselves. A cord of three strands is not quickly broken."

Find a partner whom you trust, who shares the same values as you do, complements you, and who is good at the things that you are not good at. You will share the load, and you will share the risk. Planning, which is a critical aspect of success, is a very difficult mission to undertake by yourself. A good partner, with whom you communicate well, will allow you to share ideas, analyze situations, and find solutions.

It is very difficult to overcome a storm by yourself. When you have a bad day, your partner will be there to carry the load on your behalf, and when you fail, your partner will be there to lift you up.

Factor #5: Play it smart

You must pay taxes. But there's no law that
says you gotta leave a tip.

– Morgan Stanley

My maternal grandfather, Jacob Baum, was a successful business-man and used to tell me when I was a boy: "I hope you'll have to pay millions to the taxman." At the time, I didn't understand what he meant. Now I know that this was his way of wishing me great wealth! Today, my accountant helps me pay the minimum allowed by law, and I happily pay whatever is required, grateful that my grandfather's wish for me has come true.

Tax planning and legal consultation are essential to becoming wealthy – and they often help to get you there quicker than you imagined! Having the right professional consultants, on my side, has afforded me the ability to structure the business so that I can reduce taxes, maximize net profits, all the while staying within the framework of the law.

Tax experts and legal consultants can save you a lot of money in real estate investment, tax agreements between various countries, rolling forward of accumulated losses from one year to another, and choosing between different taxation paths to maximize the bottom–line net profit.

Corporate companies enjoy many benefits, including tax defer-rals and credits, that individuals don't. For example, as a business owner, you can legally claim many expenses, which are, of course, tax-deductible. That's a big game-changer in the long run. You can also take your profits as dividends with much fewer taxes than payroll tax.

I pay my professionals hundreds of thousands, and, in return, I save millions. It's one of my best deals.

Factor #6: Money makes more money

Money makes money. And the money that makes money makes more money.

– Benjamin Franklin

Aside from working, there are many other ways to expand your wealth. I've made decent amounts of money in the stock, bonds, and commodities markets. The top investors, all wealthy, follow this factor, and, over a long period, it always works: Buy Low, Sell High!

Sounds simple? It is.

You would, however, be surprised how human nature works. The average investor buys when the markets are high and sells when they are low. When the market is hot, greed pulls the average investors into the markets where they pay irrationally high prices. When the trend reverses and the markets crash, fear pulls the same investors out, and they end up selling for irrationally low prices.

Sophisticated investors wait patiently for these special times. When fear holds the crowd, they buy the goods at (often ridiculously) cheap prices. When the fear fades and the market recovers again, they sell and reap the profits. Then they repeat.

Basically, unsuccessful investors and successful investors – the poor and the rich – behave exactly the opposite of each other.

There are always opportunities to buy low. When a stock or a market is low, everybody knows it's low. The feeling is that it's dead or it will continue to fall forever. After markets crash, after currencies crash, after oil crashes, commodities, cocoa, gold, bonds, markets in Brazil, Turkey, UK, etc., etc. The opportunities are endless.

The bond market lets your money work for you. A bond is a fixed income instrument that represents a loan made by an investor to a borrower, typically, corporate or government. Higher-quality bonds generally offer lower interest rates, while bonds that have a risk factor offer higher interest rates. Bonds pay a fixed interest rate (coupon) to debt holders. Bonds have maturity dates, at which point the principal amount should be paid back in full or you risk defaulting on it.

Playing this instrument wisely can generate a monthly income, as well as potential profit from trading value, by buying low and selling high.

Smart investments will multiply your money over time. The power of compound interest is imperceivable:

- A total amount of $100,000, with a compound interest of 10% p.a., will become a total of $1,744,940 within 30 years.
- Saving an additional $1,000 every month on the initial investment amount will give you a total sum of $3,916,261 within the same period.

Get to know and follow the wealthiest investors – people who turned millions into billions by buying low and selling high: John Templeton, Warren Buffet, Benjamin Graham, George Soros, Jack Boyle. Study their behavior. It's easy to complicate things, but it's always about simplicity.

The bottom line is that money makes more money.

Factor #7: Diversify

Diversification is a safety factor that is essential because we should be humble enough to admit we can be wrong.

– John Templeton

Almost all wealthy investors diversify, never putting all their eggs in one basket. The reason is simple:

> **Change is the only constant thing in life.**

In doing so, the investors are taking their lead from nature that has much to teach us about the value of diversification. The natural world is filled with a great variety of animals and plants. When one type of tree is infected, the disease will not necessarily impact another species of tree. The extinction of a specific species will never materially affect creation as a whole. At its essence, this is diversification in action; nature does not take risks that will impact all its creatures. Similarly, millions of sperm cells are released in a single ejaculation. All the cells work hard, in parallel, towards one mission: the conception of a single ovule, resulting in a new embryo. Diversity in nature generates survival, continuity, and success.

Nowadays, where the pace of change is so rapid, leading companies, including Amazon, Google, and Apple, have all diversified to achieve their prestigious international status. Amazon, which began in 1994, as a marketplace for books, has since expanded to sell electronics, software, video games, apparel, furniture, food, toys jewelry, and even vehicles. Today, Amazon has diversified into being a cloud provider (AWS), as well as providing entertainment and music through Amazon Prime and Music.

Where possible, you too should endeavor to spread your money around so that, should one sector decline, you have money safely invested elsewhere to make up the losses. Never base your business on a single client or a single product. Buy real estate in different locations, play in several markets, buy bonds, equities, commodities, currencies.

> **The more you diversify, the more risks you can afford to take.**

Diversification allowed me to be more comfortable when taking risks in various individual investments. As I explained earlier, my business almost went bankrupt, in 2012, when our main supplier shifted its focus and left Africa. We only had one main supplier in one country (Nigeria). It was an important, albeit expensive, lesson. Since then, I have expanded the product portfolio of my suppliers. We now have more than twenty suppliers, spread across many African countries.

The possibilities to diversify are endless. You can open an online business that works for you, invest in real estate as an asset to generate income, buy bonds, participate in your company's ESPP, or buy long-term leading stock indexes. Don't ever rely on one source of income. Many employees learned this lesson, in a very hard way, when governments imposed lockdowns as a result of Covid-19. What had once been "secure" income was suddenly not that secure anymore. If your entire existence is dependent on a single pay cheque, it is very difficult not to live in fear. Finding a legal and ethical way to generate a second income, outside of your working hours, such as a web store or another source of passive income, while remaining employed, seems to me something that businesses should be encouraging in order for employees to see the benefits of diversification.

There is, of course, a contrarian view that favors focus rather than diversification. I believe that these two contrary approaches can – and should – coexist. Focus is the key to success in each pillar of your investments while diversification is essential to eliminate total failure should one pillar crumble. The formula for building wealth over a lifetime is to diversify laterally while focusing vertically.

In basketball there is only one ball; the team that controls the ball will win the game. Don't play basketball in your financial field. Rather play golf where you have many balls to play to win the game. If you lose a ball, there is always another one inside your golf bag.

Factor #8: Never quit!

Men do not quit playing because they grow old; they grow old because they quit playing.
– Oliver Wendell Holmes

As I recounted earlier, my "early retirement" plans hit a snag when I realized that "quitting" was simply not for me. I needed to work to keep my brain sharp and to stay on purpose and connected to the world of interesting people that one meets when working.

When God created human beings, he was very clear: "By the sweat of your brow you will eat your food until you return to the ground, since from it you were taken; for dust you are and to dust, you will return." (Genesis 3:19)

Whether you work for yourself or others, don't live with the thought of "One day when I no longer have to work, I will..." Recognize that life is the journey itself. Don't make retirement (or "quitting") your target.

> **Don't think about stopping. Think about growing.**

Enjoy work, meet people, develop new skills, and improve your knowledge. Don't work hard, work smart! Once you have deployed the "formula" for wealth, you should have much more free time.

Don't wait for retirement to make time for hobbies, friends, vacations, and family. When you play the financial game correctly, the money you make will free up your time. Positive interest, income, dividends, rentals, and coupons all work in your favor to make you wealthy and to improve the quality of your life.

It's never too late to start doing the right things. Time passes anyway. The only question to ask is: "What were you doing while time was doing its thing?"

Start today, don't procrastinate. The clock is ticking, and every moment counts.

IX. THE FORMULA FOR RELATIONSHIPS

Relationships =
1. Love yourself first
2. Take responsibility
3. Make love
4. Give and don't expect to receive
5. Opposites attract
6. Communicate
7. Connect

The meeting of two personalities is like the contact of two chemical substances: if there is any reaction, both are transformed.

– Carl Jung

In the Creation Story of the Old Testament, we are told that, on the sixth day, God created the first couple – Adam and Eve. Subsequently, God said: "It is not good for the man to be alone." Right from "the beginning" then, we learn that human beings are not built for a solitary existence.

> **Humans are social creatures who depend on each other.**

Most animals live in communities; their only ability to survive is by the power of the herd. Thousands of years ago, when we lived in the savannahs, our survival as human beings depended on our ability to live in communities. Being alone usually meant becoming dinner for wild animals. Thousands of years later, we still rely on one another.

Loneliness kills.

From the moment we are born, until the moment we die, we need loving relationships. Research shows that babies born in an environment lacking in love, suffer from developmental issues. The orbitofrontal cortex is almost wholly dependent upon the environment into which an infant is born. A lack of love, emotional warmth, and physical contact slows down the growth mechanisms in the brain and body.

Put plainly, the human growth hormones are in short supply when we do not have enough love around us. The "love" (or "hugging") hormone, oxytocin, plays a crucial role. Oxytocin contributes to the growth of many of our body's cells. We often hear about elderly couples who, having been together for decades, die within a few months from each other. There is actual science behind the phenomenon. The "broken heart syndrome" is believed to occur when someone loses a close partner or spouse. Lack of love, and the loneliness that accompanies it, can cause severe damage to us at any age. In 2018, the UK appointed a loneliness minister to deal with the country's chronic loneliness problem. If this is not a sign of the times, I am not sure what is!

One of the ironies of the Covid-19 pandemic was that to save lives, we created what some psychologists see as a much greater threat to humanity than the virus, i.e. the loneliness and isolation that resulted from lockdowns and the oxymoronic concept of "social distancing." Social distancing and isolation, while critical to preventing the virus, are not "natural" human activities. Even though we may have saved lives, quality of life is no less important than quantity. The quality of your life depends on the quality of your relationships, be these life partnerships, friendships, or family connections. In nature, even the smallest particle, the atom, of which all creation is made, consists of a coupling of a proton and an electron.

The continuity of human existence lies in the connections made between human beings. The way to evaluate the strength of a connection is by the sequel it creates. In nature, when the connection between two components is "right," a third thing is born, e.g. the connection between hydrogen and oxygen creates water, while the connection between a sperm and an ovary creates an embryo. The "right" connection between people, specifically in an intimate relationship, creates harmony, love, peace, and of course, should procreation occur, the continuity of generations is secured.

As we have seen throughout this book, everything in nature works according to rules. When people in a relationship try to live without rules, acting only on instincts, or according to faulty behavior they have observed or learned, there will be chaos. In this section, I outline the fundamental rules for a successful relationship, with a specific focus on intimate relationships and, where relevant, the relationships that exist within families.

Factor #1: Love yourself first

Be yourself; everyone else is already taken.

– Oscar Wilde

You are one of eight billion unique individuals on this planet, with your own fingerprint, DNA sequence, and identity. There is no duplicate of you anywhere. Yet, we are so busy trying to change ourselves to be someone (or something) else. In the attempt to become something that we are not, we forget to celebrate the only thing we can be. Ourselves!

One of our greatest fears is to feel unloved. This is the main reason that most of us care so much about what others think of us. In our mission to be loved by others, we build masks and place shields around ourselves so that we will be seen in a positive light by the external world. If we take off the masks, if we stop being fake, if we allow ourselves to be exactly who we are, we can love and be loved without limits.

Self-acceptance is a crucial step on the journey to loving yourself.

There is no perfect weight, no perfect look, and no perfect behavior. They are all a point of view or interpretation. Pretty or ugly, right or wrong, success or failure, are all in the eyes of the beholder. You can love red today and change your mind tomorrow. One person loves skinny while another loves chubby; one loves quiet people while the other loves noisy ones. In some cultures, for example, "fat" is a status symbol for success and beauty, while being thin is regarded as poor and unhealthy. In others, "skinny" is the gold standard.

Our warped perceptions of reality shape our lives. Oftentimes, things that look like "truths," turn out to be trends and fads. Our environments influence the way we think and capture reality. Too often, we are led by consensus. Our job is to take back control of our own brains, thereby choosing our perspectives on things. Look in the mirror and love yourself with your weight, your height, the color of your eyes, and the mole on your face. Being unique is far better than being boring. We are not mass-produced in factories. We are special, unique individuals. We must learn to strengthen our self-acceptance, stand firm, and not be overly influenced by the crowd.

There is an endless range of options and possibilities on offer. You can decide not to accept yourself as you are, to be frustrated, to look for what is missing, and to care about what others think, and what they have. This is a recipe for misery. But there is another option: You can "hug" your reality and accept yourself exactly as you are.

Remember that life has two poles. It can always get better, but it can also get worse. You can lose your health, your wealth, your beauty, your talent, and, of course, your life. Be grateful for what you currently have. Accept yourself; love yourself exactly as you are.

You can't, of course, give something that you don't have. If you are looking for loving relationships, the first place to look is in the mirror! Learning to love and accept myself has been, and continues to be, a priority for me. The more I learn to accept myself, the more able I am to accept others as they are, without judgment and criticism. I have no desire to change others into something (or someone) else. I accept others despite their differences.

There is light and shade in each of us. We can choose our focus. Love allows us to accept the negative while enhancing the positive.

This applies equally to me and others. I spent many years of my life beating myself up for not being "good enough." And, of course, I judged others in the same way. When I learned to love and accept myself, I was also able to accept and recognize the things I did not like. From that place, I was able to start making changes.

> **Self-love and acceptance are not about resigning yourself to life. They are about making changes from a place of self-compassion.**

When you look at a tree, in summer, its leaves are green. In the autumn, the leaves turn gold, and in winter the leaves turn brown and fall to the ground. In the spring, new leaves sprout, and so the cycle continues. When the tree stands naked in winter, we still see the beauty of nature and our hearts can be filled with love and joy. When you accept things without judgment, when you appreciate the wonders of creation and the inevitable changes that time brings, you allow yourself to feel pure love.

We are so special just the way we are. Certainly, we have days when we look and feel better than others. But, like the tree, we are whole, part of the wonder called "life."

Factor #2: Take responsibility

Blaming the wolf would not help the sheep much. The sheep must learn not to fall into the clutches of the wolf.

– Mahatma Gandhi

The world outside of you is a reflection of your inner world. When you look in a mirror and see a spot on your face, you don't try to clean the mirror. The mirror is not the problem! Once you fix the problem at its source, the problem ceases to appear in the outside world. Healthy relationships require us to stop looking outside for solutions. Instead, we need to look within.

The imperfections which we see in others are rooted within us.

A few years ago, I was comfortably sitting on my couch, watching a football game, when Talia asked me an innocuous question. A simple "yes" or "no" was all that was required. Instead, angry at her for interrupting my leisure time with a silly question, I exploded. But here's the thing. The anger had nothing to do with my wife or the question. Talia is not an irritating woman. I was an angry person. The anger controlled my behavior and had it continued, we would have gotten divorced. This, however, would not have solved my "anger issues" or our "relationship problems."

The quality of our relationships with others is dependent on the quality of the relationship we have with ourselves. You can marry seven times or even remain single. The irritating environment around you will not disappear. When you are divorced, alone at home, and, accidentally, knock your toe on the chair that you forgot to move the previous evening, you will get angry at the chair, curse it, and probably blame the carpenter who manufactured it!

As long you do not deal with your emotions, such as anger, jealousy, or fear, they will never disappear. They will simply change form.

A simple change can completely change your life. Stop pointing your finger outwards and start pointing it at yourself. Look at your hand and notice that when you're pointing one finger outwards, three fingers are automatically pointed back towards you. Stop blaming others and begin to take full responsibility for yourself.

Once again, the importance of this lesson is illustrated in "the beginning" when Adam and Eve were living in "Paradise":

"The Lord God called out to the man and said to him, "

Where are you?"

He answered, "I heard you in the garden, and I was afraid because I was naked; so, I hid."

Then He asked, "Who told you that you were naked? Did you eat of the tree from which I had forbidden you to eat?"

The man said, "The woman You put at my side—she gave me of the tree, and I ate."

And the LORD God said to the woman, "What is this you have done!" The woman replied, "The serpent duped me, and I ate."

The blame game is in full force here: Adam blames Eve and Eve blames the serpent. Later, Adam blames God for the wife he gave him! Sound familiar? Neither of them is willing to learn from their mistakes. Instead, they blame others and do not take responsibility. And so, they are expelled from paradise.

Notice that the question God asks Adam is, "Where are you?" Scholars have debated this question. If God is all-seeing and all-knowing, he knows where Adam is. But this question is not geographical; it is a moral question: Where is your responsibility? Where are you in your relationships? Where are you with your partner, your children, your siblings, your parents? Where are you with your attitudes? What are your relationships showing you about yourself? How much responsibility are you taking?

There is no point in spending your life blaming others for what is happening, or not happening, in your life. No amount of blame, or making others feel guilty, will change the situation. When you start to take responsibility and stop blaming others, something magical happens in your life. Your "response-ability" gets stronger. Your ability to manage your responses towards events that appear in your day-to-day life changes dramatically. Where once an event would drive you out of your mind, you are now in control, able to observe the feelings of anger within you and to make a conscious decision not to respond angrily. You can count to three between the event and the response. The "angry person" that managed you is no longer the master of your life.

Take responsibility and stop pointing your finger outward. It will miraculously heal your relationships.

Factor #3: Make love

When you find that their well-being is a higher priority than your cravings, you're in love.

— Ryan Howes

Most people confuse love and passion. We say, "I love chocolate" but, in truth, we don't love the chocolate itself. We love ourselves having the chocolate. We love the feeling that the chocolate gives us. We call it love, but it's just selfishness; we love the joy it provides us. Before eating the chocolate, we craved it. When it is finished, we don't feel any emotions towards it. Where did our love for it disappear to? Once our craving is satiated by the chocolate, the true face of our imaginary love for it is revealed.

What about your partner?

Do you really love your partner, or do you love the feeling of pleasure that they give you? Is it craving or is it love? Is it conditional or unconditional love? If your partner does not return your love, do you still feel love for them?

The best example of true love, love without conditions, is the love we have for our children. The mother carries the infant for nine months in her womb and then suffers unbearable birth pains. Both parents have sleepless nights and invest many years of hard work into raising the child to maturity. This natural process creates a deep connection with the child and is the basis for unconditional love. It doesn't matter if our children return the love or not, we will always love them. That is why there is a commandment, in the Old Testament, to honor your father and mother – but there is no commandment to honor your children. There is no need for such a commandment. As parents, the effort we place into the relationship with our children creates an unconditional love that lasts forever.

At the beginning of a relationship when we find the "one," we describe ourselves as "falling in love." We feel high, there are "butterflies" in our stomach, the body releases Oxytocin into the bloodstream which keeps us "drugged," and the physical attraction is extreme. It almost feels like spiritual transcendence. We want this feeling to last forever, doing all we can to hold on to it. But it is called the "honeymoon phase" for a reason; it is temporary, created by nature for a reason. The euphoria is what creates the initial binding. And in so doing, it weakens the ego and gives us the ability to truly see someone else other than ourselves. The "falling in love phase" acts like the starter of our car. The motor needs an external force, powered by the battery, to start it. But you can't run your car for any kind of significant distance with this starting battery energy. It is not meant for long distances. This holds true for love, too. The next stage – after we have fallen in love – is to create a sustainable love that will last. This is when we need to run the car engine on fuel so that it can function effectively over a long distance.

Many people fall in love, get married, and, when the initial euphoria evaporates, they become frustrated and disappointed. And then the relationship starts to fall apart, as they struggle to keep the flame burning. It is called "falling in love" for a reason. After every fall, we should collect ourselves, put in extra effort, and continue the climb.

Just as wood is the fuel for fire, so is caring, attention, mutual respect, and open communication, the fuel that drives relationships and creates sustainable love. Preserving the relationship is an endless job. We must invest time and effort, create intimacy, and make sure that we do not take each other for granted.

> **People look for love, but love is not something we "find." Love is something we "create" through hard work and determination.**

We connect to things in which we invest our energy and effort.

For many years, my daughters tried to persuade me to get a dog. When I was seven years old, I was scratched and bitten by my best friend's cat. For years afterwards, I asked myself, "If a cat could bite me, and it was so sore, what would happen if I was bitten by a dog?" Ever since, whenever I saw a dog approaching me in the street, I would cross to the other side of the road. I kept my distance and developed a lifetime aversion to all pets. Eventually, after many years of pressure, I relented and let my daughters get a dog. My conditions were clear: "The dog is your responsibility; I'm not getting involved in raising it." For the first month, they walked Louis three times a day, played with him, and gave him water, food, and love. As time passed, the love remained, but their attention and efforts faded. Gradually, the morning trips and the feeding became my responsibility. The more investment and effort I put into the relationship, the closer I felt towards Louis. My love for him got stronger and stronger. He's a part of my family now. The effort, attention, and sweat I gave to the relationship created my unconditional love.

In Genesis 3:19 we are told: "By the sweat of your brow you will eat your food."

No sweat; no food. We must sweat to earn our bread, to earn our health, to earn our money, and, in this case, to earn our relationships.

Factor #4: Give and don't expect to receive

Don't judge each day by the harvest you reap, but by
the seeds you plant.
– Robert Louis Stevenson

In the past, in the days before self-awareness became a priority in my life, the following scenario played itself out in my home regularly. Arriving home late, after a long day at work, I would find the kitchen sink full of dirty dishes. Immediately, I'd yell at Talia. And, of course, she would yell back at me. We both wanted the other to wash the dishes. After a good screaming match, both of us were still angry, one of us lost the battle and the dishes got cleaned.

And then I discovered that there is another way...

I come home late, after a long day at work, to find the kitchen sink full of dirty dishes. I say to my wife, "I know you had a tough day with the kids, I want to assist, you rest, and I will clean the dishes." Talia responds, "No way, you just come back from a long day at work, you go and relax. I will quickly clean the dishes and then you can tell me about your day at work." We "fight" gently about who will "please" the other today, and we finally agree. The house is filled with love and peace. In both cases, the dishes were done. In one scenario, with anger and, in the other, with love and tenderness.

We always have both options. Which would you choose?

In the first scenario, all that happened is that my ego got in the way. I have learned, and experienced first-hand, that when my ego is dominant, my relationships don't work. The moment each partner agrees to give up their ego, when each side is prepared to accept that the world does not revolve around their individual needs, when your craving can be eliminated or postponed for the benefit of the other, then love can take its place and flourish.

John F Kennedy's famous maxim, "Ask not what your country can do for you, ask what you can do for your country," applies equally to relationships. Rather than asking, "What can I get from you?" begin by asking, "What can I give to you?" Rather than criticizing one another, ask, "How can I complement you in the areas that you are weak, or in the activities that you don't like?"

Stephen Covey says that we should think about our relationships as a bank account. Every time you give, you are making a "deposit," and every time you take, you are "withdrawing" from the account. Like a healthy bank account, you should always have a positive balance in your relationship i.e., more deposits than withdrawals. When your account is in overdraft, your relationship is at risk.

Factor #5: Opposites attract

When "I" is replaced by "we," even "illness" becomes "wellness."
                                                        −Malcolm X

To operate an electric device, the current must flow from the positive pole to the negative pole. Trying to connect plus with plus, or minus with minus, will not work. The opposite poles must connect precisely. If there is a contact breaker or a short circuit, the device will not function.

This simple natural law applies to relationships too. We are drawn to partners who are different from us, in the hope that they will complete our imperfections. Deep beneath our individual armors of pride, we know that we are imperfect and that we have a long journey of self-growth to reach the highest level of who we are. But with an armor of pride, who wants to change themselves? And here begins our search for the right partner, the one who has what we are missing. Initially, it is the differences that cause the attraction, then, as the relationship develops, we begin to try to change our partner.

Talia and I have been together since she graduated high school. More than twenty years later, our love is still expanding and keeps getting stronger. We have many things in common and share the same values. Yet, we are vastly different. Talia tends to be more sensitive, intuitive, and creative while I'm more logical, rational, and analytical. I'm a very practical person. When Talia wants empathy, I offer solutions.

These differences have worked in our favor. The two sides of the poles are essential when it comes to raising our children, for example. Talia is always there to hug them, to say the right thing in difficult situations, to be warm and gentle, and to spread her love and calmness. I am there, on the other side to put the limits in place. We have always played good cop-bad cop, and it has worked for our family.

Our differences were also essential to building our wealth. I thought logically and practically, taking it upon myself to support the family financially. Often, this required my leaving the family for long periods, doing whatever was needed to bring money home. Talia managed the house and acted as both parents when I was away. She was the family's "backrest." We have sustained a mutual flow that has enabled us to grow as individuals, together. Over the years, we have balanced and nourished one another. We need each other physically and mentally. We are different but complementary.

Successful relationships must have mutual flow. Each partner should contribute to the other. As long there is sufficient flow, and there is no disconnection, the partnership will prosper. Knowing that we depend on each other should change our point of view. Trying to change your partner to be like you is hopeless and illogical. The differences are just that; they are not better, or worse. Do not judge them. Do not try to change them or make the differences go away. They are essential. Accept and embrace them and thank your partner for providing what you lack.

You do not need to "correct" anything in others. Your love will expand and grow when you see, in your partner, your other half, and you see the differences as complementary to what is "missing" within you.

Factor #6: Communicate

Communication to a relationship is like oxygen to life.
Without it, it dies.

– Tony Gaskins

In the past, I used to come home late with my phone connected to my ear, or my eyes staring at the screen. My children would run to me, excited to see their dad, wanting to tell me about their day. All I saw was noise, a distraction from my '"important" business. I was there, but I was not present.

I was mentally paralyzed, unable to appreciate what was right in front of my eyes. I saw money and respect when all they wanted was attention and warmth.

Now I recognize that I was allowing my ego to place my priorities in the wrong place. Even though I paid lip service to the importance of family, by my actions, led by my ego, I placed myself first, telling myself: "I am the breadwinner, I am the important one." Judging by my actions, everything else – work, friends, money – seemed to come first. Was my family really my priority?

Nowadays, I sit in my car, outside my house, and do not enter until I feel sure that I can allocate 100% of my attention to my family. When I do, I hug and kiss my children, and pay attention. I listen to what they have to say and I'm attentive to their feelings, to the words that are not said, the things that are said in a language that only the heart can understand. Fortunately, I woke up before it was too late, before I "lost" my children due to ignorance, inattention, and egoism. Once your level of awareness increases, you stop behaving unconsciously in ways that do not serve you. Strong families find ways to allow everybody to talk about their thoughts and feelings. When you open your heart to your family, you allow for the creation of intimacy and strong connections.

> **Things that come from the heart, go into the heart.**

Strong families also spend time together. Talia insists that our whole family spends quality time together at least once a week. Every Friday evening, she cooks delicious food, which we enjoy as a family. The dinner begins with prayers. This traditional Jewish ritual, which has been practiced for centuries, is a built – in way for families to connect. No matter your religion, I highly recommend it! Sitting at our round table, each one of us shares three good things that happened during the week. It is a ritual that keeps us grateful and connected.

Epictetus, the Greek philosopher, is purported to have said, "We have two ears and one mouth so that we can listen twice as much as we speak." To strengthen communication among family members, I recommend starting with improving your listening skills. Communication is listening first, then talking and sharing your opinion.

> **Contrary to what is often thought, it is listeners, not speakers, who control communication.**

By choosing to engage with the speaker, or to tune them out, as well as by interpreting what is said, listeners hold the key to effective communication.

Give your family members your full attention; switch off your phone or put down whatever you are doing. Listen carefully to what they are saying and try to understand the intentions behind their words. Do not give advice until you are certain that you have fully understood what the person means. Most times the other side is not even interested in advice or feedback. All they want is someone to listen to them, empathy without criticism.

As Carl W. Buehner so beautifully put it, "People will forget what you said, they will forget what you did, but they will never forget how you made them feel."[36]

Although we lead very busy lives, maintaining strong relationships requires attention. Family memories are built around family activities. Rituals and routines can give your family all the time it needs – but you need to respect those times. Having dinner, celebrating holidays, going to church, or getting outside and being active, are all ways to bring everyone together.

My family used to spend our vacations with other families. I'd find myself sitting and talking to my friends, Talia to her friends, and my children to their friends.

It was all fine, and quite enjoyable. However, after we got home, and, upon reflection, I realized that our nuclear family had spent very little quality time with each other. The main purpose of the holiday, to spend quality and quantity time as a family, had not been achieved.

After this realization, we decided to limit summer vacations to our nuclear family. As a result, the relationships between my daughters have improved, they learn from and enjoy each other, and Talia and I have time to talk to each other and to be with our girls too.

---

36 This quote is often erroneously attributed to Maya Angelou (https://quoteinvestigator. com/2014/04/06/they-feel/).

When we face difficult times, we need other people to support us. When everything looks bad and life feels like a dead-end, nothing is more valuable than the support of the people we love. They encourage us to push through and stand by us in difficult times. When someone you love gives you their hand, the way forward feels easier than having to do it alone.

Imagine the following scenario: You pick up the phone, and your doctor is on the other side of the line. "I have bad news for you," he says. "You have a maximum of 90 days left to live." What would you do? Who would you tell first?

Live your life today as if you only have 90 days left:
- Who would you want to spend these 90 days with?
- What would you want to tell them during that time?
- What would you do with them?
- Will you give them your full attention?

Don't wait for the phone call. Hug your partner, your children, tell them how much you love them, how important they are to you. Look into their souls, touch them, and feel them. We are visitors here for a limited time.

Factor #7: Connect

We are what we connect to.

– Zat Rana

I've embraced technology and innovation in my life and work, so I'm very connected to the digital world in which we now live. It's a vastly different world from the one in which I grew up. The global tempo has changed, and growth is now exponential. iPods were revolutionary not so long ago. Now you hardly see them. Kodak, Nokia, and Blackberry were a phenomenon. Where are they now? That's how quickly our world changes.

This is the digital century, and we are all digitally connected now. The villages of the past have become massive cities with millions of people but with very little human interaction. The local neighborhood shops are gone, replaced by massive conglomerates that, in turn, have been replaced by online shops. The Amazons, eBays, and Ali Expresses disconnect us from the analog interface – face-to-face interaction. Even deliveries that were once done by the neighborhood postman will soon be replaced by drones that drop the goods at our front doors.

Less than 100 years ago, if you wanted to talk to friends, you had to meet them physically. After the invention of the telephone, these conversations began to occur over the "wires." Today, everything is wireless. Most of our conversations happen via text or instant message applications such as WhatsApp or Zoom calls, and, by the time you are reading this book, we may be meeting virtually over the "Metaverse." Even email now seems quaint. In-person, and even verbal, discussions have become less common. Rather, we stay "connected" by sharing our experiences over Facebook, Instagram, and Snapchat, entertaining our virtual "friends," but we miss the intimacy of the human interface.

In the digital age when there is a strong need for bonding, people are attracted to solutions like WeWork for finding shared working spaces, and in Singapore, there are already public shared vehicles. Hopefully, people will physically communicate and compensate for the damage done by the digital era. In this manner, the Covid-19 pandemic made things even worse. We were all isolated at home, forcing us to be digitally connected. When going out, we were forced to wear masks covering our mouths and noses.

We face many challenges in the digital era. This shouldn't hold us back from trying to do the right things to remain connected:

- **Spend face-to-face time, not _Face Time_:** To truly know someone, you must spend time together. There are no shortcuts. When we gain trust and are open with each other, the depth of the relationship will correlate with the time we spend together, face to face, sharing experiences. Mutual interests will strengthen and deepen the relationship further. To earn friends, invest your time in the relationships.
- **Use digital media, but don't fall into its traps:** The smartphone, like any other tool, can work for or against you. When you meet with your friends, focus on them, listen, laugh, give sympathy, open your heart, pay attention, hear what they say, and, most importantly, listen for the feelings behind their words.
- **Gain trust:** When we meet someone for the first time, we are in evaluating mode. We're looking for the answer to the very

fundamental question, "Can I trust you?" The relationship can't be established if there is not a sufficient level of trust. Give your trust with no preliminary conditions. Fundamentally, people are good, but they are covered with layers and shields. If you look deeply, you will find good intentions and love in most people.

- **Move to openness:** Only when trust is established, can the relationship progress to the next level. If I don't trust you and you don't trust me, what can we accomplish? After trust, openness is the second foundation on the way to true and strong relationships.

X. THE FORMULA FOR SPIRITUALITY

Spirituality =
1. Connect to the Source
2. Dis-cover your soul
3. The power of faith
4. Fulfill your purpose
5. Read the User Manual ("RTFM")
6. Find God

The day you were born is the day God decided that the world could not exist without you.

– Rabbi Nachman of Breslov

A man, arriving in Manhattan for an important meeting, struggles to find a parking space. Driving around, and starting to get desperate, he turns to God: "Please God, I need your help. I have to get to this meeting..." As he finishes praying, a truck pulls out, freeing up two parking spaces. The man turns back to God: "It's ok, God, no need, I just found one..."

While spirituality and faith are elusive topics, it is "reality" itself that is actually illusory.

Everything is made up of atoms. Humans, animals, plants, and inanimate objects are all made up of atoms. Every atom is about 99.999% empty space. Scientists assert that, were we to shrink all the material on earth, without the spaces, it would be the size of a golf ball! Although our eyes see a material world, the truth is that almost all reality is made up of energy and spirit. Einstein, the greatest scientist of them all stated it clearly: "Reality is merely an illusion, although a very persistent one."[37]

At a certain point in the journey of writing this book, it became clear to me that it would be incomplete if I did not address the spiritual aspects of life. For many years, I had functioned, almost exclusively, in the material world, far removed from emotions and even further from spirit. My focus had been on the accumulation of "stuff," including assets and kilograms. I believed only in what was visible and tangible – in what I could experience with my five senses. I was too preoccupied with the material and physical world to engage in any form of deep introspection.

I had accomplished my goals, but I still felt incomplete. The spiritual aspects of my life remained unsolved. I continued to ask myself questions, such as:

• Who I am? Am I my thoughts? My emotions? My character? My body or, perhaps, my soul?
• Why do I exist? What is my life's purpose?
• Is God just a manmade myth?
• What will remain of me when I'm gone? Is reincarnation real?

When I thought about tackling the spiritual chapter, I had no clue where to start, so I looked for a creative solution. Then, I had a brilliant idea – Gbade could be my shortcut! As mentioned previously, Gbade, my Nigerian business partner and friend, is a spiritual person with deep faith in God and Jesus. He talks to God and his life is guided by the Bible and his faith.

---

37 If you are interested in this topic, check out: http://www.esalq.usp.br/lepse/imgs/conteu-do_thumb/The-Illusion-of-Reality---The-Scientific-Proof-That-Everything-is-Energy-and-Real-ity-Isnt-Real.pdf

I called Gbade. "I need help to write this chapter," I said. "I know little about the spiritual side of life, and I need your experience please," I continued. I told him that I would send him a draft of the book, asked him to read it carefully, and then to write the chapter for me. I ended our conversation by asking him to send it to me when it was complete.

A few weeks went by, and I had not heard from Gbade. I called to ask how the writing was going. I was met by silence. After a few seconds, Gbade responded: "You have to write this chapter yourself. I trust you, my dear friend. Good luck."

So, in much the same way as I had done when I began the book, I decided to acquire knowledge, and find ways to simplify this elusive and intangible topic. I was not willing to give up, even if it were to delay the book's publication. I threw myself into the subject. It became a journey of years and did delay the book. But it changed my life completely.

When investigating the question of spirituality, almost no matter where you look, the big question that arises is:

Is this magnificent universe the result of a Creator or was there just a "Big Bang"?

Put differently:

Do we live in a world where everything works in perfect order, guided by supreme wisdom, or is it all completely random and chaotic?

Somehow, it is easier for human beings to comprehend the physical laws of the universe, where everything fits perfectly into precise formulae. When we see an apple fall from a tree, we recognize the law of gravity. When we hit a wall with full force, we recognize the law of action-reaction.

But then things get complicated. It is seemingly difficult for us to "see" the unseen, to "sense" the intangible, and to believe that the universal laws apply to the spiritual side of life too. Although we can't see radio waves, infrared light, or electricity, we can see their actions. The sound from the speakers or the movement of the mixer is proof of the existence of electricity. Similarly, watching leaves blowing, or feeling the wind caressing my face gently, proves the existence of wind. We can see the wind only by its actions.

Haim Bialik, the Israeli poet, expressed this perfectly:
"We don't see the wind, but she is the one that sails the ship, not the rags that fly above the mast, visible to all."

The same principle applies to the non-physical, or spiritual, universal laws. They are accurate, constant, and they appear by their actions. Unlike the physical laws, however, the non-physical laws, such as the law of attraction, are free of time and space. When I hit a wall, the pain is instantaneous. The non-physical laws, however, work like a boomerang. When I lie, steal, or hurt others, my actions initiate reactions. The boomerang has been launched. When and where will it come back to me? It can take hours, months, or years. But it will always come back; it works according to universal laws. Fortunately, the laws work both ways. When I assist others, when I contribute money, time, or love, the spiritual laws will pay it back. Some call this Karma; I call it law!

The boundaries of the spiritual world are clear, and human beings have the right and privilege to play within the framework of Creation.[38]

---

38 This is beautifully described in the following passage of Judaic text (Ethics of the Fathers, Chapter 3,16): "He (Rabbi Akiva) used to say: Everything is given against a pledge, and a net is spread out over all the living; the store is open and the storekeeper allows credit, but the ledger is open and the hand writes, and whoever wishes to borrow may come and borrow; but the collectors go round regularly every day and exact dues from man, either with his consent or without his consent, and they have that on which they [can] rely [in their claims], seeing that the judgment is a righteous judgment, and everything is prepared for the banquet."

The question to which I kept returning was:

Is everything completely random or remarkably accurate?

The answer proved crucial to my understanding of the essential nature of my life in this world. Over time, I have become convinced that the harmony, accuracy, and "intelligence" that exists in the universe simply cannot be the result of chance. Somehow, someone or something has to be orchestrating this show.

The heat of the sun, at its core, is around 15 million degrees Celsius. Outside the Earth's atmosphere the temperature is minus 270 degrees Celsius. Miraculously, the heat of the sun is just right for the living conditions on Earth. The infinite galaxies are coordinated; no galaxy ever deviates from its orbit or intercepts another galaxy's route.

As of 2022, there are almost 8 billion people on the planet, each of whom has a unique serial number, their fingerprint. Surely "randomness" would result in some duplication, somewhere? The human cell was formed 3 billion years ago and has hardly changed since. Evolution did not create the cell structure or its workings; it was there in its full glory right from the beginning.

Our bodies are made up of many different parts, each performing a vital action. The lungs provide oxygen for themselves and the other body parts; the stomach digests the food to feed itself, as well as the rest of the body. Your leg needs the knee, muscles, and blood vessels. The components cannot function independently. The heart cannot be selfish and say, "I will only beat for myself." Each part exists both for itself and for the whole body.

Everything is connected, and there is a symbiosis and harmony in all of creation. There is an overt and covert, direct and indirect, immediate and future synergy. Nothing exists solely for itself. Every individual affects someone or something else. The giver has no significance without the recipient, and the recipient needs the giver. Each creature has a purpose to fulfill and is needed to assemble the complete puzzle.

My spiritual journey changed my life. I discovered my soul and the forces that make life possible. I learned how to connect to the abundance and infinity of this universe, and to live without limitations. Now, I live with a feeling of freedom, and I surrender to whatever comes my way. I have learned to open my hands, to hug my reality, the good and the bad, and to take comfort in knowing that everything is accurate and for the best. It's all a part of my journey to fulfilling my life's purpose.

In this chapter, I will share with you the primary factors that influenced and led me towards a life of love, compassion, peace, and abundance.

I speak throughout this chapter of "God." For me, as a person of the Jewish faith, God has certain names, functions, and characteristics. Here, however, my use of the word "God" refers holistically to the "God–force," the "Creator," or the "manufacturer," whose energy suffuses the universe. Being "religious" is not the same as being "spiritual." To be religious is to embrace the dogma of a (or your) faith. I stand in no judgment of anyone's choice in this regard. To be spiritual, in my view, is to be connected to a Higher Power, and to follow rules and guidance based on a deep investigation and logical explanations, rather than following a specific leader or traditional myths.

Factor #1: Connect to the Source

If you want to find the secrets of the universe, think in terms of energy, frequency, and vibration.

– Nikola Tesla

Imagine that a magician, Houdini 2.0, comes to town with new show called "Juggling for Infinity". The magician holds three balls in his hands. He skillfully throws them in the air, and they fly up and down. The rhythm keeps flowing. Houdini 2.0 adds another ball and another, eventually managing to juggle 100 balls simultaneously, without dropping any of them.

Suddenly, he puts his hands inside his pockets. The balls continue to spin without the magician's intervention. It is an incredible sight. The international media covers the phenomenon. The whole world is enthralled by the almighty magician.

Now, think about the universe. As you read this sentence, billions of galaxies are spinning in precise orbits, and the earth is circling the sun, while simultaneously spinning on its axis. Billions of stars orbit around us, yet not a single star or galaxy falls to earth. The earth never pauses.

The universe, into which we were born, is a miracle. Yet, we take it for granted, seldom acknowledging how special it is. Human beings have reached the moon, explored galaxies, and mapped DNA. We know so much about the physical universe, but most of us understand little about the non-physical aspects of our existence.

Seemingly unlimited forces make our existence possible. Our lives are filled with endless "magic."

It may appear as if there is no order, and that things happen randomly and chaotically. Mother Nature is precise; she does not make errors. When you step back and survey the "big picture," it appears that the universe is being perfectly orchestrated. The "music" of this miraculous concert can't play by itself. Houdini 2.0 and other magic "tricks" are a wonder to us, yet the universe, and our existence within it, is "normal." It's just another day, in a mostly boring life.

This is a wake-up call!

Everything around, and within, you is an absolute marvel.

Our bodies are the most sophisticated creation of them all.. No invention will ever compare, now or in the future, to the complexity and the wonder of a single cell in your body. Each cell, the size of a few microns, is a complete "factory" that contains a power plant and a sophisticated cell replication machine (DNA), two nanometers wide, encompassing all the human features. And to add to that, there are entry and exit gates for the construction material and waste removal.

Not for nothing is the human body called a "small world"; all the details of the world are contained within it.[39]

---

39 "Man is a small world, the world is a great man" (Avot d'Rabbi Natan, Chapter 31). http://he.wikipedia.org (Hebrew)

Microscopic Human Cell Electron Microscope[40]

Allow yourself to free your thoughts. Pay attention to the magic within and around you. Stop for a minute and take a deep breath. As you inhale and exhale, ponder the following. What controls your breath? Is it you? Try to hold your breath for more than a minute. What about when you are sleeping? Can you control the pace of your heartbeat? What about when you are exercising? How does your body "know" what to do and when to do it?

**

Is this magical world, that we perceive, real or imaginary?

You and I each see a man with a gun. You see a gangster; I see a cop.

We both see a man with blood on his hands. You see a murderer; I see a heart surgeon.

A Boeing 767 crashes. All the passengers, the majority of whom are American, are killed. While the USA mourns, there are parties in the streets of Iran.

What accounts for the differences in perception in each of the above scenarios? Only the interpretation in the minds of the observers.

Thousands of years ago, people thought, intuitively, that the earth was flat. Now, we all know that it is round.

---

40 https://www.etsy.com/de/listing/1020761382/microscopic-human-cell-electron

> **The reality we perceive as "truth" is essentially a function of our perceptions.**

Yet, we believe that what we perceive is ultimately true. We believe that our "intuition" works well. But our intuition fools us. We can't trust it at all.

Our view of the world is a subjective one; we are rarely able to be objective about anything.

The earth orbits the sun at 108,000 km per hour and rotates on its axis at a speed of 1,600 km per hour. Can you feel any movement? What we "perceive" and what is "real" are not necessarily the same thing.

We experience the external world through our five senses. Our brain processes all the sensory information using circuits and networks composed of spiking neurons. But what we know, with certainty, is that the world is a reflection of our senses and an interpretation of our brain.

Human perception is extremely limited. The frequencies that we hear, and the color range that we can see are narrow. Vast radio and television broadcasting, x-ray, infrared, microwave, ultrasound, cellular, and Wi-Fi waves surround us, yet they are invisible to humans. Our phones can even be charged wirelessly by the power which moves through the air by electromagnetic induction.

The conclusion is clear. We only know what we can experience with our five senses and our limited brains.

The inherently unknowable nature of "reality" can be a difficult concept to grasp. However, the more you surrender to "not knowing," the more wondrous "reality" becomes.

> **The more you know, the more you understand how little you know!**

So, what is actually out there?

Everything in the universe is made of energy in the form of atoms. The difference between humans, animals, vegetables, and minerals is the type of atoms (the number of protons, neutrons, and electrons), and their configuration.

No one has ever seen an entire atom. Today, we know that the smallest particles of the atom are named quarks, but current technology does not allow us to understand the true nature of atoms yet. We know, with certainty that they exist, and Japan most certainly felt their impact in Hiroshima!

Although it's not intuitive to us, we are all just a form of energy, an electric field. When I shake your hand, it feels as if we are touching each other, but it is just two electric fields causing an electromagnetic induction.

> **It's all one; we are all the same. We are all simply atoms spinning in space.**

Quantum physics has proven that consciousness affects the motion of atoms. Each of us influences our own reality and collective consciousness creates the overall reality.

The modern world could not function without electricity. When we plug any appliance into the outlet, it simply starts to work. We understand that someone is responsible for generating this electricity in power plants, generated by oil, coal, nuclear energy, hydro, solar, or other natural resources. The fact that we can't see electricity, however, doesn't mean that it doesn't exist. We can only see or feel electricity by its functioning. It's inconceivable that a television set could work without power from the source. Yet, many people believe that humans, animals, and plants can live and grow without receiving power from the Source.

What is your source of life? Who generates your power?

Each one of us is connected to the grid, taking our power from the same source. With your first breath, at birth, your soul connects your physical body to the power plant. Your soul is the "transformer" of your body, receiving its power from the "grid." To live a meaningful life, with high energy and extraordinary achievements, we need to stay connected.

When you surround yourself with people whose energy is positive, they "charge" you by adding power to your battery and filling you with positive energy. On the other hand, negative people, who have drained the power in their own batteries, will consume your energy. They are "power thieves." They are consumed by negativity and usually lack faith. Stay away!

Professional tennis players, racing drivers, musicians, chess players, or any type of elite performer, achieve extraordinary results by the power of focus. They enter "the zone," losing their sense of time, where hours feel like minutes and there is a feeling of effortless ease. There is a sense of flow, they can eliminate background noise, remove all barriers, and feel the flow of their souls loudly and clearly. Having a high level of consciousness enables the soul to stay connected for longer periods, with an optimal flow of energy from the grid.

Would you choose to connect your home internet to a fibre network? Or would you prefer to stay on a dial up connection? We can all choose to connect to the grid, and to live in flow with the abundance generated from the source.

Factor #2: Dis-cover your soul

You've got to find yourself first. Everything else will follow.

– Charles de Lint

When you go on a trip, you know where you're heading, what you plan to do each day, and when you plan to return home. Embarking on a journey, however, is a completely different form of adventure. You pack a few things, set off, and then make plans on the move. Every day is a new adventure; the destination is unknown. My exploration of spirituality has been a journey. On this journey, I have discovered knowledge, peace, wisdom, love, compassion, God, and, most importantly, I have found my authentic self.

The deeper I went within myself, the clearer it became that, over my lifetime, my soul had become covered by protective layers. I was locked in a prison of my own making. Beginning in childhood, I had built up walls and layers of defenses to protect myself.

At first, children are naturally happy. They smile, even when sleeping. They are happy just by being present. They sing, dance, cry, and play with themselves and others. They are naturally curious and truly innocent. They easily connect to their imaginations, transforming a chair into a mighty stallion to carry the prince, while a simple dress can be the princess's gown.

A child's soul is wide open; it can be sensed from miles away. That is why most of us become so animated in the presence of babies and young children. They connect us to our own souls. As we grow up, our souls get covered with layers of protection. Every time we get hurt, humiliated, disappointed, or suffer trauma, we add another buffer. Over the years, we add layer upon layer, and our soul gets hidden deep within. It's unseen; there, but not there.

We are not born with bad intentions. At our source, we are pure, born to love, influence, and benefit others. We are good by nature. Trauma distances us from our natural selves. We develop an ego and layers of defenses to protect ourselves. We begin to distance ourselves from the child within us and disconnect from the soul that becomes buried deep within us.

Gradually, as I deepened my work, I began to understand that my soul too was hidden deep within me. It had become covered by shields that had protected me when I thought I needed them – when my childhood friends insulted me, when my parents chastised me, and when my first love dumped me. Over time, the real me, including my emotions, love, and compassion, began longing to burst back into the open. I came to realize that now, the shields were concealing the true, authentic, Nir.

> **Our work as adults is to peel off the layers and unleash our souls. The soul is pure; it can't change or be damaged.**

Point to yourself and notice where your hand goes when you make statements such as: "I'm really sorry, I'm responsible, I take the blame, I thank you from the bottom of my heart." You will automatically, and unconsciously, point to your heart. The soul is pure love, and the heart is the physical place in our body where we locate deep feelings. Your heart is not merely a pumper of blood. It is a powerful transmitter and receiver of energy, frequencies and vibrations. It's the gateway to your soul, the point of access to the "real" you.

I came to realize that I had to begin removing the unnecessary layers and slowly downplay the role that my ego was playing in my life. I achieved this by raising my consciousness level – I now strive only for what I really need, not for what I want, and the center of my universe has shifted from myself to others. I learned to trust myself and have gradually shed the layers and shields that no longer serve me.

The layers are like the skin of a fruit. When the fruit is growing, the skin is strong, to protect the fruit. It is hard and harmful to peel the skin at this early stage. When the fruit is ripe, and the time is right, the skin is easily peeled and the fruit appears in all its glory, full of flavor and color. Like the pit of a fruit, my gentle soul was hidden deep within me, covered by layers of defenses. I was tough, and nothing (and no one) could penetrate my elephant–like skin. Compassion, mercy, and love were seldom on display, and I rarely shed a tear.

On my journey, I came to realize that the layers weren't me.

They were pretending to be me, trying to "steal" my identity and to take control of my existence. I had been running on autopilot for so many years. My mind had become distracted by the endless voices of my thoughts. I led a restless life, chasing more and more assets, respect, achievements, and social status. The constant activity was preventing the silence from cracking through and blocking me from seeing my identity.

Previously, the layers had wanted everything for themselves. Now, my soul wanted to shine on others. Removing the layers, and exposing my soul, transformed me from an egoist into an altruist. I know that everything is connected. I began to feel within me the pain of others and I had the desire to act. This was the key to escaping the prison of my mind.

I was on a quest for the truth. I wanted to finally know the answer to the most profound question we should all ask ourselves:

Who am I?

To stop this running to nowhere, I had to learn to relax and to slow down the tempo of my life. I began to allocate a specific time every day for observation, to sit alone, with no distractions. I took deep breaths, filled my lungs with oxygen, and slowly exhaled it all out. I began to look within and simply observe my thoughts. I noticed that I have little control over them. Like pedestrians crossing the road at rush hour, thoughts come and go. Most importantly, I learned that, while I could not stop them, I did not have to engage with them either.

I learned that I was not my thoughts. I was the observer of my thoughts. Similarly, I learned to observe my emotions. I realized that I'm not my emotions either. Sometimes I feel anger, other times fear. I could not necessarily control them, but I learned that I did not have to dwell on them for longer than was necessary.

Thoughts arrive regularly and, from time to time, they bring their friends, the emotions. Thoughts and emotions play an important role in our lives. They act as advisors, mentors, friends, and devil's advocates.

I became conscious of my thoughts and emotions at an early age, mainly at night, while I was lying in bed. They told endless stories about monsters and castles, and they took me to different planets in a giant spaceship. When the stories became too boring, and I became too tired, I fell asleep. Over the years, these guests decide to extend their visits. In the beginning, they appeared a few times a day. Over the years, they began to bring more and more visitors, and it became very crowded. They talked and talked, day and night, almost without any pause, until I could barely hear myself.

My thoughts had opinions on all subjects; on some subjects, they had deep knowledge, and sometimes they knew nothing.

Sometimes they were right; sometimes they were wrong. There were times they lifted me up with good advice and there were times they pulled me down, into depression.

It's important to understand that both these entities (thoughts and emotions), while *within* you, are not *you*, even though they feel so "real."

> **You are neither your thoughts nor your emotions.**
> **Rather, you are the observer of them.**

Although they are inside you, you must learn to use them carefully. In real life, it's important to have someone external with whom to share ideas and consult. With external sources, the borders are clear, you can always welcome them in or ask them gently to go out. Your thoughts and emotions, however, are always with you. Once you recognize them as "imposters," you can learn to use them in the same way you would use any other external resource for consultation or opinion.

The ability to distinguish between your "self" and your thoughts and emotions, is essential. The way to master them is by the power of consciousness, first by silence, then by awareness. Deep meditation, while observing the thoughts and emotions gradually dissolves them.

When I was able to "hear" the sound of silence, my soul began to reveal itself. This marked the beginning of the discovery of who I am. I uncovered the real me, without masks – exposed, vulnerable, sensitive, full of love, free of my limitations – connected to the infinite. The journey returned me to the child I used to be, the one who was connected to his soul.

Connecting to my real identity and learning to become present was a journey of years. Slowly, I began noticing the beauty and wonder in everything around me; a baby's smile, falling leaves, a bird's song outside my window, and colorful flowers at every corner. Warm light began to fill the cells of my body. Fear and anger were replaced by love and compassion. I began to hear my soul, loudly and clearly, the same soul that had previously only sprouted on special occasions, when being inspired by the ocean, the stars, the universe, falling in love, or the birth of my children. These special moments, which had appeared only rarely, were becoming a regular part of my being.

> **There is no need to add happiness, to be happy.**

When the soul is exposed, it shines like a diamond, and it illuminates love and compassion for yourself and others.

Factor #3: The power of faith

Faith is taking the first step even when you
don't see the whole staircase.

– Martin Luther King, Jr.

Sight appears to be the strongest sense. It is not. If I am looking at a wall, that is all I can see. Whatever is behind the wall is invisible to me. But were a sound to emanate from beyond the wall, I would be able to hear it. Hearing is a stronger sense than sight. We can hear the unseen.

Imagination is our "super sense," it includes all five senses, thoughts, and feelings. We can imagine a sound, taste, smell, a physical sensation, or a feeling.

> **Imagination enables us to "see" the unseen and "hear" the unheard.**

Imagination knows no boundaries, distance, or time. You can imagine what is happening on the moon or how you will look and feel in two hours, two years, or two decades from now. We can use our imagination in positive ways, "seeing" ourselves living a life that is filled with trust, abundance, love, and joy. Alternatively, we can use it in negative ways, imagining a future with catastrophes, poverty, and illness. These thoughts will fill us with anxiety, worry, fear, anger, and misery.

Every human invention was created by the power of imagination and faith. They are gifts that only humans have. Whatever we can imagine, we have the power to create.

Faith is the power that converts imagination into reality, acting as a magnetic field within us, drawing energy from the future and enabling the creation of the present.

Divine Providence

When it became clear to me that the universe works in perfect order, my faith strengthened, and divine providence became a part of my wellbeing.

Divine providence operates everywhere, from meticulous oversight of the entire universe to each person's individual life. A guiding hand is leading us to fulfill our life's purpose.

The internalization of divine providence gave me tremendous peace of mind. The understanding that whatever happens is meant to be, and that whatever should occur will occur, has given me the power to overcome any obstacle. Reality has no errors and no coincidences; everything is aligned, and every event has a purpose. No results come by chance, everything has a cause and an effect.

Belief in divine providence enables you to stop fighting reality, saves energy, and reduces friction. We are here on a journey for learning, correcting, and improving.

The Creator created this world for me to fulfill my life's purpose. My parents, my wife, my children, my friends, and my community were created for me to perform my role in this creation – from the teacher who inspired me to believe in myself, my daughters who drove me crazy to modify my behavior, and even the illness that showed me what really matters in life and put me back on track.

The amazing thing is that the world – that was created solely for me – was also created solely for you, for my wife, for my daughters, for my teacher, and my entire community. From their point of view, the world was created solely for them. And indeed so. Our lives are a matrix with infinite dimensions and variables. Reality fits exactly into the pre-written script of every one of us and everything blends into everything else perfectly. There is no computer that will ever come close to the ability of the creative force that gave rise to this matrix that we call "reality."

From the day you are born, everyone you meet, everything you learn, everything you do, everything that happens to you and the people around you, are all accurate and necessary. Kindergarten, college, marriage, divorce, death, the friends you met, the news you heard, and the routes you chose. They were meant to be. It's all perfectly accurate and everything that happened is for good, even though it may not look like that, in the moment of the event. For "good" doesn't mean that everything is always "joyful." Life is not fun, fun, fun. There is torment and anguish, but all suffering has an ultimate purpose, and it is always for "good."

All the people and events of my life are a part of a pre-written script. My life's film has many different routes, every junction on the journey leads to a different script, yet all my scripts are pre-defined, and they all lead to the same place: the fulfillment of my life's purpose.

The people around us play important roles in our life, by teaching us, guiding us, allowing us to repair our faults, and to become better people. It's impossible to correct our faults without external feedback. Just as the swan needs the clear water to see its color, so too do we depend on the external world to serve as our mirror.

The reflection of my faults appears in the form of events, people, challenges, or other external incidents. It's like a private cinema projecting tailor-made movies scripted especially for me.

The movies will continue to play, in different forms, until I do my work and clear my faults.

If you have anger within you, people and events will make you angry. You will see movies with annoying people. When you learn to conquer your anger, you will barely notice annoying people around you. Similarly, if greed drives you, your life will be filled with financial challenges. Your neighbor's lawn will always look greener to you. If you are driven by pride and ego, your life's script will be full of squabbles and disagreements. By fixing the root cause, when your ego no longer controls you, your movie will become a peaceful one.

The environment around us changes as a reflection of our own personal changes. As I began to change, I was surprised at how accurate the "law of mirrors" actually is. As your inner world changes, you too will find that the world around you "magically" begins to change.

> **The only way to change others is by changing yourself.**

We all have many deficiencies to correct. As you clear one fault, its related scripts will no longer be present. But be aware that they will soon be replaced by a different scene that will require your attention!

Our life's work is internal, not external. By changing your internal world, you change your external reality.

> **You are the editor of your own movies.**

All the people and events of your life have brought you to this point, to your present. My present, my current mission, led me to write this book and to convey these messages. You are reading this book now because it is a part of your life's journey; it is the point where our paths in this infinite matrix intersect. As long I'm alive, my mission remains incomplete, and I still have work to do and a purpose to fulfill.

Even when you're very old, with little ability to move, when it looks like God has forgotten you here and you are just waiting for His mercy to free yourself from the shackles of this world, you are still fulfilling a purpose. You're an actor in someone else's movie. Someone in the matrix around you has a lesson to learn. Perhaps your son, who was so busy building his career, whose heart had hardened, will, by taking care of his father, find mercy and compassion. Your seemingly "forgotten" situation will be the door to his heart opening.

The Jewish sage, Rabbi Akiva said:

Everything is foreseen, yet freedom of choice is granted.[41]

Many scholars have debated this seemingly paradoxical statement. What is free will and what is fate?

While the end of your movie is already written, the routes you take to get there are yours to choose. Freedom of choice is the gift given to us on the way to fulfilling our life's purpose.[42]

You can choose two main routes to get there. I call them the wisdom route and the anguish route. On the wisdom route, you choose to be attentive to nature's laws, both physical and spiritual. You choose to act "morally," which is best summarized by the "Golden Rule": "What is hateful to you, do not do to your fellow." This route seems long, and, by following it, it may take you years of hard work and determination to achieve meaningful results.

Alternatively, you can choose the anguish route. On this route, you act according to your desires, instant gratification, the wisdom of the crowd, fads, or trends. This route looks shorter, is tempting,

---

41 Ethics of the Fathers, Chapter 3,15

42 Quantum theory proves that there is a built-in randomness, and that the average statistical result can be predicted out of countless random possibilities.

and, sometimes, even effortless. The anguish route provides short-term results that are seldom long-lasting.

At first glance, the wisdom route looks longer than the anguish route. For example, if you want to have money, you can steal, lie, and cheat, and make what looks like "easy money," but these "shortcuts" will eventually lead to disappointment and trouble. There are no shortcuts in life! The law of attraction is always activated. In fact, my life's philosophy and personal mantra is that, "There is nowhere to rush to as there is nowhere to get to!" Life is here and now. It is the journey that matters. Our final destination is death, so it is really better not to rush! How you get there, i.e., through the wisdom or anguish route, is up to you. Reality is misleading. Any attempt to take a shortcut in life, using the anguish route, will lead to failure. The best way to achieve your life goals is via the wisdom route. What appears to be the longer route is actually the shortest possible way.

Which route will you choose?

By choosing the wisdom route, the scenes of your movie will certainly be more enjoyable than those along the anguish route. Do whatever you can to avoid having to be the editor of your own horror movie. When you choose the wrong path, nature will force you to reroute. You will continuously get signals, in the form of "suffering," to put you back on track.

Faith allows you to accept reality as it is. Accept, appreciate and be grateful for whatever you have right now, both the good and the bad.

> **Embracing reality brings peace and calm, while resisting reality causes suffering and pain. We have the power of choice!**

When you have faith, and you know that providence exists, nothing "bad" can happen to you. Even when something "bad" happens, you trust that it's part of your intended journey.

How certain are you that the "bad" is not for the better?

No matter how hard it may be to accept, the "suffering" comes to benefit you. It is an inescapable part of life. It is a lesson, working in your favor, even though you may not be able to see or understand it at that moment.

> **The Creator created this universe, to benefit his creatures. He has no 'intention' to cause any harm, suffering, or pain.**

Illness, for example, is a "correction." Our bodies will always strive for healing. When you mistakenly eat spoiled food, your body will use all its power to eliminate it. Vomiting, diarrhea, and fever are all "corrections" by the body to recover. When this happens, is it the illness or the cure? Is it good or bad? If your body does not make this correction, the results may be fatal.

Touching fire will burn your hand, but nature doesn't want to hurt you. It has no intention to do anything "bad" to you, it is simply nature's way of preventing you from burning and damaging your arm completely. When you get burnt, should you thank nature or blame the fire?

Unfortunately, due to blindness or ignorance of natural laws, we suffer. We get many indicators during the development of disease, but we refuse to accept them as vital feedback that is working in our favor. We use medicine to suppress the symptoms. We fight nature by turning off the warning signals, refusing to acknowledge that the "bad" could possibly be working in our favor.

> **A lack of faith is the root cause of most suffering.**

Pain and illness are signs; they are begging you to change, they are not there to harm you. As with our bodies, and our lives, for that matter, so too does the earth try to correct itself at any cost.

In the last century, humans have damaged the planet, causing global warming, melting icebergs, and a hole in the ozone layer. As a result, the earth spins faster on its axis, causing drastic weather changes, such as hurricanes, droughts, and floods. The earth does not stay calm. On March 11, 2011, a 9.0 magnitude earthquake shook northeastern Japan, unleashing a savage tsunami. According to NASA, the earthquake caused the earth to slow down as it spun on its axis. More than 19,000 people were killed. The earthquake was a correction to the "illness" of the planet, caused by humans. The earthquake was nature's attempt to return the earth to its normal speed.

In the big picture view, from an immortal universal perspective, was the earthquake the illness or the cure? Was it really "bad" for humanity, or for the better?

In 2020, the Covid-19 virus shut down the entire planet. Economies froze, borders closed, and millions of people died. People were forced to slow down and stay home for months. Was the virus the illness or the cure for the mad tempo of our current life?

> **Life, and the things that happen to you, are "for you,"**
> **and not "against you."**

The Creator created nature's mechanisms which always strive for balance, health, re-creation, and stability. When you cut your finger, the body fixes itself. The blood will start to clot, white blood cells will fight against infection from germs, and begin to repair the wound. Your red blood cells will create collagen to rebuild new tissue. New skin is reborn, and your finger recovers fully. (This includes re-generation of the fingerprint, decrypted from the DNA, without any defects!)

Health does not come from the plaster, the iodine, or the nurse who bandaged your wounded finger.

> **Nature will do everything to create conditions for the survival and continuity of Creation.**

We all have faith.

Either you believe in something, or you believe that you don't have belief. In both cases, you have faith in the path you choose.

If you believe that you have luck, you are lucky; If you don't believe that you are lucky, you won't have luck.

If you believe in love, you have love; If you don't believe in love, love will not be part of your life.

If you believe your life has a purpose, there is a purpose for your life; if you don't, you live life without purpose.

If you believe in God, you have God's forces within you; If you don't believe in God, you limit God's forces from benefitting you.

> **What we believe is what we have. We attract the things in which we believe into our lives. This is the power of faith. The things we don't yet have are the things that we don't yet believe. We haven't attracted them into our lives yet. The main thing holding you back from becoming what you want to be is limited faith.**

The service center is open 24/7. The Creator is always there for you, attentive to your prayers. There is no discrimination by social status, race, or gender. We are all equal in the face of the forces of creation.

Use the power of your faith to create the life you desire.

Factor #4: Fulfill your purpose

There are two great days in a person's life – the day we are born and the day we discover why.

– William Barclay

If an egg is broken by an outside force, life ends. If it is broken by an inside force, life begins. Great things always begin from inside.

Motivation is the force that initiates, guides, and maintains goal-oriented behaviors. It is what causes you to act, whether it is getting a glass of water to reduce thirst or reading a book to gain knowledge.[43] Motivation is the generator of our life; the magnet and creator of our reality.

We are motivated by two sources:

• An inner voice, or "blueprint" which emanates from our soul; and
• External voices, which come from the environment around us.

The ability to manifest your life's results depends on your ability to distinguish between the sources of your motivation, and to ensure that you are acting based on the correct one.

Our "blueprint," or inner voice, with which we are born, contains

---

43 https://www.verywellmind.com/what-is-motivation-2795378

our "to-do" list, from which we discover the purpose (or purposes) of our life. It spurs our natural curiosity and generates passion and excitement within us. To-do lists are like personal musical notes that are embedded in our souls. They stem naturally from within us, creating the music we play during our lifetime.

We all have unique talents. We are born with these gifts, and they are given to us to fulfill our life purpose, and to share them with others. This is our gift and our obligation. If your God-given gift is a golden voice, you must be a singer. You must use your talent to influence, motivate and inspire others. That is your mission. Your talent is the musical instrument that enables you to play your melody.

If you do not pay attention to your inner voice, you have an unfulfilled mission. You received a gift, yet you threw it away. You will miss your life purpose, and emptiness may consume you from within. You can try to fill this emptiness with ice cream, chocolate, sex, movies, or any other external excitements. While they will distract you from your goal, they will all be temporary. They will not give you true satisfaction, and you will not be genuinely happy. Unfortunately, a large percentage of people are depressed, living in anxiety, and trying to suppress their feelings with anti-anxiety pills. But they don't solve the root cause of the problem.

True happiness comes from fulfilling your life's purpose. You do this when you pay attention to your inner voice.

The second source of motivation is your environment – your family, friends, colleagues, and neighbors.

Your friend lives in an opulent house, drives a luxury jeep, and enjoys high social status. Mistakenly, we interpret these influences as our real motivation.

Environmental motivation misleads us, it is fake.

We work hard, running in the rat race, sometimes for our whole lives. On this race to nowhere, we hurt our families, we sacrifice our children, and we forget our friends. When we finally reach these extrinsically motivated goals, we buy our "dream house" and a luxury jeep, then we realize the bitter truth. They do not fulfill us. We feel joy for a short while and then we fall, once again, into emptiness. It's like an oasis, an illusion. These environmental influences are no different from drugs.

We are obliged to be attentive, and to explore our blueprint and the "to-do lists" embedded within our soul. Listening to the sound of silence within you will expose your blueprint and allow you to live a meaningful life. Happiness, love, and success come from within. When your actions are based on the "right" reasons, and your motivation comes from within, there is a flow, with minimal waste of energy or friction.

> **You don't need to push yourself to be motivated. Motivation is generated by an internal flame.**

Your values are a reflection of your inner blueprint.

Which values are important to you? Which values come from your blueprint, and which ones come from your external environment? Prioritize your true values..

Be attentive to your inner voice and live your life accordingly. Create internal clarity and be honest with yourself. Once your values are clear, you can build a supportive environment around you. Choose your environment; don't let the environment "choose" you.

Choose friends who share the same values as you. Replace the friends with whom you used to gossip and waste time, with friends who pull each other upwards towards a life of value and meaning.

We can't choose our "blueprint," but we can – and should – choose an environment that supports us to live in a way that is true to ourselves. In the same way, as you need to surround yourself with friends who support you to live in truth, choose the right books, lectures, teachers, mentors, rabbis, or priests.

The Creator created simple signals to let you know if you are in the right place or not. Fear, anxiety, and sadness are signals for you to reroute. Happiness, enthusiasm, and love are the signals that you are on track to fulfill your true purpose.

How will you know if you are in your "right place"?

If you can answer the following questions with "high positive" scores, then you are on the right track:

- How much value do I generate for the benefit of others?
- How many people are influenced and inspired by me?
- How happy and satisfied am I?

Each of us has a role to play, and a purpose to execute. The Creator didn't bring us here for 80 years, just to eat, watch television series, and sleep.

> **We are all connected. Together we are one orchestra with many musical instruments. Each of us performs our individual musical notes, while the conductor coordinates the whole orchestra.**

The soul contains the notes. Your purpose is written in your soul, and it is your job to play the melody. When it is all properly in tune, a heavenly melody will sound all over, not from angels somewhere in the sky. It will arise from us, here, from heaven on earth.

Factor #5: Read the User Manual ("RTFM")

The secret of getting successful work out of your trained men lies in one nutshell—in the clearness of the instructions they receive.
— Robert Baden-Powell

When you buy a new car, it comes with so many features: autonomic drive, remote service, electrical charging, multiple driver settings, cruise control, internet connection, navigation system, multimedia, and warning lights for potential faults. The car contains hardware and software, and we need to frequently update the operating system to the latest version. Without a user manual, our ability to operate the car optimally would be impossible.

Unlike a car, life does not come with a user manual from the manufacturer. Yet, each one of us is born into a family, environment, or culture, which has its particular "user manual": Torah, Bible, Koran, Veda, etc. After Gbade's directive that I would have to write this chapter myself, I turned to the "user manual" that my birth had bequeathed me, the Old Testament (or "Torah" as it is known).

According to Jewish lore, at the revelation of Sinai, God gave the Jewish people the Torah through Moses. While I was familiar with the Torah, my upbringing had led me, mistakenly, to see God (or the "Creator") as a kindergarten teacher – someone whose role was to punish me for not listening or following His instructions.

Now, when I revisited the Torah, as part of my spiritual journey, I was not looking at it historically, or even religiously. Rather I was looking at it as a treatise on spirituality. Now, read with these eyes, I realized that the Torah is a wellspring, describing, in detail, the universe's features and functions. It contains instructions on how to use this "product" called life, optimally. Followed as a guidebook for life, rather than as a prescription from which no deviation is allowed, this manual could facilitate longevity, quality of life, strong relationships, physical and mental health, efficiency, balance, prosperity, cost – saving, and minimal failures, bugs, and errors.

The Torah contains 613 commandments to follow. There is a total of 248 "do" commandments and a total of 365 "don't do" commandments. These commandments are detailed instructions, written for our benefit.

The scripts threaten us with all sorts of punishments if we disobey the commandments. Mistakenly, people look at these threats in their literal form. Heaven and hell are not necessarily something after death. Each day we can choose how we want to live our life. We can have a life full of love and happiness, each day can be heaven. Alternatively, we can be bitter, angry, or negative, and each day will be hell. Life and death, too, are not necessarily related to the physical body. When our souls are connected to the source of life, we get love and happiness, and we feel "alive." But, when our souls are disconnected from the energy of the universe, when anxiety and fear grip you, then sadness and misery fill your life – it is called "death."

Many appliances come with two booklets: a detailed "user manual" for those interested in the bits and bytes of every feature, and a "quick guide" that is simple to read. Just plug and play. I see the Ten Commandments as a "quick guide" for life. They contain a set of clear, easy-to-use principles that are a good recipe for life. They make rest compulsory for the body and soul (on the seventh day), promote familial love ("Honor your parents"), and teach us how to behave lovingly towards each other in the last five, with their prohibitions on lying, killing, and stealing.

Read beyond the commandments, the scriptures taught me how to connect my soul to life's energy, how to feed the physical machine called my body, as well as how to behave by controlling my emotions, communicating, refueling, and resting.

In addition to reading the bible, I began practicing meditation, studying Buddhism, and investigating quantum physics. Interestingly, my study of this most modern of sciences led me to the most ancient of Jewish mystical texts, the Kabbalah.

The Zohar is the foundational work in the literature of Jewish mystical thought, known as Kabbalah. Kabbalah is a set of esoteric teachings that explain the relationship between God (the infinite, unchanging, eternal, mysterious) and the mortal and finite universe. This knowledge was hidden for thousands of years before the Zohar was made public. The Zohar first appeared in Spain in the 13th century and was published by a Jewish writer, named Moses de León. De León ascribed the work to Shimon bar Yochai (Rashbi). Rashbi was a rabbi of the second century who, according to Jewish legend, hid in a cave for thirteen years during the Roman persecution, whereupon a carob tree and a spring miraculously appeared there. During these thirteen years, Rashbi studied the Torah and was inspired by the Prophet Elijah to write the Zohar.

Undoubtedly, the Kabbalah has influenced me more than any other source of wisdom.

The bible provides guidance through stories and legends. On the other hand, the Kabbalah demonstrates the mystical teachings, the inner "secrets," of the scriptures. The Kabbalah is akin to providing the programmer access to the machine code. It's one thing to have a product's manual. But understanding the software code, which allows the product to operate, is a different ball game.

The Kabbalah provides practical guidance on how to create the future through thoughts, words, and actions, how to live a balanced life, how to manage emotions, how to raise the level of consciousness, and how to find love and compassion in any creature. It provides tools to connect to the infinite abundance of the creation. Practical Kabbalah is a set of techniques which, until quite recently, were hidden, reserved for the learned "elite" only.

The "elite" used meditation and visualization techniques, and a specific set of codes, which were encrypted inside the holy books. The meditator "tuned" himself, through the meditation, to a specific "frequency" which opened a flow of energy from the cosmic source into his soul. Each code connected into a specific "frequency" that contained the energy of the specific topic, such as, cosmic energy for health, an abundance of livelihood, courage, wisdom, or happiness.

***

A smoker may try to quit smoking over a lifetime. Each pack of cigarettes comes with warning pictures describing in detail the type of cancer it causes. But still, the smoker can't quit. The knowledge by itself is not enough. Only in the ambulance, on the way to the hospital, when the feeling of death becomes so real, will the knowledge and the feelings merge, and you will become the thing you wanted to become. The knowledge becomes faith. People who survive, can quit at that point.

Why wait until then?

The Kabbalah provides knowledge to be learned by the power of the brain, but, more importantly, it provides techniques on how to implement it in actual life: how to connect the brain to the heart. The Kabbalah taught me how to merge my thoughts, emotions, and actions. I learned how to master the brain-heart connection. It eliminated the internal conflicts and constant friction that consumed endless energy. It enabled me to live a much better life, via the "wisdom route" rather than the "anguish route." The user manual allowed me to understand the "why" and to execute the "how."

I found peace and solace in my "user manual." If you are intent on achieving the formula for spirituality, in your own life, I highly recommend that you investigate one (or several) of the "user manuals." Revisit them with new eyes, not for the dogma, but for the practices they contain. You may be surprised by how much wisdom they contain and how useful they can be to connect to the infinite power of creation.

> **Life is too complicated to guess how to operate. We have limited time to waste on trial and error.**

Factor #6: Find God

Just as a house indicates a builder, a garment a tailor, and a door a carpenter, so too does this world tell, the Holy One Blessed be He created it.

– Rabbi Akiva

A story is told about a small wave and a big wave in the ocean. The small wave looks at the big wave jealously and says, "You are older and wiser, so high, powerful, and full of confidence. I'm small, weak, and unconfident. You are so lucky; I wish I were like you." The big wave looks at the small wave and says, in a calm voice, "It doesn't matter, young wave, your job was to make romantic sounds at the shore, lovers were inspired by you, and surfers enjoyed your ride. You had a short, but meaningful life. You fulfilled your life's purpose in the best possible way. Soon we will both end our lives, and we will merge back into the infinite ocean..." The small wave shed a tear and thought to himself, "If I could only have gotten another few more seconds to live, I could have been so happy..."

Our soul is like a glass of water pulled from the ocean; the water inside the glass looks like a separate entity, but it's not. It's the ocean itself encapsulated within a glass. When you pour the water from the glass back into the ocean, the water merges and becomes the ocean again.

The Creator is infinite and contains the entire reality. And, like a drop from the ocean, our soul is not separate from the Creator. The drop has the same characteristics as the ocean. Every drop contains the entire ocean, and, at the same time, it is a single drop.

To fulfill our life's purpose, the water inside the glass and the ocean must stay connected. This connection occurs naturally. Our main job is not to disturb it, and to keep it flowing clearly.

The water should be used to benefit others, to quench others' thirst and, at the same time, the glass should always remain full of water.

Our job here is to strengthen the connection between our soul and the source, while increasing the capacity of the glass.

How can I stay connected? How do I not disturb the flow? Belief starts, firstly, in myself.

As I explained earlier, our comprehension of the external world is subjective, we all see "reality" differently. It's all in our mind, captured by our five senses. The entire external world is within us. We are the drop and the ocean.

God is not someone or something out there. God is inside us, a part of us. The soul is divine, an integral part of the Creator. We are a piece of the creation. We are part of God.

Lack of faith in God is actually a lack of faith in ourselves. You are no more separate from God than your hand is separate from the rest of your body. If your hand believes that it can operate independently, it is simply not seeing the big picture!

My faith in God gave me strength, it took me forward in challenging times and it lifted me when I was down. Faith strengthened my confidence and self- esteem.[44]

So, where does my strength come from? Am I the source of my own power, or is it something much bigger than me, coming from my connection to the infinite power of the creation?

I talk, but do I actually know how to sync my lips, my tongue, vocal cords, and the air coming from my mouth to generate a complete sentence?

It is said that the longest distance in the world is the distance between the brain and the heart. Faith closes the gap between the brain (logic) and the heart (emotion) – between the needs of the body, which wants to stay down in the material world, a finite and limited world, and the needs of the soul, which wants to go up and be connected to the infinite, the unlimited world.

> **Our soul appears at the height of its glory when there are no more gaps; when our thoughts, emotions, and actions are in harmony.**

In the Book of Joshua, the city of Jericho was the first city that the Israelites attacked upon entering Canaan (Israel). The Israelites

---

44 Be aware: There is a thin line between having high self-esteem and an inflated ego. Confidence and arrogance are not the same things!

destroyed Jericho's Bronze Age wall by walking around it for seven days, carrying the Ark of the Covenant. They circled the walls once a day for the first six days, then circled the walls seven times on the final day. Under Joshua's command, the Israelites blew trumpets made of rams' horns and shouted to make the walls fall.

The fall of the Berlin Wall, on 9 November 1989, was a pivotal moment in world history, marking the fall of the Iron Curtain and the beginning of the fall of communism in Eastern and Central Europe. The fall of the inner German border took place shortly afterwards. Three weeks later at the Malta Summit, the Cold War was declared over.

> **Our main role is to break the walls between our brain and our heart. Then, we can end our internal wars, declare victory, and live in peace.**

The formula to our spiritual life starts with the understanding that everything is inside us.

The work starts with deep observation of ourselves. Our life's purpose is to connect our soul to the infinite power of creation.

We have the power to choose between the good and the bad, between selfishness and generosity, and between life (connection) and death (disconnection). Every day, we are free to choose to stay in the dark or to open the window and connect ourselves to the endless light of the universe that lies deep inside us.

By changing our attitude, our emotions, and our desires, we change our world.

This change can happen in a blink of an eye. It requires a change in our point of view – zoom out towards a higher level of consciousness.

Your strength is not yours; it is given to you for a purpose.

Understand that everything that you have – talent, money, capabilities, life – does not belong to you. They are given to you to fulfill your mission.

We are all channels to spread the abundance of the Creator. We all have gifts (be they wisdom, money, or talents) that must be shared with others. We are a pipe to the infinite abundance of this universe. In practice, the more we give, the more we have. A pipe just passes water through itself. As long as the water continues to flow, the pipe will be full of fresh water.

When you receive in order to give, you became a carrier. The creation needs carriers to transfer the endless abundance of the universe. You receive as much as you can deliver.

When we care for nature as we care for ourselves, nature will not be exploited or damaged. It will prosper and take care of us.

When we take care of animals, they will take care to fulfill the functions for which they were created.

When we take care of one another, there will be no wars, murders, and evil.

God is not someone or something, God is everything. Every atom; everything that exists. The pieces of the puzzle should come together. We all must connect and be united, acting as one – humans, animals, plants, and nature.

Love and peace will dominate. This is the world I want to live in.

What about you? Will you stay separate, or will you get connected?

We must spread "The Formula," raise our universal consciousness to a higher level, and create a better world for our children and future generations.

Made in United States
North Haven, CT
25 April 2023

35863899R00122

A PEOPLE WHO WHO WOULD NOT KNEEL

SMITHSONIAN SERIES IN ETHNOGRAPHY INQUIRY

William L. Merrill and Ivan Karp, Series Editors

Ethnography as fieldwork, analysis, and literary form is the distinguishing feature of modern anthropology. Guided by the assumption that anthropological theory and ethnography are inexplicably linked, this series is devoted to exploring the ethnographic enterprise.

Contents

Preface

The anthropological penchant for telling other people's stories[1] carries its own hazards and ambiguities, particularly in seeming to speak for someone else. The subjects of this book, the San Blas Kuna of Panama, can speak eloquently on their own behalf, and I do not invoke anyone's name here other than my own. Nor do I offer precisely the story indigenous historians tell: mine includes too few Kuna names and too many foreign ones, and it gives less weight than they might like to the deity or their heroes of antiquity. I take heart, however, from Henry Louis Gates, who argues persuasively for the elusiveness of authenticity, especially where it is most looked for, in novels, memoirs, and histories from ethnic or tribal groups.[2] The story offered here, if not authentically Kuna, does, I hope, keep faith with what I heard Kuna say about their past and what I saw, however dimly, in the written record.

I hope, too, that the book speaks to the concerns of colleagues and students who are plumbing the impact of colonialism and nation-states on non-Western societies, but I address only some of the questions they might ask. I attempt throughout to put events and actions in anthropological context, but I also try to prevent analysis from impeding or entangling the narrative. Believing as I do that the sweep of history can be read in the lives of the individuals on whom it pulls, even seemingly insignificant individuals in small marginal societies, I have tried to tell the story in a way that any reader can appreciate.

By convention, a single name sits on the title page, but I could not have finished this project or even started it without the help of many others, and in the process I accumulated numerous debts of gratitude. They begin with the funding that made the study possible, generously provided by the National Endowment for the Humanities, the Woodrow Wilson Center, and the offices of the Provost and the Dean of Humanities and Social Science at the Massachusetts Institute of Technology.

Thanks are owed as well to the institutions that offered temporary homes at which to work and write: the Woodrow Wilson Center in Washington, my base for research in 1984; St. Antony's College and the Institute of Social Anthropology at Oxford University, where this book was begun in 1989-90; Balliol College, Oxford, host for a short research trip in 1994; and above all, the Smithsonian Tropical Research Institute (STRI), which has supported my work for the past twenty years. At Oxford, I am most indebted to Peter Rivière and Malcom Deas; at STRI to Ira Rubinoff, Jorge Ventocilla, Georgina de Alba, Audrey Smith, Olga Linares, and the late and much missed Martin Moynihan.

As an anthropologist who came late to history, I learned the indispensability of archives and other research centers, and even more of their staffs' expertise. In my case these centers include, in the United States, the Library of Congress, the National Archives, the Smithsonian Archives, the National Anthropology Archives, the American Museum of Natural History, the American Philosophical Society, the Cold Springs Harbor Laboratories, the University of Rochester Libraries, the Tioga Point Museum of Athens, Pennsylvania, the Historical Society of Hancock County, Illinois, and the District Court of St. Landry Parish, Louisiana. In Great Britain they include the Public Record Office, the British Library, the Bodleian Library, and the Pitt Rivers Museum. In Panama, the Archivos Belisario Porras, the Archivos Nacionales de Panamá, the Intendencia de Kuna Yala, the Oficina de Relaciones de Panamá con los Estados Unidos, and the Patrimonio Histórico of the Instituto Nacional de Cultura. Finally, in Sweden, the Göteborg Ethnographic Museum.

The guardians of several private document collections also made their resources available: Chany Edman, who preserves the papers of Guillermo Hayans; Hildaura López and her kin, keepers of the archive of Estanislao López; and the late Priscilla Breder, who offered me the field diaries of Charles Breder. Richard Marsh Jr. showed remarkable generosity in letting me use his father's diaries and photographs, patience in waiting for me to finish writing about them, and, most of all, forbearance in accepting what I wrote.

Others who provided research materials or guided me to them include (but are not limited to) James Atz, Leslie Barber, Gladys Barratt, Sybil Beach, Julio Benedetti, Mac Chapin, Eugene Conner, Michael Conniff, Regna Darnell, Malcom Deas, William and Katherine Durham, Frank Elder, Regina Holloman, Brian Housheal, Tylor Kitteredge, William Merrill, Elaine Mills, John Major, Alexander Moore, Edward O'Flaherty, Claude Oubre, Eduardo Posada, Jordi Roca, Robert Rotberg, Pamela Schider, T. D. Stewart, Frances Stier, and Richard Webber.

I thank the assistants who worked on this project, Ellene Felder, my mother Ellen Howe, Reinaldo Sody, Joshua Lubar, and Jaime Juárez (Lubar and Juárez supported by the MIT Undergraduate Research Opportunities Program) as well as co-researchers Jesús Alemancia, Cebaldo de León, and Francisco Herrera. Among the scholars who studied the Kuna rebellion before me, I learned most from Ricardo Falla, the late Jésus Erice, the great Kuna oral historian Carlos López, and my old friend Francisco Herrera, who has shared so many leads and ideas with me over a decade and a half that I could not say where his influence on this book begins and ends.

Those at MIT who furthered my research include the members of the Biographer's Roundtable; Helen Samuels and the staff of the MIT Archives; colleagues, administrative officers, and assistants in the Anthropology Program; Heather Lechtman as head of the Center for Materials Research in Archaeology and Ethnology; and three successive deans of humanities and social science: Harry Hanham, the late Nan Friedlaender, and Philip Khoury.

In Panama City and Kuna Yala, so many people helped me that I can mention only some of them: the former intendente Demetrio Porras; the caciques Carlos López and Leonidas Valdés; the leaders of the now defunct Centro de Investigaciones Kuna and of the very lively Congreso General Kuna and the Congreso General Kuna de la Cultura. (The two congresses will split between them half the royalties from this book.) Thanks also to Eligio Alvarado, Guillermo Archibold, Marcela Camargo, Rafael Harris, Ospino Pérez, the late Samuel Morris, and the family of the late Julio Hernandez. Special thanks to Bill Harp, who, among other things, made the book's maps. On Niatupu, where I have always counted on the community as a whole as well as numerous friends, those who helped most on this particular project were Vicente Arosemena, Amancio Brenes, David Rodriguez, Faustino Rodriguez, Gonzalo Salcedo, Ricardo Thompson, and the old men who sat and talked with me: Fernando Ponce, Francisco Hernandez, Mateo Brenes, and Miguel Hipólito, all but Miguel now gone.

I owe a special debt to the couples who took me into their homes during the research and did not complain, at least not in my hearing, when I overstayed my welcome: Mac and Carmen Chapin; Susan and Bill Harp; Olga Linares and Martin Moynihan; and Gonzalo Salcedo, Joselina Solís de Salcedo (still fondly remembered), and the whole Salcedo clan.

The friends and colleagues who read and commented on the book manuscript were Michael Brown, Jean Jackson, William Merrill, Joel Sherzer, Paul Sullivan (who provided especially thoughtful comments), and my wife, Mary June Howe, who listened to each chapter as it was written. Mary June has been a full partner in our work in Kuna Yala for almost three decades, sharing not just the hazards and pains of long-term field work but its intellectual excitement and the lifelong ties that it creates. This book is for me inextricably connected with Mary June and with that shared experience.

Lastly, a brief note about the Kuna language, which until now I have written in the orthography used by Nils Holmer and Joel Sherzer. In this work I have adopted conventions closer to those now becoming standard among the Kuna themselves, the principal difference being that the sounds rendered by Sherzer and Holmer as P, PP, K, KK, T, TT are written here as B, PP, G, KK, D, TT. (In spelling place names, on the other hand, as well as a few well-known words such as Tule, I typically follow established precedent, regardless of inconsistency.) Readers wishing to sound out the occasional Kuna words in the text will not go too far wrong if they pronounce them as they would Spanish.

Part One
THE KUNA AND THE DARIEN

1.
Sounds
Heard
in the
Distance

Two men sit side by side in parallel hammocks, swaying almost imperceptibly; their short legs hang over the hammock sides, their feet firmly planted on the floor. The hammock ropes reach up to blackened beams formed of massive tree trunks that cross the cavernous wooden building, its thatch roof peaking far above the heads of the two men. Even in the near-darkness, relieved only by flickering lanterns and torches, hundreds of men, women, and children can be seen sitting all around on low benches. The people are almost silent, however, and the light low enough so that the two seem alone, as if chanting to one another.

The first man, sharp-faced and wizened, even in the hammock noticeably bowed and gaunt, lifts his head, takes in a deep breath, and begins a long drawn-out line of chanted words. His companion—powerful, barrel shaped, with a head and body as round and solid as the old man's are thin and frail—sits quietly until the end of the chanted line, when he begins a single long word of reply, "Yeeeeessssssss," which he holds until the first man has drawn another breath and begun a new verse.

The old man begins to chant about his dreams, describing himself in another hammock and another building:

> Truly friend, I lie at home in sleep, say-and-hear-it, Mother Sleep
> holds me in the short death, I say the words.
> (Yeeeeessssssss.)
>
> Truly children, at midnight the place is silent, say-and-hear-it,
> our whirlpool is still, I say the words.
> (Thuusss it isssss.)
>
> Truly friend, at midnight in my hammock, say-and-hear-it, Mother
> comes for me, shake-shaking on my hammock.
> (Yeeeeessssssss.)

"Son, enough sleeping!" say-and-hear-it, "Son, wake up!" I say
the words.
(Yeeeeessssssss.)

Truly friend, I rolled over in my hammock, say-and-hear-it, I lay
listening to the place.
(Yeeeeessssssss.)

When I rolled over, thus it is, down on the fourth level below,
the golden snake, the archer, shook his rattle.
(Thuusss it isssss.)

Truly, far off Rrrrrrrrrrrrr, thus it is, I heard the place begin
to come alive.
(Thuusss it isssss.)

Truly, the sound of the golden snake waxed and grew, thus it is, as
if it had reached the second level below, rising toward me.
(Thuusss it isssss.)

Truly, the singing would start again, torr-torr, a great frog would
be heard singing in the underworld.
(Yeeeeessssssss.)

"What might the frog be saying to me," I thought as I lay listening
to the place, I say the words.
(Yeeeeessssssss.)

Toward the mountains a devil was shouting, "You people I will be
surrounding, surrounding."
(Thuusss it isssss.)

Friend, I lay there thinking in my hammock, "We will all be
surrounded."
(Thuusss it isssss.)

Far off underground a voice could be heard, someone was singing,
"What will become of the land?"[1]

What Will Become of the Land? What Will Become of Us?

This book tells the story of an extended encounter, one of a sort that has been
played out over and over in the past five hundred years, between indigenous non-
Western peoples on one side—societies without states, industrial production, or
modern technology—and on the other, the expansive Western world of colonies,
empires, nations, and capitalist extraction. Most variants of this story, most encounters between so-called savages, primitives, or natives and those who see themselves
as representatives of civilization and order have ended badly, with indigenous peo-

ples taken into the lowest levels of national or colonial society, their numbers diminished, their land stolen, their labor exploited, their culture flattened. Few have gone quietly, however, and some, including the subjects of this book, have won enduring victories.

In 1900 the San Blas Kuna, the inhabitants of the northeast coast of the Isthmus of Panama, had enjoyed more than a century of peace, following two hundred years of intermittent war against the Spanish empire. Within the next four years, Panama would gain its independence from Colombia, the United States would begin work on a canal across the Panamanian Isthmus, and the Kuna would be plunged into a quarter-century of conflict with outside powers who wished to subdue, exploit, and make them over, as well as a quarrel among themselves about how to respond.

They faced multiple adversaries. First to come were Black frontiersmen, people just as poor as themselves who invaded Indian territory in pursuit of natural products that could be sold on the world market. In 1907 Catholic missionaries arrived, intent on establishing a new frontier theocracy. They were followed in 1913 by a Protestant mission more opposed to Catholicism and drink than to paganism. In 1915 the government of Panama and foreign economic interests began a campaign of control and exploitation, leading after the First World War to an intensified program aimed at subduing and assimilating the Indians.

Fortunately for the Kuna, the state that confronted them was weak, its military power negligible and its colonial administration perpetually starved of arms, ammunition, paper, and funds. Its few boats were in dry dock or beached, its functionaries underpaid, its typewriter ribbons faded. For a long time the government was able to impose only a partial and tentative form of control over its rebellious noncitizens, and the outcome often seemed in doubt. The government, moreover, never inflicted on the Kuna the horrors common elsewhere: the story is one of struggle, not genocide.

The Kuna, for their part, fought back hard — or to be strictly accurate, many but not all of them did. Resistance to domination, a subject of great interest in studies of colonialism, has been detected elsewhere in the most indirect and muffled gestures: underpayment of rent, insincere deference, imitation of colonial pomp, Brer Rabbit stories, even a maid painting her toenails.[2] No such subtlety is needed to find resistance in the small Kuna villages under police domination: dissident men and women contradicted, disobeyed, confronted, and even attacked their oppressors.

By the standards of Bosnia or Sri Lanka in the 1990s, however, the violence in San Blas was small in scale and the death toll trivial. It was as agitators and activists rather than warriors that the Kuna excelled. Their leaders mastered the political processes of the national society, lobbying government offices, stalling, arguing, lying, negotiating concessions, even hiring lawyers to enforce writs and press law suits. They gave newspaper interviews, organized petitions, castigated their opponents, and complained incessantly of mistreatment, anticipating by half a century the politics of information practiced today by environmental and human rights organizations. And since Panama was by and large a democratic country, their voices were sometimes heard.

Heard but never quite heeded. When it became clear that Panama would not relent, there was what the historian John Tutino calls "a critical meeting of grievances and opportunities": along with acts of oppression, signs of government weakness had multiplied, and the Kuna finally abandoned agitation for outright rebellion.[3]

Despite the small scale of this conflict and the apparent isolation of the San Blas coast, local events were provoked and shaped by decisions and economic demand generated thousands of miles away. By its end, the drama had drawn in a large foreign cast, including scientists, journalists, explorers, diplomats, and detectives, with scenes played out in New York, Canada, and Washington, D.C. The cosmopolitan nature of the story is due in considerable part to a North American adventurer named Richard Marsh, who turned up in 1924, just when things looked most bleak for the Kuna. Marsh, who had embarked on a romantic quest for a mythical race of white Indians, combined with a more mundane search for lands on which to plant rubber, stumbled over the mountains onto the San Blas coast with an expedition almost destroyed by illness. Enlisted in the Indian cause as his expedition collapsed, Marsh took a delegation of eight Kuna, three of them with white skins, back to the United States, where they inspired public amazement and the scrutiny of the scientific establishment. Early in the following year they returned to Panama and San Blas. Marsh wrote a declaration proclaiming an independent Indian republic, and in February 1925, the Kuna rebelled against Panama, prompting immediate intervention by the United States. Perhaps most unusual of all, the revolt succeeded.

The encounter between the Kuna and the outside world consisted of more than a struggle over land and power. It was also what the anthropologist Paul Sullivan has aptly called an extended conversation, a long series of communications across cultural boundaries.[4] Through these dialogues, disparate cultures and ideologies clashed and articulated, as antagonists and allies tried to make themselves understood and to understand each other, often through a fog of mistranslation and incomprehension.

The words of this dialogue often echoed long-running debates and controversies elsewhere: polemics between a reactionary Spanish church and anticlerical liberals; disputes in North America pitting immigrants against nativists, evolutionists against fundamentalists, drinkers against prohibitionists; and in Latin America, acrimonious argument between dependent nationalism and advocates of Anglo-Saxon hegemony. As outsiders inflicted their preoccupations and obsessions on the Indians, as each one tried to make them over to fit his or her preconceptions, they replayed in small isolated villages the great issues of the modern world, along with antagonisms dating back to the Reformation.

Through this profusion of ideology and obsession several common themes emerge, the most important of which is the Indian as *Other.*[5] Each outsider took a position, explicit or implicit, on just how different the Indian was from his own kind and what that difference implied. Jesuit missionary Leonardo Gassó saw indigenous Americans as a distinct class of beings, essentially alien in their thinking and existence. His Protestant rival, Anna Coope, took a diametrically opposition position: she insisted that beneath the superficiality of difference, Indians were fundamentally like everyone else: sinners in need of redemption. Panamanian officials and the explorer Marsh both saw the Kuna as different but capable of change and thus potentially the same as themselves.[6]

Everyone who dealt with the Kuna saw them not only as the *Other* but also as the *Primitive,* one of the peoples supposedly left behind by time in a past age. For several hundred years, tribal peoples such as the Kuna have inspired intensely contradictory attitudes among Europeans and Euro-Americans, either denigrated as bestial, dangerous, uncontrollable savages, or else exalted as noble children of nature enjoying a simplicity, freedom, sensuality, and wisdom forgotten by jaded modern civilization. Concerning the Kuna, Father Gassó alternately condemned them as beasts and praised their pristine innocence. Government functionaries, who saw the Indians as barbarians, could not help admiring their fierce independence. American explorers flirted with the idea of going native, and Richard Marsh, who took up the Kuna cause, saw them both as noble primitives and as the remnants of aristocratic pyramid builders.

Positions concerning primitivism and the Kuna were in each case conditioned by other attitudes and mind-sets. Richard Marsh and Anna Coope could not disentangle their attachment to the Indians from their antipathy to others, in Marsh's case to Blacks, In Coope's to Catholics and Latin Americans. For Leonardo Gassó, the Kuna may have been gentile savages, but at least they were not Protestants or anticlerical Masons and liberals. Both Gassó and Panamanian officials worried about the Kuna affinity for Anglo-Saxon names and North American power. In each instance, dispositions toward the savage other at hand emerged in a charged field of attraction and repulsion generated by the massive North American presence on the Isthmus and by strong feelings, positive and negative, toward the modern world.

In the view of many theorists, colonial power oppresses subject peoples by "othering" them, that is, by creating and maintaining spurious distinctions between Western self and native other. What such theorists miss (apart from the stubborn reality of cultural difference) is that in certain contexts similarity or mutability can rationalize oppression just as difference or essence can.[7] What mattered most, and what all parties engaged with the Kuna held in common, was not a position on

Indian difference but a refusal to allow difference to continue. Even those who perceived Indians in the last analysis as similar rather than alien, cast the Kuna as children and themselves as parents.[8] Almost everyone treated the Kuna as blank slates to be written on at will, and even the friendliest could not resist the temptation to dominate.

The Kuna, whose slates were already full, refused the interpretations forced upon them. Some scholars doubt whether colonized peoples can effectively answer imperial discourses, whether, in Gayatri Spivak's words, they have "the ground from which they could utter confrontational words."[9] Others affirm the possibility of resistance but see dominant ideologies ensnaring their subjects even as they are rejected.[10] The would-be colonizers who actually confronted the Kuna entertained no such illusions about the native capacity for answering back, which they took as rude arrogance and insufferable pride. Their own voices, moreover, were multiple, ambivalent, and discordant, even self-contradictory, and if the Kuna sometimes listened, they also had their say. Native words and native practices, just as much as the agendas and preoccupations of missionaries and bureaucrats, set the terms of the struggle that ensued.

The Kuna insisted on running their own lives and on being left alone, but the world outside would not let them be. Nor were they consistent in their isolationism. Feeling the attraction as well as the danger of the wider world, they could not agree on what stance and strategy to take, and their arguments and ambivalence inevitably brought the external struggle into their own villages. Similarly, they might resist or deny change, but their supposedly timeless society had already been transfigured and transformed and was bound to change further. They might disavow their ties with nation-states, but in the long run ties of some sort were inescapable. The fight, as the more prescient native leaders saw, would determine not whether the Kuna and their lands would be incorporated into Panama but on what terms. Would they become landless laborers, stripped of dignity and identity, or prosperous agriculturalists and citizens able to feed their children and to stand erect?

This story, though it presents struggles and social transformations of a sort that have affected millions of people around the world, focuses on the stubbornly idiosyncratic particularity of a single small native society; on the singularity of Panama as a raw nation and the de facto colony of a world power that had supposedly abjured colonialism; on the conflicted triangle formed by Panama, the Kuna, and the United States; and on the tough-minded, outspoken, and sometimes quirky individuals who played out the story. Among the cast of characters, the leading role belongs to the engineer and explorer, Richard Oglesby Marsh, a real-life Indiana Jones who was as complex as genuine swashbucklers typically are. A willing agent of industry and development who schemed to get rich in out-of-the-way places, Marsh ultimately came to doubt the worth of capitalist expansion. Romantic and self-deluding, he felt compelled to embellish and exaggerate experiences that needed no exaggeration. Able to work his way through his own prejudices to a genuine love for the Kuna and devotion to their cause, he never succeeded in seeing them without preconceptions or separating his positive feelings for the Indians from his antipathy toward Blacks. Marsh demonstrated in the extreme the grip that ideology had on every actor in the struggle.

The story, it will become clear, belongs to Richard Marsh as well as to the Kuna. If it were fiction, one could set the plot so that this striking character appeared periodically throughout, providing narrative balance and unity as well as color, but in fact Marsh makes a brief but spectacular appearance in an early act and then steps offstage until late in the drama. Once he returns, however, he takes center stage in almost every scene.

The narrative proper covers a quarter-century from 1900 to 1925, but it is best understood in the light of the long struggles that preceded it. The story thus begins, as do many concerning the New World, four hundred years earlier, at the beginning of the sixteenth century.

2.
A
Long
Struggle

The conquest of the American mainland began in 1510 when two failed Spanish expeditions joined together at a native village named Darién by the mouth of the Gulf of Urabá, where the Panamanian Isthmus meets the South American mainland. Parties setting out from the village, renamed Santa Maria la Antigua del Darién, explored south on the Atrato River and west onto the Isthmus, where they established an outpost called Aclá. On one of these forays their leader, the famous Vasco Nuñez de Balboa, discovered the Pacific. In time, the whole eastern Isthmus came to be known as the Darién and the northern shore as the coast of San Blas.

Balboa, though anything but gentle, did spare many of the local people, who were his only source of information, gold, and provisions. In 1514, however, he was superseded by Pedrarias Dávila, who executed Balboa and embarked on a search for gold of such brutality that within ten years he had exterminated most of the population of the region. In 1524 Pedrarias moved his headquarters to a spot called Panamá, well to the west on the Pacific coast, and the open savannahs and cultivated fields of the Darién region soon reverted to forest.[1]

The stratified chiefdoms of the contact period, as sketchily described by Spanish chroniclers, seem very different from the Kuna of later centuries. Most of the names and terms recorded in the early 1500s bear little resemblance to modern Kuna words, with a handful of exceptions, notably *oba* for corn and *uru* for canoe. It seems certain that Kuna-speakers inhabited at least some of the region, but historians debate whether they were found on the Isthmus itself or only on the Atrato and Urabá. In any case, by 1541 only about a hundred Indians were left at Aclá, and in 1570 a royal census found the whole eastern Isthmus empty except for scattered camps of runaway slaves. A few miles east of Aclá, however, the same census noted the presence of "numerous warlike Indians."[2]

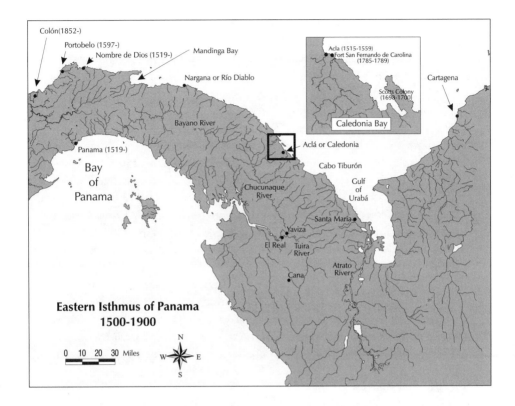

Colón(1852-)
Portobelo (1597-)
Nombre de Dios (1519-)
Mandinga Bay
Nargana or Río Diablo
Acla (1515-1559)
Fort San Fernando de Carolina
(1785-1789)
Cartagena
Scotts Colony
(1698-1700)
Caledonia Bay
Bayano River
Panama (1519-)
Aclá or Caledonia
Cabo Tiburón
Bay
of
Panama
Chucunaque
River
Gulf
of
Urabá
Santa María
Yaviza
El Real   Tuira
River
Atrato
River
Cana

**Eastern Isthmus of Panama
1500-1900**

0   10   20   30   Miles

N
W   E
S

The Panamanian Isthmus played a crucial but restricted role in Spain's New World empire as the point where silver from Peru crossed overland by mule train to the Atlantic. On the Pacific side, the small city of Panama, with a population of only about five thousand, was fed by a cattle-raising hinterland stretching off to the southwest, in the opposite direction from the Darién. The northern, Caribbean coast was unoccupied apart from a fort at the mouth of the Chagres River and two small ports, Nombre de Dios and Portobelo, which were little better than villages except during the trade fairs that took place when the silver fleet was in.[3] The lands further east between Panama and Cartagena held such marginal interest for imperial Spain that they might have escaped serious attempts at control had it not been for the Dutch, French, and English pirates preying on the Spanish Main, who visited the Isthmus with alarming frequency.

The pirates found the northern shore of the Darién, in particular, almost ideal for their purposes. Close but not too close to the route of the silver fleet and to stationary targets at Portobelo and Cartagena, the coast of San Blas offered sea turtles and manatees for provisioning, islands and coves for hiding ships and careening weed-infested hulls, and native inhabitants for guides and auxiliaries.[4] Although the earliest raiders, such as Francis Drake, recruited local support among runaway slaves rather than Indians, by the end of the sixteenth century Spain had succeeded in neutralizing the rebel Blacks; and at the beginning of the seventeenth, the Kuna, who had evidently been moving west, made their presence known by attacking Panama's eastern frontier.[5] Thereafter, Spanish authorities worried not just about Indians but about Indians in league with pirates.

With military resources stretched thin across the Americas by the demands of imperial defense, Spain depended on missionaries for help in pacifying hostile frontier peoples. In the 1630s authorities gained entrée to the Kuna through a young man named Julio Carrisolio, who had been shipwrecked on the coast and accepted by the Indians. With Carrisolio's sponsorship, a Dominican named Father Adrián de Santo Tomas succeeded in founding four missions encompassing about fourteen hundred Kuna, for which a grateful Crown rewarded the two men with titles and honors. Their charges, however, stubbornly resisted conversion, and the rest of the Kuna remained outside imperial control. Equally distressing from a Dominican perspective, within a few years rival Capuchins started to poach on their territory. In 1651, after the retirement of Father Adrián, civil authorities tried to station troops in the region, provoking the Kuna to revolt and drive out the soldiers and Capuchins, along with the miners and colonists who had come in on their coattails.[6]

Throughout the second half of the seventeenth century, the Kuna successfully resisted Spanish reconquest except at a few Dominican missions, and the pirates, who had established a strong Caribbean base on Jamaica, attacked the Spanish settlements on the Isthmus repeatedly. Henry Morgan took Portobelo in 1668 and returned to sack Panama in 1671, fighting a battle on the plains before the city in which unpacified Kuna on his side were opposed by mission Indians on the other. Spanish gold mines recently opened in the eastern Darién at Cana were attacked in 1684, 1702, 1712, 1724, and 1734, and through the 1680s parties of pirates were guided by the Indians across the Isthmus to raid on the Pacific side. The Kuna exercised caution toward these lawless men, some of whom were not above enslaving unwary Indians, and unlike the Miskitu of the Nicaraguan coast, the Darién Indians did not become professional slave raiders or mercenaries. They did cooperate regularly with parties of buccaneers, to the extent that some Kuna on the north slope began raising crops to provision foreign ships.[7]

A number of pirates published accounts of their adventures, the best of them written by a ship's surgeon named Lionel Wafer who was left behind in the Darién for several months in 1681.[8] Wafer's account, based on his observations as well as conversations in broken Spanish and a few words of Kuna, described the Indians in some detail. He found them living in hamlets scattered up and down river valleys, each cluster of hamlets centered on a fortified meetinghouse. Women wore short skirts, men only a funnel-shaped penis cover, except on formal occasions, when men

Seventeenth-century Kuna in council.

put on long cotton robes. Both sexes kept their hair long, and both ornamented their noses, women with rings, men with an oval plate of silver or gold hanging from the nasal septum. Wafer also mentioned a minority with white rather than brown skins, pallid individuals with weak eyes who seldom came out by day.

Wafer's narrative helped inspire European interest in the Darién, and in 1698 a company of Scots established a colony in eastern San Blas near the site of Aclá. The local Kuna received them warmly, but the effort fell apart within a few months, and by the time a relief force arrived, the first contingent had already departed. The disastrous colony, ultimately losing 1,700 out of 2,500 members, mostly to disease and malnutrition, was evicted in 1700 by a Spanish expeditionary force that included two hundred mission Indians led by Carrisolio's son.[9]

By this time the imperial system of silver fleets and trade fairs had all but collapsed and along with it the great age of piracy. Even as Panama slipped into economic depression and obscurity, however, the Spanish Crown, badly frightened by the Scots, worried more rather than less about the Darién. Pirates and privateers returned periodically to loot the Cana gold mines, and a number of French took up residence on the coasts of San Blas and Urabá, joining with the Kuna in raids on Spanish settlements. Moreover, a series of wars fought by European powers in the West Indies during the 1700s bestowed considerable strategic value on the Darién as a potential interoceanic crossing route, military base, or site for colonization. Although Spain succeeded in recolonizing and missionizing parts of the region, it failed to consolidate control, and in 1728 a mestizo named Garcia led the Indians in another massive revolt. Garcia was soon defeated and killed, but Kuna resistance continued.[10]

The French on the north coast eventually gave up piracy in favor of raising cacao for sale, many of them taking Indian wives, and in the late 1730s they petitioned the Spanish Crown for pardon and permission to settle permanently. Colonial authorities, eager for a buffer against growing English incursions — the British bombarded Portobelo in 1739 during the War of Jenkin's Ear and tried to take Cartagena two years later — readily agreed.[11] The British also courted the Kuna, and some strategists even dreamed of instigating a massive Indian uprising against Spain all across Central America.[12]

The Kuna, however, felt such pressure from Spanish attacks that in 1740 they sued for peace and agreed to accept new missionaries, this time Jesuits.[13] One of them, Father Walburger, left a vivid account of his unhappy experiences.[14] Among the 197 Indians in his mission at Yaviza were four *neles* or seers who opposed the missionary tenaciously, calling him the "devil in black clothing." Denying that Indians would go to hell, a destination reserved for Christians, the *neles* imitated Walburger's prayers over the dead bodies of animals and staged parodic masses in the mission chapel. In 1749, after most of his congregation had deserted the mission or succumbed to an epidemic, Walburger gave up and left.

Two years later, the whole region erupted again in a great revolt, which even menaced Panama City. The Kuna also attacked the French pirates living among them and drove the survivors off the Isthmus, refusing thereafter to marry outsiders or allow them to settle.[15] In the following years, Spanish authorities regained control of the southern Darién and brought a few hundred Kuna into mission settlements. In a report from 1774, the provincial governor noted with satisfaction success at removing noserings from women at the missions and replacing their short skirts with more modest dresses.[16] A small fort was built at Yaviza on the lower Chucunaque, effectively cutting off the pacified Kuna on the lower Tuira from their rebel kin. The latter, however, kept up hostilities for more than three decades, assisted by the British in Jamaica, who provided them with muskets, letters of alliance, canes of office, and even military advisers.[17]

In 1785 Spanish authorities elaborated a plan to defeat the Kuna once and for all. To cut the Indians off from their English allies, they built four small forts along the San Blas coast, as well as three more in the southern Darién. The garrisons held on despite fierce attacks and losses to disease, and the Kuna, having been abandoned by Britain, came to terms with Spanish authorities and once again signed a peace treaty. Two years later, however, a new colonial administration concluded that the burdens of the campaign should not be sustained, and by 1792 all of the forts had been abandoned.[18]

After nearly three hundred years, peace had finally come to the Darién. As foreign powers and freelance raiders lost interest in the eastern Isthmus, so did the Spanish Crown and church, and the Kuna were left to lick their wounds. In the last half of the eighteenth century alone, war and epidemics had cut their population in half, to an estimated five thousand, and except for a few hundred "tame" Indians on the Tuira watershed, the Kuna had been driven from the southern Darién. They left their names behind on rivers and towns occupied thereafter by Black freemen and slaves, and increasingly, by an indigenous people called Emberá or Chocó, traditional enemies of the Kuna who were in the process of migrating onto the Isthmus from South America.

At the beginning of the nineteenth century, some of the Kuna lived upstream in the Bayano and Chucunaque valleys and others on the Gulf of Urabá, but the greatest number were found in San Blas, north of the mountain spine of the Isthmus. The long arc of coast between Cabo Tiburón in the southeast and Mandinga Bay in the northwest was covered with thick tropical forest, cut by streams and small rivers running down from the cordillera ten or fifteen miles inland to enter the sea through mangroves and narrow beaches. The Kuna exploited the marine environment and coastal trade but kept their villages a few miles upstream, safe from outside threats. After 1812 the rest of Latin America was in any case too caught up in the wars of independence and the creation of new states to give much attention to backwaters such as the Darién or San Blas.

Toward the middle of the nineteenth century, the Kuna began moving down to the coast, first to sites near river mouths and then onto inshore islands, a gradual process that continued for more than eighty years. In this new niche they gained greater access to trade, along with relief from snakes, mosquitos, and endemic disease, though at the cost of increased exposure to smallpox and other epidemics. The tiny coral islands, laboriously reclaimed from thorny brush and mangrove swamps, functioned as dormitory communities, supported by agriculture and hunting on the mainland, as well as by fishing and gathering in the coastal waters.[19] Of the roughly thirty San Blas villages, the smallest held a few dozen people, the largest several hundred, while the total population was somewhere between three and ten thousand.[20]

The sea turtles with which the pirates had provisioned their ships now provided "tortoiseshell," in great demand on the world market, along with coconuts and products gathered in the forest such as dyewoods. As the century progressed, the Kuna increasingly specialized in selling coconuts, industriously planting palms on uninhabited islands and the mainland shore. In 1874 a British consul noted that the San Blas Indians accounted for a significant portion of the trade in and out of Colombia, which then included the Isthmus, and in 1890 the consul in Panama estimated (undoubtedly with some exaggeration) that in the previous year fifty tons of turtle shell, seven hundred tons of ivorynut, and five million coconuts had come out of San Blas.[21] The Kuna traded and sold these products for cloth, firearms, steel tools, and other manufactures imported by merchant captains, many of whom left goods to be retailed by native trading partners and took young men to sea with them.[22]

Kuna island village, western San Blas, 1870s.

The move to the islands and the growth of the cash economy encouraged fundamental changes in Kuna culture, particularly in the gender division of labor. As in many lowland South American societies, women had carried out all agricultural tasks other than felling and burning the forest. Now—with the increased distance between fields and village; the great physical weight of the staples, bananas, and coconuts; and the expansion of cash-cropping—men shouldered more of the burden. Women continued to fetch drinking water from mainland rivers and do a little light agricultural work and collecting but otherwise stayed at home.[23]

The system of land use also changed. Previously, fields reverted to forest and communal ownership after fallowing, but now men who cleared land alienated it permanently, and a system of private property and inheritance rapidly developed, one especially important for coconut groves and the beaches on which sea turtles came to lay their eggs. Although the original owner of each plot was always a man, daughters inherited just as sons did.[24]

In their new role as stay-at-homes, Kuna women began to dress themselves much more elaborately. Still wearing the noserings and skirts described by the pirate Wafer, as well as bead wrappings on their limbs and a piece of blue cloth over head and shoulders,[25] Kuna women gradually replaced the headcloth with an oversized trade handkerchief. They elaborated what was initially a simple blue tunic into a beautifully decorative sewn blouse, the *mola*. And they began to cut their hair short at puberty. Though their husbands and brothers—broad, short, bow-legged men with earrings and long hair—could not be mistaken for Latin American nationals, they had already abandoned nose plates and penis covers for shirts and trousers, and by the end of the nineteenth century they were cutting their hair short and wearing bowler hats. Thus it was the women who visually displayed the distinctiveness of Kuna society and its separation from the world.

Despite their reduced role in agriculture, young females formed a pivot of the economic system as the means by which families recruited and held male workers. An eligible young man first learned of his marriage on finding himself hauled off without warning to the hammock of the girl chosen for him, a ritual underscoring the power of his in-laws and the years of work he would owe them. A mature couple blessed with daughters could recruit a significant workforce of sons-in-law and a household of fifteen, twenty, or more people, all of them living in the same large thatch-roofed house.[26]

As the Kuna moved into their new coastal environment, they called on ritual as well as kinship and hard work to ease the transition. The rich ceremonial life they brought with them addressed four primary concerns: protection from supernatural danger, creation of community, their destiny as a chosen people, and the mysteries of female maturation. When a young girl reached puberty, the village devoted a week to marking the change, and within a year or so they held two more celebrations in her honor, with several days of drinking and dancing.

Much more frequent than these bashes were quieter village gatherings devoted to chanting and oratory. Each community had at least two chiefs and a gathering hall, descended from the strongholds described by Wafer; the senior village chief and his family often lived at the back. Several evenings a week the entire village would assemble after sunset to hear a pair of chiefs sing of the way to heaven and the history of their ancestors, or simply to admonish their followers about good behavior. As the chiefs sang, young village constables let out ear-splitting calls exhorting the people to listen and stay awake, and at the end of an hour or so, another leader called an *argar* would stand and interpret the chiefs' chant. While "calling to each other" in this way, the Kuna were also calling to their god, Great Father, who had given them the land, the body of his own wife, Great Mother.[27]

Before, after, and between chanted gatherings, village men used the hall as a clubhouse and forum for discussing local business. On some matters the men deferred to their chiefs and argars, elected from among themselves, but they never let leaders climb too high or acquire too much power, and any issue of consequence was decided collectively, usually after hours of debate.

If the sacred gatherings channeled relations between the Kuna and their heavenly parents, other forms of ritual repelled hostile illness spirits prone to stealing or possessing human souls. To counter these threats, the Kuna called on medicinalists, who cured with herbal infusions; chanters specialized in particular ailments; or for difficult diagnoses, seers called *neles*, who were capable of looking into the spirit world. The chanters sang to carved wooden figures representing friendly spirits; each family had its own box of figures to stand guard as well as cure. They also counted on these familiars to help them clear the way through forests and waters filled with hostile spirits, and if omens or epidemics threatened, they staged a mass exorcism, in which a specialist chanted for eight nights to a host of carved figures as well as the assembled community.[28]

In the visible human world, each village managed its affairs with little outside interference, but none stood completely alone. Sailing canoes went back and forth; villages attended each other's puberty ceremonies; men dropped in for long stays with friends on distant islands; and anyone who wished to learn ritual could spend months or years apprenticed far from home. Chiefs were expected to tour from time to time in a form of musical diplomacy, to be received ceremoniously in other villages and sing in their gathering houses. Groups of chiefs would come together to sing and orate, and through much of the nineteenth century they recognized one or another among themselves as paramount. This "great chief" emerged from among his peers, however, just as did local leaders, and he too worked to shape democratic decisions rather than impose his will.

As for foreigners or *wagas*, they were kept at arm's length: the Kuna refused to allow merchants or anyone else to settle in their villages or use debt to control them. After Isthmian independence from Spain in 1821, national and provincial governments in Panama and Colombia were too distant and too weak to exert more than intermittent influence on the Indians. Throughout the century, Colombia was by and large isolated from the outside world, internally fragmented by geography and a primitive communication system, and periodically racked by political strife. The government passed laws to end communal land tenure and integrate Indians into national society, but San Blas lay far outside the highland zone in which such laws could even partially be enforced. The Kuna periodically sent their leaders to Cartagena, Panama, and even to Bogotá, but for the most part they managed to live their lives without much outside interference.[29]

Panama, part of Colombia except during brief interludes as a secessionist state, was still oriented toward the Isthmian crossing and a southwestern hinterland. Its capital, less a city than a decrepit provincial town that burned down every few years for lack of an adequate water supply, had been caught in a depression for more than a century, and the two moribund ports on the Atlantic side had negligible effect on the Kuna.[30]

This isolation could not last, however. At midcentury, gold miners began traveling to California via Panama, and in 1855 a railroad was completed across the Isthmus. At the line's northern terminus a new port called Colón sprang up, giving Panama an effective presence on the Caribbean. Intrusions into Indian territory increased, impelled by economic demand from the Industrial Revolution and the growing economies of Europe and North America: coastal Blacks or *costeños*, the descendants of rebel slaves who since the sixteenth century had lived to the west of the Kuna, increasingly competed in San Blas for forest products and sea turtles. Over the mountains to the south, in the valleys of the Bayano and Chucunaque, mestizos and Blacks in search of wild castilloa rubber provoked a conflict with the riverine Kuna in the early 1870s known as "the Rubber War."[31]

Worse intrusions threatened. The construction of canals in Europe, North America, and the Middle East precipitated the idea of linking the Atlantic and Pacific. Among the various routes considered—which included Tehuantepec, Nicaragua, central Panama, and the Atrato—a possible Darién canal figured prominently. Attention focused particularly on a place called Caledonia in eastern San Blas, once a favorite of pirates and the site of Aclá, the Scots colony, and a late-eighteenth-century fort. In 1850 a British doctor, Edward Cullen, claimed to have crossed from one side to the other several times through a pass at Caledonia that he insisted never exceeded 150 feet above sea level. A disastrous expedition in 1854, during which a U.S. naval party was lost for more than a month on the Pacific side, found no pass under a thousand feet, but interest in the Darién route persisted.

In 1870 another North American expedition, led by Commander Thomas Selfridge, crossed at Caledonia to an affluent of the Chucunaque. In the course of a few highly uncomfortable weeks, during which unwilling Kuna guides led them through swamps and thickets, the surveyors determined that the Caledonia pass was far too high for a canal. Several years later, two French officers, Lieutenants Wyse and Réclus, investigated the Darién route once again, but the best they could suggest was a tunnel through the cordillera. Ultimately, in the 1880s, when a French company made the first attempt to build a canal, it chose the line of the traditional Isthmian crossing in Central Panama.[32]

Although the Kuna escaped the disaster of having a major waterway forced through the heart of their territory, they felt the world pressing in on them in other ways. In about 1890, Colombia moved to regulate trade with the Indians, insisting that vessels on their way to San Blas from Jamaica, the United States, Curašao, and other parts of the Caribbean pay duty at Colón or Cartagena.[33] By the end of the century, most of the sloops and schooners trading with the Kuna sailed out of the two nearby ports, even if quite a few of those based in Colón were still owned by English-speaking foreigners.

At the turn of the twentieth century, the Kuna were still keeping their distance, still holding to some of their time-honored practices and strategies. They continued to favor English-speakers, if now mostly in trade and cultural borrowing rather than war, but they realized that they had to deal with Hispanic political powers, and in the last analysis they rightly suspected all outsiders. Potential divisions were opening up in their own ranks, between stay-at-homes and veterans of work abroad; between families interested in educating their children and others adamantly opposed; and between hopes and fears directed toward Panama and Colombia. Some feared the national government in Bogotá in particular, others the Panamanians closer at hand, and a few, such as the authors of a letter presented to the British consul in Colón along with the gift of a rooster and hen decorated with red, white, and blue beads, still looked to more distant powers for help:[34]

Rio Diablio[35]

San Blas Coast

May 16th 1893

To her Majesty Queen Victoria

We William Thomson, Lewis Breakman, Emanueleta Yarso, Joseph Harvey, James Leverage, Chiefs of River Diablo do hereby beseech you to listen to our troubles and help us. We as Indian Chiefs have our families here and live in the land that God has given us, and now they intend driving us from our homes, and we have no where to make a home.

Miguel Nunis the President of Cartagena and Miguel Antonia Caro Vice President of Bogota[36] are trying to Sell our Country to the Americans. Our people have lived here for centuries. [W]e have our plantations, our Cocoanuts, we get our living by hard work. They wish to take our Cocoanuts, our rubber and everything God has given us, and drive us and our children into the mountains. We being under the Colombian flag was satisfied and well treated when Panama was a Souvereign State, but Since Bogota has become So; we are not treated well and they wish to Sell us for the gold and rubber, Even now we are well treated by Panama. The wish to keep our country to ourselves and for them to keep theirs. God gave us our wives and we do not wish to mix with other nations.

Now Most gracious Queen Victoria we beseech the[e] not to allow the Colombians to take our land and homes And drives us to the mountains to die of starvation, and we sign ourselves your most humble Subjects.

Part Two

MISSIONIZATION AND TURMOIL, 1903–1912

3.
The
New
Order

As they began the twentieth century, the Kuna made a radical distinction between themselves, the people put on the land by Great Father, and the dangerous and intrusive outsiders surrounding them. Like many indigenous societies, they simply called themselves "the people" — in their language, *Tule*. Also like many others, the *Tule* came to be known by a name not of their own choosing. *Kuna*, however, has no unpleasant connotations, and today the *Tule* readily accept that name and use it themselves. "San Blas," too, is an imposition, the name of a Spanish saint: to its inhabitants their homeland is simply *yala*, the land or mountain, or *yar suid*, the long land. Nonetheless, for the sake of clarity, simplicity, and consistency with the historical and ethnographic literature, this book refers to the *Tule* as Kuna and their territory as San Blas.[1]

Outsiders, non-Kuna, were called *waga*, a word that lends itself to being spat out as an epithet. The archetypal waga was a Spanish-speaking, dark-skinned Latin. Englishmen (called *iles* from the Spanish *Inglés*) and North Americans (*mergi*) sometimes qualified as honorary non-wagas, but in the last analysis, anyone not Tule was a waga.

As the Kuna saw it, wagas were like evil spirits: someone who dreamed of a Panamanian or Colombian was most likely seeing a devil or illness spirit in disguise. Like spirits, wagas were dangerous and sometimes hostile, prone to steal and hurt, and like spirits, they circled around on the outside trying to get in.[2] English-speaking allies and trading partners were in some ways more like the helpful familiar spirits called upon for defense, a resemblance suggested by the carved wooden figures representing the familiars, which look remarkably like eighteenth- or nineteenth-century Europeans in frock coats.[3] But familiars were still spirits, dangerous and unpredictable, and Englishmen and Americans were still foreigners.

Spirits were thought to lust after souls, wagas after land and women, both of which Kuna men jealously guarded. Women and land were in some ways equivalent, since the earth is the body of Great Mother, to be protected against mines and cattle ranches as women are from rape or seduction. Sexual fears undoubtedly followed from historical experience, from life in the Spanish mission settlements as well the years in which French pirates took Indian wives. Avoidance of sexual involvement with foreigners also followed the central strategy in Kuna domestic life, which was to control males through the seclusion of young females, with the crucial difference that parents would eventually let a few selected sons-in-law into their households, while wagas, however frequently they turned up to buy coconuts or to tap rubber, were meant to stay outside forever.[4] The inviolability of women, which elsewhere can embody the honor and exclusivity of a family, caste, or colonial power, in San Blas drew the line between the Kuna and the world.

The question of what to do about wagas, and more generally how to face the world, preoccupied the Kuna, just as it must have in previous centuries. Inevitably, the external struggle was internalized as a long-running argument between different factions and opinions, between those who thought that a little schooling or a shop in their village might be all right and others who were dead set against it. Rather than a well-oiled machine, Kuna society resembled the earth's unstable tectonic plates, shifting and realigning under increasing pressure.

The greatest potential for schism and change lay between the generations. Sons-in-law took orders from their wives' parents. In the field of ritual, they apprenticed themselves to senior chanters or medicinalists, and in politics, they started at the bottom of the ladder, as the village constables who announced meetings and kept people awake. Lacking the skill in oratory and the personal presence that would come only with practice, most young men deferred to their elders in political discussion. By no means shut out altogether, they were recognized as the most vigorous and productive members of society and in previous centuries as the leading warriors. With time they would themselves become fathers-in-law, master ritualists, and chiefs. But in the meanwhile, if youth grew impatient, if some opportunity let it overturn the age hierarchy, the temptation might prove hard to resist.

Generational tensions, questions of change, and relations between inside and outside all came to a head in 1903, when Panama broke its ties with Colombia, and in so doing brought a major world power into the Isthmus. In the next few years, the struggle would be played out in a single community known to outsiders as Río Diablo, and to the Kuna as Nargana. Christianity, schools, stores, planked houses, streets, voting, bread, dresses and shoes, gramophones, carnival, the fox trot, policemen, stocks and jails, schism and riot—all the joys of the condition its proponents called modern civilization came first to Nargana.

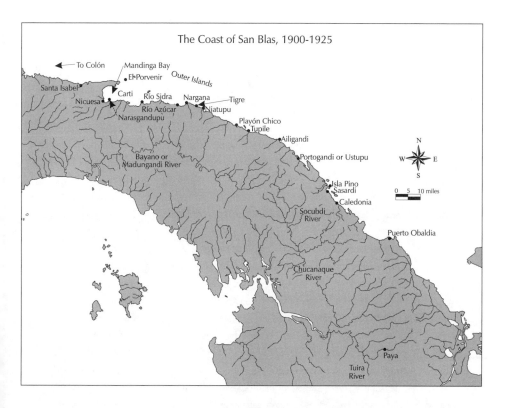

Nargana, "the Bamboos," actually encompasses two island villages located a few hundred yards apart, Nargana proper and Nusatupu, or "Rat Island." Settled in the mid-nineteenth century by Kuna from a nearby mainland village, the paired islands were separate but slightly unequal, Nusatupu living in the political shadow of its larger and more important twin.[5] After two unremarkable village chiefs, their successor, a celebrated ritualist named Inagailibalele or Abisua,[6] was elected head of all the Kuna in the late nineteenth century, making Nargana the political capital of the coast.

Abisua, who was born off the Isthmus among the easternmost Kuna, traveled west as a young man, ending up at Madungandi or Banana River in the Bayano Valley. Not long after completing studies as an exorcist, Abisua was made a chief in his new home. Later, when he was invited down to Nargana to perform an exorcism, the people there prevailed upon him to stay, and in time he was chosen first to be village chief and then to be leader of all the coastal Kuna.

At the turn of the century, Abisua, his health failing, announced his intention to retire, which prompted a regional meeting on Nargana in 1900 to find a successor.[7] According to Kuna oral history, the old chief began the convocation by singing to the assembled delegates:

He sang about finding a pole, about finding a pole with heartwood in it—in the old days the elders often sang in metaphors, in the soul of things. He sang about the essence, the soul of chiefs. He began to be singing to the men who work in the forest. "Elder forest people, over four days you will go to the forest," he said. "You will look to find where a good pole is to be found," Abisua began to be singing. . . . "In the East, I see a good white pole," he said.[8]

Supposedly no one understood Abisua's metaphor, which, given the purpose for which they had assembled and the conventional equivalence in chiefly rhetoric between poles, trees, and leaders, is unlikely.[9] As the story goes, only a delegate named Inanaginya, a leading figure in eastern San Blas and, according to some versions, already Abisua's right-hand man, grasped that their leader was singing about his preferred successor, who turned out to be Inanaginya himself.[10]

Abisua, after his choice was confirmed, continued as chief in his home village. Who would have succeeded him there and what would have happened had events continued on the same course cannot be known, but things changed irrevocably with the return two years later of one of Nargana's first literate men, Charly Robinson.[11] As a young boy, during the 1880s, Charly had been taken away by the captain of a trading vessel named Charles Julius Robinson, who came from either San Andrés or Providencia, Caribbean islands held by Colombia but populated mainly by English-speaking Protestants.[12] After four or five years of schooling and working for the family of his mentor and namesake, Charly went to sea as a sailor, and over the next several years he visited a good many Caribbean and Atlantic coast ports.

In about 1902, by then in his twenties, he returned to Nargana.[13] His parents had died during his absence, and among his siblings, only a brother survived, so on his return Charly moved into the household of an aunt. Soon afterward he married, but within a year or two he and his wife separated, as often happens in the early years of a Kuna marriage. By one account, Robinson found his wife's traditional worldview hopelessly alien to his way of thinking. According to another, he insisted they move into their own house in the North American manner, and she refused to leave her parents. The couple soon managed a compromise, however: across the street from his in-laws, Robinson built a home of a sort previously unknown in San Blas, a two-story board structure with a concrete floor. The couple and their children slept upstairs, while in the day his wife continued to work with her mother in the family cookhouse, an arrangement that allowed Charly to strike at least a small blow for modernity and civilization.[14]

Tagged as Niga Gardaduled, "Young writing-person," Robinson distinguished himself by his active participation in village gatherings and, according to several accounts, by his favor with Abisua, who was himself bilingual though illiterate. In addition to literacy, the effects of Charly's foreign upbringing were apparent in his readiness to tell Bible stories, his devotion to commerce, and his preference for the English language and things North American. (At this stage he spoke no Spanish.) Soon after his return, he opened a small store on the ground floor of his new house, and he began teaching the basics of arithmetic, reading, and writing in English to some of his friends and their children.[15]

The prodigal's return coincided closely with fundamental changes on the Isthmus.[16] For three years, from 1899 through 1902, Panama had been a principal theater for the civil conflict between Colombian liberals and conservatives known as the War of a Thousand Days, which ended in U.S. intervention and a settlement signed on board the warship *Wisconsin*.[17] With peace reestablished, attention turned again to proposals for an Isthmian canal. Following discussions with Colombia, the United States decided to take up and extend the excavations largely abandoned by the French in 1889 rather than start afresh in Nicaragua. Through intense pressure on Colombian negotiators, the Americans secured the Hay-Herrán treaty, which was completed in January 1903 and ratified by the U.S. Senate but rejected by its Colombian counterpart.

In response, Panama, a strongly autonomous region of Colombia that had enjoyed brief periods of independence during the nineteenth century, began plotting secession, with the assistance and encouragement of the North American management of the Panama Railroad. The plotters sent an emissary, Doctor Manuel Amador Guerrero, to the United States, where he fell in with Philippe Bunau-Varilla, engineer and advocate of the interests of the failed French Canal Company. After conferring with President Theodore Roosevelt and interpreting Roosevelt's wink and nod correctly as indications of U.S. approval, Bunau-Varilla sent Amador back to Panama.

On November 3 the plotters staged a successful rebellion. The United States, which prevented Colombian forces from quashing the uprising, recognized Panamanian independence three days later. The next stage went less well for Panama, however. Bunau-Varilla, having insisted that he be named special envoy for the rebel junta, negotiated a treaty with the U.S. secretary of state granting the United States sovereignty in perpetuity in a Canal Zone larger than originally envisioned and allowing it to appropriate other Panamanian lands as deemed necessary for the operation and defense of the Canal. Panamanian delegates arrived in Washington too late to take back control of the negotiations, and despite their dismay at the terms, threats of withdrawal of U.S. naval protection forced the provisional government to ratify the treaty. Thus Panama began its history as a nation without full sovereignty, a protectorate of the greatest power in the hemisphere.

Although the Kuna had played no part in secession from Colombia, their lives would be affected in far-reaching ways by U.S. hegemony as well as by Panamanian independence. How the new government dealt with the Kuna over the first quarter of the century would be strongly shaped by its fragility, insecurity, touchy nationalism, and by the presence of *two* nations on the Isthmus. How the Kuna responded would also be influenced by their perception of divided Isthmian power.

In the first few months after independence, however, Panama saw San Blas primarily as the only route by which Colombian armies might return to the Isthmus, since they could not cross the Darién overland.[18] In January the U.S. consul in Colón reported that invading troops in eastern San Blas were attempting to obtain several hundred canoes from the Kuna.[19] Military threats soon evaporated, but in the first six months of 1904 a number of diplomatic missions visited the Indian area, as both governments courted the Kuna. At the same time, indigenous leaders were taking the measure of the new order.

In January two men who evidently spoke a little Kuna were sent with letters in Spanish and English announcing Panama's national birth and inviting native leaders to the city. They were received by the chief of Nusatupu, who had Charly Robinson translate the English letter. At the end of the month a party was sent to visit the government, returning with a set of Panamanian flags for the two islands.[20] The emissaries, meanwhile, continued down the coast to Sasardi, seat of the high chief Inanaginya. After some resistance, Inanaginya was persuaded to accompany them to Panama, where in addition to flags, he was offered official support. On his return, the chief called a regional meeting to discuss the changed political situation.[21]

The issue facing the Kuna was whether Panama or Colombia should have their allegiance. Almost no one, except perhaps Charly Robinson, had any interest in becoming an active citizen of either country, but they were accustomed to offering token loyalty to a neighboring state. The governor of the province of Colón, the part of Panama closest to San Blas, commented astutely that the Indians would undoubtedly choose whichever government gave them what they wanted. Less astutely, he assumed they were after money, when what they were really asking for was to be left alone.[22] As another exasperated observer wrote a few years later:

The truth is that those Indians want to belong neither to Panama, nor to Colombia, nor to anyone. But they wish to ally themselves with anyone at all in exchange for throwing out the one that comes closest to them. Since Panama is now influencing them most closely, they turn to Colombia, as twenty years ago they turned to Queen Victoria against Colombia; and long ago they turned to the Dutch against the Spanish; and the English against the Dutch; to the French against the English; and finally, to the Spanish against the French.[23]

After 1903, if the Kuna were to decide national allegiance in terms of which power was more distant and less demanding, they would choose Colombia. But if they judged, correctly, that Panama, with the help of the United States, would soon secure its eastern border, and that Colombia's interest in San Blas would rapidly fade, then the path of realism was clearly in the other direction. Eventually, it would become clear that the Kuna, in one way or another, would have to come to terms with Panama. In 1904, however, Inanaginya opted strongly for Colombia. He sang to his followers of a well-known and reliable older spouse versus an attractive but untried younger woman:

"Now I will not divorce my old wife on you," he said. "I have a good wife," he said. "I have a hard-working wife," he said. "A wife who is up at dawn cooking me banana drink, that's what kind of wife I have," Inanaginya sang to the elders. "Not the kind who leaves me without clean clothes on the crossbeam, with clothes strewn around," he said. . . . Therefore I don't want a young wife. A wife who gets up at mid-morning, I don't want that at all," Grandfather sang, so it is said.[24]

Although definite about Inanaginya's metaphor and its political significance, Kuna oral tradition is vague about his followers' response. It may be that a majority acceded to his wishes or suspended judgment for the moment, or that the coming schism may already have been apparent. Certainly, local chiefs who wished to deal directly with Panama did not heed the high chief's preferences, which he had no means to enforce. While Inanaginya himself journeyed to Colombia later in 1904, the next most important leader, Cimral Colman of Ailigandi, visited Panama, possibly with his superior's blessing.[25] Abisua of Nargana, despite his retirement as high chief, also made the trip.

Abisua did not take the usual route, however, which was to coast down to Colón and cross the Isthmus by train. Instead, he went over the mountains on foot to his old home of Madungandi and then down the Bayano to Panama. After an interview with the president of the Republic, Dr. Amador Guerrero, Abisua returned home, and on August 8 he died in Nargana.[26]

The village now had to find a new head.[27] Under normal circumstances, it would have chosen an older or middle-aged man from among its argars and secondary chiefs, a traditionalist capable of singing in the sacred gathering as well as representing the polity. Instead, it turned to young Charly Robinson, opting in effect for a broker or mediator, someone closer to the outside forces confronting them than most of them were themselves.[28]

It is doubtful that any other Kuna village would have accepted Robinson as leader. In the decades as seat of the high chief Abisua, Nargana had been a center of trade and foreign contact,[29] and unlike most islands, it had begun letting merchants ashore during daylight hours. A number of its senior men, moreover, had spent some of their youth working on foreign boats: though most returned to a traditional life at home, they were open to a little change, especially change with a North American

Charly Robinson in middle age.

flavor.[30] Even this liberal wing of former sailors, however, was not ready to go as far as Charly Robinson himself.

The new chief carried out his first major official act almost immediately. Responding to an invitation from President Amador, Robinson went to Panama in late 1905 with a delegation that included several prominent Nargana and Nusatupu men, as well as two chiefs from Tupile and Playón Chico, villages further east.[31] During the presidential audience, Robinson and Amador had a friendly chat in English, and when Amador, after having passed out more flags, stressed his government's good wishes and readiness to help, Robinson responded with a proposal that he bring a group of Kuna boys to the city for schooling, to which Amador readily agreed.[32]

Charly Robinson was by no means the only one in San Blas interested in schools. The Kuna had little difficulty recognizing the practical advantages of being able to read, write, and do sums: several sources mention a desire to protect themselves or avoid being cheated by traders.[33] Kuna culture, moreover, lent great prestige to verbal art and esoteric learning, both of which could be acquired through modern education as well as through apprenticeship in traditional ritual. In Robinson's own case, his literacy, knowledge of English, and experience abroad took the place of his predecessor's mastery of exorcism and sacred history.

At the same time, many Kuna, even on Nargana, feared that formal education

House and store of Charly Robinson.

would import alien ideas and values. According to some accounts, the little school opened by Robinson before he became chief was closed down at gunpoint by outraged Kuna from across the mountains.[34] As seen by such conservatives, it was precisely the equivalence of traditional and modern education that made schools so dangerous. In this heated climate of opinion, the chief was wise to begin by taking the students away to school rather than bringing the school to the students.

In late October of 1906 Charly Robinson returned to Panama City with seventeen boys in tow, four of them from other islands and the rest from Nargana and Nusatupu.[35] Panama's secretary for education, summoned by President Amador on October 27, was struck by the scene in Amador's office, especially by the easy relationship between Indian chief and president, the credit for which he gave entirely to the latter:

At a telephone call from Doctor Amador Guerrero, I presented myself at the palace and I found him chatting familiarly with the indian Robinson, surrounded by fifteen indigenous [boys] . . . brought by him for the foundation of the school. . . . What simplicity of manners and what exceptional gifts as leader were those of that model president! With the same familiarity, with the same affectionate smile with which he received his secretaries and his most intimate relations, he could be seen to deal with the small urchin and the workman and even the wild savage who sought his help.[36]

The president and secretary, conferring with Amador's close friend, Bishop Francisco Javier Junguito, arranged to have the boys educated at government expense in a

Kuna boys in school with Christian Brothers.

special annex to the new Normal School run by the Christian Brothers. "This school had as its end the civilizing and christianizing of a certain number of Indian youths from the islands of San Blas, and by means of them, later on, to secure the same services for the inhabitants of all of that unexplored and barbarous region"—in plainer words, they hoped the boys would later go home and civilize the rest of the Kuna.[37] On October 31 a presidential decree made things official, and by November 3 the school was under way.

At first, the three Christian Brothers assigned to the annex had great difficulty getting through to their charges, particularly in the absence of a common language. One of the oldest boys, who spoke a little English, was called on to communicate with the others, until it was discovered that he sometimes willfully mistranslated to stir up trouble. (They expelled him.) The Brothers also perceived a great cultural and social gap between themselves and the boys, as a highly condescending report by the school director emphasized:

Much patience had to be displayed in order to give the first steps in social and moral life to these humble children of the Darién. Such sweetness and such judicious tact were necessary to capture hearts so inclined to suspicion towards those foreign to their race. One had to repeat the simplest things more than once and to descend to the most minute and vulgar details of existence. These children demanded, in things physical as well intellectual and moral, a special and painstaking education. Sea baths and showers every day, numerous and varied bodily exercises, substantial and appropriate feeding . . . they swim like fish; in the patio of the establishment they leap and play . . . frequent and long walks that they frequently take around Panama . . . one will have an idea of what is done for the health and physical development of these children, retarded up to the present. The teaching that is given them is completely intuitive and practical; and so it must be, given how extremely rebellious their minds are to the abstract, no doubt for lack of exercise. For them, above all, teaching must be made concrete; only at the cost of great efforts and with the slow action of time will the light of their uncultured brains open up.[38]

If the boys were so retarded and concrete in their thinking, it comes as a surprise to read that "the progress achieved is very encouraging," and that little more than a year and a half after their arrival "the greater part" could "read, write, calculate, and draw with appreciable perfection." After some of their homesickness wore off, the boys were easier to reach, and as they began to speak Spanish, the Brothers also learned some of "their rude dialect." More boys arrived at the school through 1907 and into 1908. A first group was baptized in October 1907, another at the end of the same year.

Although the boarding annex lasted only two years,[39] the efforts of Charly Robinson and others to arrange schooling in the city continued, and over the next fifteen years a number of Kuna boys—and, eventually, girls—were educated in secular and Catholic establishments. Moreover, the intentions of the church and government, that graduates would return to San Blas as apostles of civilization, were spectacularly fulfilled within just a few years.

At the end of 1906, however, with the boys newly lodged with the Brothers, the two most pressing questions were first, how the Kuna and Panama would progress beyond the stage of initial envoys and meetings to begin a long-term relationship and second, what Charly Robinson would do next. So prominently did Robinson and Nargana figure in both the government's calculations and the events of the following years that the two questions almost seem to be one and the same. Robinson's interest in education and trade, and his willingness to deal with Panama, offered the only realistic short-run opportunity for penetrating San Blas. The Panamanian army had been disbanded in 1904 after hints of an impending coup; the police were lightly armed; and a vessel to patrol the coast, let alone a navy, was entirely lacking. Even if the government, already in financial difficulties, had found funds in 1906 to begin pacifying the Kuna, other, more pressing needs would have taken priority. Thus voluntary measures and third-party proxies were required.

In such circumstances, national governments are often pleased to let missionaries step in, and the Panamanian constitution in fact gave the Catholic Church a special role in civilizing the country's Indians. Panama, however, suffered from a severe shortage of priests. Then in December 1906, just the person needed, Father Leonardo Gassó, turned up on the bishop's doorstep, as if by divine plan. (Father Gassó himself had no doubts at all that God had specially arranged matters.) A veteran of Indian missionization on his way from Mexico to Ecuador, where he had previously worked, Gassó needed lodging for the night and tried at the bishop's palace. Bishop Junguito, immediately recognizing his good fortune, persuaded Gassó to alter his plans, and since both were members of the Society of Jesus, he was able to square the change with their Jesuit superiors. Gassó immediately began studying the indigenous language he would be using, probably with the boys in the boarding school and Kuna men working in the city, and prepared to set out for Nargana at the first opportunity.[40]

4. Father Gassó among the Gentiles

By March of 1907 Leonardo Gassó felt prepared to enter the country of the Kuna, or, as he insisted on calling them, the Caribs. On the nineteenth the priest was aboard a small coasting steam launch in Colón harbor, ready to go but waiting impatiently for a letter of recommendation from President Amador. "I asked St. Joseph to arrange matters so that I would not go without that letter," and the saint obliged with a fierce wind that kept the boat in port until the letter arrived.[1] (Such winds are in fact quite frequent during the dry season from late December through April.) Gassó badly needed celestial assistance: when they finally headed out of the harbor, heavy seas drove them back, and when they set out again, the engine died off Portobelo. "A new mishap! We entered the bay at the mercy of the waves on either side of us, which could have dashed us to pieces. But I was carrying St. Joseph as a protector."[2]

The story of Father Gassó's adventures has survived because he wrote about them in detail in a diary covering the period from March 1907 through the end of 1908. The diary, with some additions and changes, was published in installments between 1911 and 1914 in a Spanish missionary journal.[3] Intended to be seen only by other priests and brothers, it was brutally frank as well as passionately one-sided and opinionated, and it provides a vivid and revealing picture of his encounter with the Kuna.

The journal records a series of further adventures on the little boat, including steam leaks from the boiler that forced Gassó to hide behind his umbrella and peeled the skin from his face and hands. Eight traumatic days after setting out, he finally arrived at Nargana on Wednesday of Easter week. Henry Clay, or Enrique Clair as Gassó knew him, Chief of Nusatupu, the smaller of the two islands there, came out in a dugout canoe to the launch. Despite the missionary's best efforts to give a capsule summary of Catholic doctrine, papal succession, and the dangers of hellfire,

Enrique rejected Gassó and his mission out of hand: "What? All of us burned? Hah! That will be you *wagas* . . . because we are going to see our Father-God."[4] When Gassó turned to Nargana proper, his intended destination, he had more luck, however. Taken to the little store run by Charly Robinson, Gassó gave the chief letters written in English by the president and bishop, which prompted a warm welcome: "Father, this is your house. For some time I have wanted to be instructed by a Catholic Father. . . . You shall live among us teaching us, and you shall be our father."[5]

An experienced veteran of missionary work in Ecuador and Mexico, Gassó immediately threw himself into converting the Kuna. That first night he read his letters of introduction, summarized Catholic doctrine again, read the catechism that he had translated into Kuna while still in the city, began to teach his listeners a prayer, and explained the significance of holy week, all in a single village meeting. The next day he celebrated mass — only Carlos, which was what Gassó called Charly Robinson, was allowed to participate, leaving others whispering and peering in through the wall slats — and he reexplained himself to chief Enrique on Nusatupu. On Good Friday Gassó led a procession through Nargana to the spot where he had first stepped ashore, raising a large cross to commemorate the coming of Christianity. Some of those in the procession sang prayers and knelt to kiss the cross, but some also fell into arguments with onlookers who were mocking them, which gave a taste of things to come. On Saturday an unfriendly ambassador from Carti to the west arrived to announce that on *his* island they wanted no fathers, and on Easter the priest celebrated mass again.[6]

This first stay with the Kuna lasted only two weeks. Gassó was eager to take Charly Robinson to Panama, to have official support for the mission reiterated in person, and to have President Amador, who spoke good English, explain Gassó's purposes to the chief in greater depth. (Since Robinson knew little Spanish, Gassó only minimal Kuna and no English at all, communication was not easy.) Gassó was also following a well-established pattern of repeated *entradas* or "entries," which in his case were punctuated by long stays in the city or among Afro-Panamanian costeños down the coast.

At the end of the *entrada* Gassó noted with some satisfaction that seventy boys, twelve girls, and twenty-one men had learned to sing and speak four prayers, salute the priest formally, kiss his hand, and doff their hats for both himself and the chief.[7] (This last innovation greatly pleased Charly Robinson.) Among the band of young boys to whom Gassó taught prayers and their ABCs, he thought he discerned signs of religious vocations in two of the most devoted, whom he named Leonardo and Estanislao, the first after a martyr of the Jesuit missionization of Japan, the second after his own brother in Spain. On the negative side, local resistance was already building, and rumors surfaced of impending attacks by irate Kuna from other villages.[8]

Father Leonardo Gassó, S.J.

The party left on April 7, taking Robinson's wife with them, despite considerable family opposition—according to Gassó, it was the first time a Kuna woman had left San Blas—and on the eleventh they reached Colón, whisking her off to a nunnery in a closed carriage. The next day they crossed to Panama and moved into the bishop's residence. There the visitors were impressed by the absence of women and the celibacy of the priests, reinforcing Gassó's efforts to dramatize the safely asexual nature of his mission, a point whose significance to the Kuna he had already recognized. On the thirteenth, President Amador received them and reiterated his support; the bishop baptized the chief's child as Amador Robinson, with the president and his wife standing as godparents; and Gassó and the chief took a meal at the boarding school for Kuna boys, whom Robinson admonished to stick to their studies and disregard any opposition or contrary teaching from their parents.[9]

Charly Robinson soon returned to Nargana, but Gassó stayed on for seven weeks. He had much to do, especially in managing Kuna delegations to the government, but Gassó, it later became clear, always found reasons to stay in the city.[10] Eventually, one of the delegates, a secondary chief of Nusatupu named Joe Harding or (in Kuna pronunciation) Soowadin, and known to Gassó as Soo or Sho, was prevailed upon, with much reluctance, to take the priest back with him.

Gassó's second arrival started badly.[11] He noticed that the great cross was missing, thrown into the water, he was told, by Chief Enrique of Nusatupu. One of Gassó's "little sacristans," Leonardo, immediately deserted him, in the first of several wounding rejections.[12] With Robinson away at a work camp on the outer islands to the west and many Nusatupu people aroused against Gassó, he was confined to a shack alongside Soo's house while Nusatupu debated what to do with him. At one long session to which Gassó was invited, a "demon-possessed" ritualist from Nargana named Manuel Portete took up the verbal attack, denying that the Kuna needed priests or that they would go to hell without baptism. After others had, somewhat less forcefully, repeated Portete's sentiments, Gassó told them he would not leave unless they killed him, which they said they would not do, and that if they rejected him, not only would the government be displeased but "the curse of God will fall on you; sicknesses and misfortunes will come upon you, you will die in your infidel state and descend to be burnt."[13]

With his twin threats of political and spiritual retribution, Gassó had hit on a powerful combination. Although most of San Blas lay outside effective national control, the men of Nargana and Nusatupu, who were actively trading with Panama, felt vulnerable to such pressure and inducements. As for God's anger and demonic dangers, the Kuna were already convinced of their reality, though they worried more about sickness and other spirit threats than about the hereafter, and like many missionized peoples, they apparently saw baptism as a new form of magical protection. At the end of a week, Nusatupu said Gassó could stay if he baptized its children. He immediately started performing ten to twelve of these rites a day, letting parents know that baptismal medals would repel demons, and he renamed Nusatupu Isla del Sagrado Corazón de Jesús, Island of the Sacred Heart of Jesus, though he also crossed back to his primary base on Nargana a few hundred yards away. When Charly Robinson finally returned from turtling, his public protestation of faith and support reduced the priest to tears.[14]

Gassó, it was already clear, was going to rename everything in sight. For villages, he either added a Saint's name as a prefix—Nargana became San José de Narganá in gratitude for Saint Joseph's protection—or, as with Nusatupu/Corazón, he substituted an entirely new name. To catechumens he gave Spanish Catholic names, many taken from saints and heroes of the Jesuit order,[15] and he insisted on hispanicizing anglophone names, as with Henry/Enrique and Charly/Carlos. As Tzvetan Todorov notes, when colonizers and missionizers rename so insistently and systematically, "nomination is equivalent to taking possession."[16] In effect, Gassó was remapping the San Blas coast, conquering linguistically for the church and Hispanic civilization.

During his second *entrada*, which lasted from late May to early July, Gassó threw himself in earnest into converting local Kuna by catechizing them, that is, by drilling them in prayers and basic points of doctrine, which they were to memorize and recite verbatim. The enthusiasm with which many threw themselves into learning and reciting delighted Gassó, and to increase Kuna pleasure in this new amusement he soon hit on the device of fostering competition between groups of catechumens. Gassó reluctantly offered a little instruction in the ABCs to the young boys who formed the largest and most enthusiastic group among catechumens, but he fervently opposed the Catholic Church's use elsewhere of literacy as a tool of conversion, and the essence of his method was oral.[17]

Gassó's bilingual catechism, which was modeled on an early mission text thought appropriate for the simple minds of children and Indians, was (like many first-generation missionary translations) a linguistic hash.[18] It included prayers and affirmations such as "Our Father," "Ave Maria," and the "Credo"; the decalogue, the five commandments of the church, and acts of contrition and confession; also lists of sacraments, sins, enemies of the soul, and so forth; and finally a series of questions and answers on points of doctrine to be recited in formal exchanges between priest and faithful — all of which sounded very different in Kuna than in the Spanish original. Gassó and his Kuna helpers, not knowing enough of each other's languages to work around the many theological concepts without precise native equivalents, had improvised translations, sometimes merely repeating a key Spanish term. The many garbled passages that resulted must have badly confused catechumens.[19]

The first sacrament, for instance, is rendered as "To wash, named *bautismo,*" which is not terribly informative. Since the Kuna have no precise linguistic equivalents for "pardon" and "forgive," it is not surprising that "forgiving our trespassers" is rendered as "forget" (*iege*) and heavenly forgiveness as "have pity on" (*wile dakke*), though the distinction between the two obscures the parallelism intended in the Lord's Prayer.[20] The Kuna word *sunsoged,* "true, undoubted, exemplary" is pressed into service not only to characterize Mary's virginity and the consecrated host but also to translate "glory," "redeemer," "kingdom," and "sanctified."[21] "The Sacraments of the Sainted Mother Church" is rendered ludicrously as *Dios Inna* "God's Home-brew."[22] As for the act of contrition, the first part is almost entirely confused, while the second part is not translated at all, as if Gassó's helpers simply gave up in despair.[23]

The garbled passages in the catechism reflect in part Gassó's limited knowledge of Kuna. In many places in his diary he quotes in translation long and apparently fluent exchanges with Kuna men. In other places, however, he acknowledges difficulties with what he calls "high Carib," a strongly syncopated, contracted form used, he says, in ritual.[24] In actual fact, "high Carib" is nothing other than fluent everyday speech, in which shortened word forms predominate, suffixes pile up at the end of verbs, vowels drop out, and consonants are changed. What Gassó resisted acknowledging was that by forgoing "high Carib" with him, the Kuna were communicating in baby talk, a tactic they have taken with outsiders many times since then.

Stiff-necked pride apart, there was no reason why Gassó *should* have mastered Kuna before even setting out for San Blas, and he certainly managed to plough ahead, communicating basic ideas about hellfire and papal succession as best he could. His skills must have improved with time, and meanwhile he depended heavily on Charly Robinson to explain and exemplify. Nonetheless, his authoritarian approach to life seems to have marked his language learning, leading him to over-systematize in the direction of languages he already knew and to fill in apparent linguistic gaps, thus creating his own version of the language. He persisted in his early errors, and his assistants' early garbled translations made it unchanged into the published catechism.

In any case, the details of doctrine—the six enemies of the soul and the five works of mercy—mattered less than catechism as an *event*. The mission's essence was manifested in the sessions of teaching and prayer, as they brought together the faithful, showing them who they were. Gassó appointed officers, constituting a shadow government rivaling the traditional village hierarchy, and he began timing meetings to compete with Kuna gatherings. A doorkeeper kept enemies and unsuitable individuals out, attendance was taken, and lists were drawn up dividing the faithful from their satanic enemies.

Above all else, mission meetings embodied and instilled order and hierarchy. In the beginning Gassó held back from correcting his followers' deportment, even when it drove him to distraction:

How shall I explain what one of these gentile villages is like? . . . like a cageful of loonies . . . some follow the prayer, others leave off from that and sing wildly out of tune, others suck pieces of sugar cane while stretched out belly-up, others race through the hut . . . others pinch each other, others stand up, others stretch themselves.[25]

But he began immediately to teach them proper respect toward civil and religious authorities and above all to kneel, the inability of Indians to kneel symbolizing for him their anarchic unwillingness to submit: "Today they were made to kneel rather than squat, as they are used to doing. . . . Only Christian people know how to kneel, the Bishop made me understand some time ago, and that is why for these Indians, it is almost as difficult to do so as it is for us to lie on the ground on our elbows."[26]

The question-and-answer form of indoctrination itself embodied the hierarchical relationship expected between priest and followers. Other catechisms might allow catechumens occasional substantive answers to priests' questions, but Gassó's confined them to Yes or No, or rather to Yes or No, *Father*. ("After he died on the cross, did he return to rise again living? — Yes, Father.")[27] To Gassó, catechization epitomized the proper order of society as a whole.

Kuna catechumens, however, seem to have viewed it in a different light, at least at first. The prayers they learned were undoubtedly understood as new and possibly more powerful ritual texts, like those performed by native practitioners. In traditional apprenticeship, one learned the "Way of Hot Peppers" or the "Wind Way" to control the spirits and to gain influence and prestige among humans, not to know the meaning of life, the form of the cosmos, or the nature of the deity, for all of which one went to the gathering. Such texts were composed, moreover, in esoteric languages, whose meaning students did not learn until well into the process of memorization. And while apprentices honored their teachers, that deference was not a paradigm for all proper behavior but a limited exception to the largely egalitarian nature of Kuna life. Thus, in a classic example of missionary miscommunication, Gassó and his catechumens sat in the same room, teaching and learning, but their misunderstandings did not bridge the gap between hierarchy and equality.

Catechization was to lead to baptism, but only after considerable time. Gassó aggressively sought out adult converts as well as infants and toddlers, even pushing his way into houses uninvited, and by the first week in July he had baptized 108 children.[28] He was much more cautious about offering the sacrament to adults and older children, for fear they might backslide, so except for dying people willing to make declarations of faith, he baptized only proven adherents.[29] As a test of commitment and a way to familiarize people with himself, Gassó pushed both islands to build him a combined residence and church.[30] Nusatupu delayed and resisted for years, but on Nargana adherents moved with amazing rapidity, raising a building by mid-June of 1907, and they even collected money to buy floorboards.

Despite the missionary's successes with baptism and the house-church, his presence in San Blas continued to agitate and polarize the Kuna. One night a party of men from the nearby island of Tigre landed unnoticed during an evening service, and finding the structure being built for Gassó unattended, they cut all the lashings, bringing it down.[31] Rumors reached him that attacks on Nargana were planned from eastern San Blas and from the Bayano to the south.[32] The Nargana men practiced shooting, and Gassó passed on to the government Charly Robinson's plea for arms. President Amador sent a reply promising rifles, though in much smaller numbers than requested.[33]

Enemies also appeared closer at hand. A good many people on Nargana, and even more on the other island, resisted actively or passively. Gassó saw a tendency for people to sort themselves out by age and sex, with young boys most open to Christianity, young and middle-aged men somewhat less, followed in order of diminishing acceptance by women, old men, and last, old women, who were dead set against him.[34] This generalization reflected in part shrewd observation on Gassó's part. Others have found Kuna women more conservative than men, elders more than youth. Young boys, who ran around naked, could do what they liked after fishing or helping a little in their fathers' farms, and visitors to Kuna islands were followed around by inquisitive urchins, calling out to them, taking them by the hand, and in Gassó's case, coming to catechism.

The distinctions Gassó drew in terms of age and gender also reflected the needs and attitudes of a cleric with little interest or sympathy for women (the feminine virtue he most praised was submission) and a loneliness for filial affection. They were also in line with the practice of generations of missionaries in the Americas who had struggled to capture the allegiance of young Indian boys and to set them against their gentile parents. As Ramón Gutiérrez argues concerning early missions in the North American Southwest, Catholic "fathers" have struggled to supplant the parents of their young Indian followers, to become both father and mother to them.[35] As early as his first *entrada*, Gassó was convinced that his "angels" and "delights . . . love me more than they love their mothers,"[36] and he sent numerous boys off to the city and boarded others at the mission in no small part to detach them from their gentile parents. In a more global sense, he sought to become the authoritarian but loving father of *all* the villagers, whatever their age, to make them all children.

However much Gassó depended on his smaller followers for affection, as a matter of policy he also concentrated on converting senior men, most of whom practiced one form of ritual or another. As often happens in missionization, Gassó found his most important and effective opponents, as well as a few of his strongest supporters, among the ranks of these ritualists.[37] So strongly did hostility flow between the Catholic priest and his aged Kuna counterparts that in a sermon preached to catechumens, Gassó metaphorized the motives Kuna gave for resisting baptism as five terrible old men—Señor *Yappa,* "don't want to"; Señor *Yoo,* "not yet"; Señor *Binge,* "I'm embarrassed"; Señor *Urwe,* "I'm mad"; and Señor *Budara,* "I'm tired/not inclined"—"which five gentlemen," he added, "must be put to the knife."[38]

Although Gassó did not take literally his followers' suggestion to put a number of actual flesh-and-blood old men to the knife,[39] he certainly hoped and prayed that God would destroy them, most especially the medicine man, Manuel Portete, who had spoken so eloquently against the priest on his second arrival, and who turned out to be his next-door neighbor on Nargana. Portete and his friends played their panpipes, Gassó was sure, to disrupt evening meetings, and from his doorstep the old man mocked a convert who brought food to the priest each day: "Baligiginia, *I* am servant of no one!"[40]

Gassó fought back hard. For a while he thought he had driven a wedge into Portete's family by persuading his son, named Smit, to let his children be baptized. Smit, however, changed sides or had been playing the priest along. After getting himself elected as first among the traditional, singing chiefs of Nargana, and thus second in authority to Charly Robinson, who did not sing, Smit joined forces with his father.[41] "And so today . . . he passed over to the opposite camp and . . . made himself czar of the rebels of Nargana."[42] As Smit and the sacred gathering increasingly emerged as the center of resistance, Gassó, with ingrained anti-Semitism, branded its leaders the Sanhedrin, after the priestly council of Jerusalem that had condemned Christ.

At the other extreme, some of the mission's firmest friends were ex-sailors like Charly Robinson. The problem with such supporters was what Gassó called their "great confusion of ideas," taken, he was sure, from the Yankees. "Because they detest some things from the elders, they detest them all . . . and on the other hand they admit everything modern . . . good or bad, but above all the bad." Gassó felt constrained to humor these men, without letting slip his intention, which was to keep almost everything they admired out of San Blas.[43] In many respects Gassó resembled his enemies more than his friends.

Modernity and North American ideas were not on Leonardo Gassó's agenda. Although he had not set foot in Spain since 1892, fifteen years before, he reproduced faithfully the social attitudes of Spanish Catholicism, which at the end of the century took reactionary conservatism to an extreme. Liberalism had been declared a sin by the Vatican, much of the Spanish hierarchy linked itself with the political far right, and the Society of Jesus in particular vehemently espoused the values of order, hierarchy, and submission to authority. Reactionary in the literal sense of the word, Jesuits yearned for a return to an idealized past in which Masons, liberals, and freedom of religion and the press did not menace a purely Catholic world.[44] Gassó, far from Spain, reflexively enacted Spanish Catholic attitudes and values on the San Blas coast.

Gassó's religious nostalgia focused most of all on the early New World Catholic missions, especially the Jesuit *reducciones* of Paraguay and the Orinoco—isolated, self-contained theocracies in which priests and brothers led, Indians knew how to pray and to kneel, and if they forgot, the lash reminded them. A modicum of non-Indian secular force might be needed, but religious leadership and values would predominate, and the corrupt larger world would be excluded altogether. It was not that Gassó saw himself imposing these values in addition to Christianity; order and authority, he was convinced, were inherent in true religion.[45]

The problem, of course, was that the Kuna had their own feelings about hierarchy, which were on the whole quite negative, especially about domineering outsiders. Their own chiefs, part sacred, part secular, received only mild deference, and they were watched closely to limit their power. It was not that Kuna chiefs were by nature weak, as Gassó thought, but that their independent-minded followers did not want them too strong. Social classes, similarly, were not absent merely by chance: no Kuna would let another set himself more than a little above him. Adherents of the mission might learn to kiss the priest's ring or doff their hats (though Gassó did not want to see how many stomached his pretensions in hopes of getting their children educated or Nargana's political preeminence reestablished), but they did not on the whole take well to humility. Opponents, unconstrained by such hopes, reacted vehemently. A fragment from a gathering chant attributed to chief Nele Wardada eloquently sums up the demands for dependence and subservience they recognized in the mission: "Someone wearing clothing down to the tips of his feet, 'I am your father,' someone says to me. The waga says he will make himself my father."[46] In the process of missionization there were misunderstandings and mistranslations. But in the final analysis, Kuna opponents understood what the Father wanted, and they were not about to give it to him.

5.
To
Confront
the
Stubborn

Leonardo Gassó's program does not seem to have given much attention at first to questions of sobriety. While decidedly not in favor of drunkenness, he seems to have been more predisposed to tolerate drinking for the moment than he was liberalism or unbended knees. But circumstances soon forced the question on his attention, because drinking parties robbed his sleep, his enemies featured prominently among the celebrants, and drinking brought disorder, which he hated.

The Kuna drank at puberty ceremonies, which, though given in honor of only one or two girls, drew in whole villages. The shorter ceremonies, called "night chichas," lasted less than twenty-four hours, but the "long chichas" continued until the puberty chant cycle was completed at the end of three to five days. Other activities ceased while men and women devoted themselves to ritual and to enthusiastic consumption of cane beer (*inna* in Kuna, *chicha* in Spanish) brewed in huge clay pots.

It did not help that the first ceremony to which Gassó was exposed, a short one in late June of 1907, was sponsored by his enemy Portete, or at least so Gassó thought. Not understanding that puberty ceremonies must begin at the moment that the chicha brew, laid down two weeks earlier, comes to maturation, Gassó was convinced that Portete had thrown a party expressly to thwart him. "He with a few others, playing the flute or . . . panpipe, have tried with pure jungle yells to obstruct our services today."[1]

A week later another chicha took place. "What a drinking bout last night! What savages! One must put up with it until the next voyage to see if I succeed in introducing the holy stocks for drunkards and trouble-makers, since without fear one cannot put a village in order."[2] The guests at the chicha included a hostile visitor, "who is telling them that they should throw the Father out soon, that no one should go to the Father's house to pray, that the Father is a demon. . . . They told me that the wild man was going about drunk with a machete looking for me. . . . O what a terrible mess!"[3]

As a rule Kuna villages rigorously prohibited drinking between puberty ceremonies, but Nargana and Nusatupu, perhaps because of their years of contact with traders, tolerated consumption of rum by small groups of men. In Gassó's mind, the chichas and the little parties linked Indian drinking with confusion and disorder.[4] He blamed the merchant captains and sailors, some of them North Americans, most of the rest Black West Indians, not only for rum but more generally, as the "heterogeneous element," for spoiling the uncorrupted isolation of the mission. These "ambassadors of hell" were, he was sure, fighting the mission tooth and nail.[5] In fact, though some resented his opposition to their pleasures or favored Protestantism, others believed that he was smoothing the way for their trade.

During the six weeks of the second *entrada,* support on Nargana for the mission waxed and waned, and with it Gassó's moods.[6] By early July, he felt that "the battle lines are being drawn. The bad ones are manifesting themselves more, but on the other hand, what attendance among the good ones!" According to his optimistic count, eighty families were in favor of the mission and twenty-five opposed, with a few neutrals.[7] Enemies on other islands were threatening to burn the new church or even kill Robinson and Gassó, and though the missionary did not take the threats all that seriously, he concluded that it was time for guns and stocks.

By mid-July, Gassó had convinced himself that the situation was calming and took the opportunity to visit Panama, where in addition to securing a small shipment of arms, he managed to have Chief Enrique of Nusatupu given the title of general and Robinson named governor of the San Blas coast, under Gassó's supervision.[8] By the time he returned to the field seven weeks later, however, the situation had so deteriorated that Charly Robinson was moved to plead with Gassó, "Father, every time you go to Panama the gains are undone. Stay here forever from now on."[9] In Gassó's absence a "delegation of diabolical savagery," a party of ten Kuna from across the cordillera, had visited Nargana, whipping up fears that the priest would interfere with puberty ceremonies.[10] (Since Gassó was by now referring to the rituals as "the superstitious, diabolical, dirty feasts that are crowned with a classic drinking bout," the fears were not unfounded.)

During this third *entrada,* which lasted only three weeks, Gassó's afternoon excursions through the streets of one island or the other "to visit the sick and conquer the stubborn" frequently led to a confrontation with the stubborn, notably beside the hammocks of the sick, where he attempted to leave Christian images in place of the small wooden figures used in Kuna curing.[11] In one instance, when a sick old woman refused baptism, he threatened her with Hell; two days later, when she died, he went to her hammock and, cross in hand, preached that all who had refused baptism had perished.[12] In another encounter, Gassó ended up in a virtual tug-of-war with a dying man's mother, the priest placing a picture of the heart of Jesus by the patient, the mother repeatedly taking it out again.[13]

Gassó was firmly convinced that Christian icons, baptism, and holy water saved Kuna lives. Faithful catechumens caught more fish and harvested more turtles. Just as Saint Joseph had providentially kept the priest's boat in harbor when he first set out, so on a later voyage God had made a wind just strong enough for Gassó to arrive in time to say mass. Similar Kuna beliefs he dismissed as superstition, heaping scorn on the villagers' tendency to invoke divine intervention in daily life. With each side sure of its supernatural powers, these struggles ended up as contests between rival systems of magical practice.[14]

Gassó's struggles with Charly Robinson were much more subtle and ambivalent. At moments when the chief's support kept the mission going, Gassó praised him effusively, calling him "my great Carlos." But Robinson's Americanized, modernist outlook and his inability to command obedience disturbed Gassó profoundly: from the beginning he searched for ways to impose a stronger form of control but recognized that such a move would provoke overwhelming opposition.[15] The chief in turn was "struggling within his soul," wavering between support for the mission on the one hand and the expectations of Kuna friends and his own need for autonomy on the other.[16] Having hitched his wagon to Gassó's star, Robinson was bent on becoming the dominant leader in San Blas, and others almost certainly went along in hopes of regaining the preeminence that Nargana had enjoyed under Chief Abisua. It was rapidly becoming clear, however, that Robinson and Nargana would lead San Blas only at the cost of domination by Gassó.

Ten days after Gassó's arrival, the struggle for control was played out again in the context of another drinking bout, this one involving two Black sailors from Portobelo and a noisy accordion. Despite confrontations with Gassó and mission followers, the revelry continued all night, giving the priest a terrible headache. The next night the villagers did better, putting the sailors back on their boat, "but . . . too politely, which is a bad procedure for the shameless moderns, who need neither charity nor good manners, but a cudgeling across the back."[17]

The "accursed accordion" next turned up in the hands of a Kuna ex-sailor. Gassó got little peace, either from his own efforts or those of Charly Robinson, who complained that the delinquents, having considerable public support, ignored his requests to desist. Gassó demanded that they go confront the man together, but by the time he reached the scene the chief had slipped away. The accordion passed to three Black sailors, one of whom drunkenly menaced village policemen with a knife. When the sailor made threats against Gassó, the priest laid a formal curse on him.[18]

Fortunately for Gassó, the titles granted Enrique and Charly Robinson and other evidence of government support strengthened his hand, and the menacing sailor's brother begged to have the curse taken off. The village was persuaded to suppress rum-selling, and to finish the mission building and construct stocks as well.[19] Gassó, however, would have been wise to stay on and consolidate his gains. Support was ephemeral, the situation highly volatile, and it had only been six months since he first came to Nargana. He convinced himself, however, that things were under control. At the beginning of October, Gassó set out with his little sacristan, Estanislao, who offered living proof of the great advances made by the mission.[20] Four days later the pair embarked for Spain, leaving Charly Robinson and other supporters on their own for more than eight months.

They reached Spain in early November and set out on an extended tour, the priest showing the Indian boy off to clergy and pious laymen, following a centuries-old pattern in which aborigines were brought back to Europe to be displayed.[21] The tour was a success: priests and brothers volunteered for the mission, the Jesuit order gave its approval, and they were offered numerous items for mission churches, including paintings, statues, and a marble font. In addition, Gassó arranged for the publication of his grammar and catechism, which he tried, unsuccessfully, to have set in type so unusual that Indians who learned to read the catechism could not transfer this skill to sources of contamination such as newspapers and Protestant Bibles.[22] On the negative side, Gassó had a bout of serious illness, and Estanislao began to shown signs of restiveness.[23]

After a second tour to collect all the offerings, they set sail again, reaching Colón in early May of 1908, and after long stays in the city and the coastal Black village of Santa Isabel (where Gassó was also establishing a parish and jumping-off spot), they did not reach Nargana until mid-June.[24] On his return, disarray and turbulence once again confronted Gassó. Estanislao, who as they got close to home refused to pray or wear shoes except under duress, immediately abandoned the priest, and in the next few weeks he spread rumors that Gassó would bring in more outsiders and promote race-crossing, both of great concern to the Kuna.[25] Charly Robinson was not there to greet the priest, the Indians were cool, attendance was down, and there had been numerous puberty ceremonies in his absence. The turmoil and backsliding so depressed him that he considered abandoning the effort.

Even before he reached Nargana, Gassó learned that the village had recently been convulsed by the lynching of his enemy, Portete.[26] Portete had been identified by a seer as a dream killer, or *gia dakkaledi,* someone who appeared to people in their sleep and offered a poisonous drink. Strictly speaking, it was not the accused himself who would-be victims saw but a demon in his form. Aroused villagers, however, did not always observe such fine theoretical distinctions. Accusations seem to have occurred especially in moments of social crisis, and the accused was often an arrogant ritualist like Portete.[27]

The preferred treatment for a dream killer consisted of a graduated regimen of increasingly toxic drinks that purged him of his demon or else, in a poetic reversal of the crime, eventually killed him. If the accused refused the treatment, or if people were sufficiently aroused, they might turn to more drastic and immediate measures. According to Gassó, Portete had laughed off warnings that he was being blamed for ten deaths. A mob seized him and—avoiding bloodshed, which the Kuna considered highly polluting—they placed Portete on a framework over a fire, where he died from asphyxiation and burns.

This execution fascinated as well as horrified Gassó, who saw it as divine fulfillment of his own threats against Portete for opposing the mission. Gassó was sure, in fact, that God and the saints regularly punished his enemies: a wood-cutter who worked on Sunday, for instance, was half-killed by a log; Estanislao's father died after his son's rebellion; a captain who overcharged Gassó had his arm broken; a ship's pilot who thwarted him was drowned; the chief of the men who knocked down the church was eaten by a jaguar; Inanaginya, leader of the Kuna confederacy, died of smallpox; and Portete was smoked to death over a fire—for all of which Gassó rejoiced![28]

Portete's death did not deter his son Smit, first among the traditional chiefs of Nargana. Although Gassó thought he heard Smit's adherents plotting to kill him,[29] they instead began holding singing gatherings every night, drastically cutting attendance at Catholic prayers and instruction.[30] From this point, the struggle increasingly opposed mission service to Kuna gathering, which both sides saw as equivalents and thus natural rivals.

Indeed, everything Gassó did in San Blas was conditioned by his sense of the alterity of Indians, of the radical difference between him and them. "An Indian thinks one way, a white man another; their likes are altogether different."[31] Gassó admired much in Kuna practice, especially their monogamy and hard work, and in terms of intellect, the Kuna "certainly surpass all those [savages] of America, although they are still Indians."[32] What one hand offered, the other took away, however: he credited all Kuna virtues to the eighteenth-century Jesuit missionary, Jacobo Walburger, and he frequently referred to the Indians as savages, children, and even beasts.[33] Across the cultural chasm, Gassó perceived equivalence, particularly between himself and Kuna ritualists and between his services and theirs. That equivalence, however, merely confirmed that the gathering must be suppressed.

The Kuna shared Gassó's sense of alterity, viewing wagas and Kuna as two entirely different classes of being. "God created the dog, and to this day it's a dog. . . . God created the hen, and to this day it's a hen. God created the Indian, and now they don't want to let us be Indians."[34] Like many other peoples resisting missionization, the Kuna used this sense of difference as a defense: "The English have their religion and their priests or Fathers . . . the Yankees their religion and Fathers; we have our religion and our fathers. Why don't you go to those nations and leave us alone?"[35] Most of all, Kuna opponents used their alterity to reject hellfire. In Chief Enrique's words: "What? All of us burnt? Hah! That will be you wagas . . . because we are going to see our Father."[36]

Ironically, resistance in these terms forced Gassó to argue for uniformitarianism, to insist that there was a single God with one message for all peoples. Pointing out that all descend from Adam and Noah, he put forward the frequently used claim that Blacks, Whites, and Indians stemmed from different sons of Noah, and that the Indians were cursed with nakedness and drink because their ancestor had mocked his father Noah—which implicitly reaffirms the separation and difference Gassó was supposedly refuting.[37]

At the moment when these questions were brought to the fore by the opposition plan to blanket the village with gatherings, Charly Robinson had just returned to Nargana from a work camp. When he finally appeared after a long delay, the priest felt impelled to remind him of all the benefits of the mission, including success in catching sea turtles. He also conveyed a series of letters from the government instructing Robinson and other leaders to establish a police force and jail, impose prohibition, and complete Gassó's church.[38]

Robinson himself was as ambivalent as ever, expressing support for the mission but also continuing to preside over singing gatherings and coming only intermittently to prayers and mass.[39] By the end of the month, however, the display of government backing humbled Chief Enrique of Nusatupu, and Robinson renewed his allegiance to the extent that in one prayer meeting, in his commentary following Gassó's sermon, he ridiculed Kuna religious beliefs. As opposition also continued, Gassó welcomed the division into two camps.[40]

This satisfaction was mixed with physical pain. During his stopover in Santa Isabel on his way to Nargana, Gassó had been plagued by tiny red bugs that infest the forest, tick-like arachnids called *coloradillas,* "little red ones," whose bites can itch for weeks, and by chiggers, which nested in his skin. ("Can you believe it—a living hair shirt!")[41] Although Gassó bathed regularly, his long, heavy robe cannot have helped the condition, and on Nargana his irritated skin developed pustulous boils.[42] By the end of June catechists had to hold prayers without him.

The 30th. I cannot even walk, except bent at an obtuse angle. Oh, what a way God has of tormenting me with these pains! . . . Oh what days and what nights of pain, . . . without being able to remain either standing, or sitting, or on my side for very long, or kneeling! . . . If God lets His friends here suffer this way, what will become of His enemies in hell?[43]

Gassó decided he must leave, but before he did, he summoned supporters to his bedside to extract a gift of land for the mission, despite Robinson's warnings that villagers would resist. Using his condition to gain sympathy—"It may be that I'm already dying. To suffer so—for what? For your *spiritual* good"—he got his way and had the gift formalized in a document laboriously copied out by the chief. For Gassó this donation, small but full of meaning, reversed the depredations of liberal governments—"the official thieves of Europe and the Americas"—who "steal from the bride of Christ what her children of past times gave her."[44]

On the evening of July 3, Gassó left Nargana in a sailing canoe carrying coconuts to Colón: a board was placed on top with the priest lying on the board, cushioned only by two sacks. At the end of twenty-four hours and three intense downpours, they arrived off Santa Isabel. Despite high seas they successfully shot the pass through the reefs in the dark, but finding their path on shore blocked by flooding, they spent the night anchored outside the reef. Next day, Gassó felt somewhat improved and stayed in Santa Isabel for two weeks, but when his skin broke out again, he continued on to Panama in a feverish condition.

By mid-August Gassó was well enough to leave Panama, taking with him a pair of goats and a Jesuit brother who had come to join the mission, arriving in Nargana a few days later. Charly Robinson warned that two missionaries were the absolute maximum the community would accept, and Kuna opponents were even angrier than before.[45] Gassó, encouraged by Robinson's announcement that he and several other catechumens had completely severed their connection with the gathering, began an intensive effort to separate the "good" from the "bad." He and Robinson branded the gathering hall the "House of Errors," in contrast to the mission building, "The House of God."[46]

In October another chicha puberty ceremony occurred, during which drunken opponents appeared outside a prayer session, making threats against the missionary. An even more serious incident occurred when Gassó went to beard his chief opponent Smit at the Nargana gathering house.

I asked him how did he dare to teach errors, as leader of the house of errors, and why he said that the Father was evil and demonized. He said that only he taught morality.

"Then walk with care," I said, "because up to now all those who help me have been blessed by God, and all those who hinder me have been punished by God. Remember your father, Portete . . . I said to him that for his wickedness God would give him a bad death, and in fact the Indians themselves burned him alive."

Smit, understandably, flew into a rage. Gassó ended up outside the gathering house surrounded by angry opponents, one of whom kept trying to creep around behind him with a knife. As Gassó told it, he persisted in showing them illustrations of hell as he turned to keep the would-be assassin in sight, until they responded with laughter that it was *he* would go to hell.[47]

By late October, Gassó felt he had "won" Nargana, with only five "satanic" households holding out against him—a self-serving assessment that cannot explain continued attendance at the singing gatherings, the loss of unmarried catechumens to the gentile forces, or continued confrontations with unbelievers.[48] Gassó had no difficulty rationalizing a return to the city after only a few weeks. So once again he left the field, the brother with him, only to be followed a few days later by an exultant Charly Robinson, who told him that Nargana had repelled a pagan attack.[49] United by the threat of fire, a severe danger to a mass of thatch-roofed houses, the village suppressed the small minority who refused to close ranks and easily repelled the invaders by firing government-supplied guns over their heads.

By the end of the year, the government had passed, undoubtedly on Gassó's initiative, a new measure mandating official support for Catholic missionization, authorizing Indian scholarships, and encouraging colonists on the coast (this last, something he and President Amador had repeatedly promised they would not do). The diary ends with this double triumph over gentile flotillas and liberal governments. Nonetheless, in its last lines, Gassó noted the necessity of circumspection, in order to avoid arousing the antipathy of Masons and Protestants, and in the parade on November 3 celebrating the fifth anniversary of Panamanian independence, he viewed with loathing the participation of Masonic lodges, with "their insignia and banners of Lucifer."[50]

6.
Heresy
and
Impiety

Through 1909 and 1910 Father Gassó consolidated and extended the gains of his first two years, carrying the mission past the stage of heroic individualism into institution building and spiritual conquest. He built two substantial zinc-walled mission buildings; created a boarding school for Kuna boys; and brought in more priests and brothers (for a total of eight through 1912). A number of his enemies died, notably Portete's son Smit, whose passing Gassó noted with grim satisfaction, while other opponents fled to the hamlets of Tigre and Niatupu a few miles to the east. Although some who remained refused baptism, Gassó persuaded Nargana to abandon the sacred gathering. During 1910 Charly Robinson had the village reconstructed with broad, straight streets.[1] Although Nusatupu resisted more tenaciously, Gassó forced the village to begin work on a mission building, and when the antagonistic Chief Enrique died, his successor Soo converted to Christianity.[2]

Gassó's local victories, however, could not guarantee ultimate success, since they depended on official backing, an absence of competitors, and weak regional opposition. All three conditions were about to change.

Government support had its basis in the balance between Conservatives and Liberals, a party division then found in many Latin American countries, one Panama had inherited from Colombia. Members of both parties considered themselves Catholics, but they differed sharply in their attitudes toward the Roman Church as an institution and its role in society. During a period of Liberal dominance in Colombia from 1863 to 1885, a strongly anticlerical constitution disestablished the church, but for the rest of the century Conservatives held the upper hand.[3] On the Isthmus, whose elites were on the whole less attached to orthodox Catholicism, religious issues generated less heat, and among the urban middle class, liberalism and Masonism were strong.[4]

When Panama gained its independence in 1903, the core group of secessionists, led by Miguel Amador Guerrero, were Conservatives, but several Liberals played key roles in the revolutionary junta. When they assembled to draw up a constitution, one of the subjects they debated was the role of the church. In a close vote, a minority favoring establishment lost to a small anticlerical majority: freedom of worship was proclaimed, and Catholicism was recognized only as the religion of the majority of the population. As a concession to the losing side, however, the convention passed a motion, made by Amador Guerrero, enacting government support for a seminary and missions to the Indians.[5]

Amador Guerrero, elected by the National Assembly to a four-year term as the Republic's first president, promoted ties with the church as close as the constitution would allow, entrusting to the Christian Brothers of LaSalle a newly created Normal School (the one to which the Indian boys were soon brought), as well as primary schools in a number of interior provinces. As late as 1908, at the end of Amador's term of office, the National Assembly passed Law 59, which Gassó had promoted, affirming the church's special role in civilizing the Indians.[6]

Long-term prospects for the Conservative Party and thus for Gassó's mission were much less promising. Despite their initial control of the government and favor with the North Americans, the Conservatives attracted little popular support, as municipal elections in 1904 amply demonstrated. Liberals were introduced into the cabinet early on, and the presidential elections of 1908 produced a coalition government headed by a nominal Conservative, José de Obaldía. It seemed very likely that the Liberal Party would take the presidency outright in 1912.[7]

Throughout these years, dissatisfaction with Gassó and Catholic missionization, far from a private opinion in government circles, was expressed openly. In 1908 the secretary of government and justice wrote in a biennial report:

Religious catechization, without doubt beneficial, has nonetheless lost prestige in the modern age. The new conditions of contemporary life demand new factors in the work of progress of the species. It is for that reason that the efforts of the Executive directed towards reducing those tribes to civilized life, founded in the medieval procedure of missions and religious catechization, have not up to now given practical results.[8]

During this same period, as politicians began considering alternatives to missionization, the Kuna were debating which nation deserved their allegiance. High Chief Inanaginya still favored Colombia, Charly Robinson Panama, and in the middle, a number of chiefs and villages seem to have leaned toward Panama but tried to avoid open schism. Opinions on the issue followed in a rough way positions on change and foreign influence, running from Charly Robinson's enthusiastic modernism to reactionary xenophobia on Inanaginya's part.

In 1907, the year that Father Gassó entered San Blas, Inanaginya made a final trip to Bogotá, from which he never returned, dying of smallpox in the town of Honda by the Magdalena River.[9] The following year, when Kuna delegates assembled at their late chief's village, Sasardi, to choose a successor, the election turned into a bitter referendum on the national question. Inanaginya's nephew Inabaginya (the similarity of names has caused considerable confusion) emerged as spokesman for those who favored Colombia, while the pro-Panamanian group was led by Cimral Colman, chief of Ailigandi. So acrimonious was the debate, according to oral history, that some delegates could barely be dissuaded from sailing off at once in the dark of night.[10]

The schism produced a patchwork of interspersed villages. Of those that went with Inabaginya, the largest group clustered in the East near the Colombian border, around Sasardi, but even in the very westernmost regions of Carti and Mandinga several islands stayed with Colombia, while the adherents of Chief Colman and Panama included villages scattered throughout the region, with the largest concentration on the central coast.

The two factions, now constituted as rival confederacies, did not break off relations altogether, and they still agreed on opposition to the Catholic mission. After the failed attack of late 1908, a combined force menaced Nargana again the following March, but instead of fighting their way ashore, they held another regional meeting, which charged Charly Robinson, on pain of death, with informing the government that missionaries were not wanted in San Blas. When Gassó arrived a few days later, the people of Nargana and Corazón were reluctant even to let him ashore.

Undeterred, Gassó took Charly Robinson off to Panama again, and to bolster the chief's credit with other Kuna, who were agitated by outsiders coming into San Blas to catch sea turtles, he arranged a government decree reserving the turtles for the Indians.[11] Then, rather than settling in on Nargana to rebuild support, Gassó aggressively took his mission to the island of Tupile some thirty miles to the east. Earlier visits by Tupile's friendly chief, Inadoiginya, had inspired Gassó to rename him Ignacio after Ignatius Loyola, and the village, sight unseen, as San Ignacio de Tupile.[12] Despite the chief's hesitation at hostility from other islands, Gassó was determined to establish a new Christian beachhead.[13]

At the end of April 1909, armed with official letters and carrying a boxed statue of Saint Ignatius that he had been saving for the occasion, Gassó set out from Colón in a gasoline launch along with three prostitutes bound for Nombre de Dios: "Oh stinking fruit of the Yankee civilization that . . . brings through the Republic so many of these cloacas!"[14] On the way, the captain anchored one night near the village of Ukkup Senni, or Playón Chico, a few miles short of Tupile, exposing his passengers to unfriendly visitors from the village: "I don't want Fathers, I don't want a Bishop; I don't want the Pope; get out of here! I order it."[15]

When Gassó reached Tupile the next day, Chief Inadoiginya, just back from still another regional meeting, was reluctant to let him stay, but Gassó overcame the chief's scruples. Just as during his first days on Nargana, he threw himself into activity, opening the boxed statue of the village's patron saint, celebrating mass, and teaching prayers and doctrine. Toward sunset, he set up a large cross, which the people were to kiss on entering and leaving the village. In a very busy evening, Gassó led his pupils in chanting the rosary; read the letter naming Charly Robinson governor; blessed a staff of authority for Inadoiginya; and assured the worried villagers that their enemies would not come "for the moment."

The next day an unfriendly delegation arrived from Playón Chico. His hosts could not keep Gassó from confronting the visitors and provoking a heated theological debate, in which the chief of Playón Chico rejected Catholic universalism and hellfire: "What? . . . They're going to burn us? That will be for you and yours, but not for the Indians."[16]

Afterward, Inadoiginya accompanied Gassó to Panama to visit the government. While there, word came that a flotilla of canoes headed by a chief of Playón Chico and the regional leader Cimral Colman had sacked Tupile, wounding two villagers in the process.[17] Gassó insisted on portraying this "apparent defeat" as an advance, and his account shows no remorse or even a sense of responsibility for exposing the villagers to danger, only calculation of what the incident meant for the mission.

For the government, it signaled the moment to begin imposing secular control. After experiencing some difficulty in finding suitable vessels, it sent out an expeditionary force, which rounded up the chiefs judged responsible for the attack and sent them off to Colón for brief detention. As a more permanent step, the government created a border post, named Puerto Obaldía after the current president of the Republic.[18] Since few Panamanians could be lured to such an isolated spot, the authorities had to recruit policemen among coastal Blacks on the other side of the border.[19]

Puerto Obaldía was not a great success. Some trading vessels stopped to pay duty, but others simply sailed by.[20] The small, lightly armed police force, lacking a vessel larger than a canoe, exerted so little influence over the Indians that some in the government urged that it be closed down.[21] The village did become a base for Colombians entering the forest to tap balata and gather ivorynuts, and their activities provoked conflict with the Indians. Within a few years the government began exiling convicts there, which may have given Puerto Obaldía a purpose but hardly improved its tone.[22] Panama nonetheless had planted its flag at the border.

These developments may have worried Gassó, but within a few months a much worse threat appeared from another quarter, once again menacing the island, Tupile, where the priest had just begun his new mission. The second chief of the village, named John Davis, had left a son in the city to be fostered in a Panamanian household, as a number of Kuna families were doing in this era.[23] The boy's foster father passed him on to a Methodist minister named Gray, who used him to make contact with chief Davis. Gassó, in his visits to the city, tried to check up on Kuna boys put into fosterage, even taking them out of unsuitable situations, among which households of Methodist ministers undoubtedly ranked high.[24] He learned where the boy had gone when he quizzed Davis about a copy of the Gospel of Matthew in the chief's possession. It came, Davis said, from

a Father who does not wear a cassock, and he has told us that you are bad because you are a Spanish Catholic; that the Spaniards, even today, are bad because they don't want liberty for all. . . . That you don't teach everything, but he teaches all the periodicals and books. . . . "All the Catholic Fathers are looking for women and for that reason we Fathers who don't wear cassocks have a wife in order not to need others."[25]

Gassó took immediate action. "I disabused him of all these diabolic teachings and I made him get the boy out and I put him in the school of the Christian Brothers" — only to have the original foster father pressure Davis into returning his son to Gray. What Gassó did not learn until later was that Pastor Gray had also arranged with Davis to send a woman teacher to Tupile. Although Davis undoubtedly really did want an English-language school, Gassó blamed the invitation on "cursed Yankee *mone,*" specifically on promises to compensate the chief with *mone* for his losses from the looting of Tupile. "That dolt Davis had told me nothing of this."[26]

Pastor Gray had in fact found a remarkable woman to go to the Indians, a British evangelical named Miss Anna Coope, who was as sure of God's direction in her life as Gassó was in his. As she later recounted in her inspirational memoirs, however, it had taken her a long time to get to Panama.[27] Born in 1864 in the textile town of Bolton in Lancashire, England, she was the only child of strict and moralistic but nonbelieving parents. By her own account a shy stay-at-home, as a child she read a great deal in library books carefully monitored by her father, and she never married. Although photographs show a homely but appealing face, her "pug nose," the result of an operation on a growth, "was to be all my life my thorn in the flesh."[28] "If I had not had the 'thorn' given me, I would have looked like other girls and quite probably would have married. . . . I believe God allowed that disfigurement . . . to keep me for a particular work, therefore that operation was the first lesson in my missionary training."[29]

Coope first found religion in the local Anglican school and church. After leaving school, she began to work in the mills. When a Methodist revival aroused a desire to be saved, her parents limited her involvement in religion "for fear I'd go crazy."[30] However, a serialized biography of David Livingston inflamed her further, and at age seventeen, during a low-church Anglican revival, she had an ecstatic conversion experience.[31]

Two years later her family emigrated to Rhode Island (Coope never gave up her British citizenship), where she joined a local Adventist church and again went to work in the textile industry. At a Holiness meeting in Providence, Coope experienced a second, transfiguring religious experience. Afterward at her regular church, "they exclaimed: 'Miss Coope, how beautiful you look! Where have you been?' . . . I thought 'Can this be true? If it is it only proves the Scripture: "He will beautify the meek with salvation",' Psalm 149:4. I felt the beauty within uplifting me."[32]

Inspired as well by testimony from independent missionaries, in 1897 she decided to follow their example. Then thirty-three years old, she still lived at home, giving all of her wages to her parents, minus a tenth for the church. Over her father's opposition but with her mother's backing, she set out for the West Indies, evangelizing in the islands until called home to care for her sick mother, whom Anna converted before her death in 1900. She spent another six years supporting her now aged father, until he died (a few days after *his* conversion), at which point she was finally free to return to her calling.

In late 1907 Coope set out for South America. She worked for several months in an Indian settlement on the Orinoco, locked in conflict with traders who exploited the Indians, until the local headman died and the Indians dispersed. Coope moved on to Panama, where she arrived in August or September of 1909. Hearing of Chief Davis's offer, she accepted with alacrity.

When she crossed to the Caribbean side of the Isthmus, however, she soon found that none of the trading boats would take her. Eventually, she reached Nombre de Dios and succeeded in booking passage on a gasoline launch. While waiting in Nombre de Dios, she preached in the open air and passed out tracts, observed by a priest (she never gave his name), who took the tracts and ripped them up, scattering them in the streets — which certainly would have been in character for Gassó.

Thus began a battle of missionary titans, equally matched in strength, determination, and the conviction that the other was an emissary of Satan. Both antagonists wrote about Coope's trip, she in two chapters of her memoirs, Gassó in a long letter published in a Jesuit journal.[33] The two accounts agree to a surprising extent, but not on one crucial point. Where Coope portrayed herself as heroically alone, Gassó described her with a male companion, whose existence is confirmed in a letter by Coope as one Brother Penny.[34] Apparently the demands of the inspirational missionary memoir overcame Coope's scruples and erased Penny from the story.

Both accounts agree that, when Coope marched on board the launch, Gassó tried furiously to get her ejected, with English-speaking members of the boat's crew caught in the middle. He commented acidly on the "nest of doves she wore on her head," the mountain of supplies she brought with her, and Penny's frantic efforts: "He went bustling back and forth loading his cargo, from time to time, on noting opposition, planting himself in one place, and he would repeat emphatically, 'Civilize! Civilize! Civilization!'"[35]

Once under way, Gassó resolved to return to Panama and the government at the first opportunity "to better shut the door of the mission to heresy and impiety."[36] Arriving at Nargana at eight the next morning, after a night spent with the launch aground on a sand bar, Gassó disembarked while Coope and her companion stayed aboard. In the crowd gathered at the dock was Chief Soo of Nusatupu. Coope's account has it that Soo complained of the Catholic mission and mentioned Charly Robinson, at that moment working on the mainland. Gassó, on the other hand, wrote that Soo was so alarmed at the possibility of more outsiders coming into San Blas that he sent off two of his village policemen on the launch, armed with rifles (but no ammunition). Coope claimed that the priest put the young men aboard with an admonition to "fight for me."[37]

The launch, carrying Coope, Penny, and the two village policemen with their empty rifles, but not Gassó, reached Tupile at the end of the same day. Gassó, who had to rely on what informants later told him, wrote that as soon as the pair stepped ashore they were put back aboard bodily, with such delicacy, he says, that Coope laughed. (Admiration for her toughness and strength creeps in at a few places in his narrative.) Coope's version was that after chatting with John Davis and giving him a photograph of his son, the pair were taken to the Tupile gathering house.

There was a great crowd; it looked as though the whole island was there. I was seated by the side of the chief [Inadoiginya], while John Davis . . . sat at my left. The crowd was in front of us, the two messengers, each with a rifle, at the front . . . trying to impress me. . . . But I was very busy looking at the women and babies and refused to be properly impressed.

Davis told the crowd that Coope had come to teach the Bible and reading and writing in English: "I do not know whether the whole story was told, for it seemed to me that in the middle of it there was a sudden break, the two men jumping to their feet and crying: '*Pelear! pelear! pelear!*'"[38] The meeting broke up in confusion, and Davis said the decision had gone against her. Coope thought she had recognized the Spanish verb "to fight," but it is unlikely either that the policemen would have called out in Spanish, or that they would have used the infinitive form, *pelear*. More likely, as often happens when Kuna feel an issue has been discussed quite enough, they said, *Pela!,*[39] "That's all!" meaning in effect, "Enough! No more! The matter's concluded." In any case, though Coope was loath to accept the decision, the two policemen pulled her out of the gathering house, put her into a canoe, and took her back to the launch, thoroughly soaked.

Coope and Penny had to stay with the boat all the way to Puerto Obaldía at the border. Not having learned from their previous grounding, the hard-drinking crew pushed on into the night, ending up once again, with great good luck, on a sandbar rather than a coral reef. Next day, in lightening the vessel to pull it off, they brought up one of Coope's food boxes from the hold, so she and Penny finally had something to eat. After several days they ended up back at Nargana, where Gassó came aboard.

We had not sailed more than three hours, cramped up in the launch so closely that our knees touched, when the padre spoke to me. . . . "Do you speak Spanish?" he asked, and I replied courteously: "Yes, sir," not of course using the title "father."

Then he opened the battery of his abuse. He said that I was no good; that I had no faith, no religion; that I did not eat the body of the Lord Jesus, so I had no life. He said that I had no business to come up to the Indians, that. . . . He was so excited, so angry . . . that he went over and over his statements and denunciations, not knowing how to stop.

Finally I asked the priest if he had finished . . . and then I lifted up my heart to God in prayer to help me to speak wisely, to wield the Sword of the Spirit. . . . Holding the Book out toward him, I said: "Sir, I come to these Indians to teach them to read God's Word, whose entrance bringeth light."

. . . "El Protestante!"

"Yes," I said, "this book does protest! It protests against many of the doctrines of your church. It forbids the making and worshiping of graven images. You lift up the Virgin, the Pope, scapulars, rosaries, holy water, and a wafer god."

Poor Father Gassó! Coope's memoirs continue quoting her harangue at length.

The padre squirmed and twisted, but there was no chance to get away. He did stand up as if to pass me. . . . I stood up too, and with the Word of God open in my hand I quoted passage after passage. . . . This was my hour to glorify God, to lift up Jesus to this man; he had a chance to receive the light if he would. . . . My soul seemed to be on fire for God.[40]

Coope's account ends with this confrontation, which Gassó, understandably, did not mention. He noted that he left for Panama at dawn the morning after the boat's arrival in order to reach the government before the Protestants. Although officials would not concede his argument that Law 59 of 1908 gave the Catholic Church a monopoly in San Blas, they did back him against Coope, as she later found out in interviews with the president and the secretary of government and justice.[41] It was clear that the door had indeed been shut to heresy, and Pastor Gray counseled Coope to leave San Blas alone for the moment.

Coope might have taken heart, however, had she known at the time of her second interview in April 1910 that Gassó's official backing had already begun to crumble. The month before, President Obaldía had died, and his stand-in for the next half year was a leading Liberal, Carlos Mendoza, who was also expected to be elected president in September. Mendoza and his cabinet rapidly began reducing religious influence over primary education. They transferred the Kuna boys in the Normal School to secular teachers, and within two months, closed the school altogether on the grounds that the boys kept fleeing.[42] The secretary of government and justice, Ramón Valdés, also requested a progress report from Gassó.

In his reply, Gassó claimed that the mission and Charly Robinson (characterized as "the elect of God") had made Nargana a model of peace and order, and that the Kuna as a people teetered on the brink of mass conversion. While acknowledging the attack on Tupile, Gassó mendaciously blamed it on opposition to the little Kuna-owned shops that had sprung up there. He claimed that patriotism was growing among the Indians, who now regularly flew the flag and brought their children to the city, "a relief for many households, which have never before found such cheap servants."[43]

Cabinet members must have seen through the report's half-truths, wishful thinking, and tortured facts; some at least must have doubted Gassó's feigned loyalty to Panama; and his claims for the superiority of catechization to trade cannot have impressed a group of development-minded Liberals. At best the report may have bought the mission a little time, until the administration could go see for itself.

Acting President Mendoza, during his few months in office, made a series of tours, with the announced purpose of discovering the country's needs, while at the same time consolidating his own political position. In the case of San Blas, fact-finding was to focus on "plans for the reduction of the Indians to civilized life." In addition to Mendoza himself, the large party included two cabinet secretaries, the governor of Colón, a prominent businessman, and a reporter for the *Diario de Panamá*, which published a series of articles on the trip.[44]

The party set out on August 12 on a tug borrowed from the U.S. Canal Commission. After a brief visit at Puerto Obaldía on the border, they turned westward again, stopping at Sasardi, seat of the high chief, Inabaginya, where they found Colombian flags flying. A large crowd of Indians shouted menacingly, and village leaders invited on board to meet them replied that they could not do so while Inabaginya himself was in Bogotá. After another unpleasant encounter at a second pro-Colombian island, they received a much friendlier reception in Carti and then doubled back to visit Gassó and Robinson.[45]

On Nargana they were gratified by their warm welcome and material signs of progress. Some of the dignitaries attended a prayer service, and the next day the president himself came ashore to inspect Robinson's khaki-clad force of four policemen. The only sour note came from Gassó and Robinson themselves, who acknowledged widespread Kuna hostility toward the mission.[46]

The tour was pronounced a great success. Carlos Mendoza, it was pointed out, was the first Isthmian leader since independence from Spain to visit the Indians. This rosy summary ignored obvious problems: government leaders, able to visit a large section of the national territory only in a borrowed boat, had found villages flying foreign flags and an Indian leader away conducting treasonous negotiations. Worst of all, the nation's first magistrate, the embodiment of its sovereignty, had been rudely turned away by mere savages, without his being able to do anything about it.

For all the approval lavished on Nargana, the visit did nothing to stop the movement toward secular solutions to the Indian problem. In a report published a few weeks later, Secretary Valdés noted that Charly Robinson had been named governor on the understanding he could deliver San Blas, which was clearly not the case. Valdés cast doubt on Gassó's ability to develop relations with the Indians and "to open within a short period of time to commerce and legitimate exploitation those rich regions, which the autochthonous races occupy and which they hold hostage from progress." To release San Blas from this captivity, he proposed a boat service, police detachments, and schools staffed by middle-aged married men to "extinguish the prejudices" the Indians held against lecherous outsiders.[47]

Nor was Valdés the most outspoken member of the government. In the next biennial report, the governor of Colón Province signaled the relative priority to be given to salvation and national sovereignty:

The missions established there with civilizing goals on the part of the government that sustains them have not given, nor probably will give, the slightest result, if one excepts the fact that some number of Indians give themselves to receive a baptism whose significance they do not understand, and which will probably gain many souls for heaven, but which benefits the Republic of Panama very little.[48]

Gassó's last published letters, written in October 1911, complain of persistent obstacles in San Blas: pressure on the Indians from Black sailors to accept English-language schools, and educated boys lured back to pagan "cults and devilments."[49] Even Charly Robinson, though he presented himself for baptism and Christian marriage in 1911, never gave his heart completely to Catholicism. And despite Gassó's optimistic predictions, the imminent conversion of the rest of the Kuna never materialized.

At some point, probably in 1912, Gassó left San Blas permanently for his native Spain.[50] His patron, Bishop Junguito, had died in 1911, immediately after visiting the mission, and the approaching end of government support must have been painfully clear, especially with the election of the first full-fledged Liberal administration under President Belisario Porras. One might have expected, nonetheless, that Gassó would have hung on for at least a few years more.

His departure, it turns out, repeated a pattern already set during his previous work among the Tarahumara of northern Mexico. A Jesuit historian of the Tarahumara missions notes that on his arrival there in 1902 the "zealous and vehement"

Father Gassó had produced a grammar and catechism, and that he soon began developing plans to recreate the colonial Jesuit missions, the Indians to be isolated from the surrounding population, governed by native leaders, and disciplined with corporal punishment.[51] As in Panama, Gassó took his plan to the top of the national government, to President Porfirio Díaz, and, as in Panama, when government support eroded, Gassó abruptly left, abandoning the Tarahumara to their fate.

On Nargana, Gassó's successor, Benito Pérez, soldiered on, but the obstinacy of the Kuna apparently encouraged the Jesuit order to shift attention and resources elsewhere.[52] In November 1913 Gassó, by then in Spain, registered with dismay the news that Charly Robinson had betrayed Nargana to the Protestants.[53]

After his return to Spain, Leonardo Gassó lived at a college and priestly residence in Valencia from 1913 to 1917. In 1917, at the age of fifty-two, for reasons now unknown, he left the Jesuits, becoming a so-called secular priest outside any order. Two decades later, in July of 1936, during the opening days of the Spanish Civil War, when many of the Catholic religious were massacred, Gassó and his brother, Estanislao, were taken prisoner by Republican forces. On August 27, 1936, Leonardo Gassó was taken out to the highway and shot, a martyrdom that he very likely welcomed, and one that he undoubtedly confronted with his characteristic fierce courage.[54]

7.
Colman
and
Nele

It was easy for politicians and bureaucrats to exaggerate the power of Kuna leaders. Dealing with chiefs individually, they seldom saw the meetings that advised and controlled them. Coming from a political system that was more personalistic and (despite elections and legislatures) less democratic, Panamanians tended to see Kuna chiefs as power-hungry egotists rather than as tribunes of their people. But the most active and forceful leaders *did* shape events and policy. Charly Robinson's ambitions and maneuvers, and his love of writing, trade, and the Bible, radically affected Nargana, and through Nargana, the whole coast. The skills and vision of the two great Kuna leaders of this century, Cimral Colman and Nele Kantule, their openness to change combined with an insistence on political autonomy and cultural persistence, set the course the Kuna have followed since their time.

With Colman and Nele, just as with Charly Robinson, one can see the imprint of early experience on later careers. Despite the sketchiness of the biographies preserved by their followers and occasional lapses into hagiography and legend, they tell a good deal about the experiences and training that shaped them. In the case of Cimral Colman, whose formal Kuna name was Inagindibippilele, he was, much like the mythical heroes of many cultures, tested by life while still a boy.[1]

Colman's father, a man named Machus from the village of Ailigandi, "Mangrove River," had left his wife and daughters to go to sea as a sailor. On his way home, he stopped with friends at Carti in western San Blas, and while drinking at a puberty ceremony, Machus allowed himself to be married again. As his affairs sorted themselves out, Machus ended up on Ailigandi, his second and now ex-wife back in Carti. She moved in with relatives, and at some point toward the middle of the nineteenth century she give birth to a son.

Without a father close at hand, the young boy Inagindibippilele had a difficult childhood. His uncles are said to have forced his mother to work in the fields like a man, and while she was away each day, they gave her child scalding drinks, food laced with hot peppers, and tabooed meats such as crow and pelican.[2] At about age ten, Colman began showing strong interest in myth and ritual, and like the young Jesus, in disputing with his elders. Tradition has it that he began his studies with an uncle named Akkwasus, precociously mastering two dangerous chants usually reserved for much older men, one for controlling devils and the other for calling down lightning.

A few years later Colman followed his father's example by going to sea. Out in the wide world he acquired the names by which he would thereafter be known, Cimral, or Sam, Colman. Back on the San Blas coast, Colman settled with his mother in Carti. As a young adult, he developed a reputation as a scrapper, getting into drunken brawls at puberty ceremonies and in one notorious incident outpunching an enemy he encountered on the mainland shore. His pugnaciousness so displeased his uncles that they arranged for Colman to undergo a series of medicine baths, which may have taken off some of his rough edges but did not leave him timorous or unassertive.

Although Colman married in Carti and had two children, like his father before him he divorced and moved away, marrying again on Ailigandi and fathering more children. His father, Machus, was by then second village chief, and Colman soon distinguished himself as a junior leader by speaking often and well in gatherings. To go further, however, he would have to apprentice himself to gain the knowledge expected of senior leaders.

After preliminary studies with the chief of Ailigandi and another nearby teacher, Colman crossed the mountains to a riverine village called Socubdi to study with an unusual teacher named Arrabito, said to have been the son of a Kuna mother and Latin father. Arrabito taught Colman Latin American history, with stories of Cortés, Montezuma, Simón Bolívar, and the pirates who raided the Spanish main. Colman then traveled east to the village of Paya, seat of the famous teacher Kuppi, with whom Abisua and Inanaginya had studied before him.

By apprenticing with Kuppi, Colman was linking himself with the main line of Kuna tradition. Kuppi could trace his academic genealogy, a chain of teachers and students, back to the great seers and culture heroes of the past. According to Colman's biographers, when he arrived at Paya, Kuppi counseled him, singing of all the flowers and crops he had planted, asking Colman whether he had come merely to look at those plantings or to care for them and take seeds back to grow in his own land. Understanding very well Kuppi's meaning, Colman made several long visits to Paya, gathering the seeds of Father's Way, the myths and symbols of chiefly tradition.[3]

By the end of his apprenticeships Colman had positioned himself to succeed as first chief of Ailigandi and to exercise a leading role in regional politics. In 1900, when Inanaginya took over from Abisua as chief of all the coastal Kuna, Colman was a man of fifty or more, a well-known figure with political bases in both Ailigandi and Carti, and by some accounts, Inanaginya's presumptive heir. As he waited for the old chief to die or retire, Colman may have worried about obstacles to his own succession and how many years would be left to him, but he could realistically hope to become leader of his people.

Those hopes were blasted by the schism over national affiliation, which divided the Kuna into two camps. When Colman did take over in 1907 or 1908, it was as chief of one of the two antagonistic confederacies. His leadership repeatedly contested by Charly Robinson and Inabaginya, Colman struggled to lure villages away from his rivals and to hold on to his own. For the rest of his life, Colman's efforts to defend Kuna lands and autonomy intertwined with attempts, never successful, to gain the paramount chieftanship.

Just as Colman trod on the heels of Inanaginya, so close behind him came a remarkable figure named Nele Wardada, or Nele Kantule. Like Colman, Nele was never acknowledged as leader of all the Kuna, but he eventually achieved a legitimacy and recognition that Colman would have envied, consolidating the political and cultural autonomy for which they both struggled. Famous at home and abroad, Nele became the best-known Kuna of the twentieth century — chief, seer, and master of almost every branch of ritual. If Colman emerged as leader in the context of regional struggle, Nele came to prominence through a local version of that conflict in his home community of Portogandi.

A large village of several hundred inhabitants, Putturgandi, or Portogandi as Spanish-speakers called it, was located on the shore in eastern San Baas. The village was led by a "hard" chief named Yaigun, remembered vividly even decades after his death as a fierce, uncompromising reactionary opposed to all change. At the turn of the century, probably in 1902 or 1903, Portogandi suffered two calamities in quick succession, a flood and epidemic, and in response its households began moving out, one by one, to nearby Ustupu or Agouti Island just offshore. An unpromising coral outcropping covered with brush and infested with sand fleas, its landward side a mangrove swamp, Ustupu was gradually filled in and settled over the next few years. During this period of relocation, a young man named Igwa-Ibiliginya, first elected an argar of Portogandi in 1902, came into his own as ritualist and leader.[4]

Born a seer, or *nele*, and thus endowed, according to Kuna belief, with supernormal powers to communicate with the spirit world, Igwa-Ibiliginya was most often called Nele, or to distinguish him from other seers, Nele Wardada, "Stout Seer," alluding to his thick, powerful physique. In later years, having become a puberty ceremony chanter, or *kantule*, as well, he was known as Nele Kantule, and his children eventually took Kantule as a surname in the Spanish style.

Although Nele never voyaged abroad as did Colman or Charly Robinson, he traveled widely on and off the Isthmus, mastering a wide range of ritual and knowledge. After studying Kuna medicine with his father and apprenticing briefly with an exorcist, Nele learned medicine and the role of seer with a teacher on the Gulf of Urabá. Colman's teacher, the famous Kuppi, had by this time died, but over the following years Nele was able to apprentice himself to two of Kuppi's students.[5] Like Colman, Nele also learned about the foreign world, studying with two returned sailors named William Smith and Charly Aspinwall and a man named Jesús Manuel in a Colombian town called Quibdo, where Nele was exposed to life among non-Indians.[6] Nele also picked the brains of Charly Robinson and Leonardo Gassó in visits to Nargana, and along the way he became a puberty ceremony chanter (something that normally requires decades to accomplish) and learned several more curing chants. Even as the foremost ritualist and teacher of his generation, Nele continued to gather from his students and visitors any knowledge they had of the wider world and its implications for the Kuna.

Like Colman, Nele leaned toward affiliation with Panama, and he favored moderate innovation as long as it remained faithful to Kuna identity and culture—tendencies that put him on a collision course with Yaigun, the stubborn chief of Portogandi, who kept the village, now installed on Ustupu Island, in the pro-Colombian camp. Nele, promoted from argar to third chief, gathered around him a following of mostly young men open to moderate change, and although the village politics of those years are now murky, it appears that Nele's party sometimes boycotted the gatherings presided over by Yaigun. In 1911 the village was struck by another pair of disasters, a fire followed by an epidemic. Yaigun insisted on moving to another nearby island. Less than half the population followed, however, and those left behind immediately chose Nele as their chief, ran up the Panamanian flag, and switched their allegiance from Inabaginya's confederacy to Colman's.

As it happened, Yaigun's choice of island was even less pleasant than Ustupu, and his group was soon back. Although the two factions thereafter lived with their houses interspersed among each other, they kept separate chiefs and gathering halls. At chichas, fights occasionally broke out between the two sides, and on a few occasions they tore down each other's flag. Yaigun and his followers tried to move twice again, each time driven back by sickness, until years later they established a separate village at the end of the island.

Meanwhile Nele, undisputed leader of the much larger main village, had become a major figure in regional politics, second or third in Colman's confederacy. Already a well-known ritualist and teacher, as a political leader Nele remained partly in Colman's shadow, emerging now and again in various incidents, otherwise waiting his turn and growing in influence and reputation.

The way in which experience marked Colman and Nele, in particular its imprint

Nele Wardada and Cimral Colman, 1924.

on the policy they adopted toward change and the world, stands out even in their fragmentary biographies. Like Charly Robinson, Colman ventured far from home, but unlike Robinson, Colman had reached manhood before he traveled, so Kuna values guided his appreciation of what he saw abroad. Nele Wardada, though he never went to sea, did live among non-Indians. Even their stay-at-home rival, Inabaginya, was a veteran of trips to Bogotá and Cartagena with his uncle Inanaginya and spoke a little Spanish.

What most distinguished Colman and Nele from other Kuna was the range of their learning. Many men and a few women apprenticed themselves in ritual, and every village chief learned myths, metaphors, and conventional wisdom from the body of tradition called Father's Way. But only the most ambitious of would-be leaders took long apprenticeships with famous teachers or studied the customs of wagas and North Americans with such care. Nele and Colman queried ex-sailors and anyone else who knew about the outside, building up a picture of how the world worked and how it would affect Kuna lives.

Nele, for a long time he had been conversing with his friends, his special friends. Men who had spent many years in the United States. One person's name was Charly Aspinwall. . . . A tough fellow. He came to Nele, he'd visit him off and on. . . . Nele already had been having his own thoughts, he'd been thinking ahead, so right away he asked him things: "The Americans, how did they get their land?"[7]

Aspinwall told Nele what he knew about struggles for land and self-determination in U.S. history:

"All right. I'll tell you about the Americans. The Americans got their lands with blood. If you just sit there letting yourselves be mistreated, you'll just be mistreated. You have to spill blood. The Americans are like that. . . . If you should make war, you'll need to have a flag. . . . Then you'll have a *reserva*. . . . Its limits will be measured. Then you will have your land. Then your land will be preserved." That's what he said. He was learning that history. . . .

"As for schools, you'll have to bring them in. As for schools, you'll teach your children in them. . . . If you don't teach the kids in school, who will do things for you?" . . . At that time he was telling him everything. Charly Aspinwall. . . .

William Smith came here. . . . And it was just the same, what he said. About holding the land, every last thing. "In this way the whites hold the land," he said to him. "With blood."

In terms of their experience and learning, it is striking just how much Colman and Nele resemble the leaders of rebellions and messianic movements in many other preindustrial societies. However different from the Kuna and each other these individuals might otherwise be—failed priest or clerk, lesser member of a provincial nobility, wandering merchant or beekeeper, mission-educated catechist—most had at least a smattering of learning or literacy, and they had seen something of the world and its rulers.[8]

One may wonder how well the two chiefs really understood the world. Colman, after his studies with Arrabito, probably knew little more about Simón Bolívar and Montezuma than did most Latin American schoolchildren, but he knew that the wagas, rather than an eternal fact of political life, had come from a place across the sea called *Europa,* that they had conquered most of the Americas but could sometimes be beaten, that they often fought among themselves, and that the two states immediately impinging on the Kuna were weak. Nele may not have known all that much about North American history, Indian reservations, or the U.S. federal system, but he knew that the mergis had fought the Indians and taken their land away, setting aside small parcels as native reserves, and that their national government united formerly separate entities. In sum, Kuna leaders had a rough sense of the world's scale and of its historical depth and complexity. They could read not only the peoples and states immediately before them but also the wider international environment. They had an appreciation of historical contingency, and they could draw their goals from several models. All this put them far ahead of their counterparts in the Amazon rain forest, for whom non-Indians were strange, unpredictable creatures who violated all social rules, ahead even of many peasant peoples who had been in contact with outsiders for as long as the Kuna had.

In addition to its political utility, interest in foreign lands also had a less pragmatic, more symbolically charged aspect. Knowledge acquired in Paya, Caimán Nuevo, or New York brought higher status than the same material acquired at home. (Learning away from home also prevented subordination to local teachers or overlap with the repertoires of potential rivals.) Distant locations on this terrestrial plane had prestige value similar to that of hidden realms in the spirit world, and apprenticeship with a human teacher resembled a seer's conversations with spirit helpers. (Nele, as a seer, learned from both.)

The attraction felt from the powerful Other was also evident in the eagerness with which Kuna leaders accepted the titles and perquisites of foreign office: Charly Robinson received a ceremonial staff and coat, Inabaginya a gold-braided uniform and the title of general. Despite their political sophistication, Kuna leaders seem not to have grasped that these pseudohonors insulted the recipients by portraying them as children aping the forms of civilization. They did recognize the importance of treading a fine line between the foreign and the domestic, balancing the allure of distant knowledge against the fear and hatred of foreign oppressors. Unless a chief wanted to have the epithet of *waysikkid* (waga-ish, "foreign-leaning") hurled at him, as happened with Charly Robinson, he had to combine knowledge of New York City with learning in Father's Way and Kuna ritual. He could study with marginal figures such as Arrabito or Jesús Manuel, but only if he also established his bona fides with someone of Kuppi's caliber.[9]

Whether in terms of symbolism or practical politics, the task confronting Kuna leaders was to balance the inside and outside, to accept what the outside world offered or what could not be avoided, but to protect their people as much as possible from intrusion, exploitation, and cultural homogenization. At one end of the political spectrum, even reactionaries such as Yaigun and Inanaginya sold coconuts to the world market, bought machetes and kerosene, and learned about Rome and Simón Bolívar; at the other extreme, Charly Robinson seemed to embrace foreign ways but only as a Kuna man speaking Kuna and living among his fellows in an island village. For those more toward the middle, as were Nele and Colman, their policy was not to reject innovation or the outside altogether (however much the Kuna might talk that way) but to manage the pace of change, so new things could be adopted slowly and integrated into Kuna culture. They joined in a debate still going on among the Kuna today, about how to find themselves a place to stand, one both in the world and shielded from it.

8. The Mendoza Affair

Carlos Mendoza, the acting president of Panama who was rebuffed by pro-Colombian Kuna in August of 1910, spent less than half a year in office, much of it consumed by a crisis over his right to continue as chief executive. Mendoza found himself locked in struggle with his North American overlords, and in particular with a brash young man who would, years later, become the greatest friend of the Kuna.

Mendoza, the son of a prominent attorney and government official, had followed in his father's footsteps in Colombian Panama, successively filling numerous official posts and rising to the top of the Liberal Party in an era of severe political strife. Editor successively of four partisan newspapers, he was several times jailed and several times exiled, and during the civil war at the end of the nineteenth century, he served as secretary of government for the revolutionary Liberals. In a more conciliatory role, in 1903 he had worked with the mostly Conservative junta and had been chosen to write Panama's declaration of independence.

Throughout his career a Liberal partisan and a tough, effective political in-fighter, Mendoza was also an honest, fair-minded, and unassuming public servant. The chargé at the French legation greatly admired Mendoza, remarking on his "affability and honorable nature" and his qualities of "order, method, and work." The U.S. first secretary, on the other hand, called him shrewd and anti-American, "with all the Latin lawyer's fondness for quibbles and technicalities, a racial inability to refrain long from abuse of power, and a genius for misconstruing and distorting facts" — which says less about Mendoza than about North American prejudices.[1]

Mendoza's predecessor, José de Obaldía, died unexpectedly in March of 1910. As the second of three vice presidents or designated successors, called *designados,* Mendoza had at Obaldía's death assumed the acting presidency, the first *designado* having died the previous year. In his few months in office from March through September, Mendoza, far from merely serving time, played an active presidential role, initiating reforms of education and public administration, touring the country (including San Blas), and generally giving unmistakable signs of wishing to finish out Obaldía's term, which would end in 1912.

What happened next would depend on a disputed reading of the national constitution.[2] Presidents of the Republic, elected by popular vote, served for four years, but the three *designados* were chosen for two-year terms by the small unicameral assembly of twenty-eight delegates. Since Mendoza's term as second *designado* would end on October 1, whoever the legislators then elected as first designate would hold the executive power for the last two years of Obaldía's term. Although Liberals had the majority and the party unity needed to ensure Mendoza's election, his enemies insisted that his return to power would violate the nonsuccession clause in Panama's constitution.

The question had its origin in the fear, widespread in Latin America since the time of Bolívar, of the practice called *continuismo*, by which a chief executive who controlled the electoral machinery could succeed himself term after term, accumulating dictatorial power. Mendoza's supporters argued that the nonsuccession clause did not apply, because he was technically not president but a stand-in holding presidential powers, but opponents insisted his reelection would violate the spirit and intent of the constitution. The truth was that the framers of the document (who had included Mendoza himself) had taken the clause's language verbatim from an earlier Colombian constitution without anticipating the difficulty now confronting them.[3]

The succession crisis, as it began to heat up, would almost inevitably involve the U.S. legation. Inexplicably, Washington left the legation in the hands of a newly arrived secretary, a brash, headstrong, and inexperienced twenty-seven-year-old named Richard Oglesby Marsh.

Marsh was the son of a prominent member of Congress from Illinois, Colonel B. F. Marsh.[4] Richard, born in 1883, the middle son of the Colonel's second marriage, was schooled in Washington D.C., where he spent much more of his youth than in Illinois.[5] In 1901 he entered the Massachusetts Institute of Technology (MIT). He joined ΦBE fraternity, and in his sophomore year he filled offices in the yearbook, the student newspaper, the athletic association, fencing club, the MIT Cadet Corps, and his own fraternity.[6] Grades were another matter. In his freshman year he received a mixture of Cs and Bs, with a D in chemistry and F in geometry; by the end of sophomore year, two more Ds and an F had prompted an official warning that his work was "very unsatisfactory."[7] Allowed to take the next year off, by his own account Marsh worked for the Army Corps of Engineers in Texas and later on the Mexican Railways. He returned to MIT in 1904–1905, but rather than improving,

President Carlos Mendoza.

his work deteriorated further, and in the spring, except for two Cs and an incomplete, he was marked "absent" in all his courses.

The absences, and perhaps the worsening grades as well, followed from a rapid series of personal misfortunes: a serious illness suffered by his father in January, the death of his mother in March, followed by his father's death in early June. In the fall of 1905, Richard used some of his inheritance to enroll in the University of Lausanne, Switzerland, after which he said goodbye to academic studies, setting out on several years of travel and adventure. In China he journeyed into Mongolia, and after working for the railroads in the Philippines and Bolivia, he rafted down from the Andes into the Amazon basin, an exploit that at one point left him stranded in the forest after his raft capsized.[8] The scanty information available on this period suggests that Marsh alternated between engineering work and speculative business ventures.[9]

In September of 1909, at the age of twenty-six, Marsh married a young woman named Helen Cleveland, whom he had met aboard a ship on which both were traveling. The daughter of a famous engineer and contractor named Merritt Andrus Cleveland, Helen had apparently been sent on a trip by her father to remove her

Panama City, Avenida Central, 1916.

from an onslaught of importunate suitors, only to have her meet and marry the handsome and dashing adventurer.[10]

Seemingly ready at this point to settle down, Marsh used recommendations from a maternal uncle who was chief justice of the Supreme Court and several of his late father's colleagues, including the Speaker of the House, to obtain a position in the diplomatic corps. In April of 1910 Marsh was appointed first secretary of the U.S. legation in Panama, with a salary of two thousand dollars a year, and in June he and his wife left for the Isthmus.[11]

In 1910 Panama was still a tiny country, with less than 400,000 inhabitants. Its small capital city, situated on a neck of land jutting out into the Bay of Panama on the Pacific and overshadowed by Ancón Hill and the Canal Zone behind it, had grown rapidly since the mid-nineteenth century but had only recently attained a population of 45,000. There were just 3,500 voters in Panama City, and school enrollment in the whole Republic barely passed 19,000.[12] Small as it was, however, Panama mattered a great deal to the United States because of the canal, scheduled for completion in 1915.

Despite a massive North American presence, Panama's raucous politics often mocked the tranquility and deference that the U.S. government expected. With a long history of political turmoil, Panama began the twentieth century with an unstable balance of power between the Liberal Party, which most voters favored, and the Conservatives, who initially held the presidency. However much U.S. officials wanted the fledgling government to manage its own affairs and let them get on with digging a canal, all too frequently they found themselves pulled into local quarrels.[13]

Paradoxically, it was the demand for order and stability, the keystone of its policy throughout the Caribbean, that embroiled the United States in turbulence and intrigue. Already empowered by the Panamanian constitution to suppress disorder, North American authorities soon felt impelled to announce that revolutions and coups would not be tolerated. And since nothing provoked violence as readily as electoral fraud, which had a long history on the Isthmus, they began shortly afterward to insist on clean elections as well.[14] Panamanian politicians, denied the alternative of revolution and discouraged from rigging the vote, resorted to manipulating the gringos, turning up constantly at the legation and canal headquarters. With North American power divided between diplomatic and Canal Zone authorities, schemers did not shrink from playing one off against the other.[15]

Matters had come to a head just two years before Marsh's arrival with the elections of 1908, the Republic's first real presidential contest. The campaign had pitted Ricardo Arias, who had the backing of the incumbent, Miguel Amador Guerrero, against Designado José Domingo de Obaldía. Obaldía, a Conservative whose moderation had won the backing of Liberals and dissidents in his own party, enjoyed a clear popular majority, but Amador's control of the electoral machinery ensured a victory for his protégé Arias. The Roosevelt administration grew alarmed enough to send the secretary of war, William Howard Taft, to personally deliver Amador an ultimatum demanding clean elections supervised by North American observers. Arias withdrew, and Obaldía was elected unopposed.[16]

It was all too easy to draw false inferences from this episode, especially for someone to whom confrontation and domination came as naturally as they did to Richard Marsh. Taft had certainly given Amador orders, treating Panama as a client state, and his intervention had ensured Obaldía's election. But Marsh did not recognize that, far from imposing his own preference on an unwilling electorate, Taft, whose overriding concern was stability, had made it possible for the majority candidate to win.

Marsh took up his duties as first secretary in mid-June of 1910. Within a few weeks the minister to Panama was transferred to another post, leaving Marsh as chargé d'affaires in the legation until the new minister arrived. Although a novice diplomat, Marsh had worked and traveled in Latin America, and "had already . . . formed definite opinions . . . as to conditions in those countries, particularly as to Panama where [he] had previously been four times."[17]

Marsh's first report on the succession controversy acknowledged that opinions on the issue divided perfectly along party lines but added that the best authorities and the better class of people opposed Mendoza's reelection. His line of argument confirmed that the constitutional objections merely rationalized partisan politics and racism.[18]

The objection to Mendoza, aside from the question of the unconstitutionality of his election, is of course the fact that he is half negro while his wife is a full negro. All white people, foreigners as well as natives, hesitate to have social relations with them. . . . I consider the race question involved more than mere prejudice. There is a large population of negroes in Panama, who idolize Mendoza because of his Negro blood. These negroes are mostly ignorant, and irresponsible, unable to meet the serious obligations of citizenship in a republic.

Marsh had certainly read elite prejudices clearly. In Panama, a small group of Whites and lighter-skinned mestizos tried to keep themselves apart from a much larger population of Afro-Panamanians, dark-skinned mestizos, Amerindians, and Chinese. In rural areas, especially the southwestern mestizo heartland known as the *Interior*, one ethnic group usually predominated. In the capital, however, individuals and groups of multiple shades and descent jostled and contended with one another.[19] The Conservative Party (Marsh's better class of people) appealed more to North American diplomats than to Panamanian voters, while the Liberals, who drew their leadership from a mixed group of white, mestizo, and mulatto professionals, enjoyed strong popular backing. Conservatives were sure that an Afro-Panamanian president, even one as educated, cultivated, and indeed as light-skinned as Mendoza, would brand them in the world's eyes as a "nigger country."[20] These biases were shared by the North Americans on the Isthmus, who were busy constructing a rigidly segregated microcosm of Jim Crow in the Canal Zone.[21]

In his own campaign against Mendoza, Marsh rapidly took the initiative, while leaving the impression in his dispatches that he merely concurred with the opinions of local experts such as British minister Claude Mallett and Colonel George Goethals, chief engineer and chairman of the Isthmian Canal Commission. The stern and unbending Goethals, who had just finished his second year in charge of canal construction, could wield vastly more power than a youthful legation secretary, though only when he chose. Busy from early morning to late at night on the canal, the colonel had little time for Panamanian politics.[22]

Marsh did succeed in arranging a meeting between Goethals and Santiago de la Guardia, attorney general of Panama, to promote the latter's visit to Washington to convey his vehement opinion that Mendoza's election would be unconstitutional.[23] De la Guardia, though a government functionary, was also a leader of the die-hard opposition, the small group of Amador Conservatives who, because they had sat out legislative elections in 1910 as well as the presidential contest of 1908, were in the political deep-freeze. Described by Marsh as a disinterested constitutional authority, de la Guardia was in fact a presidential aspirant and entirely without legal training.[24]

Another group of Conservatives, who had supported Obaldía in 1908, formed part of the present government coalition, though their loyalty to Mendoza and their Liberal partners was weak. Marsh decided that if Mendoza were forced to withdraw, the minister of foreign affairs, Samuel Lewis, who had proved compliant to North American wishes, would offer a likely alternative. Despite a lack of support from either Liberals or die-hard Conservatives, Marsh convinced himself that only Lewis could save Panama from the disaster of a Liberal president such as Mendoza or Belisario Porras, who would not countenance North American domination. Lewis, pleased by Marsh's backing, began feeding him confidential information from cabinet meetings.[25]

The difference Marsh saw between the two factions was real. The Conservatives, who had passed article 136 of the Constitution (over vehement Liberal opposition) giving the United States the right to intervene almost at will, often expressed privately an openness to annexation. But if the Liberals clung to their scraps of autonomy, few of them were the fierce anti-Americans Marsh perceived, and on essential points they, too, yielded to the Yankees.[26]

Marsh soon stepped up his invective against Mendoza in missives to the State Department, calling him a "grave menace" and potential dictator and alleging two mistresses and "numerous illegitimate children." Supported in Washington by anti-Mendoza memos from the previous U.S. minister and his secretary, he formally requested a legal opinion declaring Mendoza's election illegitimate.[27] Continuing to send notes and copies of his cables to Goethals, Marsh tried to rouse him into a more active role, but the colonel refused to be drawn out, politely praising Marsh's communiqués but adding, "I feel I have done everything consistent with my position in relation to the matter."[28]

As September approached, with the scheduled opening of the assembly and the election of new *designados,* the situation grew tense, and on August 18, according to Marsh, only an emergency alert prevented a Conservative uprising, though others cast doubt on the reality of the supposed insurrection. On the twentieth, informed by a delegation of Conservatives that blood would flow, he issued a public statement: "The government of the United States has entire confidence in the ability of the people of Panama and the National Assembly to elect their national officers in accordance with the Constitution of Panama, without the need of outside intervention." If these words did not hint clearly enough at his objections to Mendoza or U.S. willingness to intervene, later the same day Marsh reiterated these points in an interview with the antiadministration *Estrella de Panamá*. British minister Claude Mallett wrote that Marsh's statements and his support of Lewis "acted like a bomb-shell . . . tantamount to declaring that the Liberal Party will not be permitted to govern in the Republic of Panama after September 30th."[29]

Meanwhile, with all the rumors of intervention circulating, Mendoza's cabinet met in an emergency session. Inclined to resist, and insistent that the assembly, not Mendoza himself, should decide on his eligibility, they resolved to cable their minister in Washington, C. C. Arosemena, to query the U.S. government on its view of the matter and to complain of Marsh's meddling.[30]

The next day, Sunday, August 21, Goethals came to the legation at Marsh's request, where he was unhappy to learn that the chargé, in coming out against Mendoza, had not acted on instructions, merely on the hope that his superiors would back him after the fact. Still inclined to give the young man the benefit of the doubt, he agreed to attend a meeting at which, a go-between had promised, Mendoza would offer to step aside.[31] When the pair arrived at the presidential palace, however, Mendoza disavowed the self-styled go-between and any intention to give up his candidacy. Marsh, thoroughly embarrassed, had apparently been duped. Afterward, Goethals went off alone to the British legation, where he conveyed to Minister Mallett his disquiet at Marsh's public statements and indicated that the chargé had acted recently without his knowledge or approval; Mallett replied that Marsh had consistently claimed full backing from both Goethals and the State Department.[32]

Fortunately for Marsh, the hoped-for cable from Washington endorsing his stand arrived the next day, and others soon followed: despite a well-argued Panamanian brief pointing out the inappropriateness of foreign rulings on domestic law, the State Department had ruled Mendoza's election unconstitutional. Armed with the cables, Marsh went back to the presidential palace, and on August 27 Mendoza capitulated publicly.[33]

Whether the United States would have blocked Mendoza had Marsh not mobilized sentiment against him is unclear, but he had certainly understood the attitudes of his superiors in the State Department.[34] The undiplomatic diplomat would have done well, however, to have proceeded more cautiously thereafter. Not only had Colonel Goethals begun to have his doubts, but the instructions received in a telegram on August 24 narrowly restricted Marsh's scope of action and suggested some concern:

You are instructed that this government has no particular preferences as to individuals, and that in general any candidate not otherwise legitimately objectionable . . . will be agreeable as well as satisfactory to this government. . . . It is presumed that you have observed and will continue to observe especial caution in not discussing the affairs of the Legation with any person except the Chairman of the Isthmian Canal Commission, and you will not take part in the local politics of Panama nor express any opinions thereon publicly or privately in the absence of explicit instructions.[35]

When the acting secretary of state, Huntington Wilson, learned from Marsh that he had pressured Mendoza to support Lewis, he cabled a further caution, one that anyone other than Marsh would have heeded: "The Department does not approve of your unnecessary continuance of active mixing in local politics and active support of any political candidate."[36] Marsh, however, continued to receive Conservative delegations, to push Lewis's candidacy, and even to threaten military occupation.[37] On the last day of August he wrote Goethals a note lamenting the obduracy of the Liberals.

If the worst comes and they elect someone else besides Lewis, I will declare the whole Assembly void and null as its very existence and election is unconstitutional—of which I have clear proof—and will request the U.S. to appoint a temporary governor-general until a new Assembly can be elected. . . I think the State Department will have to uphold me. However I think we can still ram Lewis down their throats without it.[38]

Thoroughly alarmed, Goethals went immediately to the legation to object strongly, and he extracted a promise not to proceed without explicit instructions from the State Department.[39]

On the first of September, the twenty-eight deputies began their new session, though they put off the election of the acting president until the ninth. In a cable sent on the second, in which Marsh claimed to have "consulted Colonel Goethals in all things," he added: "There is a small fire started in Panama that if not promptly put out will spread into a great conflagration . . . I mean the debasing of the political organization in power . . . to the Negro, ignorant and unscrupulous element so that justice, law and order do not exist."[40] The next day he received a reply urging "the greatest tact, conciliation, and circumscription," noting that some of his most recent communication "causes the Department some concern."[41] Unfortunately, the cable added that Washington would be pleased by Lewis's election, which Marsh seized on as justification for continuing to push his candidacy.

On the fifth, Marsh met with Goethals, who upon reading the file of cables, was not pleased to discover that the State Department evidently accepted Marsh's assurances that he was working closely with Goethals. Pointing out that even the most recent cable really gave Marsh very little scope for action, Goethals once again extracted a promise not to proceed without instructions from Washington.[42]

It takes little imagination to envision his reaction three days later, on the eve of the scheduled election in the assembly, when another statement appeared in *La Estrella.*

Mr. Marsh said that there was no intention of immediate annexation of Panama. Such action depends on the choice of Vice President for the next two years. But he adds: "IF IN VIEW OF ALL THE AMERICAN GOVERNMENT HAS DONE FOR PANAMA AND ITS GREAT INTERESTS PRESENT AND FUTURE ON THE ISTHMUS, THE PANAMA ASSEMBLY AND GOVERNMENT SHOULD PERSISTENTLY REFUSE TO ACCEDE TO THE CLEAR WISHES OF THE AMERICAN GOVERNMENT, THAT GOVERNMENT CAN ONLY ADOPT SUCH MEANS TO PREVENT SUCH OPPOSITION IN THE FUTURE AS OCCUPATION AND ANNEXATION."[43]

That afternoon still another pronouncement appeared, this one published by the *Diario*.

In taking leave of us [Marsh] stated that he would not concern himself any longer with regard to the fate or destiny of this Republic, but would uphold the interests of his Government; and, moreover, that both Colonel Goethals and himself would be pleased to see the Assembly assume a hostile attitude, for in this way the United States would put an end to this Republic forthwith and forever.[44]

Marsh's threats of annexation—which Minister Mallett called "the most extraordinary acts of diplomatic bungling ever perpetrated in the Latin American Republics by United States officials"[45]—threw Panama into an uproar. An editorial in *La Estrella* entitled "At the edge of the abyss" asserted that Marsh was not bluffing and urged Liberal deputies to sacrifice party loyalties for the continued existence of Panama as a nation.[46] For their part, most of the Liberals were ready to vote for Lewis if they must but were holding out for the moment.

Goethals, after unsatisfactory attempts to communicate with the chargé by phone and letter, went to the legation once again to confront him in person. Marsh pleaded that he had been tricked into both statements. The first, he said, had been presented to him in the guise of a pro-Lewis editorial for *La Estrella*, with a request for his suggestions and corrections, only to appear next day over his own name. The second resulted from a heated confrontation with two men from the pro-administration *Diario de Panamá* outside the hospital where Marsh's wife Helen was being treated for malaria: although Marsh thought he had probably said the words attributed to him, he had not intended them as an official statement.[47] Goethals, by no means mollified, sent a cable and long letter to the secretary of war disavowing the chargé's claims and giving his own version of events.[48]

By the time Goethals acted, Marsh had already done himself in. On the seventh the statement in *La Estrella* was repudiated in Washington. Marsh was cabled next day: "The Department, of course, assumes that this outrageous report entirely lacks foundation, but you should immediately disavow and deny it."[49] William Howard Taft, now U.S. president, was drawn into the affair from his summer White House in Beverly, Massachusetts. As he learned the details of the mess and what he termed

"Marsh's fussy meddling and loquacity," President Taft pronounced him "utterly unfit to represent us there." Marsh's plotting, he added, was unnecessary: "We have such control in Panama that no Government . . . will feel a desire to antagonize the American Government."[50] All parties in Panama were informed that annexation was not contemplated and that almost any candidate would be acceptable. It was announced that a new American minister, Thomas Dawson, would soon arrive on the Isthmus.[51]

Astoundingly, Marsh would not give up. From Friday the ninth to Monday the twelfth he sent his superiors no less than six cables, chastising them for repudiating his statement and thus preventing Lewis's election; attacking the character of the assembly's choice, Pablo Arosemena (a personal friend of President Taft); insisting that the assembly "must either be dismissed as unconstitutional or be dictated to"; and urging that only Lewis's election could save American prestige.[52]

On Monday the twelfth Marsh received word that he would be sent home when Minister Dawson arrived, and two days later, the assembly elected Pablo Arosemena as acting president. On the twenty-third, Dawson arrived, and once formalities were concluded, he began investigating the former chargé's conduct. Marsh's wife, who was due to give birth in October, was still gravely ill. "Mr. Marsh's attitude . . . was manly and frank, but it was evident that he was nearly unbalanced by grief and mortification." Marsh did not attempt to obscure his actions or put the blame off on anyone else, and Dawson was inclined to be forgiving, especially in the light of Marsh's youth, inexperience, and worry over his wife's condition. The report, though devastating in detail, emphasized imprudence rather than insubordination or duplicity. Marsh wrote letters of explanation and apology to Goethals and Dawson on the twenty-fifth, and the next day he and his wife set sail.[53]

Back in the United States, President Taft, despite his disgust with Marsh, was also inclined to be merciful and recommended that he be given another post rather than dismissed. A few months later Marsh was offered the third secretary's position in St. Petersburg, which he turned down, citing a salary reduction from two thousand to twelve hundred dollars and discouraging words from the assistant secretary. His diplomatic career had ended, though not his passionate involvement with Panama.[54]

Part Three
PANAMA ENTERS SAN BLAS, 1913–1918

9.
The
Protestant
Mission

Anna Coope, after her unsuccessful sally into San Blas in 1910, bided her time for two years. After a few months working with an urban mission in Panama and apparently supporting herself by weaving linen, she left for Mexico in August of that year, moving on to Los Angeles a few months later.[1] In the circuit she made of Protestant churches to speak about her mission work, she depended at each step on donations for her upkeep and travel expenses. At the end of ten months in the United States, Coope headed south again, preaching at every island stop in the West Indies and reaching Panama in late August of 1912.[2]

Rather than entering San Blas immediately, she tried for some months to meet Charly Robinson when he came to Colón: she visited the wharf where Kuna unloaded coconuts, asking after Robinson among Indians there, and she held classes for Kuna boys, who also kept a lookout on her behalf. One of the students warned her frankly about Kuna motivations: "The Indians have their own religion; they do not want to learn about yours; they only want you to teach them to read and speak English so that they can make plenty of money like the Americans."[3] Coope, not at all discouraged, replied that she would lead the Kuna to walk on golden streets, a remark whose intent the boy probably caught, since their heaven, like hers, was all gold and silver.

During these months, she had two interviews with the newly elected president of the country, Belisario Porras, who according to Coope was horrified at her exposing herself to danger in San Blas but said she was free to go there.[4] Then, alerted to Robinson's imminent arrival in mid-January 1913, she buttonholed him at the wharf on the morning of January 17 ("My heart beat fast for joy; this was my hour!"), securing his immediate agreement to open an English-language Bible school on Nargana.[5] On February 2 Robinson sent her a letter of invitation and a canoe to transport her.

San Jose Nargana, Feb. 2nd, 1913

Dear lady I sent my 3 Indians to Bring you up
to San Blas Coas to my country My people like
to see you Dear Lady if you can By A B C Book
Engles and Bring your Piano up with you no
more for Present. Mr. Charles J. Robinson.[6]

Coope, dissuaded by friends from risking the high seas of the dry season in a dugout canoe, set out for Nargana in a trading schooner, which made a leisurely trip down the coast, taking nine days just to reach San Blas Point. Though Coope was quite accustomed to resigned waiting and passed her time by leading the English-speaking crew in Moody and Sankey hymns on her folding baby organ, by the end of February Robinson had grown impatient and sent another canoe to fetch her.

Even before Coope's arrival on Nargana, her friends and enemies had begun working feverishly to influence the government for and against her—Robinson, Soo of Nusatupu, Gassó's successor Father Benito Pérez, and Coope herself all sent off letters.[7] Father Benito, describing himself as anxious to contribute his "little grain of sand to the masterwork that the Government proposes to carry out," wrote a long letter to Porras. Along with extended observations on the region and the Indians (he called them "childish, indolent, ungrateful, timid, egotistic, and selfish"), Pérez set out a proposal for increased government support of the missionaries. His letter bears the marks of the Catholic mission's six years of hard experience, one of its principal themes being the "proverbial haughtiness" of the Kuna and the "innermost scorn (as incredible as it seems!) with which they view wagas," a word he clearly knew and hated. Father Benito also wrote Cimral Colman, head of one Kuna confederacy, not so subtly inciting the pagan Kuna against Coope: "All the Fathers told [Robinson] not to take that waga woman to the Indians, but he pays no attention."[8]

It is unlikely that Porras seriously considered the priest's proposals. Not only was he developing his own plans for advancing government control of the coast, but in 1913 the Liberals were in the midst of a program of national secularization so radical that the bishop of Panama excommunicated several legislators. Far from backing the Catholic mission, the legislature cut off the funds that it had provided since 1907.[9]

Coope says she opened her school on Saturday, the day after her arrival, and that Kuna of all ages were so enthusiastic that she went on for eight hours that day and another four that night. "The next day being Sunday, I taught them John 3:16." ("For God so loved the world that he gave his only begotten son, that whoever believes in him shall not perish but have eternal life.")

That, and: "Onward Christian Soldiers," was the order of exercises that first Sunday in San Blas. We marched and countermarched around the schoolroom; the earthen floor was humpy, but it did not matter! My school was composed of all ages. There were tottering old men . . . and wrinkled grandmothers, and middle aged and young married women also, each with a child straddled on her hip. . . . I kept them pretty lively . . . we had great times in those early days! A parrot came every day and learned to sing, "Onward, Christian Soldiers." . . . I used to spur the boys on by saying, "Dear me, the parrot has beaten all of you!"[10]

Personality clearly mattered. Every bit as tough and determined as Gassó, Coope emerges from her memoirs as warm and good-humored where he was often harsh and demanding, and she in turn seems to have inspired respect, affection, and even devotion. Thirty years later, her disciple, Alicibiades Iglesias, could still picture her vividly:[11]

Miss Coope—how well I remember her! She was a rare sight and unique character. I really don't see how anyone could be uglier in face or figure. Even with such an unpromising start, taste and interest might have worked wonders; but little did she care how she looked. She took the attitude that she had been born ugly and she wasn't going to make any effort to improve God's handiwork! Her clothes were few and all looked alike—they hung about her angular form like ruffles on a broomstick. . . . Her hair was pulled straight back from her face and fastened in a knot on the back of her head. The straight strands were forever becoming loosened and hanging limply about her face and neck.

Coope's success in these early months, as Nargana people flocked to her Bible school, cannot be attributed to personality alone, at least not in any superficial sense, because they were responding to her fundamental stance toward the world and toward them. Whereas Gassó had a keen sense of the otherness of the Kuna, of the great gap between them and him, Coope saw everyone (with the possible exception of Catholic priests) as essentially alike, all of them sinners and souls to be redeemed. When confronted by hostility from women on Tupile, she "could not help thinking of the way many so-called Christians treat a woman of the street, shrinking from even the touch of her clothing. These Indian women are made of the same sinful tendencies." And the interest of women in her clothes and hair provoked the thought: "Oh, vain woman, everywhere the same! Color does not change the natural curiosity and vanity." In her remarks on Kuna culture, she recognized women's dress as an ethnic marker—"They would not be Indians without beads"—but even there she reverted to universalism: "Dame fashion is as tyrannical in San Blas as in other parts of the world." And she concluded a chapter profiling "Some of my Boys" with the remark, "you see they are just as human as the boys in America."[12] To Coope, the Other was essentially the same.

The Kuna exhibit two sides in dealing with outsiders. Which side they show at any particular moment depends in large part on the nature of the outsider. Just as

Gassó's cold pride often provoked an equally haughty response, so Coope's easygoing informality was warmly received. With her working-class background and roots in charismatic Christianity, which rested on a direct personal relationship with Jesus, Coope was fundamentally egalitarian, and except in the case of drinking, she was content to let Kuna custom change slowly and voluntarily. Her willingness to take the Kuna as they were, to apply the same standards she had for herself, asking only that they accept Jesus and give up sin, by which she mostly meant alcohol, won her friends and converts.

Coope's accepting attitude had another side, however. Seeing everyone as essentially alike, she had little curiosity and only a superficial understanding of the Kuna. Her ethnographic observations, both in her memoirs and in notes circulated in the Canal Zone, were more perfunctory than Gassó's.[13] According to Samuel Morris, one of her students in those days, she aroused less opposition on Nargana than Gassó in part because she tolerated the Kuna sacred gathering; it is hard to believe she would have been so complacent had she understood, as Gassó did, how much the religion of the gathering competed with Christianity. Her relaxed, incurious attitude, combined with a minimal knowledge of Kuna and Spanish, seems to have left her floating on the surface of village life, aware of the currents swirling below only when warned by Charly Robinson.

Coope taught school on weekdays, with an especially heavy schedule in the first months, and Sunday evenings she held services, accompanied on her folding organ, sometimes with Charly Robinson interpreting Bible stories in Kuna. Although people of both sexes and all ages attended school at first, adults soon dropped out in favor of the children. From the beginning, Coope favored her male pupils, whom she saw as potential disciples as well as students, but she also insisted that girls attend: when parents decided to keep their daughters at home, Coope closed the school down for everyone until they relented.[14]

Along with jolly music and good-humored fun, Coope gave Nargana what it wanted, which was literacy and knowledge of a prestigious foreign language. Certainly, Kuna saw education as, among other things, a road toward economic well-being, but they were not so crass as her early student in Colón had claimed, since the Spanish language would have conferred greater benefits in commerce and salaried employment. They preferred English and anglophone culture first because of long-standing associations with English-speakers, and second because they sought a form of change that would maximize material advantage without giving up autonomy to national control, control represented by the Spanish language and Panamanian culture.

Coope seems to have made few demands, except on those she singled out for conversion, who had to accept the Bible and make a personal profession of faith. Even these converts probably did not have to undergo a major transformation: the parallels between Kuna religion and Protestant Christianity encourage a fairly superficial syncretism, in which the Bible becomes the equivalent of Kuna oral tradition, and Jesus is the most outstanding of culture heroes. Thus in large part it was Christianity that Coope's adherents adapted to their own values and goals.[15]

During the first three months after Coope arrived, a Catholic Brother continued teaching on Nargana, but according to Coope, all twelve of his pupils switched to her school, and the Brother soon departed, leaving the Catholic buildings on Nargana and Nusatupu empty. In late July of 1913, Enrique Hurtado, an official commissioned by the government to carry out a reconnaissance of San Blas, visited Nargana. Hurtado was unusually friendly to North Americans and their projects, and within a few years he had become an agent for the United Fruit Company on the coast. In his report he wrote that people there wanted secular teachers but not a return of the priests, and he praised Coope as "This lady, whose work is admirable from every point of view," laboring "in this forgotten corner of the world."[16]

Miss Cook [*sic*] is Protestant, some pious hypocrites will say, and what does it matter? That she is a foreigner and teaches English, and what does it matter? She has arrived at an abandoned spot to which neither our flashy Catholicism nor our conventional patriotism has gone. In all honesty, we need do no more than applaud whole-heartedly her activity and assist her with determination.

Coope wrote that Hurtado urged her to take over the now-abandoned Catholic mission building, with its sheet-iron siding, which after some hesitation she did in August.[17] "October 9, 1913. In my galvanized mansion—with the delightful Blue-green sea lapping at the foundations of my Big House, the Biggest House on the San Blas Coast. Red! Red! Red!"[18]

Coope felt her appropriation of the Catholic stronghold as a personal triumph over evil and ignorance.

I see that all sects have a tinge of truth, more or less . . . so far as they take the Bible and no more. The Romanist believes that Christ died for our sins, so do I. . . . But as they cover up the blood by Holy Water, rag dolls, and indulgences on scraps of paper, I cannot go further.[19]

Such slight concessions aside, Coope hated Catholicism. When she moved into the new building "built by enemies of the truth," she had all religious images taken down.[20] The statues on which Gassó had expended so much energy were thrown in the sea, with only one image saved "as an object lesson." She had the boys recite the 115th Psalm—"'They have mouths, but they speak not . . .'"—touching each part of the head as they mentioned it and finishing by stepping on the image: "Can it feel, can it help us, can it hurt me, can it get up?"[21]

Anna Coope and students.

Along with her nondenominational Protestantism, Coope instinctively disseminated the English language and the Anglo-American culture she took for granted, and she struggled to exclude the (to her) corrupt culture of the host country, as Protestant missionaries in Latin America often do. Encouraged by interest from the Kuna, many of whom already shared her prejudices, she was as energetic in bestowing anglophone names on Nargana children and adults as Gassó had been with saints' names, and she initially taught school only in English, her Spanish in this period being in any case quite rudimentary. And though she never gave up her British citizenship, she admired and identified with the United States, her second home. More than half a century later, Coope's former students, by then elderly grandparents, could still sing "The Red, White, and Blue," as well as "Jesus Loves Me."

Despite Coope's initial successes on Nargana, many other Kuna adamantly opposed her presence. On the second of November, Robinson sent an urgent letter to the governor of the province of Colón (which in theory encompassed San Blas), asking for help against an imminent attack on Nargana. President Porras wrote the that he was disposed to help Robinson, but the lack of a boat forced him to await developments. Robinson had by then dealt with the threat himself on the fifth, according to Coope by using his superior weaponry to overawe and overpower the attackers.[22] Coope, for her part, had no more qualms about provoking conflict than had Gassó before her.

November 1. . . . The wild mountain Indians came down early this morning to shoot me! and burn up the house. I was sleeping peacefully and knew not that the Indians were here.

My own brave Indians were fighting or keeping them at bay for my sake. . . . Well, I'm not the least afraid.[23]

Wednesday, November 5, 1:30. . . . Fight is on now. Chief boat challenge them — out goes seven men. Life-saver around one man (found out that belt was full of bullets) two men to manipulate the boat. My! You ought to have seen the men go in that canoe quickly. The wind blew the canoe and they fired the guns thick and fast until the enemy pulled the flag down. Hurrah! We have won! . . . Well, I have seen my first sea-fight, and mind you, it was for *me* chiefly. I prayed for my brave Indians who are fighting for the right.[24]

At about this time, Coope was joined by a woman from her own church in Rhode Island, Martha Purdy.[25] Purdy worked with Coope on Nargana for half a year, until a priest passed through the two villages and arranged to create a new school on Nusatupu. Coope, thoroughly alarmed, set to work to close the gap there: temporarily abandoning the Nargana school, she and Purdy opened a new one across the water. When the priest passed through again, he saw that he had been forestalled, and Coope was able to move back to Nargana, leaving Purdy on Nusatupu. By 1916 the Nargana school had an average daily attendance of ninety students, the Nusatupu school forty.[26]

If there was anything that Coope hated (other than Catholicism) it was liquor. Just as Gassó had brought with him from Spain a set of burning issues, preoccupations, hates, and loves, so Coope came to San Blas a missionary not only of Christianity but also of temperance. By 1913 North Americans had been debating the liquor issue for well over a century, a number of states had recently gone dry, and the Eighteenth Amendment was only six years away. Temperance, moreover, had emerged as a woman's movement, one in which women had taken prominent leadership roles since the Civil War. And just as Gassó saw hierarchy, order, and anti-liberalism as inherent in the true faith, so Coope and millions of others saw abstinence as a religious virtue.[27] She might wait a few years to bring Nargana to Jesus, but not to rid it of rum.

By this time the effects of Gassó's earlier crackdown on alcohol had disappeared. In contrast to traditional islands, where drinking was prohibited except during puberty ceremonies, Nargana and Nusatupu had a number of stores that sold rum freely, among them one owned by Robinson's brother Alfred.[28] Worse, some of Coope's own students drank.[29]

My heart is nearly broken. Seven of my brightest boys drunk. Joe, the leader among them. I feel I cannot stand this. Joe staggering and reeling drunk, hand in hand with another of my boys, with no shame, banged up against the school and all of us inside and saw it. I felt my heart would burst with grief and if I had not been near the table I should have fallen. I burst out crying and oh, had it been my own child I could not have felt worse. I sat down and wept and all the villagers came to the door to see what Miss Coope was crying about, and the boys told them. The women only laughed, as if it was nothing to them. . . . Oh, it seemed as if the foundations of my faith had an earthquake shock.[30]

Coope counterattacked on all fronts at once. To keep the boys busy and out of reach of temptation, she had them over on Saturday night for cocoa, Bible stories, and Bible picture puzzle games, and in school she hammered away on the evils of drink.[31] For the seventh birthday of Charly Robinson's eldest son — the child who had been baptized as a Catholic by the bishop of Panama, with President Amador as his godfather and namesake — Coope taught him a poem in English.

> My name is Amador Robinson,
> I am seven years old today.
> I will only drink pure water
> And learn my lesson each day.
>
> I will not drink any liquor,
> The Bible says it is bad.
> My father is Chief of Narkana
> And I am his eldest lad.
>
> Now boys and girls of Narkana,
> Will you not say with me
> That pure water is good for the Indians
> And the very best drink for me![32]

Coope laid much of the blame for the drinking on the coastal traders who sold rum.[33] Unable to keep them away from Nargana, Coope wrote the Woman's Christian Temperance Union in the United States, whose president, Anna Gordon, wrote the governor of the Panama Canal to urge that he impose prohibition on San Blas. The governor, pointing out to Miss Gordon that he lacked jurisdiction, in turn passed the letter on to the Panamanian secretary of foreign affairs.[34]

Like Gassó, Coope objected to the puberty ceremonies, called *chichas* in Spanish, with their mass drunkenness, sometimes lasting several days. (Coope, who had a tin ear, called them chee-chees.) The missionary pressured Robinson, who claimed to be sober himself and denied having an interest in his brother's rum shop, and after one extended bash, probably in early 1914, Coope persuaded Robinson to argue for prohibition. Despite calls for the chief's ouster and even a boycott of Coope's school, she got half of what she wanted: rum was not sold in stores on Nargana, and puberty ceremonies were few and short.[35] Robinson's brother Alfred resisted the ban, but Coope excluded his son from her school, turning the boy away at the door repeatedly until his father gave in.[36]

Also like Gassó, Coope worked hard at converting and controlling Charly Robinson. The latter was as ambivalent as he had been before, feeling torn between the missionary and social pressure from fellow Kuna.[37] To avoid tense situations or the necessity of taking sides or making a decision, Robinson often fled to his work camp in the outer islands of western San Blas, just as he had in Gassó's day. Toward the end of 1914, pressure mounted to relax the controls and to allow a combined long chicha for four pubescent girls. Coope pushed the chief hard to resist, with long sessions of earnest conversation. Unable to decide, Robinson became violently ill, and during his sickness and personal crisis, on November 14, 1914, he experienced a conversion. On the day the alcoholic chicha was to be brewed, Robinson had himself carried downstairs from his sickbed, ordered the brewing pots brought together and had them broken. He imposed complete prohibition on Nargana, apparently getting enough backing in the village to make the ban stick, though a pro-chicha faction, which continued to sponsor puberty ceremonies on other islands, agitated to have him removed as chief.[38] During the three months of Robinson's convalescence, "he learned lessons of obedience," and while Coope clearly meant obedience to God, her own influence over Robinson consolidated along with His.[39]

Apart from prohibition, Coope took the greatest interest in educating and converting a cohort of her brightest boys. Like Gassó before her, she seems to have taken this tack partly out of policy, with the intention of training disciples and assistant teachers, and partly out of personal need. In one letter she described at length how the chief's brother Alfred called her their mother, and she lavished maternal affection on her boys, especially Alicibiades Iglesias, whom she insisted on calling Lonny Powers.[40] "Lonnie's mother has seven children living. Her eldest boy has been in Panama city 5 years, so she has 6 children in the home, each one I have named, also named her Rachel. Her 3 boys — Lonnie, John, Paul, and the girls — Louise, Dorothea, Doris. . . . The elder brother is called Claudio, a Roman name surely."[41] Coope's disquiet over the eldest brother's Hispanic name may have been naive — did she expect him to be named Claude? — but it was well placed. Claudio had been taken by Father Gassó to Panama, where he was lodged in a Catholic hospice and training as a carpenter. When he returned, it could not be expected that Claudio would smile on Protestants or North American ways.

In May of 1914, Lonnie and two other boys "accepted Jesus." Coope began planning to send a few boys away to school, and she set herself to securing funds from mission supporters. As Lonny himself later remembered it, his parents adamantly resisted pressure from Coope, until Claudio came home on vacation and insisted his younger brother seize the opportunity. (Evidently, at this point Claudio still thought that any schooling, even Protestant, was better than none.)[42] Coope packed the eleven-year-old Lonny off to Panama in February 1916. After receiving baptism, he and another boy gave a short recitation at a missionary convention then going on in the city—like Gassó nine years before, Coope was not averse to showing off a young disciple as proof of her success. Two weeks later she sent Lonnie off on a steamer wearing a thin tropical suit and his first pair of shoes, to attend a missionary school in Nyack, New York.[43]

In these first three years, from February 1913 to February 1916, Coope, with Robinson's help and support, had made great advances in her conquest of Nargana, and her inspirational memoirs, published the following year by the American Tract Society, end with the words: "Pray for them and for me, for I am looking ahead for more land to be possessed by the saints of San Blas. We are marching on by faith."[44] Nonetheless, the train of events leading to her defeat and eventual expulsion had already begun rolling the previous year, in May of 1915, with the visit of President Belisario Porras to Nargana.

10.
Belisario
Porras
Visits
the Kuna

Fortunately for Anna Coope, her initial years on Nargana fell in between the initial period in which the government relied on Gassó and Charly Robinson to advance its interests in San Blas and the moment at which it was ready to begin acting for itself. That moment came closer in 1912, with the election of Belisario Porras to the presidency of the Republic. Porras, the dominant political figure of the era, took as his life's work the founding of a nation, a goal that in his view included the task of incorporating San Blas and civilizing the Kuna.[1]

The son of a provincial lawyer and Conservative politician, Porras was born in 1856 in the town of Las Tablas in the southwestern heartland of Panama. He was sent to school in Panama City in 1871 and on to Bogotá the following year, where he received a bachelor's degree in 1876 and a doctorate of laws in 1881. After that he studied briefly in Brussels, where he became Colombian consul. For the rest of the century, he combined law, journalism, government service, and politics, rising to prominence in the Liberal Party during an era of political turbulence. In 1896, after a failed rebellion, he went into exile in Central America, where he worked tirelessly to solicit support for the Liberal cause from the governments of Nicaragua and Guatemala.

When fighting broke out in Colombia in October of 1899, Porras was named head of the Liberals on the Isthmus, and in March of the following year, he and a small force invaded western Panama in a vessel lent them by the president of Nicaragua. Though closely supported by his friend Carlos Mendoza, Porras was forced to accept a less congenial figure, General Emiliano Herrera, as head of military operations, and the two bickered and argued as their forces advanced eastward. After defeating a government army in the field, they were routed at a bridge leading into Panama City—the debacle caused in no small part by the divisions between the two leaders. Porras returned to exile.

In July of 1901, he invaded a second time. He was joined a few months later by a small Colombian force under the command of Benjamin Herrera, who, though unrelated to Emiliano Herrera, proved just as unpalatable to Porras. After the second Herrera intercepted a letter denouncing him to the Liberal directorate, he confronted Porras in a rage, knocking him down, breaking his glasses, and almost strangling him before he was pulled off. Porras escaped to Costa Rica, and Herrera went on to decisively defeat government forces. The United States then intervened, and in November of 1902, a treaty was signed on board the warship *Wisconsin,* ending what came to be known as the War of a Thousand Days.

One year later, when Panama seceded from Colombia in a coup joined by his friend Mendoza but dominated by Isthmian Conservatives, Belisario Porras was in San Salvador. He reacted with dismay to word of independence from Mendoza, and over the next few months, "tortured and enslaved between my mourning as a Colombian and my love as a Panamanian," Porras poured out his doubts about secession in unwise letters to friends and colleagues.[2] Deciding ultimately for Panama, he returned to the Isthmus in June of 1904, to be received enthusiastically as the hope of the Liberal Party. The following year, however, a law suit challenged his citizenship on the grounds that he had initially not accepted Panamanian independence, and the Supreme Court decided against him. Porras retreated to Las Tablas until the legislature restored his citizenship.

When Carlos Mendoza became acting president in 1910, Porras was once again out of the country, this time at a conference in Argentina, and he played only a peripheral role in the crisis provoked by Richard Marsh. According to the agreement among Liberals by which Pablo Arosemena was elected acting president for the next two years, it was understood that the party would choose Porras in 1912. Although Arosemena failed to honor the agreement, Porras, then minister to Washington, returned home to popular acclaim and captured both the party nomination and the presidency, beginning (despite the country's nonsuccession law) a nearly unbroken reign over three terms, 1912–1916, 1918–1919, 1920–1924.

Dressed in an old-fashioned frock coat and four-in-hand tie, Porras conducted business in the personalistic style of a nineteenth-century caudillo, keeping the doors of the presidential palace open to interviews and petitions. It was said that in Las Tablas alone he stood as godfather to more than seven hundred children.[3] Temperate in his habits and honest by the standards of the time, he was also proud, touchy, egotistical, and unforgiving. (Given the venom of the attacks against him, he had much to forgive.) In addition to participating in several duels and ad hoc gentlemen's tribunals called "courts of honor," as president he was not above persecuting his enemies. In 1914 he broke irrevocably with his lifelong friend Carlos Mendoza, and within a few years schisms and rivalries had destroyed the old Liberal Party.

Porras made a few serious mistakes comparable to his original vacillation over independence, but overall he played the political game shrewdly. While struggling to enlarge Panamanian autonomy and his own power, he also used the Americans when he needed them. At the end of his political career, a memo by a chagrined State Department official noted that during elections in which Porras had been out of power (1912 and 1918) he had managed to provoke U.S. intervention, but during those in which he held office and thus controlled the electoral machinery (1916 and 1924), he had successfully opposed it.[4]

Despite the personalism and expediency of Panamanian politics in this era, Porras had a clearly developed program and set of principles, carried forward from nineteenth-century liberalism. An enemy to oligarchy, adherent of European and Latin American rather than Yankee culture, and a strong believer in education, development, and secular control of public life, he strove to build a set of basic national institutions, in no small part to prevent the North Americans from completely absorbing his country. By the end of his third term as president, in addition to greatly expanding primary schooling and attempting fundamental reforms of both Panamanian law and the Canal treaty, he had created national archives, a civil registry, a hospital, a modern jail and prison colony, and a national high school.

His cavalier attitude toward funding these projects drove North American authorities to distraction. Government finances, already in deep trouble by the time Porras took office, declined further with the end of canal construction, the beginning of World War I, and the uncertain postwar economy. Porras was determined to push ahead regardless in his program of nation-building, and though the U.S. vetoed his more ambitious plans and imposed financial controllers on the Panamanian government, it never got the situation or the president under control. Porras seems to have benefited personally only in moderation—unlike many politicians of the era, he left no great fortune, and during one feud he opened up his modest holdings to the scrutiny of a court of honor[5]—but he tolerated blatant graft by his colleagues, which drastically increased the cost of every project.[6]

Porras looked to economic development to reduce oligarchical power and dependence on the canal, as well as to alleviate his countrymen's poverty. Keenly aware that the Isthmus exported almost nothing other than bananas and a few natural products, he enthusiastically encouraged investment by foreigners, and he dreamed of opening up huge tracts of forestland to colonization, in order to encourage peasant smallholders and thwart the growth of vast landed estates.

Even more than development, Porras believed in schools. In a speech at the opening of a power plant, he noted that wherever they went, the Spaniards had placed a church, North Americans a factory, and "where we wish to proclaim our victory, we raise a school."[7] More than just making his country productive, Porras expected education to unify and uplift it morally, breaking down divisions of race and class. He himself, though white and a practicing Catholic, encouraged religious toleration, worked closely with non-white colleagues all his life, and he took as his second wife a woman racially and socially unacceptable to elite society.

Whatever Porras's goals and programs might have meant for Panama had he been able to carry all of them to fruition, they posed a grave threat to Kuna autonomy and well-being. Blind to Indian economic enterprise, Porras looked to North American capital and foreign colonists to open up the coast. His cultural and religious tolerance, moreover, did not extend as far as paganism, exotic dress, or other benighted practices of a backward people, all of which had to yield to modern education. Above all, Kuna separatism and pride, epitomized by their refusal to marry other Panamanians, could not be countenanced any more than could the pretensions of white oligarchs. However deluded the Indians themselves might be, Belisario Porras knew what they needed.

After Porras's inauguration in late 1912, his government began soliciting recommendations for the development of the San Blas Coast,[8] and in his first month in office, a special commission presented a draft law to the national assembly, along with a memorial on the subject.[9] The authors of the memorial, who reviewed the history of the coast from the conquest to the present, could not avoid a little admiration for the "indomitable race that bore without yielding the fire and iron of the conquistadores, jealous and conserving of its ethnic characteristics," and for "an independence so absolute . . . that in truth it may be said that it is a myth to consider the region . . . an integral part of the Panamanian nation." Ultimately, however, the memorial concluded that the Indians had to be redeemed from the state of barbarism and irrationality in which they lived, and the failure to control San Blas could only be said to have "consequences fatal for the cause of civilization and for the national treasury"—a turn of phrase that summed up nicely the government's mixed goals.

At the very end of the year the legislators passed the bill as Law 56 of 1912 for "the reduction to civilized life of the barbarous, semibarbarous, and savage tribes." Law 56 called for the formation of population centers and administrative districts; for land sales and assistance to colonists; for the creation of police posts, judges' offices, seaports, schools; and for a boat to patrol the coast—it had, in short, a great deal more to say about colonization than about the Indians.[10]

This legislative initiative coincided with a round of visits to the city by Kuna chiefs, eager to make contact with the new president. Cimral Colman came at Christmastime of 1912, and during what was apparently a friendly conference it was agreed that Porras should visit San Blas; Charly Robinson soon followed.[11] In July of the following year, an official in the Secretariat of Government and Justice named Enrique Hurtado made a reconnaissance of San Blas, visiting most of the Kuna villages on the coast, unfriendly and friendly.[12]

Hurtado, who comes across as a relaxed and tolerant person as well as a fairly acute observer, had high praise for Nargana, Coope, and Charly Robinson, though he noted that Robinson, far from having wide authority, only kept his enemies at bay through his own courage. Moving down the coast, Hurtado fell in with Colman, with whom he had an amicable visit.

In the context of Kuna complaints about the depredations of intrusive turtlers, Hurtado's report insightfully pointed out the existence of private property among the Indians. Open to the paradox of an indigenous society insisting on private property against a government claiming collective, national rights, he wondered how the Indians could be shown that such things as beaches, forests, and territorial waters could only be owned by sovereign nations. The idea that the Kuna themselves might qualify for some form of sovereignty never crossed his mind.

With his tolerance and patience, Hurtado represented the best goodwill Panama had to offer. He clearly envisioned a form of development that, though it might prejudice what the Indians deludedly considered their interests, would actually benefit them in the long run. His goodwill, however, was mixed with manipulative deception: he recommended a ban on turtling by non-Indians and the restriction of colonization to lightly populated areas, but only for the moment, until the government's foot was firmly in the door.

Hurtado's report, despite the individuality of its author's outlook and voice, echoed themes already apparent in the government memorial and in other reports, most obvious among them greed, or put more delicately and lyrically, the desire "to open . . . to redeeming progress in a district that guards in its jungles the most select display of woods—latex-bearing, resinous, for construction, dyes, and cabinet-making—veins of precious metal and natural products of value and demand in the foreign market."[13]

The reports contemplated the extraction of natural products, principally wood, rubber, balata, ivorynuts, turtle shell, and minerals. They urged that San Blas be opened up to ranches, plantations, and agricultural colonies. Even the less grandiose proposals spoke of thousands and millions of people or heads of livestock, and of the cities rather than towns that would grow on the coast.

Most of the writers anticipated that regional development would be carried out in no small part by European colonists, who would inspire the Kuna to become civilized. The government also hoped that the colonists would be a good influence on the rest of Panama, showing what hard work and devotion to agriculture could do, and even that white immigrants would lighten the dark complexion of the national population.[14] As it turned out, Panama attracted commercially minded immigrants but few yeoman farmers.

Hopes for colonization and development focused most of all on the Mandinga region of western San Blas, with its broad, deep, flat valley, its sizable river, closeness to Colón, and its great gulf, which as Hurtado pointed out, could accommodate a squadron of ships.[15] Also important, the indigenous population of the Gulf was sparse. None of the writers thought it proper that the Kuna should keep Mandinga to themselves, still less San Blas as a whole, but all of them thought it right to let the Indians hold on to their "little haciendas" to feed themselves, and Mandinga was the place where colonization could best be reconciled with Indian subsistence.

All of these dreams so far existed only on paper. The commercial reality was the trade in coconuts and manufactured goods with the Indians, much of it taken by Colombian boats. In a national economy that had little to sell, coconuts were becoming Panama's second-largest export, surpassed only by bananas. The government wanted to drive the Colombians out of the coconut market to benefit its own merchants and to bring in badly needed tax revenue. The contraband issue also had a political dimension, because the Colombian boats, coming and going at will, violated Panamanian sovereignty and demonstrated the little country's inability to secure its borders.

The Kuna, had they known the shape of government plans and dreams, would certainly have been dismayed, but some of their leaders were willing to cooperate in establishing at least titular Panamanian sovereignty over San Blas. In his communications with government officials, Cimral Colman expressed a concern to secure Kuna rights to their lands, to prevent merchant abuses, and most of all to exclude the intruders coming into San Blas after turtles, balata, and other natural products. He and his followers would help Panama set up an administrative center, if in return the officials stationed there would keep the turtlers out. As one Kuna oral history has it: "Grandfather Colman went off to Panama. He said to Grandfather Porras, '. . . I want to set up a doorway. . . . Here I'll place a cat,' he said. 'The cat that I'll put here is to catch rats for me.'"[16]

The Hurtado report noted that, in addition to catching rats, Colman had hopes of uniting all the Kuna under his own leadership. Colman saw the split over national affiliation as the major impediment to Kuna unity, and he was confident that a reunited San Blas would choose him over Inabaginya. Colman was, in any case, the government's natural choice as an ally in this period, given Inabaginya's intransigence and Charly Robinson's lack of authority outside Nargana. Although Hurtado cautioned that "it should not be believed that Colman is a paladin of civilization, as Robinson is," there were realistic hopes that he would push for gradual change.[17] In addition to showing interest in having his own sons educated, either with Miss Coope or by the government, Colman asked Porras to establish a boarding school in the city for Indian children, though he was less sanguine about schools in San Blas itself.

As it advanced its plans, the Porras administration heard at the beginning of November 1913 of an impending attack on Nargana by Kuna opposed to Anna Coope's presence. On the seventh of November the governor of Colón wrote

President Porras, passing on urgent requests from Charly Robinson for help. In the president's reply, he said that he had ordered an immediate expeditionary force to support Robinson and "to definitively occupy the Coast of San Blas and proceed with the civilization of the indigenous population," only to find that no suitable vessel was available. That same day he and his secretary of government and justice, Francisco Filos, exchanged notes on how to proceed.[18]

Filos recommended borrowing a boat from General Goethals in the Canal Zone, equipping it with a small cannon, and sending it on a tour of the coast to expel foreign vessels, haul down Colombian flags, and establish a government outpost. As inducements for Indian friends, Colman, Robinson, and Inabaginya were to be offered salaries, and turtling in San Blas was to be closed to outsiders. Porras replied positively, amplifying and modifying certain points: a machine gun would do better than a cannon, and he would go himself.

Nothing further occurred for more than twelve months, however, until the National Assembly began work on new legislation and the administration purchased a large steam launch, which alarmed the American Legation sufficiently that the chargé felt moved to lecture the Panamanian secretary of foreign affairs:

In view of the peculiar situation obtaining along the San Blas coast arising from the semi-independent state of the Indian tribes, my government could not but view with apprehension any attempt to subjugate or civilize by forceful means such a large body of involuntary citizens at the present time. I also ventured to point out the expense which would necessarily be incurred in attempting any action in the nature of a military expedition against these people.[19]

After a further exchange of letters and an interview in which Porras took offense at U.S. interference, the legation ultimately contented itself with urging special care in the choice of officials and implementation of plans.[20]

In the early months of 1915, the government passed a new law dedicated to regulating commerce on the coast and to authorizing an embargo of Inabaginya's pro-Colombian villages; issued a detailed executive decree creating a new unit called the Circumscription of San Blas; and named the unit's first intendente or head, who was Enrique Hurtado, the author of the report on the region.[21] Belisario Porras was at last ready for his presidential tour of the coast, which, it was hoped, would go better than President Mendoza's visit five years earlier.

Porras set out in the third week of May 1915. The outing, which lasted ten days, was described in some detail by the anonymous author, probably an aide-de-camp to the president, of an account published the following year by the Royal Geographic Society in Madrid.[22] In addition to Porras himself, the party included several government officials, notably the new intendente, Enrique Hurtado. The U.S. minister to Panama, William Jennings Price, was also aboard, as were J. M. Hyatt, a prominent businessman, and Narciso Navas, who had also been interpreter for President Mendoza.[23] Cimral Colman appears in the narrative at several points, but it is unclear whether he joined the party in Colón or San Blas. Unmentioned, except when pulled out of the narrator's hat to chop down trees or stand at attention, was a contingent of laborers and policemen.

The anonymous narrator wrote that they departed Colón at 4:00 p.m. on May 19, 1915. After an evening tour of the colonial ruins at Portobelo, the party left the next day at ten, reaching San Blas that afternoon. Throughout the trip the government launch, newly renamed the *San Blas,* made excellent time: by five that evening, they were anchored far into Mandinga Bay or the Gulf of San Blas, near a cluster of Kuna islands.

The narrator recorded the excursionists' surprise, a euphemism for irritation, at the sight of Colombian flags flying, and he noted that in passing the islands, the boat "sent them a benevolent and affectionate salute with its potent horn." The benevolence was debatable, but the message was clear. For a century, steam whistles and air horns on trains and boats had been used to overawe natives, perhaps most memorably in Conrad's *Heart of Darkness.*[24] In the present instance, since the excursionists had not, after all, brought a cannon or machine gun, the horn was the most potent weapon in their arsenal. The "salute" intruded into the village in a way that could not be resisted or ignored, signifying the government's will to pacify and dominate.

The next three days were devoted to exploring the Gulf. On the twenty-first, after a morning ashore, Porras returned to the boat to hear of a visit in his absence by "one of the chiefs of those tribes named Seg, who had daringly presented himself in a canoe decked out with Colombian flags, saying that he was the owner and seigneur of these lands and that he did not tolerate anyone penetrating them without his consent."[25]

"A bit put out" by the chief's audacity, Porras sent three officials and the interpreter Navas ashore on Seg's island, Narasgandup Dummad, or Great Orange Island. Taken to the gathering house, they were met by two chiefs in their hammocks surrounded by two hundred Kuna. After Navas explained the purposes behind President Porras's visit to what, the narrator ironically noted, the Indians were presumptuous enough to call "their lands," both chiefs replied that they considered themselves Colombian, that they wanted nothing to do with Panama, and that they would allow no structures to be built in their territory. They said they knew that Colman was on board, and that he was responsible for selling out their land and bringing boats with steam horns and electric lights to scare their women and children.

After an hour and a half, the four men were allowed to leave, on the condition that they send Colman ashore. Colman's son Ceferino, describing the moment many years later, said that the president asked him whether he would defend his father if he were attacked, and that when he replied that he would, Porras gave him a coat and a pistol.[26]

Thus we truly disembarked, and my father, when he got there, sat in a hammock. The Colombian flag was flying, at Narasgandup Dummad. Thus we disembarked, and my father began to speak. . . . "Now elders, you see, I want to put a door here," he said. "The coconuts being stolen from you, the turtles being caught, just as if you weren't owners of the islands, the wagas do this to the Kuna, your things are being touched—the door I will place here is so the waga won't enter like that again, so he'll only enter the right way." . . . The elders were really mad. With their faces all red, they said, "People like him are just blowhards; they only think they'll do such things." They said that to my father."[27]

According to the anonymous account, some senior women spoke too, dressing Colman down for bringing the party there with its loud and frightening horn. This persistent complaint, though it seems to have puzzled the narrator, made perfect sense in Kuna terms. A severe fright from anything powerful and unsettling could dislodge children's souls, exposing them to the evil spirits all around. In their own symbolic idiom, which equated spirits with wagas, the Kuna understood that the intrusive and unsettling horn was anything but benevolent.

In the morning, Porras and some of the others explored the nearby Mandinga River, proposed as the site of an agricultural colony and plantations to be established by the American businessman Hyatt and his backers. At midday the party turned toward the cluster of islands at Carti just to the west belonging to Colman's confederacy. In the gathering house of the principal Carti village, Suitupu, or Crab Island, Porras explained his goals, and Kuna speakers replied that they would be glad to help in the work of civilization—a diplomatic fib, since they had no intention of allowing policemen or teachers on their island.

The next day, after further exploration, the party returned to the boat and held a meeting to decide where to site the new headquarters for the coast, eventually settling on a small island off San Blas Point, which was promptly given a new and inspiring name, El Porvenir, The Future. At the end of the afternoon everyone went ashore on the island for a ceremony in which, "with the greatest solemnity and enthusiasm," they took formal possession for Panama. With dignitaries standing on the sand and a line of policemen drawn up in military formation on one side, President Porras formally handed a Panamanian flag to Enrique Hurtado, the new governor of the coast, saying,

Señor Hurtado: On taking possession of this island at the entrance of the Gulf, I put in your hands The Flag of the Republic, in the confidence that you will know how to main-

Ceremony of taking possession of El Porvenir, 1915.

tain it with dignity and with honor, guaranteeing to all in these districts their rights and as-suring for the Republic dominion over these waters and lands.[28]

A commemorative photograph was taken, and a document summarizing the pro-ceedings was drawn up and signed by everyone present, other than the policemen, laborers, and Indians. They began unloading supplies and materials for the new headquarters in the dark, and after another night spent on board, work continued in the morning.

At two in the afternoon on the twenty-fourth, the boat left the workers on El Porvenir and steamed east, reaching Nargana and Nusatupu late in the day. Photo-graphs show President Porras touring the two islands, and Coope's memoirs indi-cate that he visited her school, where he was serenaded with the Panamanian national anthem and hymns in Spanish and English. A letter she wrote the next day describes the conversation with Porras, as well as a visit by the U.S. minister to Panama, William Jennings Price, himself an evangelical Protestant.

May 26, 1915 . . . I told Mr. Price of [traders] bringing loads of rum, deluging the poor In-dians and taking their good coconuts for rum. He said I should tell the President. The Pres-ident did not come ashore next morning as he was in such a terrible hurry to get away, a fidgety Spaniard. I've met him before and he said [yesterday] "All schools in the Republic of Panama must be taught Spanish." "As far as I am concerned, it makes no difference which language they want to learn. I will teach either one or both. But my sole object is to give them God's Word and teach them the way of salvation thru Jesus only." He said,

President Belisario Porras visiting Nusatupu or Corazón de Jesús, 1915.

"Mr. Robinson has been speaking highly of you and the progress of the children." He told the chief he would build a house on this island and send a School Master to teach Spanish. See that? Mr. Price said, "But the Indians won't like it." Then Mr. Price turned to me and said, "You will teach Spanish later?" I answered, "Yes, certainly if they will learn, but the young men who have been from 2 to 7 years in Panama schools cannot read as well in Spanish as they can in English and they do not want to continue their Spanish, although I have suggested it to them. They are eager for the English. . . . There was a Spanish official with him and so he had to be careful of course.[29]

The next morning the boat proceeded east. At Tupile and Colman's seat, Ailigandi, Porras lectured friendly crowds on his civilizing program, stressing that the Indians should respect the national flag, accept government schools, and consider themselves Panamanians. The following day, at Ustupu or Portogandi, they were again confronted by Colombian flags, this time displayed by the followers of Chief Yaigun, who occupied one part of the divided island. Their reception in Chief Nele's village next door was much more satisfactory, however: a picture was taken with President Porras seated in a hammock, he gave another speech on civilization, and they were under way again.

Passing several "enemy" villages, the boat continued on to Sasardi in order to confront Inabaginya, the leader of the pro-Colombian Kuna. Inabaginya having been informed that if he persisted in refusing to acknowledge Panama, his island would be blockaded, cut off all from all shipping, "he replied in the most haughty manner that he was the absolute head of those lands and that there *he* gave the

In the gathering house of Ustupu or Portogandi, 1914. Nele Wardada and Belisario Porras in hammocks at left.

orders." Invited on board to speak with Porras, he "replied in the most emphatic manner that if the Señor President wished to confer with him, that he should come on shore, that he was as great as the president."[30] Porras, highly displeased, ordered Hurtado to put the embargo into effect immediately.

The boat passed on to the border town of Puerto Obaldía, and on the twenty-seventh, they turned west again, touching at Nargana and Porvenir, where for a few hours Porras personally directed the construction work on the new headquarters. By 6:30 the next morning they were back in Colón. In the city reporters failed to get a statement from the president, but Price obliged with some remarks on the pleasures and sights of the trip, the exoticism of the Kuna, the diplomatic way in which the president had made his case to the Indians, and "the brave, self-sacrificing and earnest work" of Coope and Purdy.[31]

Back in Nargana, the presidential visit had left turbulence in its wake. Coope describes a tumultuous meeting in the gathering house, to which she was called.[32] Since Robinson's conversion and the imposition of prohibition the previous year, a sizable faction had been out to supplant the chief, according to Coope. She says that Robinson began the meeting by relating President Porras's wishes to establish a government school and then abruptly offered his resignation as chief. Robinson's threat upstaged his enemies, creating an outcry, and the consensus of the meeting was to rename him chief. Ultimately, the village decided to accept government schools.[33]

Writing later for publication in her memoirs, Coope describes the innovation with seeming approval, while in a private letter she was much franker:

The Spaniard in any position has a string of servants and they would have to be housed and live here. They are of the low dirty class and would mix with their people [that is, with the Kuna]. The Chief and the Indians have had enough experience to know, and I would add my volume to the villainy of the Spanish people Rum and Rome ridden. They would bring their idols with them.[34]

By the middle of the following year Spanish-language schools were running on Nargana, Nusatupu, and Tupile, and a short time after, on Playón Chico. Events would show that Coope did indeed have much to fear.

11.
Colonization
and
Development

Within a year after President
Porras's visit to San Blas, the first intendente, or jefe de circunscripción, Enrique
Hurtado, had his administration under way. If by no means self-supporting, the
intendente's office, called the Intendencia, collected more than $2,800 that year in
taxes and fees, most of it from merchant vessels and balata-tappers, in addition to
almost $8,000 cleared by the government-owned launch.[1] Schools were in session
on three Kuna islands, and four new buildings had sprung up on El Porvenir.

Almost immediately, however, the administration ran up against the problems of
finance, supply, personnel, and transport that would hamper its actions over the next
decade. At the beginning of September the secretary of the Intendencia complained
that they were running short of supplies, both on Porvenir and in the survey for the
Mandinga colony, and by the end of the month the engineer in charge of the survey
sent word that they were down to one day's rations.[2] Within a short while the World
War began to shake up the government's already precarious financial situation,
forcing a budget cut for San Blas in 1917, and though modest increases followed in
later years, intendentes never stopped complaining of shortages in paper, ammunition, building supplies, and other essential materials.[3]

Even more than equipment and supplies, the administration experienced tremendous difficulties obtaining reliable transport with which to patrol the coast, carry
supplies, and respond to emergencies. The *San Blas,* a substantial ninety-three-foot
vessel bought for $45,000, made a profit when run by a private operator but lost
money when the government took it back; when leased again in 1917 it sank, leaving
the police and intendente more or less marooned on Porvenir unless they could
hitch a ride on a passing trading boat or dugout.[4] Refloated and patched up, the San
Blas was thereafter in the repair yard as often as it was at sea.

Of all the administration's difficulties, those related to personnel probably caused the most headaches. The local constabulary, given the revealing name of Colonial Police, began with ten agents and a sublieutenant.[5] By 1918 their numbers had increased, at least on paper, to twenty, still not much of a force with which to subdue and control 150 miles of coast and several thousand Indians.[6] The quality of the men recruited, moreover, was mixed at best. Unemployment in the city might ensure a supply of candidates, but forty-five dollars a month (fifteen for "indigenous police" recruited from the Indians) did not go far in an isolated and somewhat forbidding post with high expenses and none of the comforts of the city.[7] Along with some competent men, the Colonial Police ended up with a good many drunks and misfits, rejects from the national police force, whom intendentes had to weed out as best they could.

Recruitment procedures and the patronage system dominant in the Panamanian government did not make the task of weeding any easier. Presidents and cabinet secretaries, not local bureaucrats, hired and fired. Intendentes' nominations to fill vacancies were often approved, but so were those made by patrons in the government, often of unsuitable men. When an agent was fired, if he had connections higher up, he could probably get back on the force in a short time. Thus in the report on one case in which four policemen resigned after being fined for ignoring a call to drill, the lieutenant in charge, after detailing the numerous faults of all four men, pointed out that three of them had previously been fired and then reinstated.[8] In sending three other policemen back to the city for drunkenness, Hurtado wrote his superiors: "I plead with you . . . to give orders . . . that they send me sober men."[9]

One of the few ways intendentes could exercise control of the police force was to play the patronage game themselves, getting cronies and kinsmen appointed, men whom they could at least trust further than strangers. By the time Hurtado resigned, he had filled every opening at his headquarters with men related to him as kin or client. Even after Hurtado's resignation, this tight-knit network kept their loyalty to him and not to his successor.[10]

The colonization of San Blas, as essential to the government's plans as schools, pacification, and bureaucracy, also failed to run as smoothly as hoped. By the end of October 1915, work had been completed on laying out the proposed city in the Mandinga region, to be named Nicuesa after an early conquistador, and by November the final contract with J. M. Hyatt, the North American capitalist who would sponsor the colony, had been completed.[11] In return for settling two hundred colonists (later reduced to one hundred), Hyatt received 25,000 hectares (60,000 acres), which were to remain tax-free for twenty-five years.

As a city and agricultural colony, Nicuesa was a bust. Although well sited in terms of maritime access, agricultural land, and fresh water, half of the urban center's projected streets were on unusable marshy ground.[12] Immigrants, either foreign or

Panamanian, failed to appear, and by the middle of 1918, the prospective city had gathered only 250 inhabitants, mostly miners rather than farmers. An official report could not characterize the colony more positively than as an "alluring promise."[13]

As a commercial venture, on the other hand, Nicuesa was more than promising. On his 25,000 tax-free hectares, Hyatt began in 1916 by mining manganese, made quite profitable by increased demand for munitions during World War I.[14] Having worked deposits down the coast closer to Colón for some years, Hyatt was only able to begin working in San Blas after the establishment of the Intendencia, and then only in secret because of Kuna objections.[15] By June 1916 the mine had yielded seven thousand tons, worth approximately $210,000, and it continued in operation up to 1919.[16]

Hyatt's company, the San Blas Development Corporation, entered the coconut trade in a big way, planting thirty-six thousand palms by 1920, followed a few years later by bananas.[17] Hyatt was also the president of the Colon Import and Export Company, which he had founded in 1912 to compete in the coastal trade in coconuts and manufactured goods, as well as the extraction of ivorynuts, balata latex, and turtle shell. By 1915 he already had the largest string of schooners and motor vessels working the coast. In general, Panamanians might get a few crumbs or even a slice or two from the economic exploitation of San Blas—President Porras, who asked Intendente Hurtado to have a parcel of a thousand hectares near the colony surveyed for one of his children, may have gotten a slice—but North American capitalists took the greatest part of the pie.[18]

The government signed another contract, on much the same terms, for a tract in eastern San Blas, with a Spaniard named Manuel Fernandez, who proposed to establish an agricultural colony, but only after he had exterminated 90 percent of the Indians, infecting them with disease while pretending to administer vaccinations. Astoundingly, except for the proposed genocide, the Panamanian cabinet found the proposal acceptable. After Fernandez visited San Blas disguised as a merchant, he decided that perhaps the Kuna "should be treated as our fellow creatures" after all, and that they should be won over with fireworks displays, phonographs, and cinema showings.[19] The hare-brained project fell apart when Fernandez failed to secure financial backing, and he ended up in an unsuccessful attempt to convince the U.S. legation that he and Belisario Porras had been collaborating with Japanese agents to establish a secret base in the Darién.[20] For almost a decade the eastern tract lay abandoned.

The Kuna would eventually protest against the concessions on their lands, but in the first few years after 1915 they were preoccupied with a more pervasive and obvious invasion of their territory by poor Blacks. Colman's expectation that in return for his sponsorship, the government would keep intruders out of San Blas, was almost instantly disillusioned. Within a few weeks after the establishment of the Intendencia, Hurtado threw open two large tracts on the mainland, though at the same time he did reserve turtling in coastal waters exclusively for the Indians. The Colombian Blacks of Puerto Obaldía renewed their exploitation of the forests, as did the costeños from the villages between San Blas and Colón.[21] Organized into small teams of five or ten men, each with its own leader, they camped in the woods for several weeks or months while gathering ivorynuts, used for buttons, or extracting balata latex from the níspero tree, the market for which was rapidly expanding.[22] The yield from this labor was typically sold by prearranged contract to an individual or company, who would in many cases have advanced the supplies needed for the work.[23]

By the fifth month of the Intendencia, in September 1915, Hurtado had already issued monthly permits for more than 350 forest workers. Between June 1915 and June 1916, more than 2,000 barrels of ivorynuts and 29,000 kilos of latex left San Blas (along with well over 5 million coconuts).[24] Even so, Hurtado's superiors pressured him to increase the number of permits and expand the areas of forest open to exploitation.[25] The costeños might be among the most isolated and humble populations of Panama, but they were voters who knew how to use their votes to pressure the government, and as long as the Indians had little interest in such work, the buyers and exporters needed the poor Blacks to bring the balata and ivorynuts out of the forest.

Kuna resistance began again immediately. In July of 1915 news came that Inabaginya, leader of the pro-Colombian confederacy, was going through the forest with an armed band, confiscating latex at gunpoint.[26] A few months later, when a company agent refused to pay what he considered an exorbitant fee for balata hauled out of the mountains, men from the carriers' village divested his tappers of 190 pounds of the latex and all their equipment.[27] One Carti man remembers going out to confront the turtlers:

If we saw that the net-throwers had intruded, [the chief] would lead us out. . . . Twenty of us, or forty of us would go. In our midst, Chief Urdummad would lead us. The turtle-catchers would be frightened. We gathered up the nets, we'd carry off all the nets. . . . The turtle-catchers went away. . . . A month later they'd return, already they'd be coming back again, others.[28]

To be sure, resistance was uneven: some villages were induced or coerced into supplying bearers and temporary room and board for forest workers. But such arrangements often led to disputes and seizures of property by one side or the other to enforce claims, and the Kuna accused tappers of stealing crops and digging up graves in search of buried jewelry.[29] However much Hurtado portrayed himself as an impartial mediator, protecting outsiders who wanted to work in San Blas while keeping them from exploiting the Indians, neither side was satisfied.[30]

In his more positive efforts to win over the Indians and to begin the task of civilizing them, Hurtado and the government pinned their hopes on education. In mid-May 1916, one year after President Porras's visit to San Blas, schools were running on Tupile, Nargana, and Nusatupu—the latter now officially known by the name Father Gassó gave it, Corazón de Jesús—and later that year a fourth school was established on Playón Chico as well, with small police detachments on each island, ostensibly to support the teachers.[31] In his first published report, Intendente Hurtado noted that it had taken considerable effort to persuade even the friendliest villages to accept schools, which they feared would take their customs from them, a state of affairs he blamed on their bad experiences with Catholic missionaries. Soon, however, things were going so well "that I believe that in no place could a teacher more beloved and respected be found."[32]

On Nargana and Corazón, meanwhile, the teachers found themselves in competition with Coope and Purdy. As early as January of 1917, a report on examination results in the government schools noted the presence of "elements in disagreement with the uniformity of national teaching" and complained that attendance was lower on those two islands because many families sent their children to the English-language schools, which had the support of the "native chiefs."[33]

So far the government had at least tolerated Coope and her school. Intendente Hurtado had an unusually relaxed attitude toward English-speakers and Protestantism—it had been Hurtado who in 1913 had suggested to Coope that she take over the Catholic mission buildings—and very likely higher members of the administration accepted his view that her mission helped civilize the Kuna. By Coope's own account, she secured the acquiescence of President Porras by confronting him at the presidential palace, and she had an active group of supporters in the Canal Zone, probably including the American minister of the time, William Jennings Price, an evangelical Christian.[34]

Even where government schools lacked competition, they would need years to win the Kuna over. The Intendencia, moreover, had no funds for new schools beyond the four already established, even if villages could be induced to accept them. In the short run, Hurtado most needed to bend Kuna leaders to his will, a task complicated not just by Panama's military and financial weakness, but also by the egalitarian and anti-authoritarian strains in Kuna culture.

Their own customs are an obstacle to imposing on them the obligations of our laws. Their form of government in which authority is relative and no one holds it except when it is conceded by the whole people for each special case, makes them reject all other authority, which in their primitive minds will appear absurd, since one exercises it only without having adopted its trappings.[35]

Hurtado showed clear signs of ambivalence on the subject and even admiration for Kuna independent-mindedness:

Slave peoples are easy to dominate, a little kindness or rigor is sufficient to make of them what might be wanted; free peoples are indomitable and the methodical attraction, the slow evolution on the course that the superior will has predetermined is the only means of exercising its fusion with the race. The Indians of San Blas are free men.[36]

Despite his admiration, Hurtado firmly intended to take away that freedom, to make Kuna leaders the tools of his superior will. His fiercest opponent was Inabaginya, who visited Colombia twice during the first months of the new administration; Hurtado asked President Porras to find out who the chief saw on his trips abroad.[37] The Panamanian blockade of Inabaginya's confederacy, always patchy and incomplete because the government lacked the boats needed for continuous enforcement, did pressure several islands into token protestations of loyalty to Panama, and in April of 1916 the embargo was lifted on all but two villages.[38] Inabaginya himself remained intransigent, driving an exasperated Hurtado to request permission to capture the rebel by force, but the president and secretary turned him down.[39] It was undoubtedly apparent to all concerned that Colombia was not going to reclaim San Blas or send troops to support its Kuna adherents, but it suited both the rebel chief and his foreign contacts to keep up the show of alliance.

Inabaginya's principal rival, Cimral Colman, who had agreed to the establishment of the Intendencia, worked actively to encourage and consolidate Kuna allegiance to Panama, pressuring islands in western San Blas to haul down their Colombian flags.[40] Soon, however, Colman himself began showing signs of questionable loyalty and compliance, raising objections to compulsory schooling and the intrusion of non-Indians into the forest. Although he apparently avoided an open break with the government, Colman's interference angered policemen and teachers, and the potential for further rifts was already apparent.

As for Charly Robinson, although no longer the government's great hope, he still retained some official credit, as well as the rifles it had provided him. In 1918 he was awarded a monthly salary of $45 in the nominal position of indigenous policeman, and a couple of his own village constables were appointed to the official force on Nargana.[41] In the same year, the government tapped Robinson as its special emissary on a mission to Sasardi, in its efforts to persuade Inabaginya to change national allegiance.[42]

Robinson continued acting like a regional leader, especially concerning Kuna lands. In March of 1916 he sent President Porras a letter, written as usual in English, asking him "to grant us and our children" — by which he presumably meant the Kuna as a whole — "all the Islands between East of the River Man-dingali, and West of the Uah-Uah-gan-dee, also all the land inhabited and cultivated by Indians on the main-land, and in the Mountains."[43] The personal interview with Porras that followed must not have yielded concrete results, because in January of 1917 Robinson was back in the city to visit Porras's successor, Ramón Valdés. Although Valdés said he could do nothing definitive during Robinson's brief stay in Panama, he did issue a letter of intent in a newspaper article devoted to the chief's visit.

The President of the republic of Panama, makes known to all residents of the Coast of San Blas the Government of the Republic will not make any concession of lands in these regions that may infringe on the acquired rights of the members of the different tribes that live on the coast, and that he will give every protection to the Indians of the Coast of San Blas.[44]

Continuing pressure finally brought more significant results. In May 1918, Secretary Eusebio Morales wrote the intendente that after several meetings with Robinson the government recognized "the inappropriateness and even the impossibility of making concessions of land to persons not indigenous in all the territory of that circumscription."[45] After lobbying by Colman as well as Robinson, the government in January 1919 issued a decree banning cultivation by non-Indians throughout San Blas.[46] None of these measures, however, had the legal permanence of laws, and none were interpreted to exclude the colonies and plantations sponsored by the government itself.

Another success for Robinson developed out of a visit to Nargana from Nele Wardada, chief of Ustupu or Portogandi, the largest village on the whole coast. Nele, already emerging as Colman's most important lieutenant, asked Robinson for two of Miss Coope's more advanced students to teach school on his island. In place of Panamanian teachers and government schools, Nele proposed a village-run cooperative venture, for which Robinson provided two teenage boys, Freddy Phillips and Samuel Morris. Paid only in bananas, coconuts, and other produce, and teaching Spanish and English in a small thatched house, Phillips and Morris began in 1918 an enduring tradition of independent village schools. A few months later, Robinson responded to a similar request, this time from forest Kuna villages over the mountains in the Bayano Valley.[47]

These successes were interspersed with controversy. Like other Kuna leaders, Charly Robinson became embroiled in conflicts with rubber-tappers in his village's territory, and though the intendente was counseled by his superiors to handle the issue "with much moderation and restraint," Robinson was also called a "rebel Indian," not a label under which he had suffered before.[48] A few months later, the intendente dressed him down for spreading propaganda that Colman was selling all the lands of San Blas to the government.[49]

Robinson also became embroiled in disputes at home. A complaint alleges that he persuaded his followers to raise more than a thousand dollars to secure title to a large piece of unclaimed land down the coast from Nargana, and that after Robinson visited Panama they never saw the title or the money again. The complaint further alleges that Robinson drained the resources of the cooperative store he managed for the village.[50] The truth of the allegations cannot be determined, though embezzlement from cooperative stores and village treasuries has been a staple of Kuna village politics ever since.[51]

Serious threats to the chief's authority appeared, as well, personified by Claudio Iglesias, the young man whose "Roman" name had worried Miss Coope. Claudio's father, Alício, or as the Kuna rendered it, Eliseo, was throughout his life a traditional curer, which did not prevent him from embracing western schooling for his children, eventually seeing that all seven were educated. In 1912 Claudio, along with a number of other Kuna boys, received a scholarship to the Orphan's Hospice of Don Bosco, a boarding school run by the Salesian Order in Panama City, which provided each of its students with literacy, the Catholic religion, and a trade. Claudio, whose school portrait already shows the fierce will obvious in everything he did, persisted in school as all the other boys in his cohort dropped out, becoming in the process a fervent proponent of civilization and Catholicism. Even a laudatory biographical sketch by a Catholic Father uses the word "obsessed" to describe Claudio's concern with "the rapid civilization of his race," and a Salesian Brother who had been a fellow student in the Hospice later remembered Claudio dreaming of having his own motor launch in order to bring a priest to San Blas every two weeks.[52]

Claudio graduated in woodworking in 1917 and returned to Nargana soon thereafter, with the intention of working as a carpenter. Along with a handful of other young men schooled either in Panama or on Nargana and Corazón, he became the leader of a large group that began agitating for rapid "civilizing" change, and in this role he soon distinguished himself as a *tule buledi*, "tough guy." (Claudio's brother Lonny, or Alcibiades, was sent to be educated in the United States by Anna Coope and did not return until 1919.) Meeting separately from the village gatherings, which were dominated by older men, Claudio's group presented a strong challenge to Robinson's ascendancy, and it soon gained the backing of the teachers and policemen on the two islands, who found the loyalties and aspirations of the youths much more compatible than Robinson's gringophilia.

A list of the organization's initial enrollment shows 104 members, 65 on Nargana and the rest on Corazón de Jesús.[53] The organization had a plethora of officers: four chiefs, a secretary and a subsecretary, five "assessors," and four "foremen," the latter probably for work projects. Two later petitions, one with 33 names from Nargana, the other 44 from both islands, probably reflect more closely the group's active membership.[54]

As Kuna chiefs were beginning to realize, literate young men, by their very existence, threatened an established order based on seniority and oral communica-

Claudio Iglesias.

tion. In a verse from chiefly chanting often quoted in later years, Nele of Ustupu warned his followers that the "birds" (whose marks on a page seemed to resemble the scratching of claws, hence the name) would materialize a devil in the gathering house. At the same time, chiefs such as Nele, Colman, and Inabaginya needed birds to translate and write letters for them, and with almost no literate men available on their own islands, they turned to boys schooled in Nargana and Panama.[55] By giving these youths positions of influence, the chiefs co-opted them and enlisted them into the cause of Kuna autonomy. Even Charly Robinson succeeded in recruiting a number of young men less besotted with Panamanian culture than Claudio Iglesias, but there was no way that someone as ambitious or determined as Claudio himself could be co-opted.

The two factions on Nargana were distinguished as much by policy and outlook as by age, one side in its orientation Catholic, Hispanic, Panamanian, and modernist, the other Protestant, anglophone, North American, and moderately progressive. Except perhaps for Claudio himself, Catholicism functioned more as a cultural marker than a faith. The Salesians who had groomed Claudio for his civilizing role could not have taken delight from his modernism and embrace of secular Panamanian culture if they knew of it, and Father Gassó would have been dismayed at the interest of Claudio's followers in clothes, dancing, music, and money. On the other side, most of the ex-sailors and other middle-aged men who formed Charly Robinson's core support were nominal Protestants at best and less in a hurry than Robinson himself for change. The most conservative villagers, dismayed by both sides, backed the chief only as the lesser of two evils.

In some respects, of course, Claudio was merely a proxy, Charly's real enemies being Panamanian functionaries. As the chief increasingly came into disagreement with the teachers and police agents stationed on his island, someone's view had to prevail, and since Panamanian ideas harmonized with Claudio's much more than with Charly's, it was inevitable that the agents of change would ally themselves with the modernists. The scanty record for this period suggests that, for the first year after Claudio's arrival, the two sides avoided overt conflict while they organized and jockeyed for position, but a clash was inevitable.

In both Nargana and San Blas as a whole, the arrival of the Intendencia had provoked a whole series of fundamental challenges and conflicts, but for a number of reasons, notably change in the government itself, things did not come to a head for the first several years. Belisario Porras's first term as president ended in September 1916. His hand-picked successor, Ramón Valdés, an old man at the end of his political career, died in office in June 1918. During the succession crisis that followed, executive power was held for a few months by a vice president, or designate, and then in October of that year, Belisario Porras returned to office as first designate and acting president to serve out the rest of Valdés's term.[56]

Until Porras's reemergence in late 1918, it appears that the administration of San Blas just drifted, giving the Kuna a breathing space before the next government initiative. Enrique Hurtado resigned as intendente in June 1917, to resurface almost immediately as an entrepreneur, sponsoring teams of tappers and ivorynut gatherers. (Hurtado, documents show, had already gone into business before resigning.)[57] He was succeeded by Vicente Cataño, a jack of all bureaucratic trades: former chief of police in Colón, later chief census-taker, head of a prison colony, and once again chief of police.[58] The scanty record from his year and a half in San Blas leaves the impression that he was appointed strictly as a fill-in, until the budgetary and political crises could be resolved, and that he treated his duties accordingly.[59] His brief term ended in chaotic infighting, as a political operator named as his assistant tried to supplant Cataño, and the policemen appointed by his predecessor, Hurtado, ended up disregarding the orders of both men.[60]

For the Kuna, this period of anarchy and lax administration delayed the ultimate reckoning with the government. Official relations with both Inabaginya and Colman remained unresolved, as did all the issues raised by the arrival of the Intendencia and its efforts to gain control of the coast. But these issues—national sovereignty and control, capitalist penetration, intrusion into the region by non-Indians, and the contradiction between indigenous and national culture—were merely postponed, and it only required a change in national conditions and the arrival of an intendente less tolerant than Hurtado and more conscientious than Cataño to spark a conflict.

Part Four

THE CONTEST FOR CONTROL, 1918–1920

12. In the Nargana Cockpit

On the morning of January 4, 1919, the head of the police detachment at Nargana, Ramón Garrido, arrived at Porvenir to swear out a formal complaint against Charly Robinson, alleging that Robinson and a mob had threatened the teacher on Corazón de Jesús (who, as it happened, was Garrido's wife), attempted to free a prisoner from jail, and defied the authority of the Colonial Police.[1] The trouble all began, oddly enough, with a Christmas assembly in the Nargana public school.

As the teacher there, Ana Moreno de James, told the story in a letter to the intendente, she had organized a day of diversions for December 25, including pole-vaulting, foot races, and climbing a greased pole. After an evening torch-lit parade, students, parents, and teacher had adjourned to the school for recitations and a comedy performed by the children. The school assembly, an event familiar all over the Americas and Western Europe as an adjunct to public education, competed in Nargana of late 1918 with the Christmas jollity offered by the Protestant mission while communicating to parents as well as children the forms of national culture.

Sra. de James noted that she felt obliged to invite the local *jefe,* Charly Robinson, even though he and "his sort" often provoked rows in the schoolhouse, and indeed that night one of his followers got into a heated argument. To cover over the unpleasantness, after the singing of the National Anthem at the end of the regular program, she hurriedly improvised a dance of a kind called a *tamborito,* this one with the title "La Pollera." According to Ana de James, everyone enjoyed the dance except Charly Robinson, who counseled parents not to let their daughters participate.[2]

Improvised or not, Ana de James's performance was clearly meant to teach patriotism as well as raise spirits. The tamborito is a folkloric dance from the Panamanian interior, often called the national dance, and the pollera, a voluminous lace dress worn on special occasions, is the national costume.[3] The dance may have offended Robinson because it violated Kuna morality or sentiments, but Ana de James herself was sure the blame lay with the "fanatic and hypocritical" spirit of "those who profess some religious mission, whatever the sect might be to which they belong."

And it much surprises me that this tamborito, so in vogue, as much in the capital as in the provinces of the interior, should [be given] a scandalous character (according to them), and yet it is not immorality among them to bathe naked in front of my schoolhouse in class hours; this indeed, which is scandalous for whoever wants to implant morality and discipline in a school.[4]

Three days later the police on Corazón de Jesús arrested a man named Nieve for declaring publicly that the schoolgirls who danced had prostituted themselves. Soon after his arrest, Charly Robinson and a large group of his village constables carrying their staves of office crossed from Nargana to Corazón, where they demanded Nieve's freedom, pledged to seize the government policeman who had arrested him, and menaced the teacher, Elisa de Garrido.[5] Confronted by Ramón Garrido and another government agent with a revolver, Robinson backed down and returned to his own island.

Shortly afterward, however, a much larger mob armed with bayonets (probably taken from the rifles provided by the government some years before) reappeared on Corazón, causing an "indescribable uproar," during which Charly Robinson and Garrido had a verbal showdown, spoken in English. Although Robinson called out in Kuna to the people of the island, asking them to help free the prisoner, his group seems to have once again lacked the will to go up against the guns of the police.[6]

It may have seemed to Charly Robinson that a propitious moment had arrived for flexing his political muscles, since a new intendente had taken office only a few days before; if so, he badly misjudged the moment and the man, because Humberto Vaglio would never take lightly a challenge to his authority. In Vaglio's first weeks in office, however, the urgent problems confronting him in Porvenir left little time for Nargana. Told of the incident, the intendente contented himself with informing President Porras, mildly querying Charly Robinson, and counseling prudence to the government agents on the spot.[7]

Over the next few weeks, the parties to the incident contested its interpretation in communications sent to outside authorities, ending in Ramón Garrido's formal complaint.[8] Vaglio, shrewdly guessing that Robinson acted out of fear of losing ground to the militant young men led by Claudio Iglesias, vowed to visit Nargana in order to intervene on the side of youth and to impress on Robinson that all power in San Blas derived from the government and himself.[9]

The occasion presented itself two weeks later, in a petition from Claudio's group

alleging that Robinson and his followers had attacked them while they were inno-
cently playing dominos at a store owned by Claudio, merely because it sold alcohol.
According to a police report, the attackers mobbed and beat Iglesias and dragged
one of the government's indigenous policemen off to jail. The petition, exploiting
Charly Robinson's well-known preference for the United States, added: "You should
know that we are not Americans, nor are we governed by American laws, but rather
Panamanian, the same as the flag that waves above us."[10] As the struggle heated up,
Robinson was also accused of snubbing the education inspector, pressuring families
to switch to Coope and Purdy's schools, making invidious comparisons between
Panamanian weakness and U.S. strength, and asserting his authority to rule as
dictator.[11]

None of this went down well with Vaglio, who personally intervened in a public
meeting on Nargana. Asserting a government monopoly on power, which left only
residual authority to chiefs, Vaglio asked how Robinson had presumed to arrest one
of the government's agents, to which Robinson could only reply sheepishly that he
had not understood the law. Vaglio dressed him down for arbitrariness, disrespect
to the school inspector, and lack of patriotism: if Panama lacked cannons and
airplanes, he insisted, it was through trust in international law, not poverty. After
various witnesses accused the chief of violating their rights, Vaglio imposed his
settlement: Robinson was to give up his policemen, and he was to share power with
Claudio Iglesias and Ramón Garrido.[12]

After this intervention, the two factions on Nargana returned to the struggle,
organizing and plotting locally while sending out letters and reports that put their
case either to Vaglio or to his superiors in Panama. In a letter to President Porras,
Claudio's group condemned Robinson and praised the intendente for obtaining a
reconciliation of the two sides "with his characteristic adroitness like the *jefe* that he
is." (They made sure that Vaglio got a copy.)[13] The intendente's informants reported
that Robinson was holding numerous private meetings, in which he was even proposing to start a new village on the mainland.[14] Thoroughly angry, Vaglio wrote the
chief a long reprimand in shaky English, with a copy to President Porras.

Your promises for me worth nothing since you haven't try to fulfil them with good will
and sincerity. I am tired of so many words: to be or not to be, sir Robinson. . . .

Have you ever thought sir Robinson in the great satisfaction that afford the remem-
brance of the well-doing made in a town as an honest and equanimious commander . . .
sowing amidst the villages the seed of the wright . . . tell me if your conscience don't re-
proach you nothing.[15]

At this point Coope was drawn into the struggle as well. Through this period she
had been raising money from North American supporters to construct new mission

buildings on the two islands, with President Porras's permission. The police on Nargana reported, however, that Coope was inciting Robinson against the government and using the new buildings as propaganda to attract students away from the government school. Vaglio, who proposed eliminating Coope's schools altogether, sent her a letter halting construction. In addition, Porras ordered the Catholic mission buildings taken by Coope in 1913 turned over to the government.[16] Coope received the word just as construction began.

April 16, 1919. . . . A beautiful morning. I have been busy with my housework and now a few minutes to rest. Looking out at my door I can see the carpenters. Twenty-eight concrete pillars are going up and there are to be thirty-six. Think of it! We are preparing for other missionaries who will come. . . . Oh, the enemy has been busy. On April 1st, a truly remarkable day, three Panamanian policemen came to my house, gave me a very official letter to stop building this house. Well, you can imagine my feelings.[17]

After communicating those feelings in strong terms to Ramón Garrido, by 10 a.m. the same day Coope was in a canoe on her way to beard Vaglio (whom she called "the old Dago"), arriving at Porvenir the same afternoon.[18]

He said, "Well, if you have been telling them that all these six years, they ought to be converted." I told him some of them were. He said he was a free thinker, and I said, "So am I. Whom the son of God makes free is free indeed, and the Bible is the only Book that gives us freedom."[19]

The upshot of their confrontation was that Coope gained permission to continue building but only by signing a contract severely restricting the scope of her work: she was forbidden to teach school, and even her missionizing activities were to be conducted outside of school hours, at night and on Sundays.[20]

During these same weeks the issue of schools became mixed with a seemingly unrelated matter, that of the dress of Kuna women and girls, specifically the gold rings worn through the septums of their noses and the bead ligatures with which they wrapped their arms and legs. At the beginning of the year, when Cimral Colman had complained that Charly Robinson had punished a couple for piercing their infant daughter's nose, the intendente assured Colman that despite his appreciation of just "how ugly and unhealthy this custom is," he favored toleration of noserings on adult women and a gradual, noncoercive phasing out for young girls, "to the contentment of all."[21]

Gradual, however, turned out in practice to mean weeks rather than years, and contentment was far from universal. In early April President Porras ordered Vaglio to ban the wearing of noserings and leg-bindings by Indian schoolgirls, and in May he sent the same order directly to the schoolteachers on Nargana and Corazón.[22]

Soon all of the schoolgirls attended classes with unbound limbs and unadorned noses.[23] Detachment head Garrido formally recorded the support of Charly Robinson as well as Claudio Iglesias, and in a letter he noted approvingly "Robinson is as smooth as silk; I can assure you that this time it is not a farce."[24]

Toward the end of May, however, on his return from another island, Garrido found that the farce had resumed. Three itinerant jewelers who made gold ornaments for Kuna women had stirred the Indians up, asserting that every Panamanian could wear anything she wanted and promising to defend anyone who resisted the order.[25] Even without outside meddling, many schoolgirls missed their noserings: at the beginning of June some began wearing them outside school hours, and Ana de James complained that Anna Coope was allowing their use in mission services.[26] At the beginning of June, while Garrido was again away, opponents of the ban held a meeting to organize resistance.

It appears that many of these men had initially been complacent on the dress issue, perhaps until their wives and daughters woke them up. Charly Robinson, for his part, clearly disliked noserings, but as the battle lines were drawn, he could hardly throw his lot in with Claudio and his group, while the men on the other side, some of whom wanted noserings saved and some simply to have them phased out more slowly, included many key supporters of the Protestant school and Charly's leadership. Whether Robinson liked the issue or not, he had little choice concerning which side to take.

Much more was at stake than mere ornamentation or one chief's declining power: for both Indians and Latins, women's dress symbolized in a fundamental way the ethnic identity of the Kuna and their separation from national society. Both friends and enemies of noserings came to understand that an attack on women's dress was merely the opening battle of a general war against all of indigenous culture.

The government had not begun with the centerpiece of women's dress, the reverse-appliqué *mola* blouse, which has since emerged as a key symbol of Kuna identity.[27] They began instead with noserings and limb bindings, because these ornaments modified and distorted the body much more radically and thus, much like foot-binding as seen by westerners in China, epitomized everything barbarous-seeming about indigenous culture. In 1910 a newspaper article on President Mendoza's visit to San Blas asserted that Kuna women lived shorter lives than men because of limb binding,[28] and Enrique Hurtado's report from 1913 noted that Nargana appeared civilized, except for the women, with their "legs cinched up with cords and laces."[29] Thus government functionaries could argue that they were freeing female bodies rather than constraining them, and that in general they were liberating the Kuna from barbarity.[30]

As the dress issue heated up through the month of June, Charly Robinson tried to obscure his connection with the pro-nosering faction. Despite Garrido's efforts to keep him on-island, in the early hours of the fifth of June, Robinson left for Porvenir, where he convinced Vaglio of his innocence, asserting that he had wanted to suppress those who spoke out on noserings but did not dare do so while Garrido was away.[31] Informed of Robinson's end run, Garrido replied scathingly that Charly did his agitating "secretly . . . in order to be able later to [claim] that the village rose up against him because the police weren't there."[32]

In mid-June, while Garrido was again off-island, Robinson sent off a delegation to President Porras, the party slipping away in the night to avoid the police. A reporter for the *Panama Star and Herald,* intrigued by the issue, spoke in the city with Robinson's four English-speaking delegates, Jim Phillips, Jack Archibold, Charles Smith, and Joe Harvey: they said they supported the gradual phasing out of noserings but not instant elimination or the fining of recalcitrant women. After a week waiting in vain for an interview, the four gave up. Meanwhile, as soon as Garrido returned to Nargana, Claudio and several of *his* supporters left for Panama with police blessings, where presumably, they received a warmer welcome.[33]

On the nineteenth, Coope wrote in a letter:

Well some policemen come up and arrested the Chief's brother and a young married man because Alfred, the Chief's brother, whose eldest girl came to my school, and all the girls have to take the ring out of their noses by order of the President. Well, I heartily approve of it and have done my very best to get them to do it; so has the Chief and he has set them the example by not having his two little girls' noses or ears pierced. Well the government is doing it in such a fighty way, demanding that they do it, that of course the Indians are mad clear thru. And while they have taken out the ring from the smallest girls, the big girls would not take out the ring, not even those who had been going to the public school. Ever since this order was issued they left school. Force work will never do like love. They love us and when we talk of anything that is bad and tell them, they agree and talk and think and change, so that before Government orders, many of the babies had no noserings.[34]

Things came to a head on June 29, just as Garrido left the island on another trip.[35] The police tried to arrest three agitators, one of them Charly Robinson's brother Alfred, only to be attacked by a large body of men armed with staves, machetes, and guns. Alfred boasted that they were not afraid of the government, adding that from then on, all the schoolgirls would wear noserings and attend the mission school. A group of rebels crossed over to Corazón de Jesús to attack the indigenous police, who had to be rescued by their Panamanian colleagues and several forest workers. Stores in the village refused to sell to teachers, and rebels threatened to burn down the house where an agent boarded unless his Kuna landlord threw him out.[36] Many years later, one Nargana man remembered the day vividly.[37]

People were making such a noise, a great racket. . . . Off we went, running. . . . Claudio was an unusual man, tall, and strong, strong. Two men were holding him by the arms . . . Aii! well look! . . . old men were fighting on the ground with youths. . . . . On and on and on. Then they pried him loose. Then they got him out. Fierce, Claudio was, umh! On the point, on Nargana's point.

Alicio Iglesias did not take kindly to his son's capture. "He was a tough old man. He got a piece of iron. 'The person who seized my son, I'll finish him off!'" Claudio himself was in the little jail, "smashing at things, crash! that's what he did. Knocking things down." Quieted by his followers through a window, he got free that night and fled to Porvenir in a canoe. As the immediate furor died down, teachers and police sent off urgent requests for relief, and they holed up "arms at the ready, waiting for the attack."[38] In her plea, Ana de James alluded to "these regions where duty has placed us as true heroes of civilization and conquest," and she expressed a willingness to die like a martyred saint "so long as you defend the blood of the innocent."[39]

A relief force set out from Porvenir, but no motor launch being available, it consisted only of Lieutenant Antonio Linares and two police agents in a canoe. Linares began an inquiry into the incident, only to be slipped a note urging him to suspend proceedings because a large mass of armed Indians had gathered behind him. When he persisted, Agent Guillermo Denis came close and pointed out that their little group could never resist if such a mass of men attacked. Linares gave up for the moment, sending an urgent request for men, weapons, and ammunition.[40]

After a further delay of two days, reinforcements finally arrived, led by the intendente himself. Summoning Charly Robinson, Vaglio dressed him down "as strongly as might be for the reprehensible conduct of his indians. . . . Robinson spoke hardly at all, he was stammering."[41] Having made sure that children went back to school, the girls without noserings, Vaglio held a meeting. His discourse on dress and obedience, which he himself termed "prolix," was briefly interrupted when his agents confiscated a gun being aimed at his back through a cane wall.[42]

On the basis of his investigation of the uprising, Vaglio imposed a total of $147.50 in fines on nineteen of the rebels, prominent among them the chief's brother Alfred. Although Charly Robinson's own involvement in the attempted coup could not be proven, he was held responsible nonetheless for payment of the fines. As Belisario Porras approvingly wrote to Vaglio, "The imposition of these fines . . . is one more proof of the complete submission of these Indians. There is no bad from which good does not come."[43]

As damaging as the aborted uprising was to Charly Robinson's failing fortunes, hopes for complete submission were premature. Consolidating the victory, the government gave Claudio Iglesias the title of honorary police chief and threw

Robinson's men off the force.[44] Robinson, however, visited Porras in September and briefly persuaded the president not only of his own improved behavior but also of undue harshness on Vaglio's part. He had not reckoned, however, with Vaglio's skill at bureaucratic hardball: he was summoned to Porvenir for a formal deposition, in which relentless questioning forced him to deny everything he had previously affirmed, with the result that his standing with the president sank even lower than before.[45]

Vaglio advertised his triumph in the published report of the Ministry of Government and Justice, announcing that "today Robinson has had to accept that I am his *Jefe.*"[46] Claudio and his group, in contrast, had "struggled with daring against the rancidness of the old ones," constituting "a palpable example of the good that schools provide us, . . . since these youths educated by the government, who have learned to love their flag and its hymn . . . are today those who truly love Panama."[47]

Vaglio blamed Coope in the report for inciting the chief to rebellion and troublemaking. At the end of the year he wrote Porras again, alleging that Coope continued holding out the hope to the Indians that the United States would annex San Blas and guarantee their liberties. President Porras, angry at the "antipatriotic proceedings" and "the efforts of Miss Coope to sow anarchy on that coast," urged Vaglio to keep her in check, though he did not heed his subordinate's advice to eject the mission altogether, probably because he feared the reaction of Coope's North American and British supporters.[48]

In July of 1919, the return of Coope's foremost disciple, Alicibiades, or Lonny Iglesias, brought her as much pain as joy. Coope had sent Lonny off in 1916 to Nyack Bible Institute in New York State. World War I had closed the school, and along with a few other Kuna boys, Lonny had been sent to a Protestant mission school in Venezuela, where the boys had been mistreated. When Lonny and two other boys reached home, Claudio Iglesias and his father Alicio, already enemies of Coope, blamed her for what had happened. Although Lonny did not break off relations with her, he did fall under his older brother's sway. To all appearances, Coope had lost her prime convert forever.[49]

If the struggles of 1919 had been confined to the two islands, Robinson and Coope might have triumphed. But national power, however tenuous in San Blas, tipped the scales in the other direction. More than numbers of supporters and local maneuvering, what mattered was success in external communication, success especially in what sociologists call labeling, meaning efforts to attach moral judgments to actions and personalities. The party won that best communicated its version of what was happening, painting the situation in colors favoring itself over its opponents. Despite the facile persuasiveness that had served Charly Robinson so well since 1904, the young modernists were able to play on his weaknesses, especially his alliance with Coope and his gringophilia, persuading first the police and teachers, then the intendente, then the president, that Robinson was not the "paladin of civilization" and friend of the government he had once been considered but an obstructive, power-hungry rebel manipulated by a meddlesome, anti-patriotic foreigner.

The outcome of the struggle had far-reaching effects. Beyond the fortunes of Coope's mission or Charly's Robinson's political career, beyond even the trajectory of change on which Nargana was now moving, the turbulence there affected the way in which the government's representatives in San Blas understood their struggle with the Kuna. The police and modernists had been opposed on Nargana by an ad hoc alliance of pagan conservatives and moderates thrown together with Yankee-loving Protestant progressives. However ephemeral that coalition and incompatible its members, it established a connection in the official mind, which feared "the denationalization of a large and important portion of the national territory by means of the tolerance of the government and the implantation of customs, senti-ments, idiom, and religion completely different from national ones."[50] After 1919 the problem as seen from Porvenir and the presidencia was not just to civilize and pacify half-savage Indians but at the same time to eradicate the seditious effects of North American influence in San Blas.

13.
Humberto
Vaglio
Takes
Charge

Belisario Porras, inaugurated for a new term in October of 1918, soon received reports of disarray in San Blas. To clean up the mess and to implement his plans for civilizing the Indians, he appointed a new intendente, an out-of-work foreign-born engineer named Humberto Vaglio.[1] On his arrival in Porvenir, Vaglio, never one to mince words, reported that he found the intendente's office in "total chaos," with accounts and other essential records in disarray or missing altogether. The buildings and dock were falling down, the launches were out of commission, and discipline was so lax that one agent, thought to be stationed in Carti just a few miles away, had actually been in Colón for the past four months. "The administration is a veritable absurdity."[2]

Vaglio set immediately to putting things right.[3] After straightening out the books, he moved to strengthen the embargo on the rebel chief Inabaginya, to exclude Colombian boats from the coastal trade, and to tax and regulate Panamanian vessels.[4] He reorganized his domain into three districts, each with its own police detachment, and supervised the administration of the national census in San Blas. (The census-takers counted seventeen thousand Kuna.)[5] When the next election came around in 1920, he organized balloting in the villages ready for national politics: clubs with the name "Fatherland and Porras" were formed in several communities, and Nargana and Corazón de Jesús unanimously returned 194 votes for the Liberal Party ticket.[6]

Most of all, Humberto Vaglio worked to impose control. Over the first half of 1919, while he was bringing Charlie Robinson to heel, he also cooperated with Chief Cimral Colman to overcome the resistance of several islands in Carti and Mandinga Bay that four years previously had defied Belisario Porras and that still flew the Colombian flag—an intolerable insult to Panamanian sovereignty and his own authority. Colman, for his part, undoubtedly worked with Vaglio partly in hopes that the villages might be induced to give up on Inabaginya as well as Colombia, something that ultimately did not happen.

What the intendente did not tell Colman was that he intended to play him off against his rivals, Inabaginya and Charly Robinson, and to impose his will on *all* of them.[7] As he wrote later that year:

Slight or rather almost null was the Sovereignty and Authority of Panama on the Coast; I noted with distress in what small regard the Saguilas [that is, chiefs] and indigenous people held the authority of the Jefe of the Circumscription, and it is clear that the authority of the government could only be null so long as the indigenous tribes did not understand that the true Great Saguila of the Coast cannot be nor should be other than the representative of the government.[8]

Vaglio began his campaign with a visit to a village called Chucumbali, "In the Bay."[9] After lecturing villagers about commerce and education, he complained about the Colombian flag flying overhead, only to be told that it was their flag, and besides, the Panamanian flag was ugly. He returned the first thing next morning with a squad of police, who knocked a few heads with their rifle butts, tore down the flag, and took the island's chief off to Porvenir to sign a declaration of loyalty to Panama.[10] Soon all the villages in western San Blas capitulated, and the intendente put in an order for new flags.[11]

President Porras's reaction to Vaglio's struggles against rebel Indians revealed a contradiction in official thinking between persuading and coercing. At one point, Porras urged "soft and convincing measures, which demonstrate that we are civilized men, because in no other way will we justify ourselves in aiming to carry civilization to . . . an inferior race." But a few weeks later he congratulated Vaglio for the success of the measures taken in Chucumbali, which if persuasive, were anything but soft.[12] For his part, Vaglio had no ambivalence about either means or ends so long as Kuna chiefs "recognize and reconcile themselves to the fact that they are no more than mere honorary employees of the Government and . . . agree that their traditional divine rights pass into history."[13]

The next step was to overcome the great rebel Inabaginya himself. On a visit to Ustupu or Portogandi at the end of May, a hostile crowd told him the pro-Colombian chief Yaigun was with Inabaginya at Sasardi, daring Vaglio to follow him there.[14] The thought that "perhaps this was said to me . . . to test my valor and character" convinced him to take up the challenge. Once in Inabaginya's presence, Vaglio pointed out that nothing more could be expected from Colombia in San Blas and that Panamanian patience would eventually wear thin. He proposed a deal by which Inabaginya would gradually change national allegiance, and in return the

Panamanian government would confirm his titles as chief or *saguila* and "honorary general," the commercial blockade would be lifted, and no more concessions would be granted for exploitation of forest products in eastern San Blas.[15] After further contacts, Inabaginya made the change, whose inevitability he now recognized, and he later visited the government in Panama.[16] Vaglio, who was surprisingly ready to like and admire his adversary, thereafter cultivated the chief as an ally and informant.

Despite these early successes, many things went badly for the new intendente. He soon ran up against the same obstacles that had hampered his predecessors — shortages of equipment and supplies, insufficient funding, unreliable transport, and, regarding his employees, problems of both quality and quantity. Although he received an extra ten men in early 1920, he never had nearly enough agents to do all that was expected of him, and of those he did have, some were competent, honest, and sober, and others were anything but.[17]

The problem with finding enough good men was, first of all, that intendentes had little to offer them. In his first days Vaglio was greeted by a police petition asking for a much needed raise: half their salary, the petitioners said, went to food; clothes washing was ruinously expensive; on special missions they had to pay their own costs; and in return they were stuck with a "monotonous and sedentary life."[18] They could have added that 5 percent was deducted from salaries during election years, and that paychecks were often late and hard to cash. Vaglio did what he could, but he had no direct control over salaries and conditions.[19]

He could attempt the augean, and ultimately sysyphean, task of disciplining the force and eliminating its worst offenders, who included officers as well as regulars. After firing four "worthless" policemen and the corregidor of Puerto Obaldía in his first few weeks in office,[20] later that year Vaglio had to deal with a sublieutenant who rejected his orders and criticized him to the newspapers, another who made off with sixteen hundred dollars, and still another who in three drunken days successively threatened his fellows with a revolver, a bayonet, a club, and nitric acid.[21]

If anything, 1920 was worse. One agent quit immediately on arrival, dismayed, according to Vaglio, at finding that he was actually expected to work. A detachment head complained of two subordinates who were habitually drunk, undisciplined, scandalous, and menacing toward other policemen and the people of the village. And in November Agent Ramón Ramos was transferred from Porvenir, where he had been refusing work, mistreating prisoners, and offending his colleagues, to Playón Chico, where he promptly slandered the teacher.[22] Other requested firings in 1920 included Diego Arosemena (said to be habitually drunk), Enrique Barsaillo (insolent to superiors), Francisco Lombardo (lazy, a liar), Manuel Amores (lazy, insubordinate), J. M. Tejada ("worthless"), Cristobal Cuenca (cut a blanket in two and stole half), Isidro Junca (multiple offenses), and Mario Luzcando (drunk).[23] In addition, all the agents at Puerto Obaldía were punished for going off to a dance and leaving the barracks in the charge of prisoners, who promptly cleaned out the detachment's funds from a drawer.[24]

Supply and transport problems also persisted. Vaglio scrounged materials for a little construction on Porvenir during 1919, but at the end of the following year police on the four pacified islands were still living and working downstairs in the village schoolhouses (which were all in need of repair), without barracks of their own.[25] By hook or crook, he managed to get a few revolvers and to retire some of the most decrepit rifles, but as late as mid-1920 a few of his men still had no firearms at all.[26] He pleaded in vain for a navigation light at Porvenir, pumps for fresh water, and even a decent typewriter—he was told that all he needed was a change of ribbon.[27] The official boat, the *San Blas,* alternated between disrepair and complete breakdown, and a more recently acquired launch, the *Santa Isabel,* had never been much even in its youth twenty-five years before. As a result, when the intendente needed to confront rebellious Indians, as often as not he had no way to get his men to the scene of the trouble.[28]

The source of these problems was all too apparent: insufficient funds. The two-year budget for 1919-1921, adopted over Vaglio's protests, was $36,000, an amount, he noted scathingly, less than the aggregate salaries of the Circumscription's employees. He managed to get this figure increased by $15,000, still not enough to cover salaries completely, and at the end of 1920 he calculated that more than $13,000 was needed just to limp through to the end of the fiscal period.[29]

Vaglio also discovered that villages amenable to hauling up a Panamanian flag were not necessarily willing to accept teachers and policemen. His plan to station men on Carti, Ailigandi, Ustupu, and two other islands was so firmly and successfully rebuffed that two years later he had not succeeded in imposing either barracks or schools in any of them.[30] Even on the islands where teachers and police were already stationed, conflict erupted when they began enforcing school attendance, especially when they banned chichas and noserings.

Vaglio, who took being thwarted very personally, soon came to identify Cimral Colman as the source of his troubles, a conclusion that, while it neglected the broad base of Kuna resistance, correctly singled out his most formidable opponent. During the months that Inabaginya metamorphosed in the intendente's eyes from the great rebel to a friend of the government (if a somewhat unreliable one), Colman went through a reverse transformation, from ally to rebel.

At first Vaglio tried to shrug off criticisms of Colman for the sake of their alliance, calling him "the best friend of Panama" and "a likeable old man."[31] The goodwill began to dissipate within a few months, after an apparently successful meeting in early April with Colman and his lieutenants. Vaglio thought he had come away with an agreement to prohibit the importation of alcohol, to limit chiefs to one-year renewable terms of office, and to begin removing limb-bindings from women and realigning houses into orderly rows. In return, Vaglio suggested arrangements for patrolling the western border of San Blas to keep out costeño interlopers.[32] His satisfaction evaporated on hearing of Colman's claims that the prohibition on liquor did not include homemade chicha (an oversight on Vaglio's part, soon remedied), that the intendente had backed off on imposing schools (mostly true), and that Colman had intimidated Vaglio, this last a claim that greatly offended Vaglio. He also heard that Colman was traveling around encouraging resistance to schools and changes in custom.[33]

Relations deteriorated still further a few weeks later, when Colman temporarily derailed the effort to get schoolgirls out of noserings. Belisario Porras had sent the orders to suppress traditional ornaments in April and May directly to the intendente and to the schoolteachers on the four pacified islands, apparently without informing his secretary of government and justice, Ricardo Alfaro. In response, Colman went directly to the secretary, who without knowing that he was countermanding a presidential order, sent instructions that Kuna girls should be allowed to wear whatever they wanted. Vaglio quickly straightened out the confusion, getting the ban on noserings reinstated, and the upshot of Colman's action was to alienate the president as well as the intendente.[34]

By the time Vaglio submitted his first biennial report a few weeks later, his mind was made up about his ex-friend. His anger, sense of betrayal, and personal antagonism burn on the page.

Simral Colman, whom I supposed would be a help to the government when this past January he offered me his friendship and support, is the one who is most resistant to everything that might be called civilization and progress. What most mortifies me about this rancid old Indian is his character, as false as it is fickle, that desires to continue exploiting his villages with absurd and ridiculous tales that he calls traditions of his race. In everything and for everything he invokes the God of the Indians, and to him he attributes everything he wants to do or what suits him that the superstitious indigenous people should believe.

Of slight intelligence, of no personal value and of little character, rather he is allowed to dominate by the Saguilas who have him as head. Vain . . . General Colman would like to cover his body with a brilliant uniform and burden it with a multitude of decorations, even though these are of copper and have no value. . . . What can we expect of this Saguila? Nothing. But I will entreat Colman and put an end to his Saguila-ship . . . and I will leave him so that in the future he bears no more than the name of Saguila, just as I have done with his like Robinson.[35]

The intendente especially hated being lied to. In his tactless belligerence, he told one Kuna chief, "It is true that lies are innate in Indians, just as it pleases them to be the carrier of everything bad and uproarious."[36] His accusations, however prejudiced, were not completely wrong. The Kuna, who felt strongly about truthfulness among themselves, had no qualms about lying to wagas. Colman, while less devious than Charly Robinson, was quite willing to placate the government with false promises and once back on the coast, to distort what officials had said to him.

Vaglio, to be sure, could not see the beam in his own eye. He did not tell his ally Colman of his plan to reduce all Kuna chiefs to figureheads, nor that he cultivated Colman "in order to obtain through his conduct in an indirect, dissimulating, and efficacious manner the faithful execution of our dispositions without [the Indians] noting any imposition on our part."[37] Vaglio also felt free to denigrate Kuna leaders in published reports while seeming to respect them face-to-face, and the government blithely disregarded its promises to exclude rubber-tappers and turtlers. Deception, in short, was hardly a Kuna monopoly.

Equally important, Vaglio and others in the government failed to understand that Kuna leaders put them off with false assurances because they felt they had no other options apart from outright defiance or complete capitulation. Promising to accept schools or prohibition without any intention of doing so was merely good policy, forced on them in what they saw as an unfair struggle against largely illegitimate power—a point of view Vaglio was incapable of even recognizing.

Kuna leaders, nonetheless, would have done themselves a service by lying less often and more adroitly. They seem not to have realized, at least at first, how frequently the intendente communicated with his superiors, how effective his intelligence gathering was, and thus how easily their lies would be detected. When they were caught out, they lost respect, not only from Vaglio but also from President Porras and Secretary Alfaro, and in the ongoing political game, disrespect reduced influence.[38]

Ultimately, however, Vaglio came to detest Colman less because he lied than because he thwarted his plans. As Colman began to understand Vaglio's goals in San Blas and his absolute unwillingness to compromise, noncompliance hardened into active resistance, antigovernment agitation, and especially on the issue of land, a search for private solutions.

Saving Kuna lands was a major preoccupation for Cimral Colman, just as it had been for Charly Robinson. At the beginning of the new administration, Colman had pinned his hopes on cooperation with the government, and President Porras did in fact issue a decree in early January 1919 prohibiting non-Indians from cultivating land anywhere in San Blas.[39] The measure, however, did not exclude rubber-tapping or agricultural colonies sponsored by the government, and as a decree rather than a law or legal title it offered little long-term security. Colman wrote Vaglio in February urging him to have a boundary line cut in the forest at the western end of the territory, because costeños from nearby villages continued making farms on land reserved for the Indians, and in their April meeting Vaglio suggested stationing a border guard.[40]

José de la Rosa.

Within a short time, however, Colman gave up on the government. He hired a lawyer from Colón named José de la Rosa, who became his *apoderado general,* a legal role combining aspects of a general counsel and the power of attorney. De la Rosa drew up a memorial to President Porras, a formal petition asking him to grant the Kuna collective title to their lands, and the latter, in a memo to his attorney general requesting a legal opinion, indicated that he was "in principle in favor of this measure to guard these peoples from the rapacity of strangers."[41]

In the end nothing came of the petition, and de la Rosa devised a scheme to secure land titles for the villages in Colman's confederacy. The contract they drew up obligated Colman to pay $12.50 in five installments for each of one thousand Kuna participants, in return for which de la Rosa would have their lands surveyed and title secured. If for any reason Colman's group backed out on the contract, the money already paid would not be returned.[42] Not only was the scheme unlikely to succeed, but its terms strongly favored de la Rosa.

In a meeting at the presidential palace at which the intendente was present, the lawyer presented the plan to Belisario Porras, who not only approved but spoke in its favor to Colman. Porras, however, seems to have had in mind merely that the Kuna would register ownership of the coconut groves they were actually using, while Colman had the more ambitious goal of gaining title to all the land in the domain of his confederacy's villages or even to all of San Blas. According to the rumors that reached Vaglio's ears, Colman's agents were also claiming that once having obtained title, they would be able to throw out the Intendencia, police, and schools and continue with chichas and noserings.[43] To raise cash for their quotas, Colman's followers began assiduously gathering coconuts and even going into the forest after ivorynuts, and since not everyone in Colman's group was overjoyed by the titling scheme, his agents had to pressure villagers to contribute.

Vaglio's initial worries soon turned to outrage. In September of 1919 he communicated his concerns to his superiors, enclosing complaints from Colman's enemies and suggesting that the titling be supervised in Porvenir. Contradicted by Porras, who reiterated his support for the scheme, Vaglio hastened to explain that he had no interest in a "war" against de la Rosa, desiring only that the program be properly supervised and that it not encourage disorder and sedition.[44] As the heavy-handed collection of money continued, however, a verbal war did ensue. Not only did the initiative challenge the intendente's position as maximum authority on the coast, but it implicitly abrogated functions such as taxation and territorial control that any good bureaucrat would consider properly the government's. From late 1919 all through 1920, Vaglio and his police lieutenant, Antonio Linares, kept up a stream of communications denouncing the scheme while reporting on Colman's obstinacy and his agents' depredations.[45] The president and the secretary, however, somewhat reluctantly renewed permission, as long as collections were voluntary.[46]

Conflict over land titling, rather than a war to itself, constituted one front in a wider struggle to control the flow of information in and out of San Blas. Just as the factions on Nargana had struggled to get out their versions of what was going on there, so when Cimral Colman got no satisfaction from Humberto Vaglio, he made end runs around him to the city, complaining that a certain policeman was mistreating people, that costeños were invading the forests, or that women were being arbitrarily deprived of their noserings. Although the complaints sometimes distorted events, he seldom had the need to lie, because the police and intendente did not want those higher up the chain of command to know everything that went on, and because Vaglio and his immediate superior, Secretary Alfaro, had distinctly different viewpoints and dispositions. Alfaro was a moderate and distinguished aristocrat, soon to be secretary of foreign affairs and later briefly president. He and (to a lesser extent) President Porras really did expect to civilize the Kuna primarily through persuasion and pressure, as they insisted repeatedly, whereas the men on the spot, frustrated by Indian intransigence and perfidy, felt quite justified in using force.

In their struggles to get the word out to Porras, Alfaro, and the public, the players in the game of information politics had a great deal to say about each other as well as about events in San Blas. In sociological terms, they tried to label each other. From mid-1919 on, Vaglio kept up a stream of vituperation against Colman, portraying him as an unprincipled monster of incredible deviousness interested only in his own power. In this effort he was assisted by Inabaginya, who, soon after pledging allegiance to Panama, began sending letters to the intendente denouncing his rival and reporting on his activities. The following example is unusual only in its brevity.[47]

This is exclusively to inform you [about] the propaganda that Señor Colman is making, now in [his] arrival [back in San Blas], well to reunite all the villages that are with him, and he said to them: That a minister had come from every foreign nation to speak with him, in order to lend him support in the matter of the purchase of the lands, that everything is now arranged, only five thousand pesos is lacking. And to that end, those villages are paying. With regard to you, he says that he absolutely does not have to have anything to do with you, since he says that you are trembling with fear of the attitude that he has taken in this matter, which I believe to be a lie.

> Your Friend,
> Inapaquiña

From one perspective, Vaglio did quite well in this game. President Porras accepted the intendente's unflattering portraits of Colman and Charly Robinson, and although Colman sometimes succeeded in getting the ear of Secretary Alfaro, the intendente was generally able to fend off questions from the Secretariat about Kuna complaints by instituting a perfunctory inquiry, quibbling with details, or dismissing the matter out of hand. Whether or not Alfaro always bought Vaglio's version of events, in most cases there was little he could do without calling his subordinate a liar or overriding him altogether. Moreover, just as Colman made end runs around Porvenir, so Vaglio—who counted Belisario Porras as a godfather of his child and who in their more personal correspondence addressed the president as *compadre*— was able to exploit his relationship with Porras, sending him copies of his communications to the secretary and sometimes bypassing Alfaro altogether.[48]

Despite this success, Vaglio fumed at Colman's ability to put obstacles in his way, and he felt, quite correctly, that his superiors' willingness to listen to Kuna leaders undercut his own power. In September of 1919, in the wake of several visits to Panama by Colman, Nele, and Charly Robinson, Vaglio wrote Alfaro and Porras:[49]

This cannot continue in this way, and since it is necessary that I have the authority among the Indians that I ought to, I beg you that you do not receive them any more dealing with administrative matters concerning this Coast, and that you oblige all of them to come to an understanding with me. This is the only way to make them obey and respect the orders of this headquarters, and that they should understand that the Jefe of the Circumscription is not a mummy whom they can mock, because his excellency the President of the Republic is his friend and attends to him well.

Porras, who as an old-style caudillo, kept an open door at the presidential palace, was unsympathetic:

What you ask of me is impossible. The executive cannot abandon the administration of the Coast to your single will, nor is it possible for me to refuse to hear the indians when they come to see me. What you should seek is to join the legal dispositions that prevail on the Coast to the kindness and persuasion indispensable in order to treat with inferior peoples as the indians are.[50]

Vaglio was forced to backpedal rapidly, denying that he wanted autocratic powers or to cut the president out of decision making. Thus, at the end of 1919, the struggle to dominate the Indians that had begun a year before and the game of information politics it had generated, far from ending, continued to grow and intensify.[51]

14.
Confrontation and Embitterment

By late 1919 Humberto Vaglio had been in office for the better part of a year. He had soundly defeated Charly Robinson and Anna Coope, assuring the dominance of Claudio Iglesias and his young followers on Nargana, and he had induced Inabaginya to abandon Colombia in favor of Panama. But things were going less well with Cimral Colman, who was emerging as his most formidable opponent. Colman and Vaglio, like two boxers in their opening rounds, had traded a few jabs and taken each other's measure, but no one had yet landed a really solid blow, and Colman's tenacity had so far thwarted the intendente's hopes for an early knockout. (Vaglio would also have added, vehemently, that his handlers, the secretary and president, were not always in his corner, and that they had tied one hand behind his back.) By the end of 1920, one year later, a series of confrontations and violent incidents had embittered both sides, and though Humberto Vaglio had been knocked out of the ring, the victory did Cimral Colman little good.

The first incident took place just a few miles to the east of Nargana, in a small village known both as Tikantikki, "Strong River," and Niatupu, "Devil Island."[1] In November 1919 Niatupu was little more than a large hamlet of one or two hundred inhabitants in about fifteen houses, most of them strung out in a row facing the beach along the inner side of the island. The coconut palms around the houses gave way on the outer side to a mixture of brush, low seagrape thickets, mangroves, and some tall trees.

Originally a work camp, Niatupu had become a refuge for dissidents from Nargana. Some hated all teachers and missionaries, others had enrolled their children in Coope and Purdy's schools. Most kept up ties with kin left behind. But all of them detested what was happening in their old home. After the unsuccessful uprising in

Niatupu or Tigantiki.

June 1919, one of the ringleaders, a man named Kilu, had fled to Niatupu with his household, including an unmarried pregnant granddaughter; when she gave birth, the baby was killed.[2]

Humberto Vaglio, who now had a justification for showing rebel Kuna he was boss without fear of contradiction from his tender-hearted superiors, immediately blamed the "atrocious" crime on Kilu himself. Kuna oral tradition on the other hand, says the girl concealed her condition from housemates and secretly gave birth out of doors.[3] "Someone heard an infant crying in the seagrape. He said, 'Why is there crying there? Where is a baby coming from?'. . . He went to Grandfather [probably the village chief]. 'Grandfather, someone is crying. Why is someone crying there? A little person is crying.' Then grandfather said, 'Go get it for me, you hear!'" Once the mother's identity had been discovered and the baby had died and been buried, the incident might have ended, if gossip had not carried the news to Nargana. "By the end of that same day . . . the police already knew. . . . Someone who had been here was a big mouth."

Detachment head Ramón Garrido sent off an arresting party. Since the four agents arrived at midnight, a full eight hours after setting out, either they took their time, or else they were waiting until everyone was asleep. They arrested Kilu, still in his hammock, but a struggle ensued, in which Kilu's brother-in-law shot one of the policemen with his shotgun. The others fled east in their canoe, away from Nargana, leaving the lightly wounded agent behind in the brush, where he was found next morning. Village elders, vetoing suggestions to finish him off, sent the policeman with an escort in a sailing canoe to Carti, where other Kuna took him on to Porvenir.

Meanwhile, the three fleeing policemen had made it back to Nargana, and an armed party, led by Lieutenant Antonio Linares, set out for Niatupu in a launch, supposedly in search of the missing agent, though informants had told them he was on Porvenir. Linares's report claims that the Niatupu men fired at him first from the beach, and when he forced a landing, the thatch-roofed houses caught fire from dynamite thrown by the Indians and burning wads from their shotguns. The Kuna claim, much more plausibly, that the police came to retaliate.[4] The young men of the village wanted to fight, but their elders persuaded them to take the women to outer islands. When they went down to the shore to parlay, the police shot one old man dead on the spot, scattering the others.

The motorboat unloaded nothing but kerosene. Suach-suach-suach! they poured out the kerosene. Then they finished off the place. [The flames] flash-flash-flash-flash. . . . Over that way there was a big shop. . . . Wiped out! Gone! . . . The people had lost it all! The big pigs there, the pigs were all fried—tiiii!—the pigs were bubbling and frying. . . . Like burning off old forest, that's what happened, you hear. The place was giving off smoke, smoking, smoking, it was like that all day! We got up the next day and it was still burning like that.[5]

In the aftermath of Niatupu's destruction, Vaglio and his enemies struggled to interpret its meaning. The intendente seized on the incident to plead for more resources and power, and to castigate Colman, who had in fact not been involved.[6] He also made sure the police version of events was prominently reported in the *Panama Star and Herald* under the headline "San Blas Redskins on Warpath over Quilo's Arrest."[7] Colman's lawyer countered with a contrary version in *El Diario*, prompting Vaglio to expel de la Rosa's informant, an itinerant jeweler, from San Blas.[8]

The next incident, which took place a few weeks later, grew out of tensions between the Kuna and outsiders exploiting the forests and coastal waters of San Blas, tensions that rose as extraction intensified. The intendencia's figures for 1919 indicate that in addition to more than five million coconuts and just over a thousand pounds of turtle shell, both produced mostly by the Kuna themselves, 251,000 pounds of ivorynuts, 169,000 pounds of balata latex from the níspero tree, and 2,000 pounds of *raicilla*, the plant from which the medicine ipecac is produced, were legally shipped out of the Circumscription.[9] (In the other direction, $93,000 worth of merchandise was imported into the district to be sold to the Kuna.)[10] Friction also developed at Mandinga, as work on the Hyatt banana plantations got under way.

The intendente and his subordinates acted in what they saw as an even-handed fashion, forcing Kuna villages to let forest workers into their territories and to supply them with porters, while also punishing tappers and plantation workers who stole from Kuna farms.[11] Neither side was appeased. The situation deteriorated further toward the end of 1919, with a number of hostile confrontations, one involving Inabaginya personally.[12] Although Vaglio decreed a complete ban on the sale of firearms, several villages in eastern San Blas colluded with pliable merchant captains to smuggle in guns and ammunition.[13]

Then on January 15, 1920, a rubber tapper staggered down to the shore a few miles west of Sasardi with the story that his party, camped at the headwaters of the Navagandi River, had been fired upon from out of the dark one night as they finished cooking their latex.[14] The police could not respond, being short of arms and men and for the moment without a seaworthy vessel. The corregidor of Puerto Obaldía railed against the Indians, proposing that "a single man in an Airplane [could] destroy these peoples who will never in any way become civilized."[15]

By the time the story reached the city, it had taken on lurid coloration, with a newspaper report that Indians had massacred seventeen on Porvenir itself.[16] A later article offered the comments of "a San Blas Chieftan" in Colón: "Tuli sogi chippoo arabi mai sholie," which was translated as "we don't want white men there." Since the speaker actually said something more like "People say the white [boat], the Arabia, isn't there," the reporter seems to have exercised some creative license in his translation.[17]

The dead, it turned out, only numbered five, but their bodies had been mutilated.[18] Vaglio, who most blamed Inabaginya for instigating the attack while offering his friendship to the government, wrote the secretary: "You should know that these Indians must be treated with rigor, especially in cases like these, since with sweets we will never get anywhere."[19] In March, he arrested the chief.[20] Frustrated by a lack of proof—no Kuna would make a statement—he nonetheless proposed forcing him to pay reparations to the family of each dead tapper, but Secretary Alfaro ordered Inabaginya freed unless proof was forthcoming.[21] Inabaginya, somewhat chastened but eager as ever to get his rivals, suggested that Nele Wardada be arrested just as he had been.[22]

The struggle over outside intrusions would not end. Not only did the forest workers return, but the government soon opened turtle fishing to non-Indians for the first time since 1915. During the months before the presidential contest of 1920, the costeño men of Santa Isabel threatened to sit out the election unless the ban on turtling was lifted, in which case they promised to vote en bloc for Porras. The latter quickly gave in, noting that "their vote in this matter does not leave room for doubt."²³ Although Vaglio tried to defuse the issue by reserving turtling on beaches and islands for the Kuna and the open sea for non-Indians, the compromise satisfied no one. Armed parties of Kuna attacked turtlers or confiscated their catch and equipment, and both Inabaginya and Colman complained repeatedly that outsiders were taking all the turtles and looting their island coconut groves.²⁴

Colman had not been involved in the attack on the rubber-tappers, but he got no credit from Intendente Vaglio, and the two kept up their game of information politics, in which the primary move was calling foul. After a visit to Panama by Colman, Vaglio pulled in his escort for questioning, and the chief's secretary had to flee to Colombia.²⁵ The antagonists traded accusations concerning Mandinga, Colman alleging that plantation workers were invading Kuna lands, Vaglio that Indians were menacing the workers, and when Secretary Alfaro came in person to verify the company's compliance with its government contract, Colman turned up uninvited to lodge further complaints. Vaglio and his subordinates — who blamed all problems on "the obstacles that without any good reason whatsoever are presented by those most obstinate in vice and wickedness" — stepped up pressure against the land-titling scheme, while also pushing hard to establish police posts on the islands of prominent rebels.²⁶

Finally, in May, after Nele Wardada absolutely refused to allow police on Ustupu, Vaglio turned to stronger measures, sending Nele and two other holdouts to Puerto Obaldía for six months' confinement.

That cruel waga was living at The Point [that is, at Porvenir]. He called to Nele. "You will come here to discuss an issue." . . . When they crossed over there, the wagas didn't let Nele talk at all. "Come here." Wham! into jail. Oh! Nele was truly mistreated. His followers got mad, they say. Whew! "Don't fight them! You'll just make them punish me worse. If you do, if you fight them, I'll disappear."²⁷

A few days later Vaglio ordered the same for Colman and four village chiefs, instructing the corregidor of Puerto Obaldía, "All the vigilance and restrictions that you may have with them is not too much, and I trust that you will make them taste the penalty that they themselves have sought by their own hands."²⁸ Nele later said that he was beaten while in confinement.²⁹

Vaglio had not reckoned on the speed of communication to the city from little Puerto Obaldía, which since the year before was the site of a U.S. radio post forming part of the canal defenses. Colman immediately radioed out word of his detention, and within a few days José de la Rosa had obtained a writ of habeas corpus from a judge in Colón ordering the release of the prisoners.³⁰ The freed chiefs returned deeply embittered. "So Nele came home again. And thus they angered Nele. 'The waga trifled with me. . . . He treated me like a criminal, when he threw me in jail. An outrage.' Then he began to gather his thoughts."³¹

In the wake of the jailings, both sides began to play a rougher game. Just out of jail, Colman, along with his lieutenant, Olonibiginya of Carti, and thirty followers paid a visit to Porvenir on a day Vaglio happened to be away. When the police attempted to arrest one of Colman's men who was declaiming against the wagas, his comrades mobbed the office, stopped only by armed reinforcements.[32] That same night, a newly appointed indigenous policeman named Pedro Paniza, who was from another Carti village, reported hearing of a plot to ambush him early next morning on his way to work on the mainland. At 4 a.m. a police squad led by Lieutenant Linares surprised a small flotilla of canoes close to the shore and captured Olonibiginya.[33]

In early June the judge who had issued the writ of habeas corpus, Rodolfo Ayarza, summoned Colman, Olonibiginya, and eleven others to Colón.[34] Any records of the proceedings have been lost, but Colman was soon back on the coast.[35] In mid-June Colman presented a memorial drawn up by de la Rosa asking that Vaglio be removed from office, complaining that though President Porras had promised to reduce the use of noserings gently and gradually, Vaglio was carrying out a campaign "as if against a horde of savages," and that the Indians, "persecuted and oppressed," had resolved to flee into the mountains.[36] The Secretary rejected the petition but asked Vaglio to respond.

Colman next alleged that the head of the second detachment, Isidro Junca, was mistreating people under his control. Secretary Alfaro displayed some sympathy for the Indians and suspicion about his own subordinates: "This is not the first time that the Indians of San Blas have complained of being outraged by the functionaries that the National Government has sent to that Circumscription to protect them and their interests, and it is now time that measures are adopted to the end that the Indians are treated with benevolence and affection."[37]

In response, Vaglio conducted a pro forma investigation with a fixed set of questions presented to collaborationist village leaders: Were there any complaints against Agent Junca? (No) In what community was Colman chief? (Ailigandi) Was Colman empowered to represent this village? (No) Were they happy with the government, schools, and the teacher? (Yes).[38] Using his report as the occasion for an impassioned philippic against Colman, Vaglio heaped on reports from Inabaginya and Pedro Paniza, whose house Colman's followers had burned down after they failed to kill him.[39] To all appearances the rebuttal was successful.[40]

Over time, however, Vaglio's vehemence and his obsession with Colman damaged his own credibility as much as his enemy's reputation. Moreover, his patron and *compadre,* Belisario Porras, had resigned the presidency in January as a ploy to circumvent the nonsuccession clause in the constitution. Out of office for a few months, Porras the candidate won reelection, but he had to wait until October for his inauguration, and in the meanwhile, First Designado Ernesto Lefevre exercised executive power. When Lefevre received Colman's protest against Junca, he passed it on to Secretary Alfaro with a covering note:

> I include for you another complaint from Colman. Despite what Vaglio tells us, I believe that this good friend does not have the patience of the case towards the Indians.
>
> So long as the Intendente considers some Indians as enemies, we are going to have difficulties in San Blas. On the other hand, if the authorities of that circumscription keep in mind that those poor peoples cannot change customs in a day, things will proceed better.
>
> Perhaps this will make up my mind to write Vaglio because I want the tension that seems to exist in the relations of Colman and his Indians and him to cease.[41]

The next time that Vaglio went to Panama he did not come back. The available documents do not indicate precisely what happened, but a letter alludes to the "judgement given against Vaglio," and it seems clear that he was eased out of office.[42] With Colman's forces exultant at the intendente's defeat, Lieutenant Linares, left in charge at Porvenir, wrote a succession of letters as bitter and vituperative as any of his superior's, complaining of Olonibiginya and the "unbearable" Colman, "who, befouled by de la Rosa, hate us to death since it was attempted to confine them in Puerto Obaldía as bad ones and rebels."[43]

The final and in some ways worst incident of 1920 occurred after Vaglio's removal, this one on the island of Playón Chico or Ukkup Senni (both names mean "small beach"), some twenty-five miles east of Nargana. As the ultimate government-controlled villages all the way to the border, Playón Chico and Tupile formed the last outpost of "civilization," with Colman's headquarters, Ailigandi, only ten miles beyond. The two islands had been among the first both to "grasp the Panama flag" in 1904 and to accept schools and policemen in 1915 and 1916. Chief Inadoiginya of Tupile was the most important early modernist after Charly Robinson: in addition to welcoming Gassó to his island, he had sent his children to both Catholic and Protestant schools.[44]

The arrival of police and teachers on both islands was apparently peaceful, but after a year or two, as they began enforcing school attendance and interfering in village life, they stirred up controversy, and on Playón Chico, the first chief, Olonabdiler, led a breakaway group of about ten households to a nearby uninhabited island. With the secessionists only a few hundred yards away and other dissidents still in its midst, Playón Chico found little peace.[45]

Through 1919 and 1920, the two islands went through much of the same turmoil as Nargana. In July 1919 the usually compliant Chief of Playón Chico, Olobanikke, wrote President Porras that the suppression of noserings and bead bindings—which a few days previously had sparked off a revolt on Nargana—was endangering progress on his island, where despite the village's previous commitment to education, "we are resolved not to send our children to school."[46] Colman's agents agitated on both islands when the Colonial Police were away, recruiting older boys as anti-government village constables and pressuring parents to pull their children from school.[47] Intendente Vaglio visited Tupile personally in October, getting most of the children back into class.[48] But agitation continued, with rumors that Playón Chico would soon move to the mainland.[49]

At the end of 1920 the police further agitated the situation when they began enforcing a ban on alcohol announced by Vaglio earlier in the year. When an agent had Olobanikke call a meeting to get children into school and discourage chichas, the speakers who openly contradicted him and encouraged resistance included the chief's own brother.[50] After months of turmoil, things came to a head on both islands in late September of 1920. Agitation by Colman's forces had picked up after his release from jail, and again after news came of judgments against the intendente. Colman himself met with supporters on Playón Chico in August, appointing an alternative, rebel government for the village; school attendance afterward dropped by a half, and Colman's adherents began menacing the lone government agent on the island.

Antonio Linares, the police lieutenant in charge at Porvenir, reacted to the alarming news by sending a special force, headed by Sublieutenant Santiago Castillo, to reestablish control.[51] On September 23, according to later Kuna testimony, Castillo held the men of Tupile captive in their gathering house while his agents went house to house confiscating firearms. He announced that all noserings were to be confiscated as well, leading, it was claimed, to a wild scene in which fleeing women even jumped in the water and tried to swim away.[52]

Late the next afternoon, Castillo and four agents, one of them Claudio Iglesias of Nargana, arrived on Playón Chico. A meeting was called, and at about eight Castillo and his men entered the gathering hall, accompanied by the local schoolmistress. Only Castillo carried a firearm into the meeting, a .38-caliber revolver. With Claudio Iglesias translating, Castillo addressed the large crowd, beginning with the subject of sanitation. His audience kept silent all the way through his next remarks on strengthening school attendance, until he reached the explosive subject of chichas, announcing that puberty ceremonies and their associated drinking were banned.

In the ensuing uproar, an outspoken rebel named Susu could be heard outside denouncing Castillo. Agents were sent out, according to the Kuna, to arrest Susu; according to the police, to bring him in to discuss the issue. Everyone agrees that Susu resisted and a general melée resulted in which, the police alleged, one agent was mobbed and dragged off. As Castillo started outside to assist him, he encountered Colman's head policeman, Oloingikke, in the doorway. Castillo's enemies claimed that he knocked Oloingikke down, and when the latter struck back, Castillo shot him dead. According to the police, Oloingikke and a large mob overwhelmed the policeman: as Castillo was knocked to the ground, Susu and another man called loudly to *gingi sedage!* "Bring guns!" Oloingikke's son ran home and fetched his rifle but could not get a clear shot at Castillo. A mass of men mobbed Claudio and the other police, and in the words of the teacher, "The disorder was phenomenal."

According to Castillo's testimony, he fired his pistol once into the air and then into the men on top of him, mortally wounding Oloingikke. The others fell back, giving Castillo space to scramble up and back away toward the schoolhouse, where he was joined by the other policemen. Noticing that the schoolmistress was not with them, they had just decided to venture out to find her when she turned up, having slipped out the back of the meeting.

As Castillo and his little band hurriedly sent off a policemen in a canoe to Tupile for help, Chief Olobanikke came to the door of the schoolhouse. Begging their pardon for the incident, he inquired about police intentions. Told that they would defend themselves but not counterattack unprovoked, he went back to the gathering house and in a reconvened meeting persuaded the assembled men to abandon hostilities, despite threats by the fiercest rebels to renew the attack.

The moment passed, and the next day the police, backed by prompt reinforcements, began reestablishing control. To prevent communication with Colón, no one was allowed off the island. Holding the men in the school building and threatening them with imprisonment, they went from house to house stripping the village of guns and bows, after which they challenged the men to fight. Hearings on the incident were held on Playón Chico and later at Porvenir, with twenty-four witnesses interviewed over two weeks.

Meanwhile, some of the rebels slipped away to Carti and then to Colón. On the twenty-seventh of September, only three days after the incident, one of them filed a complaint against Castillo before the Second Circuit Court in Colón.[53] The next day Colman's lawyer, José de la Rosa, denounced the killing of Oloingikke to the Secretariat of Government and Justice in a memorial that noted the presence of eight Indian witnesses in the city.[54] Although Lieutenant Linares fulminated against the "slanderous [and] implausible" memorial,[55] he could not stop the proceedings already in motion, and Sublieutenant Castillo was summoned to the city and arrested. Thereafter, however, his fortunes revived rapidly, and a judgment by the Supreme Court on October 21 found that he had acted in self-defense. Though the verdict may have disappointed Colman's forces, they had at least succeeded in making Castillo's actions the issue rather than those of his attackers.[56]

The incident must have disquieted the police profoundly. No one had come to their defense, and the pro-government second chief (and probably the first chief Olobanikke as well) knew beforehand that an attack was planned. The second chief, asked why he had not warned Castillo, lamely pleaded that the conspirators moved much more decisively than he had anticipated, and that he had not dared to denounce them in public. Even the meeting after the attack in which Olobanikke persuaded the others to desist should have frightened the police by its implicit ethnic solidarity: despite fierce disagreement between the opposed factions, at a moment of divisive conflict they were nonetheless in one building debating the fate of the police in the other.

When Humberto Vaglio began as intendente, the government had already found three leaders — Robinson, Nele, and Colman — willing to accept Panamanian sovereignty, to tolerate some change, and in effect, to begin the slow process of incorporating the Kuna into the Republic. Two years later, one of the three had been suppressed in favor of a ruthless fanatic, and the other two had been jailed, beaten, and embittered. Both police and Indians felt alienated and betrayed.

At the end of 1920 Humberto Vaglio was still writing memos about San Blas, but he never returned to his post, a fate he seems to have anticipated.[57] Earlier, in the aftermath of the ambush of the rubber-tappers, he had quoted a proverb, "El que se mete a redentor sale crucificado" (He who puts himself forward as redeemer ends up crucified), adding, "And sooner or later I expect my cross."[58]

Part Five
THE CONQUEST OF SAN BLAS, 1921–1924

15. The Death of Claudio Iglesias

Any hopes that the departure of Humberto Vaglio might signal a change toward cooperation and harmony were dispelled immediately when his replacement, Andrés Mojica, took office in January 1921. Colman and a number of followers came to Porvenir to greet the new man and sound him out, a visit on which the intendente reported in detail.[1] Colman began by expressing his readiness to cooperate and forget past conflicts. Mojica replied, ominously, that he intended to be their friend but only "within the rule of law" based on respect for the government and his own authority. Moving directly to particulars, Mojica reprimanded his visitors for having knocked down a house in Carti two days before solely because it had been measured as a potential barracks.

The interview proceeded in the same edgy, hostile tone, covered over by a paper-thin veneer of amiability. Colman asked hopefully whether other government personnel had been changed; Mojica said no. Colman offered to send some of his own policemen to help out, but Mojica refused. Mojica then announced that he would be putting schools on Carti, Ailigandi, and Ustupu. (He did not tell them that he had yet to find money for even one.) Colman answered that schools were all very well, but they inevitably led to the suppression of noserings and chichas and the graduation of self-important young men all wanting to be chief. Mojica countered with praise for education and young men's ambitions. After more imperious orders from the new intendente, the interview finally ended, with the delegation again offering protestations of friendship as it departed. In reporting on the encounter, Mojica condemned Colman as an obstacle worse than a frank enemy, because he resisted while seeming to comply, a back-handed compliment to the old chief's tenacity.[2]

Mojica, then thirty-eight years old, was already a veteran of sorts on the coast, because he had been corregidor of Puerto Obaldía for a few months in 1915. Thereafter a legislator, vice president of the Municipality of Panama, subsecretary in various branches of the government, and briefly acting secretary of development, he was a self-avowed socialist and, like many politicians in the Liberal Party, a Mason. Why such an up-and-coming official would volunteer for bureaucratic exile, a mystery even to President Porras, was later clarified when Mojica confessed he was fleeing from harassment by a superior as well as from an accumulation of debts that he hoped to eliminate through spartan living.[3] In their extensive and genial correspondence, the president used the familiar pronoun *tu,* while Mojica kept to the more formal and respectful *usted.*[4]

If Mojica was smoother and less choleric than his predecessor Vaglio, he was just as imperious and authoritarian, just as eager for "the conquest of the Indians."[5] His appointment signaled the importance that Porras attached to pushing ahead with the program in San Blas: as Mojica indicated to Cimral Colman, he brought with him a mandate to establish more schools and police posts, and, as soon became clear, to get noserings off Kuna women. This time, in fact, the president demanded a complete change of dress.

On Nargana and Corazón, Mojica seems to have started this process almost at once, and by the end of March the detachment head, Ramón Garrido, was able to write the intendente a ceremonial letter announcing success.[6] Mojica congratulated him in even more fulsome language for measures "carried out with such happy success and in such a mild and judicious manner that instead of rancor between the tribes and yourselves—in abandoning these ugly but traditional and beloved customs—there was put in place the most perfect harmony."[7] The reality was quite different, as Anna Coope noted in a letter.

Jim Phillips, one of our Christian men, had trouble. The police came and told him to tell his brother's wife, who is old, to take her ring out. He said something about it was not his wife, he couldn't do that, whereupon [a policeman] struck him on the back with his Billy stick . . . and he was put in the stocks. . . . Well, all the men of forty years old and over, his chums and equals, vowed vengeance on the Spaniards.[8]

What resistance did occur on Nargana was repressed through fines, jailing, and time in the stocks. If Charly Robinson did not promote the dress change, as Garrido claimed, he certainly did not stop it. Already weakened by the events of 1919, he was in no position to mount serious opposition.[9] Those who objected most strenuously departed, joining the exodus to as-yet unpacified villages.[10]

Although Garrido was able to keep the lid clamped down tight on Nargana, when the conflict over women's dress spilled over to neighboring islands, he lost control of events. This time the problem was a small village two and one-half miles to the southwest, easily visible from Nargana, called Kwebdi, or Río Azúcar (Sugar River). The incident began when a woman of Nargana, a widow or divorcée, visited her brother on Río Azúcar. Typically, no account of the events that followed bothered to identify her by name, but her brother was called Charly Nelson or just Nelsin. Nelsin, an argar or vocero of Río Azúcar and already a known opponent of Panamanian rule, came home from the forest on the afternoon of April 21 to find his sister weeping because the nosering and leg bindings had been taken from her and she had just spent two or three days in jail, apparently for having resisted police orders.[11]

That afternoon Garrido twice sent the woman's son-in-law to fetch her, but even after he threatened to jail the young man in her place, she refused to return to Nargana. As Anna Coope noted, Garrido made good on his threat:

Her brother [Nelsin] was so vexed that his old sister had taken the ring out to please the Panamanian, that he said his old sister should not return to her daughter's house. The spies heard it and the Chief of Police sent [the son-in-law] to bring back the old woman and the brother would not let her go, so when [he] came home he was imprisoned and his wife also. For two nights he sat with feet in stocks, the little children left to look out for themselves, and the baby cried so the first night (11 months old) they took it to prison with its mother.[12]

By evening both villages were stirred up, and a Nargana man who had married on Río Azúcar told Garrido that during the afternoon he had heard several men in the house next to his plotting to kill the police if they came there.

Garrido held off sending his men until past midnight. Why he waited so long, an issue soon to be hotly contested, is unclear. Most likely he hoped to get the drop on Nelsin at a vulnerable moment when the village was sleeping, in effect repeating the tactic that had gone so badly awry on Niatupu. At 12:55 a party set out in a sailing canoe for Río Azúcar to arrest Nelsin and another village leader, with instructions (as each police witness later carefully noted) to use peaceable means if possible but to defend themselves if attacked. Led by a tough policeman named Miguel Gordón Herrera, the party included Claudio Iglesias, along with three more agents, two indigenous and one Panamanian.[13]

On reaching Río Azúcar, the police party landed at one corner of a little cove. They were immediately spied by a lookout, who started through the streets rousing out the village men. The arresting party had to ask the way to Nelsin's house, only a few yards away, and once inside amid all the hammocks, they were able to find their quarry only by threatening his son-in-law with a pistol. An indigenous policeman named Agustín Gonzalez began explaining Nelsin's arrest to him, while Miguel Gordón, who did not understand Kuna, stood by. By this time the house was packed with villagers standing and watching, while another group began gathering in a house next door.

Claudio Iglesias and an agent named Benigno Ospina, who were watching the house next door, arrested a suspicious individual on Gordón's orders and Iglesias was left in charge of the prisoner. Gordón had another suspicious individual arrested, and when Agent Ospina took him outside, according to his testimony, he found Claudio wrestling with an armed man. Ospina said he grabbed the barrel of the man's gun and was about to fire his own, but Claudio called out not to shoot. Another man then tried to wrest Ospina's revolver from him. As Miguel Gordón later testified:

At that moment I heard a row outside Nelsin's house, and they were sounding a [conch-shell trumpet]. I went out immediately to see what was happening, and seeing that the village was coming in a mass with machetes against us, I called to Agent González to come out, which he did not do, believing he could calm their spirits in their dialect.

When I went out the door, an Indian came at me with a machete, and with my revolver I made five discharges at him without scoring a hit, and with the last of the shots remaining to me, the Indian came on top of me with the machete as I too advanced, and I believe that with this shot I wounded him. Another of them clasped me, knocking me to the ground, and in the struggle my glasses and hat were broken. I suffered several scratches on my hands as well as my face, but with such luck that I defended myself from him without shooting him, since I had no more shots left.

When I got up off the ground, I was called by Ospina, who was saying to me, "Get this man who has me fucked off of me!" Hurriedly coming to his defense, where an Indian had him with his head bent over a canoe struggling to take away his revolver, with the handle of mine I gave [his attacker] three blows to the head, thus succeeding in saving [Ospina] from the claws of death. Another who had already made three machete cuts at Ospina and who was coming on top of him, I don't know who shot him, whether it was Ospina, Sanguillen, or the other one.

I looked in every direction calling to Iglesias and González, but all was in vain, because they didn't answer the call that I made them, and in view of the fact that the village was coming on top of us shooting at us and with machetes and poles, Ospina was able to get into the canoe where Sanguillen was, wounded, I stayed on land because it pained me to leave two good friends and government servants who might perish, but I could do no more.

Ospina, for his part, remembered that from the canoe, "I saw an Indian with machete in hand coming against Miguel Gordón . . . to whom I shouted, "Get in! We're wounded and they're going to kill you! and on seeing the machete over Gordón, I fired and the Indian fell."[14] As Gordón testified:

Ospina insisted, calling to me and telling me that he too was wounded and that I should get in, which I did, the party of savages continuing to shoot, hitting me, though only with very small shot, a bullet wound from behind.

With the sail of the canoe in which we had come shot full of holes, and without knowing how to steer the canoe, we left, resolved to die in one way or another, with two wounded men invalided by the blood rushing from their wounds.[15]

The agent Domingo Sanguillen, who as the only Kuna among the three police survivors did know how to manage the canoe, had the steering paddle, but with bullet wounds in his head and body, he was in considerable pain. As for the two men they left behind, if Claudio Iglesias and Agustín Gonzalez were still alive at that instant, they were certainly dead moments later.

How the melée began is a matter of dispute. According to one version, Claudio first shot the man he was supposed to arrest and then was attacked by others in return, while police witnesses said that he had merely defended himself.[16] Whatever the case, the casualties, in addition to Claudio and Agustín, included four dead Río Azúcar men and a number wounded.

On Nargana, people had worried about the possibility of violence since the police party went off, and, according to the oral history of Carlos López, they saw the flash of gunfire in the night. In the morning, only a few people ventured out, the rest staying close to home. One man, fishing in the waters between the two islands, saw a canoe coming in the distance and wondered why its progress was so erratic — "That person, why can't he steer straight?"[17] — and as it came closer, he saw the three survivors of the mission, all of them wounded, with Miguel Gordón now steering. At 8:30 a.m., long after fleeing Río Azúcar, the three reached Nargana and reported to Garrido.

During the same hours, another Nargana man out in his canoe met an emissary from Río Azúcar, who told him where the bodies of Claudio and Agustín could be collected, warning that only women should be sent.[18] Miss Coope, though she had little pity for her enemy, shared in Nargana's consternation.

The whole village is mourning and in fear. Lonnie's brother Claudio and his chum Augustine are both lying in their homes, dead, killed by Indians. God has comforted dear Lon. He feels as I do that Claudio is now in hell, but he has lived such a bad life, was drunk last Sunday and has scorned at God's Word and vowed that soon he'd be chief and then he'd shut up this school.
. . . I went to Lonnie's house and they had Claudio on the floor trying to get his clothes either on or off. . . . He was so limp looking I said, "Lon, is he dead?" And Lon said, "Yes, feel his pulse." I took that soft, clammy hand and was quite sure he was dead. It seems to me I've never felt death so ghastly as now, especially because I knew the man and his life. . . . As I write the dead body of Claudio is going in the canoe to be buried.[19]

On Río Azúcar, three village policemen had set off well before dawn for Porvenir to inform the intendente of the incident. As a bureaucrat's bureaucrat, Mojica's first action on hearing the news was not to send troops but to take depositions, after which he arrested the three messengers as prime suspects.[20] Only after writing to the secretary of government and the chief justice and drawing up a resolution outlining the steps to be taken did the intendente set out late that afternoon for Nargana with a squad of police.[21] (Despite his fears, this time a boat was in working order.) He reached Nargana at nine that night and immediately began taking more depositions. The next morning, having towed Claudio's burial party to the river as a mark of respect, he proceeded to Río Azúcar, where he summarily arrested Nelsin, Chief Kantule, and several others, in a roundup so indiscriminate that it caught one returning traveler who had only reached home a few minutes before.[22]

After several days of interrogations on Porvenir, Justice Rodolfo Ayarza of Colón arrived to carry out further investigations on Río Azúcar itself.[23] Some witnesses insisted they had not been present—one even claimed to have slept through the shouting and gunfire—and most said it was too dark to see who did what. Chief Kantule tried to put responsibility for killing Claudio and Agustín onto the four dead Río Azúcar men, who were safely out of reach of Panamanian justice. But he and others did name a few combatants, and the three men sent to Porvenir had all admitted being present. The investigating force indicted Nelsin for sedition and four others for homicide. Miguel Gordón was also indicted, very likely because of pressure from Colman's lawyer, José de la Rosa, but in Gordón's case the indictment seems to have been quashed within a few weeks.[24]

The killings stirred up the situation on the coast. Of the four teachers in San Blas schools, only one, Elisa de Garrido, returned to work after vacation, and she was already present as wife of the first detachment head. When the intendente asked the secretary of public instruction to hire substitutes, the latter could not find even a single teacher brave enough to serve.[25]

Just as bad for the Intendencia, news of the killings encouraged disobedience, especially on volatile Playón Chico. Mojica, impatient with delays in getting women out of noserings, himself carried out the transformation on Tupile; at the same moment, Colman was on Playón Chico whipping up resistance, after which the village constables, who had recently been banned, defiantly resumed parading with their staves.[26] A few days later, a troublemaker on Playón Chico tried to foment an uprising, while on the little secessionist island next door, "the men say that they are waiting for the police as on Río Azúcar."[27] Agents on Playón Chico freely punished men for giving their wives traditional haircuts or carrying a constable's staff, but control was so tenuous that detachment head Castillo refused to investigate turtlers for fear of what the Indians would do if left alone.[28] The crisis came to a head when Mojica learned that dissidents were about to burn construction materials and even the school in order to prevent the police from building barracks on the island. In a lightning raid, he held the men in the schoolhouse while their homes were searched for weapons. The ringleaders were packed off to jail, and this broke local resistance, at least for the moment.[29]

On a broader front, Colman's forces continued pushing hard, collecting money for the purchase of land titles and holding regional meetings in which speakers made death threats against the police.[30] In his campaign of complaints and propaganda, Colman wrote a memorial against the violent suppression of native dress, which prompted an inquiry from the Supreme Court. Mojica wrote a long and huffy reply, praising the dress change as "one of the principal bases for civilization" and insisting that the consent of husbands was always obtained — the wishes of the women themselves presumably being irrelevant.[31] A letter from Colman to *La Estrella* called for the removal of authorities in San Blas, to be replaced by candidates whose description sounded remarkably like his lawyer, José de la Rosa.[32]

In the courts, meanwhile, de la Rosa had taken over the defense of the five accused Río Azúcar men, counterattacking fiercely and doing his best to make police conduct the issue. He made much of what he called Miguel Gordón's "confession" to having shot one man and struck another with the butt of his pistol. More tellingly, he attacked the lack of prudence and care shown by sending a party in the middle of the night and the illegitimacy of arresting, without a warrant, men who had not yet committed any crime.[33]

The case went to trial on September 23. Witness testimony and a review of previously collected depositions took only two hours, and after a break for lunch, the rest of the day up to 9:20 p.m. was devoted to legal arguments. The records do not indicate how long the jury stayed out, but when it returned, the verdict was for acquittal of the Kuna accused.[34]

The judgment and the incident itself left relations between the Kuna and the Intendencia even worse than before, with both sides embittered and unwilling to yield. On Nargana, Claudio Iglesias's successor as leader of the young turks, Estanislao López, enthusiastically entered the fray against Protestants and Yankee-lovers. The modernists and the Intendencia felt Claudio's death as a serious loss, but they made the best of it. His siblings, already the recipients of several scholarships, were awarded several more after his death.[35] As a martyr to civilization, Claudio was commemorated in the names of several new youth groups on pacified islands, as well as a monument on Nargana.[36] The hopes that Claudio might prove useful even in death were expressed in a perfervid eulogy from the journal of the Salesians who had groomed him for his civilizing role. "Sleep in peace, Oh Claudio! The blood shed for the good of the Church and of the Fatherland, like the blood of the first Christians, will regenerate the land bathed with the sweat of your apostolic labors."[37]

16. The Noose Tightens

After the death of Claudio Iglesias in April 1921, Intendente Mojica pushed ahead rapidly with his program to gain control of San Blas, civilize the Kuna, and crush his enemies. Despite the same problems of transport, supply, and personnel that had hampered his three predecessors, and despite tenacious and sometimes successful resistance by his Kuna opponents, Mojica gained more than he lost, and within a short period victory seemed within reach.[1]

The first enemies the administration set out to conquer were the sources of anti-Panamanian corruption, the odious Protestants on Nargana and Corazón de Jesús.[2] In September of 1921 Anna Coope wrote President Porras to complain of mistreatment by the head of the indigenous police and young men's group, Estanislao López, and by the detachment head, Ramón Garrido, who had closed down her Bible classes by forcing all able-bodied villagers to attend nightly dances in the schoolhouse.[3] On the fourteenth of August, Coope added, a meeting was held in front of Charly Robinson's house in which López loudly threatened to kill her. Never inclined to passivity, Coope set off with Purdy two nights later to lodge a protest. On their return, having missed Intendente Mojica in Porvenir, they were grilled by Garrido on their temerity in going around him to his superiors. He put Coope's paddlers in the stocks as punishment for leaving the island without permission, refusing her offer to pay their fines, and then jailed Charly Robinson for telling her of López's threats.

In visits to Nargana two weeks later, Mojica managed to avoid Coope, leaving her a note informing her that a village meeting had decided to restrict her Bible classes to Sundays only. Afterward, she said, Estanislao López grew more high-handed than ever, and Charly Robinson, "threatened with prison if he comes to my house or my meetings and if he doesn't dance every night," gave up the fight.[4]

Coope, by now a scarred veteran of the information wars, followed up with complaints to the Methodist mission conference in Panama and the head of the American legation. Because she was a British citizen, the American minister in turn sent a copy on to the British legation, and all three bodies wrote the Panamanian Secretariat of Foreign Affairs demanding protection for Coope. In early December the secretary communicated the results of an investigation that, not surprisingly, found all of Coope's accusations groundless.[5]

Her fortunes declined even further in 1922, as a priest began visiting Nargana at three-month intervals. In a letter thanking Porras for supporting this miniature counterreformation, the bishop of Panama indicated that church and state could defeat a common enemy:

Yes, my good friend, this is the truly efficacious medium, and perhaps the only one, to civilize those hordes and secure national interests in that region against the invasion of alien elements, who in everything will think less about civilizing our unhappy Indians; and who, under the hypocritical mantle of civilizing them, what they really pursue are self-interested ends to do with lucre, if not political ones.

I judge it opportune and proper . . . that you place or name some police agents to instill respect and fear in the Yankees, since I fear that when the Father returns to Colón, the gringos will try to attract the Indians once again and to wreck the work of the missionary.[6]

The bishop need not have worried, because Garrido had already communicated to Coope a decision, according to him reached democratically by the men of Nargana, to enforce attendance at Catholic services and forbid participation in Protestant ones.[7] Purdy described the isolation into which she and Coope were thrust:

A policeman is stationed on every side of my house to watch if any one comes on meeting nights, and if any one does come, the parents are ordered to take them out, or go to prison. That is Rome for you. However, some of the boys come in the darkness; they do not want to give up. You see, they have been saved. . . . If it were not for the presence of the Invisible One I would be miserable.[8]

Purdy succeeded in smuggling one of her young followers named Peter Miller out of San Blas and sending him to a Protestant school in North Carolina. According to her account, Garrido filed charges for removing a minor from his home without parental permission. A judge was sent to Nargana to investigate (very likely the much put-upon Judge Ayarza). When he pointed out to Purdy that Miller's parents denied having given permission for their son to travel, she answered that they had been threatened with jail. "He looked kind of wise at the secretary and smiled, then thanked me and dismissed the case."[9]

Coope herself was evicted from Nargana in late 1922.[10] She recorded a meeting in Panama with the president in December of that year, in which, she says, Porras spoke warmly to her but endorsed a Catholic monopoly in San Blas. Coope did not give up, of course, and by the end of January 1923 Porras had surrendered, granting her permission to return to Nargana, so long as she worked exclusively in Spanish.

March 9, 1923. . . . First meeting in eleven months last night. . . . House packed, Jesus is victor. Enemies said, "Miss Coope can never open that school again; never. That bell shall not ring." But it did; it did. Ah! Blessed is she that believeth. . . . Last night was a victory. When the secretary told me I went to Chief Robinson. He wept for joy. The people ran out to meet me . . . said "Miss Coope our great friend, not afraid of Policemen, not afraid of President, God is with her."[11]

Her enemies, however, reimposed a quarantine on the mission, punishing anyone who visited or assisted Coope, and she seems to have spent much of 1923 and 1924 under virtual house arrest.[12]

At the same time that the administration was consolidating its hold on Nargana, it initiated an aggressive campaign of expansion. Mojica, forced to bide his time with the principal rebel strongholds, which were too large and powerful to subdue, reluctantly turned to smaller, easier targets.[13] He began with Wichubwala, a new village on a little island next to Porvenir. In June 1921 Mojica reported with evident pleasure on a meeting with immigrants to Wichubwala the previous day, in which he laid out streets and house sites, and a flag-raising ceremony in which they lined up respectfully with their hats off opposite a rank of policemen. The next year he found them a teacher, and in December he was able to announce that the village women had given up on native dress.[14]

This compliant new community was an artificial creation, entirely recruited at the intendente's urging by Pedro Paniza, the government's principal agent in western San Blas. The dozen households attracted to Wichubwala by the prospect of schooling and unclaimed forestland chose as chief a man who just happened to be Paniza's father-in-law and the owner of all the land on the island. The intendente, for his part, intended Wichubwala as a means to encourage defection and "divide the prevailing opinion in neighboring places, especially Carti."[15]

The same divisive tactics were used against the more vulnerable rebel islands, where Mojica and his agents began promoting agitation by disaffected young men.[16] In early 1923, Estanislao López shepherded a youthful delegation from several islands to the city to ask for teachers, and by the end of the year schools and police posts had been established on Tigre, Río Azúcar, and Río Sidra. Construction of a youth club, social dancing, and dresses for women followed soon after, as did voting in the next presidential election. With the pacification of several more villages in 1924, the government had gained control of a long strip of coastline stretching all the way to Tupile. The next island beyond this frontier was Colman's seat, Ailigandi.[17]

In this same period, economic threats also intensified. Preparations for large-scale capitalist exploitation of San Blas increased rapidly, spurred on by problems elsewhere. The largest producer of bananas in the country was the United Fruit complex at Bocas del Toro in northwestern Panama: attacked by a blight called Panama disease, production at Bocas dropped from five million bunches in 1919 to three million in 1922. Small plantations continued to spring up around Lake Gatún on the canal and at the mouth of the Chagres, and local banana production quadrupled between 1922 and 1924, but there, too, Panama disease began making inroads. Attention thus turned strongly toward uncontaminated stretches of coast, including San Blas.

The San Blas Development Company, which already had thirty-six thousand coconut palms at Mandinga, began planting bananas in large numbers, expected to begin yielding in 1924. Construction got under way on a large dock for deepwater cargo ships and sixteen miles of narrow gauge rail line. By the end of 1924, almost six thousand hectares were said to be under cultivation, and the company claimed to have invested more than a million and a half dollars, suggesting that the operation would soon rival the largest plantations in South and Central America. During 1924 the Development Company was formally taken over by the United Fruit's principal rival, Vaccaro Brothers of New Orleans, soon to be renamed Standard Fruit, and the contract with the government was renegotiated and expanded.[18]

In 1923 the formation of a second firm was announced, the San Blas Panama Banana Company, with a government concession of five thousand hectares. Exploration and preliminary work began in 1924 on a parcel of three thousand hectares near the Colombian border, while a further grant of two thousand hectares in central San Blas was saved for later development. United Fruit, which held a large block of shares in the new company, was to supervise planting and ship all production for the first ten years. Still more ominously for the Kuna, the company's Panamanian agent, former intendente Hurtado, signed a contract with the government to build a rail line from Caledonia over the mountains to the Pacific side. If built, the railroad would open up both slopes to mining, logging, bananas, and rubber.[19] The boom was reflected in a syndicated article calling San Blas the potential "gold coast" of Central America.[20]

The expanding Mandinga plantations drew unemployed laborers from elsewhere in Panama and Central America. In early 1924 several hundred West Indians were said to have left Bocas for San Blas,[21] and in one three-month period later the same year more than 600 Jamaican laborers, as well as 350 Panamanians, Colombians, Central Americans, and others came to work.[22] By August of that year, the company was asking for police help with labor unrest.[23]

The capitalist conquest of San Blas, although it left the Kuna enough land to meet their immediate needs, posed a serious threat. It might take years or decades before the loss of land hampered the Kuna in feeding their children, but the villages nearest the two plantations soon complained of encroachment on their farms and theft of bananas and coconuts by laborers.[24] More important, the plantations dismembered San Blas, destroying any hope of securing an undivided Kuna homeland.

Meanwhile, on a smaller scale, outsiders continued to invade the forests and coastal waters in search of ivorynut, balata latex, and sea turtles, provoking periodic confrontation.[25] The volume of each product taken out varied from year to year, depending on international prices and local conditions, but the return was always enough to draw poor Blacks into the region. In the second half of 1924, for instance, declared cargos at Porvenir included 103,600 pounds of ivorynuts, 3,232 pounds of turtle shell, and 2,780 pounds of balata latex, figures that take no account of smuggling and false declarations.[26] Ivorynuts, which were collected in several parts of Panama, had a total national production of 3.8 million pounds in 1922 and 2.5 million in 1923. In 1924, 2 million pounds of ivorynut, worth $46,000, were exported, along with 36,000 pounds of balata latex ($11,451) and 14,500 pounds of turtle shell, worth $50,000 — all significant sums in 1920s' dollars in a tiny, impoverished Latin American country.[27]

The politics of this extractive economy was based on the triangular relationship between costeño Blacks, the Kuna, and the government, which persisted into the 1920s, with Blacks and Indians pressuring the government from either side, one to promote turtling and forest gathering, the other to stop them.[28] The government tried out various arrangements, regulating, limiting, or suspending one activity or another, and it made efforts to protect Indians from theft and other depredations, but it insisted throughout on the right of Panamanian citizens to support themselves on national lands.[29]

National lands. Here, in the official mind, was the crux of the matter. It was not merely that bureaucrats supported the economic claims of Black costeños and their backers. It was that Kuna insistence on territorial sovereignty — their "deeply rooted belief that they are the absolute owners of the lands, waters, etc. and that the government lacks the right to issue such permits" — deeply offended nationalist sentiment.[30] Indians, from this viewpoint, could and should be allowed the means to support themselves, but they must not claim sovereignty or the right to control the "national forests" and "territorial waters," a right that pertained only to sovereign states.

Despite the obstacles the Kuna posed to development, they already played an active part themselves in the national economy, both as producers and consumers. Coconuts, almost all of which were shipped in the shell to the United States, constituted Panama's most important export after bananas, and American consuls consistently attributed well over one-half the country's production to San Blas. The total amount exported annually from Panama declined somewhat after the late 1910s, from more than 19.5 million nuts in 1917 and 1918 down to 13 or 14 million in 1924, following a drop in prices from an average of about $60 per thousand in 1918 to $46.60 in 1920; throughout the rest of the 1920s the average price per thousand never rose above $30. Output from Kuna palms continued at high levels, however — out of 14 million nuts exported by Panama in 1924, 8 million were credited to the North Coast and thus in large part to the Kuna — and a small set of companies, of which Colon Import and Export was the largest, continued to buy up most of what the Indians produced.[31] The income from coconuts, in turn, made San Blas an attractive market for metal tools, kerosene, cloth, and other goods.

In Latin America more often than not, trade of this sort victimized native peoples and peasants: store owners, commissaries, and itinerant merchants grossly over-charged their illiterate and powerless customers, and in many instances their debts (which the merchants made sure were never paid off) held them in perpetual servitude. The Kuna, in sharp contrast, avoided entanglements and crippling obli-gations. They might complain of sharp dealing by coasting merchants (a compli-ment the latter returned), but they never let anyone set up shop on their islands, still less gain control. In the first decades of this century, moreover, the Kuna themselves began to sell to each other in little stores owned by cooperative groups and whole villages, as well as by entrepreneurs like Charly Robinson.

In 1923 and 1924, however, this economic self-sufficiency began to erode sharply, as the government extended and strengthened its hold on San Blas and outsiders increasingly took over trade with the Indians. The largest interest, Colon Import and Export, acted in a relatively benign fashion, anchoring schooners and decommissioned World War I subchasers off several islands as floating trading posts. More ominously, the police on pacified islands closed down Kuna-owned stores, opening the way for new shops tended by Antilleans and mestizos. Many or most of these shops were owned by a single man, a police agent named Rafael Morales.[32]

Even more ominously for the Kuna, Morales breached the protection, however partial, that their land had enjoyed since President Valdés's decree of 1918. Outsiders might be allowed in for turtling and forest work, but except for the government-sponsored plantations, non-Indians had been prohibited from acquiring land or planting anywhere on the coast — before Morales. At Río Sidra, where he was sta-tioned for a while as police agent, Morales established a plantation, worked by a few foreign laborers, with a dock for shipping bananas.[33] However small this operation compared with the two giants run by Standard Fruit and United Fruit, it set a grim precedent.

The plantation, Morales's chain of shops, and his freedom to combine police work with business all suggest protection by his superiors, and more than one source points to Intendente Mojica as his silent partner or controller.[34] In another sign of corruption, Elisa de Garrido, until recently schoolmistress on Nargana, in March 1923 formally denounced a clandestine trade in liquor, offering the testimony of twelve past and present employees of the Intendencia. Without naming names, the memorial said the trade was carried out "principally in El Porvenir, which is the headquarters of the Circumscription," hinting broadly at Mojica's involvement.[35]

Ultimately, the question of who profited, and whether they did so legally or illegally was of secondary importance. What mattered was that by 1924 large pieces of Kuna territory had been alienated, outsiders roamed freely through their forests and waters, policemen told them what to do, and their way of life was rapidly coming to an end.

17.
Pacification
and
Resistance

When the government first stationed police on four Kuna islands in 1915, oral tradition notes that they treated the populace with some moderation and restraint. By the end of 1921, however, six years of hard experience had taught police agents caustic and ignoble lessons. They learned that freedom of speech and movement encouraged resistance, that unpunished dissidents redoubled their insolence, that opponents would never recognize the superiority of national civilization, and that, in general, the Indians were ungrateful, dishonest, and dangerous. Especially dangerous. Since 1919, rebels had fought the police on Nargana, Niatupu, Playón Chico, and Río Azúcar, the last skirmish leaving two agents dead; worse, the killers had gone free. Thus when cabinet secretaries gave orders to pacify and civilize the Indians in short order, but only through sweet persuasion, the men on the spot paid little attention. Petty tyranny undoubtedly came more naturally to the drunks and bullies who all too often found their way onto the force, but after 1921 even the honest men, men who believed sincerely in their civilizing mission, took a hard line.[1]

In gaining the upper hand, the police moved to clamp down on movement and communication. Having learned what ensued when Colman stirred up his adherents on Playón Chico or witnesses to an incident testified in city courts, they began cutting off pacified islands altogether from the outside.[2] "If you went off during the day . . . you'd be caught, they'd pursue you in a motor boat. They'd catch you, and wham! in you went."[3] Kuna visiting other communities had to produce a pass from the police of their home village, and to keep men from using their daily work off-island as a pretext for flight or external communication, authorities ended up requiring them to check in each day.

Even communication within the village became suspect.

Now if you were sitting on the front porch . . . if you were sitting and talking to each other, your friend and you, about where your friend had been, what you had done in the forest, sitting asking each other—you couldn't do that, that's what happened. Someone was listening behind your back. . . .

The elders would say, ". . . we're just chatting about nothing in particular. About how I went to work in the forest." . . . When they had spoken to the waga like that, the waga wouldn't say anything but "No. . . . "You're talking against us. . . ." The elders would end up arrested.[4]

The police eventually grew so worried about seditious talk that they required agriculturalists—who were accustomed to leaving before dawn and returning in midafternoon—to stay away all day. "If the men who go to work in the forest, if a few of them arrive home early, . . . the police would send him off again to work. The police didn't want the Indians to stay in their homes to talk with their wives in insolent words."[5]

In the village, the official gaze fell on everyone. "The wagas patrolled in the streets, they kept watch on the place, you couldn't sleep well. At night, like spying on you, like keeping watch, that's how the wagas were."[6] What the police didn't see or hear themselves, they learned from informers: "Someone was listening behind your back. There were still many on the wagas' side who would repeat what you said, who would distort it on purpose, someone who was mad at you. Someone who didn't like you would have a lot to say about you."[7]

Disobedience or disrespect was not tolerated, especially not by hard-bitten agents such as Miguel Gordón. One had to do things "according to what friend Gordón said. Gordón got mad easily. If people didn't do what he said, he'd get mad. I saw that he wanted things his way. The elders couldn't say anything. The elders couldn't get angry. Who could answer back? The wagas are brutal, we said. The wagas were always angry."[8]

To enforce their will, the police had an array of sanctions, first among them fines, some of which were listed in their own records: "April 4.— Maniquine, married, Playón Chico.—for cutting his wife's hair [in a traditional short haircut], that being prohibited. $5.00 fine." Next up the ladder of discipline came jailing, used to punish women as well as men: "[June] 14th.—Francisco Gonzalez.—For taking the name of Agent Sanchez, for having a girl bathed [in a puberty ritual] . . . punished with 29 days of arrest."[9]

The stocks, first introduced by Father Gassó, combined restraint with public humiliation and pain. Unlike their colonial North American equivalents, these log contraptions held the prisoner splayed backward, rear end on the ground, legs pulled forward and up. "Bam! they did it, he was caught. . . . In Tupile. He was thrown down there with his legs raised, with his feet, wham! pinned between poles. . . . He had to piss where he sat on the sand. We were suffering."[10]

Colonial police agent, Nargana, 1925.

Obdurate resisters would eventually be packed off to El Porvenir and Puerto Obaldía for longer terms: "Then one last time, my grandfather really went away, he was taken off to Porvenir. . . . Grandfather was gone six months, in Porvenir. Tossed in the calaboose. I was there when grandfather came home again. Oh my, his clothes were dirty, his clothes were in tatters!"[11] By early 1924 so many Indian prisoners had accumulated on the border, thrown in with hardened convicts and forced to sleep under the eaves of houses, that the corregidor of Puerto Obaldía was moved to write President Porras about the strain on his resources.[12] Finally, if all else failed or if sufficiently angered, a police agent would simply administer a beating on the spot—though not, the evidence suggests, torture or execution.[13]

Even after pacification seemed complete, the Kuna fought back in subtle ways, using what James Scott calls weapons of the weak.[14] Exasperated references crop up in official reports to deceit, inconsistency, noncompliance, and "the bad faith with which the natives always proceed."[15] Writing to a detachment head, Mojica observed, "You well know that they give the appearance of accepting every government order even though they never think to comply with it."[16] A month later, the detachment head, clearly driven to distraction, complained: "These people never say the same thing twice; they frequently come to make complaints against other Indians, but when they see that their countrymen could be punished, they deny with the greatest brazenness what they had previously said."[17]

A stronger form of resistance, one practiced since the turn of the century on Nargana, was flight. An elderly man in the 1970s remembered vividly having escaped from Corazón de Jesús as a boy: his mother paddled a canoe across to the local river in the predawn darkness, her family lying flat in the bottom among the water calabashes. Speaking with people in nearby canoes and letting them think she was on her way to fetch water and wash clothes, she turned east toward Niatupu at the last moment, her family egging her on from concealment until they were out of sight.[18] During the early 1920s, as the police clamped down, the exodus grew, dissidents voting with their feet or their paddles, reaching a climax in 1924 with a mass desertion from Playón Chico.[19]

A few of the most obdurate dissidents, finally, continued to disobey, confront, and even attack their oppressors. In late 1923 on the island of Río Sidra, an agent who went out on night patrol received a machete blow in the dark, and even as late as December of 1924, a year and a half after the police first arrived on that island, a list of twenty-four offenses, punished in most cases with jail, included lack of respect for authority (three cases), lack of respect along with resistance (one case), disobedience (four), traveling without permission (twice for the same man), and being "pernicious" (one case).[20]

No matter how hard the police worked to seal off each village, in the last analysis they depended entirely on outside support. Everyone on both sides well knew that the handful of agents on each island, despite their monopoly on pistols and rifles, could not control several hundred restless natives if they could not count on reinforcements to suppress uprisings and recidivism, and equally important, if they did not have the intendente to stand between them and higher officials.

It was not that Mojica or Vaglio condoned all their subordinates' actions. Whatever the Kuna might think, intendentes did not turn the police loose to rape and plunder. In 1924, when a number of policemen proposed a party, Mojica set strict guidelines, urging the local detachment head to

maintain order in such a way that there is no troublesome case to lament and all is decency and moderation. You will exert yourself in all this and you will try to prevent any person from turning up with arms of any kind, machetes, revolvers, pocketknives, straight razors, etc., or that the natives are mistreated under any pretext.[21]

In another instance, Mojica ordered a detachment head to reprehend an accused agent if found guilty, "since such conduct greatly demeans the good name of the government and the confidence that its representatives should inspire in all the natives of the Circumscription of San Blas."[22] In still another, he even ordered an arrested Kuna man sent to Porvenir with a report justifying his detention, since he had previously been jailed on dubious grounds.[23] In quite a few cases he disciplined, transferred, or investigated agents for bad behavior, including "abuse of office" as well as personal faults such as drunkenness.[24] There was just so much an intendente could do, however, without damaging police morale or opening too wide a rift between himself and his men. When he fired corrupt or brutal subordinates, moreover, all too often patronage brought them back again like some persistent weed.

On the other hand, as long as Mojica believed that an agent's actions served the cause of civilizing or pacifying the Indians, he was willing to look the other way or even lead the cover-up. When two intrepid young men of Niatupu traveled all the way to the presidential palace in 1923 to complain of police abuse, Mojica scoffed.[25] An accusation that traditional dress was suppressed through "violent and barbarous means" provoked a furious denial, in which he quoted at length from detachment heads' reports—which he knew to be false—crediting the change entirely to free choice.[26] In his report for 1922, he claimed that restrictions on movement imposed on Nargana by the previous administration had been removed, and even more implausibly, that police agents "are already considered, not a menace but rather as comrades or friends . . . due to the tenacious interest of this office always to respect the rights of the natives."[27]

The lengths to which the intendente would go to suppress resistance was perhaps most apparent on Río Azúcar, where Claudio Iglesias had been killed in 1921 at the beginning of Mojica's administration. The following year a group of twelve young men began building a clubhouse, despite, in Mojica's words, "the tenacious opposition of the old men, enemies of civilization, and of the threats of which they are the objects."[28] In May 1923, a teacher requested by the young men was reluctantly accepted onto the island by Chief Kantule.[29] Two months later, youthful witnesses who had been eavesdropping on Nelsin (the dissident whose actions had precipitated the 1921 incident) accused him of plotting to kill them.[30] In August, modernists and the teacher clashed with drinkers over a chicha.[31]

Finally, in November the intendente sent a large force to pacify the village at one stroke, to forestall, he said, an uprising planned by "bandits" such as Nelsin.[32] As Kuna petitions later described the incident: "Then . . . a drowning of sadness arrived. All the Indian men being in the forest, the gasoline launch of Señor Mojica came to catch all the Indians, and when an Indian came from the forest they caught him and tied him up."[33] Chief Kantule was pulled from his canoe and beaten as severely as the others.[34] "On arriving at the village of Corazón de Jesús, they grabbed them tied up and threw them onto the shore like a piece of cane to burn in the oven."[35] The next day, back on Río Azúcar, the police first summoned all the young boys to the school and then lined the women up in the center of town to change their clothing.[36] The men were banished.

And then they sent us to Porvenir and then we saw that we suffered greatly in the body . . . and then they sent us to Puerto Obaldía, and then . . . Señor Kantule, he got sick, and when he was on the point of death, . . . they sent him home. And . . . when he arose he had all over his hide wounds from the blows the police gave us. Thus it is that you know very well that we are not animals that they should do that to us, that they should tie us up like that.[37]

Within a few years, such measures had effectively quelled most resistance. They had also deeply offended and alienated the Kuna, not just diehards such as Nelsin but vacillating moderates such as Chief Kantule — who died shortly after his return home from detention — and even many of the modernists and collaborators. A few indigenous policemen themselves began subverting official restrictions and punishments.[38] By the end of 1924, the police were firmly in control, but they had few Kuna friends left.

Like pacification, resistance depended on outside support. The pacified Kuna, no longer able to come and go at will or to receive visitors, kept up contact with their comrades on Carti, Ailigandi, and Ustupu in secret.

Those who loathed the wagas . . . they secretly sent news to Grandfather [Colman], they'd come at night. "I'm going fishing," they would announce, at home. But not really, they'd carry a message. And then they'd come back the same night. The police would be mad: "Where have you been wandering about?" they'd confront me. "Nowhere. I went night fishing along the coast."[39]

Eventually rebel leaders set up a network of spies: "Colman said, 'We'll put lookouts at every knoll [i.e. village]. What the wagas call "spies."'The elders say 'lookouts. . . .' 'You will keep watch on the place,' it was said to him. Ukkup Senni's was Igwa-dinuydiginya, along with Susu; they became spies. . . . Kwebdi's was Nersin. Kantule too."[40]

This web of watchers and subversives led back not just to individual leaders such as Colman and Nele, but to their gathering houses. The sacred gathering was the true font of resistance, the organization that linked islands and leaders together and the source of the symbols that inspired them to endure. Though gatherings on pacified islands were invariably suppressed, captive Kuna depended on the gatherings of the rebel strongholds to continue the fight.

Leaders, first of all, knew each other in large part through the gathering. Chiefs were expected to travel frequently to other villages, where they would sing morning and night.[41] A visitor spent the day in a hammock in the gathering house, where he had nothing to do but talk, except when taken out to eat at someone's home, and at night after the last meeting, he would usually sleep at the local chief's house. By the end of a successful visit, a properly loquacious touring chief had made himself known to the host village and created warm personal ties with the men who kept him company. In the case of a regional leader such as Colman, he also reanimated his influence and authority among his followers.

Chiefs and argars also traveled to learn the traditional knowledge, called Father's Way, that they performed in the gathering.[42] Unlike medicine and major curing chants, which could take years or even decades to master, each element of chiefly tradition—one set of instructive metaphors, a narrative about the seers and heroes of sacred history, a description of one level of the underworld and its spirit inhabitants—could be learned in a few sessions with a knowledgeable chief, typically late at night after the gathering had ended. Although ambitious men learned from a variety of teachers, most acquired at least some of their repertoire from the high chiefs who led them. Thus many of Colman's lieutenants, even those now trapped on pacified islands, were also his students.

High chiefs would also convoke regional gatherings, sometimes in response to a crisis or new development, sometimes simply to bring their leading followers together to chant and talk. Delegates would arrive in sailing canoes, or in Colman's case, in a larger vessel such as a schooner or launch he would rent for the occasion. "They'd arrive, crammed full! in the dry season wind. . . . They'd come land here. Crammed full! forty or sixty of them, they'd pour out."[43]

The result was a constant stream of visitors between islands, especially to the Ustupu and Ailigandi gathering houses.

The Carti people were coming and going, the chiefs. Tibin. He was coming and going . . . from Carti Suitupu, Olonibiginya. Olonibiginya's father, he was named Urdummad. He and his father came and went together. . . . They were all truly coming and going to Colman. Another who came and went was from Kwebdi [Río Azúcar], Kantule. . . . One from the mountains, from Madungandi, they called him Kantur Sippu. . . . Another was coming and going, someone from Tigre.[44]

The long-standing ties, built on student-teacher relationships and past regional gatherings, formed the basis for resistance all across San Blas; the visits and meetings that continued through the early 1920s and the clandestine ties to those trapped on police-dominated islands sustained the struggle when the waga seemed poised to swallow up the whole coast.

The gathering also nourished resistance in another way, as the setting in which chiefs sang to their followers, telling them of the struggle and what it meant to be Kuna. President Porras and his minions were trying to dominate them in terms that were moral and ideological as well as material, denigrating "our Indians" as an inferior people and dismissing their way of life as savagery. In the face of this powerful assault, Kuna leaders had to make an answer, to create what has been called a counterhegemonic discourse, naming the enemy and reaffirming their own place in the universe.[45] Much of this discourse was already at hand, in the histories and conventional wisdom of Father's Way, but leaders such as Colman and Nele were also expected to put their own stamp on it, creating a set of metaphors identified with their leadership, metaphors that are still remembered today in oral tradition.[46]

Colman, like all chiefs, reminded his followers of their dependence on Great Father and Great Mother.

Grandfather would sing about how Father had given them the land. About the rising of Tad Ibe, the Sun, how Tad Ibe came renewing his headdress . . . he came waking up the trees. "The birds respond, 'A great person is coming, Great Father is coming,' the birds respond. . . . He is the one who gave us bread, he is the one who gave us drink, he has cared for us,' they sing. . . .

"We people, we are here too," he said. As for us, Father put us here too. "In the whole world . . . only through the Sun do they have food to eat. Only through Father can they eat. We are the same. . . . He came to give us the world. . . . He put peccary here, we came to hold the land. 'This you will eat,' following Father's words.

". . . Great Mother is here. She sits in a hammock. Mother sings: 'You who are coming here, children, I see you with pleasure . . . would that you not suffer. Would that I might lead you for a long time,' Mother sings. She sings to the animals, she sings to all of us. 'This is what Father left me for,' Mother sings from her golden hammock." Thus Grandfather would sing.[47]

Colman's seemingly bland theological message was in fact highly pointed and political, because the land, as the body of Great Mother, had come to the Kuna as a gift from Great Father, one that mere human institutions such as nation states could not abrogate. Similarly, childlike dependence epitomized the proper relationship with the deities, but *only* with them, not with waga policemen, Catholic priests, or upstart youths, who had no legitimate claims to deference or obedience: "Now then, we are caring for the land, no one else has been watching over it, only we have been watching over it. [Father said]: 'That someone else would end up caring for you, that someone else would give you food, it won't happen like that. It is I who will be giving you food.'"[48]

Against this moral baseline of Father's generosity, Mother's bounty, and the ability of the Kuna to provide for their dependents, Colman elaborated a series of ugly and frightening images representing the waga threat. Many were presented as phantoms from his dreams:

". . . Then I lie down, I sleep. No sadness," he said. . . . "I just lie thinking of Father. . . . When I sleep, would that Mother puts good dreams on me, that I wake from sleep having seen only good things in the spirit of the place. . . . I'm not sad," he said . . . "I've been feeling fine. . . . I have eaten, I have gotten things for my children, I have worked on the land, I have worked in crops. . . . I foresee more children coming."

"Now then, elders, while living like that I thought, 'From where might suffering come upon us? What might come to sadden us?'"[49]

As Colman's dream chants progressed, they would turn frightening and oppressive, beginning with the ominous sound of a pit viper's half-heard rattle, which, for a people who hate snakes as much as the Kuna do, summoned up the most negative feelings:

"I am lying in hammock. I am lying in hammock at home. It is the midnight, I am fast asleep. Having reached midnight, the place is all still, the place is all silent. At midnight in my hammock, I feel as if my mother were giving me a shake-shake-shake," thus he sang.

"'Great boy, enough sleeping!' I hear mother call to me," he sang. "I woke up," he said. "When I woke up, I didn't feel sleepy any more," he said. "I rolled over in the hammock," he said. "I lay listening hard to the place," he said.

Grandfather Colman was singing, at Ailigandi, by himself, they say. "When I rolled over, in the still of the night, down on the fourth level, the golden archer snake shook his rattle. 'Porrreee!' that's what I began to hear far off. On the fourth level, the place was being brought to life. Then it sounded as if things were happening on the second level," he said.

". . . The phrase 'Golden archer snake,' that refers to the *waga*. The waga first began to intrude here, the place first began to come alive—*that* is what the golden archer snake making the sound 'poorree' on the fourth level, that's what it means. It was about how the waga first began to bring the place alive."[50]

Other spirit intruders approached.

"Now then . . . the singing would start again, from time to time. A frog would truly be heard singing underground. The frog, toorr, toorr, a great frog came rising up, through the levels of the underworld. 'What might the frog be saying to me,' I thought," he said. "'What does it say to me?' I lay listening. When I listened well again, I dreamed," he said, "and toward the land something else could be heard. A devil was shouting," he said. "A devil came shouting. 'You Kuna I will be surrounding-surrounding'—I lay thinking that it would surround us all."[51]

The effort needed to hear the viper's rattle and the frog's croak far off underground suggested the difficulty in recognizing the initial signs of danger, while the gradual increase in sound as the specters moved up through the levels of the underworld evoked the inexorable approach of the Western world.

Colman devised images for each enemy and danger. Intrusive workers felling trees for their latex were dogs running through the forest at their master's calls. Turtle-fishers were cormorants and other diving birds. The police, as they molested Kuna women and deprived them of their native dress, were leaf-cutter ants stripping cacao trees of their greenery. Indecisiveness and defeatism were represented by toucans, with their heads turning one way and another. But it is the most general images of danger—the serpent, the frog, the shouting devil—that are most remembered today.

To encourage resistance, Colman invoked the great hero Tad Ibe, who before ascending into the sky to become the sun, had with his celestial brothers repeatedly fought the demons of antiquity.

Colman was touching on the place, at Ailigandi. "Therefore children, do not sleep too much. Stay awake," he said. He was strengthening his followers. "Tad Ibe, on the tips of arrows, he put torches with names. That's how I'll do things for you," he was saying. He meant guns. He was chanting metaphorically. "I will fight for you. Great Father made us Kuna men, we come here as the great-Kuna owners of the land. . . . We come being persecuted, that's how the place is. . . . For whom will I be acting? I will be acting for my grandchildren, acting for my children."[52]

Colman's students and visitors to Ailigandi would learn these images as they sat listening and then go home to their own islands to tell them to their followers, and if their gathering house still functioned, to sing them themselves. The men who remember him have no doubts that over time he formed their thinking.

Thus I saw the visitors, the visitors who came and went. "That's what they're here for" I—didn't think about that at all. I supposed that "Grandfather sang to the visitors for no particular reason. For no special reason he has begun to inform them about things." As for me, I still went around naked then. I always lay down at the end of the bench [in the gathering house]. From there I saw the chief sing to visitors, about how things were about to go bad, sometimes I heard him singing like that. He sang about that it seems, and later, well little by little I thought about it; I really began to take it in.[53]

There was, after all, considerable danger that people would *not* take it in, that they would fail to rise to the challenge: resistance was by no means inevitable. It was quite possible that the villages under Colman's leadership would adopt Inabaginya's strategy, countering further incursions but avoiding responsibility for the inhabitants of islands already dominated by the police, or that the political struggles between Colman and Inabaginya would be seen as discrediting the cause of Kuna autonomy. Danger, too, that if the police came to Ailigandi or Ustupu or Carti, they might uncover the same rifts between young and old as elsewhere, or that people would not be sufficiently motivated for the coming battle. Colman needed to seize people's imaginations, to evoke and represent as well as name the enemy, to remind people what they had to lose, and to find a level of discourse that would ennoble the struggle and prepare for its culmination. "Therefore, he did well. We sat listening with pleasure. . . . One and another sat taking it in. To make his children act, that is what Grandfather worked for. If Grandfather had not worked in that way, well where would we be? Well the place would be nothing but wagas."[54]

And in the afternoon he brought together all the women of the village. He brought them together there in the park. He put them in a line, one after the other. He was taking things off them. He put a big table there, then they called them, one by one, to take all the beads off them, their molas, and the noserings they wore. They broke them and gave them back again. Then they gave them a length of cloth that they got from the store of a certain Morales. They got it from the store, they gave each one a length, and off they went. "Make that dress, use it from now on. From today onwards you have to wear that dress. Don't use your traditional clothing." Well, off they went, even the oldest women, to their homes.[1]

18. Dancing and Civilization

The police and their superiors wanted more than control. Ever since April 1919, when Belisario Porras decreed that Nargana schoolgirls could no longer wear noserings, it was clear that the government's prime goal was ethnocide, the destruction of a culture. Its agents would not be content until they had eradicated the "semisavage" or "barbaric" customs of the Kuna, turning them into good Spanish-speaking Panamanians.

This preoccupation with cultural practice often turns up among colonial and modernizing governments, but it is by no means universal. Quite a few states and empires have been content to let subject peoples wear colorful costumes and speak unintelligible languages as long as they submitted to authority and provided the labor needed in mines or plantations. Panama's very different stance, its insistence on transforming Indian culture, was in part strategic and opportunistic. Lacking the guns, soldiers, funds, and bloodthirstiness needed to effect instant submission, the government could conquer the Kuna only by changing them. Necessity, however, does not fully explain the fervor that politicians, bureaucrats, and policemen brought to the civilizing mission, the affront they felt at the presence of an unashamedly non-Latin culture within the national borders.

The cultural conquest of the Kuna formed part of a program of nation building, the creation of a new republic out of an isolated and impoverished Colombian province. The obstacles in the way included a volatile, precarious political system, a heterogenous national population, and most of all, domination by a foreign power. The United States reserved the right to take land and conduct military maneuvers, to enforce sanitation in the terminal cities, and intervene in civil conflict. It kept a monopoly on radio and telegraphic communication and veto power over the financing of any major government project. Possessing the only military force on the Isthmus, in 1916 the United

States further insisted on disarming the Panamanian police. Inevitably, despite its fervent wish that Panama would learn to manage its own affairs, the U.S. legation was repeatedly dragged into local conflicts and problems.[2]

In some respects the situation had improved by the 1920s. Talk of annexation had all but ceased, President Porras and his allies increasingly asserted themselves, and both sides moved toward realization that the canal treaty needed renegotiation. The North American establishment brought economic opportunity, though never as much as was hoped for, and the United States had dramatically improved public health. Elites were willing to learn English and collaborate with foreigners, and even the liberals, who resented American domination but worshiped progress and economic development, could not help being impressed by the wealthiest and most powerful nation in the hemisphere. Panamanians, nonetheless, were repeatedly reminded of their dependent status, of the hollowness of their claims to sovereignty, and of the scorn in which the gringos held them.

In these circumstances, the Kuna, by loudly and successfully rejecting national control and Hispanic culture, poured salt on the wounds of injured nationalism. Politicians and bureaucrats could not help but perceive their frustrations on a small stage like San Blas partly in terms of more fundamental national dilemmas. For the sake of the canal, they had to put up with the loss of territory and the presence of thousands of aliens unable to speak the national language, but it was insupportable to endure the same insults from a tribe of semisavages.

The Kuna only made matters worse by showing a preference for names such as Smith and Davis and for schooling in English. A few officials, including the first intendente, Enrique Hurtado, may have been indifferent to anglophone influence, and the foreign minister, Narciso Garay, later claimed that he had argued in cabinet meetings for tolerance of Indian custom.[3] To Belisario Porras and Andrés Mojica, however, the struggles on Nargana with Anna Coope and Charly Robinson only served to confirm the suspicion that the Kuna resisted Panamanian civilization out of seditious foreign loyalties as well as barbaric obduracy.

The government's ultimate goal in San Blas was total transformation of the Indians. In the short run, police, bureaucrats, and their young Kuna allies concentrated on particular targets, creating a coherent program of symbolic domination, a package of meaningful, highly charged tokens of Panamanian hegemony. By no means merely symbolic in the sense of something decorative or ineffectual, the effort to destroy indigenous culture was understood by both civilizers and their opponents as the heart of the matter.

First and last, the government strove to eliminate difference, to make Indians the same as everyone else. Any noticeably distinct practice could be targeted, especially if the Kuna struggled hard to defend it, but early on, female dress emerged as the prime embodiment of alterity. Belisario Porras and his subordinates simply could not imagine how Indians could be turned into good citizens so long as women bound their arms and legs and stuck rings in their noses. The campaign that began in 1919, which was expanded in 1921 to include all aspects of female dress, was further extended in 1922 to encompass newly pacified islands and the old grand-mothers who had previously been exempted.[4]

The police also singled out indecency and barbarism. Bathing naked out of doors, chewing chicha mash to encourage fermentation, picking lice out of hair, checking agriculturalists' bodies for ticks, burying defective newborns, piercing septums, de-forming limbs — all had to stop in the name of decency and decorum.[5] This revulsion at savage practice, however deeply felt, had an element of calculation: by taking noserings or infanticide as representative of native practice as a whole, government agents implicitly asserted that all difference was barbaric.

Closely linked to the question of decency was hygiene. It did not seem to matter that the Kuna bathed frequently or wore spotlessly laundered clothes, or that many outsiders found their villages neat and clean. The disorder and filth perceived by the police were blamed for a series of epidemics that swept through San Blas in this era, including several waves of smallpox and the worldwide influenza pandemic of 1918-1919.[6] What the Kuna needed most was immunization against smallpox, but the government found vaccine for only a handful of islands. The paramedic assigned to San Blas, who seldom had enough of the most basic remedies even for the police and teachers (and whose position was more often than not left vacant) did next to nothing for Kuna well-being.

Instead, government functionaries tried to improve health by making the Kuna neat and tidy. Organizing householders to sweep the streets and collect trash, they ordered them to fill up wells (whose brackish but mostly untainted water was used for washing) and to do away with pigpens (which, however backward in official eyes, did little harm to health). As police control consolidated, they had kitchen gardens and medicinal shrubs uprooted, coconut palms and breadfruit trees felled, houses rebuilt along straight, broad streets, and islands swept bare of obstacles and shade.[7] These measures replicated ones that only a few years before had been imposed on urban Panama by the North Americans in a high-handed but highly effective cam-paign that had all but eliminated the threats of dysentery, malaria, and yellow fever.[8] In San Blas the police succeeded in passing on the insult the American sanitarians had imposed on Panama (It is not *we* who are unclean but the Indians). Against smallpox, however, the cleanup had no effect whatsoever.

The wagas didn't want the place looking bad. They wanted . . . everything neatly in row after row, things were happening that way. "These coconut palms are just spoiling the place. Cut down the palms. Put things in rows," the wagas said. The elders did what they were told. The place was being remade that way, wide streets were being laid out. . . .

They felled a big grove of coconut palms. Palms wiped out!. The elders' coconuts were gone. . . . What could their owners say? . . . Well if you called out, you'd come to grief. The elders had been despoiled. Something good had ended.[9]

Sanitation, in sum, enacted order more than it promoted health. Unable or unwilling to recognize the discipline and control in Kuna life, the intendente and police were going to put their barbarous subjects in order by means of right angles and straight lines, as had other colonial authorities since the time of Cortés.[10]

Order was also imposed through paper. Boats and cargos were recorded on manifests; Indians were counted in a national census; and each police post established a registry of births and deaths. (The police on Nargana, greatly offended by a similar list kept at the Protestant mission by Miss Coope, interpreted it as an encroachment on national sovereignty.)[11] Each notation and piece of paper had an obvious instrumental goal, contributing to domination of the Indians; at the same time, each was a token of national hegemony, an assertion that the people whose names were recorded belonged to Panama.[12]

Order and disorder were also the essence of the police campaign to suppress drinking and puberty ceremonies. Like Leonardo Gassó before them, the government forces experienced chichas as chaotic and dangerous.[13] "The greatest part of the disorders, disregard, and punishable deeds that have occurred among the Indians, above all in those who, unfortunately, are still under the pernicious influence of Colman, have been produced by alcohol."[14] Except on bibulous Nargana, the Kuna did not drink at all between chichas (something for which the police gave them no credit), but during festivities they pulled out all the stops, men, women, and older adolescents going on for hours or days. Bunches of men sometimes wandered through town, even past schools in session, and until 1919, visitors from unpacified villages would attend chichas on islands where the police were stationed, adding their voices to those of local dissidents. As one pro-government man later remembered:

Those of the [unpacified] villages, who did not yet share with us the ideas of advancement, would give free rein to their unrestrained sentiments, loosing their tongues in mortifying words, face-to-face with the police, who armed as they were, and carried along by the current of the *fiesta*, at times did not know how to keep a clear head. One day an altercation of very bad tone took place, in which one of the disputants, a member of the outpost, let off various pistol discharges. In spite of having done them in the air, they caused annoyance and strong commentaries against the servants of the government.[15]

Thus in March 1919 the administration decreed prohibition for all of San Blas.[16]

The ban by no means settled the issue. For the Kuna, puberty ceremonies promoted the maturation of young girls and the ritual equilibrium of the community as well as individual enjoyment, and they were not about to abandon them without a struggle. Colman repeatedly defended chichas as time-honored custom.[17] His followers smuggled in rum (which supplemented the home brew),[18] and on the unpacified islands they went on sponsoring puberty rituals despite raids from Nargana to smash the giant clay pots in which the cane beer matured.[19]

Along with order and decency, the administration also imposed signs of modernity and progress, at least to the extent that its meager budget allowed. It was important that, as much as possible, official buildings be constructed of boards, with raised floors, and in 1923, kerosene street lights were installed in several pacified villages, for the sake of progress as well as security against rebel attacks.

Most important, perhaps, and certainly inherent in everything else, was national sovereignty, represented by the flag. The first Kuna chiefs to visit Panama in 1904 and 1906 were sent home with the national banner. Intendente Vaglio, as one of his first acts in 1919, forcibly raised the flag on rebel islands. And during the 1920s, as each island submitted, the Intendencia ordered more flags. The Kuna readily understood and used this language, as their defiant display of Colombian banners during presidential visits made clear.

Everything American or British, all the reminders of foreign domination, had to go. In their place, the government imposed distinctively Latin, Hispanic institutions: Catholicism, saints' names, and especially the Spanish language. In a nation dominated by English-speakers, it was essential that Indians take names such as López and not Smith, and that they speak Castillian rather than English.[20]

In addition to the generically Hispanic, the Kuna were to learn specifically national and mestizo custom. In the jumble of different populations of urban Panama and Colón, it was agreed that true national identity—the elements of dress, cuisine, song, and festival that everyone recognized as quintessentially Panamanian—was to be found in the southwestern interior among the mestizo peasants of Coclé, Herrera, Los Santos, and Chiriquí. The Kuna might not be ready to wear the lacy pollera, but they could certainly learn to dance the tamborito.

The mass, on the other hand, was not a priority. The administration took no special interest in making Christians out of the Indians except on Nargana, and even there, it promoted Catholicism less to save souls than as a token of Hispanic identity, a response to the anglophone threat posed by Anna Coope's Protestant mission. Nor did the police and bureaucrats pay any special attention to Kuna religion. Once they had pacified an island, the sacred gathering had to go, along with the rest of indigenous practice, but officials never expressed the same fear and scorn as they did toward chichas.

Among all the elements of national culture imposed on the Indians, schools and dancing were probably most important. Schools were the ideological weapon for overcoming Indian resistance, the substitute for the army Panama lacked. In the words of an official report: "We the employees of the Circumscription of San Blas are the sappers who clear the terrain for Public Instruction, but the employees of Public Instruction are those who will establish themselves in the conquered position and hold it."[21] As the medium by which civilization and nationalism could be instilled, schools taught young Kuna bodily discipline, patriotic sentiments, literacy, and the Spanish language. They were also themselves the message: they embodied the liberal cult of schooling as it had developed in nineteenth-century Europe and the Americas, what the historian Eric Hobsbawm has called "the secular equivalent of the church."[22] For citizens of modernizing nations—and in this instance, for almost everyone involved in civilizing the Kuna, from Belisario Porras on down—formal education was a token of value, marker of social class, and source of individual and collective improvement. Not surprisingly, they all endorsed Intendente Vaglio's sentiments: "Without schools there is no civilization."[23]

The Kuna, for their part, reacted to schools in complex and ambivalent ways. Conservatives opposed them tenaciously, recognizing that schooling would supplant traditional socialization and overturn the age hierarchy. Others, especially on Nargana and Corazón, wanted their children educated, for the prestige of new knowledge as well as the practical benefits of literacy. Colman and Nele represented a middle position held by many people who recognized the utility of schooling but feared its potential for harm: Colman sent his own sons away to be educated, and Nele promoted a small educational plant on Ustupu, staffed by Kuna and controlled by the community. But both recognized the government's schools as a tool of domination, one they opposed as tenaciously as the most reactionary traditionalist.[24]

The most curious feature of the acculturative program was social dancing, which began with the tamborito performed by Ana Moreno de James at Christmas of 1918. In early 1920, Nargana held its first carnival, with dancing, a parade, and a ceremonial carriage bearing the Queen of Carnival, who was Claudio Iglesias's sister Luisa.[25] At about the same time, the youth group established itself in a newly built clubhouse and began sponsoring dances to the music of wind-up victrolas, first for schoolchildren but soon for other young people, even married couples as well. Attendance was obligatory, and a young woman who refused to go, or a husband or father who kept her home, was fined or even jailed. Starting in 1922, centers with names like "Club Civilización" and "Centro Claudio Iglesias" were inaugurated on Playón Chico, Tupile, and Río Azúcar.[26] Everywhere police and teachers went, clubs followed.

In Urgandi [Río Sidra], then, they put a club. . . . The old men, the masters of the place, got angry . . . the old men didn't want it, they didn't want a club. On the other side, those who had brought it were dancing. Dancing. Little by little the followers began to be taken over . . . the young men were in control. . . . The old men said, "I'm sick of dancing in the club. The women said the same thing. . . . They'd say to them, "If you don't dance in the club, I'll throw you in jail."[27]

By December of 1922 the intendente had some second thoughts, concluding that dancing needed regulation: students who were up every night until eleven or twelve had little energy left for schoolwork the next morning. Although dances were henceforth to be held on Saturdays and holidays only, no doubts were entertained about the "excellent results in our civilizing labors" provided by the tamborito and the two-step.[28]

The obvious question is why dancing, rather than religion or labor? Resistance itself certainly encouraged the police and modernists, as also happened with chichas and women's dress. Dancing, moreover, offered a powerful diversion to restless young men and women, a much more exciting way to pass an evening than singing mission hymns or listening to chiefs chant, and as a source of distress to the senior generation, it powerfully subverted the age hierarchy. At the same time, dancing, clubs, and carnival, as complex, layered symbols, imposed a form of domination that both sides intuitively understood.

The clubs where it all took place seem to have been modeled on the political organizations then prominent in Panamanian urban life, which provided recreation for their members as well as votes for party candidates.[29] Carnival was the culmination of each year's dancing, the year's most important event. Many social theorists, following a line of analysis that begins with the great Russian literary critic, Mikhail Bakhtin, identify carnival with excess, rebellion, and reversal of the social order.[30] While Panama's version of the pre-lenten festival certainly had its Rabelaisian aspects, it was above all the master symbol of national identity. Combining rural and urban elements and dominating the ritual and social year in the capital as much as the interior, carnival was an obvious token of Panamanian civilization to impose on the Indians.

As for dancing itself, this was hardly the first or last time that it provoked social change or generational conflict: the waltz had shocked Europe and the Americas as thoroughly in the 1830s as rock and roll would in the 1950s. During "the jazz age" following World War I, the so-called Dance Craze swept the World, and like the great influenza pandemic, it eventually reached the remotest corners, even Nargana and Tupile. When young men and women did the *tamborito,* the national dance, they enacted Isthmian patriotism, just as Ana de James had in 1918. But they also danced the foxtrot, the waltz and two-step, jazz steps, and even the *danzón cubano,* the precursor of the mambo— all tokens of international, North American-tinged modernism.[31] The two formed an uneasy mixture.

To Kuna opponents, what most dismayed them was the sexuality of social dancing.[32] They objected to couples holding each other as they moved around the floor, and they feared dances as occasions at which women and girls were open to the advances of the police. A complaint by the chief of Tigre, taken down by a secretary in English, said:

First carnival on Nargana, 1920. Claudio Iglesias's
sister Luisa as queen of carnival.

You see and they doing wrong and touch My girls and put my women in the jail they
doing Touch my women you see now they building a Club and State [that is, start] to
dance the girls you see by and by police do jealous with my women you see when any
girls can speak with his husband and young men can speak with his wife . . . you see
panameño people want to take all the lady.[33]

Kuna fears about lecherous policemen were not limited to clubs. In terms of
sexual danger, jails were worst of all, because women as well as men could be
arrested, and in the cells a woman was alone and unprotected. "They even throw
the women into prison in order by violence to have relations with them and the
women cannot defend themselves nor can their men defend them because they are
so terrified. Thus it happened in the village where the policeman Herrera lives.[34]

Official records confirm two cases of sexual violence by the police. In June of
1921, the detachment head on Nargana, Ramón Garrido, wrote the intendente that

an agent named Daniel Pomareda had tried to violate a woman in jail while drunk. "In view of the gravity of the offense . . . I request from you his immediate transfer and to that end he follows under arrest to headquarters."[35]

The second case occurred two years later, in October 1923. The agent in charge on Playón Chico wrote the detachment head on Tupile:

I inform you that yesterday the Colonial Agent, Sr. Etanislao Hinestroza, on guard in this Section, taking advantage of the fact that I was on a mission to the [detachment] headquarters, penetrated the room that serves as jail for prisoners, where the indigenous woman [name omitted] was under arrest for police offenses, making use of her by force. . . . As I consider this a grave offense and that there can be no pardon for it, I make you aware of the case so that you in turn may inform the Intendente if you consider it appropriate.[36]

In a formal investigation, the victim testified that since she had been arrested, Hinestroza had pestered her to live with him, which she had no interest in doing, until one night he tied her up with a belt and raped her. The detachment head, Miguel Gordón, a hard-bitten agent with no tolerance for Kuna back-talk, nonetheless readily concluded that his accused colleague was guilty, despite an absence of eyewitnesses.[37] The disposition of both cases may well have fallen short of ideal — Hinestroza's name disappeared from police rosters but Pomareda's did not. There is no sign, however, that their superiors condoned their actions or allowed them to continue.

It would be naive to assume that no rapes escaped detection or report, and the surviving records are incomplete, but there is also little reason to believe that the two cases were the visible tip of a monstrous iceberg. Not only were at least some superior officers firmly opposed to molestation of the Indians, but it is highly unlikely that the schoolteachers, who did complain several times about police misconduct, would have tolerated blatant sexual violence. It is much more plausible that a handful of shocking incidents came to epitomize for the Kuna, to sum up in the most powerful manner, sexual predation that was for the most part more diffuse.[38] Consensual relations and seduction undoubtedly occurred much more often than rape, and coercion seems to have been directed for the most part against male Kuna rivals and would-be protectors of sisters and daughters.[39] For Kuna men, knowing that women and girls were willingly conducting affairs or marrying outsiders was in some ways even more upsetting and threatening than forced sex.

For that reason we don't want the Panamanians, because each man wants his women, and some have the idea about their wife, as they were at the dance and when they know that his wife has done wrong, the husband is angry, then the policemen put him in the jail and so the husband cannot speak about how his wife has done wrong because they put him in the jail one or two months.[40]

If rape was infrequent, the police were hardly chaste. A few brought their wives, but the single men in the majority were looking for spouses or lovers. In 1920 a Tupile man complained that his teenaged daughter had been made pregnant by a police agent, Guillermo Denis. The culprit satisfied national law and his superiors by offering to marry the girl, though her father was by no means happy about a poor policeman as son-in-law.[41] Other incidents of misbehavior involving indigenous as well as colonial agents, such as elopement, adulterous affairs, obscene language, and insult to teachers, also appear in the records.[42] But many or most of the police, as long as they acted within the bounds of national law, probably saw little wrong in their love affairs.

It might be argued that the struggle over sex resulted from individual desire rather than official policy. But policy actually played an important role: the government was determined to break down all aspects of Kuna separatism (even if, as always, higher-ups convinced themselves that it could be done peacefully). Everyone knew that the Indians called Panamanians *waga*, that (incredibly) they believed themselves superior, and that they expressed their superiority and difference by refusing to marry outsiders. As far as Panamanians were concerned, such attitudes were mere prejudice, deserving of destruction rather than respect.[43]

In 1920 a police agent discussed with Inadoiginya, the collaborationist chief of Tupile, the possibility of intermarriage.

I said to him that in keeping with this, Wagas[44] will arrive in a place where [the local people] liked them, and that should they would want to marry it could be done and the Intendente had ordered me to offer every protection in this matter and this would bring progress and Civilization, and otherwise it would be much delayed. . . . I said if some policeman asks some girl to marry him, he being a good man, I believe it can be allowed him . . . it is necessary . . . in order to achieve the aims that we are pursuing, to transform San Blas into a civilized place, that the pretensions of the Indians of being superior in race disappear.[45]

The following year, after agent Denis married the girl he had impregnated, she gave birth to a mixed-race child, an event announced with a flourish in a letter to the intendente:

I have the honor to inform you that with the date of the 18th of the present month, there has been registered in this office the birth of the minor José Guillermo Denis, child of Colonial Agent Guillermo Denis and the Indian woman, [name omitted]. This is the first such case that has happened, being in agreement the parents of the Indian woman, who show themselves very content. As you will see, little by little there have been fulfilled the desires of our illustrious chief executive, Dr. Belisario Porras, which is the crossing of the races.[46]

In 1924, when the intendente wrote the secretary of government and justice to respond to charges that the dance clubs promoted immorality and the seduction of young girls, he pointed to the marriages contracted by Indian women with police agents and other wagas, marriages that were not only moral, he said, but were "succeeding in destroying the ill will that since time immemorial the indigenous peoples of all countries have felt against the Castillian element."[47]

Clearly, rape was not policy but intermarriage was. As government officials saw it, to integrate the Kuna into national society, they had to break down barriers as well as erase differences, and the sexual barrier was one of the highest and most strongly defended. Kuna defenders, moreover, were obviously right about the dances: they *were* mixers, designed to bring men and women together for romance and to weaken the senior generation's control of marriage. Even the change in female dress made women more accessible and desirable as well as more civilized.

The program carried out in the San Blas microcosm was conditioned by the national and international macrocosm, in this instance by Panama's complex mix of races and ethnicities. Whereas the Conservative Party stood for white domination and racial exclusivity, the Liberals appealed widely to people of color. They were committed to a national population as well as a national society, to a people who combined formerly distinct races and ethnicities. Racial divisions, whether set by white elites or separatist Indians, impeded that goal and had to be overcome.

This process was being repeated all across Latin America, as emerging elites tried to come to terms with their mestizo, "mixed," background, to see themselves not as exclusively Indian or European, but as a new, distinctively American fusion, what one Mexican theorist grandly called "the cosmic race."[48] Laudable in its inclusiveness and intent to break down caste barriers, the mestizo synthesis had several blind spots, notably concerning Indians and Latin Americans of African descent. It embraced the Indian ancestry of national populations but not the indigenous peoples who survived—"an inert Indian past provid[ed] the raw material for a resolutely mestizo future"—and like most melting pot philosophies, it had little tolerance for groups reluctant to jump into the pot.[49] No one could see a way to create nations in which component peoples also preserved distinctive identities, still less one that holdouts such as the Kuna refused altogether to join.

With another few decades in San Blas, the police would very likely have had their way. Many young people enjoyed the dances, and at least among the modernist minority, a few would tolerate intermarriage. When the police quizzed Chief Inadoiginya of Tupile on the subject, he answered that he and his followers had no objections, though they much preferred their daughters to marry rich shopowners rather than poor policemen.[50] By the mid-1920s, quite a few merchants as well as police had taken Kuna wives and begun raising families. In doing so, however, they provoked resentment and even fury, whose full force they would feel when their domination of the captive villages unraveled.

19.
Friends
and
Agitators
Frustrated intendentes often blamed their troubles on pernicious outside agitators such as Anna Coope and José de la Rosa. This patent rationalization, which allowed officials to ignore the reality and depth of Indian grievances, did have a germ of truth: the Kuna looked to sympathetic outsiders for information, advice, and in the case of de la Rosa, for critical assistance in defending themselves against outside threats, particularly threats from the government. Apart from Coope, Purdy, de la Rosa, and the many laborers and merchants with business in San Blas, quite a few outsiders passed through during the early 1920s: sportsmen, travelers, drifters, fugitives from justice, deserters from U.S. forces, the writer Rex Beach, even a Colombian novelist, Miguel Acevedo y Pinilla.[1] One of these visitors, a veteran of the Mexican Revolution named Olivo Olivares, presented just the kind of threat that intendentes feared.

Olivares, then a sailor on a coasting merchant vessel, turned up on Nargana in March of 1922. Claiming to have been stranded accidentally, he was allowed to stay until his boat returned.[2] During his few days on the island, he was agreeable and loquacious, discoursing to all who would listen on his native country, its indigenous peoples, and the Mexican Revolution. A few days later, an order arrived from Porvenir for his arrest as an alien without means of support or official permission to stay, but by then Olivares had used the pretext of a brief visit to Tigre to fly the coop.

Worse, rumors came back that Olivares was spreading sedition, encouraging resistance to the government, and playing on fears that the police would burn Tigre as they had Niatupu.[3] Colman's group began holding regional gatherings, and a "disrespectful and menacing" letter, said to have been penned by the Mexican, was sent to the intendente. Word soon came that he had moved to Ailigandi, where a merchant captain was said to have observed him supervising firing practice and teaching Kuna how to make defensive trenches.

Intendente Mojica, thoroughly alarmed, embargoed Ailigandi and dispatched another arresting party in a launch, led by Lieutenant Francisco Cabeza. The launch's engines began giving trouble almost immediately, the first sign of a jinxed voyage typical of the difficulties facing the government in subduing the Kuna. After a brief stop at Tigre, Cabeza spent two days trapped on Nargana by high seas and mechanical troubles. When he set out again, the engines failed altogether, and the launch was swept onto a reef. It took three days to refloat the boat and nine more to patch its hull and tow it home, leaving Olivares free to continue spreading subversion.

Cabeza set out in late May on a third attempt just as Colman's lawyer came into San Blas on one of his periodic visits. Informed of the embargo on Ailigandi, de la Rosa continued his trip there regardless.[4] Cabeza, meanwhile, stopped at Tupile in order to arrive at Ailigandi early in the morning, when Kuna islands were most vulnerable, while able-bodied men were away working. The pause gave rebel spies time to get word to Colman, who, when Cabeza arrived, was waiting with all his men.[5] The ensuing confrontation, recorded in oral tradition as well as an official report, typifies the tense encounters, halfway between violence and conversation, in which rebels and police met each other in the early twenties.

As one witness, then a half-grown boy, remembered the occasion, the Ailigandi men worried about their lack of firearms:

The elders said, "what can we use? . . . We'll make lances. . . . We'll make them an arm's span long. If the waga starts to fight, we'll beat the wagas with them, those of us without guns." . . . Colman admonished them. "The wagas will come. Before they get here you assemble, all of you . . . have the sharpened boat poles buried beneath you. . . . Sit with your feet on top, with its cord just peeping out of the ground. . . . If you see the wagas start to fight, whssssht! you pull it out, and immediately you've got it in your hands. Right away you begin to hit them."

Women and children were sent to the windward side of the island, to crouch among rocks there. The men who did have hunting guns lurked in nearby houses or hid their arms close at hand in the thatch. "As for Colman, he sat in the middle. Right smack in the middle there was a chair, and he sat in that. Friend Ceferino, he stood behind his father. . . . He was ready too: now he had a gun too, ready in his pocket. A little pistol."[6]

Cabeza arrived and was taken to the village meeting hall, where he encountered Nele of Ustupu, as well as Colman. Under questioning, Colman insisted that they had disregarded Olivares's advice to arm themselves against the police, and concerning the flurry of regional meetings, that they had merely been called to admonish people about working hard and acting morally. As for Olivares himself, he had started cursing, staying out late at night, and propositioning women, so they fobbed him off on a delegation of Colombian Kuna on their way back across the border. Although not in the least convinced by Colman's deceptions, Cabeza gave up on the interrogation, contenting himself with a demonstration of police firepower on his way out.

In the next few days, Cabeza learned from Inabaginya—who as always was ready to inform on Colman—not only that Olivares had been hidden upriver at Ustupu, but also that Cabeza himself had come close to death. On his way back west, he stopped again at Ailigandi, to find the chiefs of all the islands in Colman's group assembled, along with José de la Rosa. Mindful of warnings from Inabaginya, Cabeza stationed agents to watch his back and guard the doorways. Colman's forces, in turn, assigned men to shadow the police.

The lieutenant and the lawyer launched immediately into a heated argument, with the result that Cabeza arrested de la Rosa on the spot for defying orders to stay away from Ailigandi. Though oblivious to the lawyer's protests, Cabeza was persuaded to release him by Colman, who promised to come to Porvenir within a few days. Prudently resisting the urge to arrest Colman himself, Cabeza tried to question Nele, who refused to reply except by shaking a carbine, which the police promptly confiscated.[7]

Back on Porvenir the following day, Cabeza drew up a formal complaint, which in addition to authorizing the arrest of Colman, Nele, and the Chief of Tigre for fomenting sedition, fined de la Rosa fifty dollars for violating the embargo.[8] A week later, when de la Rosa, Nele, and three representatives of Colman turned up on Porvenir, Nele and two others were taken into custody as hostages, while Cabeza went off again to capture Olivares at Ustupu.

Olivo Olivares disappeared into Colombia before Cabeza could find him, but José de la Rosa's troubles had just begun, because his circling enemies smelled blood in the water.[9] In a meeting on Nargana in mid-August, he was confronted by Charly Robinson and other angry Nargana men, who complained vociferously that Indians from Colman's group were meeting their quotas with de la Rosa by stealing coconuts.[10] A memorial signed by more than one hundred names from Nargana denounced de la Rosa for fomenting "antipatriotism,"[11] and in hearings held on the island, a witness from Río Azúcar claimed to have heard de la Rosa state that the president wanted to make them intermarry with wagas and promise to prevent the government from taking off noserings or punishing Kuna who attacked policemen.[12]

At the end of October the newspapers published a presidential order permanently banning de la Rosa from San Blas, on the grounds that he was defrauding the Indians as well as fomenting rebellion. His protests were in vain, as was a memorial signed by more than seventy Kuna leaders. Porras, far from relenting, ordered a judicial investigation with an eye toward indicting de la Rosa. The investigation apparently failed, and de la Rosa briefly went on the attack once again, suing Estanislao López, unsuccessfully, for calling him a thief.[13] As late as 1924 he was still petitioning to be let back in San Blas.[14]

By depriving Colman of de la Rosa's services as propagandist, spokesman in government offices, and defense attorney, the administration scored a great victory. Beyond the specifics of his advocacy, Joselito, as a lawyer among bureaucrats, thwarted intendentes by promoting the rule of law over administrative fiat—by insisting that police could not arrest without warrants, that individuals should not be jailed or held hostage without legal justification, and that only judges and juries could convict for crimes. Since judges usually agreed—and since Panama was democratic enough to heed judicial orders—his view often prevailed. In other respects, however, Mojica and Porras did Colman a good turn by ending the land-titling scheme, which if not technically fraud, was indeed a deception, one with no chance of securing Indian lands, still less of evicting police and schools.

Few visitors to San Blas stirred things up as vigorously as José de la Rosa or Olivo Olivares. Some, however, left much fuller records of their goals and experiences. Even those who had trouble telling the truth, as was the case with the next pair of outsiders to arrive, revealed a great deal about themselves and the Kuna, about the encounter between Western sensibilities and the exotic Other. Lady Lilian Richmond Brown was an unconventional, cigarette-smoking British aristocrat who came to Panama at some point during 1922 (she was quite vague on dates) with F. A. Mitchell Hedges, a noted hunter and fisherman.[15] Having heard wild stories of San Blas and the Chucunaque, Mitchell Hedges organized a trip down the coast on a borrowed yacht, while Richmond Brown nursed an illness at the Hotel Tivoli.[16] On his return, Mitchell Hedges and Richmond Brown, now recovered, bought the yacht and headed back to San Blas on their own.

Knowing just what happened on their outing is somewhat difficult, since the lies and exaggerations in Richmond Brown's book written a few years later begin with the title, *Unknown Tribes, Uncharted Seas*. In her narrative, Indians perpetually teeter on the brink of attack, stingray tails can kill within minutes, and man-eating sharks are everywhere, making the briefest dip in shallow water suicidal. The pair did have adventures, most of them near-disasters of their own making, but the seas were charted and the Kuna friendly and well known.

After touching at Porvenir, Nargana, and Niatupu, the pair stopped in an isolated anchorage, where on a jaunt upstream Richmond Brown wrote that they were menaced first by a bushmaster and then by a caiman. "Crash! went the rifle. An enormous burst of water rose into the air close to where we had been leaning over drinking. 'A damned great crocodile,' he said. 'I saw its head stealing out from under that bush. Jolly place, isn't it?'"[17]

Richmond Brown's romanticized interest in the Kuna, occasionally tinged with empathy or admiration, tended much more to unabashed condescension and revul-

Frederick Mitchell Hedges and Cimral Colman, 1922.

sion. She praised the Indians for defecating in the ocean, a practice she found noteworthy, given "how appallingly dirty some of their other habits are." Finding the Indians "pathetic and childlike in their simplicity," she casually concluded that they were often incestuous and "really incapable of any of the finer feelings as we know them."[18] The pair attempted to overawe the natives with flares, firepower, and simple medical remedies, some of which, she freely admitted, were placebos. She baldly asserted that the Kuna had never before seen firearms or motor vessels, and—fulfilling one of the most tired myths of colonial writing—that the flares convinced the Indians that she and Mitchell Hedges were gods.[19]

At Ailigandi, after initially avoiding a meeting ("A pow-wow would mean hours in a smelly hut, stinking like nothing on earth"), they conferred with Colman.[20] As a Kuna chronicler remembers the encounter, the chief pumped them for information:

First an Englishman came here, an Englishman. . . . He was visiting for pleasure. He spoke here . . . about his origins, his fathers and where they lived, their customs, he spoke about what he had learned about others' things. Back then Colman always wanted to hear about wagas' ways. If a waga came here, he'd ask him a lot of things, to learn from him.[21]

In Richmond Brown's version:

The Chief appeared to me to be quite an intelligent man. Among other things, he told us that their gods had ordered them not to change their mode of dress, or do away with their anklets and nose-rings.

He was very anxious to know whether the land from which we came had got a name — did a great spirit dwell there, and who were we? Midge did his best to answer these questions, telling him that the name of the land was England, where there was a great white Chief who was called a King.

The Indian mind is very curious, seeming to confuse the spiritual with the material. . . . It was difficult to keep a straight face. . . . His next query was a poser. Were we the children of the King? I hope our reply will not be considered *lèse-majesté*, for there was nothing for us to do but claim the greatness thrust upon us![22]

(Colman, who had seen the world as a sailor, had words in his own language for kings and Englishmen, and was undoubtedly trying to ask the pair whether they were the subjects, not the biological offspring, of George V.)

After more coastal cruising, Richmond Brown claims that they crossed the mountains to the Kuna of the Chucunaque — "I knew I had been plunged from the twentieth century into a prehistoric age" — though nothing she wrote substantiates the claim.[23] They then blundered back down the coast toward Colón, on the way getting lost in the forest and running aground. They crossed through the canal to the Pacific, spending some months catching large sharks and running aground again. Richmond Brown returned to England in April of 1923, where she was made a fellow of the Linnean Society, the Royal Geographical Society, the Zoological Society, and the Royal Anthropological Institute, presumably in return for donating her collection of molas and artifacts to several British museums.[24]

The next foreign visitor to San Blas brought with him a very different set of expectations and a different set of literary models for writing about his experiences. The only thing he shared with Richmond Brown and Mitchell Hedges was the assumption that with the Kuna he had found a primitive remnant of past ages. A native of Pennsylvania employed by the Panama railroad, William Markham saw Indian men — and once, "the queerest looking woman I had ever seen" — at the docks in Colón, which sparked his curiosity.[25] He gradually made friends with a man from Nargana whom he called Jake, and after two visits to Markham's home, Jake returned the invitation.

In May 1923 Markham set out in the Colon Import Company's boat, the *Arabia*, equipped with cot, blankets, food and cookware, camera, guns, and gifts for the Kuna. To judge by the manuscript account he wrote after his return, he was a man of modest education, and he shared many of the preconceptions and prejudices of his time, but they did not keep him from watching and listening attentively and reporting on his experiences.

Markham presented his papers at Porvenir and then went on directly to Nargana,

Lady Richmond Brown and friends on Ustupu or Portogandi, 1922.

which impressed him as "the cleanest place that I ever saw."[26] He visited Charly Robinson and a baseball diamond, and noting that Anna Coope's establishment was closed down, he stopped in at the public school, where the teacher, who seemed about eighteen to Markham, willingly lined up her students for a photograph. That evening he attended a dance:

There was quite a good floor and fairly good music, but poor lighting system as they use the lantern of the hayburner type, and you could scarcely see across the room, and I will never be able to tell whether it was a waltz two step or just plain hop, but the young folk were having the time of their lives so why worry about the step.[27]

His friend Jake being away from home on an offshore island, Markham set off the next morning with Jake's brother Richard to Niatupu. In a conversation with the Niatupu chief, he was lectured about how Spaniards had always fought the Kuna, robbing their land and women.

He said the Great Spirit had made the land for the Indian alone and had placed the fish and turtles in the Ocean and Turkeys in the trees, the wild pig in the Bush, the Plantain,

William Markham with Kuna women, 1923.

Yam, and Banana all for the Indian. . . . Well a whole lot of his argument was true and my heart went out to him and his people when I thought of the way the Americans treated the Indians years ago, but I hope that the Panamanian Government in civilizing them would do as the American Government had done in the late years.[28]

When Markham asked permission to take pictures, the chief refused, saying that outsiders sold pictures in Colón of Kuna women with bare legs. Markham, in his naive way, showed the chief pictures of bathing girls and women's underwear in the Saturday Evening Post, pointing out that the women in the pictures had not objected. Whether through these arguments or several gifts, he got the chief to relent and let him make photographs and buy molas. Later he went hunting on the mainland. Far from being attacked by bushmasters and crocodiles, he and Richard wandered around for three hours without seeing any game, suffering nothing worse than blisters on Markham's tender feet.

Markham crossed to nearby Tigre, and after again winning over the village chief, he ended the day in a long discussion of Kuna custom. Told by his host to sleep where he wanted, he put his cot down on the sand amid the hammocks of the house's permanent residents.

It was a long time before I went to sleep. . . .

I thought of the race of human beings I was with, not a policeman or a soldier. I thought of my home State Pennsylvania during the recent coal strike . . . then to think here were no jails or road-gangs, and near my home is [a] reformatory containing 2,200 young men between the ages of eighteen and twenty-five. . . . Then there was no churches of any kind. These people have one faith and are apparently happy. No Army or Navy. . . . How quiet the village was, not a dog barking, not a Baby crying, just a little noise of waves breaking on the reefs, . . . and the man running the gang saw [that is, snoring] next to me.[29]

Markham's sympathetic musings were ultimately no more spontaneous or clear-eyed than Richmond Brown's prejudices. Where she arrived ready to find foreign exoticism and social inferiority, he brought with him a centuries-old stereotype of primitive nobility and innocence that ill-suited the tough-minded Kuna. Having gone through a day marked by bustle, complexity, and suspicion, in a region seized by turmoil and struggle, Markham represented Kuna life by the sound of waves beating on the reef at midnight, a supposed peace and simplicity he saw as a critique of his own civilization, much as had Rousseau and Montaigne before him. The waves, nonetheless, do beat peacefully at night on Kuna islands, sleep in a crowded extended-family household is much as he describes it, and the Kuna would have endorsed his dislike of armies, jails, and churches.

Markham returned to Nargana, eventually moving on to Río Sidra, where people seemed receptive to schools and civilization, and after a few days, to Carti Suitupu, where they were not.[30] Markham was strikingly ambivalent about change and the Kuna, alternating in his account between impatience or criticism and long rambling paeans to primitive simplicity. His naiveté was sometimes quite remarkable: in a conversation one night with a man who enthused over a prospective son-in-law, "I told him I was a good fisherman, what San Blas girl do I get? The Indian got mad and said I did not want Indian girl I had two women in Colón." Aware of Kuna sensitivities about lustful outsiders, Markham nevertheless concluded, "They don't seem able to take a joke."[31] He seems to have compensated for such rough spots, however, through generosity, lack of pretension, and a willingness to sit and talk as an equal with the people he met, all of which the Kuna greatly appreciated.

A day later Markham returned to Colón, by now a committed partisan of the Indians. Although his hosts and friends had unburdened themselves of their grievances, they would not have told him that violence was about to erupt again, and indeed that the men of his last stop in Carti were about to raid the island he had just come from, Río Sidra.[32]

Río Sidra, or Urgandi, comprised two islands, which were separated only by a shallow channel. The establishment of a police post and school in 1923 threw the community into turmoil and drove out several opponents, including the island's chief. Rebel Kuna blamed the indigenous policemen on the island, especially Pedro Paniza, and they feared that Carti Suitupu, Colman's base in the west, would be next.[33]

Colman's followers already hated Paniza for his work on behalf of the government in western San Blas, for which three years previously they had burned down his house on Carti Yantupu and tried to ambush him. The cluster of islands at Carti held a gathering, and with the blessing of Río Sidra's exiled chief, they resolved to eliminate their enemies there, lest they use the new outpost as a stepping-stone toward Carti itself.

On the night of June 22, villagers on Río Sidra retired at about midnight, after one of the police-sponsored dances. Two or three hours later, a large party of men with faces painted red crossed silently to the windward island and fired volleys into the barracks, killing Pedro Paniza. Witnesses claimed that two of them then cut out Paniza's heart and drank his blood. Several other indigenous policemen and their supporters saved themselves by fleeing in the dark, another managed to slip loosely tied bonds, and the teacher and the sole Panamanian policeman on the island were let go, because the raid had targeted Kuna collaborators only.

As happened after previous incidents, the Intendencia had little success in punishing the attackers. Three Kuna men were arrested in Colón but later set free when witnesses could not identify them, and though people on Río Sidra had recognized several of the raiders, the police failed to flush them out of hiding in Carti. Eventually the investigating authorities simply gave up.[34]

William Markham went back to work for the Panama Railroad, but he did not forget his new friends. In the narrative of his trip that he wrote during the following months, he glossed over the troubles in San Blas, saving anything controversial for a letter to Belisario Porras. The letter, after being revised by someone else in more elevated literary style, went to the president in February of 1924.[35]

Markham tried hard to be tactful: he conceded the need to civilize the Kuna, praised the government school on Nargana, and acknowledged the bad record of the United States with North American Indians. The letter told Porras that many Kuna had great faith in him, and while decrying the persecution of Coope, it also criticized her for teaching in English and for muddying the waters by introducing a foreign religion. Markham urged that, treated properly, the Kuna "will be as loyal and true as any other Panamanian subject."[36] Throughout, he adopted the stance of adviser and helper to the government in a worthwhile task.

His criticisms, nonetheless, were clear. He described an incident at Río Sidra in which police had dragged people from their homes to pose for his pictures. "Now the home to the American, Panamanian or to the Indian is the most sacred thing on earth, and should be respected. . . . This little act stirred up more hatred than you will be able to overcome in a number of years." While euphemizing the question of police sexuality—"These young men are human and they are continually looking for a girl or a mate and the Indians know it and it keeps them agitated and suspicious"—he asked Porras to send married agents only, or better yet, to send teachers without policemen. Without saying that Kuna lands were in jeopardy, he suggested that the government provide documentation to set their fears at rest. And most of all, he urged an uncoercive, nonviolent approach to civilizing the Indians.

Noting the deletion of controversial material from the account of his trip, Markham promised not to embarrass Porras's administration by publicizing the letter, though his language may be taken to imply that silence was contingent on reform. In a subsequent interview with Porras, the president assured him that Indian lands would be protected, while in a reply to the letter dated March 10, Porras wrote that the cabinet was deeply interested in Markham's suggestions, and that "within a few days my Government will take the necessary steps to straighten out matters there."[37]

Markham's intervention had come at a critical moment. Recent signs that all was not well in San Blas included the raid on Río Sidra, a petition protesting an illicit trade in alcohol, a lawsuit between a former detachment head and the intendente, and various assorted complaints. A new letter alleging mistreatment came from Colman in early 1924, and the day before Markham's interview with the president the intendente had to report that a police agent had killed an unarmed man on Río Azúcar.[38] It was no longer possible to turn a blind eye. After Porras's interview with Markham, the president wrote his current secretary of government and justice, Rafael Neira, ordering that police abuses be stopped. Secretary Neira, already disturbed by Colman's complaints and the recent killing, responded that he, too, thought something had gone wrong in San Blas and that Porras should investigate personally. The president told Neira to organize a trip of inspection to the coast, a decision the secretary communicated to Mojica in a harshly critical letter a few days later.[39]

As it turned out, Porras's good intentions came to nothing. He may have been distracted by election-year maneuvers to pass on the presidency but keep power, as well as by controversy over renegotiation of the canal treaty, or he may have let Mojica's importance in getting out the vote in San Blas override his scruples. In any case, he never made his promised trip. Porras's hand-picked successor, Rodolfo Chiari, won the election but shrugged off his predecessor's attempts to control him, and Belisario Porras, though remaining for years a prominent public figure, never regained office. Despite another petition alleging mistreatment of the San Blas Indians (very likely inspired by Markham), this one sent by the Woman's Club of Cristobal in the Canal Zone, Andrés Mojica continued as intendente.[40] The school and police post on Río Sidra were reinstated immediately after the raid, and every few months a new village fell under police control.[41] "'If we just sit here, we won't survive,' Colman said. 'We won't survive, if we just let ourselves be persecuted. We must fight back.'"[42]

Part Six
THE WHITE INDIANS, 1923–1924

20.
A Glimpse
of White

Indians Richard Marsh, undiplomatic diplomat, impolitic politician, and gentleman adventurer, returned to Panama in 1923. During his six weeks there Marsh saw Indians (though not Kuna), and he underwent an experience, a highly charged but ambiguous encounter with legendary beings, that started him on a path to San Blas. He arrived in mid-June 1923 on a fruit company steamer at the port of Colón, where he set up a headquarters in the Hotel Washington. He deposited a letter of credit for $25,000 at a local bank, letting it be known that he was looking for land on which rubber could be planted.[1]

The thirteen years since Marsh had left Panama had not been uneventful. Settling first in his family's hometown of Warsaw, Illinois, Marsh worked for a year and half on a large dam being built nearby on the Mississippi.[2] With the completion of the dam in 1912, Marsh turned to business, promoting several projects at once: a waterfront industrial district, a bridge over the Mississippi, and an electric train line. Initially, the bridge and railroad showed promise, but all three projects ultimately failed for lack of financing.[3]

In 1915 Marsh announced his candidacy for mayor of Warsaw. Elected by a wide margin on an antiprohibition plank, Marsh lasted only a few months in office. His plan to build a sewage system and extend the town's water mains provoked heated opposition, and after a tumultuous public meeting, he abruptly resigned in disgust and left town.[4]

In another abrupt shift, Marsh moved south and bought a bankrupt cypress timbering company in Port Barre, Louisiana. This highly speculative deal, which required him to produce a great deal of lumber within a few months, left Marsh financially exposed, and a former employee and stockholder named Schee filed claims against the company, hoping to collect after throwing it into bankruptcy.

When sabotage struck Marsh's timbering equipment, he knew who to blame. He found Schee at breakfast on the porch of his boardinghouse and shot him five times. Indicted for manslaughter, Marsh pleaded self-defense, and though Schee had been unarmed, the Louisiana jury evidently felt the man had provoked his own death, because they acquitted Marsh after a brief trial.

The logging company nonetheless went bankrupt in 1918. Marsh tried again in 1920, buying back the establishment from its receiver, but by early 1922 he had fallen fifty thousand dollars behind in payments and the seller foreclosed.[5] With his remarkable capacity for landing on his feet, by 1923 Marsh found a position in a New York City firm of consulting engineers headed by the famous former general, George Goethals, who had been in charge of canal construction during Marsh's short-lived diplomatic career. Given that Goethals, who was not known for a forgiving nature, had put a large part of the blame for the Mendoza affair on Marsh, his willingness to hire him thirteen years later says a great deal about the latter's powers of persuasion.[6] By 1923 Richard Marsh was ready for new adventures.

Marsh, it could be said, was back in Panama because of Herbert Hoover and Winston Churchill.[7] In 1922, the year before Marsh's trip, a British government committee appointed by Churchill, then secretary of state for the colonies, recommended a system of mandatory quotas for colonial rubber plantations to keep production down and prices up. When the plan won parliamentary approval, most American tire manufacturers went along, but the maverick entrepreneur Harvey Firestone launched a patriotic crusade, persuading Secretary of Commerce Herbert Hoover that the rubber producers' cartel and other foreign monopolies in raw materials posed a threat to U.S. industry and national security. Among other measures, Hoover and Firestone began a drive to promote American-controlled rubber production, leading to wide-ranging field surveys by the Department of Commerce and private teams backed by Firestone.[8]

In terms of production costs, few parts of the tropical world could compete with cheap Asian labor, but Latin America's proximity to the United States seemed to offer countervailing strategic advantages as well as low transport costs. Panama, close to North American ports, located on a major trade route, and dominated by the United States, in some ways seemed ideal.[9] According to Marsh, he enthusiastically discussed the possibilities in Panama with General Goethals, who sent him to Hoover, who sent him to Ford and Firestone, who sent him to Panama.[10]

After three weeks on his own, he was joined by two representatives of his backers, Marmond Freeman and Walter Noble, men of a very different sort from Marsh himself.[11] Freeman, in Marsh's opinion, "was a Firestone rubber-buyer, whose experience had consisted of sitting in the bar of the elaborate Raffles Hotel in Singapore, changing into his thirty-five white linen suits (so he said) and examining sheets of crude rubber brought in for his approbation. His qualifications as an explorer ap-

The Darién and Eastern San Blas
1923–1925

proached the vanishing point. The very sight of the jungle made him ill." As for Noble, who was sent to check out land titles, "nothing is more pathetic than an American lawyer in Latin America."[12] The pair seem to have returned Marsh's disapproval and dislike.

Marsh had been sent to reconnoiter lands along the northern, Caribbean coast of Panama, west of the canal in the opposite direction from San Blas. These lands proved unsuitable, however, so Marsh turned his gaze toward the Darién.[13] He set off along the Pacific coast by boat, with Freeman and Noble reluctantly on board, both with coats off but ties still knotted. In a book he later wrote about his experiences, Marsh depicted the party as alone on board with a mutinous Black crew, failing to mention the presence of the provincial governor and a squad of police.[14]

As the boat crossed the Bay of Panama toward the Gulf of San Miguel, a crew member described by Marsh as an Indian (more likely, a mestizo Panamanian) appeared on deck in a drunken frenzy and began threatening others with a knife. In his book, Marsh could not resist romanticizing the event, claiming that the attacker was from the tribe at the headwaters of the Chucunaque, who hoped to take over the boat and thus protect his homeland from intruders. The man was quickly subdued and thrown into the hold.[15]

After a brief stop at La Palma, the tiny capital of the Darién, where the governor and policemen disembarked, taking the prisoner with them, Marsh's party started up the Tuira River. Their destination was Yaviza, a few miles up the Chucunaque, site of the eighteenth-century fort that had broken Kuna control of the southern Darién, now a small village of about 350 inhabitants.

Although the Panamanian Isthmus as a whole runs east-west, it takes the form of a shallow S lying on its side: east of the canal the land increasingly curves toward the south, so by the Gulf of San Miguel, it heads roughly southeast. As one ascends the Tuira, a few miles above its mouth the river turns sharply south toward Colombia, while the Chucunaque turns in the other direction, leading north-by-northwest along the length of the eastern Isthmus. It was on the Chucunaque above Yaviza that Marsh hoped to find flat lands, low but above flood level, that would be suitable for planting rubber.

Like many visitors to remote areas, Marsh was confused about the identities of the local peoples, which in his case affected the outcome of the trip. In addition to hearing of the reputedly ferocious Indians guarding the headwaters of the Chucunaque and the San Blas Kuna on the north coast, Marsh encountered peoples on this excursion he called Chola and Chocó, and he was told of wilder Indians called Chocoi. In fact, all three names referred to the same people, who call themselves Emberá but who were known to outsiders as Chocó.[16] While most of the Chocó lived in widely scattered hamlets along the rivers of the Darién, they visited the towns to sell plantains and buy trade goods, and a few lived for varying periods of time on the outskirts of Yaviza.

Marsh was later scornful of Yaviza—"a straggling collection of some fifty ramshackle bamboo huts beside the stream—black babies everywhere, flies, mangy dogs, garbage, rubbish, and mud"—and even more of its inhabitants: "degenerate blacks, less civilized than when they came from Africa."[17] During a tour of the village, Marsh spied something much more interesting, however:

Across the narrow clearing were walking three young girls, perhaps fourteen to sixteen years old. They wore nothing but small loin-clothes. And their almost bare bodies were as white as any Scandinavian's. Their long hair, falling loosely over their shoulders, was bright gold! Quickly and gracefully they crossed the open space and disappeared into the jungle.

I turned to the negro headman in amazement. *White Indians!* The one tale of Latin America in which no respectable explorer dares to believe![18]

The "White girls," Yaviza, 1923. To the right of this photo in Marsh's journal, he wrote "The three Chucunaque—light brown hair, fine texture, skin tanned but distinctly a white or 'ruddy' skin."

Told that the girls lived with an Indian man on the edge of town, and (so he later claimed) that they came from a tribe, part dark-skinned, part light, who lived well up the Chucunaque, Marsh followed down the path they had taken.[19] He arrived at a small clearing by the river, where he found an open-sided house, with a living platform raised about six feet off the ground. He overcame the girls' apprehension with smiles and a gift of dimes, and although they did not respond to his Spanish, they let him photograph them in front of the house.[20]

This encounter thrilled Marsh's romantic soul. A reader of popular anthropology and social theorizing, much of which was permeated by racialism and social Darwinism, Marsh explained the girls to himself in terms of evolutionary and diffusionist theories about races progressing or degenerating. He concluded that the three were representatives of an ancient white race, either primitives or else the regressed remnants of an archaic high civilization, and in either case distant relatives of modern Europeans. In a letter to his son, he wrote:

Poor little indians—waifs and children of God and of nature—I can't get them out of my mind. . . . For son, these Indians are of a fine and old race—not mere degenerates or low bred people like some races—but the survivors of Neolithic man in the present generation. They are the same people as our ancestors in Europe 15,000 or 20,000 years ago, before the coming of the dark-white Mediterranean races—they have much the same blood as we have—I know I have much in common with them—only they got into a side eddy of progress, and didn't develop or "evolute" as our Caucasian and the Mongolian races have done.[21]

Through the cloud of fantasy and speculation, Marsh was right about one thing: there *are* white Indians in Panama, the same ones described by the pirate-surgeon Lionel Wafer in the seventeenth century. The Kuna, in both San Blas and the Darién, have the highest known rate of albinism anywhere in the world. Although albinos make up only a fraction of 1 percent of the Kuna population (and in that era albino babies were often subject to infanticide), all other human populations have fewer still. Rather than forming a separate race as Marsh thought or even a distinct social group, Kuna albinos are scattered among all their communities. They have no special formal or ritual role on the basis of their albinism, other than being sent out to shoot arrows at eclipses. Disfavored as marriage partners and tending toward sedentary indoor occupations because of their sensitivity to the sun, many die earlier than other Kuna.[22]

The three females encountered by Marsh, however, were neither Kuna nor white.[23] (Nor, for that matter, were they all girls—one was obviously an adult.) The open-sided house with its raised living platform is typical of the Emberá Chocó, many of whom still live today on the outskirts of Yaviza, and his photographs show two typically dressed Chocó girls and one woman, with coloring that is moderately dark or moderately light, depending on one's reading of Marsh's black-and-white photographs. The putative golden hair and Scandinavian-white skin, moreover, sounded less extreme in Marsh's letters, which described "bodies as light as a sun-burned white girl on a bathing beach, and decidedly *light brown hair.* . . . The young American mermaids who frequent the bathing pools on the Canal Zone . . . are . . . darker."[24]

The "girls" were remarkable only if one took for granted, as Marsh did, that different biological populations of humans, so-called races, are both entirely distinct from one another and internally uniform—in this case, that all true Indians have identical dark skins and coarse black hair. In fact, skin and hair shade sometimes vary among different Indian individuals as well as among populations, depending on exposure to the sun, diet, skin disease, and genetic variation. And members of different populations—tanned mermaids and forest Indians—can and do overlap in skin shade.

The initial encounter with the supposed white Indians was, in short, an illusion, a combination of preconception, romantic folklore, racist theorizing, and wishful thinking. As Marsh himself noted, he was by no means the first to entertain this notion. The Mandan Indians of the North American great plains were identified as lost Welshmen, and a number of Indian groups such as the Aché of Paraguay have been touted as the descendants of Vikings.[25] Rather than testifying to the reality of long-range voyages by Madoc or Leif Ericson, the persistence with which explorers and travelers kept finding traces of lost white races demonstrated the strength of romanticism, nationalism, and racism in Western thought. In Marsh's case the illusion was doubly ironic, because the objects of his fantasy, blond Indians, did in fact exist, but not in Yaviza.

However prone to wishful thinking, it is hard to believe Marsh would have set so much store by this brief and ambiguous encounter unless it fit something he already knew. In his book he mentions rumors of white Indians in eastern Panama, which he said he connected with similar stories heard in the Philippines and in other parts of Latin America.[26] More to the point, Marsh talked during his weeks in Panama with William Markham and Frederick Mitchell Hedges, both of whom had seen albino Kuna in San Blas. In a manuscript written a few months later, Marsh made much of Mitchell Hedge's theory that the supposed hieroglyphs on San Blas molas derived "from strange unknown tribes in the interior . . . remnants of a very ancient and at one time highly developed and powerful people."[27] Thus the waifs of Yaviza, rather than the unique origin of Marsh's quest, were interpreted in the light of information gained from other sources.

Not forgetting his original goal, Marsh was determined to look further for rubber lands. Any enthusiasm Freeman and Noble may have had for the trip, however, had disappeared with seasickness, heat, and the incident with the sailor who had run amok. Up to Yaviza, they had seen nothing but hills and swamp, and crew members who had gone ashore were warned that fierce Indians at the headwaters killed intruders who went too far upstream. Marsh, however, insisted on a one-day round-trip in an outboard-powered dugout canoe to survey the low valley he was assured (correctly) lay just around the next bend.

After trying out the outboard, Marsh went to bed on deck, while Freeman and Noble bunked down in the cabin, according to Marsh with their clothes and shoes on and the portholes tight shut. In his book, Marsh felt obliged to keep up the atmosphere of mystery. He described himself descending into the hold to visit the prisoner. Struck, he said, by the man's obstinate courage and his determination to guard the independence of the Upper Chucunaque, Marsh set him free: "I motioned to the hatch, and he plunged through it into the river with a clean splash."[28] In more prosaic fact, the prisoner was not there to be liberated, because he had been left behind in police custody at La Palma.[29]

The next day, Marsh and his reluctant companions had an uneventful tour up the Chucunaque, in which Marsh at least, concluded that the country upstream did indeed have great potential for planting rubber. Late that afternoon, as the launch crew prepared to drop downstream from Yaviza, Marsh was visited by the girls from the previous night, now more completely clothed and accompanied by a young man.[30] The visitors were entertained with sweet biscuits and fizzy water and impressed by the show of firing up the engines, and just as the boat was leaving, "a full grown Chucunaque white man, with two women and a child in his canoe, swung into view."[31]

The "White chief," Yaviza, 1923.

The canoist, "the most magnificent and gorgeous specimen of human male, civilized or primitive, the writer has ever seen," "as white as any white man . . . with long, very light hair, almost yellow" inspired a lengthy rhapsodic description of his physique and colorful decorations. This brief glimpse, lasting just a few seconds, led Marsh to conclude that the man must be "a fearless, independent, masterful, leader, . . . a chief, a king, or merely an independent member of a proud and democratic people."[32] Once again, however, his own photographs undercut Marsh's claims: despite the explanation that "the hair, of course, photographs dark, as always with brown or yellow," the pictures show, not a forest Aryan, but a quite typical, if impressive, Chocó man wearing Chocó clothing and decorations.[33]

On the return trip from the Darién, Marsh was filled with enthusiasm for the Indians, the beauties of the Chucunaque Valley, and the possibilities for planting rubber, along with considerable worry about the harm that development could do to "these wonderful, primitive, loveable, children of Nature."[34] Freeman and Noble, on the other hand, seem to have felt an overpowering urge to get out of the backlands and away from Marsh.

On the thirty-first a group of Panamanian Rotarians, who were interested in financing a road between Panama and Colón with the proceeds from leasing land, arranged for Marsh to meet with President Porras and his cabinet.[35] Recognized as the notorious meddler in Panamanian politics, Marsh was called to account for his actions in keeping Carlos Mendoza from the presidency, a task he apparently carried off with some success. According to Narciso Garay, Marsh passed the blame to his superiors in the U.S. government.[36] Making a smooth transition into his own pitch, he told the cabinet that disillusionment over such high-handedness had convinced him that only visionary entrepreneurs like Henry Ford could bring the United States and Latin America together.

Belisario Porras, for his part, may not have cared much, since Marsh's intervention in 1910 had paved the way for his own election two years later, and he and Mendoza had subsequently fought bitterly for control of the Liberal Party before the latter's death in 1916.[37] Porras, moreover, greatly favored foreign investment. The upshot was that Marsh reached a provisional agreement with the government to acquire a huge tract of land, totaling, according to different versions, four hundred thousand hectares, a million acres, or even two million.[38] He had three months in which to advance the Panamanian government one hundred thousand dollars as deposit. Two days later, on the second of August, Marsh sailed home.[39]

Despite his haste, Marsh did not forget the white Indians. In calls paid on the Governor of the Canal Zone and the commanding U.S. army general on the Isthmus, mention of his discoveries elicited polite skepticism from the Governor, but according to Marsh, General Babbit said that an American pilot had flown low over a riverine village in the Darién inhabited by Indians with white skins. When Marsh expressed an interest in returning to explore further up the Chucunaque, Babbit offered support.[40]

Even before Marsh left the Isthmus, the Panamanian government cabled its Legation in Washington requesting an investigation of Marsh's claims to backing by Henry Ford. The Legation replied that Ford spokesmen disavowed any connection with Marsh.[41] In an exchange of letters, President Porras and his Foreign Minister, Narciso Garay, argued for and against the deal.[42] Marsh, in fact, had indeed come to Panama with backing from both Ford and Firestone, who were ready to invest large sums in rubber production. (Within a few years Ford had established a plantation in Brazil, Firestone a massive complex in Liberia.)[43] On Marsh's return to the U.S., however, they declined to back his project, and the Panamanian government's time limit for the down payment expired at the beginning of November.[44]

Marsh did not give up. He conceived the idea of a dual-purpose expedition up the Chucunaque, to look for both white Indians and rubber lands. He wrote and circulated a long manuscript, with a history of eastern Panama and its Indian peoples as well as a narrative of his own recent experiences, arguing for the existence of a lost White race. In a search for new patrons, Marsh was turned down by George Eastman but found success with Lammot Du Pont, who had been a fraternity brother at MIT.[45] The Du Ponts, who a few years later bought up controlling interest in U.S. Rubber, may or may not have cared much about white Indians, but they knew their raw materials.[46]

Marsh began recruiting scientists for the expedition at the University of Rochester, not far from his wife's family home in Brockport, New York. His choice, Herman L. Fairchild, an emeritus professor of geology, was elderly and rotund, but Marsh assured the president of the university that he had no intention of subjecting Fairchild to any hardship, and it was eventually arranged that he should go.[47]

When Marsh wrote the Smithsonian Institution in search of an ethnologist, a specialist in the cultures of primitive peoples, they checked out his references and background before committing themselves.[48] The head curator for anthropology, Walter Hough, reported:

So far as I can learn, Mr. Marsh is reliable man. I suppose he is more or less a soldier of fortune, that is, he is engaged in a great many pieces of work for industrial concerns and for the government.

As to his "white Indians," I have little interest except to say that it is probably much exaggerated. Nevertheless, this is the one place in the world under the domain of the United States from which the Museum has almost no specimens. My interest is in getting out specimens from this region.[49]

The Smithsonian, lacking an available ethnologist, proposed John L. Baer, a young man who had filled several temporary positions at the National Museum in archaeology and physical anthropology.[50] Marsh, in addition to agreeing to turn all artifacts collected by the expedition over to the museum, contracted to pay Baer's expenses, as well as a monthly stipend of $225. The American Museum of Natural History nominated Charles Breder, aquarist at the New York Aquarium, whose salary and expenses would also be paid by Marsh.[51]

Breder was young and fit, and Fairchild was not expected to strain himself, but Baer presented a problem. Obese and out of shape, he also suffered from a chronic kidney ailment. Marsh later claimed that he pressured the Smithsonian for an alternative in better physical condition, but the Institution had no one else to offer.[52] For both Baer and Breder, the Darién expedition was their first big break, a chance to make a name in their fields, and both made themselves available on short notice.

Expeditions such as Marsh's had for a long time been ventures in publicity and self-aggrandizement as well as discovery, and Marsh, like others before him, established close ties with a newspaper.[53] The *Rochester Times-Union* and the North American Newspaper Alliance sent a reporter, Paul Benton, and Pathé News a cameraman, Charles Charlton.[54] Finally, Marsh asked the Commerce Department to provide a representative from its rubber survey, and though the survey's director had received mixed reports on Marsh's activities in Panama, he agreed that if in its first few weeks the expedition produced evidence of suitable land in the Chucunaque, the head of the survey's Caribbean party would be sent to join it in the field.[55]

The party assembled in New York City and sailed on January 16. After a stormy trip, they arrived in Colón a week later, ready to begin their search.

21.
In the
Darién

Marsh and his party spent two weeks in Colón, Panama City, and the Canal Zone preparing to go to the Darién. North American authorities in the zone offered military supplies and equipment as well as men, and President Porras conferred official Panamanian blessings. Expedition members were honored at a Rotary Club meeting and went tarpon fishing with William Markham, the railroad employee who had become an advocate for the Kuna.[1]

The biologist, Breder, however, allowed little time for such diversions. Within a few hours after docking in Colón, he was out on the grounds of the Hotel Washington observing gekkos, and the next morning, before clearing his baggage through customs, he went off to the city fish market to view the catch. Thereafter, he kept at his research until the expedition left for the field, even making notes on a tiny fish found in a puddle under a dripping spigot.[2]

The expedition's scientists were less happy with its notoriety than were its boosters and publicists. In one of his newspaper articles chronicling their exploits, Paul Benton echoed Marsh's theorizing about the white Indians:

Are they the lost remains of a forgotten blond race which once held sway as emperors and kings over their darker aboriginal neighbors, lost survivors of some great Nordic invasion before the dawn of history in the western half of the world? Are they, and they may be, fragmentary survivals of a Paleolithic culture, so ancient that its very monuments have crumbled into the eternal dust? For there still are mysteries in the world.[3]

John Baer wrote home to his mentor in a different vein: "We have been receiving lots of undesired publicity. I have refused to make any statements until we come back and work up our data. Most of these [reporters] have all kinds of crazy ideas. . . . It is amazing how ignorant some newspaper men can be and get away with it."[4]

Amidst all the speculation, one letter published in a local paper pointed out, quite correctly, that there was no separate race of white Indians in the Republic, merely albinos scattered throughout the Kuna population.[5]

If Marsh read that letter, he did not let it deter him. Eager to scout the expedition's route from the air, he secured the use of two open-cockpit military planes. On the morning of January 29, they flew east up the Bayano River. Since Marsh planned that the expedition, traveling in the opposite direction from the planes' track, would ascend the Chucunaque to its source and then continue down the Bayano toward Panama City, he was pleased to find only a low pass between the two headwaters. His intention to fly over the entire Darién had to be abruptly scrapped, however, when the pilot pointed to oil leaking from the plane's radiator.[6]

Once back in the city, Marsh found that he had offended the U.S. Army commandant, who forbad any further flights.[7] Eager to make maximum use of the dry season, which in most years runs from about late December to April, Marsh gave up further aerial surveying after an uncharacteristically brief struggle, and in a few days he had completed preparations for the field.

The expedition embarked from the Pacific end of the Canal on February 5 at a few minutes before midnight on a vessel rented from the U.S. Signal Corps. The group on board included the six men who came from the United States with the expedition: the three scientists, Fairchild, Baer, and Breder; the reporter Benton; Charlton the movie cameraman; and Marsh himself. They were now accompanied by several others recruited on the Isthmus.[8] President Porras sent Raoul Brin, a botanist and agronomist from a prominent Panamanian family. The U.S. Army seconded a young lieutenant in military intelligence, Glen Townsend, the Canal Zone Administration an engineer and topographer, Omer Malsbury. Marsh also hired an expatriate American taxidermist and ex-policeman named Harry Johnson.[9] The lower ranks of the thoroughly hierarchical expedition included Townsend's Puerto Rican orderly; a corporal from the U.S. Army Signal Corps; a mestizo cook and cook's helper; and two black laborers. In the Darién they were joined by a policeman and more laborers. It was a large and heterogeneous crew.[10]

The expedition set up base camp in a coconut grove on the Chucunaque about a half mile below Yaviza. Lieutenant Townsend, assigned the task of laying out the camp, soon had it set up in military order, with a neat line of thirteen army tents and steps cut down a steep bluff to a floating dock of balsa logs.[11]

In his book, Marsh claimed that the coconut grove was empty and abandoned, "planted by no one knows whom," possibly by a mysterious survivor of a secret German radio station from World War I. In more prosaic fact, the palms belonged to a local businessman, whose plantation buildings stood a few yards behind the camp.[12] This little deception typified Marsh's efforts to turn the Darién from a backwater into a howling wilderness. He claimed to have discovered not only an unknown valley, which was merely the combined Chucunaque and Bayano basins, both well known, but even two hidden cordilleras, which he dubbed the Porras and Marsh ranges. Forgetting the provincial governor and a huge British mine abandoned a few years before, Marsh insisted that the Darién lay far outside national jurisdiction. And like many others, he dismissed and ignored his predecessors in the field.[13]

Apart from erasing competition and signs of civilization, Marsh's account of these weeks, published ten years later in his book, *White Indians of Darien,* combined and simplified episodes, making them follow in order for the sake of narrative coherence; facts were edited, suppressed, exaggerated and occasionally invented; and to hold reader interest, events were endowed with an atmosphere of danger, mystery, and mild sexuality.

The party spent two months based at the camp below Yaviza, carrying out research, exploring the surrounding area, and preparing for the main event, the ascent of the Chucunaque. Though the ever-energetic Marsh covered a great deal of ground, what mattered in these months was less where he went than whom he encountered. While chasing from one end of the Darién to the other after a non-existent white tribe, Marsh repeatedly came into contact with the region's black and brown inhabitants, and it was these ethnic encounters that came to dominate the experience of most members of the group. The expedition dealt with Indians and Blacks socially, hiring and trading with them, but also intellectually, by observing, sorting into types, judging their relative merits, explaining, imagining, and even fantasizing about them. Though the objects of all these thoughts stood before them, it is striking how thoroughly the explorers imposed the preconceptions they brought with them about the natural simplicity, sexuality, freedom from restraint, and nobility or lack of it of the natives.

Only one member of the expedition, who cared more about the animal inhabitants of the region, seemed mostly unaffected by the natives. Biologists had worked in the Darién but not on the Chucunaque, and Charles Breder was going to make the most of the opportunity to record the fish, amphibians, and reptiles.[14] He spent his daylight hours in pursuit of fish, seining, dip-netting, hooking, trapping, dynamiting, and poisoning them as required. (What science did not keep, the expedition ate.) His great passion, however, was nocturnal and amphibious: after dark he observed frogs and toads by lamplight along a nearby stream and occasionally photographed them by flash.

The biologist's preoccupation eventually came to seem "egotistical" to Marsh: "All are showing a splendid spirit, except Breder, who perhaps is so interested in his own work as to be a bit useless & selfish in other respects."[15] All the scientists, to be sure, pursued their callings, but not to the exclusion of white Indians. Baer collected artifacts and made notes on native customs but devoted himself primarily to shooting monkeys for Smithsonian collections and measuring the skulls and body form of as many Indians as possible.[16] The elderly Professor Fairchild, relieved that oil company geologists seemed to have done his work for him, contented himself with keeping records of temperature, humidity, precipitation, and tides (which come upriver past Yaviza each day). Fairchild avoided even the forest behind the camp for fear of bugs.[17]

The others in the expedition also had their specialized functions, as well as outside constituencies and audiences to whom they reported: Malsbury, who stayed only a few weeks, made celestial observations, sent off passenger pigeons, and tried unsuccessfully to establish radio contact with the Canal Zone. Johnson hunted and preserved birds and mammals and assisted Baer and Breder; Charlton filmed, Benton wrote newspaper articles; President Porras's representative, Raoul Brin did a bit of botanizing; and Townsend, presumably, wrote reports for U.S. military intelligence.[18] These differences did not, however, keep most of them from joining Marsh in what he called his flying squadron.

Spurred on by a geologist's report of having seen Indians "white as any white man," Marsh began his search the day after settling into his base camp.[19] He was told that the girls encountered six months previously had left town for a home up the Río Chico across from Yaviza, a tributary with Emberá Chocó homesteads all along its length.[20] Two days later Marsh made a day trip up the Chico with Charlton, Benton, and Townsend. He did not find the girls, but he did see a few children with "towheads" (probably the result of dietary deficiencies) and one person with lighter than average skin.[21] Over the next several weeks, expedition members noted similar variation in skin and hair color, but Marsh never expressed doubts about his sightings the year before, and he rationalized the lighter-skinned Chocó he kept meeting as crosses with "my white Indians."[22]

Within a few weeks, even the canoeist who had so impressed Marsh was identified from his photograph by local Chocó: he was a visitor from the Sambú district well to the southeast, currently staying on the Chico.[23] Marsh also heard of a white Indian woman at a Kuna village called Pucro and scattered white Indians on another river. Though he resolved to visit them, he kept his main efforts focused in the other direction, at the headwaters of the Chucunaque, where he still hoped to find all-white villages.[24]

If the pale ghosts remained elusive, relations with corporeal Indians progressed rapidly. The expedition hired Indian laborers to help unload its supplies, and others came in over the next few days.[25] These Emberá Chocó were relative newcomers to the Yaviza area. Originally from the Pacific coastal forests of South America, they had begun migrating onto the Isthmus in the eighteenth century, taking up lands vacated as the Kuna retreated northward. Culturally very different from the Kuna, the Chocó lived in scattered homesteads, planting crops, hunting and fishing, and raising plantains to sell in towns such as Yaviza. Although families visited one another extensively and kept up an active ritual life, they never joined together in villages or recognized any formal political leaders. Their bare-bones technology, seeming lack of organization, and minimal clothing encouraged Westerners to interpret them in evolutionary terms as representatives of an early stage of humanity, as *Truly Primitive Man*. But the Chocó kept their tools and social organization simple not because they were stuck in some past era but because they worked beautifully in the present, allowing them to expand and prosper on the Darién frontier.[26]

One aspect of Chocó primitiveness that made an immediate impression was nudity. (The elderly Professor Fairchild in particular seems to have had difficulty adjusting to bare breasts.) On the level of imagination and ideology, exploration has often been figured in sexual terms, as the penetration of "virgin" lands. So, too, interethnic relations in remote areas are often played out in terms of illicit but alluring liaisons between white men and native women, and conversely by a rigid prohibition on sex between white women and native men.[27] If expedition members refrained from physical relations with the Indians—Marsh said he forbad sexual contact, and Chocó women generally deferred shyly to their men—*thinking* about the Indians was sexualized by the discovery that they were polygynous, as well as by their disconcertingly powerful and attractive bodies. Benton wrote about Chocó affairs for his newspaper readers in the arch style often adopted by travel writers:

The Indians who visited us today included one wrinkled old sinner, most gorgeously arrayed in an elaborate set of beads which encircled his middle and criss-crossed over his chest. He was, in addition, brilliantly painted. . . . When we inquired about his painting we were informed that he was courting a girl whom he sought for his third wife, and he painted himself to be "beautiful." He was alright. No fifth avenue flapper ever bedaubed herself more vigorously in that sacred cause. . . . The old buck evidently is wealthy in those things which go to make wealth among the Indians, as his wives are both young and pretty. Late in the afternoon another group of Indians came in, one of the girls being a particular belle. She wore her dowry around her neck in the shape of [a] necklace of Panamanian quarter dollars.[28]

Marsh was ready for his Indian visitors, both "bucks" and "belles," with a tent full of goods brought from Panama and the United States, which Fairchild, Johnson, and Benton all compared to a ten-cent store.

If the reader can imagine someone walking into a dime store and buying everything in sight with a sweep of his hand, then he will have some idea of the heterogeneous display the indians presents made: mouth organs, toy balloons, bird whistles, tinkling bells, countless trinkets, several dozen imitation leather hand purses—in all three large cases of guady and ingenious trifles designed to excite the cupidity of primitive man.[29]

Richard Marsh and Emberá Chocó women and children listen to a gramophone, Marsh Expedition base camp, 1924.

As Benton's patronizing remarks suggest, these gifts were saturated with invidious meaning. Since the beginning of European exploration, the eagerness with which local peoples sought guns and hatchets — "the irresistible magnetism of white commodities" — had been taken as proof of Western superiority, and their willingness to accept beads and mirrors as proof of their childishness.[30] In this case, at least, it is doubtful that Primitive Man and Woman really were overwhelmed by these trinkets — more substantial items such as tobacco, cloth, machetes, shotguns, and cash seem to have aroused much greater interest. But the Chocó, by accepting gimcrack items that the givers despised, seemed to be implicitly assenting to their portrayal as shallow, childish, and greedy.

The largesse, along with a concert played on the phonograph, rapidly made friends just as had been anticipated, and Charlton filmed Marsh (in Fairchild's words) "seated among a lot of squaws and papooses."[31] A Chocó couple was signed on as hunter and washerwoman for the camp, and for the rest of the expedition's stay, Indians kept bringing in live parakeets, dead jaguars, and other animals and skins to sell or barter.[32] Marsh got on especially well with a man named Avelino, who he decided was a chief, though in fact the Chocó had no chiefs.

This misunderstanding was typical of Marsh's limited and ideologized conception of the local peoples. He greatly admired the Chocó and got on well with them, at least at first, but he never saw through the seeming transparent simplicity of their

manners to the real complexity of their lives. Even Marsh's admiration was ideologized in that he praised the Chocó for virtues that were juvenile, natural, and
physical. Calling them "a happy trusting childlike race," he first introduced them to
the readers of his book through several pages of wonderment at the strength of a
man who single-handedly carried ashore a huge trunk.[33] His understanding was
ideologized, as well, in assuming the inevitable destruction of a group that was
actually thriving and expanding: "Poor little children—somehow it makes me sad
to see their impossible condition, and I fear their race is doomed—They are few in
number, and the negro is continuously encroaching upon them."[34] Most of all, it
was ideologized in that Marsh insistently paired Chocó virtues with Black vices and
deficiencies: one was clean, the other dirty; one poled skillfully upstream, the other
fell in the water. Like many colonial writers before him, Marsh saw one ethnic group
less in its own terms than as foil for another—Natural Man and Noble Savage
(whatever his ultimate limitations) revealing the deficiencies of the ignoble semiciv-
ilized African.

To treat the Chocó as noble savages encouraged brief flirtations, not with Indian
belles but with the dream of going native, of adopting the apparent spontaneity, the
freedom from civilization's restraints and discontents that many westerners perceived in primitive society. A few days after the first Chocó visit to camp, Marsh
accepted an invitation to come up the Chico again and spend the night.[35] Arriving
late in the day at Avelino's house, a large open-sided rectangular building with a
living floor raised about eight feet above the ground, Marsh passed out several more
presents and played the phonograph. "Then I fear I forgot my white man's training."[36] Taking off his wet clothes, he made himself a loincloth from a towel and
suggested that the Chocó paint his body with designs like their own.

With the spirit of foolishness prevailing, we staged an impromptu affair. A big circle was
formed facing the victrola. Our party mustered half a dozen electric flashlights—I took
one, and started hopping and jumping and whirling to the jazz music—the flashes shot on
and off—the circle of amused [and] intensely interested indians of all sizes was an inspiration. Soon Breder stripped to a face towel and joined the dance—then Benton and Brin—
Baer played the victrola—and such giggles and laughter and applause my dancing (?) never
brought before, and I think never will again.[37]

The next day, after continuing up the Chico and finding no traces of white
Indians,[38] Marsh dropped Baer and Breder off at Avelino's on his way back downstream, returning himself two days later for what he decided was a "harvest festival,"
actually a curing ritual and dance.[39] This time everyone in the party was painted.
"Then we hung necklaces of Woolworth's glass beads about our necks. . . . All in
all, with our painted bodies . . . we made quite a gay looking crowd for staid?,
civilized? whites."[40]

Marsh Expedition members painted by Chocó. Left to right: Johnson, Breder, Marsh, Benton, and Baer.

After dark, Avelino, who was in fact not a chief but a shaman, began a long chanted seance, in which spirits were invoked to cure a sick child and women danced slowly around the enclosure in which he worked. In the morning, after a not very successful attempt to have the dancing restaged for the movie camera, the party returned to base camp, working much harder than usual because their boatmen had not yet sobered up from a drinking bout the night before.[41]

As mysterious and primitive as the Chocó seemed, it was clear that they could offer few if any white individuals, and they refused to consider going to the headwaters of the Chucunaque into the territory of their traditional enemies, known locally as the "wild, fierce Kuna" or *Cunas Bravos*. It was said that the wild Kuna would not allow anyone further up the river than the mouth of a sidestream called the Membrillo, at what Marsh melodramatically called "the deadline." The explorer, however, was eager to scout out the route they would soon be taking, so two days after returning from the Chocó ritual, he set out upstream in two outboard-powered canoes, with one of the black boatmen "in the very bow—where he will present a good target."[42]

Although Marsh did not in fact anticipate any serious threat, each white member of the party was armed with a rifle and pistol and each canoe held two shotguns. As it turned out, they encountered Kuna almost immediately, in the undramatic form of six or eight men in two canoes who passed them going downstream.[43] In the five-day circuit, nothing worse occurred than a few mysterious noises in the night, except that Marsh accidentally discharged a shotgun in his canoe, slightly wounding a Chocó boatman.[44] Later, in mid-March, Johnson escorted Baer and Breder on scientific trips of a few days each up the Chucunaque. They met aloof but not overtly hostile parties of Kuna, who they believed were shadowing them, whistling in the night and even, Baer was convinced, creeping up on him as he slept.[45] The signs all seemed to indicate that when the expedition started upriver in earnest, they might well be opposed.

In the meanwhile, there were Kuna much closer at hand, even if they were "tame" rather than wild.[46] In his book, Marsh claimed that while he was away on the Río Chico, enigmatic visitors had appeared at dusk on the hills behind base camp, causing considerable apprehension. The more prosaic truth was that these not-so-mysterious Indians had actually turned up on the day after the expedition first arrived, and from much closer at hand, since they were working as laborers on the plantation a few yards away.[47] The visitors were from Pucro, a Kuna village to the southeast on an affluent of the Tuira; their leader, José Mata (who really was a chief), invited Marsh to pay a visit. On February 29, after only a day's rest from his last trip, Marsh set off with Benton, Charlton, and three boatmen, reaching Pucro four days later.

The Pucro Kuna, who told Marsh a story of population loss from epidemics, asked for medicines, and he sent a runner back to base for quinine. "These Cunas are a sad people — not the joyous irresponsible savages the Chocoi are." Despite the appearance of gloom (which may have been merely the cool reserve Kuna adopt before strangers), Marsh's hosts inspired favorable comparisons with the Chocó, in the kind of ethnic distinctions drawn by colonial writers. The Kuna may not have been robust, but they were natural ladies and gentlemen:

There is a self respect — a modesty — a courtesy and a sense of appreciation among the Cunas that does not exist among the Chocoi — first, the men have but one wife, and treat her much more respectfully — second, the men wear the hair short, have shirts and trousers, and leather sandals. Third, the women cover the whole bodies, with shirt and skirt, and in some cases very artistically decorated. . . . They are very polite, always shake hands, and always return a present with a present, or apologize if they have nothing. The Chocois took everything, like greedy children, but *never* offered us anything for nothing.[48]

Marsh arranged to visit another Kuna community, Paya (the same Paya at which Chief Colman and others from San Blas had studied with the famous teacher Kuppi), where, he had been told, he could see a white Indian woman. As it turned out, the woman was so frightened by their interest that she fled into the forest.[49] In his book, Marsh compensated for the quiet visit by composing an entirely imaginary adventure among hostile injuns, in which his party was set upon and robbed of half their equipment. The fictional Marsh forced his way into the house of the local chief. "Behind him, sprawled flat on the ground, was an almost naked woman, very voluptuous, light skinned and good looking, but completely drunk." In the tale, Marsh got his baggage back by threatening to shoot the chief and burn down the village.[50] On the real trip, after a peaceful overnight visit, Benton and Charlton were ferried down to the Tuira, while Marsh returned to Pucro by trail.

During a wait there for the runner to return from Yaviza with medicines for the Indians, Marsh played his phonograph to break the ice, as he had at each stop of the trip.[51] That night he gave a dance lesson in the fox trot. The chief's pretty teenaged daughter, whom Marsh and his companions had dubbed "the Princess," apparently received more attention from Marsh, Benton, and Charlton than her sisters, and she developed a crush on the explorer. When Marsh showed her pictures of his wife and daughter, "she went off in a perfect tantrum of rage." This harmless flirtation (much safer with a "modest," well-clothed Kuna girl than with "brazen voluptuous Chocoi maidens") and the Princess's brief infatuation, were blown up into something larger in the book, which had it that José Mata offered his daughter for Marsh to marry, even suggesting he could take another local woman as a second wife and become chief of all the Tuira Kuna. The story, as embroidered upon for publication, perfectly embodied the archetypal colonial fantasies of the savage chief's dusky but comely daughter and the white man who goes native and becomes a local monarch or deity. Significantly, in Marsh's case the intrepid explorer only flirted with sexual temptation, enjoying the frisson of forbidden pleasures but ultimately putting them virtuously aside.[52]

A few days after Marsh returned to base camp, a second party headed by Baer, Brin, and Johnson left for Paya and Pucro to study the Kuna for a few days. They met the albino woman who had eluded Marsh, although she found the attention so upsetting that she painted herself black with the same long-lasting black dye used in Chocó body painting. Afterward Marsh depicted this nine-day trip as a test of Baer's fitness for the coming "big push": although he was told the portly anthropologist came through well, it later emerged that he had struggled to keep up.[53] Meanwhile Marsh made several more short trips around the Darién, the only result of which was to confirm his growing disenchantment with the directness and seeming lack of manners of the Chocó.

During these weeks, he was also visited by a Kuna chief from another affluent of the Tuira called the Capeti. Unlike José Mata of Pucro, the new man was on good terms with the Kuna of the upper Chucunaque. Marsh established that they were located on two sidestreams, the Sucubdi (or Socubdi) and the Morti, and at a place called Wala. Although all three villages were actually inhabited by ordinary Kuna with brown skins, Marsh convinced himself that only the Socubdi Indians were Cunas Bravos, and that his white Indians were to be found at the third village. These Wala Indians were neither Kuna nor Chocó but "a very different race, with a different language," fitting perfectly with his sighting in 1923 of the Yaviza canoe-

Anthropologist John Baer measures a Chocó man.

ist, who he was now sure, must be from Wala. Precisely how Marsh arrived at these distorted conclusions, through what combination of preconception, credulity, misunderstood Spanish, and pressure on the chief for the desired answers, may be obscure, but the result was clear: Marsh had now fixed his goal, the supposed white Indians of Wala.[54]

Toward the end of the month, the composition of the group for what Marsh called "the big push" began to sort itself out. Brin and Charlton returned from trips to the city bringing supplies, and Townsend was able to go after all, bringing another army lieutenant, Dwight Rosebaum ("who in spite of his name seems the right sort of fellow").[55] Malsbury had left some weeks before, and Dr. Fairchild was preparing to go home.[56]

As the party took final shape, the decisive practical question was who would work, because the Whites could not be expected to do their own poling and hauling. Although Marsh much preferred the Chocó, they refused to go into Kuna territory, which left the local Blacks. Among expedition members, Marsh was perhaps the most outspoken on the subject, but the others shared the overt racism of the time, routinely identifying themselves as "the white men" and in Breder's case, referring to Yaviza as "a vile nigger town." Of necessity, Marsh put together a crew of Blacks, mostly recruited from communities other than Yaviza: "picked men . . . tough, hard-boiled pirates—but they say they will 'go to hell' with me."[57] Those with the expedition the longest had begun to be recognized by some version of their names: Justo was rendered as Hoosa, and an English-speaking Black was referred to as Dirty Dick to distinguish him from Dick Marsh. Most important among them was an old frontiersman named Barbino, who had been guiding the expedition for weeks, and who knew the region intimately, including the supposedly unvisited upper Chucunaque. Barbino had no desire to go, but Marsh, who learned that the old man had been a fugitive from justice, coerced him into staying on by threatening to have him arrested.[58]

Just before the group's departure, an incident was supposed to have occurred that epitomized the mixture of fact and fantasy in Marsh's version of events and tied together the themes of sex and race woven all through his account. When Marsh first listed the members of the party in his book, he alluded to a Panamanian army captain, who thereafter disappeared from the story until the last moment, when according to Marsh the man disgraced himself by attempting to lure a "very beautiful young Chocoi girl" to return to Panama with him.

Panama in fact had no army, and no captain appears in anyone's field notes, Marsh's included. This fantasy figure seems to have been loosely based on a humble local police agent assigned by the provincial government to guard the base camp. Whether or not this man tried to seduce a Chocó woman, the episode as depicted forms a pair with Marsh's flirtation at Pucro: the mythical captain makes lustful advances on the naked and overtly sensual Chocó, while Marsh receives an offer from the more refined and fully clothed Kuna, which he reluctantly turns down. Here the crucial distinction was between Panamanians and Americans, figured as an opposition of lust and restraint, of blackness against whiteness.[59] Later in San Blas, the element of Panamanian lust, and the triangle of Whites, Blacks, and Indians would reappear.

The real-life policeman was in any case replaced by another man named Villamarino, a tough mestizo, "white in character if not entirely so in color," with a knife scar across his face and an automatic on his hip: "a typical tropical frontiersman . . . quite a man, and fearless and efficient—even in Panama some fine men are developed." Equally to the point, he was, in Marsh's assessment, "the only competent English-Spanish interpreter in the party."[60]

At the very end of March they were ready to go. The base camp was disassembled, Fairchild left for Panama, and at noon on the twenty-ninth the party, now numbering twenty-four—eleven Whites, eleven Blacks, and a mestizo cook and helper—started upstream in six canoes, two of them equipped with outboards pulling the other four.

22.
Up the
Chucunaque

Marsh's goal was to ascend the Chucunaque, first to the Socubdi then to Morti and on to Wala, where he hoped to find his white Indians. From there, most of the boatmen would return downstream, while the rest crossed the low divide to the headwaters of the Bayano, which they would follow downstream to its mouth. Only afterward would he and a few others visit San Blas.[1]

They found the going smooth and easy, at least at first, to the extent that Breder was able to spend the day editing his notes as they went along.[2] Marsh established a routine of breakfast at 6:00, getting under way at 7:30, and continuing without lunch until 3:00 in the afternoon or a little later, when they would make camp on a sand or gravel bar. While other members of the party cleaned their weapons, washed, and mended, Breder spent the next hour or two collecting fish and frogs, before an early dinner.

At night they took turns standing guard, one white man and one black for each watch, 9:00–12:00, 12:00–3:00, and 3:00–6:00. At any sign of danger, the watchkeepers were to rouse the camp with a gunshot or whistle blast, though Breder noted that the guard was intended as much to prevent Black desertion as Indian attack.[3] Marsh was sure that the Indians were many fewer than claimed and armed only with shotguns. The Indians of Wala had been described to him as magically powerful, as well as ferocious,[4] but Marsh, like other explorers and colonizers before him, trusted in modern technology, not just for its objective effects but as the West's form of magic, to dazzle, overawe, and cow the natives.[5]

They may try their "Magic." . . . But if we whites . . . with a pretty good group of hard-boiled half-breeds . . . with our high power rifles, three new rapid fire army automatic machine guns . . . our canoe Elto motors, our victrola, electrical equipment, wireless, numerous trench hand grenades, plenty of dynamite, weird army sirens and whistles, and abundant presents and medicine—cannot produce more "Magic" than the primitive Wallas, well, we ought to wallow before the Wallas.[6]

Restless natives were slow to show themselves, but illness struck immediately. On the first day out Baer developed a headache and was allowed to skip his watch. The next day, March 30, Brin, who had complained of fever just before the journey began, felt sick again. Until that point the party had been remarkably healthy. Insects had proved scarce during the dry season, Marsh's flying squadron had several times camped out under the stars, and daily doses of quinine had kept everyone fit. On the thirty-first, however, Brin insisted he felt ill enough to turn back. Marsh, whose private diagnosis was "cold feet," was reluctant to let him go but felt that he had no choice with President Porras's personal representative, so he sent him downriver in a small canoe with two boatmen.[7]

That same day, the expedition began to encounter obstacles. In the absence of human habitation anywhere along the Chucunaque, great trees grew down to its banks; as the river narrowed going upstream, some of the trees that had been undercut and felled by flooding were washed away, but others, spanning the river, were lodged for months or years—on one of the earlier jaunts upriver, Barbino had pointed out a deadfall that had held for a quarter-century.[8] Small canoes could be readily hauled around or over most obstacles, but with two dozen men and all their equipment, Marsh had opted for heavy cargo dugouts, the three largest of which were more than forty-five feet long.[9]

On the thirty-first the Black boatmen had to dig a canal around one fallen tree. Thereafter open sections of smooth water and rapids alternated with increasingly frequent stops at natural barricades. On the third of April Marsh started using dynamite on the largest trees, an opportunity that Breder exploited to collect the fish killed by the shock waves. On the fourth a single tree required three sticks of dynamite and arduous chopping. The distances covered each day kept dropping, from about twenty-five miles on March 30 down to only two and one-half on April 5: that day it took them five hours to clear three logjams. On the sixth, one huge tree by itself cost them a two-and-one-half-hour delay and three sticks of dynamite, leaving a reserve of only two sticks.[10]

So far no one had seen any Indians, not even after passing the "deadline" at the mouth of the Membrillo early on April 2, but it was assumed that they were shadowing the expedition. As early as the night of March 30, Charlton thought he heard signals while on guard duty. In an article written the following year, Johnson commented sarcastically: "Our lads, who started the day like so many impregnable arsenals, were now annoyed by hearing strange whistling noises in the night. Was

Camping below log jam, Upper Chucunaque, 1924.

it bird or Indian?"[11] Two nights later, on the midnight-to-three watch just below the Membrillo, the unexcitable Breder noted: "It is not unpleasant to sit under the stars listing the sounds of the tropical night. This is the first time I ever mounted guard for 'wild' indians. A new & interesting experience, but I imagine a bad one for a person with an 'imagination.'"[12] The next morning, fresh tracks of barefoot humans were discovered not far from camp. To make the expedition's presence felt by their watchers, Benton fired a volley with his automatic, while Marsh set off a rocket. That afternoon they found a Kuna campsite, and the next day they encountered another, with a row of feathers stuck in a line in the sand, which they took as a warning.[13]

Breder observed: "Life is rather intense here.—In the air we have to watch for insects & indians—in the water for Characins [small fish that nipped at bathers's legs] and Crocodilians."[14] Nonetheless, Marsh felt that his party was, apart from a little peevishness on Benton's part, doing "splendidly."[15] The Black boatmen, on the other hand, seemed unhappy: on the morning of April 6, one man took after another with an axe. The same afternoon the expedition camped a few miles from their first goal, the mouth of the Socubdi, just downstream from a huge logjam. That night, after the camp had recovered from a scare caused by an opossum, three boatmen were overheard planning to defect. Marsh confronted them and by invoking government authority and threatening to shoot deserters, extracted promises that they would stay on as far as the first Indian village.[16]

The next day the camp did not move. The lieutenants and Villamarino went ahead with two boatmen in the smallest canoe (a full thirty-five feet long) to find the Socubdi while Marsh took seven Blacks to attack the logjam. With Marsh driving them on, they cut through in only an hour. But as they moved on to other jams, the boatmen's strength gave out. It turned out that, unknown to Marsh, they had been starting the day with tea and three crackers—he promised to make sure they were fed a hearty breakfast thereafter. At three the scouting party returned to say that they had found signs of human habitation as well as the mouth of the Socubdi just a few miles beyond.[17]

The group passed the last barrier on the Chucunaque with great effort ("even the whites worked") and arrived at the Socubdi on the ninth, where they camped for more than a week. Marsh congratulated himself on reaching territory unexplored by anyone else, with the sole exception of the Selfridge Expedition fifty years earlier, which had given up and turned back. "So far as we have been able to ascertain, no white man . . . has ever been above the Sucubdi."[18] Marsh wanted badly to believe he was first, or at least second, but he had in fact been preceded over the previous four centuries by soldiers, pirates, rubber tappers, travelers, and explorers, of whom Selfridge was only one.[19]

On the tenth, a scouting party surprised several Kuna youths, who fled upstream. The river, although largely free of barriers, was only fifteen feet wide and a foot deep near its mouth, to all appearances much too shallow for Marsh's dugouts, and it seemed obvious he would have to get suitable transport from the Kuna or failing that, to move the expedition upstream in relays in its least heavy canoes. Thus on the eleventh an advance party set off to find the Socubdi Kuna.[20]

The party spent three hard days traveling upstream, dragging their canoes through each set of rapids. At night they rigged a rocket to set off if attacked, but Marsh was by now ready to dismiss the fearsome reputation of the wild Kunas as "bosh." On the fourteenth, they surprised three frightened Kuna boys, who were relieved to find the party friendly and agreed (one of them spoke some Spanish) to take them to their chief. Marsh and Rosebaum went ahead, while Villamarino went back for the rest of the advance party.[21]

After an hour's walk, they entered a small hamlet, where they were greeted in English by an old man: "How are you, boys. Glad to see you." The chief, named Salisiman, a kuna-ized form of Charly Seaman, had been a sailor for many years. He said he had been sending out young messengers to warn them of an attack planned by the Morti and Wala people and to invite the expedition to save itself by passing rapidly through to the coast, but the messenger boys had all taken fright. Marsh replied that he would be sending down to the coast for supplies and would then decide where to go next.[22]

Soon after the rest of the advance party arrived the next afternoon, they were told that an attack was imminent on the main expedition back at the mouth of the river.

Marsh, amused at the timidity of the Kuna boys and learning that epidemics had recently ravaged the region's population, was not too alarmed. (The threat may in fact have been real: even today Wala and Morti retain a reputation for tough opposition to incursions.) However, he sent Kuna runners to warn Townsend and then followed himself in canoes with Villamarino, Rosebaum, and a number of Blacks and Kuna, leaving Benton, Charlton, and the laborer dubbed Dirty Dick at Socubdi.[23]

They reached camp late the next morning, to find that Baer had a high fever. The next day the whole expedition started upstream, with Baer in a bed rigged in one of the canoes. His condition inspired mixed reactions. Already nicknamed *macho monte,* or "tapir," by the group, he was told by Marsh that in his canoe-bed he was the Queen of Sheba, and the others referred to him as "Sleeping Beauty." Although Baer's suffering was real enough, Marsh's instinct was to blame it on physical and nervous exhaustion rather than illness.

I hate to see a white man, in these surroundings – amongst negroes & indians – even though sick – so utterly loose all his morale. . . . I have ceased to worry about him for his own sake – but he is a heavy drag on our party. . . . I have feared from the beginning that just this thing would happen. But we must make the best of it.[24]

Baer had certainly been a poor choice for the expedition. In addition to his obesity, he suffered from what was in those days called Bright's Disease, a chronic kidney ailment. But he had also contracted a serious condition in the field. One of his most onerous tasks at the base camp had been to dissect the howler monkeys shot for him, weighing and preserving their organs. Just before the big push, in a letter to Aleš Hrdlička, his sponsor at the Smithsonian, Baer had written: "I have been having some trouble with bites from flies which infected the monkeys and caused great parasites about their throats."[25] As Marsh himself later recognized, Baer was apparently bitten by a screwfly or botfly, which leaves its larvae in a mammalian host. Although botfly bites in themselves seldom cause mortal harm, they can lead to serious infection.[26]

By the second exhausting day up the Socubdi they could hardly go further with the big canoes. It had rained several times, but the dry season hung on, and water levels remained low.[27] In the middle of the night, however, the seasons changed, as Breder discovered: "About 2:00 a.m. a distinct sensation of dampness overcame me and I awoke to find an inch or so of water in my cot."[28] As the downpour continued, Marsh recognized how exposed they were camped on a river bar, and at nine that morning, with rain coming down in sheets, he ordered everything loaded into the boats except the sleeping patient. When the rising river reached Baer's tent fly, he was rushed to his canoe bed, and at eleven they started upstream again.[29]

The crisis came about noon: "The 'bore' of the flood from the cloudburst in the mountains near by came upon us in one terrible rush, as if a dam had suddenly burst."[30] The last two canoes, one holding Breder and his boatmen, the other Marsh and his boatmen with Baer under a canopy, managed only to get a little out of the main current on opposite sides of the river. In Breder's words:

Here we lay for some time "climbing" hand over hand up into the branches of riverside trees as the water boosted us up. At one time by actual measure the water was rising at a rate of 3 3/8" in 5 min, but it rose faster a little later. Great tangled masses of logs and brush rushed down at a rate that could not have been less than 15 miles an hour! The dislodged spiders, centipedes, ants, frogs, etc. swarmed over us in startling variety.

Even in these desperate circumstances, Breder did not forget why he was there. "I collected a good series . . . 2 others with bright yellow broken hairs and an equally yellow belly which have darker spots. . . . A *Bufo* of a different sort than seen before was taken in numbers. I chopped down numerous large banana trees and succeeded in taking 2 frogs."[31] Marsh, meanwhile, was in a much more exposed position on the opposite bank, with logs scraping against the side of his canoe and Baer tossing and turning under his canopy. Eventually Townsend came down in a small canoe to check on them, bringing the news that the rest of the expedition was camped on dry ground a few hundred yards ahead. Marsh did not feel he could move his canoe without endangering or soaking Baer, so he sent Townsend back up for food. After Townsend returned, the canoe with Baer was worked into more protected water and its cargo unloaded.

Their success encouraged Breder to attempt a crossing to Marsh's side, which ended in disaster. Swept downstream toward rapids, Breder's two boatmen panicked, clutching onto vines and snags, and then as the boat was pulled on, they abandoned it to the current. It was run broadside onto the protruding branch of a submerged tree, and as the canoe filled with water, Breder, too, had to let it go, watching his supplies, most of the specimens collected in the last three weeks, and all his notes go off downstream. The elderly head canoeman, Barbino, leapt into Townsend's canoe with three others and shot off in pursuit, which greatly impressed Marsh despite his prejudices: "Never have I seen such quick action and fire — seldom such courage."[32]

Marsh managed to lower his canoe down to the snag on a long line, with the sleeping Baer still aboard under the canopy, to fetch the soaked and exhausted Breder. "Stripping off and warming myself over Marsh's fire I counted my remaining possessions; 1 milk can of specimens, 1 40' seine . . . 1 wrist watch, 1 blue athletic shirt, 1 pair underpants." As they tried to protect themselves from the snakes and insects driven onto their little island by the flood, a tarantula jumped onto Breder's neck but failed to bite. Even the indefatigable biologist "did not quite have the ambition to go frog hunting."[33] Toward dusk they heard a yell from downstream, and Barbino appeared with almost all of the contents of Breder's canoe, which had been so carefully wrapped that they survived the soaking. After receiving Marsh's congratulations, Barbino's crew pulled Breder's second boatman out of the branches of a half-submerged tree, where he had been left in disgust since the accident. As the skies cleared and the river began to drop rapidly, exposing the branch to which Breder had clung now twenty feet in the air, they sent most of the boatmen up to the camp, afterward celebrating their survival and the day, which was Easter Sunday, with a punch improvised from sugar, canned milk, and some of Breder's grain alcohol.[34]

They reached Socubdi late the next day, able to use the outboards again in the now-deep water. Marsh was still determined to continue on to Wala and the Bayano, but first they had to get Baer out and replenish their food supplies. After a day's rest, he sent Benton and Rosebaum with six Kuna over the cordillera into San Blas to a floating store belonging to the Colon Import-Export Company, a schooner that Salisiman informed him was anchored twenty miles down the coast.[35]

For the next few days, the expedition stayed in the hamlet, kept company by Salisiman and a few men and boys. Marsh queried Sali about a comb he found with a few light hairs in it: he was told that three white Indians lived in the valley, two women and a man, the latter evidently a *nele* or seer. Marsh seized on this response to extend and elaborate his fantasies, abetted by Sali's minimal English and his willingness to tell him what he wanted to hear.[36] Marsh concluded that the white Indian man, whom he and Sali ended up calling Sakla Cheepu, "White Chief," could be none other than the canoeist encountered in Yaviza the year before. Sakla Cheepu, as the wandering leader of all the interior Kuna, had been organizing the resistance to the expedition, or so Sali said. When Marsh asked to meet this elusive figure, Sali claimed that he had left for the coast and suggested the expedition should try to catch up with him there. Although Marsh readily grasped that Sali was trying to get rid of him, and that much of what he said was "superstition, legend, exaggeration, and plain lies," he eagerly accepted those parts that fit his preconceptions.[37]

During these days, Breder managed to go out collecting along a nearby creek, but no one was allowed into the main village just downstream, still less a second village some way upstream. Marsh was inclined to go along with Kuna wishes for the moment, despite his great advantage in firepower, since the expedition depended on the Indians for food, lodging, and bearers.[38] Townsend, sent to reconnoiter the second village, was stopped on its outskirts, and when he and Marsh tried again a few days later, Sali implored them not to enter and then leapt out of their canoe into the river. The evidence suggests that the Socubdi Kuna, disturbed by epidemics and a recent small earthquake as well as by the expedition, were holding an eight-day exorcism, during which the village had to be closed off.[39] Sali, probably a secondary chief, had been sent to keep the visitors company while the exorcism proceeded.

Marsh, however, decided that Sali was an imposter, a stand-in for Sakla Cheepu, who was hiding in what Marsh now dubbed "the Forbidden City."

On the twenty-seventh, Rosebaum returned from the storeship in San Blas alone — "*no Benton.*" His absence was worrisome: in January, Marsh and Fairchild had written Benton's employer to complain of the newspaperman's behavior in Panama, and a letter of reprimand had caught up with Benton at base camp, provoking a vow to have it out with Marsh sooner or later.[40] The group decided that someone should go to Colón to procure transport for Baer and supplies and at the same time to forestall anything Benton might plan — Rosebaum volunteered again. A day or two later everyone but Johnson, Villamarino, and the sick man would hike to San Blas, where they would arrange to get Baer out.[41]

Marsh wrote the text of a cable to be sent to the *Rochester Times-Union* warning them against Benton, as well as a letter to the governor of the Canal Zone requesting a seaplane or boat to evacuate Baer, and, on the chance that Rosebaum might find him still at the storeship, a letter that exhorted Benton to play fair and threatened if he did not "to take such course to protect my own just interests as seems necessary."[42]

The day after Rosebaum left the second time, it rained heavily again, and the high water blocked the trail to the continental divide, which crossed and recrossed the upper Socubdi more than twenty-five times. After Marsh's attempt to enter the second village, the Indians left them alone, which they found ominous, and with more rain, the level of the river stayed high. The boatmen wanted to return to Yaviza, and Marsh was growing "desperate."[43]

The next day he adopted desperate measures. Taking a leaf from Balboa and Cortez, he swore to destroy the canoes if he heard any more talk of turning back, and with Blacks armed for the first time as well as whites, they cut a trail up to and through "the Forbidden City." After this show of force, they were met on their return to their quarters by Sali and his brother, who was evidently a seer or nele as well as a chief, but not white. Now anxious to appease Marsh, they readily agreed to provide the twenty-five bearers he demanded for the trek to the coast. At the same time, Marsh learned that a mysterious black powder had been sprinkled on the party's cots. When confronted, Sali claimed that it was nothing but a little friendly magic — except for airing out their bedding, Marsh conspicuously ignored it.[44]

On the first of May, a month after leaving base camp at Yaviza, Marsh, Breder, Charlton, and Townsend and his orderly set off on the "long, hard, wet trail up the Pacific slope" along the upper Socubdi, accompanied by ten Black boatmen and twenty-five Kuna carrying tents and cots, personal equipment, victrola, presents for use in San Blas, and even one of the outboard motors.[45] After camping that night in rough shelters cut by the Kuna, they crossed the continental divide at eleven the next morning and a few minutes later, reversing Balboa, gazed out on the Atlantic.

23.
On the
Coast

Marsh and his followers emerged onto the coast at a historic spot. Called Magemmulu, "Face-paint Point," by its Kuna inhabitants, it was known to the world as Caledonia, after the short-lived Scots colony that had been located just across the bay at the turn of the eighteenth century, or alternatively as Aclá, the name it had held as a Spanish outpost in the early sixteenth century. At various times in its history, Caledonia Bay had been the origin of the expedition on which Balboa discovered the Pacific, the favorite jumping-off point of pirates crossing the Isthmus, and the most frequently proposed terminus of a Darién canal.

In 1924 Caledonia was a small village set on a beach facing onto a sheltered corner of the bay. Its inhabitants, though reserved when the expedition first arrived on May 2, warmed up over the next few days, and Marsh established a good relationship with their chief, who soon sported a pith helmet from the expedition.[1] Marsh planned to spend ten days: after a visit to the Colon Import floating store anchored about twenty miles away at Isla Pino, where with luck he might catch up with Rosebaum and Benton, he would send supplies back to his followers still in Socubdi. He would visit and film Chief Inabaginya, Colman's rival.[2] He would then bring Baer out and send him to Colón, and finally return to the Chucunaque and Bayano to complete his trip.

At the storeship, Marsh found Rosebaum down with malaria and Benton demoralized and complaining of stomach problems but without animus against Marsh or the expedition. It was arranged that when they reached the city on the company ship, Benton would gather new supplies and personnel and arrange transport for Baer. On his return to Caledonia, Marsh spoke with former intendente Hurtado, now an official of the new United Fruit plantations a few miles to the east; Hurtado told him that the expedition had already lost one member, Raoul Brin, who had died of malaria a few days after reaching Panama City.[3]

Expedition members at Caledonia Village, 1924.

On May 7, Marsh paid a visit to Inabaginya on New Sasardi, an island village a few miles down the coast from Caledonia. For the rest of May, Marsh returned to Sasardi every few days, using gifts, phonograph concerts, and medical treatment to cultivate the chief's friendship. During Marsh's third visit, Inabaginya asked to have his people vaccinated against smallpox, which had been ravaging the coast as well as the interior.

In their conferences, Inabaginya expressed disquiet at recent intrusions – the new banana plantations, a proposed railroad across to the Chucunaque, the storeship anchored at Isla Pino, the plantations at the other end of San Blas, and now Marsh's expedition.[4] Later Marsh learned of Kuna troubles with rubber-gatherers and of conflict with Black plantation workers, particularly a recent case in which two laborers had tried to rape an Indian woman and girl. With a deep-seated antipathy to Blacks, reinforced by his years in the American South, Marsh was all too ready to interpret the rape as emblematic of the threat faced by the Indians.[5]

From their first encounter, Marsh lectured Inabaginya vehemently on the situation of the Indians and what they had to do:[6] "I saw no use in beating around the bush – so I told him, that while the indian was dying off of smallpox, fever, etc, because he was too ignorant, too lazy, and too superstitious to know how to live and keep well, all the rest of the world was growing and increasing."[7] Marsh gave Inabaginya a stiff dose of social Darwinism, talking of races evolving and competing, and the destruction of those that failed the test. He rejected out of hand Inabaginya's claim that the Kuna held their land by divine right.

I told him that idea was all wrong. . . . That God did not give any particular part of the world to any particular people. . . . That where worthless people refused to use the land to good purpose, they had to give way to better people. . . . That ten thousand years ago all the Indian ancestors came from Asia & Polynesia. . . . Not a country in the world but what was peopled by races that came from other lands, conquered or stole the land.[8]

Marsh's feelings toward the Kuna were at this point quite ambivalent. He found them vastly preferable to Blacks and capable of great improvement, but still a pretty mixed lot, especially on days when Salisiman or someone else was making life difficult for him.

I have gotten over any sentimental idealism of the indian—the grown men are, as a rule, lying, deceitful, lazy, ignorant, superstitious, bestial, and degraded—though there are some notable exceptions of fine character among them—but the children are a very bright, intelligent, friendly, normal class of children who if given a show might develop into a worthwhile people . . . but as between the Indian and the Latin Negro—I infinitely prefer the indian.[9]

Marsh was especially negative on economic questions. Apparently unaware of the millions of coconuts that the Kuna produced each year, he had gotten the erroneous idea (very likely from weeds in Kuna fields and the coconut husks littering their groves) that they "did not take care of one twentieth part of their coconuts, bananas, coffee or chocolate already growing."[10] Marsh's faulty observations merely confirmed what every proponent of capitalist expansion held on faith, namely that the natives underutilized their lands. Marsh insisted to Inabaginya that "the indian must open his country to outside commerce and intercourse," and that if they did, they should be able to secure their farms.[11] The policy must then be *"vaccination, sanitation, and education."*[12]

There is no way to know how much of this Inabaginya took in through a double translation from English to Spanish to Kuna.[13] He would certainly not have agreed to accept schools, abandon Kuna medicine, or give up their claims as original owners of the land. But he recognized Marsh as a potential ally, one who disliked wagas and the Panamanian government just as he did, and who might be able to get support for Kuna territorial claims as well as protection from smallpox.

Marsh, who began by urging Inabaginya to seek guarantees from the government, offered to take him to the city to petition both American and Panamanian authorities. With his facility for juggling two balls at once, Marsh began planning an ethnological tour of the coast, with stops at each island to make films and buy artifacts, combined with a mission on behalf of the Kuna. Soon the plan expanded to include a visit to the United States.[14]

Marsh also began formulating in his mind a scheme for a protectorate over San

Blas, to be headed by an American commissioner, who sounded very much like himself— "No Panaman will handle it efficiently or honestly." Anticipating that he would have to conceal this plan at first from Inabaginya and President Porras, he expected to set it out in detail to U.S. Secretary of State Hughes in Washington: land in San Blas was to be leased or sold to outside interests, who would pay fees to the government and the Kuna, establishing a fund for scholarships, schools, and so forth. Since "the indian will not work, of course," the native population was to become, in effect, a "landed gentry."[15] He still failed to grasp that the very last thing the U.S. government would welcome was another chance to get caught up in Panamanian internal affairs.

Before he could start to put his schemes into effect, Marsh had to get Baer out and then finish the journey originally planned. When he returned to Caledonia on May 8, the expedition debated what to do about the sick man. Townsend volunteered to take Baer back down the Chucunaque. Marsh, who thought the hardships of the river trip would prove even more difficult than a mountain crossing, also doubted he had enough money left for a boat to pick Baer up on the Pacific side. He decided to let Townsend go back for the equipment and to follow soon afterward himself to fetch Baer. On Townsend's way in, however, he crossed with a messenger bringing news that Baer was worsening, so Marsh sent a note saying to bring him out immediately.[16]

In the ten days since the expedition had left Socubdi, according to Johnson, the men left behind had begun to feel abandoned. Baer had developed sores from the botfly bites. Johnson managed to keep Villamarino from taking Baer downriver, according to his account provoking him into a frenzy, in which he shouted over and over "Tu no eres jefe mío! Tu no eres jefe mío!" (You aren't any boss of mine!). Johnson let Villamarino and three boatmen go, because he feared that the agitated policeman would begin shooting with his automatic. Marsh later claimed that the four men were never seen again, though in fact Johnson ran into Villamarino in the city and was told that, going with the flood, the four had made Yaviza in thirty hours.[17]

On the fourteenth Townsend started across from Socubdi to San Blas with a party of twenty-four Kuna bearers, two teams of four each taking turns carrying Baer in a hammock suspended from a pole. They arrived in Caledonia on the sixteenth, with Baer in better shape than had been feared. Marsh still saw his condition as a physical and mental breakdown rather than illness, a diagnosis Baer's weeping and moaning only reinforced. In light of his collapse, however, the plan was to get him to Colón in two or three days on the next supply vessel from the Import-Export Company.[18]

It ought to have been obvious to anyone that the expedition was falling apart, but Marsh clung to the notion that after sending Baer out and resupplying, he could return to the Socubdi and finish the river journey with the remnants of his party, whom he now called "the old guard": "We are just on the point of real accomplishment. I hope to do for these Indians in a small way what Perry did in Japan."[19] But the attrition continued. A couple of days later in Marsh's absence, Breder, who had been feeling seriously ill for several days, went aboard a passing vessel on its way to Colón, and Townsend followed a week or so later. Marsh privately condemned each "desertion" and blamed it on the departing man's weakness. As soon became clear, they all had excellent excuses: in addition to Rosebaum's malaria, Benton's stomach pains ended in appendicitis, and Breder had to be treated in hospital first for typhoid fever and then for malaria. Even Marsh himself was hit by several days of malarial fevers.[20] Nonetheless, Marsh would not let go of the idea that "most of my party have shown the 'white feather' in the extreme tests."[21]

On the seventeenth, the day after Baer was brought to Caledonia, Marsh traveled down the coast to Puerto Obaldía, where he knew a U.S. radio station was located. He stayed there four days, trying to communicate with Rosebaum, Townsend, and Panamanian and American authorities while guiltily enjoying clean sheets, bread and jam, and other comforts of the station. The U.S. military radioed that they had no smallpox vaccine, but on the twenty-first, President Porras promised a boat and doctor to treat Baer and vaccinate the local population. Rosebaum had also recovered and was on his way back.[22]

In Caledonia on the twenty-second, Marsh found that Charlton had missed an opportunity to send Baer out on a passing launch. As Baer's condition worsened, they waited. On the twenty-seventh, Marsh heard that the doctor promised by President Porras had arrived on Sasardi and was administering vaccinations. Hurriedly fetched by Marsh, the doctor declared that Baer was suffering from the effects of botfly bites exacerbated by his obesity and kidney disease and would not last much longer outside a hospital. A few minutes later, the fruit company launch arrived with Enrique Hurtado and a surprise visitor, the army pilot from Marsh's aerial survey of the Darién in January, who had come out to see the expedition. At the pilot's suggestion, Hurtado promised to radio a request next morning for one of the American seaplanes that had just arrived on the Isthmus.

At the end of the following day, May 28, a seaplane flew in and landed in front of Caledonia. Baer, however, had died just a few moments before. The plane was followed the next day by a naval vessel, the USS *Curlew*, but by that time it was too late even to take back Baer's body, which had joined the bones of Balboa and the Scots in the Caledonian sand the day before.[23]

Marsh's enemies and critics later tried to heap blame on him for Baer's death, which was only partly justified. Before starting up the Chucunaque, the explorer had warned his followers of the dangers and of his determination to press on regardless. Baer, in particular, insisted on going despite Marsh's reservations. After Baer sickened, a series of difficulties largely outside Marsh's control hindered the patient's evacuation. On the other hand, someone as decisive as Marsh could likely have moved more quickly to evacuate Baer if he had not been preoccupied with picking up the pieces of his expedition, and if he had not dismissed Baer's condition as the man's own fault.

Two days after Baer's death, Marsh finally had to call it quits when a message arrived saying that Rosebaum's superiors would not let him return after all.[24] By no means ready to give up altogether, Marsh simply moved on to the next phase of his schemes, the proposed trip by Kuna delegates to Panama and the United States. A message from Inabaginya, who announced that he was willing to travel soon if Marsh would abandon the dash to the Bayano, solidified the plan.[25] And then, at the last possible moment, the sad remnants of the expedition unexpectedly achieved its original goal, the discovery of the white Indians:

Johnson located them for me, and has seen and interviewed them. . . . So, we will reach Panama in two or three weeks, and then . . . will sail for New York—I with my Indian King of Kings and two attractive full-blooded White Indians. Charlton says it will be the greatest stunt of the century—that interest in old Tut will be as dead as old Tut is. . . . Then all go to Washington, where we will be presented to the President and Secretary [of State] Hughes, and Ina & I will put our plans before them, while the scientists can examine my "White Indians" with their own eyes—and then probably we will tour the country raising funds for the betterment of the Darien Indians. . . . I have "opened" the Darien.[26]

Marsh radioed the news of his success to Benton in Colón, and on June 14, the *Rochester Times-Union* displayed a banner headline, "MARSH FINDS WHITE INDI-ANS," relegating news of the great Johnstown flood to type one-third as large. The *New York Times* also covered the story, though more discretely.[27]

A few loose ends had to be wrapped up before leaving. Marsh, Johnson, and ten bearers crossed to Socubdi to retrieve the rest of their equipment, coming back out on June 2. Marsh arranged to borrow a sailing yawl from the fruit company in which to cruise down the coast, and Inabaginya, having grasped Marsh's interest in white Indians, promised to find some more.[28] The chief himself proposed to follow Marsh to Colón in a few days. After meeting with the assembled chiefs of Inabaginya's confederacy on Sasardi and going through his proposal with them, Marsh set out.[29]

On the first night of the trip, the yawl anchored at Portogandi or Ustupu, where Marsh, Charlton, and Johnson examined a white Indian boy and walked through the streets, mobbed by friendly Kuna. Of the two mutually antagonistic villages on the island, Marsh was undoubtedly supposed to visit the one affiliated with Inabaginya. However, Nele, who was by now heir-apparent to Colman, invited Marsh to *his* gathering house. Marsh treated several sick people, he was told about the government ethnocide and its employees' sexual misdeeds, and he lectured the crowd at length concerning the germ theory of disease, the value of sanitation and education, and the evolution of races. While on Ustupu, Marsh's professed interest

Richard Marsh with Albino Kuna Boy, 1924.

in artifacts unleashed a flood of gifts, and Nele rounded up several albinos for his inspection. (Marsh later left the impression that crowds of white Indians appeared—Johnson counted five.)[30]

Two Kuna joined the delegation at Ustupu, Nele's son Alfred, an ex-sailor who spoke some English, and a young albino called Sippu, or in Marsh's spelling, Cheepu, which simply means "white." Taken to Cheepu's home, Marsh was surprised to find that the boy's parents were brown-skinned, which is in fact usually the case. Albinism is a recessive trait, appearing only in individuals with a pair of the appropriate genes. Since the Kuna discouraged albino adults from marrying, most white babies were born to parents with brown skin, each parent having a single gene for albinism. Someone else might have found this irrefutable evidence that the whites did not constitute a separate race discouraging: Marsh, however, rationalized it as support for the theory that white races everywhere originated through a process of partial albinism.

At Ailigandi they were met by Colman, now a stooped old man with a bad palsy, and again by Nele, who had undoubtedly gone ahead of them to brief Colman on the great opportunity presented by Marsh. Colman complained of Panamanian persecution, producing copies of letters of complaint sent to the government, and

Marsh said he would try to get American schools for San Blas. According to Marsh, "When we left the house, we saw many more white Indians in the street—whole families of them." (Johnson saw eleven.)[31] Marsh convinced himself that most of the white Indians had come from the mainland, and being told of the stigma suffered by albinos among the Kuna, he somehow concluded that white Indians were routinely banished to live by themselves in isolated places, which reinforced his fantasy of an all-white village at Wala.[32]

Colman had fully recognized the opportunity for outside help that Marsh represented and called a meeting to organize participation in the mission. He sent as his personal representative an up-and-coming ritualist and politically ambitious Ailigandi man named Igwa-Nigdibippi—reduced to "Igwa" by Marsh. Cheepu was joined by an older albino boy, whose name evidently began (as do many Kuna names) with the prefix Olo- "gold"; he was thereafter simply called Olo. And as interpreter and third political delegate, a man from Niatupu or Tigantikki named Philip Thompson was chosen.

Thompson was one member of a loose network of literate young Kuna men who had been recruited as secretaries for the rebel chiefs. A son of Chief Joe Harding (Gassó's "Soo") of Corazón de Jesús, Philip had been sent as a young boy to Panama to be fostered and had ended up traveling with the family of a Panamanian diplomat to Washington, where he studied for several years in an orphan's school. As a young married man, he had sided with Charly Robinson against Claudio Iglesias and later fled to Niatupu.[33] Thompson's son recalled how his father described being picked for the delegation.

Before they went to American-land, there was a big meeting on Ailigandi, he said. . . . "I went to Ailigandi. . . . The birds [that is, literate men] were brought there, ahead of time. All the birds in San Blas, they brought us there. With all that, I believe there were as many as twenty-three or twenty-four of us there. The gathering house was full. . . .

Masta Mas, as we called him, he was already there. . . . He was the one who helped us," he said to me. "He came to show us a hand. . . . Then the leaders said to him, 'These birds sitting here, you talk with each one. Talk with each of them, to find out which one as you hear it translates best for us into American-speech.'"

The bilingual and trilingual men among whom Marsh was to choose included a good many ex-sailors, quite a few of them heavily tattooed. The spectators watching from the sides began joking that the man with the most tattoos would be chosen. "That one who is most spotted and speckled, he has to be the one who will be chosen to go to American-land."

Then Masta Mas said, "This one. This one will go on your behalf to American-land. . . ." "What do you know, it wasn't one of the speckled ones! It turned out to be someone with unmarked skin! So the kids were all making lots of noise at each other: 'You were fooled!. . .'"

Right. Then with that, when they were all there, then Nele said, Nele: "I'll tell you. My son, he will carry my spirit. He will *represent* me." Then Colman said, "Igwa-Nigdibippi, he will bear the spirit of my speech.... Then this Felipe Thompson, he will be the interpreter."[34]

The political half of the delegation was thus complete. To round out the "scientific" side, an appealing teenaged albino girl named Margarita from Nargana was recruited, along with her nonalbino parents, Jim and Alice Berry.

Marsh, Charlton, and Johnson arrived in Colón on the evening of June 16, along with nine Kuna, the expedition's two cooks, the guide Barbino, and three laborers who had stayed with the party to the very end. Taking cars to the Hotel Washington, Marsh booked rooms for the Indians and whites and found clothing for the tattered explorers.[35] Benton cabled an article to the *Times-Union*, which it published under another banner headline.[36] The next day Marsh bought Palm Beach suits for the Kuna men, and Margarita had her hair bobbed.

On the eighteenth Marsh and Charlton visited Breder in the hospital. (Even while recuperating, the biologist recorded the case of a fellow-patient who had been bitten by a barracuda, carefully plotting the teethmarks.) Allowed out for part of the day, Breder met the white Indians.

They are curious indeed. There are two boys, partial albinos (?) Light hair [illeg.] blue eyes, white tender skin, many liver spots and an abundance of hair on the arms (white). . . . The curious part is not the apparent Albinism but the fact that the[y] have immense round heads quite different from the more narrow ones of the typical San Blas.[37]

For the rest of their time in Colón and Panama, controversy swirled around Marsh and his discovery. The very first article to appear in *La Estrella* and the *Star and Herald* struck an antagonistic note. It described the explorers coming ashore as "a sorry sight," and the white Indians as "apparently no different to the well known type of Albino which is often seen on the streets of Colón."[38]

Marsh had by this time worked out a complicated racial classification typical of that era. Racialists had no qualms about simultaneously assigning supposed races to particular regions, merely on the basis of visual impressions, and at the same time picking out individuals as representatives of distant stocks. Theorists spun elaborate fantasy histories of waves of races, representing different evolutionary levels, those races migrating, conquering, displacing, interbreeding, progressing and degenerating.[39] In this vein, Marsh identified six separate races, ranging from "the true Cuna very closely resembling the Japanese" to a "splendid North American type" found only among chiefly families, and a paleolithic type, who sounded very like Sakla Cheepu. The white Indians apparently sprang from this paleolithic stock.[40]

If Marsh made much of the Indians through typological distinction, Panamanians belittled them by lumping them together under a derogatory label. *La Estrella* referred to Marsh's companions not as Kuna or Tule or even *indios* but as *machikwa*, a Kuna word meaning "boy." As far as *La Estrella* was concerned, even the females and adult men in the party were all "boys."[41]

In making his case in Panama for the existence of a race of white Indians, Marsh faced the difficulty not only that albino Kuna had been seen in the city, but that a few excursion parties from the Canal Zone had visited Nargana in recent years, so the teenager Margarita in particular was immediately recognized. Worse for Marsh, Townsend's employers insisted on an exclusive, offending the touchy local papers.[42] The next article in the *Star and Herald* attacked every weak point the reporter could find. Since Marsh invoked Breder's standing as a scientist, the paper pointed out that Breder was a youth in his twenties and an ichthyologist, not an anthropologist. Marsh claimed that the blond Indians' skulls were 15 to 20 percent larger than those of an average White man—the reporter extracted statements from Breder and Johnson that the Indians had not been measured yet. Perhaps most embarrassing, it recounted a fracas in which a cameraman from Fox News was chased across the grounds of the Hotel Washington by Marsh and Charlton when they caught him poaching on them filming the Indians in what the paper termed a "fake jungle scene."[43]

After a heated letter to the editor from Marsh,[44] on the twenty-fifth the paper rolled out heavier artillery, in a long interview with one A. Hyatt Verrill. Played up by the paper as an anthropologist at the Museum of the American Indian in New York, Verrill was merely a free-lance artifact collector on contract to supply the museum. Author of popular books and articles, in Panama Verrill had also been involved in dubious mining ventures. Dismissing the larger heads of the albinos as an optical illusion, he denied that the whites had any "scientific value whatever. . . . They are only freaks, the same as a three-legged chicken."[45]

Marsh hit back hard. An article published a few months before, which claimed that American flyers had discovered a lost city in the Darién, included an illustration showing Verrill with his hands tied, supposedly captive to wild Kuna. Gloating that the Indians in the picture were actually Chocó, who were "about as dangerous as a pet canary," Marsh savaged the errors in Verrill's article, which included placing the colonial ruins at Yaviza on the wrong side of the river. More to the point at hand, Marsh insisted that whatever the white Indians might turn out to be, they were not true albinos, who have "white hair, pinkish eyes and blue gums."[46]

Although each antagonist attacked more successfully than he defended, in retrospect both made valid points. The white Indians are indeed albinos, not a separate population, as subsequent research has established beyond doubt. On the other hand, the rate of albinism in the Kuna population, the world's highest, is anything but trivial scientifically, and if as Marsh himself admitted, he was not the first to notice the white Indians, he did take the lead in posing them as a scientific problem.

The embarrassments did not end there. In the same edition of the *Star and Herald* as Verrill's attack there appeared another article entitled, "Marsh Helpers to Sue for Wages Due." The expedition's cook, Francisco Pinzón, was acting as spokesman for the last six of its crew, who together claimed $808.50 in back pay. Having, they said, been brushed aside by Marsh at his hotel, they had engaged a lawyer to pursue their claim.[47]

The most devastating attack, however, came from the United States, from Aleš Hrdlička, head of the Anthropology Division of the Smithsonian's Natural History Museum, Baer's sponsor and the leading physical anthropologist of his generation. Irascible and outspoken, Hrdlička issued a statement branding the white Indians "impossible" and "a shameless hoax." "I am disgusted with the whole affair."[48]

With much to do besides rebutting newspaper attacks, Marsh spent a week and a half in Colón and Panama packing up his collection of artifacts, showing the Indians around and seeking passports for them, which required President Porras's personal intervention. In the case of Inabaginya, who arrived with his secretary and a grandson, the government refused to allow him to go and even detained him briefly, estranging the embarrassed chief from Marsh.[49]

On the day the party sailed, the *Star and Herald* published a bit of racist humor at Marsh's expense entitled "White Negroes Now Discovered, claim of Hendem D. Line." Professor Line:

F.O.W.B. Frogologist of the Ecuadorean Dinosaur Institute who arrived on the Isthmus yesterday with forty-five moving picture camera men . . . said he discovered one hundred and forty-four different races of white negroes. "In the upper reaches of the Hornswoggle . . . we found . . . the Tick Tocks. In the Cukoo regions we found the Honeywrigglers, Jazzawallas, Bambinos, Fidgetys, Comebacks, Xylophones, Swinettes, Criscos, Three-in-ones . . . and Pie-eyed Picklers."[50]

Marsh may have been relieved to get away.

24.
The
White
Indians
on Tour

On the sixth of July, Marsh, Major Johnson, and the eight Kuna arrived on the ship *Calamares* in New York City, where they were met on board by Mrs. Marsh, two of their children, and a number of reporters and photographers. The press paid most attention to Margarita, recording the details of her outfit, the powder on her face, and the bob in her hair. It was noted that all three white children avoided the open sun, and that none of the Indians seemed as impressed as they should have been by the New York skyline.[1]

The reporter covering the story for the *New York Times* managed to pack an impressive amount of condescension and misinformation into one short article. He rendered Alice Berry's Kuna name as Dingalingadinga Bo and noted that for the duration of the trip she and her husband had abandoned their usual costume of animal skins. Marsh, for his part, stressed that the white Indians were *not* albinos. "I confidently believe they are offshoots of the ancient paleolithic type, from which the first Nordic differentiation occurred perhaps fifteen thousand years ago."[2]

The white Indians, despite their novelty, joined a centuries-old tradition, by which New World natives (many of them kidnapped) were brought back and displayed as curiosities. They included such well-known figures as the helpful Squanto and Darwin's Fuegians—York Minster, Jemmy Button, and Fuegia Basket.[3] North American Indian delegations had also been visiting Washington since the founding of the Republic, and in recent years, each World's Fair featured native villages in which Algerians, Dahomeans, and Ilongots portrayed themselves, demonstrating the evolutionary superiority of white civilization.[4]

These displays built on the fascination of encountering the exotically different near at hand. The frisson of reversed expectations, of savagery ensconced in the heart of civilization, worked whether the visitors wore their picturesque animal

Kuna delegates on board ship, New York Harbor, 1924. *Left to right:* Inez Berry, Margarita Berry, Olo, Cheepu, James Berry.

skins or put on suits and ties. The same reversal or inversion informed the fascination with the white Indians (as well as their literary cousins in the pulp fiction of H. Rider Haggard and Edgar Rice Burroughs): natives were by definition dark-skinned, it was part of their essential nature, yet here were *natives with white skins.*

Skin color and race were very much on the American mind when the Kuna party docked. During the early 1920s, racial and ethnic fears surged in response to Black migration from the South and a renewed postwar wave of European immigration. Anti-immigrant literature often characterized newcomers in supposedly scientific racial terms, as "Alpines" and "Mediterraneans," deficient, dark-skinned peoples, who along with the Jews, threatened to overrun and even "mongrelize" Nordics and Native Americans — this last a term that referred not to Cherokee or Navajo but to old-line white Protestants. In April of 1924, less than three months before the Kuna visit, Congress responded to nativist sentiment by passing a bill drastically curtailing immigration.[5]

Marsh had his own immigration problems, because authorities would not let the Kuna disembark until he came up with a five-hundred-dollar bond for each of them as surety that they would not become public burdens. It was not until the end of the day after their arrival that he got them off the ship and installed in the Waldorf

Astoria. The next day the Kuna were taken on a ride around the city and a visit to the zoo. Marsh's son remembers the fun of shooting blowgun darts into the mahogany doors of their rooms until the management made them desist.[6]

That evening, Charlton's employers, Pathé News, sponsored a banquet in the hotel. A number of eminent scientists listened for two hours as Marsh told the story of the expedition, after which they were allowed to examine the three white children. Although several anthropologists were present, when the gaggle of savants offered its verdict, the medical men had prevailed. Marsh was gratified that they ruled out albinism but less pleased that they rejected his racial theories, diagnosing the white Indians as sufferers from an abnormality or tropical ailment they proposed calling "Marsh's Disease."[7]

The next day the Kuna were taken to the American Museum of Natural History for more investigation, this time by Clark Wissler and other anthropologists on the museum staff. The faces and bodies of the delegates were measured and their skin, hair, eyes, and teeth closely examined. A report delivered to the press afterward declared that the white Indians were absolutely typical albinos, though of scientific interest because so many were concentrated in one population. Editorials in the *Times* attacked the tropical disease theory and came down firmly on the side of albinism.[8]

Marsh did not yield. He invoked the verdict of the banquet scientists; he seized on minor errors in the museum examinations; most of all, he insisted albinos looked very different from his charges. He settled on the idea that the whites displayed some form of partial albinism, and that as such, they could still constitute the beginnings of a new race.[9] A few days later, he told a Rochester audience that the only point on which all agreed was that the whites were *not* ordinary albinos, which would have surprised Wissler and his colleagues.

The party, meanwhile, had moved to the Marsh family residence, Helen Cleveland Marsh's childhood home in Brockport, New York, outside Rochester. The Kuna, said to be "tired of being examined, photographed, prodded by scientific fingers and their gums examined as though they were so many horses," enjoyed family parties and pony rides in Brockport and put up with more photo sessions and interviews.[10]

Marsh then moved the group to a large summer house belonging to his wife's family just over the Canadian border on the Saint Lawrence. The Kuna men and boys sailed, swam, fished, and hunted with Johnson and Marsh's twelve-year-old son, Richard Junior, and on one occasion, Jim Berry hauled young Marsh out of the river when he hit his head on a rock. When Nele's teenaged son Alfred tired of the water, he would, according to Johnson, walk into the nearest town, exploiting his celebrity to chat up local girls.[11] The three young albinos were posed outside for misleading photographs decked out in animal skins, and Igwa-Nigdibippi drew on cloth a huge map of the San Blas coast.

Kuna delegates in bathing costume on the Saint Lawrence, 1924.

In mid-August more scientists came to see the Kuna, this time from the British Association for the Advancement of Science, which was meeting in Toronto. In the final session of the association's anthropology division, the white Indians were discussed and Marsh was invited to speak. He later claimed support for some of his views from a scientist named F. C. Shrubsall as well as the famous Julian Huxley. According to the *New York Times,* however, Shrubsall articulated the majority opinion that the white Indians, though very interesting, were albinos, a judgment later reiterated in the British journal *Man.*[12]

Among the institutions that had so far had a crack at the white Indians, the Smithsonian was conspicuously absent. Having furnished John Baer to the expedition, the Institution had been promised control of all anthropological materials collected. But Aleš Hrdlička's press statement in June branding the white Indians a fraud had so incensed Marsh that he snubbed Washington and left the crated materials with the American Museum instead.[13] Marsh said he finally yielded after a personal visit and a promise of a public apology. Hrdlička's less than abject retraction, apparently spoken at the Toronto meetings, acknowledged that "Mr. Marsh deserves the thanks of . . . anthropologists for having brought to their attention a subject of considerable scientific interest and importance."[14]

An end to the feud was in everyone's interest. Hrdlička and the Smithsonian undoubtedly wanted the materials promised to them, and Marsh could not bring his plans to fruition outside Washington. An agreement was reached that the materials would be sent to the Smithsonian; that the Kuna would come to Washington to be studied; and that a blue ribbon committee consisting of Hrdlička, Charles Stiles of the Public Health Service, and Charles Davenport, director of the Department of Genetics of the Carnegie Foundation, would supervise further study of the white Indians.[15]

The composition of the committee — who was kept off it as well as who was on it — was one result of the turmoil in and around anthropology in the 1910s and 1920s. This seemingly esoteric subject, concerned with primitive peoples and the ancient past, was in fact thoroughly caught up in the great social issues of the times. As the field changed from a gentleman's pursuit to an academic discipline, tensions over professionalization and competition between rival centers, especially Cambridge, New York, and Washington, further stirred things up. The Kuna visitors were unknowingly swept into these currents.

Charles Davenport, the second member of the committee, a biologist who thought he knew all about anthropology, was the leading American spokesman for eugenics, the movement dedicated to saving and improving the genetic composition of humanity.[16] Eugenics had originally attracted some liberal and radical followers, but in the United States it was a reactionary movement by the 1920s. Believers insisted that crime, poverty, and immorality were all caused by defective genes, with the implication that social legislation and other nongenetic remedies were doomed to failure. In addition to encouraging reproduction by the biologically fit in the middle and upper classes, eugenicists proposed sterilizing the unfit, and within a few years both their propaganda and the sterilization programs they encouraged directly inspired Nazi "race hygiene."[17]

To prove scientifically the genetic basis of prostitution, feeble-mindedness, and other conditions, Davenport sent out assistants — young women minimally trained but thoroughly coached in expected results — to collect family histories. With public and private funding, he built laboratories and a "Eugenics Record Office" in Cold Spring Harbor on Long Island.[18] His right-hand man, Harry Laughlin, vigorously promoted sterilization of undesirables and acted as scientific expert for the drafting of anti-immigrant legislation. Davenport also worked closely with Henry Fairfield Osborne, the aristocratic and bigoted head of the American Museum of Natural History, and with Madison Grant, author of the anti-immigrant bible, *The Decline of the Great Race*.[19]

On the other side, the foremost opponent of eugenics and scientific racism was Franz Boas of Columbia University, a German Jewish immigrant and outspoken liberal. In addition to attacking the assumption that nations, races, cultures, and languages were identical or homologous, Boas showed in a famous study that second-generation immigrants differed in head form from their parents, suggesting that even the supposedly invariant physical features used to distinguish one race from another responded to environmental change. Most of all, by developing the culture concept, Boas offered a plausible and sophisticated alternative to hereditarianism.[20]

One front in the struggle against racism was fought at the borders of the discipline itself. Davenport, Osborne, Grant, and their allies wanted to tie anthropology closely to biology, genetics, and psychology, making it essentially the study of racial difference. In 1918 they founded a new organization, the Galton Society, open only to socially and politically acceptable native-born Americans and intended to rival the existing anthropological societies dominated largely by Boas and his followers.[21]

Hrdlička, by no means native-born, fell between the two camps. A critic of eugenics and no friend of amateur race theorists, Hrdlička also resented Boas and entertained doubts about his commitment to physical anthropology within the wider discipline. For all his reservations about the soundness of Davenport's crew, Hrdlička needed to preserve good relations for the sake of future funding, and their view of anthropology as a discipline centered on human biology fit his own ideas better than did Boas's cultural emphasis.[22]

Boas had in fact stepped on a great many toes. In his efforts to professionalize the discipline, he had offended not only rich amateurs such as Grant, but the volunteers and self-trained professionals at the Bureau of American Ethnology and National Museum in Washington. Many of these men still adhered to nineteenth-century social evolutionism, which Boas attacked relentlessly. Apart from the culture of North American Indians, still the prime subject matter for both camps, rivalry between the Boasians and "the Washington crowd" focused in particular on Mexican and Central American studies. Not least, the Anglo-Saxon and partly patrician establishment resented the intrusion of Boas and his students, many of them Jews and immigrants. In several respects, then, the struggle to set the boundaries and center of anthropology as a field of study replicated wider conflicts in the country as a whole.[23]

After a contentious decade of bruising factional fights, things came to a head in 1919, at the end of World War I. Boas, pacifist, pro-German, and vocally critical of U.S. entry into the war, wrote a letter to the *Nation* condemning four unnamed anthropologists for spying in Central America under the cover of research. (The charge was true.) His vitriolic letter, which also called American democracy "a fiction," gave his enemies, including Hrdlička, the patriotic justification to move against him. At a special meeting of the Council of the American Anthropological Association, a large majority — in which Washingtonians and Central Americanists featured prominently — voted to censure Boas. In the aftermath, the secretary of the Smithsonian, Charles Walcott, privately tried to have Boas fired from Colombia and investigated by the Department of Justice.[24]

By the time the white Indians visited a few years later, the Boasians had regained control of the association and its journal, and the move toward professionalization and the dominance of cultural anthropology was well advanced. Neither the old guard nor the old antagonisms had disappeared, however, and the eugenicists and scientific racists were at the peak of their public influence. Thus, whether or not Hrdlička really believed in the white Indians, it behooved him to get them to Washington, away from Boasians, even marginal ones such as Wissler. And whatever Hrdlička's feelings about Davenport, it made sense to put him on the committee, along with another prominent biologist, C. W. Stiles, thus fixing the biological nature of the subject matter.

The committee's correspondence through the fall of 1924, in which it tried to pin Marsh down concerning control, responsibility, and plans for future work, did not endear the explorer further to Hrdlička.[25] It was arranged that when Marsh returned to Panama in January, he would take a scientist or scientists with him to study the white Indians in the field. Davenport proposed two candidates, with a clear preference for one of them, Reginald Harris, the director of the Biological Laboratory at Cold Spring Harbor. Harris, ideologically to Davenport's taste, had written an article for the *Eugenical News* that blamed the backwardness of several South American countries on race crossing and pointed out the superiority even of shiftless Hispanic whites to Indians and Blacks.[26] Davenport praised Harris in his letter to Hrdlička without mentioning that the young man was also his son-in-law. Once chosen, Harris and his wife, Jane Davenport Harris, went ahead of Marsh to Panama to work at scientific facilities in the Canal Zone.[27]

Marsh and the Kuna party, meanwhile, came to Washington in mid-October, moving into the Willard Hotel. Marsh delivered a talk on the radio, with chanting by Igwa-Nigdibippi, and the next day hosted a large dinner, to which forty scientists, including Hrdlička, were invited. In articles and press releases by an organization called Science Service, Igwa-Nigdibippi increasingly received star billing as the supposed crown prince of the Darién, fulfilling the stereotyped expectation that visiting natives should be royalty in their own country. A reporter for the *Post* obliged with remarks on the visitors' "deep innate sense of refinement," as well as their suits, pocket watches, "tastefully selected" ties, and nonchalant smoking, "the royal heir using an amber cigarette holder."[28]

On October 18 the white Indians visited the Smithsonian, where they were measured and examined yet again, this time by Hrdlička himself, who decided that they were closely related to the Maya of Guatemala and southern Mexico.[29] Within a few days the party moved from the hotel to a large rented house in Chevy Chase, where they stayed through the end of the year. Life there must have been hectic, with crowds of visitors, linguists, anthropologists, and hangers-on in attendance at different moments. The teenager Alfred continued to use his fame to meet girls, now at the local soda fountain.[30] Otherwise the Kuna mostly stayed at home or were taken out to assist with meetings, publicity, or studies of their language and culture.

The most active investigators were two linguists, John Peabody Harrington of

Alfred Kantule, James Berry, and Margarita Berry with
linguist J. P. Harrington at the Smithsonian, 1924.

the Bureau of American Ethnology and Paul Vogenitz from the Post Office Department.[31] Harrington was a strange character, depicted years later by his ex-wife as a
driven man obsessed with saving American Indian languages and fearful that his
colleagues, especially Jews, were stealing his material.[32] With his co-worker
Vogenitz, who shared his fascination with linguistic structures, as well as his anti-
Semitism and hostility to religion, Harrington exchanged bantering letters written
in a variety of languages and phonetic scripts ("Bai dhis xwndwrful sistm wiy kaen
rait inglic xidhaut dhw yux get w litl yuxzd tux it luks prutiwr dhaen qrdineri
inglic)."[33]

For the most part, Harrington's investigations were devoted to the Kuna lexicon:
names of animals, objects, places, kinsmen, and parts of the body. To collect animal
names, he and Vogenitz visited the zoo and National Museum with informants, and
for parts and emissions of the body, he stood with the men in front of a museum
exhibit of human figures. Harrington noted that Philip did not enjoy saying taboo
words, and Igwa-Nigdibippi walked away from the museum case whenever he heard
one, "but Alfred gives them to me with great pleasure."[34]

Vogenitz, who ended up spending more time working with the Indians than did

Harrington, also mastered more of the grammar, even learning to speak simple Kuna. As an amusement and exercise, he wrote Harrington a satiric letter in the Indian language on evolution and religion: "I don't know why our friend Lorenso [evidently a fellow Washingtonian] doesn't believe in *eboluci*. He said to me, I don't believe in *eboluci*. . . . The *kristianos* don't believe in *eboluci*. God is not our friend. God is not a friend of the Kuna either. . . . *Eboluci* is good. God is bad. Lorenso is bad too."[35] (The Kuna, who considered Great Father much more than a friend, and who, when they heard of it years later, did not like Darwinian evolution at all, would not have been amused.)

The only published result of all this work was a curious press release and a couple of newspaper articles, which claimed that many Kuna words came from early European and Sanscritic languages.[36] Of the different alleged influences on Kuna, Vogenitz pointed most insistently to Germanic languages such as English and Norse, for which the clincher was the resemblance between *Tule,* the Kuna name for themselves, and *Ultima Thule,* the New World location sought by Norse voyagers (even though the first is pronounced Doo-lay and the second Thool).

Harrington and Vogenitz, both Viking enthusiasts, had combined their knowledge of various languages with romanticism and a great deal of wishful thinking. They were following in a tradition, which had begun with Columbus, of finding traces of presumed pre-Colombian visitors to the New World, visitors whose identity—wandering apostle, Welsh prince, survivor of Atlantis, lost tribesman of Israel—depended on the education, preoccupations, and national identity of the beholder. Such romantic diffusionism (today incorporating space aliens), was already scorned by most professional anthropologists, but Harrington, who had little interest in serious theory but a penchant for offbeat notions, fell into an amateur's trap.[37]

Like all such fantasies, the Nordic strain in Kuna disappears under close scrutiny. Among numerous errors, Vogenitz said the Kuna for howl was *ulue,* which in fact means "be mad, fight," whether howling or silent, and that *parbatti,* actually "spotted," meant "colored." Even vaguely plausible pairs meant very little, given that just as a matter of statistical probability, any two languages, each with thousands of words, will have dozens or hundreds that sound vaguely alike, and of those, a few dozen with related meetings. Ironically, some of the borrowings were quite real— *musue* "headcloth, handkerchief," for instance, was probably once the French *mouchoir*—but they came from traders and pirates in recent centuries and not from Eric the Red.

Harrington and Vogenitz's Viking fantasy, which except for wasting a little government money, did no discernible harm, would hardly merit discussion except that it derived from a not-so-benign mind-set, the Nordic or Teuton myth. Since the late nineteenth century, American nativists, reacting against the waves of southern and eastern European immigration, had insisted that Anglo-Saxon America was essentially Germanic—an idea reaching its culmination in Madison Grant's *Passing of the Great Race*. Claims that Vikings had discovered America or founded Maya and Aztec civilization, in some respects harmless romantic diversions, could also function as coded assertions of Anglo-Saxon priority and superiority. It is not surprising that in interpreting the Kuna visitors, Harrington and Marsh both called on Teutonism.

Another example of ideologized science occurred in December, when Charles Davenport and one of his assistants, Miss Grace Allen, administered a battery of intelligence tests to the Kuna. The tasks assigned lay completely outside the experience of the delegates, most of whom had never been to school, and Allen's article, published the following year, describes the Indians as perplexed and bemused. She and Davenport, nonetheless, had no qualms about confidently computing Kuna mental abilities, all of them abysmal, ranging from a low of five mental years for Margarita to a high of 9.5 for Cheepu, Olo, Philip, and Igwa-Nigdibippi.[38] These ludicrous results—which Marsh subsequently distorted—reached an extreme of foolishness with Igwa-Nigdibippi, who was in later life a famous teacher of tradition, able to memorize thousands of lines of poetry.

Two more studies were carried out. A museum staffer named Herbert Kreiger brought out a monograph on Kuna and Chocó material culture based on the artifacts collected by the expedition, and an ethnomusicologist, Miss Frances Densmore, wrote a short work on Kuna music.[39] During the two weeks that Densmore worked with the Kuna in early December, Igwa-Nigdibippi dictated a text in Kuna to Vogenitz devoted mostly to his experiences with her:

Now we are living in Washington. Now in Washington my friend Pablo [Vogenitz] comes to me every day. He is learning Kuna. Now an American woman is collecting Kuna ways. She is collecting Kuna songs. As for her, she comes to get me in the day. She takes us to her place. . . . She is collecting the way of our Kuna seers. . . . Now our drinking chicha, I talk about all of that. . . . Our photographs are being taken. "Four hundred years from now, your name will still remain here in Washington . . ." the American says that to me. So every day I go to her place.[40]

Harrington privately savaged Densmore's study. Commenting on the manuscript of the monograph she wrote soon afterward, he dismissed her song texts, translated by Alfred, as "the dressed-up . . . bilingualism of a 19 year old boy who has a reputation among his fellows for loose statements."[41] (He might have added that Densmore misunderstood much of what was told her: the chicha in Igwa-Nigdibippi's text, for instance, somehow became a wedding in her monograph.)

The tensions and difficulties at the house on Pennsylvania Avenue seem to have gone well beyond sniping between colleagues. Though much of what happened that autumn was not recorded, suggestive bits and pieces indicate serious trouble.[42] Densmore's pocket diary for December 15 reads, "warned against Mr. Marsh," and for the next day, "Mr. Marsh arrested." It turned out that the explorer was briefly detained after his check to the Willard Hotel bounced, but he promptly cleared the matter up.[43] More consequentially, the tensions in anthropology, particularly the animosity between the Washington anthropologists and Franz Boas and his students, surfaced in a ferociously anti-Semitic letter from Vogenitz to Harrington.[44]

There is nothing on earth that is too low for that bunch of New York Jews to stoop to; and . . . we have incurred their enmity through our activities with Indian languages and our friendship with Gates and Morley [prominent Central Americanists and anti-Boasians]. . . . You saw what they tried to do to Marsh. . . . That skunk Boas, his right-bower Goldenweiser and the rest of his scurvy crew have the idea that Central America is their territory, and resent what they are pleased to call the "intrusion" of Gates, Morley, Marsh, ourselves and others.

The letter accused a man who had spent time at the house in Chevy Chase of spying for the Boasians, and noted that "Marsh told me the last thing before he left that he would support us unqualifiedly, in spite of all that the Kikes might try to do to us." Given Harrington and Vogenitz's paranoia on the subject, it is hard to know just what happened, but Marsh and his white Indians had clearly been recruited to the cause of Anglo-Saxon anthropology.

After recovering from another bout of malaria, Marsh seems to have devoted himself to lobbying on behalf of the Kuna. Although Kuna folklore has it that the party was received by the U.S. president, a State Department cable indicates that Marsh wrote letters at the end of December to the White House and the department but was denied an interview at both places.[45] According to Marsh, a number of scientific societies passed pro-Kuna resolutions, and an informal support group was formed, with prominent officials and scientists—in fact, both occurred the *following* year, 1926, and the group seems to have consisted only of Harrington, Hrdlička, and Davenport.[46] However much support Marsh elicited, which seems to have been less than claimed, he had done what he could, and in early January, he set out for Panama, accompanied by Harold Johnson and all the much-studied delegates, except for Cheepu, who stayed behind to be educated in Marsh's family. In a letter written a few weeks later, Hrdlička expressed satisfaction to Davenport at having rid themselves of the difficult explorer.[47]

Part Seven
THE KUNA REBELLION, 1925 AND AFTER

25. The Republic of Tule

Marsh and his party landed in Colón on January 10. Although he later wrote that he slipped quietly into the country and on to San Blas, he and the delegates actually met the press more than once.[1] Reginald Harris and his wife Jane had already been in Panama for several weeks, doing a little research, and had heard a great deal of skepticism about Marsh's claims, especially about the originality of his discovery and the existence of all-white Indian villages.[2]

Marsh spent a week in the city, continuing his campaign to promote intervention in San Blas with both the U.S. military and the legation. The chargé d'affaires, Mr. Howell, cabled Washington on the twelfth that Marsh had told him "there may be uprisings by the San Blas Indians when they learn that he has brought them no assurances of relief from Washington." Howell requested permission from State to speak with Panamanian officials but was told that Marsh was not considered reliable enough to pass on his warnings.[3]

During Marsh's absence in the United States, his friend, Belisario Porras, had been succeeded as president of the Republic by a new man, Ramón Chiari. According to Marsh, Porras sent a warning that he would not be allowed to return to San Blas, and a few days later Chiari called him to the Presidencia.[4] If Marsh did receive such a summons, he ignored it, setting out without official permission on January 19 on a Colon Import and Export Company vessel, the *Impco*.

The party spent several hours ashore at Nargana, where they visited with Jim, Alice, and Margarita, who had preceded them into San Blas.[5] The next day, January 21, the *Impco* reached Ailigandi, where Marsh's party was met by Igwa-Nigdibippi, Olo, and Alfred. Marsh, Johnson, and the Harrises were put up in a large house belonging to Olo's family, and Jane Harris, who was supposed to return to Colón, persuaded her husband and Marsh to let her stay until the boat came back ten days

Nele Wardada, Igwa-Nigdibippi, and other Kuna leaders on return of delegates from the United States, 1925.

later. Reginald Harris jumped into studying albinos, Marsh into nightly political meetings with Nele, Colman, the men of Ailigandi, and a stream of visitors from other communities.[6]

Marsh's arrival on the island exacerbated an already tense situation. It is unlikely that the government seriously feared a mass insurrection, given the fractious divisions among the Kuna, their lack of arms, and the Intendencia's past successes in containing local outbreaks. But a nasty incident could readily occur again. Intendentes had learned to blame their trouble with the Indians on outside agitators, and just as happened three years before with Olivo Olivares, word undoubtedly reached Mojica that Marsh was spreading sedition.

Mojica had passed Ailigandi traveling east to Puerto Obaldía on a vessel called the *El Norte,* which belonged to the plantations just getting underway in eastern San Blas, and two days after Marsh's arrival, the boat anchored below Ailigandi on its return trip, with Mojica and Inabaginya on board, the latter on his way to express opposition to Colman and Marsh as well as to a new wave of rubber-tappers and plantation workers. Marsh and his companions stayed out of sight, and an envoy was sent out to the boat. According to Marsh, the police began beating the envoy when he would not reveal the Americans' whereabouts, while another account has it that the defiant messenger ended up tussling with Claudio Iglesias's successor, Estanislao López, who later claimed he won. All versions agree that in the face of an infuriated crowd on shore, Mojica released the man and the boat steamed off westward.[7]

Jane Davenport Harris on Ailigandi, 1925.

The incident had certainly put the fat in the fire, but for the moment the four North Americans were able to settle into village life. The next day the community held a chicha, which Marsh claimed to be the first outsider to witness. Worried about a police attack during the revels and offended, like many others before him, by the drunkenness and apparent disorder, he did approve of the lack of fights and the abstinence of the better class of Indian.[8]

The house provided to the Americans, if sparsely furnished, was large and airy: the Harrises slept upstairs in a loft, Marsh and Johnson downstairs. Their interpreter had the village build them an outhouse over the water, and they took their meals on a boat owned by the Import Company anchored just off the island. Throughout their stay the Harrises drank only coconut water, except when compelled by politeness to accept "slimy" Kuna drinks. In late afternoon, they often bathed at the river, sometimes accompanied by Igwa-Nigdibippi, and some evenings after the gathering they played bridge.

Jane Harris, who was an artist, made sketches and oil paintings, and she got enough clay locally to sculpt a number of heads, including Nele Wardada's. Wearing Kuna dress, minus nosering and leg-bindings and keeping her shoes and stockings on, she went around the island freely with the women and children. Marsh, highly impressed, called her "a splendid addition to the party" and gave her much of the credit for their warm acceptance on Ailigandi.[9]

Reginald Harris's studies of the white Indians promptly resolved most disputed questions. Concerning the mountain villages to which white Indians were supposedly banished at adulthood, Harris questioned Nele and others, all of whom emphatically denied their existence.[10] Nonetheless, the three American men held to their plan to walk in to the Bayano to see for themselves, and Jane Harris insisted on going too. In the meanwhile, Reginald Harris pursued other lines of inquiry. In addition to measuring and examining albinos, he tried to work out their total numbers and proportion in the Kuna population (he estimated 0.7 percent, the highest known anywhere), and especially to collect family histories to determine how the albinism was inherited and genetically controlled. He recorded twelve whites on Ailigandi and ten more on a visit to Ustupu.[11]

Harris's results seemed to confirm the hypothesis that Kuna albinism was a recessive trait, meaning that for each pair of genes controlling it, only individuals with both genes would be white. The further supposition that it was a simple recessive, that is, that a single pair of genes determined its appearance (which is in fact the case), Harris assumed but could not confirm. By implication, although fewer than one Kuna in a hundred was white, many others in the population carried the gene for albinism.

Except for pushing the scientific importance of the white Indians, in which he too now had a stake, Harris gave little comfort to Marsh's claims. Like Marsh, he did call them partial albinos, though he merely meant that, unlike albinos in some populations, the white Indians showed a trace of color in their hair and eyes. Similarly, he entirely ruled out the supposition that Kuna whiteness could have resulted from some past intermarriage with non-Indians. Though he waffled a bit on the race question, allowing that the white Indians "hold potentialities for race production," it was clear they were part of the Kuna population.[12]

Marsh's capacity for wishful thinking, combined perhaps with delicacy on Harris's part, seems to have obscured the bad news. As Marsh understood it, Harris's work, except perhaps in a few trifling details, was "a complete vindication and corroboration of my own theories."[13] And if the Kuna denied the existence of all-white villages, well, they had previously denied the existence of white Indians. In a cable he arranged to send from Colón, he wrote, "Harris says positively not albinos," and he attributed his own ideas to the biologist: the white Indians resulted from an unusually high mutation rate, or more likely, "Darien Indians formerly extensively mixed with unknown prehistoric white race."[14]

Marsh should have known better. Especially after living with three white Indians for six months, how could he miss what subsequent studies have amply demonstrated?: Kuna albinism, rather than a sign of biological superiority, is a debilitating condition that shortens and blights the lives of its sufferers.[15] Reporters had remarked on the aversion to sunlight of the three white Indian children, and in Brockport Marsh had tried to have something done for Cheepu's bad eyes.[16] Although Marsh could not have known that many male albinos die prematurely of metastasized skin cancers, he must have seen how readily Cheepu and Olo's skin reddened in the sun. For his purposes, however, Marsh needed paleolithic survivors or forerunners of a new race, not stigmatized sufferers from a genetic condition.

While Reginald Harris studied the albinos and Jane Harris painted and sculpted, Marsh politicked. Nele, Colman's designated successor, came and went several times. Delegations came to Colman and Nele from Carti, from other coastal communities, and even from the Bayano and Chucunaque. Marsh readily grasped the importance of the meetings in building consensus, but he tired of the endless talk. "It yet remains to be seen if these indians really have the courage to fight for their rights."[17]

Rumors circulated that Mojica was training loyal Kuna for a strike against Ailigandi. (In the end the unwilling militiamen, who were from Nargana, refused to go.)[18] The rebels were eager to strike first, but Marsh counseled patience. He saw clearly that the scattered police detachments could be overcome, but that if Panama counterattacked in force, the Kuna would have to abandon the islands for the forest and a long drawn-out struggle. Pinning his hopes on American intervention, which was by no means assured, Marsh advised his friends to present themselves in a good light by observing diplomatic and military conventions and by sparing any whites in parties they might attack.

On January 29, two U.S. Army planes flew over Ailigandi, which Marsh interpreted to mean that word of unrest in San Blas had reached the city.[19] When the *Impco* returned on February 2, Marsh wrote the commanding general in the Canal Zone to feed his presumed concern.[20] The long missive stated that a great many abuses (Marsh put special emphasis on arbitrary jailing and rape) had put the Indians "in a very bitter and belligerent frame of mind," though they would take no aggressive action for now unless attacked. While claiming to have discouraged rebellion, Marsh added that he had told them "that no race and no people in the world had to submit meekly to such treatment." He formulated a list of eight demands, foremost among them guarantees for Kuna lands, local self-government, and protection from abuse.

The letter took close to a week to reach the general, who wrote a cautious reply on February 10 expressing interest in Marsh's plans for exploration and reminding him to communicate with the U.S. legation, not the military. Marsh's warning, forwarded to the legation, would not have been seen by the American minister, John Glover South, until after he returned to Panama from abroad on the thirteenth.[21] South sent copies of both letters to Washington on the eighteenth, adding that, as the State Department had instructed the month before, he would take no action without further orders.[22] By the time the packet of letters reached Washington, the Kuna had already revolted.

On Ailigandi, news that Mojica might return in force persuaded Marsh to put off plans for a trip to the Bayano. A clash of some sort began to seem inevitable: "The Indians were aroused to a frenzy, and there was no use attempting to pacify them — the best I could do was to induce them to make their actions legal and formal."[23] A flag was designed, presumably by Marsh, featuring a large swastika.[24] A traditional motif in Kuna basketry, the swastika was associated in some North American minds with Aryans and Aryanism, but not yet with Nazis. Marsh also wrote up a lengthy "Declaration of Independence and Human Rights of the Tule People of the San Blas and Darien," which was approved in the Ailigandi gathering house on February 12.

This remarkable document, twenty-five handwritten pages in length, consists of a summary of Kuna history and society, a catalogue of abuses said to annul Panamanian claims to sovereignty over the Indians, a formal severing of ties, and the proclamation of a Republic of Tule. Supposedly taken down by Marsh from dictation and translated into English, the document assumes the voice of the Kuna; in fact, it was Marsh who spoke throughout.[25]

He began by identifying the Kuna as "the direct descendants of the ancient Mayan people," echoing Aleš Hrdlička, who had noticed a resemblance between the Kuna delegates and modern Maya populations. Marsh had undoubtedly read that Classic Mayan cities had fallen into ruins long before the Spanish conquest, and he accepted the erroneous idea that the people who built the cities had disappeared. Marsh was in this way characterizing the Kuna as "the last remnant of a once great and highly developed people." He pointed to supposedly hieroglyphic picture writing, to pyramids he was sure he had seen in the forest, and to the testing of the Kuna delegates, which, he claimed, revealed great intelligence. If now simple villagers, the Kuna lived a life notable for democracy, peace, and especially for "personal chastity and conjugal fidelity . . . practiced . . . to a higher degree perhaps than among any other living people."[26]

In some of the words Marsh put in their mouths, the Kuna regretted their descent from greatness, and in others took pride in their present simplicity. "Only in material and scientific development have we fallen behind. . . . The vainglory of complicated, artificial, material civilization . . . passed from our minds. . . . Perhaps the pendulum of our fate swung back too far." In this ambivalent language, Marsh was trying to reconcile Kuna tribal life with his own version of social Darwinism, which required that the Indians, if he was to defend them, be elevated and advanced as well as pure in heart.

Marsh also had difficulty with Kuna religion: his apologetic allusion to "universal mystical conceptions . . . representing the same groping of the developing finite mind to pierce the infinite" was not one the Kuna themselves would ever offer. The Kuna deity, Marsh wrote, was called A-oba, a mystery god the Kuna themselves have never heard of—Marsh had simply misunderstand his informants, who were comparing Great Father to Jehovah.[27] Not surprisingly, he described A-oba as white, implicitly equating him with the figure Quetzlcoatl in ancient Mexican religion.[28] Quetzlcoatl, often described as a light-skinned, bearded wanderer, was a favorite of

Viking theorists. Marsh also wrote that the Kuna had worshiped the first Spaniards because they associated their light skins with A-oba—another idea borrowed from Mexico, and as Ganath Obyesekere forcefully argues, one of the most enduring myths of European colonialism.[29] The Kuna, for their part, would have been shocked to hear that they had venerated wagas, even briefly.

When Marsh's account reached the twentieth century and the current situation, Kuna input was apparent in details such as compulsory dancing and black turtlers, though Marsh got many of the details wrong. Kuna fears and preoccupations were apparent, as well, though only those that coincided with Marsh's own. Concerning sex, for instance, Kuna men worried about consensual as well as forced interethnic relations, but Marsh was obsessed with the violation of women in jail. Similarly, in the matter of race, the Kuna certainly disliked Blacks, with whom they had struggled for centuries in both the Darién and San Blas, but they recognized that powerholders were typically white, and they feared encroachment by any outsiders, regardless of skin color.[30] Marsh, on the other hand, fulminated obsessively against "a race, who but a few years back were degenerate and degraded savages in Africa." He insisted that the police were Black, though even his own photographs taken on Nargana show, not Afro-Panamanians but mestizos, men of mixed Indian-White ancestry. In his fixation, he could not admit that it was White leaders, especially his friend Belisario Porras, who had ordered the subjugation of his now-beloved Indians.[31]

The total picture presented by Marsh, though assembled from scattered bits and pieces, was coherent and meaningful: a noble race that had seen better days, one if not exactly white then at least associated with whiteness, was being overrun by degraded dark-skinned interlopers. The resemblance to the self-image of nativist WASP North Americans, especially idealogues such as Charles Davenport and Madison Grant, was no accident. These descendants of the founding fathers saw their national role diminished by competition from recent immigrants, and they feared worse to come, with genetic dilution, even "mongrelization" by dark-skinned, sexually loose Slavs, Italians, Jews, or even newly mobile Blacks.[32] Marsh, by portraying the Kuna predicament in a way that he himself found affecting and that would, he hoped, appeal to North American authorities, ended up with a symbolic self-portrait, a representation of the hopes and fears of old-line Anglo-Saxon America projected onto the Darién Isthmus.

At the end of the twenty-five pages, the Declaration concluded by announcing that "the Republic of Panama . . . has forfeited any further just claim to sovereignty over our race," setting the territory of the Tule nation, pledging to accept schools and international trade, promising to allow established plantations to continue but barring any others (a ploy on Marsh's part to avoid alienating the fruit companies), and petitioning for a U.S. protectorate. By the time the Declaration was completed, it had become clear that if Marsh wished to play a role in events, he must give up crossing the mountains into the Bayano. Nonetheless, he encouraged Johnson and the Harrises to stick to the plan, if nothing else to get them away from danger. Having decided that he himself could be most useful in Carti, "in the hopes of aiding in intercession for the Indians by American forces from the Canal Zone,"[33] Marsh set out in a sailing canoe in the late morning of February 14.

Marsh had a wild trip. The Kuna were quite accustomed to sailing small canoes long distances over open water, one man steering with an oversized paddle and bailing as needed, one or two others hiking out to windward with lines from the masthead; in the rough seas of the dry season, however, crew and passengers seldom stayed dry. After four hours bounding from wave to wave, Marsh and his companions came abreast of Tupile, the first pacified village. Surprised by a canoeload of police, with whom they exchanged shots, they escaped only because the man tending the mainsheet of the police canoe accidentally let it slip.

At about one in the morning during a squall, they ran up on a reef, fortunately at its leeward end, and were just able to back off, half swamped. Afterward, in characteristically Kuna fashion, the crew dealt with the mishap by laughing hilariously, a display of spirit that greatly impressed Marsh. An hour later, as the sky cleared and visibility improved, they stopped on an uninhabited island for a fire and coffee; continuing on, they reached Carti at dawn.[34]

Carti, rather than a single community, comprised several island villages at the mouth of the Carti River, two affiliated with Colman, two with Inabaginya. Marsh was taken to Carti Suitupu, seat of Colman's chief lieutenant, Chief Olonibiginya. The chief's "dignified, commanding appearance," and the beauty and self-possession of his wife and daughters greatly impressed Marsh: "Certainly some wonderful blood and breeding runs in these chiefs' families."[35] Marsh was put up in the gathering hall, along with a great many Kuna who had flocked from other villages into the western rebel center.

Marsh learned that four U.S. submarines had visited Carti, their officers asking for Marsh, which he took as another indication of American military concern. As in Ailigandi, the Kuna held at least one gathering a day, and with the help of an interpreter, Marsh addressed a packed house the morning after his arrival. "So I told them a long story about themselves—It was much the same as that of the 'Declaration of Independence'—starting with the great Mayan race and recounting all their experiences down to the present."[36] At the end of the speech, a message arrived from Colman: the *El Norte* had turned up soon after Marsh left Ailigandi, and Mojica had vowed to attack the principal rebel islands if they did not hand over the Americans. Colman's people said they would fight. The news put the Carti gathering into an uproar and set off preparations for war.

Marsh had by now been won over to belief in the Kuna as well as their cause. "Never have I been so obsessed with the idea there was a job to do—& that only I

could or would do it."[37] His months with Kuna friends had overcome earlier prejudices about the Indians and doubts about their strength of will. In his devotion to
the Kuna cause, he left behind his plans for rubber and other commercial ventures,
to the extent that he began to see the banana plantations as well as the Black
rubber-tappers as enemies. Unfortunately, the ideological association of Indians
with nature, childhood, and antiquity were less easily discarded, still less Marsh's
deeply ingrained racism:

I simply can't sit still and see these Panaman negroids exterminate these wonderful people.
. . . What a wonderful little group out of a dim and unknown past — so childlike and
naive — I always feel like being amongst our own ancestors of long ago. . . . I can't see
them go under before the negro — what an abhorrent crime.[38]

Marsh had the Carti Kuna bring in their firearms, many old shotguns and a few
rifles, to be cleaned and readied. Learning that they had little ammunition, he visited
the floating store of the Colon Import Company just off the island, where he found
ample powder, shot, shells, and even a few shotguns, but no caps or primers, which
were stored in a safe. Fortunately, he spied the combination written in pencil on the
wall, allowing him to liberate everything they needed. (He paid cash.)[39]

On Thursday the nineteenth the *Impco* turned up briefly with the Harrises and
Johnson. They told Marsh they had started into the forest toward the mountains the
day after he left, only to have their guides turn back because they were worried
about an imminent attack on the island. On their return, the women and children
of Ailigandi and Ustupu were sent to the mainland, but Mojica, though he embargoed the two ports, did not attack. When the *Impco* arrived, the Americans
embarked, Johnson "forgetting" to bring his rifle and ammunition with him. At
Tupile, they encountered Mojica, who quizzed them about Marsh and showed off
two machine guns. Harris and Johnson, however, noticed the clumsy way the police
fired the guns and a severe lack of ammunition. On Nargana they were told that
Jim Berry and Philip Thompson had been jailed in Porvenir for praising the United
States.[40]

The *Impco* left Carti that afternoon with Johnson and the Harrises and reached
Colón next day. Harris, who carried copies of the Declaration of Independence,
delivered them to the manager at the Washington Hotel, with instructions to pass
them on to the press and American authorities, but the manager, fearing Panamanian ire, sent all of them to zone authorities, who passed them on to the legation.
Although the Panamanian government refused to accept officially the copy addressed to President Chiari, it did pass on another copy to the *Star and Herald,* which
published the document in its entirety on February 27, after news of an Indian
uprising had already appeared.[41]

On the twenty-first, two days after the departure of Johnson and the Harrises, a large flotilla of canoes from Carti was to attack Porvenir after midnight, and Marsh, his face painted red like the others, was going with them. The "only chance," he wrote in his diary, was "a quick swift blow—cleaning up the coast, and then American intervention—Will it come!" At the last moment, however, spies reported numerous men and several machine guns at the Intendencia, so the Carti forces decided to hold off. Then on Sunday they received word that their counterparts in the east had liberated Tigre and Playón Chico.[42] The Kuna, in their own phrase, had "brought out war," and as Marsh well recognized, the question was how, once it was out, anyone could contain it again.[43]

26.
Bringing
Out War

The Kuna of Colman's alliance, now fully committed, had set their revolt for Sunday, February 22, 1925, the beginning of Carnival.[1] An attack of this sort, occurring simultaneously in several places, poses problems of coordination and communication beyond those of local uprisings, especially for rebels without telephones, radios, or even much experience with calendar dates.[2] That Sunday offered a prominent landmark, one with special significance for the Kuna, since Carnival, with its drinking and dancing imposed by the police, called to mind the exorcisms by which communities periodically rid themselves of spirits by getting them drunk. The rebel Kuna were about to exorcize the human world.[3]

In eastern San Blas, Colman and Nele's forces planned to liberate the two nearest captive islands, Tupile, home of the modernist chief Inadoiginya, and Ukkup Senni, or Playón Chico, scene of perhaps the greatest turmoil on the whole coast. They began by sending out scouts and spies. About a week before the planned attack, Colman sent home a refugee from Playón Chico, with a canoeload of household goods and a plausible cover story that poverty had driven him back to where his coconuts were.[4] He was followed a few days later by two notorious dissidents, Igwa-Dinuydiginya and Susu. All three survived initial police skepticism and intensive grilling, leaving them free to scout the ground and open the way for the coming attack.[5]

As in Carti, the Kuna had to arm themselves as best they could. The Ailigandi people had some shotguns, as well as a few small-caliber rifles and one fine hunting gun, which had been left behind by Harold Johnson. The rifles went to men with reputations as hunters, Johnson's gun to a crack shot named Joe Brown. Ustupu had almost no guns, because Mojica had recently staged a raid one morning when most men were off-island at work and confiscated every firearm his agents could find. Many men had to make do with wooden staves or machetes. It was not much to go up against rifles, pistols, and machine guns, especially for a people who had not fought a real war in well over a century.[6]

On the morning before the attack, the contingent from Ustupu arrived at Ailigandi, jamming a little cove on the island with dozens of beached canoes. To identify the rebels and keep them from shooting each other, they all wore white hats woven from palm fronds, with strips from women's headcloths as hatbands. Their faces were painted bright red for war, a color hated by evil spirits, and to build up their vital forces, the warriors had all been treated with jaguar teeth, hawks' hearts, and other powerful medicines.[7]

The combined war party came together in the Ailigandi gathering hall.[8] There was no possibility that Colman, old and sick, would go, and even Nele was expected to stay back on Ailigandi with other elders. In their place they named several younger men as field commanders, first among them an imposing young leader of Ustupu named Olodebiliginya: "The way was given to Olodebiliginya. . . . 'You yourself will stand in the bow. . . . If you are the first to die, you will die, it doesn't matter.'"[9]

Colman and Nele exhorted their followers, Colman making the gesture of offering to join them: "Then grandfather stood up. To his friend Yobliga he said, 'You and I will go. You and I will lead. Get us some guns.' Then all the people made noise, 'That's it!!!'"[10] Nele grasped his crotch, saying, "If I am a Kuna man, I will fight!"[11] "Nele stood up, Nele. In Ailigandi. He stood up . . . dancing there, stepping, and stepping. He hit Yobliga, bam, bam, bam. 'I'll do you, then you'll fight,' he said. . . . Then the troops did it too, Oh!" Emerging outside in the late afternoon, the men continued working themselves up, yanking on each other's arms. "There were many men on the beach dancing around in eagerness, with their faces just the same, all red, every last one."[12]

Then the flotilla embarked, with a few shots fired into the air, each canoe paddled by a group of friends. After they had pulled away, Colman, Nele, and the elders went back to the gathering house, and in the evening they assembled all the women and children.

And truly Colman was singing to them, as evening came, Nele Kantule and he. . . . "Girls, don't think of things away from here. Send your thoughts only to Father, send your thoughts to Great Mother. Don't let your heart be fixed on things away from here. . . . Your boys have gone, your men have gone. . . . If Father says, 'This is the last time you will see your men's faces,' your men will all die over there on you."[13]

The women were eventually sent home to sleep on the ground with their worries and their children, all lights extinguished. Half-grown boys too young to go with the warriors were sent out to sound the alarm if boats approached.

Out on the sea, the canoes spread apart. Coming abreast of Tupile in the middle of the night, half stopped there while the others swept on. Tupile was lit up by kerosene torches recently provided by the government, and carnival festivities had begun a day early. When the raiders waded ashore at the very end of the island, their local contact, who had gotten cold feet about abetting a bloodbath, told them the police were waiting with arms ready. The raiders, huddled in the dark on the point, rapidly called off the attack. As they later discovered, several policemen from Playón Chico *were* visiting on Tupile, but they were not on guard and could most likely have been overrun.[14]

The rest of the flotilla continued on in the dark toward Playón Chico, where the lead boats rendezvoused with their agent Susu. Beforehand, the dissidents on the island had been quietly organizing. One man later remembered getting the news, along with a warning not to let it slip to his brother-in-law, because he *wakkad,* "belonged to the wagas." Late in the night the Playón Chico rebels gathered with what weapons they could muster, all of them wearing white hats. As the first of their allies came ashore, the local men put the plan into operation without waiting.[15] An Ustupu man remembered: "We didn't go in on our feet but splashing, one dropping in, splash, another splash, more splashes, all together. All six of us . . . the guns, they carried them ashore overhead, in their arms. A gun was firing, bang-bang-bang. Off we went, creeping and creeping."[16]

The only policemen then on Playón Chico were Gregorio Gordón, brother of Miguel Gordón the detachment head on Tupile, and two indigenous agents, Benito Guillén and Pedro Estocel. The local rebels rousted Gordón and Guillén out of bed, telling them that men from Ailigandi and Ustupu were invading. Gordón started off down the street, pistol in hand, when one of his feigned supporters grabbed him from behind; Gordón got off several shots, wounding one attacker, but they pinned him down, and the invaders who just then came on the scene continued beating and shooting him with his own gun even after he died.

The native policeman, Benito Guillén, stood rooted in one place in fear and amazement, his gun in hand. Guillén, who had served for ten years in his home village, had been accused by his superiors of going easy on dissidents, and now, rather than resisting, he pleaded for his life. The local rebels had yet to do him serious harm when the Ustupu and Ailigandi men stormed onto the island, but despite orders from the field command to kill only wagas, the invaders mercilessly beat Guillén to death with their staves.

Amid the gunshots and tumult, the most prominent collaborators fled through the darkness, one hiding in a corncrib, another in water up to his neck in a well.[17] All of them survived with nothing worse then a severe tongue-lashing, as did the crew of a trading boat tied to a dock, the wife of a Spanish shopowner, and a West Indian couple working on the island. Less fortunate were the four small children that Panamanian policemen had fathered with local women, all of whom were killed.[18]

Meanwhile, the second indigenous policeman, Pedro Estocel, roused by the noise, came onto the killing ground a few minutes late and had a second or two to take in the scene before someone raised a cry against him. Despite taking a hard blow on the shoulder, he managed to run away among the houses, pulling his shirt off to make himself less visible in the partial darkness. He reached the beach, ran a canoe into the water, and paddled hard for the mainland, untouched by shots fired after him. Once on shore, Estocel continued on into the forest, climbing the slope of a nearby hill. That night he came back down to the coast and slept on the beach, covered with banana leaves, which cannot have given much protection from sand fleas or cold to a man wearing only his trousers. The next morning, he surrendered in a nearby shore hamlet, and by evening he was back in Playón Chico, where he too was pardoned.[19]

One reason the rebels had secured Playón Chico so easily was that several men usually stationed there had gone off to Tupile. It remained to be seen whether the police could be picked off as they returned, a tactic the Kuna compared to hunting animals attracted to a fruiting tree.[20] A few hours after sunrise, the rebels spotted a canoe sailing from the direction of Tupile, so those with guns ran to prepare an ambush.[21]

The canoe, sailed by three pro-government men, was bringing two Panamanian policemen, one of them married to a local woman, and the son of a Spanish storeowner. As it crossed the shallows, a volley killed one agent outright and left a paddler and the Spanish youth mortally wounded. The second policeman staggered to shore. "The waga wasn't soft. He'd fall and then get back up. It was hard to finish him off."[22] Finding his Indian brother-in-law among the gathering crowd, he clutched his knees, begging for mercy, but someone else ran up and shot him dead. Despite orders from Olodebiliginya, some of the raiders were so worked up that they began chopping the police bodies into pieces, sparing only the Kuna paddlers and the body of the Spanish youth. Other rebels, frightened and disgusted, refused to participate. "'Well,' I said to them, 'you're drunk [with blood lust]. How do you think I could do that?'"[23]

That evening just at sunset, patrols spied another canoe from the direction of Tupile coming in on the mainland side of the island. "They came on with a conchshell blowing. . . . 'Call to them in Spanish, . . .' Olodebiliginya said. . . . 'If they're wagas, they'll call in Spanish. But if they're Kuna, they'll call in Kuna.'" Joe Brown the marksman was put upstairs in the schoolhouse, and other men hid themselves among the canoes pulled up on the beach. They called out in the gathering night, receiving an answer in Spanish, and the ambushers fired a volley, only to find that their victims were Kuna. "'*An Tuleee!* We're Kuuuna!!' they said."[24] It was a boatload of six young men pressed into service to find out why no one had reported back from Playón Chico. Although several were wounded, all but one survived.[25]

As the rebels now knew, the detachment head on Tupile, Miguel Gordón, had sent both boats to Playón Chico, and he had to be wondering what had happened. Gordón, a tough, competent, and sometimes brutal policeman, the hardened survivor of the shoot-out at Río Azúcar four years before, was feared and hated on Playón Chico. "'A fierce waga lives there,' the friends said. 'A ferocious person.'"[26] Counting Gordón, only three Panamanian agents remained on Tupile. With luck, even the fiercest animal would be drawn to the fruit tree.

Early the next morning they saw a boat coming from the direction of Tupile.[27] As it approached the leeward shore near the school building, they saw Gordón, as well as a Panamanian agent named Castillo, an indigenous policeman, Antonio Orán, and four Kuna paddlers. With Joe Brown again at a window upstairs and other gunmen lying by the building outside or mingling with a large crowd, they staged an elaborate charade of Carnival, with music, dancing, and men weaving through the streets, bottle in hand. As the boat came in, they even let out a cheer, "Viva Miguel Gordón!"

Whether Gordón was taken in (accounts disagree), he stood up while the boat was still some distance from shore, and Joe Brown, seeing his opportunity, shot him through the neck. In the ensuing fusillade, Gordón got off several pistol shots, as did Castillo. But the boat was rocking back and forth, and their shots went high. The native policeman, Antonio Orán, took two slugs in his right arm and one in his left hand;[28] he was saved from death by Olodebiliginya himself, and the paddlers all escaped serious injury. The last man, Castillo, threw himself in the water, still clutching his gun, and swam away hard, only to be overtaken by a pursuer in a canoe and shot.[29]

When the shooting stopped, Miguel Gordón was just barely alive. "The people really whaled away at him—he was the one they were most after, the one they most wanted."[30] Even Gordón's death was not going to cheat them of their revenge, especially not a few men from a shore hamlet he had recently subdued.

The waga had been mistreating them. Some of them had been punished by him. . . . So when those men learned that the waga had been shot, they rushed over there. Then they did all that, with machetes, chop-chop-chop, all the same, just furious. "You made us suffer terribly. You dragged me off. . . . You made me suffer. Take that! Take that! Take that! Well, they completely finished him off. There was nothing left of him.[31]

The anger gripping the butchers must have been tremendous to have so completely overcome Kuna aversion to shedding blood, which polluted anyone who touched it. The killers, and even more the men who cut up bodies, put themselves at terrible risk from the souls of the dead men. In later years, whenever one of the ex-combatants sickened, curers were likely to diagnose the effects of 1925, and it was said that many of those stained with blood died before their time.[32]

Eventually, the leaders in the field decided that they had done all they could on Playón Chico, leaving the village in the charge of local rebels. On the way home, they decided to have another try at Tupile. Although the one remaining policeman there had already fled, the man sent ahead as scout soon let the cat out of the bag, and when the would-be invaders reached the island that night, they saw all its torches lit and groups of men patrolling. They ended up just as before, meeting their man in the dark and letting him persuade them to call off the attack.

The returning canoes, tightly massed, swept into Ailigandi, where they were warmly greeted. Nele and Colman counseled their followers to leave the killing behind, not to adopt violence as a problem-solver or way of life: "'Truly said. For a short time I have sent you to make war. Later on, in a month or two months, don't turn into the kind of fierce person who sees others as his food. The path does not lie that way' — Nele said that to us."[33] The Ustupu people then continued on toward their own island, arriving at dawn, only to find they could not go home.[34] In both villages, the fighters were sent to isolated corners of their island for several unpleasant days of purification to rid them of the pollution of blood and danger from their victims' souls, detaching them from war and effecting their reentry into life.[35] The men slept scattered on the sandy ground in little shelters, observing a laundry list of taboos: "Nele said, 'Don't sit on stools. Get sea stones, make them your stools. . . . Don't use hammocks. Smooth out the sand, and lie on that.' Owww! The people were suffering. . . . 'Don't scratch yourselves with your hands. Get pieces of cane.'"[36]

Despite their discomfort, the rebels had so far done remarkably well. They had killed or driven out all the police in eastern San Blas (except at Puerto Obaldía), sustaining no deaths themselves and only a few wounds. They had liberated Playón Chico, and a few days later they finally entered Tupile, burning down the school and dragging the pro-government chief, Inadoiginya, off to Ustupu for a long course of lectures on improving his behavior.

At the opposite end of the coast, the western insurgents in the Carti and Mandinga region had massed on Suitupu with Olonibiginya and Marsh: their eyes were focused on Porvenir and possible friends or enemies coming from Colón. In between was a string of pacified villages that, for the moment at least, were left on their own to throw off Panamanian rule without outside help. In several villages, the police fled when news of the rebellion spread. That left Nargana and the two islands a few miles to its east, Tigre and Niatupu.

Both islands had been pacified for little more than a year. The program first worked out on Nargana had by then been routinized into a standard operating procedure, and both villages rapidly received a school, police barracks, a dance club, and a chance to vote for the Liberal Party. In late February, everyone on both islands was preparing for carnival.

Río Tigre, which the Kuna call Tigir, was run by two police agents, neither of whom had endeared himself to the village. The indigenous policeman, Roberto Estocel, had gotten a local girl pregnant, while Luis Mojica, the intendente's nephew, had recently married on another island but also pawed at Tigre women. "He wanted to be the only one who could call to the women. That's how Luis Mojica did things. If you resisted just a little, instant punishment! . . . With no hesitation he'd put you into darkness."[37]

On Saturday evening, February 21, a canoe arrived inconspicuously from the east carrying three exiles.[38] Village men heard the news that rebellion was about to erupt throughout San Blas, and that they were expected to do their part. "They said to us, 'Now at noon you kill the waga. If you don't kill him, . . . we'll come shoot you too. . . . You hear?'"[39] The three exiles went off to spend the night on the mainland.

It was the young men of the dance club who were supposed to take the lead. Some had invited the police and school onto their island two years previously but now regretted their action, while their president, a former student of Miss Coope, had secretly worked as Colman's secretary the year before. Now given a chance to redeem themselves, the young men met to plan their attack.

The next morning they assembled in their clubhouse, a building of boards with a thatch roof and steps leading up to a raised dance floor. Although Carnival should not begin until Sunday noon, the young men, undoubtedly feeling the pressure from the three waiting at the river, decided to begin early.[40] "The women were being taken to the club. . . . 'Dance,' they said, 'dance.'"[41] An invitation was sent to Luis Mojica, who was passing the time in a store by the water. Mojica, however, would not come. "It was as if he understood what was happening. We called and called and called to him. Then we began to make music, to bring him to us."[42]

Soon one of the ringleaders called to the club president to tell him that the three exiles had started across the water to the island. "'Quick-quick,' he said, 'Be quick and finish them off. . . .' Then I went over there where Luis was and invited him. . . . 'You're missed. The party is starting. Carnival is under way. . . . The food is almost cooked.' Three times I called to him."[43] Whatever his misgivings, Mojica eventually came to the club. As he entered the dance floor, one of the plotters grabbed him from behind and brought him down. "Then we all rushed at once, hitting and hitting him, bam! bam! bam!"[44] The mob went to find the Kuna policeman, Roberto Estocel. Since Mojica had not been able to shout, Estocel was easily lured out: "Then he was coming, they were bringing him in their midst, then someone struck him with an axe. He was brought down, just like threshing rice."[45]

The revolutionaries stopped with the two policemen, sparing a Black storeowner and his son. They also left a trading boat, called the *Ambition*, which had a clear view of some of the mob's actions.[46] Within a few days, the boat's captain, Edison Whitaker, was in the city offering a report to the *Star and Herald* in which the two dead policemen had grown into a multitude of murdered innocents: "Indians, bloodthirsty and crazed, began slashing Panamans on every hand. The helpless natives tried in vain to flee from the Indians but the surprise was complete. . . . The streets of Tigre island were strewn with dead Panamans before Whitaker got away."[47] Whitaker also reported, more truthfully, that the bodies were violated.[48] Estocel was buried on the mainland, but the remains of Luis Mojica were taken to a little island, chopped into pieces, dropped into an open pit, and left for the vultures.

Whitaker's lurid account in the *Star and Herald,* along with the principal victim's connection with the intendente, gave Tigre a special notoriety, and since the killers proudly announced that similar events were taking place all along the coast, he brought news to the city of a general insurrection.[49]

Niatupu, visible a few miles to the east of Tigre, was also controlled by two policemen, one Latin and one indigenous.[50] Both men, Marcelino Herrera and Samuel Guerrero, had brought their wives with them. They were assisted by a volunteer helper, a Nargana man named Sosip. Two Black Antilleans, a storekeeper and canoe-builder, also lived on the island.

Like the Tigre plotters, the Niatupu rebels could not bring themselves simply to overwhelm the police, no matter how greatly they outnumbered them: they felt the need not only to work themselves up but also to devise a stratagem, and as on Tigre, they took pains to make their actions collective and thus to generalize responsibility. Several of the men most embittered by police actions took the lead, while Philip Thompson, back from the United States, played the role of eminence grise. The head of the dance club, another graduate of Miss Coope's school and one-time secretary to Cimral Colman, was not expected to take part in the killing, simply to keep the festivities going.

By Sunday, a good many people knew what was to happen. As had occurred on Tigre, the police locked up almost all the guns from the village in the barracks, and dancing began at midday. Soon afterward during a break in the festivities, the plotters saw their opportunity, a canoe some ways off traveling east to west. It was a party of Tigre men who had set to communicate with Ailigandi but had capsized their canoe. Soaked and discouraged, they had turned toward home, and when first sighted, they were heading toward the channel between two uninhabited islands that lie just out to sea from Niatupu proper. The plotters called out to alert the police, telling them it was rebels coming from the east.

The policemen reacted just as had been hoped, rushing off to intercept the rebels. They launched a canoe on the back side of Niatupu and crossed the narrow channel to the next island, which they traversed on foot to the channel between it and the outermost island. Catching sight of the canoe just then emerging from the pass in the direction of Tigre, they fired several times, shivering its sail and hitting the boom; the crew lay down in the canoe bottom, however, and soon sailed safely out of range.

The plotters, meanwhile, seized control of the village. Herrera had entrusted the barracks to a man named Lupos, who was in fact a ringleader. The guns were liberated, and many of the women and children were bundled off to a couple of houses where they could be kept safe, but the revelers continued dancing and making music to maintain the illusion of normality. Several young men ran up to the windward side to ambush the police on their return from the outer islands, hiding in a cookhouse, a bath enclosure, and the brush nearby.

The plotters instructed a man named Manuel on how to set up the police. "Go meet them. They'll tell you, 'Pull up the canoe.' You say to them, 'No, I won't pull it by myself, just a second and I'll go call them at the club to pull up the canoe.'"[51] Manuel did as he was told, leaving the three policeman standing by the canoe smoking and waiting for someone other than themselves to do the work of hauling the heavy dugout ashore. The ambushers fired on them, but raggedly, because one man's gun went off before the others were ready. Herrera shot back, and then "it was nothing but guns firing."[52] Almost everyone missed: Herrera was hit in the arm, but otherwise the skirmish did little damage.

The three policemen scattered, each fleeing toward his own house. Sosip was run down at the water's edge. The native policeman, Samuel Guerrero, was tackled by a hotblood named Jimmy Smith. "He threw Jimmy Smith over, Samuel was a big man. . . . The two of them were going at it." Jimmy Smith's supporters, seeing that he seemed to be getting the worst of it, clubbed Samuel repeatedly, but he wouldn't give up until someone fetched an ax: "He came running with it and planted it between his shoulders . . . whack!"[53]

As the pursuit began, the wife of agent Herrera was being watched by youths assigned to her.[54]

Over there guns went off. The woman . . . started to come out on me. Whew! A Devil woman. She began to scream and scream and scream. . . . I grabbed her. . . . I stood in the middle holding her. . . . I saw Herrera come running, wounded a little. Not dead at all. He was coming holding a gun, he came running toward me. I stood there holding his wife. . . . I took fright and ran off, I was scared. . . . The waga fell as he came close to the barracks. . . . Kuna, older men, came rushing after him.[55]

Herrera frantically tried to climb into the loft of his house. "He was climbing up, and they grabbed his shoe. . . . Then they fell on him, cutting and cutting with their machetes, and someone ran up and shot him with his own gun."[56]

During these struggles, chaos reigned. "There were lots of people here, women. One whole house full of them. The women were screaming and yelling, I tell you."[57] Despite the best efforts of their mothers, young boys ran around everywhere, watching the men dispatch the policemen. One man remembered:

Sosip was hung up upside down. You hear. He wasn't lying on the ground. . . . I was standing there, standing and watching. . . . I would have run over, but my mother saw: "Why would you touch those things?. . . Don't touch those things! The spirits will come take you away. It's all bloody. . . ." Off I went! I ran off home. I took fright. When I was sitting at home, the elders called out: "Everyone go bathe!"[58]

Some of the fiercest rebels wanted to kill every last Panamanian and collaborator, but the elders insisted on sparing the policemen's wives, as well as the storekeeper and canoe-maker and the villagers who had previously sided with the police.[59] Philip Thompson shielded Herrera's Panamanian wife, and an old woman saved Samuel's wife, a Kuna, by cutting her hair and restoring her to native dress. "Snip-snip-snip, they did a rushed job on it, and it was all in clumps . . . they changed her dress."

Jimmy Smith was coming, Lupos was coming. They were coming to get her, to kill her. The old lady said. . . . "Come here, girl." She took hold of her. She held her arm, like this. So she stood her up. . . . "Who do you see standing here? Look, it's Samuel's wife, she stands here wearing Indian clothes, you see her headcloth? She looks exactly like us."[60]

As on Tigre and Playón Chico, the enraged rebels desecrated the dead bodies, later taking all three to the shore and burying them there. That night everyone slept on the ground rather than in their hammocks, with no lights showing anywhere in the village. The streets were empty, except for the ghosts of the policemen. "When the place was heard, well, it was a place of spirits, full of noises, as it became night. In the streets, well a *garbe* spirit called, bibitbit! you hear. Just like someone running. It was their spirits, at night."[61]

Nargana, as always, was different.[62] The police had held the upper hand not for months but six years, and most serious dissidents had fled. As for Charly Robinson, he knew that his past resistance to the police and Claudio Iglesias would bring him no credit with the rebels to the east, who hated him almost as much as they did Claudio's successor, Estanislao López.

According to Erice, the rebels seized a Nargana man named Antonio who had the misfortune to stop on Tigre, sending him home with instructions to organize an uprising. They also sent a foolish ultimatum to Estanislao López telling him to kill the Panamanian police if he wished to be spared; López, predictably, rejected the demand and instead fled in a large canoe, taking with him the family of Claudio Iglesias. As rumors spread through Corazón and Nargana, Carnival dancing in the club ceased abruptly. Charly Robinson crossed to Corazón, where he found government supporters frantically packing belongings into canoes and the detachment head, Horacio Méndez, preparing a defense. Méndez gave Robinson a pistol, which came in handy almost immediately when he returned to Nargana and was confronted by a crowd of angry men blaming him for the attack that everyone assumed was coming.

Few slept that night. The next morning, some of the local merchants, aware that Méndez, too hung over and demoralized to defend the community, would himself attract rebel hostility, rolled him up in a large piece of canvas and sent him off in the bottom of a canoe. Children of Kuna mothers and Panamanian fathers were hidden away, one of them in a barrel. Charly Robinson, taking up an offer of shelter from Anna Coope, concealed himself in a wardrobe, clutching his pistol. Later that day a small flotilla arrived from Tigre and Niatupu. The police on Corazón wanted to fire at them but were persuaded by merchants and local people to hide instead in the mangroves of a nearby swampy island. The insurrectionists roamed around for a few hours, doing not much other than roughing a few people up, but warning that another force was coming the next day.

That night the men of Nargana, in good Kuna fashion, confronted the crisis by holding a meeting. Having resolved to appeal for outside help, they asked Anna Coope to take down a petition to the American minister on their behalf:

Panama — San Blas — Feb., 24, 1925
To the American Government.

We the San Blas Indians in Republic of Panama appeal to U.S.A. for protection from the imposition and brutality of the Panama Gov't as represented by the men who have brutalized us for over six years. Their treatment is getting worse we cannot and will not stand it any longer. Please listen to our plea and help us at once. . . . If you will send help at once all the Indians are ready to submit to the American rule.

The names taken down in Coope's hand included William Markham's friends Jake and Richard, "Charles R.," and sixty-nine others.[63]

Whether Charly Robinson truly stayed for the meeting, he certainly did not hang around to see what the returning revolutionaries would do the next day. He left in a canoe for Santa Isabel far to the west, as did the remaining government police, and in the morning the foreign merchants fled as well. The men left behind decided to send the women and children to the river, where they camped for several nights in the houses built for the dead in the cemetery. The men armed themselves as best they could and waited for the invasion from the east, just as they had in 1908 and 1913.

On Wednesday, the second flotilla arrived, bearing men from Ustupu, Ailigandi, and Playón Chico, with the intention not of attacking but of reestablishing the old order of things. Allowed ashore unopposed, apparently in return for a commitment not to kill anyone, they held a meeting on Nargana and named Markham's friend Richard chief. As on the day before, the invasion petered out after a few hours.

By this time, Estanislao López, having fled two days earlier, had reached the city and communicated the news of a general uprising. López and the Iglesias family had sailed through the dark from Nargana on Monday night, reaching Porvenir just before dawn Tuesday morning. Sentries there, already on the alert, fired at them but stopped when they called out. When the secretary in charge heard the news, he sent López and Alcibiades Iglesias on to the city along with Jim Berry, who was being held prisoner on Porvenir. They set off again, arriving in Colón after dark and sleeping at the police station.[64]

The first thing the next morning, Wednesday, February 25, they had an interview with the alcalde of Colón, who read the letter from Porvenir and by nine had sent them off on the train to Panama. According to Estanislao López, at the Secretariat of Government and Justice, Secretary Carlos López initially read their note with some skepticism, doubting the ability of the Indians to mount a full-scale rebellion, and he dismissed the three men until the next day. That afternoon, however, after newspaper reports appeared and Miguel Gordón's sister turned up with a telegram from Puerto Obaldía reporting her brother's death, they were taken more seriously. As angry crowds gathered and Indians in the city went into hiding to escape mob violence, the government began to assemble an expeditionary force to go confront the rebels.[65]

27.
Cruiser
Diplomacy

In three or four days the rebellion had almost run its course. Playón Chico, Tigre, Niatupu, and Nargana had been liberated, and the remaining police on Río Sidra, Tupile, and finally on Porvenir itself fled.[1] In one or two places where would-be rebels lacked police victims, they demonstrated their devotion to the cause in ugly killings of non-Indian workers and storekeepers or Kuna collaborators, people who otherwise were spared. The total number of deaths, less than thirty, was low, and Marsh played no direct role in the attacks.[2]

A decade later, when Marsh wrote a book on his adventures, the minimal casualties and his own noncombatant status evidently seemed too tame, so he spiced up his account with several imaginary battles.[3] Previously he had merely embellished and trimmed his account, or else, as with all-White villages in the mountains, he had convinced himself first; here, much more blatantly, he fabricated two amphibious landings against garrisons armed with machine guns and rifles.

While the fictional Marsh rampaged up and down the coast, the real one awaited developments at Carti. Late on Tuesday, February 24, word came that the police on Porvenir just across the bay had murdered Jim Berry and Philip Thompson — both were actually alive — as well as a rebel spy named Peter, who had been shot in his cell as the police abandoned the post.[4] To the chagrin of Marsh, who had been pressuring the Carti Kuna to spare civilians, they reacted to Peter's murder by killing four foreign workers at Río Sidra and a shopkeeper on another island. The shopkeeper's wife, brought to Carti, was so terrified despite Marsh's assurances that she refused to leave his presence and had to sleep on a cot at the foot of his own cot.[5]

On the twenty-fifth, just after dawn, Marsh and a large party of Carti Kuna landed at Porvenir. The last police had in their haste left clothes on the line, official papers on Intendente Mojica's desk, and a number of rifles still in their rack.[6] Marsh encouraged the men to burn the thatch-roofed dwellings of the police but persuaded them to spare the frame administration buildings.[7] In the absence of bodies, he still held out hope for Jim and Philip, though in the days to come Marsh trumpeted their murder as fact. On the return to Carti, the sadness of Peter's death lightened as they traveled home bearing loot, "hilarious indians reclining in rocking chairs on top of heavily laden boats."[8]

The next afternoon a small fruit company vessel, the San Blas, turned up at Carti with the manager of the Mandinga plantations, a Mr. Perino. Ushered into the gathering house, Perino asked about their intentions toward the plantations, to which Marsh replied that they would not be disturbed if they remained within their legal rights. Marsh then gave Perino two "executive statements" of the "Tule Nation," one announcing the formation of a provisional government, and the other decreeing that the law of the American Canal Zone would hold in San Blas. Before leaving, Perino told them that the fruit company launch, La Isla, would arrive the next day with a large force of Panamanian police, and Marsh replied that the Kuna would resist any attack.[9]

Marsh would have been relieved to know that La Isla was not coming alone, and that he had indeed inspired intervention in the crisis, though not by the proclamation of a republic, which had only inspired ridicule,[10] but simply by creating a messy diplomatic situation as a foreign national involved in a domestic conflict.[11] The current U.S. minister to Panama, John Glover South, had returned to the Isthmus on February 13 and read Marsh's letter to General Lassiter. According to South, he received the copies of the Tule Declaration of Independence on the twenty-fourth, and on the twenty-fifth, the Panamanian secretary of foreign affairs, Horacio Alfaro, sent South a note informing him of the revolt. Alfaro, whose sources said Marsh was claiming U.S. government backing, announced Panama's intention of expelling the explorer and his American companions as "undesirable elements," a task for which he requested U.S. assistance to avoid unnecessary violence.[12]

South, who had been minister to Panama since 1921, was, like his predecessor W. J. Price, a Kentuckian. A prominent physician and past president of the state medical association and state board of health, he was married to the daughter of an important Republican leader who had been governor and senator.[13]

Alfaro and South met that evening: South suggested they rush Marsh out of the country, while Alfaro insisted that his offenses demanded trial and punishment.[14] South offered to take a mixed party to the scene of the trouble in an American vessel, and the navy supplied a cruiser, the USS Cleveland, from what was called the Special Service Squadron—five ships used to patrol the Caribbean and Central American coasts, protect U.S. interests, intervene on occasion, and generally demonstrate who was the dominant hemispheric power. The squadron flagship, the Cleveland, an elderly and outmoded vessel only four years away from the scrapyard, nonetheless projected vastly more firepower than any Latin America military could hope to counter.[15]

The Panamanian government was not going to be seen putting all its trust in the Americans. As word spread of the uprising on the twenty-fourth, large demonstrations in Colón and Panama City demanded action. The government put together a force of 160 policemen, leaving the firemen to patrol city streets. At noon on the twenty-sixth a cheering crowd saw the Panama City contingent off on the train to Colón. There the troops marched to the docks, and at 5:30, with the city band playing and more cheering crowds, *La Isla* embarked for San Blas with many rifles, two machine guns, all the boxes of ammunition that could be rounded up at short notice, and four cows—but not, as it soon turned out, enough tents, food, or water.[16]

Both the American legation and the Panamanian Secretariat of Foreign Affairs, meanwhile, had been in cable communication with Washington: the secretariat answering questions from its legation in the United States, which had read reports of the revolt in the *Washington Post*; Minister South apprising the State Department of the situation and later announcing that he was off in a hurry to San Blas.[17] In a reply to South on February 26, Secretary of State Hughes took a harder line than the minister had:

URGENT. Make thorough investigation Marsh's connection with uprising. If satisfied he is responsible inform him Department cannot countenance any attempt of American citizen to foment disorders in foreign territory, and that it will not be disposed to intervene to prevent his just punishment by Panaman authorities.

Last paragraph your No. 22, Department prefers that Panaman authorities handle matter independently and provide for Marsh's transportation to Colon. It is believed that presence of United States war vessel will be sufficient to deter natives from further resistance.

Keep Department fully informed of all developments.[18]

On the evening of the twenty-sixth, Minister South's party got under way a few hours behind the boat carrying the police. In addition to South and a legation secretary, the passengers included Carlos López, the Panamanian secretary of government and justice; an assistant secretary of foreign relations; the British consul in Colón (to see to the protection of Anna Coope and other British subjects); a senior official of the national police, Colonel Arango; a reporter for the *New York World*; and William Markham, who had been recruited as unofficial Indian expert.[19]

After running all night, the *Cleveland* anchored off Porvenir the next morning, at about 8:30, soon after passing *La Isla*, which was rolling hard in rough seas. A party went ashore from the *Cleveland* to inspect the Intendencia, and the Panamanian troops began to disembark. Shortly afterward, Perino of the fruit company showed up in a launch to say that Marsh was at Carti with several thousand well-armed Indians. He also handed over Marsh's "executive statements," which both the Pan-

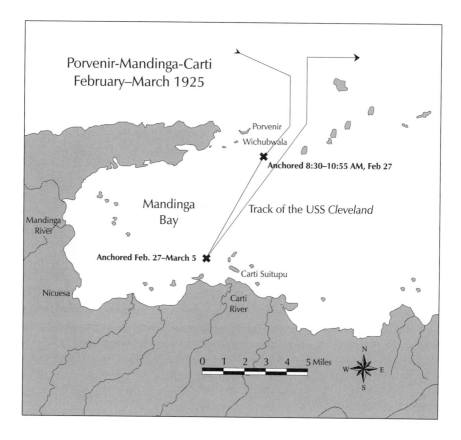

amanians and South took as evidence of the explorer's complicity in the rebellion. As the *Cleveland* steamed on toward Carti across the Gulf, leaving the Panamanian forces setting up camp, South told Markham that it looked bad for Marsh. "I replied 'better wait until you hear Mr. Marsh's story and it may look different.'"[20]

For Marsh and the Kuna on Carti Suitupu, the appearance of a large ship's masts in the early morning, even while the *Cleveland* was still hull down over the horizon, caused rejoicing. As Marsh saw it from eight or ten miles away and his quite subjective point of view, the *Cleveland* appeared just in time to cut off *La Isla* and physically block it from carrying out an immediate attack on the Indians. "It was as if a small terrier dog, intent on reaching its prey, suddenly looked up and perceived a huge Great Dane blocking the way."[21]

The *Cleveland* anchored off Carti Suitupu at 11:30, and Markham, who was well known there, was sent ashore. Taken to the gathering house, Markham conveyed Minister South's invitation for Marsh to come aboard under safe conduct, which was accepted. When Markham asked him about his involvement in the rebellion, Marsh replied:

"Bill, you know what their grievances are and any red blooded American would do the same as I have done. I did not start this rebellion but I did their writing for them and I will take my chances with the Indians and give up my life if necessary for their cause." "Well" I replied "You have a big heart but I don't think you will have to do the fighting alone. We have several million Americans that will help you when they know the truth of this disturbance."[22]

In a long conference between Marsh and South in the early afternoon, the minister explained that the Panamanians wished to try him for his part in the insurrection, and that the legation had received instructions not to stand in their way if his participation could be proved. First, however, he wanted to hear him out. Marsh recited the list of Kuna grievances, along with an edited version of his own role in events, which started to erode the minister's preconceptions.[23]

At Marsh's suggestion, South agreed to meet the Indians at a meeting arranged by Markham. After telling the Kuna massed in the Suitupu gathering house that he hoped to be of help and to hear their side of things, South listened to translations of speeches by Olonibiginya and other leaders detailing the wrongs they had suffered. At Markham's prompting, the Kuna said they would defend themselves but would not attack Panamanian forces without provocation. South offered to do his best to resolve the situation working through the Panamanian government but not to take them under the direct American protection they had been seeking. When he questioned them about the explorer's role in the rebellion, they insisted that he had merely taken down their grievances and demands, and that he had tried to restrain rather than incite them.[24]

Kuna eloquence, stage-managed by Markham, won the minister over. "I was greatly impressed by the intelligence, forcefulness, sincerity, and honesty displayed by the Indian leaders during my talk with them."[25] Over the next few days the rebels followed up on the meeting with a series of letters in broken but expressive English reiterating their suffering and grievances.

Meguecanti 1 of March of 1925
Dr. South, Dr. La Osa, William Markham
    S.S. Clevland
My dears Sir:
    I write this letter to make know you what police men made of us when they are in my place. First they made to take the ring noise, beans and change the sut of my wifes, and after that they start to put prisim of my mien uithout doing nothing bad things Sometime they want to do bad thing of my wife and my young ladies and such other bad thing. Dr. South, that things that made the police men my men not wanted because they made of us like a Slaves men.
Chief of indians of place Maguebcanti
    Luis Bran, Santiago Perz[26]

The Kuna version of events was also confirmed in the city by Reginald Harris, as well as by a fact-finding mission that had gone down the coast in an American tug. The party on board stopped at Ailigandi, where Nele and other chiefs absolved Marsh of all responsibility for the rebellion, to which, they said, they had been driven by unbearable oppression. Colman made a particularly strong effect by producing a set of handcuffs allegedly used to hold a woman for seventeen days.[27]

In Carti, after returning to the ship, South conferred with Panamanian officials. In addition to bringing them up to date on his meeting with the Indians, the minister again proposed that if Marsh could be expeditiously removed from Panama, the revolt might be peacefully concluded. Although Secretary López rejected once again the idea of letting Marsh escape punishment, South cabled Washington twice in the next eighteen hours promoting this solution.[28]

South invited Marsh to spend the night on board ship, very likely to get him away from the Indians. Marsh settled in and made friends with the cruiser's officers, who in the next few days passed on to him information circulating on board. The British consul, Hugh Ford, finding his American companions sympathetic to Marsh and the Indians, took private offense at what he called "the peculiar belief of the American people that they are entitled to dictate the policy, from a moral point of view, of all lesser nations." Two hours of listening to Marsh, moreover, convinced him that he was "mentally unbalanced."[29]

That same day the Panamanian National Assembly decreed martial law in San Blas, and the *Star and Herald* published the full text of the Tule Declaration of Independence. On the diplomatic front, the Panamanian minister in Washington cabled home that the State Department emphatically denied ever supporting Marsh's subversion, and that Marsh and the white Indians had been refused interviews with the president and secretary of state while in Washington.[30]

In San Blas that next morning, Saturday the twenty-eighth, it seemed as if the police were about to go on the offensive. Police Commandant Arango had told Markham that with the arrival of troop reinforcements, they would be ready the next day to subdue the Indians, who could not go unpunished for killing policemen. British Consul Ford doubted "that the Panamanian government would . . . abandon their proposed punitive expedition, owing to the adverse effect . . . on the political career[s] . . . of the cabinet."[31]

Marsh and Markham went ashore to warn the Kuna leaders, who evacuated noncombatants to the mainland. By late afternoon the crisis had dissipated, and in retrospect it is clear that no attack was imminent. The Panamanians had already agreed not to go on the offensive for the moment and were soon persuaded to forgo seizing Kuna vessels, not a major concession, since they lacked boats to enforce the blockade.[32] By this time, moreover, they knew that they would be going up against a force dug in behind rock walls. Their intelligence, failing to discover Kuna ammunition shortages, vastly overestimated Indian strength. Police machine guns could presumably have raked the Kuna defenses, but they had no small boats with which to effect a landing.[33]

Radio messages, U.S. and Panamanian, went back and forth between the *Cleveland* and Panama City all day and into the evening. South informed the State Department that Marsh had formally petitioned the captain of the *Cleveland* for asylum. Learning that the Panamanian chief justice, Francisco de la Ossa, would arrive the next day to conduct an investigation, South provided Markham with a ship's launch to confer with Kuna leaders and recruit witnesses and delegates. Then at the end of the day on February 28, South received the message from Washington for which he had been waiting, approving his proposals for resolving the crisis.[34]

The next day, Markham continued playing impresario. He persuaded the Kuna, as a politic concession, to take down the swastika flag. (He kept it as a souvenir.) To accompany the male witnesses, he chose several young women, including Olonibiginya's daughter, who had impressed him with her outspoken forcefulness. A ship's cutter fetched Justice de la Ossa from Porvenir at two, and the Indians came aboard at two-thirty, being greeted by Captain W. B. Wells at the top of the gangplank and escorted to the stern, where the session got under way.

Markham portrayed de la Ossa, an elderly oligarch, as biased and obtuse in his questioning, asking the delegates whether they had anything to do with writing the Tule Declaration of Independence and taking their negatives to mean that Marsh had done it on his own. South insisted that the Kuna did not understand what de la Ossa was getting at. Even when Markham's queries made it clear the document had been written on Ailigandi many miles to the east, de la Ossa clung to his preconceptions — which, it should noted, were correct, at least concerning Marsh's authorship of the declaration. Having complained of his inability to interrogate Marsh himself, the justice was taken aback when the great devil was produced for questioning. The explorer explained that he had written down the declaration from Kuna dictation on Ailigandi, and when de la Ossa complained about being so far from the scene of the crime, Minister South proposed to take him there on the *Cleveland,* an offer he declined.

The delegates then gave testimony on police abuses. At one point, Markham led Olonibiginya's daughter up to the justice and asked him what was wrong with her costume, even lifting off her headcloth to better show her ornaments, after which she spoke eloquently through the interpreter about how the police had mistreated her people. When de la Ossa raised the question of the goods looted from the Intendencia, Markham got a promise from the Kuna delegates to bring everything back immediately except the rifles.[35]

The justice later told reporters he had asked to have Marsh turned over, but Minister South said he would have to wait for word from Washington. A week later

Kuna interpreter addressing U.S. minister John Glover South and Panamanian chief justice Francisco de la Ossa, on board the cruiser USS *Cleveland*, 1925.

in a brief report, the justice noted that circumstances had prevented a proper investigation. Marsh's complicity in the rebellion was evident, but because the Indians covered for him, it was impossible to prove. De la Ossa duly noted the complaints of the Indians but also accused the Protestant missionaries of conspiring with Marsh, on the basis of a report (apparently true) that Anna Coope had passed out American flags.[36] The session on board the *Cleveland* ended at about quarter to five, when de la Ossa left for Porvenir. Captain Wells, who in Markham's words was "there with bells on" for the Kuna, arranged a tour of the ship and a photo session.[37]

Having decided that the "Indian's cause is just," South kept pushing for a peaceful solution. The Panamanians, though holding off for the moment, were unwilling to let the situation continue indefinitely. Secretary of Foreign Affairs Alfaro hoped that with Marsh gone, the Indians would return to peace, but if they did not, the government was in the process of hurriedly buying a gunboat. South, on the other hand, thought that any campaign against the Indians would be an expensive failure. As for Marsh, the Panamanians indicated they would request his extradition when the *Cleveland* returned to the Canal Zone.[38]

On the day after the inquest, South decided he could make more progress with Secretary of Foreign Affairs Horacio Alfaro, who was "the most likely to see the justice of the Indian's case and the necessity for adopting conciliatory measures."[39]

Minister John Glover South, Justice Francisco de la Ossa, and Richard Marsh seated, on board the cruiser USS *Cleveland*.

At one-thirty that afternoon, South and Markham flew off to Panama in a navy seaplane. In a long meeting, South and Alfaro came to an understanding that the whole episode could be brought to a close if the rebels would pledge to return to peace and allegiance to Panama before officials on Porvenir, with South acting as mediator. The next afternoon, March 3, the two diplomats flew back to San Blas, and in the morning the minister went ashore again and "after great difficulty" persuaded the Kuna to attend a peace conference that afternoon.[40]

It is unclear just what conjunction of forces, personalities, and circumstances brought the Panamanian government to the negotiating table. On some issues, especially those concerned with canal security, the Americans simply insisted. In this case, however, nothing suggests that South issued an ultimatum, and the Panamanians may simply have decided that if public opinion would allow it, they should follow the path of least resistance. Certainly, the government found itself in a difficult position. It might be able to make the rebels suffer, especially when the new gunboat arrived, but a successful assault on Carti could not be guaranteed, still less any kind of extended campaign. Whatever the police did, moreover, there would be witnesses. Concerning Marsh, his proclamations might be enough to convict him in a fair trial, but he could not be scapegoated for the entire rebellion, because too much had come out about mistreatment of the Kuna. Marsh was threatening, moreover, to use any proceedings to publicize official corruption in San Blas.

The group that assembled on Porvenir on the afternoon of March 4 included

U.S. officials and Kuna witnesses pose for photographer on board the USS *Cleveland.* Minister John Glover South at right rear.

Secretaries López and Alfaro; Justice de la Ossa, dragged back to San Blas almost immediately on his return to the city; and a Kuna-speaking Panamanian and sometime adviser on San Blas, Narciso Navas.[41] The other side consisted of chiefs from thirteen western communities, supported by twenty-eight other men and women. The extended proceedings, mostly translated back and forth between English and Kuna, were later summarized by South.

The Panamans listened to the tale of Indian grievances; admitted the truth of most of the complaints; and promised that these abuses would be corrected and the Indians would be accorded better treatment in future. The Indians rejoined that similar problems had been made many times in the past but never honored; and said frankly they had no faith that they would be kept this time. The Panamans agreed to remove from office Senor Mojica, the Governor of San Blas whose illegal acts were largely responsible for the recent uprising. . . . The Indians rejoined that Governors had been removed in the past, sometimes at the request of the Indians themselves; but that each new Governor had been worse than his predecessor.

After four hours of discussion, during most of which time the conference seemed to be at a deadlock, an agreement was drawn up and signed by the Panaman officials and the Indian chiefs which guaranteed to the Indians the same rights and privileges which are accorded to all other citizens of Panama.[42]

By about three the document, in effect a peace treaty, had been typed up and

Sailing canoes at Carti under the guns of the USS *Cleveland*.

signed by López, Alfaro, de la Ossa, and by Minister South as witness, with the names of the thirteen chiefs written at the bottom and their marks alongside. The rebels agreed to submit to the authority of Panama and return the arms they had captured but not to give up their shotguns. The government would install authorities as needed but otherwise allow the Indians to maintain order among themselves. Schools would not be imposed. It also undertook to "protect the Indians in their manners and customs" and to extend them the same rights and privileges as other citizens; in return, the rebels promised to respect other Kuna who wanted schools or different customs.[43]

Two crucial points did not become part of the written record. South argued that the Indians should be forgiven for acts committed during the rebellion. Alfaro promised that his government had no intention of punishing them, but the Panamanians refused to allow a written amnesty clause. South, in theory an observer and mediator, did not feel he could insist, and the Kuna delegates did not pick up on the point.[44] On native land rights, as well, the document is silent.

In his report to the State Department, South underlined Kuna distrust of the agreement and the critical nature of his own intervention:

It is quite clear that the Indians do not trust the Panamans, nor consider their promises worth the paper they are written on. That the Indians were willing to treat with the Panaman officials at all, was due entirely to my efforts, and the Indians accepted the Porvenir agreement only because I explained to them that it was . . . a public promise made before the whole world, and especially before the United States Government, and was in the nature of an assurance to the United States as well as a promise to the Indians themselves.[45]

Following the signing, Justice de la Ossa again tried to investigate Marsh's actions, with no more success than before. (Marsh himself was apparently confined to his bunk on the *Cleveland* with another bout of malaria.) In a radiogram sent a few minutes later to President Rodolfo Chiari, Secretaries López and Alfaro recommended that since Marsh's guilt could not be established, the government should expel him from the Republic rather than attempt to secure him for trial.[46]

Minister South's labors had not ended. At six the next morning, Chief Olonibiginya came aboard; and before seven they were at Porvenir, where the rifles surrendered by the Kuna were sent ashore. A party of Panamanian officials came aboard, including, strangely, former intendente Mojica, but not Secretaries López and Alfaro. The cruiser steamed east, and before two that afternoon it was anchored off Ailigandi. In South's words, "I went ashore at once to urge the Indians to receive and confer with the Panaman officials; but it was only with the greatest difficulty and after a discussion lasting more than two hours that I succeeded in accomplishing my object."[47] Finally, with great reluctance, Colman assented to the agreement reached in Porvenir and even shook hands with Panamanian officials.[48]

At six-fifteen South and his party came back aboard. As they got under way, the *Cleveland* fired a one-gun salute for Cimral Colman. After picking up Alfaro and López the next morning at Porvenir, by late on the afternoon of Friday, March 6, they were in Colón harbor, and all the ship's passengers except Richard Marsh disembarked, with nineteen guns for López and Alfaro, fifteen for Minister South. The cruiser continued the next day to its anchorage on the Pacific side with Marsh, who stayed aboard until the sixteenth.[49]

The press, both Panamanian and international, had followed events closely day by day, and it had a good deal to say. The local opposition papers, expressing the unforgiving sentiments of many Panamanians, criticized the Porvenir agreement, especially the lack of punishment for murderers of the nation's policemen. The *Diario* and the *Star and Herald* were more ready to acknowledge the justice of Kuna complaints and to praise South, López, and Alfaro. An English-language columnist for the *Star and Herald,* taking to an extreme the pro-Indian sympathies found among many resident North Americans, went so far as to praise the Kuna for rejecting civilization: "No single instance can be cited where contact with civilization has brought to the Indians anything but loss and degradation. . . . Ultimately, I suppose, they will have to swallow the dose, but let us not be so hypocritical as to pretend they ought to like it."[50] Almost no one in the press, however, had kind words for Richard Marsh.

On the twelfth, de la Ossa's report was printed in the papers, and on the thirteenth, *El Tiempo* published a long, rambling defense of his administration by former intendente Mojica, who suggested that behind Marsh lurked sinister powers plotting to take over San Blas — a view that even members of the cabinet were prone to credit. The *Star and Herald* columnist, more realistically, pointed out that capitalist forces would not have insinuated themselves in such a spectacular and clumsy fashion, but his alternative explanation of Marsh's actions, that he was a bit touched, was equally unflattering.[51]

Marsh himself kept his peace at first, refusing to make any statements except for remarks praising the Harrises and Coope.[52] Over the following ten days, however, he opened up, disavowing an article that had recently appeared under his name in a North American magazine and then giving an interview to a local publication.[53] Finally, just before leaving, he wrote a long letter to the *Star and Herald* warning that the country was in danger of being taken over by its negro majority, who would in turn be dominated by foreign corporations.

There are just two human elements in this country which in my blunt opinion are worth saving. One is the Tule race of Indians—which in the fundamentals of human character is one of the noblest races in the world. The other is that rapidly diminishing group of old, white, aristocratic, cultured, romantic families. . . . The negro, of course, is inevitable and cannot be eradicated. . . . There is just one solution, one escape. In your innermost hearts you know it as well as I do. That is voluntary annexation to the United States.[54]

The publishers of the *Star and Herald* decided that the statement was too inflammatory to publish.

On March 14, President Chiari issued an order expelling Marsh from Panama.[55] He was transferred directly from the *Cleveland* to a steamer bound for New York, and on the seventeenth he departed Panama for good, in the same cloud of adverse journalistic comment as twice before.

28.
The
Fruits of
Rebellion

The rebel Kuna had been very lucky. The success of their insurrection depended on chance as well as their own tenacity, courage, and organizing capacity. They would have revolted even without Richard Marsh (regardless of what generations of Panamanian commentators have since claimed), but their actions would not necessarily have attracted such widespread attention, still less official U.S. intervention. A different American minister might not have been so well disposed to the Kuna or so willing to forgive Marsh. Other Panamanian cabinets might not have contained men so ready to admit their government's fault and to accept compromise. Even with the same cast of characters, any number of things could have turned out differently.

The victory won in February and March of 1925, moreover, was partial and tentative. The rebels had cast off police domination and regained their autonomy. But they had not secured their lands against future threats or settled how they would relate to Panama. It remained to resolve this ambiguous condition and to secure the fruits of victory.

Within two weeks after John Glover South returned from San Blas, his hopes for a lasting peace were shaken by news that Panama had imposed an embargo cutting off all the rebel villages from the coastal trade, and that it had bought a second-hand steam trawler, renamed the *Panquiaco,* and equipped it with machine guns to patrol the coast. Revenging themselves for the well-publicized killing of the intendente's nephew, the police fired a fusillade into Tigre early one morning, wounding a woman and throwing the village into panic. South, who called the punitive policy "the most tactless and fruitless method possible of dealing with the Indians," worried that it would lead to a protracted guerrilla war.[1] He received periodic bulletins from William Markham in Colón, along with troubling letters from the Kuna pleading for his help.[2]

Things were actually not quite so bad as they appeared, however. Although the government made punitive gestures, no doubt partly to appease public opinion, Secretary López refused the new intendente's request to subdue Colman by force. For the most part, pacification consisted of a game of flags, in which rebel villages were forced to take down the Tule and American banners, and at least while the police were present, to fly the Panamanian.[3]

Nargana, however, could not be left in rebel hands. After a raid in mid-April in which a heavily armed party of police found the Tule flag flying and Charly Robinson's house and store in ashes, they recaptured the island a few days later, and at the end of the month, Ramón Garrido and his wife returned as detachment head and schoolmistress.[4]

At the end of May the intendente announced that San Blas had been pacified, a judgment reiterated by the governor of Colón, who visited the coast twice during June, bringing Inabaginya to the city to denounce the rebels and pledge his loyalty to Panama. On the other hand, the captain of the USS *Galveston*, which also paid a visit, found Ailigandi abandoned, its inhabitants in the hills, and Colman's forces agitated by a recent cruise of the *Panquiaco*, in which the boat's guns had raked three villages.[5]

Anna Coope returned briefly to Nargana in July to turn over her school, which she had been induced to sell to the government. As soon as she stepped ashore, she and her old enemy Ramón Garrido returned to the fray, prompting him to confine her to quarters to suppress antipatriotic agitation.[6] The government officials on the trip were much more favorably impressed by the already reorganized young men's group on Nargana, which held a dance during their stay, so impressed that they suggested that such youths and dances were just what was needed to pacify and civilize the rest of San Blas.[7]

For the rest of the year, rebel leaders kept smuggling letters of complaint out to the American legation, but Minister South was on leave for most of that time, and the less sympathetic chargé felt that the Indians must inevitably submit to Panama and so did not respond. In February, the government sent a North American spy into San Blas; having won the confidence of rebel leaders, the spy returned to the city with a representative from Colman. At the legation, despite an eloquent appeal to American traditions of liberty and self-determination, the delegate was firmly told not to expect help against Panama.[8]

During all this time Marsh had kept quiet, except for a vociferous exchange with Panama's minister to Washington, Ricardo Alfaro, on first arriving home.[9] At the end of 1925, however, he returned to the attack. Together with Davenport and Hrdlička, Marsh offered a resolution at the meetings of the American Association for the Advancement of Science expressing concern for Kuna welfare.[10] A few weeks later, he testified before the House Committee on Interstate and Foreign Commerce, proposing that America respond to foreign rubber monopolies by planting in the Chucunaque Valley and shipping the latex out to the coast on a railroad through the Caledonia Pass—which, he was sure, the Kuna would allow in return for protection of San Blas. "But do you understand that I want to save my simple, straightforward, honest, and quite noble-minded Tule friends not only from mongrelization by vile degenerate Latin American negroes, but also from the machinations of money-mad, materialistic, and quite selfish captains of industry of Modern 'highest human civilization'?"[11]

In March, the explorer announced plans to return to Panama, where he expected to act as broker for the Indians in land negotiations with the government, as well as to start a school for the Kuna like Indian schools in the United States and to continue looking for lost tribes and cities. Minister Alfaro promised that Marsh would be treated as an outlaw, but the latter vowed to go regardless and challenged Panama to catch him.[12]

Minister Alfaro was concerned enough to hire a detective agency. For two weeks an operative engaged a room a few doors down the street from the Marsh home in Brockport, New York. The bogeyman himself was seldom sighted, but neighbors were glad to depict Marsh in unflattering terms as an overly proud, self-aggrandizing sponger.[13] Within a few weeks, the Federal Bureau of Investigation also dispatched an agent to Brockport at State Department request: his report, equally negative but much more complete, touched on everything from Mrs. Marsh's inheritance to the Mendoza affair and the homicide years before in Louisiana.[14]

At the beginning of April, a London-based group holding large mining concessions in Panama announced a major gold strike. Within a few weeks Marsh was back at work, raising a hue and cry to the effect that the British were attempting to tie up millions of acres to keep the United States from planting rubber on the Isthmus. A long inflammatory memo he circulated provoked a congressional resolution demanding that the State Department report on whether Britain was gaining control of the lands and natural resources of Panama.[15]

The controversy soon subsided, as it became clear that neither Britain nor the United States had any interest in Isthmian rubber.[16] In the aftermath, Marsh finally seems to have given up on returning to San Blas, though not on exploration or white Indians. The following year he began organizing an expedition to the Venezuelan Orinoco and the Matto Grosso of Brazil to find a lost American pilot, a missing British explorer Colonel Fawcett, and the hidden white civilization Fawcett claimed to have discovered. He recruited a large party, supposedly to include Harris, Breder, Harrington, Rosebaum, and Cheepu, the latter to act as translator. As announced in a newspaper article entitled "Back to the Jungle," Marsh expected to ensure a friendly reception through the use of seaplanes, which would "literally pour presents on the startled natives below." The effort collapsed before it got under way.[17]

In 1927 Marsh went to work for Du Pont, first at a textile plant in Buffalo, then in New York City, and finally in Washington; in 1929 he set up as an independent consulting engineer.[18]

While Marsh was moving from agitation to regular employment, the stalemate between the Kuna and the Panamanian government dragged on through the rest of the 1920s. The government maintained the commercial blockade on Ailigandi and Ustupu for some time but did not try to reimpose police posts or interfere with Kuna custom, except on Nargana. In 1928 priests and nuns arrived to staff the Nargana public schools, welcomed by Charly Robinson, now returned to the Catholic fold.[19] The rebel Kuna dreamed of liberating Nargana by force but prudently held back, as did the police on their side.

Before the stalemate could end, both sides needed a cooling-off period and a change of leadership. Nele Wardada, or as he was now called, Nele Kantule, had effectively led the rebel forces since the 1925 uprising, but Colman, though retired and ill, clung to life, and it was not until after the old chief's death in 1929 that Nele moved.[20] His agents made contact with a recently formed labor union, the Federación Obrera, which acted as go-between, and in August of 1930 the government in turn sent Estanislao López and another man to represent it at a Kuna congress. Afterward a delegation of fifteen chiefs and secretaries came to town to meet with President Florencio Arosemena, offering their allegiance to the Republic, along with a list of demands.[21]

Arosemena, who received them cordially, entertained the delegation with a meal, an outing, and a visit to the movies. He then sent them away to draw up a formal petition. They returned three days later to ask for the same civil rights as other citizens, as well as suffrage, revival of scholarships for Indians, a new administration in San Blas, free trade, and most of all, security for Indian lands.[22] Privately, they also promised to vote for Arosemena's party, and Nele and several others were put on government salary. Arosemena also sent the delegation on to the commandant of the U.S. military in the Canal Zone, General Preston Brown. Their meeting resulted in an arrangement by which Kuna men have ever since done K.P. duty on U.S. bases. The understanding, which eventually led to the formation of a Kuna labor union, also regularized the relationship between the Indians and North Americans in a form that Panama could live with.[23]

Inabaginya, as jealous of Nele as he had been of Colman, arrived in Colón two weeks afterward to denounce the whole thing. In a newspaper interview branding his rival a murderer of policemen, Inabaginya played up his own preeminence and loyalty. "And all modesty aside, I can offer assurances that I have prestige and that I am sincerely loved by my comrades and subordinates."[24] He must soon have learned from the president that the deal stood, however, because a few days later he reversed himself, announcing support for Nele's petition.[25] At a government-sponsored meeting of reconciliation held a few weeks later in San Blas, the two leaders signed a joint letter thanking President Arosemena and urging passage of legislation to protect Kuna lands.[26]

A bill passed by the end of the year, and though it inadvertently excluded some of western San Blas, the error was corrected a few years later.[27] By this time, the fruit companies had already vacated their lands. The Mandinga plantations, ravaged by banana blight, ceased operations in 1929, and the plantations in eastern San Blas succumbed to disease and the worldwide depression soon afterward.[28]

Over the next several decades, the Kuna and the government extended the negotiations begun in 1930. In 1938, San Blas was reorganized as a special *comarca*, or district,[29] and in the mid-1940s, after the deaths of Inabaginya and Nele, a sympathetic intendente helped broker a reconciliation of the two confederacies and the creation of a unified political system for the comarca, with semiannual meetings of a representative body called the Kuna General Congress and a hierarchy of three ranked high chiefs, or caciques. The new system was confirmed by the government in legislation passed in 1953.

Richard Marsh returned to adventure in 1931, working on reconstruction efforts in Nicaragua following an earthquake. In October of 1932 he briefed a State Department official on the situation there, following up with a long outspoken memo. Marsh tactlessly condemned the actions of the U.S. Marine Corps in Nicaragua, even those of General Henry L. Stimson, who was by then secretary of state. In other respects, however, Marsh's point of view had changed greatly. Professing his support for the common people and opposition to the corrupt ruling class, he dismissed the conservatives as useless relics, in Panama as well as Nicaragua. Warning the State Department against Somosa and Chamorro, among others, he vehemently defended the rebel Sandino and proposed a plan that would lead to a Sandino presidency — advice the United States was not about to heed.[30]

In 1933 the adventurer, now fifty, settled into a quieter existence, going to work for the government, among other tasks designing agricultural catchment dams for sites all over the country. During World War II he worked with the army as a civilian engineer in North Africa and later in Ethiopia, from which he returned, according to family legend, with treasure. He retired a few years later to Vero Beach, Florida, where he died quietly at the age of seventy in 1953.[31]

Nele Kantule, although he never became leader of all the Kuna, eclipsed his rivals in the postrebellion years. He reorganized village government in his sector, and throughout his life he promoted initiative and self-help, insisting that the Kuna run their own schools and cooperatives. Having learned to exploit connections with sympathetic foreigners, Nele built an alliance with Swedish anthropologists, using their publications to cement his reputation as the foremost Kuna leader and traditionalist of the century.[32]

Alcibiades, or Lonny Iglesias, made up with his old mentor, Anna Coope, in the year after the rebellion and was sent again to the United States. He returned in 1932 with an American wife, and together with an ex-student of Miss Purdy's, he established a nondenominational Protestant Kuna church, which many years later joined the Southern Baptists. Attaining the leadership position for which his dead brother Claudio had always hungered, in the 1940s Alcibiades helped engineer the political reorganization of San Blas.[33]

Charly Robinson, though never again the political force he had once been, received in old age Panama's highest honor, the order of Vasco Nuñez de Balboa, awarded for his services in bringing civilization to San Blas. At his death, a newspaper photograph showed his old enemy Estanislao López, long since reconciled, sitting in mourning at the end of Robinson's coffin.[34]

As for López himself, once a youthful firebrand and enemy of traditional culture, his later career was characterized by moderation and compromise. By 1930 he was working closely with men who would gladly have killed him in 1925, and in the mid-1940s he was elected third high chief of San Blas. Elevated to the first position in 1971, he was soon named leader of all the indigenous people of Panama, in which role he established a system of congresses and high chiefs for the Emberá and Guaymí. Unforgiving enemies, who gave him the derisive nickname of *Ia Way*, Older Brother Waga, feared he would sell the Kuna out, but in fact López generally worked hard to protect indigenous interests as he understood them. In later years even seen enjoying himself at chichas, López, too, received the order of Balboa before he died.[35]

Today, almost three-quarters of a century after the events of 1925, most of the islands that joined in the revolt hold annual commemorations in late February, with parades and bloody reenactments. The last handful of veterans, who tottered out wearing red shirts to speak at the sixtieth anniversary in 1985, had by the seventieth in 1995 almost all gone to Great Father.

The things they fought for, however, have for the most part survived. The Kuna still feed themselves largely by their own efforts from their own land and water. Most Kuna women still wear molas, noserings, and limb bindings, and even those who do not wear them sew molas to sell. Villages still call to Great Father and Great Mother in sacred gatherings, though attendance has gotten sparse, and San Blas— today officially called Kuna Yala—still belongs to its indigenous inhabitants.

But much has changed. Having resolved their historic ambivalence about education, the majority of Kuna today have completed primary school, many of them secondary school and university as well. Out of forty-seven thousand Kuna in the Republic, as many as nine thousand live in Colón and Panama City, where women in molas walk confidently through city streets. For those still in Kuna Yala, tourism has grown tremendously as a source of income. Every few days in the dry season,

Portrayal of police abuses, commemoration of Kuna rebellion, Niatupu, 1985.

cruise ships unknowingly trace the track of the warship *Cleveland* past Porvenir and Carti; airstrips and small hotels are dotted along the coast; and even eastern villages far from the cruise ship circuit produce thousands of molas a year for the international market.[36]

At both ends of the coast, almost every village has at least one church, Protestant, Catholic, or both (and sometimes Mormon and Bahai as well). Anna Coope, however, might not recognize or endorse the Kuna version of Christianity, and Leonardo Gassó would be appalled. Converts see little contradiction between church religion and the one practiced in "Father's House"; Kuna preachers invoke the culture hero Ibeorgun as well as Jesus; one foreign nun goes around in mola; and two priests, themselves Kuna, vehemently defend traditional belief and practice.[37] When Gassó's best-loved successor, a Spanish priest named Jesús Erice, was on his deathbed in 1992, visitors found that in his final delirium, Jesús would only speak Kuna; when he died, the people of Tupile, where Gassó had planted his cross eighty years before, took the Father's body back and buried it with full gentile honors.[38]

Some of the old divisions and differences from the early years of this century are still apparent. Nargana and Corazón, where no one has worn molas since the 1930s, have gone their own way, embracing education, progress, and salaried employment. Community festivals on Nargana for many years commemorated, not the Kuna revolution, but the arrival of civilization and the flag of Panama. Even Nargana, however, felt moved to build a gathering house in the 1970s after a half-century lapse, and Corazón de Jesús, today a hotbed of traditionalist sentiment, has been renamed Akkwanusatupu.[39]

Nearby Tigre, where rebels killed the intendente's nephew in 1925, revived its tough reputation in 1962, when it fought a gun battle with a government patrol boat attempting to capture a Colombian contraband schooner.[40] Ailigandi, Colman's seat, created a national scandal in 1977 by flying American and Tule flags during the plebiscite on the Torrijos-Carter Canal Treaty, on which San Blas voted an emphatic no.[41] Inabaginya's successors in far eastern San Blas continue to combine cultural conservativism with intermittently pro-government politics.

The old antagonists of the Kuna, the Afro-Panamanian costeños, have been replaced by other intruders. Landless mestizo peasants from western Panama began pouring into the Darién in the 1960s, clearing the forest and putting cattle to pasture. By the time the Kuna woke up in the 1970s to the danger this hungry pastoral army presented, its advance guard had already crossed the mountains into Kuna Yala. In response, a union of Kuna workers in the Canal Zone organized a project to demarcate the boundaries of Kuna territory and create a forest reserve along the cordillera. Outside San Blas, the colonists have stripped the land bare, recreating the savannahs last seen five hundred years before, advancing all the way to Yaviza, where the Panamerican Highway ends, at least for now.[42]

Other intrusions the San Blas Kuna have yet to deal with satisfactorily. Black Colombians have been coming over the eastern border to pan for gold, and troubles in the Atrato region threaten to spill over into San Blas and the Darién. Cocaine passes up the coast, just as other contraband has for centuries, and some Kuna have become involved in the drug trade. Others have responded to national and international demand by diving for spiny lobsters, octopus, and reef fish, rapidly depleting marine resources.[43]

As for the national government, most of the time it deals with indigenous peoples more respectfully and honestly than other states in the Americas, but especially when issues of development or national hegemony arise, somehow Panamanian politicians never learn. In the mid-1990s the government granted mining concessions covering more than three-quarters of Kuna Yala, and it was insisting, over vehement Kuna objections, on installing a naval base at Caledonia.

As this book went to press, the Kuna were mobilizing to meet these latest threats, invoking as always the example of 1925. At the same time, they were also struggling to come to terms with themselves, to balance their desires for cash income with the declining health of their natural environment, to reconcile their emerging identity as educated citizens with ethnic and cultural difference. Kuna curers still treat numerous patients but they attract few students. Young educated defenders of Kuna tradition present street theater about the evils of Christopher Columbus and write poems in Spanish about militant culture heroes, but they seldom attend the gathering or work in the forest. Women in traditional dress bring up little girls in slacks and shorts, and many young women in their twenties put on molas only for dances and chichas. Although the annual commemorations of 1925 depict the struggle as us against them, Kuna against Waga, people quietly acknowledge that then and now, they have always struggled among themselves and within themselves, and that while defeat may be permanent, victory is never final or complete.

Abbreviations in Notes

819, 847   File numbers for Records of the Department of State Relating to Internal Affairs of Panama. File numbers beginning with 819 cover the period 1910-1929, those beginning with 847 years prior to mid-1910. RG59, U.S. National Archives.

ABP   Archivos Belisario Porras, Universidad de Panamá

AEL   Archivos de Estanislao López, Nargana and Panamá

AmLeg   (Records of) the U.S. Legation in Panama, RG84, U.S. National Archives

AMNH   Archives of the American Museum of Natural History, New York

AI   Archivos de la Intendencia, El Porvenir, Kuna Yala [San Blas]

ANP   Archivos Nacionales de Panama

BL   British Library, London

CMBd   Field diary and notes of Charles M. Breder Jr., 1924, American Museum of Natural History, New York (Numbers refer to notebook and page.)

Correg.   Corregidor (Regional administrative official, Republic of Panama)

Corresp.   Correspondence

Dec.   Decreto (decree)

Destac.   Destacamento (police detachment)

Diario   *El Diario de Panamá* (newspaper)

Disp   (Diplomatic) Dispatch

enc.   encargado (temporarily in charge of office)

encl.   enclosure to diplomatic dispatch

Est.   *La Estrella de Panamá* (newspaper)

Exts.   Departamento de Relaciones Exteriores, Government of Panama

FO   (records of) British Foreign Office

GO   Gaceta Oficial (official gazette), República de Panamá

Hac.   Secretaria de Hacienda (Secretariat of Finance) Government of Panama

HLFd   Diaries of Herman L. Fairchild, Department of Rare Books and Special Collections, University of Rochester Library: HLFd1, small pocket diary, "Darien Expedition, January-March 1924"; HLFd2, in the *Rochester Alumni Review* 2:4, pp. 79-82; HLFd3, "Notes and Collections on Marsh-Darien Expedition"

Int.   Intendente (governor of the Circumscription of San Blas)

intv.	Interview
Jefe	Head, usually of police detachment (identified by ordinal number)
LC	U.S. Library of Congress
MAE	Ministère des Affaires Etrangères, Consulat et Agence Diplomatique, Panama, Direction Politique et Commerciale 13.128.2, Government of France (held by ORPE, Universidad de Panamá)
MGJ	Memorias de Gobierno y Justicia (biennial report, Secretariat of Government and Justice) Government of Panama
NAA	National Anthropological Archives, National Museum of Natural History/National Museum of Man, Smithsonian Institution
NARS	U.S. National Archives and Record Service
NYT	*New York Times*
OH	Oral history (see listing in bibliography)
ORPE	Oficina sobre Relaciones de Panamá con los Estados Unidos, Universidad de Panamá
PanLeg	[Records of] the Legation of the Republic of Panama in Washington
PC	Panama Canal Executive Office, Records Bureau, General Records 1914-1934, RG 185, U.S. National Archives
POb	Puerto Obaldía
PRO	Public Record Office, Kew, United Kingdom
Res.	Resolución (resolution or declaration, Government of Panama)
RG	Record Group (U.S. National Archives)
RGHd	Field notes of Reginald G. Harris, January-February 1925, Davenport-Harris Papers, Cold Springs Harbor Laboratories (numbers refer to page)
ROMd	Diaries of Richard O. Marsh, 1924 and 1925 (numbers and letters refer to year, notebook, and page)
RTU	*Rochester Times Union*
RU	Record Unit (Smithsonian Institution Archives)
SD	U.S. State Department
S&H	*Panama Star and Herald*
SecGJ	Secretario de Gobierno y Justicia, Government of Panama
SecHac	Secretario de Hacienda, Government of Panama
SecIP	Secretario de Instrucción Pública, Government of Panama
State	State Department/Secretary of State, U.S. Government
SIA	Smithsonian Institution Archives
Ten.	Teniente (lieutenant)
Tomo	Volume
USNM	United States National Museum, Smithsonian Institution

Notes

Preface

1. The phrase comes from Sara Suleri (1992).
2. Gates (1991).

1. Sounds Heard in the Distance

1. This chant excerpt has been freely adapted from a text by the eminent Kuna historian, Carlos López (OH López).
2. See Adas (1992); Bhabha (1985); Jean Comaroff (1985); Guha (1983, 1984); Parry (1987); Scott (1985, 1990); Spivak (1988); and insightful discussions of resistance by Brown (1996) and Keesing (1992:199-241).
3. Tutino (1986:20-23), following Skocpol (1979), Brinton (1938), and others, links insurrection to weak or inconsistent repression (Tutino 1986:20-23) as well as to "rapid and severe deteriorations of rural social conditions." Also apposite here are Adas (1979:80-91); Coatesworth (1988); Little (1989:124-186); Stern (1987a, 1987b); and Tilley (1978:98-142).
4. Sullivan (1989). Also Comaroff and Comaroff (1991:200).
5. In the voluminous literature on alterity, see especially Berkhofer (1978, 1988); JanMohamed (1985); McGrane (1989); Mitchell (1988); Pike (1992); Said (1978); Spivak (1988); Taussig (1993); Thomas (1994); Todorov (1984).
6. As will become clear, these attitudes were shot through with ambivalence and contradiction. See Thomas (1994); Stoler (1985, 1989, 1992); Stoler and Cooper (1997); and Comaroff and Comaroff (1991:118).
7. See especially Stoler and Cooper (1997), and in a different context, Chomsky (1979:88-93).
8. On infantilization, see Thomas (1994:132-137); Comaroff and Comaroff (1991:117).
9. Spivak (1988:307).
10. See Comaroff and Comaroff (1991); Guha (1983, 1984); Gramsci (1971); Keesing (1992:199-241); Thomas (1994:55-58); Scott (1990). In a form of this argument that unfairly belittles the Kuna, Michael Taussig

(1993) depicts them as colonial puppets or mimics, implicated in the prejudices of dominant groups and engaged with them in an infinite regression of mutual emulation and imitation.

2. A Long Struggle

1. Andagoya (1865); Castillero Calvo (1995); Castro (1996); Las Casas (1992); Sauer (1966).
2. Castillero Calvo (1995:37-40, 74, 77); Oviedo (1944, 1950). For disputes on whether the Kuna descend from the contact period chiefdoms, see Helms (1979); Herrera (1984:14-28); Howe (1977a); Langebaek (1991:373); Romoli (1953, 1987); Smith (1981:249-270); Stier (1979:40-48,110-115); Torres de Araúz (1975:73-136). For the sake of simplicity, I ignore Kuna populations off the Isthmus (Severino 1956; Vargas 1993).
3. Castillero Calvo (1984); Earle (1981:135); Jaén Suarez (1978:45); Mena Garcia (1984:148-170); Ward (1993).
4. The criteria are Galvin's (1991).
5. Castillero Calvo (1991:72-73, 1995:122); Herrera (1984:29-30); Olivardía Rangel (1963:55-59); Rodriguez (1979); Rojas y Arrieta (1929:38-39); Romero (1975); Severino (1956:30); Castillo (1995).
6. A. E. Ariza (1964:54-62); Castillero Calvo (1995:168, 171-177, 210, 225-227, 245-265, 287-288, 337-362); Requejo Salcedo (1908 [1640]); Rojas y Arrieta (1929:44, 48-50); Severino (1956:27-72, 81-101, 174-195, 260); Stier (1979:68-69).
7. A. Ariza (1971:112); A. E. Ariza (1964:62-64); Araúz and Pizzurno (1991); Castillero Calvo (1991, 1995); Dampier (1927); Davis (1934[1704]); Earle (1981); Esquemeling (1924); Galvin (1991); Hoffman (1980); Jaén Suarez (1978:78-80); Kemp and Lloyd (1960); Luengo Muñoz (1959, 1961); Pares (1936:94-95); Piedrahita (1971 [1684]); Restrepo (1888a); Ringrose in Esquemeling (1924:299-331); Rojas y Arrieta (1929:48-50, 109-112); Severino (1956:12-25, 67, 74-75, 81-101, 174-261); Stier (1979:61-71); Wafer (1970); Ward (1993:161-185); ms. "An Account of our Intended Voyage . . . ," Add.11,410, BL.
8. Wafer (1970).
9. Prebble (1968); Rojas y Arrieta (1929:84-90); Stier (1979:75-77).
10. A. Ariza (1971); Castillero Calvo (1995:228-229); Davis (1934 [1704]:156-161); Galvin (1991:99); Langebaek (1991:375-376); Luengo Muñoz (1959:147, 1961:346-353); Pares (1936); Rediker (1987); Ward (1993:150-155, 161-185).
11. Alcedo y Herrera (1972 [1743]); Anonymous (1960); Castillero Calvo (1995:204-206); Davis (1934:156-161); Holloman (1969:411-413); Jaén Suarez (1978:81-82); Langebaek (1991:375-377); Pares (1936:552); Remón (1985 [1754]:137-138); Severino (1956:255-256,301-306); Stout (1947:52); Wassén (1949:29.
12. Bladen to Harrington, 6/12/1739; Bladen to Lords of Council, 9/10/39; Tapel to Walpole, 9/11/39; "Sir Charles Wager's Abstract of Several Schemes under Consideration, Oct. 1739"; "Mr. Dundas's Paper to Sir Charles Wager," 12/13/39 — all Add.32,694, BL. Knight to Newcastle, 11/20/1739, Add.22,677. Vernon to Dennis, 4/13/42, 7/03/42, 7/06/42; Vernon to Newcastle, 4/27/42, 6/30/42; Vernon to Trelawney, 6/22/42 — all in Vernon (1744:91-120). Wager to Vernon, 6/10/40, 7/09/1740, 6/21/41, 8/18/41, 8/20/1741, in Vernon (1757:13-14, 16-17, 44-47). Assembly of Jamaica, for 5/04-7/13/1741, 1747, pp. 562-563. Pares (1936:70-77, 93-97); Richmond (1920:30-31).
13. Castillero Calvo (1995:229); Luengo Muñoz (1961:35).
14. Castillero Calvo (1995:215-224); Severino (1956:279-86).
15. Castillero Calvo (1995:206); Severino (1956:256, 301-306); Rojas y Arrieta (1929:133); Stier (1979:81-82); Langebaek (1991:377).

16. A. Ariza (1971 [1774]).
17. Alcedo y Herrera (1972 [1743]); A. Ariza (1971:95, 107); M. Arosemena (1972); Castillero Calvo (1991:89; 1995:260-264, 327-330, 345-357, 444-450); Cuervo (1891); Langebaek (1991:377-378); Luengo Muñoz (1961); Olivardía Rangel (1963:61); Rojas y Arrieta (1929:102-103, 152).
18. Breuer (1993:109-141); Castillero Calvo (1995:328-335); Gil y Lemos et al. (1977 [1789]); Herrera (1984:40-45); Horton (n.d.); Jaén Suarez (1978:82-83); Luengo Muñoz (1961); Rojas y Arrieta (1929:158-160); Severino (1956):313-329); Stier (1979:84-85); Torres de Araúz (1977).
19. See Cullen (1853:71-74); Jaén Suarez (1978:155-159); Selfridge (1874:14, 25, plates facing 2, 14, 22, maps 1, 2, 12); Stout (1947:54). I rely also on numerous conversations and interviews with Kuna on this topic.
20. Cullen (1853:74); Stout (1947:59); Selfridge (1874:10). Only the roughest of estimates are possible. Jaén Suarez (1978:77-83, 141-159) is entirely too confident in his sources.
21. Consular reports, Mr. Bunch, 1873-1874, LXXIV; C. Mallet, 1890, LXXXV, Accounts and Papers, Commercial Reports, PRO. I am indebted to Eduardo Posada for copies of consular reports.
22. Dunham (1850); Olien (1988); Roberts (1965 [1827]).
23. Discussed by Brown (1970), whose chronology is skewed. The Kuna of today are aware of this historical change.
24. Howe (1976a).
25. Roberts (1965 [1827]:43-44).
26. For a comprehensive review, see Howe (1985). See also Helms (1976); Holloman (1969:136-197, 1976); Prestán (1975:61-106); Stier (1979:212-22, 291-347. We can be fairly confident about Kuna culture and social organization in the late nineteenth century, despite a lack of contemporary accounts: Gassó's observations (1911-1914:X, XI) date from 1907, and several of my oldest informants were born before 1900.
27. Chapin (1970); Gassó (1911-1914:X); Howe (1974, 1986); Sherzer (1983, 1990); Howe, Sherzer, and Chapin (1980). In the nineteenth century, nonchiefs also chanted in the same fashion to greet each other after long absences. On chanted dialogue in lowland South America, see Fock (1963); Rivière (1971); and Urban (1986).
28. Chapin (1983); Nordenskiöld et al. (1938); Howe (1976b); Stier (1979); OH, Gonzalo Salcedo.
29. Bushnell (1993). I ignore here the successive changes from Gran Colombia to New Granada to Colombia. In 1870 Kuna delegates travelled 125 days to Bogotá, securing an agreement that they hoped would protect them from incursions and abuses by forest workers and merchants (Jorge Morales Gómez, "El convenio de 1870 entre los cunas y el estado Colombiano," *Revista Colombia de Antropología* XXXII; also Turpana 1985, Guionneau-Sinclair 1991:53-56.
30. Jaén Suarez (1978:45). Consular reports, Consul Mallet 1875 and 1876, LXXXIII); Acting-Consul C. Chamberlain (1883, LXXIII), Commercial Reports, Accounts and Papers, PRO.
31. Drolet (1980:31-60); Hayans, ms. "Isla Pino," Edman Archive); Herrera (1984:55-65); Olivardía (1963:63-68); Selfridge (1874:36, 50). Consular reports, Acting-Consul Crompton (1874, [volume unknown]); Consul Mallet 1875-76, LXXXIII, Commercial Reports, Accounts and Papers, PRO, courtesy of Eduardo Posada.
32. Cullen (1853); Gisborne (1854); McCullough (1977); Selfridge (1874); Réclus (1881).
33. Consular report, Acting Consul-General Mallet 1890-91, LXXXV, Commercial Reports, Accounts and Records, PRO.
34. FO 135, "From Consuls," 1893, 204, PRO. Thanks to Malcom Deas for pointing me to this document.
35. That is, Río Diablo, Spanish name for Nargana.
36. That is, Rafael Nuñez and Miguel Antonio Caro, presidents of Colombia. *Nunis* is the Kuna word for milk.

3. The New Order

1. The name Kuna Yala, which the Kuna adopted in the 1980s for their territory, would be anachronistic in a historical work.
2. See Severi (1981, 1988).
3. Cf. Taussig's hyperbolic interpretations of these figures (1993:3–14, 100–111, 186–188, *passim*).
4. This argument is developed more fully in Howe (1991). On sex and social boundaries, see Stoler (1985, 1989, 1992, 1995).
5. E. López, ms. "Nombres de los personajes," misc. mss. concerning Nargana; Wassén (1938:20–24, 72–76; 1949:25); personal communication, Freddy Filos, 3/21/72; intvs., Francisco Hernandez, 1/14, 1/15/71.
6. OH, Carlos López; E. López, ms. "Fechas de los Caciques Generales . . . : Inacailipler Abisua, Numero 1, 1800–1904," "Nombres . . . ," AEL; Ayarza (1981:10–11; Inakeliginia (1997:54–57); Moore (1983:100).
7. E. López, mss. "Algunos relatos . . . de los congreso generales," "Fechas," "Nombres"; Moore (1983:98).
8. OH, Carlos López; Inakeliginia (1997:55–57).
9. On poles and chiefs, see Howe (1977b:145–149); Sherzer (1983:97, 1990:64–117).
10. Several authors suggest that Inanaginya succeeded Abisua as first regional chief *in 1880* (Herrera 1984:77; Holloman 1969:419, 422; Moore 1983:105; Stout 1947:84), an inference from a confused text in garbled English (Nordenskiöld et al. 1938:208). This is much too early: E. López (mss.) dates the succession precisely at 1900; Carlos López (OH) gives a vivid account of the succession meeting based on oral testimony; and Abisua was still politically active up to his death in 1904. Estanislao López introduces another confusion (mss. "Fechas," "Nombres," "Relatos") suggesting that Abisua was nominated high chief for the *first* time in the 1900 meeting but declined on the grounds of old age (see Ayarza 1981:10–11) and indeed that there were no high chiefs or congresses before then.
11. Coope (1917:107–108); Gassó (1911–1914:II, 203–205); Holloman (1969:421–423); E. López, "Algo sobre la vida de Saila Charles Robinson," in Wassén (1949:99–101), and mss. "Fechas," "Nombres," "Relato del Señor Alfredo Inaediguine Robinson"; G. Medina, *Est.*, 8/22/61; Moore (1983:100–101); OH, Samuel Morris; Puig (1948:143–149).
12. Some sources say Robinson was raised on San Andrés (Puig 1948:144–145), others Providencia (Coope 1917:107; Gassó 1911–1914:II, 204; E. López in Wassén 1949:99–100). Possibly both are correct.
13. While sources differ on when Robinson returned, his election as chief in 1904 makes a date later than 1902 implausible.
14. Coope (1917:165–167); Gassó (1911–1914:II, 204).
15. Estanislao López mentions this school (ms. "Fechas"), which one of my informants, Francisco Hernandez, attended (intv., 1/17/71). See also Moore (1983:100).
16. Conniff (1992); LeMaitre (1971); McCullough (1977); Major (1993).
17. Pizzurno Gelos (1990); Porras (1973); Ricord (1989.)
18. I lean heavily on Herrera's insightful discussion (1984:68–71).
19. Herrera (1984:69–71).
20. Malmros to Buchanan 1/25/04, in Herrera (1984:75).
21. Araúz (1958), in Herrera (1984:68); E. López, mss. "Fechas," "Nombres," "Algunos relatos."
22. O. Malmros to W. I. Buchanan, 1/22/04, in Herrera (1984:73).
23. Gassó (1911–1914:VI, 85).

24. OH Carlos López. Inakeliginia (1997:57-59).
25. Ayarza Pérez (1981:18); Nordenskiöld et al. (1938:210, 212). Puig, however (1948:199), says that Colman began visiting the presidencia from 1906 on. A recent source (Inakeliginia 1997:58) suggests that the schism began at this time.
26. E. López, ms. "Fechas"; Ayarza (1981:17).
27. The succession of chiefs on Nargana may have been more protracted and difficult than most accounts indicate (Gassó 1911-1914:II, 204; López in Wassén 1949:100). Several accounts misdate the succession in 1903 (Falla n.d.:19; López in Wassén 1949:100; Stout 1947:85).
28. Coope (1917:108); Gassó (1911-1914:II, 204); E. López, ms."Nombres"; Puig (1948:146).
29. See Holloman (1969:421).
30. E. López, ms. "Nombres."
31. E. López, ms. "Nombres."
32. Some sources give Robinson credit for the idea, others Amador. It may have been both (Gassó 1911-1914:II, 205).
33. Gassó (1911-1914:II, 205); E. López, ms. "Nombres."
34. Intv., Francisco Hernandez, 1/17/71.
35. Erice (1961); Gassó (1911-1914:II, 205); E. López, ms. "Nombres"; Puig (1948:173-178); Rojas y Arrieta (1929:246-248). Most sources say seventeen boys, some—confused by additional drafts sent in 1907—mention twenty or twenty-two. The most reliable list, with sixteen names for 1906, comes from Puig (1948:177-178). Estanislao López gives three discrepant lists (mss.), which agree with Puig on about thirteen names.
36. Melchor Lasso de la Vega, 6/01/20, in Puig (1948:175).
37. Anonymous, archives of Colegio La Salle, quoted by Puig (1948:173).
38. Hermano Venero Carlos, report, 6/12/08, in Puig (1948:175).
39. Res. 55, 6/30/10, GO 1910, p. 565.
40. Gassó (1911-1914:II, 205).

4. Father Gassó among the Gentiles

1. Gassó (1911-1914:I, 157). Hereafter, in citations from Gassó's diary, the author's name and the year will be omitted; roman numerals refer to volume or chapter numbers and Arabic numbers to pages *within a particular volume* of the serial. The translations in this chapter and chapter 5 of passages from Father Gassó's diary are my own, although I also checked them for error against a draft translation of the diary by Ned F. Brierley. I am editor and director of the translation project.
2. I, 157.
3. Gassó (1911-1914).
4. I, 203. *Waga* is *huaca* in the original.
5. II, 204.
6. II-III, IV:235-236.
7. V, 58; also IX, 162.
8. IV-V.
9. V; VI, 59, 85.
10. VI, 85-87; VII, 132.
11. This episode is narrated twice: in VI, 87ff., and VII, 132ff.
12. VI, 87.
13. VI, 88.

14. IX, 161-162; VII, VIII, IX.

15. IV, 236.

16. Todorov (1984:27).

17. XII, 275; VI, 85; XV, 64. See Beidelman (1982:14).

18. XVIII, 186. Gassó (1908a); Burkhardt (1989); Nida (1966); Rafael (1988). I use the term "catechism" more broadly than Gassó, who reserved it for the question-and-answer section of the document.

19. When a successor to Gassó read some of the worst passages to helpful Kuna, they were stumped (Puig 1948:151).

20. Gassó (1908a:21, 8-9). This is not to say that as a matter of *behavior* they are incapable of forgiving or pardoning.

21. Gassó (1908a:9, 11, 19, 21, 25, 31, 35).

22. Gassó (1908a:20-21, 26-27). *Dios ina,* "God's medicine," which may have been intended, would be only marginally better.

23. Gassó (1908a:20-21).

24. V, 57; VI, 77; VII, 134; XII, 274: XIV, 43. See also Gassó (1908b).

25. IV, 236.

26. V, 56. On kneeling, see Axtell (1985:121-122); Gutiérrez (1991:49); Sweet (1995).

27. Gassó (1908a:32).

28. XIV, 42.

29. V, 56; XIV, 42; XVI, 89, 106.

30. IX, 182-184; XII, 273; XIII, 16; *passim.*

31. IV, 88; IX, 183.

32. IX, 181; XIV, 41, 44.

33. IX, 183; XII, 274. It is often assumed that Robinson got all one hundred rifles he requested, but Gassó seems to have separately specified twelve or fifteen.

34. IV, 237.

35. Gutiérrez (1991:71-81); Thomas (1994:133).

36. V, 56. I see nothing to suggest that Gassó was sexually attracted to the boys.

37. IX, 163; XIII, 16.

38. XIV, 44. I have changed Gassó's spelling and glosses of two of the words.

39. XIV, 42.

40. XII, 274; XIII, 16.

41. XIV, 17, 41.

42. XIV, 17, 41.

43. VI, 86.

44. Callahan (1984); Lannon (1987). On missionary antipathy or ambivalence toward the modern world, see Beidelman (1974, 1982).

45. IV, 56; XIII, 16; Sweet (1995).

46. OH, Carlos López.

5. To Confront the Stubborn

1. XII, 15.

2. XIV, 18.

3. XIV, 18, 41.

4. XIV, 41.

5. XVI, 106; XIII, 17.
6. For example, XIII, 17.
7. XIV, 18, 42.
8. XV, 65–67.
9. XVI, 88.
10. XVI, 88.
11. XVI, 89.
12. XV:65. This particular encounter occurred late in the second *entrada*.
13. XVI, 89; XVI, 90, 106–107.
14. I, 57; IX, 162; XX, 16; XXI, 39, 136–137.
15. IV, 56; V, 58; VI, 86; XIII, 16.
16. XVI, 90.
17. XVI, 106.
18. XVI–XVII.
19. XVII, 135.
20. XVII.
21. Brandon (1986).
22. XVIII, 186.
23. XVIII, 137–187; XIX, 231.
24. XIX, 231–279; XX, 279–280.
25. XXI, 66.
26. XIX, 259, 279; XXI, 39.
27. I rely here in part on Chapin (1983:115–117).
28. VII, 132; IX, 132; XIV, 43; XVI, 67; XX, 280; XXI, 39, 66.
29. XX, 16.
30. XXI, 40.
31. Gassó (1909b:237); VII, 133; X, 206; XXI, 39; XXII, 112.
32. X, 206; XI, 250; X, 204, 206, 227; XI, 228–229, 250.
33. For example, IV, 56; XIV, 18, 43; XXI, 39, 66.
34. VI, 86.
35. Gassó (1910a:334); VI, 86; XX, 280; XXI, 66–67.
36. I, 203. In the original, waga is *huaca*. The souls of Kuna wrongdoers could be punished for a while in the underworld, but not in one single place and much less systematically than in the Christian hell.
37. XIV, 42, 43; XV, 64; XVI, 89.
38. XX, 16–17.
39. XX, 17; XXI, 39.
40. XXI, 66–67.
41. XIX, 259.
42. XXI, 102–103.
43. XXI, 68.
44. XXI, 90, 91.
45. XXII, 112, 133–134.
46. XXII, 134–135.
47. XXII, 136.
48. XXII, 136.
49. XXII, 181.

50. XXII, 181; Gassó (1909a:211); Fernandez (1911:100).

6. Heresy and Impiety

1. Canduela (1909); Erice (1961:68); Fernandez (1911); Gassó (1911-1914:IV, 236; XXII, 134; 1911b:29); Gurruchaga (1909); E. López, ms. "Fechas"; Mejicanos (1914); Puig (1948:152); Valanzuela (1912).
2. Gassó (1911-1914:VI, 88, 109-110; 1911b; 1913:346-348, 355).
3. Or, to be precise, a coalition of Conservatives and ex-Liberals. Bushnell (1993:120-139); Bushnell and Macaulay (1988); Deas (1986).
4. A. E. Ariza (1964:7); Rojas y Arrieta (1929:233, 248).
5. Isaza Calderón (1982:302-305); Mega (1958:297); Rojas y Arrieta (1929:242).
6. Mega (1958:298-303); Mellander (1971:37-69); Rojas y Arrieta (1929:242-249).
7. Isaza Calderón (1982:307-321); Major (1993:116-124); 819.00/447-515; Mellander (1971).
8. MGJ (1908:LIV-LV, in Herrera 1984:94).
9. Gassó (1911-1914:vi, 85, 86; ix, 182; xv, 64). Some accounts claim that the Colombian government jailed or even executed Inanaginya, but Estanislao López agrees with Gassó that the chief died while on his journey (ms. "Nombres").
10. OH, Carlos López; Inakeliginia (1997:58). The latter source puts the schism in the time of Inanaginya and says that Inabaginya's accession to the chieftainship merely reinforced the division.
11. Gassó (1909b, 1910a, 1910c).
12. Gassó (1911-1914:VI, 59; XII, 275).
13. Gassó (1909a:237; 1910a:319).
14. Gassó (1910a:321-322).
15. Gassó (1910a:326).
16. Gassó (1910a:333).
17. Alcalde de Portobelo to SecGJ, 5/20/09, in Anexos de la Sección de Gobierno, no. 198A, GO 1910; Sec enc Gobernador Provincia de Colón to Unknown, n.d. 1909, in notes of Francisco Herrera. See Herrera (1984:90-91).
18. S. Lewis, Sec. Relaciones Exts. to J. Blackburn, Canal Zone Dept. of Gov., 5/29/09; Blackburn to Goethals, 6/01/09; Blackburn to Lewis, 6/01/09, 80A-15, PC, NARS; Int. Vaglio to SecGJ, 6/04/19, ABP; *Diario*, 8/17/10; Ayarza (1981:31).
19. *Diario*, 8/17/10; Herrera (1984:91); report by Ramón Valdés, MGJ, 1910, in Puig (1948:224-228); note by Francisco Herrera concerning MGJ, 1910:315-41.
20. Eduardo Navas, 12/31/09, "Movimiento marítimo por naciones habido in Puerto Obaldía durante los meses de Junio a Diciembre de 1909," GO, 1909:1000.
21. The original force numbered sixteen; it fluctuated thereafter. Herrera (1984:91); MGJ, 1910, in Herrera (1984:92); notes by Francisco Herrera on MGJ, 1910:315-341; MGJ, 1912:102-105; Dec. 21 of 3/26/10, GO, 1910, no. 1094, p. 289.
22. Jefe 3d to Int., 11/15/19; Int. to Subinspector National Police, 11/24/(19); Int. to Jefe 3d, 11/24/(19); Subinspector to Int., 11/29/(19).
23. See Holloman (1969:169-170).
24. Gassó (1911a).
25. Gassó (1911a:284). I have altered Gassó's punctuation and formatting.
26. Gassó (1911a:285). *Mone* as in the original. A letter from the Alcalde of Portobelo following the 1909 attack on Tupile published in the official gazette (Anexos de la Sección de Gobierno no. 198A, GO) notes that Davis assessed his losses to the raiders at $300, out of a total of $1,400 claimed by four Tupile men.

27. Coope (1917, 1931).
28. Coope (1917:3).
29. Coope (1917:4).
30. Coope (1917:8, 10).
31. Coope (1917:15).
32. Coope (1917:27).
33. Coope (1917:79-103 [1931]); Gassó (1911a).
34. Coope to Jeffrey, 2/02/10, in Keeler (1956:152).
35. Gassó (1911a:283).
36. Gassó (1911a:283-286).
37. Coope (1917:84).
38. Coope (1917:85-86).
39. Or depending on one's Kuna orthography, *Bela*.
40. Coope (1917:94-98). Some paragraph breaks have been changed.
41. Coope (1917:100); Coope to Jeffrey, 4/26/10, in Keeler (1956:152).
42. GO, 1910, no. 1161, p. 565; no. 217, p. 1122.
43. Gassó (1910b:164).
44. Isaza Calderón (1982:331-333); *Diario,* 8/12, 8/17, 8/18, 8/19/10; *Panama Journal,* 8/10, 8/11, 8/12, 8/17, 8/18, 8/19, 8/20/10. S&H, 8/18/10, cited in Herrera (1984:100).
45. *Diario,* 8/17/10.
46. *Diario,* 8/19/10.
47. MGJ, 1910, as cited in Puig (1948:224-228).
48. MGJ, 1912:103. See Herrera (1984:96).
49. Gassó (1913:346; 1911-1914:VI, 85, 109).
50. Misioneros Hijos del Corazón de Maria (1939:114). Gassó's last letter from the field (Gassó 1913) seems to hint at continuing health problems.
51. Ocampo (1966:81-93). I am grateful to William Merrill for providing this source.
52. Misioneros Hijos (1939:114).
53. Gassó (1911-1914:XXI, 40).
54. Catalogus Provinciae Aragoniae, Societatis Iesu; P. Jordi Roca, S.I., personal communication, 6/16/92; Mendizabal (1972); Nordenskiöld et al. (1938:5); Torres de Araúz (1961:74).

7. Colman and Nele

1. Anon., n.d., "Biografía del Cacique General John Colman (Inakintipipilele)" [courtesy of William Durham]; Juan Colman, "Documento original, breves biografías de nuestros antepasados abuelos que conocían las ciencias religiosas," in Wassén (1949:96-99); López and Colman, ms. 7/28/77, "Breve biografía de Inakkintippippilele Colman, 1840-1929"; E. López, ms. "Fechas de los caciques generales . . . : Olokintupiler [*sic*] Colman," AEL; Puig (1948:197-199); Iguaniginape Kungiler (1994); Matutino, 8/n.d./76; Panamá América 8/04/90, "Se recuerda a gestor de la Revolución Tule." Intvs., Gonzalo Salcedo, n.d./70; Francisco Hernandez, 1/11/71; Horacio Méndez, 9/27/71.
2. These uncles were presumably his mother's sisters' husbands, with whom she would normally have lived. As noted in chapter 2, Kuna women then worked more in the fields than they do now.
3. I omit a story told by Colman's enemies, which claims that he was thrown out by Kuppi before completing his studies because he had made love to Kuppi's daughter.
4. The voluminous material on Nele and the Ustupu schism leaves many points unclear. Published

sources include Chapin (1983:17-24), 444-482; Hayans, "The Life of Nele de Kantule," in Wassén (1938:31-44); Rubén Pérez Kantule, "Una resumen de la vida de Nele de Ustup," in Nordenskiöld et al. (1938:89-91); Puig (1948:193-195). I have discussed the schism previously (Howe 1986:238-239).

Pamphlets and unpublished manuscripts include Holloman, n.d., "Nele Kantule: A Study of San Blas Cuna Leadership in a Period of Transition" (courtesy of the author; see also Holloman 1969:439-454); Efrain Castillero [López] and Enrique Obaldia, n.d. [c. 1966], "Biografía del Cacique Nele Kantule"; Castillero López and Obaldia, ms. 9/03/75-76, "Biografía de Nele Kantule, Sahila Tumat (Cacique General) de San Blas (1868-1944) con motivo del XXXI aniversario de su muerte"; Estanislao López, ms., "Fechas de los caciques generales . . . : Iguahibiliguile Nele Kandule, Numero 7, 1929-1944," AEL.

The archives of Chany Edman on Ustupu contain undated manuscripts, all or most by Guillermo Hayans: (1) "The Life of Nele de Kantule" (the basis for the biography printed by Wassén); (2) "Biografía del gran caudillo Yaicun"; (3) "Palabra de Jaicun"; (4) "Gran incendio . . ."; (5) "Biografía del Sr. Iguanibinape"; (6) "La Historia de Ogobsucun . . ."; (7) "Algunas obras. . . ." I am especially grateful to Regina Holloman for allowing me to make use of her unpublished study of Nele. More generally, all students of Kuna society are indebted to Holloman's doctoral thesis (1969) for her analysis of leadership and learning among the Kuna. I also depend on my own interview with Horacio Méndez, 9/27/71, and fragments from several interviews with other informants.

5. Also identified as Nitippilele.

6. Some versions say Manuel Jesús.

7. OH, Sir Willis; Inakeliginia (1997:65).

8. See Adas (1979); Cohn (1970); Lawrence (1964); Wallace (1969); Wilson (1972).

9. On the antiquity and significance of the equation of distance, learning, and prestige, see Helms (1979, 1988); also Cooke (1984:115-116), and Langebaek (1991).

8. The Mendoza Affair

1. Isaza Calderón (1982:152-159, 186-192); Scoullar (1916-1917:113); Westerman (1956: 5-24); Barré-Ponsignon to MAE, 3/03/10, MAE; Weitzel to State, 3/03/10, 847/230.

2. I have benefited from writing on the Mendoza episode by Michael Conniff (1985:41-43, 1992:76) and John Major (1993:125-127), as well as from their great generosity: both provided photocopies of notes on relevant documents.

3. Hitt to State, 6/11/10, 847/236; La Palabra, 5/21/10 (in Hitt to State, 6/11/10); Manifesto [against Mendoza], 7/20/10, in 847/240; PanLeg, Wash., to Wilson, 8/24/10, 819.00/290; Est., 7/03, 7/19, 7/30/10 (letters by M. Herrera and J. A. Henriquez). See also Fábrega and Galindo (1981).

4. Warsaw Bulletin, 6/09/05; Hancock County Biographical Review, 1907, p. 61; History of Hancock County, 1921, v. 2, p. 1379 (all courtesy of Barbara Cochrane, Hancock County Historical Society).

5. National Cyclopedia of American Biography, v. 40, 1955, pp. 573-574; Explorer's Journal, Autumn 1953:55; Who's Who 1948; intv., Richard Marsh Jr., 5/01/84, 1/86.

6. Information courtesy of George Fan, ΦBE alumni scribe.

7. Grade sheet, Registrar's Office, MIT. Grades have been translated from the system then in use.

8. Richard O. Marsh, photograph albums, inscription to book of Greek mythology, courtesy of Richard Marsh Jr.

9. Marsh to Davenant Rogers, 11/17/10, R. O. Marsh personnel file, 123.M35, Division of Latin American Affairs, Department of State, NARS; intv., Richard Marsh Jr., 5/01/84, 1/86.

10. Intv., Sybil Cleveland Beach, 4/17/83; Richard Marsh Jr., 5/01/84, 1/86.

11. R. O. Marsh personnel file, 123.M35; name card file, Diplomatic Division, NARS.

12. GO, 7/16/10, VII:1174; GO, 9/06/10, VII:1217; Jaén Suarez (1978:20, 22, 32).

13. Major (1993:116-125); Mellander (1971:106-109); Sands (1944:58, 65-66).

14. Healy (1988); McCain (1937:62-70); Mellander (1971:87-88). For a recent and authoritative analysis, see Major (1993:116-154).

15. For example, Weitzel to State, 2/18/10, 847/221. Also McCain (1937:62-92); Mellander (1971); Sands (1944:3-68).

16. Major (1993:122-124); Mellander (1971:143-186).

17. Marsh to Dawson, 9/25/10, in Dawson memorandum, 11/10/10, R. O. Marsh personnel file, 123.M35. Barré-Ponsignon to MAE, 8/20, 8/22, 9/02/10, MAE; Mallett to FO, 9/10/10, FO 35714/50, PRO.

18. Marsh to State, 7/28/10, 847/240. Barré-Ponsignon to MAE, June through Sept. 1910, MAE.

19. Biesanz and Biesanz (1955:202-235); Conniff (1985:16-44); Figueroa Navarro (1978, 1987); Isaza Calderón (1982:132-133); Jaén Suarez (1978:233-278).

20. Hitt to State, 6/11/10, 847/236; Hitt memo, 8/12/10, 819.00/297; Weitzel memo, 8/10/10, 819.00/298. Chalkley to FO, 3/14/10, FO 371.944/1516; Barré-Ponsignon to MAE, 4/01, 6/29/10, MAE. Also Mellander (1971:87-88, 99); Sands (1944:18-20).

21. Conniff (1985); Franck (1913); McCullough (1977:574-588); Hitt to State, 6/11/10, 847/236.

22. Marsh to State, 7/28/10, 847/240; Griffin (1988:278-280); McCullough (1977:508-543).

23. Goethals to SecWar, 9/13/10; de la Guardia to Sec State Knox, 8/04/10; Marsh, cable to State, 8/05/10; Marsh to Goethals, 8/05/10 — all in Box 10, 1910, General Correspondence, G. W. Goethals, Ms. Division, LC, also 819.00/241, 244.

24. Marsh to State, 8/05/10, 847/241; Hitt to State, 6/11/10, 247/236; Weitzel to State 3/19/10, 847/233; PanLeg, Wash., to Wilson, 8/24/10, 819.00/290.

25. Weitzel to State, 3/19/10, 847/233; Hitt to State, 6/11/10, 847/236; Marsh to Goethals, 8/10/10, in Goethals Corresp; Marsh to State, 8/15, 8/17/10, 847/248, 253.

26. Major (1993:116-122); Mellander (1971).

27. Marsh to State, cables 8/17 and 8/19/10, letter 8/15/10, 847/248, 250, 253. Hitt memos, 8/10, 8/12/10, 819.00/196, 197; Weitzel memos, 8/11/10a&b, 819.00/294, 298.

28. Marsh to Goethals, 8/10, 8/16, 8/18/10; Goethals to Marsh, 8/17, 8/20/10 — all in Goethals Corresp.

29. Marsh to State, cable 8/20/10, 819.00/251; *Diario*, 8/20/10; *Est.*, 8/21/10; Mallett to FO, 8/22/10, 371.944/33140 PRO.

30. Barré-Ponsignon to MAE, 8/22/10; Mallett to FO, 8/24/10, 371.944/33141, PRO.

31. Marsh to State, 8/20/10, 819.00/251; Goethals to SecWar, 9/13/10, in Goethals corresp.; Marsh to Dawson, 9/25/10, and Dawson to State, 9/28/10, 123.M35.

32. Goethals to Mendoza, 8/23/10; Mendoza to Goethals, 8/23/10; Goethals to SecWar, 9/13/10; Dawson to State, 9/28/10, 123.M35 — all in Goethals corresp. *Panama Journal,* 8/23/10; Mallett to FO, 8/24/10, FO 371.944/33141, PRO; Mendoza to PanLeg, Wash., 8/23/19, in C. C. Arosemena to Wilson, 8/24/10, 847/254.

33. State to AmLeg, 8/22, 8/23, 8/24/10, 847/251, 251A, 254; Marsh to State, 8/24, 8/26a&b, 8/29/10, 847/252, 255, 256, 819.00/258; Memo, "JRC" in Office of Solicitor, 8/24/10, 819.00/288; Hitt memo, 8/25/20, 819.00/295; Marsh to Goethals, 8/24/10, and Mendoza to Marsh, 8/26/10, in Goethals corresp.; Mallett to FO, 8/25/10, FO 371.944/31161, PRO.

34. Hitt to State, 6/11/10, 847.236. Marsh undoubtedly knew of his predecessors' dislike of Mendoza, and probably of the scorn for everything Latin American of the secretary of state, Philander Knox, and his chief assistant, Huntington Wilson (Healy 1988:145-147).

35. Wilson to AmLeg, 8/24/10, 847/254A.
36. Marsh to State, 8/29, 8/30/10, 819.00/258, 259; Wilson to AmLeg, 9/01/10, 819.00/259.
37. Sherill, Buenos Aires, to State, 8/31, 9/01/10, 819.00/260, 264.
38. Marsh to Goethals, 8/31/10, Goethals corresp.
39. Goethals to SecWar, 9/13/10, Goethals corresp.; Dawson to State, 9/28/10, in 123.M35/14.
40. Marsh to State, 9/02/10, 819.00/265.
41. Wilson to AmLeg, 9/03/10, 819.00/265; Dawson to State, 9/28/10, 123.M35/14.
42. Goethals to SecWar, 9/13/10, Goethals corresp.
43. *Est.*, 9/08/10, also in Goethals corresp., also in Dawson to State, 9/28/10, 123.M35/14; Goethals to SecWar, 9/13/10, Goethals corresp.
44. Herrera and Morales, "La Situación" (broadsheet), in Goethals to SecWar, 9/13/10, Goethals corresp.
45. Mallett to FO, 9/10/10, FO 371.944/35714, no. 49, PRO.
46. Editorials; letters by de la Guardia, Arias et al.; Ycaza; Narciso Garay; Anon., in *Est.*, 9/08, 9/09, 9/10/10.
47. Dawson to State, 9/28/10, and Marsh to Dawson, 9/25/10, in 123.M35/14; Marsh to Goethals, 9/25/10, Goethals corresp; Marsh to State, 9/10/10, 819.00/272.
48. Goethals to Marsh, 9/08, 9/09/10; Thatcher to Goethals, 9/09/10; Goethals to SecWar, 9/13/10a&b — all in Goethals corresp. SecWar to State, 9/14/10 819.00/282. Mallett, caught between the contradictory claims of Marsh and Goethals, was loath to give up the idea that the colonel and President Taft were behind the campaign to impose Lewis, and he leaned toward seeing Marsh as a "scapegoat," left holding the bag after carrying out an American plan in a clumsy and overenthusiastic manner (Mallett to Grey, 9/10, 9/15/10, FO371.944/35714, PRO). Conniff's interpretation of the episode (1985:41-43, 1992:76) seems to follow Mallett closely. I find Mallett an interested and sometimes biased witness. To my mind, though Marsh obviously acted in the overall context of American domination of Panama, the evidence strongly indicates that he took the initiative in the campaign against Mendoza, and that in attempting to impose Lewis he acted entirely on his own.
49. Wilson to Taft, 9/07/10, 819.00/277A; State to Marsh, 9/08/10, 819.00/268A.
50. Taft to Wilson, 9/07a&b, 9/08a&b, 9/09, 9/10, 9/12/10a&b; Wilson to Taft, 9/07a&b, 9/08a&b, 9/09, 9/11/10.; Pan National Assembly to Taft, 9/09/10, 819.00/268, 271, 274-277, 279-281, 283, 285.
51. Wilson to Taft, 9/07, 9/11/10, 819.00/277, 279; Taft to Wilson, 9/08, 9/09, 9/10, 9/12/10, 819.00/277, 279, 280, 285; Wilson to AmLeg, 9/08/10, 819.00/268; Taft to Mendoza 9/12/10, 819.00279. GO, 9/16/10, VII:1225.
52. Marsh to State, 9/09a&b, 9/10, 9/11a&b, 9/12/10, 819.00/269-270, 272-274, 278.
53. GO, 9/29/10, VII:1236; *Est.*, 9/25/10. Marsh to Goethals, 9/25/10, in Goethals corresp.; Marsh to Dawson, 9/25/10; Dawson to State, 9/28/10, 123.M35/14.
54. Taft to Knox, 10/20/10; Knox to Taft, 10/22/10; Marsh to State, 3/09/11 — all in 123.M35.

9. The Protestant Mission

1. Vandervelde and Iglesias (1983:20).
2. Coope (1917:101-105). Although Coope states that she left Panama in August 1911 (1917:102), she later states that when she returned in August 1912 she had been away two years.
3. Coope (1917:106).

4. Keeler (1956:153).
5. Coope (1917:106).
6. Coope (1917:109).
7. B. Pérez to Porras, 1/29/13; B. Pérez to Sec F. Filos, 2/14/13, AN(?) (courtesy Francisco Herrera); Robinson to Porras, 3/n.d./13; F. Sho to Porras, 1/12, 3/09/13; Coope to Porras, 3/15/13.
8. Colman to B. Porras, 1/31/13, ABP(?); B. Pérez to General Corman [*sic*], 3/02/13 (all courtesy of Francisco Herrera). The originals have *huaca*.
9. Mega (1958:313).
10. Coope (1917:112-113).
11. Morgan (1958:36-37). Although this description undoubtedly derives ultimately from Iglesias, the words cannot be the exact ones he supposedly used in 1933 but rather a re-creation for publication twenty-five years later.
12. Coope (1917:87, 91, 174-175, 147).
13. Coope (1917:165-175); "The San Blas Region," 80A-15, PC, NARS. These notes clearly derive in one way or another from Coope. At times they seem to be written by her, at times written by someone else on the basis of information from her.
14. Dietrick (1925:15).
15. See Lane (1983:75-86).
16. E. Hurtado to SecGJ, 8/15/13, ABP.
17. Coope (1917:116-117). She does not name the official in question, but Hurtado's report and a later letter on the subject (Porras to Int. Vaglio, 4/02/19, ABP) leave no doubt that it was he.
18. Coope to Jeffrey, in Keeler (1956:154).
19. Coope to Jeffrey, 8/12/14, in Keeler (1956:150).
20. Coope (1917:94).
21. Coope (1917:118).
22. C. Robinson to Governor Colón, 11/03/13, AN(?) (courtesy Francisco Herrera). Joaquín Valencia to R. Arcia, 11/03/13; Arcia to Porras, 11/07/13; Porras to Arcia, 11/08/13, ABP; Coope (1917:163-164); Keeler (1956:154, 162).
23. Coope to Jeffrey, 11/01/13, in Keeler (1956:154).
24. Coope to Jeffrey, 11/05/13, in Keeler (1956:162). Keeler misdates this passage.
25. Coope (1931:128-129). A later volunteer, Annie Beaver Pugh, died in Nargana in 1919 (Keeler 1956:164-166).
26. Coope (1917:124-129).
27. Blocker (1976, 1989).
28. Coope (1917:120).
29. Coope (1917:120-123, 139-141).
30. Coope to Rev. Hartman, n.d., in File 80A-15, PC NARS.
31. Coope to Rev. Hartman, n.d., in File 80A-15, PC, NARS.
32. Coope to Jeffrey, n.d. [1913-1914], in Keeler (1956:154-155).
33. Coope to Rev. Hartman, n.d., in File 80A-15, PC NARS.
34. File 80A-15, PC NARS.
35. Coope (1917:120-125).
36. Dietrick (1925:15); Coope (1917:123-124).
37. Dietrick (1925:15).
38. Coope (1917:149-155).
39. Coope (1917:155); MGJ 1920.
40. Coope to Jeffrey, early 1914, in Keeler (1956:155).

41. Coope to Jeffrey, 2/15/n.d., in Keeler (1956:155).
42. Morgan (1958:38-39).
43. Coope (1917:132-136); Keeler (1956:157-158).
44. Coope (1917:180).

10. Belisario Porras Visits the Kuna

1. This tag comes from Sisnett's *Belisario Porras o la vocación de la nacionalidad* (1956). I depend on Sisnett (1956); Bushnell (1993:140-154); Isaza Calderón (1982); Major (1993:127-146); Ortega (1965:27-31); Porras (1931, 1973); República de Panamá (1942); Ricord (1989). I have read letters in the Porras Archives (ABP), as well as State Department files (SD), although I do not cite either here.
2. Sisnett (1956:179); also Isaza Calderón (1982:311).
3. Sisnett (1956:1520).
4. Memo, "Previous Interventions in Panama Elections," 7/24/28, Records of Francis White, SD, RG59, NARS.
5. Sisnett (1956:159, 312).
6. John Major's jaundiced view of Porras (1993:127-146) is too influenced by U.S. diplomatic sources. The projects Major depicts as frivolous were mostly basic institutions, which Porras wanted badly to complete while in office.
7. Sisnett (1956:151, 252, 257).
8. Narciso Navas (1909, "Estudio sobre la cria de tortugas y careyes en la costa Atlántica"; 1910, Informe no. 9; 1910, Informe no. 10 de 1910. N. Navas to Governador de Provincia de Colón, 9/04/09; N. Navas to B. Porras, 2/08/13. N. Navas and Eduardo Navas, 1/15/13 (untitled report). Stavros J. Pilides to B. Porras, 4/12, 10/22/13; S. J. Pilides, 10/20/13, "Memoradume Notorio sobre San Blas; n.d., "Continuación de mi Memoradume sobre San Blas de 20 de Octubre de 1913." Father Benito Pérez to B. Porras, 1/29/13; B. Pérez to Francisco Filos, SecGJ, 2/14/13. All at AN(?) (courtesy of Francisco Herrera). See also the report by J. D. Arosamena, MGJ (1912:102-105), discussed by Herrera (1984:96-98).
9. GO, año IX, no. 1801-1805, pp. 3827-3849, 11/02, 11/08/12; año X, no. 1850, p. 4035, 1/24/13. Herrera (1984:103-104) notes that the document was composed by Juan Sosa.
10. See also Minister Dodge to State, Desp. 350, 3/05/13, Div. of Latin Am. Affairs, NARS.
11. Colman to Porras, 1/31/13; Manuel Hernandez for Colman to Porras, n.d., ABP. S&H, 3/19, 3/20/13.
12. Enrique Hurtado to SecGJ, 8/15/13, ABP.
13. GO, año IX, no. 1801, 11/08/12, p. 3849. I have added dashes to clarify the sense of the passage.
14. South to State, 5/04/26, 819.52G31.
15. Hurtado to SecGJ, 8/15/13; Narciso Navas, Informe no. 10 of 1910, ABP.
16. OH Carlos López; Inakeliginia (1997:72). Luis Walter (OH) gives much the same account, with a lock metaphor. Castillo (1996).
17. Hurtado to SecGJ, 8/15/13, ABP.
18. C. Robinson to Governor Colón, 11/03/13, AN(?) (courtesy Francisco Herrera); Joaquín Valencia to R. Arcia, 11/03/13; Arcia to Porras, 11/07/13; Porras to Arcia, 11/08/13, ABP; Filos to Porras, 11/08/13; Porras to Filos, 11/08/13, ABP.
19. W. P. Cresson to State, Disp. 366, 12/28/14, 819.00/481, NARS.
20. W. J. Price to State, 1/12, 3/26, 3/30/15; W. J. Price to E. Lefevre, 2/01/15; E. Lefevre to W. J. Price, 2/18/15, 819.00/481-485, NARS.

21. GO, año XII, no. 2169, p. 5336, 1/29/15. 819.032/22, NARS; GO, año XII, no. 2187, pp. 5411-5413, 3/12/15.

22. A passage (Anonymous 1916:6) suggests that the author was Carlos de Diego, Juan B. Chevalier, Justo Arosemena, or Carlos Endara. Many episodes on the trip are confirmed in narratives by Estanislao López (ms., "Nombres") and Carlos López (Inakeliginia 1997:72-74).

23. Porras to Price 5/17, 6/08/15; Price to Porras, 6/05/15, AmLeg 846, NARS.

24. Adas (1989:162-163, 223-224); Conrad (1902:82, 89-91, 109-110). The narrator, who seems well educated, may have read Conrad's novel, published thirteen years earlier.

25. Anonymous (1916:6).

26. OH, Carlos López.

27. These are not the exact words used but a reconstruction by the Kuna oral historian Carlos López, based on what Ceferino Colman told him (OH, Carlos López).

28. Handwritten document, with heading "I. de San Blas," ABP (courtesy of Francisco Herrera).

29. Coope to Jeffrey, 5/26/15, in Keeler (1956:155-156). Coope's narrative is in places confusing as to speaker and audience.

30. Anonymous (1916:12-13).

31. S&H, 5/30/15.

32. Coope (1917:158-161); Keeler (1956:156).

33. In a letter written on the twenty-sixth, Coope said government schools were rejected, which reflected either a misunderstanding on her part or a changed decision thereafter (Coope to Jeffrey, 5/26/15, in Keeler (1956:156); Coope (1917:158-161).

34. In Keeler (1956:156).

11. Colonization and Development

1. MGJ, 1916:LXXXIII-LXXXIV, 459, 463.

2. Navas to Hurtado, 9/02/15; Navas to Inspector of Port, Colón, n.d.; Navas to Governor Colón 9/07, 9/10/15; Exploración de Navagana y Mandinga, Federico Gutierrez B., Sept.-Dec. 1915; Int. to SecGJ, 11/10/15, AI.

3. For example, Informe Semestral, Int. Mojica to SecGJ, 1/21, 7/21, AN(?) (courtesy Francisco Herrera).

4. MGJ, 1916:LXXX-LXXXI, LXXXVI, 473-474; MGJ, 1918:LV-LVI.

5. Int. to SecGJ, 9/11/15, AI.

6. MGJ, 1918:LVI.

7. Documents bearing on a policeman's lot in San Blas include a petition to the intendente, 1/03/19, and Junca to Int., 6/25/20.

8. Linares to SecGJ, 2/14, 2/21/21, AI. Averiguación sumária formada para esclarecer las faltas cometidas por el Agente de Policía, no. 140, Sr. Enrique Barahona, el día 4 de Julio del presente año [sic], AI. John Major (1993:116-154) makes it clear that the condition of the national police also left much to be desired.

9. Int. to SecGJ, 10/31/15; SecGJ to Int., 11/11/15; see also SecGJ to Int., 8/12, 8/14/15; A. Mojica to B. Porras, 8/29/15, ABP; Muro to Int., 11/19/15, AI.

10. Ramón Garrido, Antonio Linares, Arturo Pérez, and Guillermo Denis, all of whom later played prominent roles in San Blas. Garrido had spent time in prison (GO, no. 1214, 9/02/10; Res. no. 129 of 8/31/10; Herrera 1984:113-114).

11. F. Gutiérrez to B. Porras, 11/09/15, ABP; MGJ, 1916:LXXXV-LXXXVI, 464, 471-473.

12. F. Gutiérrez to B. Porras, 11/09/15, ABP.

13. MGJ, 1918:LV.

14. MGJ, 1916:471-473.

15. MGJ, 1916:461.

16. MGJ, 1916:466; file 863, Corresp. of U.S. Consulate in Colón, 1925, RG84, NARS; Int. to Major Loring, 1/28/19; Int. to Manager, Colon Import and Export Co., 3/31/20, AI.

17. File 861.5, Corresp. of U.S. Consul in Colón, 1920, 1922, 1924, RG84, NARS.

18. B. Porras to E. Hurtado, 11/10/15, ABP.

19. File 890.602 F39, 1916-1917, NARS.

20. Ironically, the Japanese *had* secretly approached the Panamanian government, but the Panamanians had immediately notified the Americans and cooperated with them in dealing with the Japanese (E. Morales to B. Porras, 6/30, 7/10, 7/13/15; Morales to SecGJ, 6/30, 7/08/18; Porras to Morales, 7/24/15, ABP). I omit a brief episode in which a less erratic but unsavory Hungarian tried to revive the project: Memo, SecWar to State, encl. in State to W. J. Price, 1/08/17; Disp. 1244, W. J. Price to State 1/29/17, 890.602 F39. See also MGJ, 1916:LXXXVI, 476-481; MGJ, 1918:LVII.

21. MGJ, 1916:LXXXII; Drolet (1980:50).

22. Vander Laan (1927:45).

23. The archives of the Intendencia in Porvenir contain several such contracts from 1911. Some crews apparently worked directly for companies or individuals.

24. Hurtado to B. Porras, 10/04/15, ABP; MGJ, 1916:466.

25. Hurtado to B. Porras, 10/04/15, ABP; SecGJ to Int., 10/21, 11/08/15, AI; MGJ, 1916:467.

26. L. F. Muro to N. Navas, 7/21/15, AI.

27. L. F. Muro to Int., 11/19/15; A. Ayarza to Navas, 11/24/15; E. Sanchez to Navas, ll/24/15; C. Delisse to Navas, n.d. Also Navas to Correg. Santa Isabel, 8/16/15; A. Anderson to Navas, 9/06/15; Correg. Santa Isabel to Int., 9/16/15; Int. to Correg. Santa Isabel, 9/14/15; Correg. Santa Isabel to Int., 9/23/15 — all AI.

28. OH, Luis Walter. Correg. Santa Isabel to Int., 12/03/17, AI.

29. Hurtado to B. Porras, 10/04/15, ABP. C. Luis to Int., 11/09/15; A. Anderson to Navas, 9/06/15; Navas to Correg. Santa Isabel, 8/16/15; Int. to Correg. Santa Isabel, 9/14/15; Correg. Santa Isabel to Int., 9/16/15; Correg. Santa Isabel to Int., 9/23/15; L. F. Muro to Int., 11/19/15; statements in Porvenir 11/24/15a, 11/24/15b, n.d.; Navas to Correg. Santa Isabel, n.d./15; Sec. de la Circunscripción to Correg. Santa Isabel, 8/16/15; A. Anderson to Sec. de la Circunscripción, 9/06/15; Int. to Correg. Santa Isabel, 9/14/15; Correg. Santa Isabel to Int., 9/16, 9/23/15; Alfonso [illegible] to Cataño 10[?]/02/17, AI. OH, Carlos López; Inakeliginia (1997:75-76).

30. Hurtado to B. Porras, 10/04/15, ABP; MJG, 1916:467.

31. Hurtado to B. Porras, 5/17/16b, ABP.

32. MGJ, 1916:467-468.

33. Report to Inspector of Public Instruction, 1/16/17, AI.

34. Coope (1917:99-101); Keeler (1956:152-153, 161).

35. MGJ, 1916:461-462.

36. MGJ, 1916:462.

37. Int. to B. Porras, 12/20/15, ABP; SecGJ to Int., 9/24/15, in Ayarza (1981:41-42). The governor of the Colombian Department of Bolívar recorded a visit by Inabaginya in 1916: Ramón Rodriguez D. to José Vicente Concha, 11/25/16, J. V. Concha, Caja 13, Academia Colombiana de Historia, Bogotá (source courtesy of Eduardo Posada).

38. MGJ, 1916:LXXXV. Four years later Colombian boats were still sneaking into San Blas. Puyol to Int., 1/14/19; Int. to SecGJ, 5/20/19, AI.

39. SecGJ to Int., 8/12/15, AI; also 9/24/15, MGJ, in Ayarza (1981:40). Sec GJ to Int., 9/24/15, AI; MGJ, 1915 [?] in Ayarza (1981:40-42); Int. to SecGJ, 10/04/15, AI. B. Porras to Hurtado, 9/26/15; Hurtado to B. Porras 10/04/15; Hurtado to B. Porras, 9/15/15, ABP. Int. to SecGJ, 9/18/15, AI; MGJ, 1916:464.

40. Navas to Int., 8/26/15, AI.

41. Toma de posesión, 6/01/18, AI.

42. E. López, mss. "Algunos relatos," "Fechas de los caciques."

43. Robinson to President, 3/14/16, AN(?) (courtesy Francisco Herrera).

44. S&H, 1/26/17, encl. 2 in W. J. Price to State, Disp. 1244, 1/29/17, 819.602 f39, NARS. The article is in English. The language in which President Valdés's letter was originally written is unclear.

45. MGJ, 1918, as quoted in Ayarza (1981:58).

46. Porvenir, Circular no. 12, to Alcalde of Palenque, 1/11/19, AI.

47. Samuel Morris, intv., 1/28/89; conversations, Freddy Filos; E. López, misc. mss.; Hayans in Wassén (1938:42-43); Anon. ms. Stout's dating of the early 1920s is in error (Stout 1947:90). An intendente salaried a later teacher to encourage the school (Ten. Linares to Garrido, 6/09/20; MGJ, 1920:243).

48. Narciso Garay to Hurtado, 6/20/17, and MGJ, 1918, as quoted in Ayarza (1981:57-58).

49. Int. to Robinson, 9/17/17; Int. to Belisario Díaz, 9/18/17, AI.

50. C. Iglesias et al. to SecGJ, 1/30/21, AI.

51. Holloman (1969:263-264); Howe (1986:138).

52. Puig (1948:188-191).

53. E. López, ms. on Nargana: 49-50.

54. C. Iglesias et al. to SecGJ, 1/30/21, AI.

55. Colman, while firmly blocking the establishment of schools on Ailigandi, arranged for his own sons to be schooled elsewhere.

56. Herrera (1984:121); McCain (1937:73-75, 202); Major (1993:133-134, 138-139). As noted in chapter 8, vice presidents or designates were elected every two years by the National Assembly: Porras was elected first designate and thus acting president.

57. MGJ, 1918:LVI, 434; Registros de un poder especial, no. 89, 3/20/18; no. 64, 5/01/17, AI.

58. Herrera (1984:124); Diario, 8/25/10; S&H, 1/31/20; Int. to Correg. P.Ob., n.d./17, AI.

59. Int. to B. Porras, 12/23/19, ABP; Herrera (1984:124). Herrera detects veiled accusations of embezzlement in complaints by Cataño's successor (Herrera 1984:125; MGJ, 1920:244; and see Int. to Navas, 3/19/19).

60. V. Cataño to B. Porras, 11/14/18, ABP.

12. In the Nargana Cockpit

1. Complaint by Ramón Garrido, Porvenir, 1/04/19, AI.

2. Moreno de James to Int., 1/07/19; Int. to Maestra Escuela Mixta, 12/31/18, AI. I have made a few changes in the punctuation and grammar of Sra. de James's somewhat convoluted prose. Samuel Morris (Intv., 1/28/89) confirmed these events and even sang a little of the song.

3. Chenille and Chenille (1977); deLeón Madariaga (1980); Zarate (1962).

4. Moreno de James to Int., 1/07/19, AI.

5. Arturo Pérez to Int., 12/28/18, ABP. Some witnesses affirm that Robinson's police were already armed with bayonets. Garrido's complaint mentions only garrotes (untitled testimony, 1/13-1/14/19, untitled complaint by Ramón Garrido, 1/04/19, AI).

6. Untitled testimony, 1/13-1/14/19, AI. There are discrepancies in the testimony, which I have attempted to reconcile.

7. Int. to Porras, 12/29/18; Porras to Int., 1/03/19; Int. to C. Robinson, 12/29/18, ABP. Int. to A. Perez, 1/04/19, AI.

8. B. Porras to Int., 1/03/19, ABP.

9. Int. to SecGJ, n.d. [1/19/19 or 1/20/19], pp. 15-16, ABP.

10. Pérez and Denis to Int., 2/05/19, ABP; Claudio Iglesias et al. to Int., 2/05/19, AI. I have assumed that *somos regidos* rather than *regimos* was intended.

11. Int. to SecGJ, 2/15/19, ABP.

12. All Kuna islands had local village constables, but only Robinson's had been recognized as government agents during the time of President Valdés.

13. C. Iglesias et al. to Porras, 2/08/19, AI.

14. A. Pérez to Int., 3/27/19; G. Denis to Int., 3/30/19; Int. to Robinson, 3/31/19, ABP. G. Denis to Int., n.d./12/19, AI.

15. Int. to Robinson, 3/31/19; Porras to Int. 4/05/19, ABP.

16. G. Denis to Int., 3/30/19; Int. to Porras, 3/31/19; Int. to Coope, 3/31/19; Porras to Vaglio, 4/02/19, 4/05/19; Porras to Coope, 4/05/19, ABP.

17. Coope to Jeffrey, 4/16/19, in Keeler (1956:158).

18. Coope to Jeffrey, 9/19, in Keeler (1956:159); Garrido to Int., 4/01/19, AI.

19. Coope to Jeffrey, 4/16/19, in Keeler (1956:158).

20. "Convenio," 4/01/19, AI, ABP. Int. to Jefe 1st, 4/01, 4/07/19; Circular 1 of 1919, Porvenir; Int. to Coope, 4/07/19; Int. to SecIP, 4/11/19, AI. Porras to Int, 4/08/19; Int. to Porras, 4/13/19, ABP. Garrido to Int., 4/1/5/19; Int. to Jefe 1st, 4/12/19, AI. Int. to Porras, 4/25/19, ABP. Inspector General de Enseñanza Primaria to Int., 4/24/19, AI.

21. Colman to Vaglio, 2/01/19; Vaglio to Colman, 2/03/19, AI; Int. to SecGJ, 2/15/19, ABP.

22. Porras to Int., 4/02/19; Int. to Porras, 4/13/19, ABP. Porras to teachers, in Garrido to Int., 5/09/19, AI.

23. Garrido to Int., 5/09/19, AI.

24. In Vaglio to Porras, 4/17/19, ABP.

25. Garrido to Int., 5/23/19, AI. C. Iglesias to Int., 5/28/19, AI—the letter is erroneously dated April.

26. Moreno de James to Int., 6/02/19, AI. Coope called nose piercing "that horrible custom" but was otherwise fairly tolerant of native dress (1917:170, 173-175). See also S&H, 6/24/19; Moreno de James to Vaglio, 6/29/19, AI.

27. Hirschfeld (1977); Parker and Neal (1977); Salvador (1978); Sherzer and Sherzer (1976); Tice (1995).

28. *Diario*, 8/17-8/20/10.

29. Hurtado to SecGJ, 8/05/13, ABP.

30. See Vaglio to Colman, 2/03/19, AI. Arnold (1993); Foucault (1979).

31. Garrido to Int., 6/05/19; Int. to Garrido, 6/06/19, AI. Int. to SecGJ, 6/11/19, p. 5, ABP.

32. Garrido to Int., 6/21/19, AI.

33. S&H, 6/24/19.

34. Coope to Jeffrey, 6/19/19, in Keeler (1956:158).

35. For the sake of simplicity, I omit a brief episode at the end of June in which Vaglio had the ex-chief of Corazón, whom he had deposed in April, arrested and beaten (Int. to Porras, 6/29/19, ABP; OH, Alberto Campos).

36. Julio Carles to Int, 6/29/19; Guillermo Denis to Int., 6/29/19; Moreno de James to Int., 6/29/19, AI, ABP. Int. to SecGJ, 7/06/19, ABP.

37. Int. Samuel Morris, 1/28/89.

38. Julio Carles to Int., 6/29/19, AI, ABP.
39. Moreno de James to Int., 6/29/19, AI, ABP.
40. Linares to Int., 6/30/19, AI, ABP.
41. Linares to Int., 7/02/19, AI, ABP; Int. to SecGJ, 7/06/19, ABP.
42. Untitled interrogation of C. Robinson at Porvenir, 9/18/19; Int. to Porras, 6/04/19; Porras to Int., 6/09/19; Int. to SecGJ, 7/06/19, ABP.
43. Garrido to Int., 7/06/19; Circunscripción de SB, untitled, undated list of fines, AI, ABP. Porras to Int., 7/17/19, ABP.
44. Int. to Jefe 1st, 7/19/19, AI.
45. Garrido to Int., 8/21/19; Int. to Porras, 8/23/19; Int. to Porras, 9/05, 9/16, 9/18/19; Porras to Int., 9/11, 9/12, 9/26/19; untitled interrogation of C. Robinson at Porvenir, 9/18/19, ABP.
46. MGJ, 1920:240-241, 243-244. Vaglio began writing the report before the uprising, but since he let it stand, it presumably reflects his opinions afterward as well.
47. MGJ, 1920: 242.
48. S&H, 11/20/19. Int. to Porras, 12/02/19; Porras to Int., 12/10/19, ABP. Also Int. to Jefe 1st, 7/15/19; Int. to Coope, 4/07, 8/21/19, AI. When Purdy returned from leave, her complaints were to no avail: Purdy to Jeptha Dunca, SecInstPub, 1/29/20; Int. to Duncan, 2/16/20; Duncan to Int., 4/09/20; Int. to Duncan, 2/16/20; Duncan to Purdy, 3/08/20, AN(?) (courtesy Francisco Herrera). Int. to Duncan, 4/20/20, AI.
49. Iglesias and Vandervelde (1977); Keeler (1958:158-159); Morgan (1958:46-47); Vandervelde and Iglesias (1983:30-31).
50. Informe semestral, Int. to SecGJ, 6/30/22, ABP. Also SecGJ to Int., 6/30/23, AI.

13. Humberto Vaglio Takes Charge

1. Porras to SecGJ Ricardo Alfaro, 11/06, 11/09, 11/11/18; SecGJ to Porras, 11/09/18, ABP.
2. *Verdadero adefesio*, Vaglio to Porras, 12/23/18, 1/20/19; Vaglio to SecGJ, c. 1/20/19, ABP.
3. Int. to SecGJ, c. 1/20/19, ABP; MGJ, 1920:236-256;
4. Int. to SecGJ, 2/01, 5/20, 5/31, 6/22, 6/31/19; Int. to Jefe 1st, 4/16/19; Jefe 1st to Int., 4/19, 4/23, 7/08, 9/10/19; Int. to Enc. 3d, 5/17/19; Colman to Int., 7/07/19; Enc. Porvenir to Capitán Puerto Colón, 7/23/19; Decree no. 5, 5/27/20, AI.
5. Decree 28, 2/25/20; Int. to SecGJ, 1/19, 1/27/20; Int. to Dir. Genl. Censo, 4/01/20; Int. to Jefe 1st, 4/24/20; Int. to Jefe 3d, 3/29, 4/24/20; Jefe 2d to Ten., enc. 5/08/20; Jefe 3d to Int., 5/10, 5/20/20; Inap to Int., 5/12/20, AI. The official census total for San Blas was 17,716; Vaglio said his men had counted more than 30,000 the year before. The first figure is more plausible.
6. Int. to Jefe 3d, 1/05/19; Int. to Jefe 2d, 1/05/19; Jefe 2d to Int., 1/15/20; Jefe 3d to Pres. Directorio Liberal, 2/08/20; Int. to SecGJ, 8/04/20, AI. Given the small number of voters overall, a few hundred votes from San Blas could influence totals in the province of Colón. In 1924 an opposition party charged that the 1920 vote in San Blas was illegal (in 819.00/1126). In the 1924 elections Kuna voted on several pacified islands.
7. Int. to SecGJ, c. 1/20/19, p. 14, ABP.
8. MGJ, 1920:236, 241.
9. A name no longer in use today, perhaps the community otherwise known as Narasgandup Dummad, "Big Orange-Grove Island," which had defied Porras and Colman in 1915.
10. Int. to SecGJ, 1/29/19, ABP. Colman to Int., 2/01, 2/02, 2/04/19; Statement, 1/28/19, AI.
11. Colman to Int., 2/01, 2/02/19; Int. to SecGJ, 1/30/19; Ten. enc. to Colman, 3/12/19; Colman to

Ten. enc., 3/11/19; Int. to Jefe Almacén General, 11/04/19, AI. Int. to Porras, 2/03/19; Int. to SecGJ, 2/03/19, ABP.

12. Porras to Vaglio, 1/03, 2/03/19. The ambivalence is also marked in Porras to Vaglio, 4/29/19, ABP.

13. MGJ, 1920:236, 241.

14. Vaglio to Porras, 6/08/19, ABP.

15. *Saguila* is Vaglio's spelling for *sagla*, the Kuna word for chief.

16. MGJ, 1920:241; Jefe 3d to Int., 6/07/19; Jefe 1st to Int., 6/21/19; Inabaginya to Int., 10/28/19; Int. to Inabaginya, 6/23/19, AI.

17. Int. to SecGJ, 1/28/20, AI.

18. Petition to Int., 1/03/19, AI. Also Int.[?] to Andreve, 11/16/16, AI.

19. Int. to Administrador Provincial de Hac, 2/01/19; Int. to SecGJ, 1/21, 2/01, 6/22/19; SecGJ to Int., 2/10/19, AI.

20. Int. to SecGJ, 1/11/19; Int. to SecGJ, 2/03/19, AI. Int. to SecGJ, 1/07, 2/04/19; Correg. to Int., 1/04, 1/20, 4/18, 5/01/19; Int. to Auxibio Puyol, 4/08/19, AI.

21. Int. to Porras, 2/06, 2/07/19; Porras to Int., 2/10/19, ABP. Int. to SecGJ, 2/07/19; Enc. Porvenir to SecGJ, 3/08/19, AI. Int. to Sub-Agente Fiscal, 11/18/19, AI. Porras to Int., 1/23, 7/07/19; Int. to SecGJ, 6/28/19; Int. to Porras 5/07, 6/28/19, ABP.

22. Int. to SecGJ, 4/17/20; Linares to SecGJ, 7/20, 11/20/20, AI.

23. Jefe 3d to Ten., 2/26, 3/06/20; Int. to SecGJ, 3/20/20; Investigation, 6/25/20, Pérez to Ten., 7/15/20; Int. to SecGJ, 7/03/20; Head 3d to Int., 9/16/20; Int. to W. Powelson, Mandinga 3/n.d./20; Linares to SecGJ, 10/19/20; Linares to SecGJ, 11/16/20; Linares to SecGJ, 12/18, 12/30/20; AI.

24. Int. to Jefe 3d, 1/17/20; Jefe 3d to Int., 2/26/20, AI.

25. Int. to SecGJ, 4/04/19, 11/14/20, AI.

26. Int. to SecGJ, 4/26/19, 3/21/20, 5/10/20; Jefe 1st to Int., 5/16/20; Jefe 3d to Int., 5/20/20; Ez. Pérez to Ten. Jefe, 3/23/20, AI.

27. Int. to SecGJ, 3/25, 5/16/19, 3/27, 5/10/20; SecGJ to Int., 5/24/19, AI.

28. Int. to SecGJ, 1/20, 5/04, 5/n.d., 6/12/19, 1/28, 2/25/20; SecGJ to Int., 2/10, 2/20/19; Ruan, Agente Fiscal to Int., 6/16/20, AI. Int. to Porras, 12/18/18, 4/21, 5/04/19; Int. to SecGJ, 12/23/18, 4/21, 5/04/19; Porras to Int., 1/06, 4/29/19, ABP. MGJ, 1920.

29. MGJ, 1920:244-252; Int. to SecGJ, 5/31, 6/22/19, 6/08, 11/14/20, AI.

30. Ten. enc, to Jefe 3d, 5/11/20; Vaglio arranged to pay the salary of the teacher on Ustupu/Portogandi, but the school was controlled by the community, not the government.

31. B. Guillén to Int., 1/03/19; Int. to B. Guillén, 1/06/19, AI. Int. to SecGJ, c. 1/20/19; Vaglio to Porras, 2/03/19; Porras to Vaglio, 2/10/19, ABP.

32. Vaglio to Porras, 4/10/19; Vaglio to SecGJ, 4/10/19, ABP.

33. Jefe 1st to Int., 4/15/19, AI. Vaglio to Porras, 4/21/19; Porras to Vaglio, 4/29/19, ABP.

34. Vaglio to Porras, 6/04/19; Porras to Vaglio, 6/07/19, ABP.

35. Informe semestral que presenta el Jefe de la Circunscripcíon de San Blas al Señor SecGJ 7/19, ABP; MGJ, 1920. Paragraphing has been modified.

36. Int. to Olonibiginya and Tibin, 7/17/20; Int. to SecGJ, 7/20/20; Jefe 3d to Int., 5/20/20; Jefe 2d to Int., 5/17, 5/26, 6/06/21, AI. Vaglio's successor complained in similar terms: Report, Mojica to SecGJ, 7/21, AN(?) (courtesy Francisco Herrera).

37. MGJ, 1920:241; Int. to Porras, 4/21/19.

38. For example, Colman to Int., 3/22/20, AI.

39. Int. to Alcalde Palenque, 1/11/19, AI.

40. Colman to Int., 2/04, 2/09/19, AI. Porras to Vaglio, 1/07/19; Vaglio to Porras, 4/10/19; Vaglio to SecGJ, 4/10/19, ABP.
41. B. Porras to Santiago de la Guardia, 9/15/19, Tomo 13, Folio 308, ABP (courtesy Francisco Herrera).
42. Contract between C. Colman and J. de la Rosa, seen at intendencia in Porvenir, 5/29/20, copy dated 8/13/20; date of contract unclear, possibly 3/05/19.
43. Int. to SecGJ, 9/01/19; Vaglio to Porras, 1/16/19, ABP.
44. Int. to SecGJ, 9/01/19; Vaglio to Porras, 1/02/19; Porras to Vaglio, 1/06/19; Vaglio to Porras, 1/16/19, ABP.
45. Int. to SecGJ, 5/14, 7/13, 7/20/20; Linares enc. Porvenir to SecGJ, 5/29, 10/18, 11/27/20, AI.
46. SecGJ to Colman, 8/12/20, AI.
47. Inabaginya to Int., 5/23/21, AI.
48. For example, Vaglio to Porras, 1/11/19; B. Porras to Vaglio, 1/16/19, ABP.
49. Int. to SecGJ, 9/02/19; Int. to B. Porras, 9/05/19, ABP.
50. B. Porras to Vaglio, 9/12/19, ABP.
51. Vaglio to B. Porras, 9/16/19, ABP.

14. Confrontation and Embitterment

1. Sources include interviews (especially intv. Alberto Campos, Eliberto Gonzalez, et al., 2/23/91), some of them summarized in Howe (1974:66-67); two oral narratives (OH, Camilo Porras, Alberto Campos); a narrative of the incident by Padre Jesus Erice (n.d.) found in the archives of Porvenir and apparently written on the basis of documents in mission archives and perhaps interviews with one of the policemen involved; a contemporary newspaper article (S&H, 11/18/19); a letter by the missionary Anna Coope (Coope to Jeffrey, 11/19, in Keeler 1956:159); several letters and reports in the archives of the intendencia (Garrido to Int., 11/11/19a&b; Int. to Colman, 11/12/19; Garrido to Int. 11/16/19; Carles to Linares, 11/16/19, AI); and several more in the Porras archives (Int. to Porras, 11/12a&b, 11/15, 12/16/19; Int. to SecGJ, 11/12a&b, 12/01/19; Porras to Int., 12/22/19). See also Herrera (1984:196-198).
2. Infanticide did occur from time to time among the Kuna, always in secret: midwives would bury an infant that emerged deformed or albino. No one took the practice lightly, however.
3. OH, Alberto Campos. Kuna women, in their loose blouses, can conceal their condition so well that children and sometimes even adults may not be aware.
4. OH, Alberto Campos.
5. OH, Alberto Campos.
6. Int. to SecGJ., 12/01/19, ABP.
7. S&H, 11/18/19.
8. Int. to Pres., 12/16/19; Acosta to Int., 12/12/19; Res. no. 1 of 12/26/19; Porras to Int., 12/22/19, ABP. Int. to Acosta, 12/27/19, AI.
9. Productos exportados de la Circunscripción de San Blas para el puerto de Colón durante los años de 1919 y 1920, AI. The figures should be taken as very rough indicators only.
10. Guillermo Denis to Int., 4/19/19; Int. to Jefe 1st, 4/21/19. Also Jefe 1st to Int., 5/03/19, AI. As always, these figures do not include products extracted illegally or smuggled out without paying tax.
11. Decree 2, 3/05/20. Linares to J. Molinar, 4/05/20; Int. to Comisario enc. Santa Isabel, 8/20/19, AI.
12. Agent J. Sanchez to Int., 12/06, 12/12/19; Jefe 3d to Int., 3/21/20, AI.
13. Int. to Jefe, 3d 12/03/19; Jefe 2d to Int., 1/19, 1/20/20, AI.

14. Jefe 3d to SecGJ, 1/17/20; Jefe 2d to Int., 1/20/20; Int. to SecGJ, 2/04/20, AI.
15. Jefe 3d to SecGJ, 1/17/20; Int. to Jefe 2d, 1/20/20; Int. to SecGJ, 1/22, 1/28/20; Int. to Jefe 3d, 3/09/20; Jefe 2d to Int., 1/18/20, 1/23/20, AI.
16. S&H, 1/31, 2/02, 2/03/20. Jefe 2d to Int., 1/20/10; Jefe 1st to Int., 1/21/20; Int. to SecGJ, 1/22/20, AI.
17. Rendered more accurately, "Tule soge, sippu Arabi masuli" (S&H, 2/14/20). The sentence is telegraphic, probably because it had to be repeated slowly to the reporter. "The white man's boat, the *Arabia*" could also have been intended. The *Arabia* belonged to the company in Mandinga.
18. Jefe 2d to Int., 1/27/20; Int. to SecGJ, 2/04/20, AI.
19. Int. to SecGJ, 1/22/20; Inabaginya to Jefe 3d, 1/n.d./20; Jefe 3d to Int., 1/17/20; Jefe 2d to Int., 1/19, 1/20/20; Int. to Jefe 2d, 1/20/20, AI.
20. Ten. enc. to Jefe 3d, 3/06/20; Int. to Jefe, 3d 3/16/20, AI.
21. Int. to SecGJ, 3/31, 4/10/20; SecGJ to Int., 4/05/20, AI.
22. Linares to SecGJ, 5/29/20; Int. to Jefe 3d, 5/14/20, AI.
23. Int. to Colman, 3/26/20; Int. to Jefe 1st, 4/06/20, AI. Linares to Porras, 10/12/19; Porras to Int., 11/12/19, ABP.
24. Int. to Jefe lst, Jefe 3d, 6/20/20; [Illeg.] Sta. Isabel to Int., 4/13/20; Jefe 1st to Int., 5/17/20a&b, Colman to Int., 3/22/20; SubsecGJ to Jefe, 3d 7/07/20; Inabaginya to Jefe 3d, 5/10, 8/28, 9/01/20; Jefe 3d to Int., 9/08/20, AI.
25. SecGJ to Int., 1/29/20; Int. to SecGJ, 2/05/20; Jefe 2d to Int., 1/30/20, AI; intvs. Mateo Brenes 1970-1989.
26. Int. to Jefe 1st, 3/22/20; Jefe 1st to Int., 3/23/20; Int. to SecGJ, 3/26/20; Int. to Colman, 3/26/20; L. Person to Supt. Plantation, n.d.; R. Elliot to M. Tiernan, Mandinga, 3/11/20; M. Tiernan to Int., 3/11/20; Int. to Tiernan, 3/12/20; SecGJ to Int., 3/09/20; Int. to SecGJ, 3/13, 3/20/20; Int. to SecGJ, 5/14/20; ? Tupile to Int., 5/19/20; Ten. to Jefe 3d, 6/05/20; Int. to Jefe 2d, 4/24, 5/11/20, AI.
27. Int. to SecGJ, 5/14/20, AI; OH, William Archibold. Inakeliginia (1997:65).
28. Res. 3 of 5/13/20; Int. to Jefe 3d, 5/14/20; ? Tupile to Int., 5/19/20; Jefe 2d to Int., 5/23/20; Jefe 3d to Int., 5/20/20, AI.
29. Nele to AmLeg, n.d./25, AmLeg R800-San Blas.
30. Juez 2d Circ. to Int., 5/17, 5/24/20; Ten. to Jefe 3d, 5/19, 5/20/20; Jefe 3d to Int., 5/26/20; Ten. enc. to Jefe 3d, 5/20/20; Enc. Tupile to Ten. enc. Porvenir, 5/27/20, AI.
31. OH, William Archibold. This extremely useful text illustrates the strengths and weaknesses of oral history, since some details are correct, others wildly off.
32. Ten. enc. to SecGJ, 5/29/20, AI.
33. Ten. enc. to SecGJ, 5/30/20, AI.
34. Segundo Juez de Circuito to Int., 6/02/20; Int. to Colman 6/07/20, AI.
35. Agent E. Pérez to Jefe 2d, 5/24/20; Jefe 2d to Int., 7/07/20, AI.
36. MJG, 1920, in Ayarza (1981:50-51).
37. SecGJ to Int., 7/10/20, AI.
38. Int. to SecGJ, 7/16/20; Acts of Investigation, Tupile and Playón Chico, 7/18/20, AI.
39. Int. to SecGJ, 7/20/20, AI.
40. Several months later, after Junca had angered his superiors, many of the previously rejected accusations were trotted out again and confirmed. SecGJ to Int., 7/10/20; Int. to SecGJ, 7/16/20; acts of investigation, Tupile and Playon Chico, 7/18/20, AI; Junca to Int., 4/28/20; Int. to Junca, 5/07/20; Linares enc. to SecGJ, 11/16/20. SecGJ to Colman, 8/12/20, AI.
41. Pres. E. T. Lefevre to Sec. Alfaro, in SecGJ to Int., 7/06/20, AI.

42. Ten. enc. to SecGJ, 9/25/90, AI. Informe Semestral, Int. Mojica to SecGJ, 1/21, AN(?) (courtesy Francisco Herrera).

43. Ten. enc. to SecGJ, 10/06/20, AI.

44. OH, Antonio Orán.

45. Interviews and oral narratives from Manuel Paredes, Manuel González, Simon Avila. Manuscripts include "Biografia del Sr. Manuel González" (provided by the late Sr. González), and E. López, "Biografia del Saila Olonabdibler," "Biografia del Saila Olobanique," AEL; G. Hayans, "Reseñas históricas . . . ," Archives of Chany Edman.

46. Olobanikke to President, 7/01/19, AI. For the sake of simplicity and consistency, in citing letters to and from Kuna with traditional names, I stick to the spelling used in the text of this book (here Olobanikke), even if a different spelling (Olopanique) is used in the letter.

47. Jacinta Aguilar to Int., 9/02, 9/06/19; Int. to J. Aguilar, 9/05/19; Manuela Frago to Int., 12/10/19, AI.

48. J. Aguilar to Int., 10/31, 12/n.d./19; Int. to J. Aguilar, 9/05/19, AI.

49. Int. to Olobanikke, 11/10/19; Juan Sanchez to Int., 11/21/19; 12/06/19. To keep the narrative focused and short, I have omitted several episodes that occurred during these months.

50. E. Pérez to Jefe 2d, 5/24/20; M. Frago to Jefe 2d, 5/24/20; Jefe 2d to Ten. enc., 5/24/20, E. Pérez to Ten. enc. 6/n.d., 6/05/20; Ten. enc. to SecGJ, 5/27, 6/10/20; Jefe 2d to Int., 7/07/20, AI.

51. The most complete source on the incident is the record of police investigations, "Las declaraciones tomadas sobre el ataque de los agentes de Colman en Playón Chico contra la Policia Colonial destacada en la misma isla," 9/25-10/10/20, and the record of judicial proceedings found in the same file from the Panamanian national archives—received courtesy of Francisco Herrera. Also useful are Linares Ten. enc. to SecGJ, 9/25, 10/06/20; SecGJ to Ten. enc. 9/29/20, AI. The latter letter includes a memorial by José de la Rosa, 9/28/20, and letters by Eduardo Montecer, 9/23/20, and Olonibiginya to J. de la Rosa, 9/27/20. Also Informe Semestral, Int. Mojica to SecGJ, 1/21, AN(?) (courtesy Francisco Herrera), also in Herrera (1984:273-282). I have benefited greatly from Francisco Herrera's detailed and insightful analysis of the incident (1984:149-160). See also Inakeliginia (1997:82-83).

52. Letter from Eduardo Montecer, Tupile 9/23/20, AI; 2d Juzgado Colón, 9/27/20, complaint by Sosip Harris, in "Las declaraciones," reproduced in Herrera (1984:152, n. 226). Jefe 2d to Int., 5/17/21, AI. A report from the following year does mention twenty-three noserings confiscated from Tupile women in 1920 (Int. to SecGJ, 5/02/21, AI).

53. Juzgado Segundo del Circuito de Colón, "Denuncio presentado por el indio Sasip Harris contra el agente de Policia Colonial de apellido Castillo, por el delito homicidio perpetrado en la persona del indio Olo Inquique," 9/27/20, AN.

54. SecGJ to Ten. enc., 9/29/20, AI.

55. Linares to SecGJ, 10/06/20, AI. I have cleaned up slightly Linares's grammar.

56. Testimony by second witnesses (name unknown, page missing), Iguaniaitiquinape [Igwaniadiginappe], Iguaniciquina [Igwanigiginya], Quilo Cerrety [Gilu Serredi], Fabricio Arosemena. The judicial review probably reached the correct conclusion. Even hostile Kuna witnesses tended to corroborate police allegations, and a number of plausible details, such as the medical practicant's enumeration of the bruises on Castillo's body, are quite persuasive. While one may doubt whether agents were hauling Susu into the gathering house for a friendly discussion, a number of Kuna witnesses testified that Colman and other rebels had encouraged an attack, and that hours before the incident, Susu, Oloingikke, and others had met to plan their actions.

57. The last memo that has come to light is dated 1/07/21, AI.

58. Int. to SecGJ, 2/08/20, AI.

15. The Death of Claudio Iglesias

1. Int. to SecGJ, 1/17/21, AI.
2. Int. to Jefe 1st, 1/17/21; Int. to Jefe 2d, 1/17/21, AI.
3. Mojica to B. Porras, 10/13/22, ABP; Andreve (1926:342); Scoullar (1916-1917:389). No. 44, "Leaders," no. 128, 2657-M-39, Series 64-65, General Records 1906-1948, Office of Director of Intelligence, NARS; 819.00/447-515, NARS. Ortega (1965:31).
4. For example, Porras to Mojica, 9/08, 12/22/21; Mojica to Porras, 10/19/21, ABP.
5. Int. to SecGJ, 5/23/21, AI.
6. Int. to SecGJ, 1/24/21, AI. Jefe 1st to Int., 3/27/21, AI.
7. Int. to Jefe 1st, 3/29/21; Int. to C. Iglesias et al., 3/29/21; Int. to SecGJ, 4/02/21, AI. MGJ, 1922.
8. Coope to Jeffrey 4/21, in Keeler (1956:160).
9. C. Iglesias et al. to SecGJ, 1/30/21; Int. to SecGJ, 1/31, 6/20/21; SecGJ to Int., 2/14/21, AI.
10. Jefe 2d to Int., 6/06/21; Int. to SecGJ, 1/31/21, AI.
11. Erice (1951), in Herrera (1984:169).
12. In Keeler (1956:160). Also Erice (1951:6), in Herrera (1984:168).
13. Juzgado Segundo del Circuito, Colón, Diligencias en averiguación del autor de los hechos de sangre ocurridos en la Isla de "Río Azúcar" entre los indios y la Policia Colonial e Indígena del Primer Destacamento, Circunscripción de San Blas, 29 de Abril de 1921. Also OH, Carlos López; OH, David Díaz; OH, Sir Willis; Keeler (1956:160); Herrera (1984:160-181); Intv., Samuel Morris, 1/89. Inakeliginia (1997:79-81). I have not seen Erice's article (1951) on the incident; many of its essential points are summarized by Falla (n.d.:41) and critically examined by Herrera (1984:160-181), whose painstaking unraveling of the action I have used extensively. Carlos López's oral history, though mistaken on a few points, has considerable useful detail. The oral account by David Díaz is clear and generally reliable. Coope's letters (in Keeler 1956:160), though subjective and in places confused, are vivid and useful. The hagiographical biographies of Alcibiades and Marvel Iglesias (Morgan 1958:47-48; Iglesias and Vandervelde 1977:15; Vandervelde and Iglesias 1983:32-33) offer distorted and fanciful accounts.
14. "Diligencias."
15. Gordón offered both a written report (in Jefe 1st to Int., 4/22/21) and a statement like that of other witnesses (in "Diligencias"), which differ only slightly. The quotations are from the written report, with a few interpolations from the statement. I have changed Gordón's punctuation and grammar in a few places and added paragraph breaks.
16. Erice (1951), as cited by Herrera (1984:172-173).
17. OH, Carlos López.
18. OH, Carlos López; Morgan (1958:47-48); Iglesias and Vandervelde (1977:15); Vandervelde and Iglesias (1983:32-33).
19. The letter or letters from which this passage derives are incorrectly dated "April 24th, 1920" by Keeler (1956:159). Several sources have it that Claudio and Agustín's bodies were "in pieces" (*goagwar*) (OH, Sir Willis, Carlos López), "mutilado" (Vandervelde and Iglesias 1983:33), or "ferozmente macheteados" (Falla n.d.) An official later claimed that one man had cut open Claudio's chest and chewed his heart into pieces (Alba to Garay, 11/30/23, in Castillo and Méndez 1962:58). These claims are probably exaggerated. Coope's letter precludes the possibility of dismemberment, and Samuel Morris, who viewed the body, stated in an interview (1/28/89) that it was in one piece. The depositions indicate that, in addition to inflicting machete wounds (in killing him, not afterward), the perpetrators chopped off two of Claudio's fingers to remove rings, whether to steal them or to save them for his family is unclear.

20. "Diligencias."

21. Int. to Juez Superior, 4/22/21, AI.

22. "Diligencias"; Int. to SecGJ, 4/22/21; Int. to Juez Superior, 4/22/21; Int. to SecGJ, 4/24/21, AI.

23. Unfortunately, I have not been able to obtain records of the judge's investigations, which are alluded to by José de La Rosa (in "Diligencias").

24. Juez 2o del Circuito to Int., 5/10/21; Int. to SecGJ, 5/11, 5/14, 6/20/21; Int. to Jefe 1st, 5/10/21, AI.

25. Int. to SecIP, 5/14/21; SecIP to Int., 5/23/21, AI.

26. Int. to SecGJ, 5/02, 5/09, 6/20/21; Jefe 2d to Int., 3/30, 4/25, 5/01, 5/06, 6/04, 6/06, 6/30, 7/09/21; Int. to Jefe 2d 4/05/21; Int. to SecGJ, 6/20/21; SecGJ to Int., 5/09/21; B. Porras to Int., 7/22/21, AI.

27. Jefe 2d to Int., 5/17, 5/26, 6/06/21; Int. to Jefe 2d, 5/31/21, AI.

28. Jefe 2d to Int., 5/03, 5/24, 5/26, 5/30/21; List of prisoners and punishments from 3/21 to 6/21, 2d Destac., 7/n.d./21; Int. to Jefe 2d, 5/26/21, AI.

29. Int. to SecGJ, 6/30/22, ABP.

30. Jefe 1st to Int., 5/18/21; Diligencias con motivo de las amenazas contra Ramón Garrido D. y Santiago Castillo Jefes del 1er y 2o Destac. respectivamente, 6/04/21; Int. to SecGJ, 6/20/21, AI.

31. Int. to Juez Superior, 8/15/21, AI. Only the intendente's reply has come to light.

32. *Est.*, 9/30/21, discussed in Herrera (1984:180).

33. "Diligencias."

34. "Diligencias."

35. Int. to SecGJ, 2/10/21; Int. to SecIP, 4/13/21, 4/28/21, 4/29/21; SecIP, 5/10/21, AI.

36. Int. to B. Porras, 7/23/21; B. Porras to Int., 7/28/21, AI.

37. "Claudio Iglesias ha muerto," *La Acción: Organo de los Cooperadores Salesianos de la República de Panamá,* attached to "Diligencias."

16. The Noose Tightens

1. For example, Int. to SecGJ, 2/01, 2/14, 3/28, 5/17/21; Int. to SecIP, 4/13, 5/02, 5/14/21, AI; Int. semiannual report to SecGJ, in Herrera (1984:281).

2. Int. to SecGJ, 6/30/22, ABP.

3. Coope to Porras, 9/07/21, in Castillo and Méndez (1962:37-44).

4. Coope to Porras, 9/07/21, in Castillo and Méndez (1962:43).

5. Coope and Purdy to Porras, 9/07/21; Price to Bennett, 9/12/21; Graham to Garay, 9/15, 10/22/21; Oliver and Kingsbury to British Legation, 9/15/21; Garay to Graham, 9/19/21; Garay to SecGJ, 10/24/21; Garay to [?] Legation, 12/08/21 — all in Castillo and Méndez (1962:33-50).

6. Bishop [Rojas y Arrieta] to Porras, 6/n.d./22, in Porras to Mojica, 6/20/22, ABP.

7. Garrido to Int., 6/19/22, in Mojica to Porras, 6/22/22, ABP.

8. Purdy to Unknown, 9/19/22, in Keeler (1956:165).

9. Purdy to Unknown, 9/19/22, in Keeler (1956:164-165); Vandervelde and Iglesias (1983:34-35).

10. Coope says Porras wrote suggesting she sell her mission to the government, a measure Mojica had urged in his annual report. Coope to Jeffrey, n.d./22, in Keeler (1956:157). Int. to SecGJ, 6/30/22, ABP.

11. Coope to Jeffrey, 3/09/23, in Keeler (1956:161). The account in Vandervelde and Iglesias (1983:34-35), though unattributed, is taken directly from Keeler.

12. Marsh diaries, 1925, pp. 11-12; Guardia Vega to Int., 6/30/23, AI.

13. Int. to SecGJ, 10/04, 11/14/23, AI.

14. Int. to SecGJ, 6/20/21; SecGJ to Int., 6/29/21, AI. Int. to Porras, 3/11, 5/06, 6/30, 10/10/22; Int. to SecGJ, 3/11, 6/30/22; Porras to Int., 3/18, 5/10, 10/14/22, ABP.

15. Int. to Porras, 3/11/22; Int. to SecGJ, 6/30/22, pp. 12–13, ABP. Ms. Guillermo Hayans, "Reseña histórica de la Isla Wichuwala . . . ," Archive Chany Edman. The island was later resettled by a different group of Kuna immigrants.

16. Int. to SecGJ, 10/11/22, ABP.

17. Int. to SecGJ, 10/11/22. ABP; Int. to SecGJ, 12/07/23, AI; OH, David Díaz, 10/06/85.

18. "Increasing Exports of Bananas from Colón/Cristobal," 4/21/23; "Increasing Banana Production in Colón Consular District," 10/03/23; "Review of Commerce and Industry for Quarter Ending 6/30/25"; "American Foreign Service Report" 9/06/24, 2/03/25; "Banana Production in Colón District," 8/20/25; "New Panaman Port of Entry in San Blas," 8/25; Confidential no. 6, 2/15/34— all in file 610, 861.5, Corresp. of U.S. Consul in Colón, RG84, NARS. *Panama Times*, 3/21/25.

19. Though linked to two different fruit companies, the plantations were not entirely separate. John Popham, successor to Jesse Hyatt, was president of both firms, and the treasurer of the eastern operations was an employee of Colon Import and Export, closely linked to the western plantations. In this era, before United Fruit and Standard Fruit merged, banana production was based on a complex and often impenetrable web of subsidiaries, partial subsidiaries, and other contractual arrangements. "Increasing Banana Production in Colón Consular District," 10/03/23, file 610, Corresp. U.S. Consul in Colón, 861.5, RG84, NARS. *Panama Times*, 3/21/25. Contrato 49, Ley 6a de 1923, GO 4100, 2/27/23, pp. 3151–3152. Porras to Int., 1/09/22, ABP. Jefe 3d to Barria, enc. Porvenir, 2/03, 2/16/24; Jefe 3d to Unknown 5/07/24; AEL. Hurtado to SecGJ, 11/23/25; Pres. Chiari to T. G. Duque, 11/30/25, AN(?) (courtesy of Francisco Herrera).

20. *Est.*, 8/28/24; American Foreign Service Report, 9/06/24, file 610, Corresp. of U.S. Consul in Colón, 861.5, RG84, NARS.

21. *Est*, 1/13/24.

22. Passenger lists, Porvenir, 7/01/24–9/30/24, AI. Lists include 279 "laborers," 179 of them Jamaican or "Inglés," 51 Panamanian, and 110 other nationalities. Passenger lists without occupational breakdowns include 335 Jamaicans and 184 Panamanians and other nationalities, all or almost all laborers. (Merchants and plantation management are excluded from these totals.) There were 47 female passengers, 32 Jamaican, and 15 Panamanian and other passengers, most classed as "domestico." The lists are inconsistent and sometimes unclear, so the totals are not exact.

23. San Blas Development Co. to Int., 8/06/24, AI.

24. Correg. POb to Int., 5/07/24, AI.

25. Jefe 2d to Int., 5/31/21; Int. to SecGJ, 6/08/21; Int. to Inabaginya, 4/11/23, AI. Jefe 3d to Int., 3/26/24, AEL.

26. Declarations of Cargo, Porvenir, 1924, AI. The corresponding figures for the second half of 1920 and the first half of 1921, respectively, were 604,600/118,450 pounds ivorynut, 904/2590 pounds turtle shell, and 7,968/3,425 pounds balata (Informe Semestral, Int. to SecGJ, 1/21, 7/21, AN(?), [courtesy Francisco Herrera]).

27. "Export Products from Colon, 1924"; "Annual Declared Export Return, Exports, Colon to U.S., 1923," "Review of Commerce and Industry for Quarter Ending 6/30/25," table, "Exports for Colon District, 1924-25," 1926, file 610, Corresp. U.S. Consul Colón, 861.5, RG84, NARS. American Foreign Service report no. 10, "Tagua Nut Trade," Corresp. U.S. Consul Panama, RG84, NARS. It should be noted that figures vary from one source to another, and even from one consular report to another, and so should be treated as approximations.

28. Jefe 2d to Int., 5/17, 5/20/21; Memorial by men of POb. to Int., 5/15/24; Int. to memorialists, 5/n.d., 6/24/24; Int. to Gordon enc. 3d, 6/24/24, AI.

29. Int. to SecGJ, 4/16, 5/01, 5/10/21; SecGJ to Int., 4/23, 5/09/21; Int. to Jefe lst, 4/29/21; Jefe 1st to Int., 5/22, 5/23, 5/28/21; Int. to Jefe 2d, 5/01/21; Jefe 2d to Int., 5/09, 5/19, 5/26, 5/31/21; Correg. P.Ob to Int., 5/06/24; Int. to Men P.Ob., 6/24/24—all in AI.
30. Int. to Porras, 5/10/23, AI.
31. Bulletin, "High Prices of Coconuts at Colon," 10/02/19; "Coconut Industry in Colon Consular District," 10/11/22; Consul to H. M. Black, 11/25/24; American Foreign Service Report no. 19, 2/03/25; "Reduced Coconut Exports from Colon," 4/04/25; "Coconut Production, Colón Consular District," 3/01/30, 861.3-861.5, Corresp. U.S. Consul Colón, RG84, NARS.
32. Erice (1975:380); Jefe 1st to Int., 4/01/24, AEL. Morales seems to have had fingers in several pies: a letter from 1924 lists debts owed him by police agents on Nargana, and a roster of cargos declared in Porvenir the same year shows him as consignee between August and December for a total of 55,000 coconuts (Declarations of cargo, Porvenir, 1924; M. Herrera, Nargana, to Int., 4/01/24, AEL).
33. Erice (1975:379-380).
34. R. Marsh, ms. "Declaration of Independence." Erice (1975:380).
35. E. de Garrido to SecGJ, 3/08/23, AI.

17. Pacification and Resistance

1. Even the Black inhabitants of Puerto Obaldía, who, as civilized Spanish-speaking citizens, escaped most of the interference experienced by the Kuna, complained of mistreatment (Memorial, 10/10/24, AI).
2. Unknown, Ailigandi to Unknown, AmLeg 4/03/25A, 1925, v. 6, R800 San Blas, NARS. Manuel Levid et al., Río Sidra, to Unknown 2/27/25; Olonibiginya to Unknown, 3/03/25; in Castillo and Méndez (1962:164-165, 168).
3. OH, Willy Archibold.
4. OH, Ailigandi Anon. 2.
5. Unknown [possibly Colman], Ailigandi to Unknown, 4/03/25, AmLeg, 1925, v. 6, R800 San Blas, NARS. I have changed the distracting "insolence" in the English original to insolent.
6. OH, Carlos López.
7. OH, Ailigandi Anon. 2.
8. OH, Ailigandi Anon. 2.
9. List of prisoners and punishments from 3/21 to 6/21, 2d Destac., 7/n.d./21. See also Olonibiginya to Unknown, 3/03/25, in Castillo and Méndez (1962:168). Keeler (1956:160).
10. OH, Willy Archibold.
11. OH, Ailigandi Anon. 2.
12. Jefe 3d to Sec enc., 1/16/24, 2/16/24; Int. to Jefe 3d, 1/07, 2/23/24; Jefe 3d to Int., 3/24/24; AI. Int. to Jefe 1st, 2/18/24; Serracín enc. 3d, to D'Croz enc., 2d 11/?, 11/18/24, AEL. Olonibiginya to Unknown, 2/n.d./25, in Castillo and Méndez (1962:162).
13. Inakeliginia (1997:90). The frequency of corporal punishment (never mentioned in official documents) is hard to assess: in the dramas with which the Kuna commemorate the 1925 rebellion, loud and bloody police violence dominates almost every scene. A few killings occurred, but not as summary executions.
14. Scott (1985, 1990). On resistance, see Adas (1992); Guha (1983, 1984); Keesing (1992). Also the discussion and references in chapter 1.
15. Int. to Jefe 2d, 5/31/21, AI.

16. Int. to Jefe 2d, 4/12/21, AI.

17. Jefe 2d to Int., 5/26/21, A1.

18. Intv., Fernando Ponce, 11/27/70.

19. Report, Int. to SecGJ, July 1921, AN(?) (courtesy Francisco Herrera); Jefe 2d to Int., 10/25/24, AI. OH, Willy Archibold. RGHd.

20. Cuadro de Presos, Río Cidra, Diciembre 1924, 12/31/24.

21. Int. to Garcia and Morales, 9/03/24, AI.

22. Int. to Jefe 1st, 3/28, 6/03/24, AEL.

23. Int. to Jefe lst, 9/04/24, AI.

24. *"Extralimitacíon de funciones,"* Int. to Jefe lst, 9/08/24a, AI. Also Int. to Jefe lst, 9/08b, 9/08c, 9/17, 9/19/24; Méndez to Int., 9/19/24; Méndez to Alberto Sandoval, 9/05/24, AI. Jefe 3d to Int., 3/22, 3/25, 3/27/24; Jefe 3d to Blackwood, 4/17/24; Int. to Herrera enc. 1st, AEL.

25. SecGJ to Int., 1/29/24; Int. to SecGJ, 2/18/24, AI. Also L. Salazar and Punapippi to Pres. Chiari, 2/27/25, in Castillo and Méndez (1962:166). Olonibiginya to Unknown, 2/n.d./25, in Castillo and Méndez (1962:162).

26. Int. to Juez Superior, 8/15/21, AI.

27. Int. to SecGJ, 6/30/22, ABP.

28. Int. to SecGJ, 10/11/22, ABP.

29. OH, David Díaz.

30. Investigation, 7/04/23, AI.

31. OH, David Díaz, 6/10/85. Minutes of meeting, 8/15/23, in Judicial file, lst Circ. of Colón, 12/14/22, pp. 12–13, AN.

32. Jefe 3d to Sec. enc., 1/16, 2/16/24; Int. to Jefe 3d, 1/07, 2/23/24; Jefe 3d to Int., 3/24/24; AI. Sec. enc. Porv. to Jefe 1st, 1/23/24; Int. to Jefe 1st, 2/18/24; Jefe 3d to Unknown, 2/15/24; Jefe 3d to Blackwood, 2/17/24; Jefe 3d to Sec. enc. Porv., 2/03/24, AEL. OH, David Díaz. Alba to Garay, 11/30/23; Olonibiginya and Oloaynayginya to Narciso Navas, in Castillo and Méndez (1962:55–64). Herrera (1984:200–201).

33. Chief of Río Azúcar to Unknown, 2/27/25, in Castillo and Méndez (1962:73–74).

34. OH, David Díaz. Oloaynayginya and Olonidiginya to Unknown, 11/28/23, in *Onmaked* 2:1.

35. Unknown [possibly Colman], Ailigandi, to Unknown, 4/03/25, AmLeg, 1925, v. 6, R800 San Blas, NARS.

36. OH, David Díaz.

37. Chief of Río Azúcar to Unknown, 2/27/25, in Castillo and Méndez (1962:73–74). Also in *Onmaked* 2;11.

38. Jefe 2d to Int., 5/01, 10/25/24; Dec. 5, 11/01/19; Dec. 7, 9/15/20, AI.

39. OH, Sir Willis. Also OH, Willy Archibold.

40. OH, Carlos López; Centro de Investigaciones Kunas, ms. I have corrected the first spy's name to fit the form given by most other sources.

41. See Howe (1986:72–75); Sherzer (1983:91–95).

42. See Howe (1986:83–84).

43. OH, Jimmy Solís.

44. OH, Samuel Morris of Ailigandi; OH, Jimmy Solís.

45. See Gramsci (1971); Guha (1983, 1984); Hendricks (1991); Keesing (1992:225–238); Taussig (1980); Urban and Sherzer (1991).

46. For a fuller presentation, see Howe (1994).

47. OH, Jimmy Solis. The sun is Great Father's helper or agent.

48. OH, Jimmy Solís.

49. OH, Jimmy Solís.
50. OH, Carlos López.
51. OH, Jimmy Solís.
52. OH, Carlos López.
53. OH, Jimmy Solís. The sentence that begins, "I supposed that . . ." actually came at the end of this passage, representing in effect an afterthought on the speaker's part. I have taken the liberty of interpolating it into its present place earlier in the passage.
54. OH, Samuel Morris of Ailigandi.

18. Dancing and Civilization

1. OH, David Díaz, in Spanish, concerning Río Azúcar in late 1923.
2. McCain (1937); Major (1993); Mellander (1971).
3. Garay (1982 [1930]:5–32).
4. Int. to Jefe 2d, 4/05, 7/09/21, AI. Int. to Porras, 10/10, 12/20/22, ABP. Denis to Int., 9/22, 10/01/23; Serracín to Int., 10/21/23; Int. to enc. Río Cidra, 10/02/23; Int. to SecGJ, 11/14/23, AI.
5. These aspects of the police program appear prominently in oral history and commemorative dramas.
6. Colman to Int., 7/07/19; Int. to Jefe 1st, 1/07/20; E. Pérez to Ten. enc., 6/05/20; Inabaginya to Jefe 3d, 8/28/20; Int. or Ten. enc. to SecGJ, 9/14, 10/06/20; SecGJ to Int., 1/13/21; Int. to SecGJ, 5/06/24, H. Méndez to Unknown, 9/03/24, AI.
7. Int. to Olobanikke, 11/10/19; Juan Sanchez to Int., 11/21, 12/06/19; Jefe 2d to Int., 12/16/19, AI.
8. McCullough (1977:464–468).
9. OH, Ailigandi Anon. no. 2. I have taken the editorial liberty of reversing the order of these two passages.
10. Adas (1989:260); Foster (1960); Mitchell (1988:63–94).
11. Jefe 1st to Int., 6/08/20; Int. to Coope, 6/10/20, AI.
12. For example, Decree 28, 2/25/20; Int. to SecGJ, 1/19, 1/27/20; Int. to Dir. Genl. Censo, 4/01/20; Int. to Jefe 1st, 4/24/20; Int. to Jefe 3d, 3/29, 4/24/20; Jefe 2d to Ten. enc., 5/08/20; Jefe 3d to Int., 5/10, 5/20/20; Inabaginya to Int., 5/12/20, AI.
13. Testimony, M. Frago, Acts of Investigation, 9/28/20, ANP (courtesy of Francisco Herrera). Although I emphasize the direct experience of police and teachers, the association of danger and disorder with drinking by subordinate peoples is old and widespread (Axtell 1985:64–67; Taylor 1979:28–72; Williamson 1984:209–211). Intendentes and higher administrators may also have been influenced by the example of North American Indian reservations and by the Canal Zone, which went dry in 1915. Mojica wrote of "the vice of alcohol, against whose use and abuse are today pledged governments and societies" (Int. to SecGJ, 2/22/21, AI). The struggles over drinking and prostitution involving U.S. soldiers in Panama, discussed by John Major (1993), may also be relevant.
14. Int. to SecGJ, 2/22/21; Jefe 2d to Int., 5/01/20; Int. to Jefe 2d, 5/07/20, AI. Alba to Garay, 11/30/23, in Castillo and Méndez (1962:57). Once prohibition had been decreed in San Blas, moreover, it was feared that any retreat on the issue would be taken as a sign of weakness.
15. In Erice (1975:287–288).
16. Int. to Porras, 4/10, 4/21/19; Int. to secGJ, 4/10/19; Jefe 1st to Int., 4/15/19; Porras to Int., 4/29/19, ABP; Int. to Jefe 1st, 4/02/19, AI.
17. SecGJ to Int., 9/29/20; Linares enc. to SecGJ, 10/06/20; SecGJ to Int., 2/04/21; Int. to SecGJ, 2/22/21, AI.

18. Int. to J. Bartling, Playa de Damas, 9/08/19; J. Bartling to Int., 9/10/19; Colon Import Co. to Int., 9/12/19; Garrido to Int., 5/01/19; Int. to SecGJ, 6/13/21, AI.

19. Junca to Int., 5/01/20; Linares enc. to SecGJ, 10/18, 12/20/20, AI. A raid on Niatupu is reenacted in its annual commemorations.

20. SecGJ to Int., 5/13/19; Vaglio to Coope, 6/10/20, AI.

21. Int. to SecGJ, 6/30/22, ABP. Semiannual report of Int. to SecGJ for 7/31-12/31/20, in Herrera (1984:278).

22. Hobsbawm (1983:271, 293-297; 1987:174-179).

23. Vaglio to Sec. Alfaro, 11/14/20, AI.

24. Arias (1996); Smith (1981).

25. E. López, ms. "Nombres."

26. Int. Mojica to SecGJ, 10/11/22; Int. to Pres. Porras, 10/11/22, ABP.

27. OH, Luis Walter, 6/08/85.

28. Res. l of 12/18/22, in Int. to Pres, 12/21/22, ABP.

29. For example, Biesanz and Biesanz (1955:378). The first club on Nargana was probably a hybrid between the youth faction and the evanescent Liberal Party clubs organized by policemen to support Belisario Porras in the 1920 elections.

30. Bakhtin (1984).

31. Sources on kinds of dancing on Nargana: Int. to SecGJ, 10/11/22, ABP; Markham, ms. IF/2905; S&H, 8/07/25; Garay (1982:13, 28). My wife June and I attended dances of this sort on Nargana in 1970.

32. Versions of this discussion of sexual predation were presented as talks at the Institute of Social Anthropology, Oxford University, November 1989, and the MIT Seminar on Peoples and States, December 1990. Among many useful comments and suggestions, I benefited especially from the remarks of a discussant, Gail Hershatter.

33. Chief of Tigre to Unknown, 3/25, R800-San Blas, AmLeg, NARS.

34. Guillermo Hayans, in Wassén (1938:54); see also Nordenskiöld et al. (1938:218, 222). The strongest accusations came through Richard Marsh, who was not objective concerning race and sex: Declaration of Independence and Human Rights of the Tule People of San Blas and the Darien (see chapter 27). Also Marsh to General Lassiter, 2/02/25, p. 2, Disp. 645, 819.00/1163; Marsh (1934:202, 232).

35. Garrido, Jefe 1st to Int., 6/07/21, AI. Estanislao López wrote that a policeman named Pomadero (that is, Pomareda) had in 1917 arbitrarily killed a male Kuna dissident (ms. Sucesos sangrientes).

36. E. Pérez to M. Gordón, Jefe 2d, 10/06/23, AI.

37. Record of investigation, Tupile, 10/[24?]/20. In a third incident not involving the police, two West Indian employees of the eastern banana plantations were accused of attempted rape. The case was immediately investigated, and the accused were arrested and sent to Porvenir. Cabeza, Jefe 3d to Intendente Mojica, 5/05/24; Int. to Jefe 3d, 5/15, 5/16/24, AI.

38. John Major (1993:148) has characterized the police reign in San Blas as "an orgy of rape and torture." My conclusion that rape occurred less often than claimed may be suspect or unpopular. I can only say the evidence overcame my initial assumptions. Apart from Richard Marsh, accusations of rape appear mostly in complaints to North American officials in early 1925. The Kuna could have learned from Marsh about North American attitudes and played up rape in their complaints to American officials (Gail Hershatter, personal communication). A complaint by the Woman's Club of Cristobal, probably engineered by William Markham (see chapter 19) mentions the seduction of minors but not rape (Mojica to SecGJ, 9/01/24, AI).

39. Oral testimony concerning two neighboring islands, for instance, suggests that the agents on

Tigre in 1924 were predatory but those on Niatupu, married men, were not (OH, Ceferino Villaláz, Mateo Brenes). Kuna today are usually less specific, saying that the police "touched the women" (*omegan ebusa*). Recorded complaints in the records of the U.S. legation in Panama (NARS) include notes by a legation officer on an interview with a Kuna chief, 2/25; Luis Bran and Santiago Pérez to Minister South, 3/07/25; Coope to U.S. Consul, Colon, 2/26/25; Anon 1, Ailigandi, 4/03/25; Letter Anon 2, Ailigandi, 4/03/25.

40. Letter Anon., Ailigandi to Unknown, 3/03/25, R800-San Blas, AmLeg.
41. Jefe 2d to Int., 5/03/20, AI.
42. Serracín enc. 3d to Int., 11/19/24; S. Guerrero to J. S. Garcia, 6/14/23; Int. to Frago, 1/14/21; Frago to Int., 1/25/21; Jefe 3d to Int., 9/16/20, AI. Porras to Neira, 4/08/24; Neira to Porras, 4/10/24; Porras to Neira, 4/21/24; Neira to Porras, 4/22/24, ABP (courtesy of Francisco Herrera). Int. to Jefe 1st, 9/08/24; Int. to SecGJ, 10/06/24, AI.
43. In contrast, a great many foreign observers have approved of Kuna sexual separatism, seeing it as a worthy example of "race consciousness."
44. Spelled *guacas* in the original.
45. Jefe 2d to Int., 1/28/20. The word "being" is my interpolation for a small gap in the microfilm.
46. Castillo to Ten. enc. Porvenir, 3/20/21, AI.
47. Int. to SecGJ, 9/01/24, AI.
48. Vasconcelos (1948).
49. Hale (1996:45). As with many of the topics covered in this chapter, there is a great deal more to be said on mestizoization. See esp. Gould (1996); Hale (1996); Smith (1996).
50. Jefe 2d to Int., 1/28/20, AI.

19. Friends and Agitators

1. OH, Carlos López, 3/85, and Mateo Brenes, 4/12/85; Ailigandi Anon. 1; Beach (1917); Herrera to Int., 6/21/24; Cabezas to Blackwood, 4/16/24; Gordón to Int., 10/13/24; Serracín to Int., 10/31/24, AEL. Seracín to Int., 9/10/24; Jefe 2d to Int., 9/28/24; Gordon to Int., 10/31/24; Jefe 1st to Sec. enc. Porv., 8/16/24, AI. Inakeliginia (1997:93).
2. Int. to SecGJ, 6/30/22, pp. 64-65; Cabeza to Int. informe, n.d. [5/22]; Cabeza to Int. informe, n.d. [6/22]; Int. to Porras, 6/07, 6/14/22; Porras to Int., 6/13, 6/17/22, ABP. Judicial file, 1st Circuit of Colón, 12/14/22, AN. Cabeza, Jefe 3d, investigation report, 7/n.d./22, in Castillo and Méndez (1962:n.p.). E. López, ms., "El origen," in Castillo and Méndez (1962:n.p.). Herrera (1984:181-188). OH, Ailig Anon. 1. Cabeza's report is reproduced in Panamá America, 2/15/76, with an erroneous date.
3. E. López, ms. "El orígen." Herrera (1984:182) shows that López's dates are erroneous, but his meeting transcripts appear reliable.
4. Cabeza to Int. informe, n.d. [6/22]; Res. 15, 6/04/22, in Judicial file, 1st Circuit of Colón, 12/14/22, AN.
5. OH, Ailigandi Anon. 2. It is my inference that the warning mentioned in this text was of Cabeza's mission. See note 7.
6. Presumably the pistol given him by President Porras in 1915.
7. Though the original says, ambiguously, "He limited himself just to replying with a carbine," I assume the consequences would have been more drastic if he had pointed the gun at Cabezas. Primary sources for the encounters on Ailigandi and Cabeza's second trip are OH, Ailig Anon. 1, and Cabeza to Int., 6/n.d./22, in Int. to Porras, 6/07/22, ABP. (See also Res. 15, 6/04/22, in Judicial

file, lst Circuit of Colón, 12/14/22, AN.) Despite differences in detail, agreement on crucial points persuades me they describe the same events.

8. Res. 15, 6/04/22, in Judicial file, lst Circuit of Colón, 12/14/22, AN.

9. Cabeza, Jefe 3d, investigation report, 7/n.d./22, in Castillo and Méndez (1962:n.p.).

10. Minutes of meeting, 8/15/22, in Judicial file, lst Circuit of Colón, 12/14/22, pp.12-13, AN.

11. C. Robinson et al. to Porras, 8/23/22, ABP, in Judicial file, lst Circuit of Colón, 12/14/22, pp. 12-13, AN. Porras to SecGJ, 9/07/22, AN.

12. Judicial file, lst Circuit of Colón, 12/14/22, AN.

13. The only available material on this suit is a manuscript fragment by Estanislao López (ms. untitled).

14. Porras to SecGJ, 2/23/24, ABP.

15. Mitchell Hedges (1923); Richmond Brown (1925).

16. Johnson (1958).

17. Richmond Brown (1925: 80-83).

18. Richmond Brown (1925: 65, 102, 155, 94, 156, 148).

19. Obeyesekere (1992).

20. Richmond Brown (1925:97).

21. OH, Ailigandi Anon. 1.

22. Richmond Brown (1925:99-101).

23. Richmond Brown (1925:119). See the acid review by Frank Speck (1926). A picture of Richmond Brown with the supposed daughter of a Chucunaque chief, for instance, was obviously taken on a coastal beach.

24. Richmond Brown (1925): title page; Pitt Rivers Museum, accession records 1924.46.

25. Markham, ms. untitled, Tioga Point Museum, Athens, Pa., cat. no. IF/2905, 28 pp., p. 1.

26. Markham, ms.IF/2905, p. 4.

27. Markham, ms.IF/2905, p. 5.

28. Markham, ms.IF/2905, p. 7.

29. Markham, ms.IF/2905, pp. 16-17.

30. Markham got the names for the two islands reversed in his narrative.

31. Markham, ms.IF/2905, p. 27.

32. Juzgado Superior, 8/18/23, "Sumario en averiguación del o los responsables del motín o levantamiento de los indios en RIO SIDRA, Circunscripción de San Blas, el 23 de junio de 1923," AN; untitled records of interrogations, Porvenir, 6/23-8/06/23, AN(?) (courtesy of Francisco Herrera); OH, Carlos López; OH, Luis Walter; Inakeliginia (1997:78).

33. OH, Luis Walter.

34. Chiari to Int., 7/03, 7/11/23; Int. to SecGJ, 7/03, 7/16/23, AI. Also sources given in note 32.

35. Markham to Porras, 2/01/24, with ms. IF/2905, Tioga Point Museum. Markham to Porras, Encl. 4, Disp. 659, 3/13/25, 819.00/1180.

36. Markham to Porras, 1/01/24.

37. Porras to Markham, 3/10/24, with Markham ms.IF/2905.

38. Int. to SecGJ, 3/07/24; Int. to Jefe 1st, 9/18/24, AI. Int. to enc. 1st, 3/07/24; Herrera enc. 1st to Int., 3/07/24, AEL.

39. Porras to SecGJ, 3/22, 4/26/24; Int. to SecGJ, 2/25, 4/24/24; SecGJ to Porras, 3/24/24, ABP (courtesy of Francisco Herrera); SecGJ to Int., 3/31/24; SecGJ to Int., 5/12/24; Porras to Int., 7/22/21, AI.

40. Int. to Jefe 1st, 9/19/24; Int. to Jefe 2d, 9/17/24. A long document from an opposition party (in 819.00/1126) includes accusations that in 1920 Mojica, then an important operative in the city, had helped rig the election, and that the voting organized on several Kuna islands was illegal.

41. Int. to SecGJ, 10/04/23, AI.
42. OH, Ailig Anon. 1.

20. A Glimpse of White Indians

1. G. Johannes, Chief of Police and Fire Div. Canal Zone to J. G. South, 80A-15, PC, NARS, date unclear; also in Treadwell to Whiteford, 10/22/23, file 861.7, AmLeg.
2. Marsh to State, 4/09/11, Marsh personnel file, 123.M35, DLAA, NARS; *Warsaw Bulletin,* 2/10, 2/24, 4/07/11, 1/19, 8/11/12. For material on Marsh and Warsaw, I am indebted to Barbara Cochrane of the Hancock County Historical Society, and especially to research by my mother, Ellen V. Howe.
3. *Warsaw Bulletin,* 1/31, 10/04, 10/11, 11/29, 12/13, 12/27/12; 1/17, 1/24, 2/07, 2/14, 4/25, 7/04, 10/03, 11/29, 12/12, 12/13/13; 1/02, 1/16, 3/07, 4/13, 4/20, 4/27, 5/15, 6/19, 7/03, 10/09, 10/23/14; 1/01, 4/05, 4/23/15. *Carthage Republican,* 1/28, 4/01, 7/01/14; Moore (1982).
4. *Warsaw Bulletin,* 2/05, 2/12, 2/19, 2/26, 4/05, 4/09, 4/16, 4/23, 5/28, 6/04, 6/21, 6/22, 7/02, 7/09, 7/23, 7/30/15.
5. Intvs., Richard Marsh Jr., 1/86; Charles Dejean Jr., Leon Haas, 3/21/88. *St. Landry Clarion,* 6/09/17, 12/08/17; *New Orleans Times-Picayune,* 6/07/17; *Warsaw Bulletin,* 5/24/12, 4/23/15. Clipping probably from the *Warsaw Bulletin,* Hancock County Historical Society. Norgress (1947:60, 63–69). Special thanks to Frank Elder. Records of 16th District Court, St. Landry Parish, Opelousas, Louisiana: Vendee Record no. 77374, J. U. Holse to R. O. Marsh, 6/06/16; no. 77796, Richard O. Marsh to Port Barre Timber and Tie Co., Ltd., 10/17/16. Vendor record no. 86072, Edwin J. Bomer to Richard O. Marsh, 5/01/20. Docket no. 22277, *Bomer-Blanks Lumber Co. vs. Richard O. Marsh,* 3/17/22. Docket no. 20809, *J. C. Schee vs. Port Barre Timber & Tie Co.* Docket no. 20813, *J. C. Schee vs. Richard O. Marsh.* Criminal Docket no. 8296, Inquisition of Coroner's Jury no. 607, 6/08/17, Inquest Book 2, p. 257, District Court Minutes, pp. 340, 381, 388, 415, 417, 419, 420. Docket no. 21114, *Dugos and LeBlanc Ltd. et al. vs. Port Barre Timber & Tie Co.,* 10/05/18. Vendor record no. 91966, correction of sheriff's sale, Port Barre Timber and Tie Co. to Dugos and LeBlanc Ltd., 10/16/19. Contract and Lease no. 86266, R. O. Marsh and E. J. Bomer to J. O. Nessen Lumber Co., 6/04/20.
6. Griffin (1988:276–277).
7. Brandes (1962:63–128, 1981); Burner (1979:183–189); Chalk (1970); Coates (1987:205–263).
8. Chalk (1970:63–64).
9. Chalk (1970:50); Treadwell, Hill, and Bennett (1926); Julius Klein to Sec. Commerce, 2/04/24, 621.2, RG-151, NARS.
10. Marsh (1934:7–10).
11. G. Johannes to Minister South, 80A-15, PC, NARS; Marsh, ms. "Primitive White People."
12. Marsh (1934:22–23).
13. Marsh (1934:10); Marsh photographic album. British capitalists had in fact already tried planting rubber elsewhere in the Darién (Méndez 1979:57; Treadwell, Hill, and Bennett 1926:188).
14. Marsh (1934:5); R. Marsh to R. Marsh Jr., 7/24/23; R. Marsh photographic album.
15. R. Marsh to R. Marsh Jr., 7/24/23; Marsh (1934:5–6).
16. The Spanish plural of Chocó is Chocoes, and some Spanish-speakers will refer to an individual as Chocoe. Marsh and other English-speakers misheard this as Chocoi. Chola is the feminine form of Cholo, a derogatory word for Indians or halfbreeds. The Wounán, another group called Chocó, do not figure in this story.

17. Marsh (1934:25).
18. Marsh (1934:26).
19. Marsh originally described the three as a mother and two girls (R. Marsh to R. Marsh Jr., 7/25/23); the photographs show that one is considerably older than the others.
20. In a contemporaneous letter, Marsh treats the encounter with the young women more matter-of-factly (R. Marsh to R. Marsh Jr., 7/25/23).
21. R. Marsh to R. Marsh Jr., 7/26/23.
22. Arosemena (1980); Harlan (1932); Keeler (1953, 1964a, 1964b, 1966, 1968); Keeler, MacKinnon, et al. (1963); Quinan (1924).
23. Torres de Araúz (1973) pointed out that the girls were Chocó not Kuna.
24. Marsh, ms. "Primitive White People," pp. 19, 21, 22. In letters written in Yaviza, Marsh also describes the girls as having "light-colored" skins like a tanned white person and brown rather than blond hair (R. Marsh to R. Marsh Jr., 7/25/23, p. 8; 7/26/23, p. 18).
25. Pistilli S. (1978).
26. Marsh (1934:19–22), and ms. "Primitive White People."
27. Marsh, ms. "Primitive White People." Markham, ms. IF/2905, p. 14; Richmond Brown (1925:64). In his manuscript from late 1923, Marsh mentions Markham and Mitchell Hedges without specifying when he spoke with them. In his book (1934:21–22), Marsh mentions wondering, while on his way to the Darién, whether Kuna picture-writing held the key to Maya hieroglyphs, which, if true, suggests he had already spoken with Mitchell Hedges. On the other hand, Marsh's reaction at the time to the Indian girls, as recorded in letters home (R. Marsh to R. Marsh Jr., 7/25, 7/25/23) seems less dramatic than the version later given in his book, suggesting that his interpretations solidified on return to the city. It is also likely that in 1923 or before Marsh was exposed to the imaginative ideas about Kuna albinos of Harold Johnson, who accompanied Mitchell Hedges to San Blas and later joined Marsh's expedition (Johnson 1958).
28. Marsh (1934:29–31).
29. R. Marsh to R. Marsh Jr., 7/24/23–7/28/23.
30. In a letter to his son (R. Marsh to R. Marsh Jr., 7/26/23), Marsh does not indicate unambiguously that they were the same girls as the previous night.
31. Marsh, ms. "Primitive White People" p. 30.
32. Marsh, ms. "Primitive White People," pp. 31–32.
33. The man was poling rather than paddling, which indicates that he had just emerged from the Río Chico, along which many Chocó lived. In a letter written that evening, Marsh said the man was "also light colored [that is, like the other indians in Yaviza], with long light brown hair" (R. Marsh to R. Marsh Jr., 7/26/23). The next day's installment (R. Marsh to R. Marsh Jr., 7/27/23) also indicates that his remarks about light skin and hair and nobility encompassed *all* the Indians of the Chucunaque and not just certain individuals. For some reason, this man is not mentioned in Marsh's book (1934).
34. R. Marsh to R. Marsh Jr., 7/26/23.
35. G. Johannes to Min South 80A-15, PC, NARS; Porras to Garay, 7/23/23, ANP; McCain (1937:180–183).
36. Garay to Porras, 8/09/23, ANP; G. Johannes to Min South, 80A-15, PC, NARS.
37. Isaza Calderón (1982:347–355); Marsh (1934:53); Westerman (1956:60–62).
38. Porras to Garay, 8/08/23; Garay to Porras 8/09/23, ANP. Whiteford to Treadwell, 11/19/23, 621.2, RG-151, NARS; G. Johannes to Minister South, 80A-15, PC, NARS. Reed to State, 8/21/23; Treadwell to Whiteford, 10/22/23; Johannes to Am. Minister, 11/07/23; South to State, 11/23/23, file 861.7, AmLeg. The deal may have conveyed exploitation rights rather than ownership.

39. G. Johannes to Min South, 80A-15, PC, NARS.
40. Marsh (1934:36-38). Surveying lands vital to canal security probably mattered most to the general.
41. Exts. to PanLeg Washington, 8/01/23; Alfaro to Exts. Panama, 8/06/23, ANP.
42. Garay to Porras, 8/07, 8/09/23; Porras to Garay, 8/08, 8/11/23, ANP.
43. Chalk (1970:153, 176-195); Coates (1987:233-234).
44. Whiteford to Treadwell, 11/19/23, 621.2, RG-151, NARS.
45. R. O. Marsh Jr., intvs., 5/84, 1/86.
46. Chalk (1970:153-154).
47. Marsh to Rush Rhees, Pres. U. of Rochester, 10/03, 10/11, 11/02, 11/19/23, n.d.; Rhees to Marsh, 10/08, 10/11, 11/20/23, Department of Rare Books and Special Collections, University of Rochester Library.
48. Marsh to "Director, Smithsonian Inst.," 11/01/23; W. de C. Ravenel to Marsh, 11/14, 11/27, 12/21/23, 1/07/24; Marsh to Ravenel, 11/20, 12/07, 12/17/23; W. Hough to Ravenel, 11/09/23, File 84900, Accession Records, Registrar 1834-1958, USNM, RU 305, SIA.
49. W. Hough to Ravenel, 11/09/23, File 84900, Accession Records, Registrar 1834-1958, USNM, RU 305, SIA.
50. J. L. Baer personnel file, Records of Dept. of Anthropology, Inactive Personnel, 1921-1964, USNM, NAA; OH, T. D. Stewart.
51. G. Kingsley Noble to G. H. Sherwood, Acting Director AMNH, 1/14/24; G. H. Sherwood to Marsh, 1/14/24a&b; Marsh to Am.Mus., 1/14/24, AMNH. Atz (1986). Intvs., Priscilla Breder, 10/84; James Atz, 7/09/87.
52. Marsh (1934:134).
53. Herbert (1989); Riffenburgh (1994); Rotberg (1970).
54. E. Cohen, Pathé News, to Ravenel, 12/13/23; Ravenel to Cohen, 12/18/23; article of agreement signed by Paul Benton, 1/04/24; RU 305, USNM Registrar, 1834-1958, Accession records, file 84900, SIA; RTU 1/10, 1/16, 1/26/24.
55. Klein to Sec. Commerce, 1/08, 2/04/24; H. N. Whiteford to R. Marsh, Brockport, N.Y., 1/12/24; Whiteford to J. Treadwell, Balboa, 1/12, 1/15/24; Cable, Whiteford to Treadwell, Buenaventura, 1/18/24; Julius Klein to Sec. Commerce, 2/04/24, 621.2, RG 151, NARS.

21. In the Darién

1. CMBdI:4-18; Baer to Hrdlička, 1/25, 2/22/24; Baer to Hough, 2/01/24, Hrdlička files, NAA; *The Campus* (Rochester Univ.), 2/29/24; Marsh (1934:39-57).
2. CMBdI:4-18
3. RTU, 1/10/24. Paragraph divisions deleted.
4. Baer to Hrdlička, 1/25/24, Hrdlička files, NAA.
5. S&H, 1/31/24.
6. Marsh to Mrs. Marsh, 1/29/24a&b; Davis, ms. pp. 5-6; unpublished map with airplane route traced; aerial photographs of Darién; Marsh (1934:42-50).
7. I have found nothing on the dispute with military authorities except Marsh's book and a manuscript from late 1924 (Davis ms.).
8. Marsh (1934:40-41); ROMd24a:9-10; *The Campus* (Rochester Univ.), 4/11/24.
9. Johnson (1958).
10. Since first writing this chapter, I have taken account in a few places of Michael Taussig's discussion of Marsh and the expedition (1993:144-175, passim). Insightful and in places brilliant, Taussig in

these pages is also frequently slapdash and misleading, and his remarks on the Kuna are demeaning.

11. Johnson (1925:30); Marsh (1934:66); *The Campus*, 4/11/24; ROMd24a:15-18; Townsend, RTU, 3/29/24.

12. Marsh (1934:64-65); ROMd24a:13,104; *The Campus*, 5/02/24.

13. Compare Taussig's remarks on this point (1993:156-60), which are characteristically both perceptive and—in the claim that "much of the population of the Darién . . . turns out to be a *lumpen*-refugee mass fled from the city"—exaggerated. See also Thomas (1991:178).

14. CMBd; Breder (1925, 1927, 1946).

15. ROMd24a:174, 93-94.

16. ROMd24a:32, 97, 190; Baer to Hrdlička, 2/22, 3/11, 3/28/24, Hrdlička files, NAA.

17. *The Campus*, 5/02/24; Fairchild diaries, 1, 2 & 3; ROMd24a:32, 203, 205.

18. O. E. Malsbury Report to Governor of the Canal Zone, 3/20/24, 67-C-80, PC, NARS.

19. ROMd24a:11.

20. ROMd24a:18.

21. ROMd24a:23ff.; RTU, 3/21/24.

22. ROMd24a:24-26, 122, 147, 149, 153-155, 158-161; *The Campus*, 5/02/24; Baer to Hrdlička, 2/22/24, Hrdlička papers, NAA.

23. ROMd24:101, 143ff., 185; HLFd3.

24. ROMd24a:20, 57, 92, 102.

25. ROMd24a:26.

26. Faron (1961, 1962); Harp (1994); Herlihy (1985, 1986, 1987); Kane (1994); Lowen (1972); Torres de Araúz (1975, 1980).

27. See esp. Stoler (1985, 1989, 1992, 1995).

28. Benton, RTU, 3/29/24.

29. Johnson (1925:30); HLFd2, p. 80; RTU, 3/17/24. "Indians presents" and "guady" are as in the original.

30. Adas (1989:159-165); Spurr (1994:35); Thomas 1991:87, 83-124.

31. HLFd2, p. 85.

32. Rochester Alumni Review, p. 82.

33. Marsh (1934:66-68); ROMd24a:26, 45, 55, 148. Taussig, in his florid discussion of Marsh and his expedition (1993:151-175, 193-199), makes much of Marsh's admiration for this man; for the sake of balance, it should be noted that Chocó rivermen do show remarkable strength and agility.

34. ROMd24a:31.

35. ROMd24a:33ff.

36. ROMd24a:41.

37. ROMd24a:43.

38. ROMd24a:51. For his book (1934:85), Marsh invented a sighting of white Indian footprints.

39. ROMd24a:60ff.

40. ROMd24:63-64.

41. ROMd24a:60-70; CMBdI:39-43; Johnson (1925); Marsh (1934:93-99).

42. ROMd24a:74.

43. Malsbury Report, p. 3.

44. Malsbury Report, p. 3; ROMd24a:74-88. In his book (1934:129-131), Marsh combined the accidental shooting and the encounter with the Kuna into one dramatic incident and put the trip up the Chucunaque back to late March in the narrative.

45. ROMd24a:137-138; HLFd2:88: Baer to Hrdlička, 3/11/24, Hrdlička Files, NAA.

46. S&H, 3/02/24; RTU, 3/14/24.
47. Marsh (1934:88-89); ROMd24a:13; HLFd2:80; RTU, 3/19/24.
48. ROMd24a:115, 110.
49. ROMd24a:120-121, 132.
50. Marsh (1934:112-120).
51. ROMd24a:101, 109, 124, 130. Interested readers should look at Taussig's fascinating discussion of the phonograph (1993).
52. Marsh (1934:121-123); ROMd24a:130, 169, 187-190.
53. ROMd24a:95, 143, 168; Johnson (1925:32, 34); Marsh (1934:134-136).
54. ROMd24a:179-187; Marsh (1934:124-127). Wala and Morti have both been visited repeatedly since Marsh's time.
55. ROMd24a:193.
56. ROMd24a:85, 89, 95, 135, 140, 197.
57. ROMd24a:197.
58. ROMd24a:161, 171-172; Marsh (1934: 133, 144-145); Malsbury Report, p. 3.
59. Taussig's remarks on Marsh and sexuality are feverishly hyperbolic (1993:162-173). While it is true that in some frames the Kuna are figured as female and sexually threatened, this is one of several representations, not the overwhelmingly dominant trope that Taussig alleges. By the end of Marsh's book, the figure of Kuna as male standing up for his rights and his women is primary, and both male and female representations appear throughout. The crucial association with whiteness for Marsh was *sexual restraint,* just as it was in the literature of eugenics.
60. ROMd24a:196, 253.

22. Up the Chucunaque

1. ROMd24a:96,98.
2. CMBdII:3.
3. CMBdI:2,4; ROMd24a:208-211, *passim*; Marsh (1934:142).
4. ROMd24a:183-186.
5. See Adas (1989:159); Taussig (1993).
6. ROMd24a:186-187. *Sic* "weird." The machine guns and grenades ultimately were not provided by the army.
7. ROMd24a:206-207, 211, 215-18; Marsh (1934:144); CMBdII:9.
8. O. E. Malsbury, Report to Governor of the Canal Zone, 3/20/24, p. 5, 67-C-80, PC, NARS.
9. ROMd24a:220,245; Marsh (1934:141, 145-146); CMBdII:12-13.
10. ROMd24a:215-230; CMBdII:14-15; Marsh (1934:141-149).
11. Johnson (1925:34); ROMd24a:213-214, CMBdII:8-9; Marsh (1934:143).
12. CMBdII:12. *Sic* "listing."
13. ROMd24a:213-214, 224-226; Marsh (1934:134-135, 143, 147-148); CMBdII:8-9, 12-14.
14. CMBdII:16.
15. ROMd24a:228-229, 231.
16. ROMd24a:234-237; CMBdII:17-18; Marsh (1934:149-151).
17. ROMd24a:238-241; Marsh (1934:151); CMBdII:19.
18. ROMd24a:244-245.
19. The river shows up on maps under several names, including Sucubdi, Sucuti, Chucuti, Chucurti.
20. ROMd24a:238-245; CMBdII:21-23; Marsh (1934:152-156). For the sake of simplicity, I omit a small rebellion by Townsend: ROMd24a:252-256; CMBdII:17-24.

21. ROMd24a:257–267; Marsh (1934:153–158).
22. ROMd24a:267–273; 1934:159–162.
23. ROMd24a:271–273, Marsh (1934:162–165).
24. ROMd24b:9–14. *Sic* "loose." CMBdII:34–35.
25. Baer to Hrdlička, 3/11, 3/28/24, Hrdlička Files, NAA.
26. Marsh (1934:187); transcribed intv., Watson Perrygo, 1978, RU 9516, SIA.
27. ROMd24a:263–273; CMBdII:29–32.
28. CMBdII:38.
29. ROMd24b:17–19.
30. ROMd24b:19.
31. CMBdII:39. "Hairs" is a guess at a semilegible word.
32. ROMd24b:28.
33. CMBdII:40, 41.
34. ROMd24b:16–33; CMBdII:38–41; Marsh (1934:166–172).
35. ROMd24b:36–38, ROM24c. The third and fourth notebooks of Marsh's 1924 diaries have no page numbers.
36. Marsh's claim that Sali spoke perfect English, of which Taussig (1993:158) makes much, is contradicted by both Johnson and Breder (Johnson 1925:36; CMBdII:35).
37. Marsh (1934:160); ROMd24c; Marsh ms., projected revisions for Marsh 1934, pp. 5–8. Sakla Cheepu was omitted for some reason from Marsh's book, but according to a manuscript, he planned to reinstate him in a second edition (Marsh ms., projected revisions).
38. CMBdII:42–61; ROMd24c; Marsh ms., projected revisions.
39. Sali said that they had been chanting for four days in the second village, and he asked for tobacco (used in exorcisms) to confront an evil spirit that was threatening them. The earthquake had occurred on the twenty-sixth, the day before they began chanting. ROMd24c; CMBdII:56; Marsh ms., projected revisions, pp. 13–16.
40. ROMd24c.
41. CMBdII:57.
42. Marsh to Benton, 4/27/24; Marsh to *Gannett-Times Union*, n.d.; Marsh to J. M. Morrow, 4/27/24 (courtesy of Richard O. Marsh Jr.).
43. ROMd24c; Marsh ms., proposed revisions, pp. 10–11.
44. ROMd24c; CMBdII:60–61; Marsh ms., projected revisions, pp. 13–16.
45. ROMd24c; CMBdII:61.

23. On the Coast

1. CMBdII:64-65; Marsh (1934:177).
2. ROMd24d.
3. ROMd24d:1–4; Marsh (1934:178).
4. ROMd24d:12–13; Marsh (1934:178–179).
5. ROMd24d:70–74, 77–78; Marsh (1934:190–192). In a shocking commentary in his journal, Marsh noted that to keep Blacks in check, experience in the United States had shown that if the law failed, then lynching was necessary.
6. ROMd24d:13–14, 15–18, 25–28, 62–64, 78–79, 80–81, 88–89; Marsh (1934:179–180, 194–196).
7. ROMd24d:13.
8. ROMd24d:26–27.

9. ROMd24d:75; Marsh (1934:189-190).

10. ROMd24d:13,56; Marsh (1934:195).

11. ROMd24d:16.

12. ROMd24d:78.

13. ROMd24d:32,78.

14. ROMd24d:4-16, 23-29, 32-35, 60-62, 88-89.

15. ROMd24d:62-63. Marsh's plan is similar to what has since happened on many North American reservations. Marsh contemplated doing well as he did good: knowledge of fruit company plans to build a narrow gauge railroad to the Chucunaque inspired dreams of combining bananas and rubber, which he planned to submit to the head of United Fruit on his return to the United States (ROMd24d:49-51; Marsh 1934:189-196).

16. ROMd24d:19-22; Marsh (1934:182-183).

17. Johnson (1925:36); Marsh (1934:182); ROMd24d:30, 40, 66.

18. ROMd24d:14-15, 30-31.

19. ROMd24d:15, 43.

20. CMBdII:78-91; ROMd24d:39-40, 65-66, 68-70

21. ROMd24d:68.

22. ROMd24d:36-57; Marsh (1934:185-186).

23. ROMd24d:54-86; Marsh (1934:187).

24. Marsh vowed to try again the following year. Sensibly, he anticipated starting from Yaviza in early January, when river levels would still be high; not so sensibly, he decided he needed more equipment rather than less (ROMd24e, p. 10-11).

25. ROMd24e:10-11.

26. ROMd24e:11-12. Paragraph break deleted. It is not clear in which village Johnson discovered the Indians: two possibilities are the village on Tuppak or Isla Pino next to the storeship, or Navagandi, nearby on the shore.

27. RTU 6/14/24; NYT 6/15/24.

28. In his book (1934:196), Marsh has it that Inabaginya himself first revealed the presence of white Indians on the coast. At this point in the narrative, my copy of Marsh's diaries, kindly provided by Mr. Richard O. Marsh Jr., gives out, and since Charles Breder had already left for the city, I am largely dependent on Marsh's book (1934) for the account of his trip down the coast.

29. Marsh (1934:193-1960).

30. Marsh (1934:198-204); Johnson (1925:37).

31. Marsh (1934:207); Johnson (1925:37).

32. Marsh (1934:205-209).

33. OH, Ricardo Thompson.

34. OH, Ricardo Thompson.

35. S&H, *Est.*, 6/18/24; Johnson (1925:37).

36. S&H, *Est.*, 6/17/23; RTU, 6/23/24.

37. CMBdII:93-94. Paragraph break deleted.

38. S&H, *Est.*, 6/18/24.

39. ROMd24d:11; ROMd24f:20; Marsh ms. proposed revisions; intv., R. 0. Marsh Jr., 5/84.

40. RTU 6/23/24; S&H, 6/21/24.

41. A shorter version of the same word, *machi*, is still in wide circulation in Panama today (see Leis 1992).

42. Marsh (1934:212-213).

43. S&H, 6/21/24. Marsh was right: the heads of Kuna albinos tend to be larger than average.

44. S&H, 6/22/24.
45. S&H, Est., 6/25/24, 819.63, NARS. Marsh (1934:213); Verrill (1921).
46. S&H, 6/26/24. Verrill's scorn for the subject did not keep him from rushing an article into print, "Hunting the White Indians" (Verrill 1924) only three weeks after the delegates' arrival in New York.
47. S&H, Est., 6/25/24.
48. RTU 6/21/24; Marsh (1934:213-214).
49. Marsh (1934:215-216); CMBdII:95-102.
50. S&H, 6/30/24.

24. The White Indians on Tour

1. NYT, 7/07/94; RTU, 7/07/94.
2. NYT, 7/07/94; RTU, 7/07/94.
3. Brandon (1986:14-15); Browne (1995:235-269).
4. Rydell (1984, 1993); Viola (1981).
5. Chase (1977:252-301); Cravens (1978:176-178); Degler (1991:32-83); Higham (1966); Kevles (1985:32-83); Perrett (1982).
6. NYT, 7/08/24, Intvs., R. O. Marsh Jr., 5/84, 1/86.
7. RTU, 7/09/24; NYT, 7/09/24; Fairchild (1924); Marsh (1934:216-217).
8. Examination forms filled in for Kuna delegates, n.d., Dept of Anthropology, AMNH; NYT, 7/10, 7/11, 7/12, 7/14/24; RTU, 7/12/24; Science Service (1924a); Wissler (1924).
9. Marsh (1934:217); RTU, 7/12/24.
10. RTU, 7/11, 7/12, 7/18, 7/19/24.
11. Intv., Richard Marsh Jr. 1/86; Johnson (1958:179-180).
12. Fairchild (1924); Marsh (1934:218-219); Shrubsall, Haddon, and Buxton (1924); NYT, 8/14/24; S&H, Est., 8/07/24.
13. Marsh to Ravenel, 11/20/23, 1/07/24; Pindar to Sec. Smithsonian, 10/29/24; Phipps to Smithsonian, 10/27/24; Cable, Marsh to Smithsonian, 6/19/24 — all RU 305, USNM Registrar, Accession records, SIA.
14. Science Service, Daily Science News Bulletin 185C, 10/08/24; Marsh (1934:219); NYT, 8/14/24; Science Service (1924b).
15. Science Service (1924c); Science Service, Daily Science News Bulletin 185C, 10/08/24. Marsh to Ravenel at Smithsonian, Kellogg at National Research Council, Merriam at Carnegie Institution 10/17/24, RU 305, USNM Registrar, Accession Records, SIA; also in Misc. Subjects, Hrdlička files, NAA. Hrdlička to Marsh, 10/20; Hrdlička to Stiles, 10/20; Hrdlička to Davenport, 10/20; Correspondence 1903-1925, 1909-1945; Hrdlička papers, NAA. Marsh (1934:219-220).
16. Chase (1975:114-120); Cravens (1978:49-51); Davenport (1911); Kevles (1985:41-56); Paul (1984); Rosenberg (1961:89-97).
17. Kuhl (1994).
18. Chase (1975:120-124); Cravens (1978:49-51, 314 n. 8); Kevles (1985:41-112); Rosenberg (1961).
19. Chase (1977:163-75, 291-300); Degler (1991:48-51); Grant (1916); Hellman (1968:194-197); Higham (1966:155-157, 271-277, 313-314); Kevles (1985:75, 102-104).
20. Boas (1911a, 1911b, 1928); Chase (1975:181-189); Degler (1991:59-83); Higham (1955:125, 153); Hyatt (1990:83-122); Kevles (1985:134).
21. Chase (1977:165-166); Spencer (1979:624-713); Stocking (1968:287-292).
22. Spencer (1979:624-737); Stocking (1968).

23. Hyatt (1990:43-82); Spencer (1979:624-737); Stocking (1968).

24. Hyatt (1990:123-138); Spencer (1979:713-723,791-796) Stocking (1968).

25. Marsh to Ravenel at Smithsonian, Kellogg at National Research Council, Merriam at Carnegie Institution, 10/17/24, RU 305, USNM Registrar, Accession Records, SIA; also in Misc. Subjects, Hrdlička files, NAA. Hrdlička to Marsh, 10/20, 11/17/24; Hrdlička to Stiles 10/20, 11/17/24; Hrdlička to Davenport, 10/20, 10/25, 11/05, 11/11/24, 1/20/25; Davenport to Hrdlička, 10/20, 11/03, 11/11, 11/13/24, 1/10/25; Davenport to Marsh, 10/23, 11/11, 11/13/24; Davenport to Stiles, 11/03/24; Stiles to Davenport, 11/06/24; Marsh to Hrdlička, 11/08/24. Hrdlička's letters are in Correspondence 1903-1925, 1909-1945, Hrdlička papers, NAA; Davenport's in correspondence, Davenport files, American Philosophical Society. Copies of letters between the two men are found at both locations.

26. Harris (1922); Harris to Davenport, 5/01, 11/08/21; Davenport to Harris 5/06, 12/06/21, Correspondence, Davenport papers, American Philosophical Society. Science Service (1924c).

27. Marsh paid Harris's fare and expenses (Contract between Marsh and Harris, N.Y., N.Y. 12/01/24, Davenport-Harris papers, Archives of Cold Spring Harbor Laboratory).

28. Watson Davis to Hrdlička, 10/14/24, Hrdlička correspondence, NAA; *Washington Post*, 10/16, 10/17, 10/18, 10/26/24; *Washington Evening Star*, 10/14, 10/16/24.

29. Measurements of Kuna in Misc. Subject File: Cuna Indians, Hrdlička Collection, NAA; unidentified newspaper photograph, Harrington Collections, NAA; Hrdlička (1926); *Washington Post*, 10/18/24.

30. Intvs., Richard Marsh Jr., 5/84, 1/86.

31. Daily Science News Bulletin no. 187A, 10/20/24; *Washington Evening Star*, n.d. [Oct. 1924], in Harrington papers, NAA; *Washington Post*, 10/19/24.

32. Laird (1975: esp. 3, 5, 8, 10, 25, 32, 46, 68, 81, 86-87); Stirling (1963:370-381). His voluminous field notes have recently been issued on microfilm: The Papers of John Peabody Harrington in the Smithsonian Institution, 1907-1957, Kraus International Publications.

33. Harrington to Vogenitz, 10/05/24, Harrington Papers, NAA.

34. Harrington notes, 10/19/24, *passim*, NAA.

35. Vogenitz to Harrington, n.d., Harrington papers, NAA.

36. Science Service, Daily Science News Bulletin 195C, 12/17/24; *Washington Evening Star*, 12/19/24; Vogenitz notes, n.d., Harrington papers, NAA; Marsh (1934:220).

37. Laird (1975:68).

38. Allen (1926); Davenport to Hrdlička, 10/14/25, Hrdlička Correspondence 1909-45, Box 10, NAA.

39. Densmore (1926); Krieger (1926).

40. Text dictated by Igwa-Nigdibippi, 12/09/24, transcribed by Vogenitz, 12/10/24, Harrington papers, NAA.

41. Harrington, untitled notes, Harrington papers, NAA.

42. Marsh's book gives few details; his diaries stopped when he left Panama, and a recurrence of malaria put him out of the picture for several weeks.

43. Diaries, 1916-1950, Personal Papers, Frances Densmore, 4250:2, NAA; *Washington Evening Star*, 12/15/24.

44. Vogenitz to Harrington, 1/14/25, Corresp., Harrington papers.

45. Cable, Sec. State to AmLeg, 1/14/25, AmLeg Panama, NARS.

46. Res. before the Am. Assoc. for the Advancement of Science, Kansas City, Missouri, 12/28/25-1/02/26, in Davenport Papers, Am. Philosophical Soc. Library, also Hrdlička Papers, Misc. Subjects, NAA. Marsh to Davenport, 12/17/25, Am. Philosophical Soc. Library. *Science* 1/29/26, p. 115; NYT, 1/02/26.

47. Hrdlička to Davenport, 1/20/25, Corresp. 1909-1945, Hrdlička papers, NAA.

25. The Republic of Tule

1. S&H, 1/12, 1/13, 1/16/25; Marsh (1934:224); E. López ms. "Sucesos Sangrientes"

2. J. Harris, ms.; R. Harris (1926a:21); Walker to Zetek, 3/09/25; V. Kellogg to Barbour, 3/04/25; Governor Walker to SecWar Weeks, 3/04/25, 80-A-15 PC. Report on use of Barro Colorado Island, conveyed 5/08/25, 892.6, AmLeg.

3. Howell to State, 1/12/25, Div. of Latin American Affairs 819.4016/1; Hughes to AmLeg, 1/14/25; Lassiter to Am. Minister, 2/10/25, AmLeg. Herrera (1984:250–252).

4. Herrera (1984:248); Marsh (1934:224).

5. ROMd25a:9–12, Marsh (1934:224–226).

6. ROMd25a:13–15, 18–20.

7. ROMd25a:15–18; Erice (1975:291); Garay (1982:10); E. López "Sucesos sangrientes"; Marsh (1934:227–229).

8. ROMd25a:20–24.

9. ROMd25a:20, 45; J. Harris, ms., *passim*.

10. RGHd:3; Harris (1925a:460).

11. RGHd; Harris (1925a, 1925b, 1926a, 1926b).

12. Harris (1925a:460, 1926a, 1926b).

13. ROMd25a:20, Marsh (1934:227).

14. Science Service to Davenport, 2/07/24, Harris papers. Also Marsh to Lassiter, 2/02/94, in ROMd25b:46–47, and 819.00/1162.

15. G. Arosemena (1980); Keeler (1953, 1964a, 1964b, 1966, 1968); Keeler, MacKinnon, et al. (1963).

16. Sybil Beach, personal communication.

17. ROMd25b:5–6, 10.

18. ROMd25b:5. Anna Coope later confirmed that the Nargana detachment head spent several weeks drilling village men with rifles (Coope to Am. Consul Colón, 2/26/25, AmLeg R800-San Blas; Paul Kelley [?], "Memorandum for Chief, Police & Fire Div," 3/02/25, 80-A-15, PC.

19. ROMd25a:28.

20. Marsh to Lassiter, 2/02/25, in ROMd25b:46–57, also 819.00/1163.

21. S&H, 1/14/25.

22. Lassiter to Marsh, 2/10/25; South to State, 2/18/25, 819.00/1163.

23. ROMd25b:11.

24. One Kuna source, eager to counter claims that the Kuna were manipulated by outsiders, has it that the flag was designed by Colman, Nele, and others the previous August (Iguaniginape 1994:29). Marsh's diary, which was intended to be read, reproduces the flag but does not specify its authorship (ROMd25a:59; ROMd25c:27) and several pages are missing from Jane Harris's narrative. The Nazi swastika is the reverse of the Kuna one.

25. Found in State Department Central Decimal Records (Enclosure 4, Disp. 651, 2/28/25, 819.00/1176); also S&H, 2/27/25; ROMd25g; and discussed by Guionneau-Sinclair (1991:20–21) and Martínez (1996). It is remarkable that some commentators have accepted the document as purely indigenous.

26. The Kuna, though clothed as well as monogamous, are hardly the frozen prudes Marsh depicted.

27. In pronouncing Spanish words, the Kuna often drop "J," a sound absent in their own language, and the Spanish "H" is silent. For Spanish words such as "Jehová," with the accent on the final syllable, the Kuna also shift the emphasis to the penultimate syllable: for "José" they say "óse." Thus they would have pronounced "Jehová" as "Eeoba," or in Marsh's rendering in English, "A-oba." Harris's notes (RGHd) also mention "A-oba."

28. Two Kuna culture heroes were white, but not the two greatest, Ibeorgun and Tad Ibe, and Great Father's skin color is not a subject for theological discussion. Like many other afficionados of White Gods, Marsh may have been influenced by Lew Wallace (1873), Hubert Howe Bancroft (1883), and their followers.

29. Obeyesekere (1992).

30. Michael Taussig's tendentious and offensive discussion of Kuna racial attitudes (1993:144-150, 271-273) accuses them of "complicity" with racist white Americans, even though the Kuna did not begin working in the Canal Zone in significant numbers until the 1930s. Amazingly, he mentions the treaty from 1741 in which the Kuna called for the exclusion of Blacks from the Darién, as well as my claim that the police in the period 1915-1925 were mostly mestizos without noticing that both undercut his argument. He also claims support from my work (Taussig 1993:271), asserting that I deny economic competition between Kuna and Blacks as a source of Kuna antipathy, a categoric argument I do *not* make in the works he cites. The centuries of conflict and competition have obviously conditioned Kuna racial attitudes. Similarly the generalized Kuna distrust of strangers is no mere extension of antipathy to Blacks, as Taussig's argument implies.

31. Francisco Herrera (1984:110-115) was the first to point out Marsh's error concerning the ethnicity of police agents, an error repeated by several recent scholars. Since then, Herrera and I have both pursued this issue in written sources and oral interviewing. Although the first policemen in 1909 in Puerto Obaldía were all Colombian Blacks, the Policía Colonial was from the beginning composed largely of mestizo men from Panama City and the southwestern *Interior*. One or two individuals, notably the Kuna-speaking police agent Guillermo Denis, may have been Black or mulatto. Marsh (Declaration of Independence) was also confused about the ethnicity of Black forest workers, who were predominantly costeños and Colombians and not West Indians.

32. Higham (1966).

33. ROMd25b:13.

34. ROMd25b:13-25; Marsh (1934:237-241).

35. ROMd25b:26-27.

36. ROMd25c:3-4; Marsh (1934:242).

37. ROMd25b:29-30.

38. ROMd25b:29-30.

39. ROMd25c:9-12; Marsh (1934:244-245).

40. ROMd25d:8-17; Marsh (1934:250); Coope et al. to Am. Consul Colón, 2/26/25, in R800-San Blas, AmLeg.

41. Marsh to Lewis, 2/12/25; Marsh to Science Service, 2/12/25; Lewis to Watson, 2/20/25; Walker to South, 2/21/25; South to Lassiter, 2/25/25; South to Walker, 2/26/25, AmLeg R800, also PanCanal 80A-15. S&H, 2/27/25; ROMd25d:17-22; Marsh (1934:251).

42. ROMd25d:22-26.

43. *Bila onosa.*

26. Bringing out War

1. The classical account of the rebellion itself, by Jesús Erice (1975), is not invariably correct. For Playón Chico, I also depend on an interview (Intv., anon., 8/12/75) and three oral histories (OH, Simón Avila, Manuel Gonzalez, Manuel Paredes, 1975). Most important are accounts taped by my co-workers, Jesús Alemancia and Cebaldo de León. Unfortunately, several speakers from Ailigandi (Anon., 1, 2, 3, and 4) are not identified by name on the tapes. Chronology poses a difficulty.

Erice, who worked forty years before me, places the Playón Chico uprising a day later than I do. I hold with Sunday for three principal reasons: (1) the plan would likely call for simultaneous uprisings in each village; (2) Marsh records in his diary hearing news of the liberation of Playón Chico on Sunday night; and (3) an excellent informant from the Playón Chico rebels was clear and explicit on the point (Int., Anon., 8/12/75).

2. See Stern (1987b) on coordinating regional rebellions.

3. The connection between exorcism and the 1925 rebellion, often pointed out by the Kuna today, was first mentioned in print by Alexander Moore (1983).

4. OH, Samuel Morris, 1985. As always with Kuna oral histories, these are the narrator's reconstruction of dialogue. *La Prensa,* 3/03/95.

5. Erice (1975:292-294); OH, Willy Archibold, Carlos López; Intv., Ukkuppa, Anon., 1975; Inakeliginia (1997:95-97).

6. OH, Ailigandi, Anon., 1, 2, 3, and Samuel Morris, Carlos López, Sir William, Willy Archibold, Saly William.

7. Ailigandi, Anon., 1; Saly William; Inakeliginia (1997:66-67).

8. Ailigandi, Anon., 1.

9. OH, Sir Willis. Inakeliginia (1997:66-67).

10. OH, Sir Willis.

11. Heard in speech by Carlos López, 2/85.

12. OH, Ailigandi, Anon., 1.

13. OH, Ailigandi, Anon., 1.

14. OH, Ailigandi, Anon., 1, 3, and Saly William, Samuel Morris, Willy Archibold. Erice (1975:294-295); Inakeliginia (1997:98-99).

15. Intv., Ukkuppa, Anon., 8/12/75; OH, Sir William, Saly William, Willy Archibold; Inakeliginia (1997:97).

16. OH, Saly William.

17. Intv., Ukkuppa, Anon., 8/12/75.

18. Erice (1975:304); OH, William Archibold.

19. Several sources mention Estocel's flight (Int., Ukkuppa, Anon., 8/12/75; OH, Willy Archibold), but most of the details come from Erice (1975:297, 300-302).

20. Inakeliginia (1997:99).

21. Another problem in chronology: Erice (1975:297-299) places this windward ambush before another that took place on the leeward side, as does one oral history (OH, Saly William). Two other oral histories and an excellent informant reverse the order, however (OH, Sir William, William Archibold; Int., Ukkuppa, Anon., 8/12/75). I follow Erice, though with some hesitation.

22. OH, Saly William.

23. OH, Saly William. Almost all the oral histories mention the butchery, as does Erice: OH, Ailigandi, Anon., 1, 2, 3, and Saly William, Sir William, Willy Archibold, Carlos López; Int., Ukkuppa, Anon., 8/12/75; Erice (1975:298, 300); Inakeliginia (1997:102-103).

24. OH, William Archibold.

25. OH, Ailigandi, Anon., 2, 3, and Saly William, Samuel Morris, Carlos López, Sir Willis, William Archibold; Int., Ukkuppa, Anon., 8/12/75; Erice (1975:299); Inakeliginia (1997:100-101).

26. OH, Sir Willis.

27. OH, Ailigandi, Anon., 2, 3, Saly William, Samuel Morris, Carlos López, Sir Willis, William Archibold; Int., Ukkuppa, 8/12/75; Erice (1975:299-300); Inakeliginia (1997:101-102).

28. Orán to SecGJ, 9/16/26, AN(?) (courtesy of Francisco Herrera).

29. Ailigandi, Anon., 3; Erice (1975:300).

30. OH, Ailigandi, Anon., 3.

31. OH, Ailigandi, Anon., 3. I have taken the liberty of interpolating the take-thats from another text. Also Sir Willis, Willy Archibold; Erice (1975:300).

32. OH, Ailigandi, Anon., 3.

33. OH, William Archibold, Sir Willis.

34. OH, Sir Willis.

35. Erice (1975:303); OH, William Archibold, Sir Willis, and Ailigandi, Anon., 3; Inakeliginia (1997:107-108).

36. OH, Willy Archibold.

37. OH, Juan Pérez 6/13/85. See also the letter from Tigre to Americans on board USS *Cleveland*, 2/n.d./25, AmLeg R800-San Blas.

38. Here, too, sources disagree on chronology. Several suggest that Tigre and Niatupu rebelled later than eastern villages (OH, Juan Pérez, Manuel Grado); two specify the twenty-fifth (OH, Ceferino Villaláz, Vicente Arosemena). Erice (1975:364-368), on the other hand, states that envoys arrived on Saturday and the killing happened on Sunday; the *Star and Herald* says Sunday the twenty-second.

39. OH, Ceferino Villaláz.

40. S&H, 2/26/25.

41. OH, Juan Pérez.

42. OH, Ceferino Villaláz. Erice (1975:365-366) has it that the young men threw a dance in defiance of Mojica's wishes, thus provoking him into coming to the club, an implausible scenario contradicted by all other sources (OH, Ceferino Villaláz, Juan Pérez, Manuel Grado); intv., Milton Parks, 1/89; Moore (1983). Parks says that Mojica was not wary but absorbed in what he was doing.

43. OH, Ceferino Villaláz.

44. OH, Juan Pérez.

45. OH, Ceferino Villaláz.

46. This boat, later mentioned in telegrams whose sentences ended with "stop," is known in some Spanish-language accounts as the "Stop Ambition," in others as the "Stoop Ambition" or "sloop Ambition": Castillo and Méndez (1962:76); Paez (1941:33).

47. By "native," English-speakers on the Isthmus usually meant dark-skinned Panamanians, not Indians.

48. S&H, 2/26/25.

49. S&H, 2/26/25.

50. Sources on the Niatupu uprising include interviews with Gonzalo Salcedo, 11/03/70; Fernando Ponce, 11/27/70; Francisco Hernandez, 1/08, 1/11/71; Abran Escobar, 1/17, 10/19/71; Mateo Brenes, 2/23, 4/12/85; Camilo Porras, 2/25/85; Ricardo Thompson, 2/25/85. Taped oral narratives include OH, Manuel Campos, 2/25/91; Camilo Porras, 11/71, 2/25/85; Ricardo Thompson, 4/14/85; Vicente Arosemena, 5/04/85; Miguel Hipolito, 2/22/85, 2/20/91. I also observed dramatic reconstructions of the uprising in February of 1985, 1991, and 1995; I assisted in filming the 1991 drama. I have also used Erice's published account (1975:368-370).

51. OH, Miguel Hipolito.

52. OH, Miguel Hipolito.

53. OH, Vicente Arosemena.

54. OH, Camilo Porras, 11/71.

55. Intv., Camilo Porras, 2/25/85.

56. OH, Miguel Hipolito, 85.

57. OH, Miguel Hipolito, 85.
58. OH, Miguel Hipolito, 91. Bathing removed or reduced spiritual pollution and danger.
59. OH, Camilo Porras, 11/71.
60. OH, Miguel Hipólito, 85.
61. OH, Vicente Arosemena.
62. Here I depend heavily on Erice (1975:371-377).
63. Petition to U.S. minister to Panama, 2/24/25, AmLeg R800-San Blas, NARS.
64. E. López, ms., "Sucesos Sangrientes"; "Entrevista Personal," in Castillo and Méndez (1962:257-260); Erice (1975:385).
65. E. Lopez, ms., "Sucesos Sangrientes"; Erice (1975:385-386).

27. Cruiser Diplomacy

1. U.S. radio station POb to Commandant 15th Naval Dist., 2/27/25, AmLeg R800-San Blas. Exts. to PanLeg, 2/27/25, in Castillo and Méndez (1962:152). *Diario*, 2/27/25.
2. Falla (n.d.:63-64) arrives at a total of 27, including 8 colonial police and 4 indigenous police. Carlos López (OH) says 9 policemen. A government resolution of 3/19/25 lists 7 colonial and 4 indigenous agents, though one of the latter had actually survived (unidentified clipping, AEL).
3. Marsh (1934:254-262).
4. Erice (1975:384-385)).
5. ROMd25d:28-33, 38-39; Erice (1975:381); Markham, ms. IF/2907, p. 4.
6. ROMd25d:33-38; Marsh (1934:261-262).
7. Among other things, Marsh's restraint saved the records of the Intendencia and made this book possible seventy years later.
8. ROMd25d:38.
9. Marsh to [?] Perino, 2/26/25, in Castillo and Méndez (1962:147-148); ROMd25d:40-42, ROMd25e:n.p.; Marsh (1934:263-264); Memo, Kelley [?] to Chief [?], 3/01/25, 80-A-15, PC.
10. Castillero R. (1946).
11. The most important sources on the ensuing events include: (1) Records of the Department of State on the Internal Affairs of Panama, files 819.00/1154-1187, U.S. National Archives (NARS); (2) the Records of the United States Legation in Panama (AmLeg), R800-San Blas, RG84, NARS, which include documents not found elsewhere; (3) Panamanian diplomatic documents from the Secretaria de Relaciones Exteriores (Exts.), reprinted in a master's thesis (Castillo and Méndez 1962; supposedly from the Memoria[s] de Relaciones Exteriores, they may in fact come directly from diplomatic files); (4) Records of the British Legation in Panama (FO288/202, PRO); (5) Records of the Panama Canal, File 80-A-15, PC, RG185, NARS; (6) Log Books for the USS *Cleveland*, RG45, NARS; (7) newspaper articles in the *Panama Star and Herald, Diario de Panamá, Tiempo de Panamá, Panama Times*, and *New York Times*; (8) Richard Marsh's diaries, courtesy of Richard O. Marsh Jr. (ROMd25, sections a-f); (9) William Markham's narrative, catalog no. IF/2907, Tioga Point Museum, Athens Pa.. (10) *White Indians of Panama*, Marsh (1934:254-276); (11) Erice's chronicle of the Kuna revolt (1975), which is wildly wrong concerning U.S. diplomatic and military involvement. I am grateful to my research assistant, sponsored by the MIT UROP Program, Jaime Juárez, for his very useful chronology of events and documents. For other accounts using some of this same material, see Chardkoff (1970); Herrera (1984, 1987); Iglesias (1993); Jones (1986). Kuna oral historians unanimously aver that U.S. intervention was arranged in Washington before Marsh and the delegates returned to Panama. Erice (1975) accepted this interpretation, and later commen-

taries often rest on the assumption that the fix was on. As I hope is clear from this chapter, the documentary evidence does not support this claim.

12. Alfaro to South, 2/25/25, 819.00/1176, also in Castillo and Méndez (1962:146-147). Marsh to Lewis, 2/12/25, 819.00/1176; Lewis to Watson, 2/20/25; Walker to South, 2/21/25, 819.00/1176; South to Lassiter, 2/25/25; South to Walker, 2/26/25; AmLeg & 80A-15, PC; South to State, 2/18/25, 819.00/1176; Walker to Weeks, 3/04/25, 80-A-15, PC.

13. Personnel file, J. G. South, 123 SO85, Records of the Dept. of State, 1910-29, NARS. *Kentucky Medical Journal*, XVII:11; Women's Auxiliary to the Franklin County Medical Soc., ms. "Doctors of Franklin County," 1948 (both courtesy of Dr. Eugene H. Conner). [Kentucky] *State Journal*, 5/14/40. Personal communications, Mrs. Edgar Hume, Dr. Eugene Conner, Martin South.

14. Alfaro to South, 2/26/25, 819.00/1176. The note is dated February 16, but everything indicates that it was written on the twenty-sixth. Other small puzzles in chronology: Governor Walker sent the packet from Marsh on the twenty-first after speaking with South on the phone, but South says he did not receive it until the twenty-fourth. South says Alfaro wrote him the same day, the twenty-fourth, but the latter's note is dated the twenty-fifth (South to State and enclosures, 2/28/25, 819.00/1176); Walker to SecWar, 3/04/25, 80-A-15, PC). Unlike Herrera (1984:198; 1987), I see no reason to interpret either South's slowness in contacting the Panamanian government or these small discrepancies as evidence of a State Department conspiracy in favor of Marsh or the revolt.

15. File on USS *Cleveland*, OS-United States Naval Vessels, Subject File 1911-1927, Office of Naval records and Library, RG45, NARS. Department of the Navy 1963. South to State, 2/28/25, 819.00/1176.

16. S&H, 2/26, 2/27/25; Johannes to Walker, 2/227/25, and Walker to SecWar, 3/04/25, 80-A-15, PC, NARS; "Entrevista personal con Etanislao [sic] López," in Castillo and Méndez 1962:259. Concerning the number of policemen, I follow Governor Walker rather than the larger figures in some other sources.

17. South to State, 4 p.m., 10 *p.m.*, 2/25/25, 819.00/1154, 1155; R. Alfaro, Washington to Exts. Panamá, 2/26/25, Exts. to PanLeg 2/27/25, in Castillo and Méndez (1962:148-149, 169-171).

18. Hughes to South, 2/26/25, 819.00/1154.

19. Log of *Cleveland*, 2/26/25, NARS; Markham, ms. IF/29072, p. 1; Ford to BritLeg, 4/03/25, PRO; S&H, 2/27/25.

20. Markham, ms. IF/2907, p. 2; Log of *Cleveland*, 2/27/25, NARS; López to Chiari, 2/27/25, AmLeg.

21. ROMd25f:3-4; Marsh (1934:265-266).

22. Markham, ms.IF/2907, p. 2; ROMd25f:4; Marsh (1934:266).

23. ROMd25f, p. 6. Someone kept notes on part of the interview (AmLeg).

24. Markham, ms.IF/2907, p. 2-3; ROMd25f:7-10; South to State, 4/13/25, 819.00/1180; Marsh (1934:267-268).

25. South to State, 3/13/25, 819.00/1180; South to State, 10 p.m., 2/27/25, 819.00/1157.

26. Bran and Pérez to South, de la Ossa, and Markham, 3/01/25, AmLeg. Careful not to close off any paths, Olonibiginya and several village chiefs sent similar letters in Spanish to Panamanian President Chiari. Olonibiginya to Unknown 2/n.d., 3/03/25; Levid, Sami, and Salazar to Unknown 2/27/25; Luis Salazar to Pres. Chiari, 2/27/25—all in Castillo and Méndez (1962:161-169).

27. South to State, 2/28/25; Memo of Harris/Morgan Interview, 2/26/25, 819.00/1176; S&H, 2/27, 3/02/25; Lamb to South, 2/26/25; Davis, Scotia to Commandant 15th Naval Dist., 2/27/25, 2/illeg./25, AmLeg; Log of *Cleveland*, 2/28/25, NARS; S&H, 3/02/25. Markham also gave South a copy of his letter to President Porras (Markham to Porras, 2/08/24, appended to South to State, 3/13/25, 819.00/1180).

28. Exts. to PanLeg, 2/27/25, in Castillo and Méndez (1962:150). South to State, 10 p.m., 2/27/25,

819.00/1157; South to AmLeg, 9 a.m., 2/28/25, AmLeg; South to State, 11 a.m., 2/28/25, 819.00/1160. Chiari to López, 8:38, 2/n.d./25, p. 90, AmLeg. Markham, ms. IF/2907, p. 2-3; ROMd25f:10-11; Marsh (1934:269).

29. Ford to BritLeg, 3/03/25, FO 288/202, PRO. On the minister's reevaluation of Marsh, see South to State, 3/13/25, 819.00/1180. Away from San Blas, meanwhile, José de la Rosa hypocritically condemned Colman's subversive actions and his disregard for "the great services" that Panama had provided the Indians (*Diario*, 2/27/25). Charles Davenport sent diatribes to several branches of the government in support of the "chaste" Kuna, who were seeking "to maintain the purity of their blood" against "licentious, thieving negroes" (Davenport to Reed, 2/28/25; Davenport to Wadsworth, 2/28/25; Bacon to SecSt, 4/03/25; Davenport to Coolidge, 2/28/25, 819.00/1159, 1162, 1166-1167).

30. Res. 7, Asamblea Nacional, 2/26/25, 819.00/1177; also in Castillo and Méndez (1962:153); S&H, 2/27, 2/28/25; R. Alfaro to Exts., 2/27/25, in Castillo and Méndez (1962:151); *Diario*, 2/28/25, in Castillo and Méndez (1962:158).

31. ROMd25f:14; Markham, ms. IF/2907, p. 3; Ford to BritLeg, 3/03/25, FO288/202, PRO. The telegram quoted by Marsh in his book (1934:270) – "Attack and capture Carti immediately (signed) [President] Chiari" – is spurious.

32. Chiari to López, 12:45 p.m., 2/28/25, 9:08 p.m., 2/28/25[chk]; Alfaro to Morales, 9:06 p.m., 2/28/25; South to AmLeg, 9 a.m., 4 p.m., 2/28/25; Morgan to South, 8 p.m., 2/28/25; South to State, 10 a.m., 2/28/25, AmLeg. South to State, 1 p.m., no. 26, 819.00/1158. Exts. to PanLeg, 2/28/25, in Castillo and Méndez (1962:160-161).

33. ROMd25f:13-16; Exts. to PanLeg, 2/28/25, in Castillo and Méndez (1962:160-161); Marsh (1934:270-272). Marsh's account of the supposed exchange of telegrams between Chiari and his forces in the field has no basis in fact.

34. South to AmLeg, 9 a.m.; South to State, 10 a.m., 2/28/25, AmLeg. *Cleveland* to SecNavy, 3/03/25, 819.00/1157; South to State, 11 a.m., 819.00/1160; South to State, 1 p.m., 819.00/1158; Hughes to AmLeg, 5 p.m., 819.00/1157; AmLeg to South, 8:00, 8:28 p.m., AmLeg. Morales to H. Alfaro, 2/28/25, in Castillo and Méndez (1962:171-172).

35. Markham, ms. 2, p. 6-8; South to AmLeg, 5 p.m., 3/01/25, AmLeg; South to State, 10 p.m., 3/01/25, 819.00/1161; Log of *Cleveland*, 3/01/25, NARS; ROMd25f:11-12; Marsh (1934:269); S&H, 3/03, 3/13/25; *Diario*, 3/12/25.

36. De la Ossa, report, 3/09/25, in *Diario*, 3/12/25; S&H, 3/13/25.

37. Markham, ms. IF/2907, p. 8.

38. South to AmLeg, 5 p.m.; AmLeg to State, 10 p.m., 819.00/1161; AmLeg to South, 11 p.m., 3/01/25; South to AmLeg, 9 a.m.; Morgan to South, 11 a.m.; State to AmLeg, 5 p.m., 819.00/1161; South to State 9 p.m., 3/02/25 – all in AmLeg. R. Morales to H. Alfaro, 3/01/25; H. Alfaro to Morales, 3/01/25; R. Alfaro, Washington, to Exts., 3/02/25; Exts. to PanLeg, 3/02/25 – all in Castillo and Méndez (1962:174-179).

39. South to State, 4/13/25, 819.00/1180; AmLeg to South, 11 a.m.; South to State, 9 p.m., 3/02/25, AmLeg.

40. South to State, 4/13/25, 819.00/1180; Exts. to PanLeg, 3/03/25, in Castillo and Méndez (1962:183). South to Commander *Cleveland*, 11 a.m., 3/03/25; South to State, 2 p.m., 3/03/25, AmLeg. South to State 9 p.m., 3/02/25, 819.00/1164; Log of *Cleveland* 3/02-3/03/25, NARS; S&H, 3/04/25.

41. Eusebio Morales, SecHac, to López and Alfaro, in Castillo and Méndez (1962:181-182).

42. South to State, 4/13/25, 819.00/1180; South to State, 4 p.m., 3/04/25, AmLeg; López and Alfaro to Chiari, 3:40 p.m., 3/04/25, in Castillo and Méndez (1962:184-185); S&H, 4/05/25.

43. The Porvenir treaty is appended to South to State, 3/13/25, 819.00/1180. A copy with Panamanian signatures is in AmLeg. Copies are also found in S&H, 4/22/25, and Braithwaite-Wallis to Foreign Office, 5/14/25, FO288/202, PRO. Paraphrases are found in S&H, 3/05/25; López and Alfaro to Chiari, 3:40 p.m., 3/04/25, AmLeg, also in Castillo and Méndez (1962:184-185); Wassén (1938:62-63); South to AmLeg, 3:50 p.m., 3/04/25, AmLeg; South to State, 4:00 p.m., 3/04/25, AmLeg, also 819.00/1168. Guionneau-Sinclair's summary (1991:21) is misleading, as are a summary by Markham (ms. IF/2907) and various versions given by Marsh (ROMd25f, p. 21-22; Marsh (1934:272-273); Marsh, "A Statement," *Panama Times*, 3/21/25). Other copies have continued to circulate in typed and mimeographed forms in San Blas (anon., ms. "La Paz para San Blas.") President Chiari's enthusiastic reply (Chiari to López and Alfaro, 9:46 a.m., 3/05/25) is in Castillo and Méndez (1962:235).

44. South to State, 4/25/25, 819.00/1185; S&H, 4/22/25.

45. South to State, 3/13/25, 819.00/1180.

46. South to State, 3/13/25, 819.00/1180; South to AmLeg, 3:50 p.m., 3/04/25, AmLeg; López and Alfaro to Chiari, 3:40 p.m., 3/04/25, AmLeg, also in Castillo and Méndez (1962:184-185); de la Ossa report in *Diario*, 3/12/25; ROMd25f:20; Marsh (1934:272); Corporal Bolling, USMC, list of surrendered arms, AmLeg.

47. South to State, 3/13/25, 819.00/1180; Log of *Cleveland*, 3/05/25, NARS.

48. South to State, 3/13/25, 819.00/1180; South to State, 7 p.m., 3/05/25, 819.00/1169; Exts. to PanLeg, 3/07/25, in Castillo and Méndez (1962:186); Estanislao López, "Entrevista personal," in Castillo and Méndez (1962:259).

49. Log of *Cleveland*, 4/05-4/07/25, NARS; Exts. to PanLeg, 3/07/25, in Castillo and Méndez (1962:186).

50. S&H, 3/02/25; also 2/27/25.

51. S&H, 2/27, 2/28, 3/02, 3/05, 3/12, 3/13/25; *El Tiempo*, 2/27, 3/05/25, in AmLeg. *El Tiempo*, 4/13/25, in 80-A-15, clippings, PC; South to State, 4/19/25, 819.00/1182. Braithwaite-Wallis to Foreign Office, 3/14/25; Ford to Braithwaite-Wallis 3/03/25, FO288/202.

52. Harris himself was quickly and quietly ejected from the Isthmus by Canal Zone authorities, who felt that he had deceived them about his plans and intentions (Walker to Zetek, 3/09/25; V. Kellogg to Barbour, 3/04/25; Gov. Walker to SecWar Weeks, 3/04/25, 80-A-15, PC).

53. S&H, 3/05, 3/08, 3/10, 3/14/25; *Panama Times*, 3/21/25; Marsh (1924:272-273).

54. R. O. Marsh, statement, 3/14/25, appended to South to State, 3/19/25, 819.00/1182; South to Duque, 3/19/25, AmLeg.

55. H. Alfaro to South, 3/16/25, 819.00/1182; expulsion order, dated 3/14/25, in 819.00/1182, also AmLeg; S&H, 3/15/25.

28. The Fruits of Rebellion

1. South to State, 3/19/25, 819.00/1182. Anon. Kuna to U.S. Legation, 3/11/25, AmLeg; S&H, 3/30/25.

2. Markham to South, 3/31, 4/17, 4/22, 4/24/25; South to Markham, 4/01, 4/21, 4/27, 5/26/25; Igwa-Nigdibippi to South, 5/01/25, AmLeg. Colman, Nele, et al. to South, 4/20/25. Lyons to South, 4/17/25; Iguainch Qui Quinya [Igwa-ingiginya?] to Dahl, 4/20/25; Colman and Nele to Dahl, 4/30/25, 819.00/1189.

3. S&H, 5/30, 5/31, 6/02/25; Int. to SecGJ, 5/28, 6/03/25, AI.

4. Int. to Ten. Huertas, Nargana, 4/18/25; Int. to SecGJ, 4/17/25; Int. to Ten. enc. Nargana, 4/29/25, AI.

5. Commander Galveston to Commander Special Service Squadron, 6/22/25, in South to State, 6/25/25, 819.00/1194; Log of the U.S.S. *Galveston*, 6/17/25-6/21/25, RG45, NARS.

6. S&H, 8/06, 8/07/25.

7. S&H, 8/06, 8/07, 8/09/25.

8. In 819.00/1245, 1248, 1252, 1253, 1272.

9. NYT, 3/24, 3/30/25; S&H, 3/25, 3/27, 3/28, 6/12/25.

10. Res. before the Am. Assoc. for the Advancement of Science, Kansas City, Missouri, 12/28/25-1/02/26, in Davenport Papers, Am. Philosophical Soc. Library, also Hrdlička Papers, Misc. Subjects, NAA. Marsh to Davenport, 12/17/25, Am. Philosophical Soc. Library. *Science*, 1/29/26, p. 115; NYT, 1/02/26. Copy of Res. delivered to State Dept., 1/21/26, in Livingston to SecSt, 4/09/26, 819.00/1262. Committee mentioned in notes on interview with Marsh, in 819.00/1244.

11. 819.6176; S&H, 1/23/26

12. *Washington Evening Star,* 3/10, 3/12/26; NYT, 3/12/26; S&H, 3/12, 3/13, 3/19/26; *Rochester Evening Journal,* 3/29/26; *El Tiempo,* 4/01/26, in 819.00/1273. Pan. Minister Washington to State, 3/15/26; Grew to SecWar, 3/29/26; Asst. SecState to Attorney General, 3/29/26; Flint to Governor Canal Zone, 3/31, 4/08/26; SecWar Davis to State, 4/06/26; Flint to Martyn, 4/05/26—all in 80-A-15, PC, NARS. 819.00/1260, 1267, 1268, 1272, 1273, 1274.

13. "Marsh. Expediente Investigacion, Agencia William Burns, Marzo 15 a 31 de 1926. Expediente sobre la Rebelión de Tule, Relaciones Exteriores, 1925" (courtesy of Francisco Herrera).

14. Grew, State to Attorney General, 3/29/26, 819.00/1260; J. E. Hoover to Grew, 4/26/26, Bureau of Investigation Report, 4/21/26, 819.1275.

15. Marsh, ms. "British Influence," Pamphlet file "Panama," NAA. NYT, 4/05, 4/07, 4/11, 5/16, 6/04, 6/05, 6/06, 6/08, 6/18/26. Memo of conversation w/Marsh, Division of Latin American Affairs, 819.6341, 819.602, 819.6126/2, 819.6341, 819.676/2. Major (1993:186).

16. NYT, 6/06, 6/08/26.

17. File 93957, RU 192, SIA, especially Marsh to Smithsonian, 8/31/27; Wetmore to Marsh, 9/01/27; Marsh to Wetmore, 9/03, 9/09, 9/30/27; Marsh to Little, 9/20/27; Ravenel to Marsh, 8/13/27. *Washington Evening Star,* 9/08/27; NYT, 8/31, 9/07/27; *Washington Post,* 12/04/27.

18. Intv., R. O. Marsh Jr., 5/84, 1/86; obituary, *Explorer's Journal,* Autumn 1953, pp. 54-55; *National Cyclopedia of American Biography* v. 40, 1955, pp. 573-574.

19. Hernández (1996); Lane (1983:27-29): Misioneros Hijos (1939:116-145).

20. According to Hayans (ms. "Algunas obras"), Nele formally succeeded Colman in 1927. In a letter to Harrington from November 1927, Colman describes himself as "cacique de la tribu" and Nele as "el segundo" (Colman, Nele, Slater, Davis et al. to Harrington, 11/03/27, Harrington Corresp., courtesy of Elaine Mills). In a continuing search for support, Colman and others sent letters and cables from Colón to Cartagena to Marsh, Harrington, and presumably others (Colman to Harrington, 8/24, 11/24/27, 12/25/28, courtesy Elaine Mills).

21. S&H, 8/08, 8/12/30; Davis to State, 8/22/30, 819.00/1516; Cruse, report no. 856, 8/25/30, 819.00/1522. According to Estanislao López (ms. "Congresos Generales"), Nele began trying to deal with the government on specific issues as early as 1928. According to Samuel Morris (intv., 1/28/91), Nele was motivated by rumors of a new concession on the coast.

22. S&H, 8/15, 8/16/30. Group of Kuna leaders to Pres. F. H. Arosemena, 8/13/30, in Nördenskiold et al. (1938:115-117), in S&H, 8/15/30, also in Guionneau-Sinclair (1991:21-23). Davis to State, 8/22/30, 819.00/1516.

23. Intv., Samuel Morris, 1/28/91.

24. S&H, 8/26/30. Davis to State, 819.00/1517.

25. S&H, 8/30/30.

26. Nele and Inabaginya to F. H. Arosemena, 9/08/30, in Nordenskiöld et al. (1938:117-118). S&H, 8/16, 8/n.d./30. 819.00/1516, 1517, 1518, 1522. Mensaje dirigido por el presidente . . . , 9/01/30, in 819.032/135.

27. C. Robinson to F. H. Arosemena, 10/29/30, in Nördenskiold et al. (1938:118-119). "Mensaje dirigido por el presidente . . . ," in 819.032/135. Ley 59 de 1930, GO 5901, Año XXVIII, 1/07/31; also in Nordenskiöld et al. (1938:112-114); also in Guionneau-Sinclair (1991:21-23). "Mensaje dirigido por Primer Designado . . ." in 819.032/140.

28. "Bananas in Panama and Canal Zone," 11/08/34, in Corresp. U.S. Consul Colón, 861.5, NARS. S&H, 5/n.d./34; Confidential Corresp. no. 6, no. 23, Colón, 852. 819.6156/5,6. In 1934 Standard Fruit transferred all its holdings in Mandinga back to the government, which meant in effect to the Kuna.

29. Ley 2 de 1938, GO 7873, Año XXXV, 9/23/38.

30. Marsh ms. [1932], untitled, Marsh to Stimson 10/22/32 (courtesy R. O. Marsh Jr.). These are the ancestors of more recent Somozas and Chamorros.

31. Intv., R. O. Marsh Jr., 5/84, 1/86; obituary, *Explorer's Journal*, Autumn 1953, pp. 54-55; *National Cyclopedia of American Biography*, v. 40, 1955, pp. 573-574; obituaries *Miami Herald, Washington Star, Washington Post*, 9/06/53.

32. Nordenskiöld et al. (1938); Hayans, ms. "Algunas obras"; Chapin (1983:17-24, 444-482); Holloman, ms.; Holloman (1969:439-454). See also material on Nele's life cited in chapter 8.

33. *Panama American*, 4/29, 5/06, 5/09, 6/03, 6/04/33; S&H, 4/29, 5/06, 5/09, 6/03/33; Holloman (1969:346-348); Hudgins Morgan (1958); Iglesias and Vandervelde (1977); Keeler (1956:169-176); Lane (1983:39-47); Vandervelde and Iglesias (1983).

34. Estanislao López, ms.; *La Hora*, 2/12/66.

35. *Panamá America*, 6/17/75; *Matutino*, 8/27/75; *Est.*, 8/27/75.

36. Swain (1977); Tice (1995).

37. Lane (1983:75-86).

38. Chapin (1992).

39. Moore (1981).

40. Olivardía (1963:88-94).

41. *Est.*, 11/01/77.

42. Breslin and Chapin (1984); New Scientist, 6/24/82; Wali (1989, 1995).

43. Ventocilla, Herrera, and Nuñez (1995); Ventocilla et al. (1995).

Bibliography

Unpublished Manuscripts

Anonymous
  "Biografía del Sr. Manuel González" (courtesy of Sr. González).
  "Biografía del Cacique General John Colman (Inakintipipilele)" (courtesy of William Durham).
Breder, Charles M.
  (1924) "Marsh-Darien Expedition: Journal of the Representative from the American Museum of
  Natural History, C. M. Breder, Jr." (CMBd) (Archives of American Museum of Natural History),
  divided into volumes: CMBdI, 1/16/24-3/26/24; CMBdII, 3/26-7/06/24.
Castillero [López], Efrain, and Enrique Obaldia
  (c. 1966) "Biografía del Cacique Nele Kantule."
  (1975-1976) "Biografía de Nele Kantule, Sahila Tumat (Cacique General) de San Blas (1868-1944)
  con motivo del XXXI aniversario de su muerte."
Centro de Investigaciones Kunas
  (c. 1986) "Nombres míticos de los centros de insurrección de 1925."
Davis, Watson
  (1924) "The Discovery of the White Indians of Panama, as told by R. O. Marsh, their discoverer, to
  Watson Davis." Science Service, Washington D.C.
Jane Davenport Harris
  (c. 1925) Untitled narrative of her experiences in San Blas (incomplete).
Harris, Reginald G.
  (Jan.-Feb. 1925) Untitled field notes in San Blas (Davenport-Harris Papers, Cold Springs Harbor Lab-
  oratories).
Hayans, Guillermo (Archives of Chany Edman, Ustupu, Kuna Yala)
  "Algunas obras que hizo el Dr. Nele Kantule después de la Revolución de 1925."
  "Antes de la Revolución de San Blas de 1925."
  "Biografía del gran caudillo Yaicun."
  "Biografía del Sr. Iguanibinape."
  "Gran incendio en la comarca de San Blas."
  "Isla Pino."

"La Historia de Ogobsucun y su orígen."

"Historia de la Revolución de San Blas de 1925."

"The Life of Nele de Kantule"

"Palabra de Jaicun."

"Reseña histórica de la isla Wichuwala que hoy es pueblo y su fundación."

"Reseñas históricas de los primeros sahilas que fueron del pueblo Aguayoi en Río de Ucucenis y en la Isla Carnirtupo y su funadador."

Holloman, Regina

(1970s) "Nele Kantule: A Study of San Blas Cuna Leadership in a Period of Transition" (courtesy of the author).

López, Arnulfo Jr., and Juancito Colman

(7/28/77) "Breve biografía de Inakkintippippilele Colman, 1840-1929."

López, Estanislao (Archives of Estanislao López, Nargana and Panamá)

"Algunos relatos reseñas históricos de los congresos generales celebrados en la Comarca de San Blas, los abos que han tenidos en varios lugares de los pueblos."

"Apuntes históricos de los sucesos sangientas de la Comarca de San Blas de años de 1908-1917-1921-1923-1925-1952-1959-1962-1976-1977."

"Fechas de los caciques generales muertos, sus duraciones, administraciones estuvieron, y labores, sus relaciones."

"Nombres de los personajes olvidados de forjadores que dío alumbramientos de la Comarca de San Blas, actualmente que se encuentra en progreso en San Blas."

Untitled: Various village histories.

Untitled: Biographies of various village leaders.

Untitled: Various historical materials on Nargana.

William Markham (Tioga Point Museum, Athens, Pa.)

Untitled narrative of Markham's experiences in San Blas in 1923 (IF/2905) Tioga Point Museum, Athens, Pa.

Untitled narrative of Markham's involvement in events following the Kuna rebellion of 1925 (IF/2907) Tioga Point Museum, Athens, Pa.

Richard O. Marsh (privately held by Richard O. Marsh Jr., unless otherwise indicated)

(1923-24) "The Primitive White People of Eastern Panama" (also at NAA).

(Probably late 1924) "The Marsh-Darien Expedition of 1924" (NAA).

(1924-25) Diaries in San Blas and Darién (ROMd), in the nominal form of an extended letter to Helen Cleveland Marsh (NAA), divided into notebooks: ROMd24a, 2/05-4/15/24; ROMd24b, 4/17-4/23/24; ROMd24c, 5/01-5/02/24; ROMd24d, 5/06-5/28/24; ROMd24e, 5/29-5/30/24; ROMd24f, 5/31/24-6/04/24; ROMd25a, 1/22-2/05/25; ROMd25b, 2/09-2/15/25; ROMd25c, 2/17/25; ROMd25d, 2/18-2/25/25; ROMd25e, 3/02/25, with copies of documents from 2/25 and 2/26/25; ROMd25f, "Conclusions," written 6/25.

(1925) "Declaration of Independence and Human Rights of the Tule People of San Blas and the Darien."

(c. 1925) "Scientific Aspects and Matters of Interest of the Tule People, Concerning Which Further Investigation is Desired and Contemplated."

(1926) "British Influence, and Control of the Future Industrial Development of, Panama" (NAA).

(1926) "The Trail of the White Indians."

(1932) Untitled: On the situation in Nicaragua.

(c. 1934-35) Untitled: Projected revisions for a new edition of *White Indians of Panama*.

(1935) "Lost Colony of Greenland Norsemen: Are They the White Indians of Darien?"

Tape-Recorded Oral Histories and Interviews

Recorded by Jesús Alemancia (JA), Cebaldo de León (CdL), and James Howe (JH).

Anonymous, Ailigandi No. 1, 2/20/85 (JA).
Anonymous, Ailigandi No. 2, 2/85 (JA).
Anonymous, Ailigandi No. 3, 2/85 (JA).
Anonymous, Ailigandi No. 4, 2/85 (JA).
Anonymous, Tupile, 2/23/85 (JA).
Archibold, Willy. Ustupu, 2/22/85 (CdL).
Arosemena, Vicente. Niatupu, 5/04/85 (JH).
Avila, Simón. Playón Chico, 7/11/75 (JH).
Barratt, Gladys. Vero Beach, Fla., 10/14/84 (JH).
Breder, Priscilla. Venice, Fla., 10/10/84 (JH).
Brenes, Mateo. Niatupu, 2/23/85, 4/12/85 (JH).
Campos, Manuel. Niatupu, 2/25/91 (JH).
Díaz, Ricardo. Río Azúcar, 6/10/85 (JA).
Garrido. Carti Yantupu, 6/n.d./85 (JA).
Gonzalez, Eliberto. Niatupu, 2/24/91.
Gonzalez, Manuel. Playón Chico, 7/12/75 (JH).
Grado, Manuel. Achutupu, 5/19/85 (JH).
Guillén, Benito. 6/n.d./85 (JA).
Hipólito, Miguel. Niatupu, 2/22/85, 2/20/91 (JH).
López, Carlos. Tupile, 2/85 (CdL).
López, Sra. de. Tupile, 2/85 (CdL).
Martinez, William. 6/n.d./85 (JA).
Morris, Samuel, of Ailigandi. 2/n.d./85 (JA).
Morris, Samuel, of Nargana. Panama City, 1/28/89 (JH).
Orán, Antonio. Tupile, 2/23/85 (JA).
Paredes, Manuel. Playón Chico, 7/11/75 (JH).
Pérez, Elena. Ailigandi, 2/85 (JA).
Pérez, Juan. Tigre, 6/13/85 (JA).
Porras, Camilo. Niatupu, 11/71, 2/25/85 (JH).
Salcedo, Gonzalo. Niatupu, 10/07/74 (JH).
Sir Willis. Ustupu, 2/20/85 (CdL).
Solís, Jimmy. Ailigandi, 2/85 (JA).
Stewart, T. D. Washington, D.C., 10/31/84 (JH).
Thompson, Ricardo. Niatupu, 4/14/85 (JH).
Villaláz, Ceferino. Tigre, 4/12/85 (JH).
Walter, Luis. Carti Suitupu, 6/08/85 (JA).
William, Saly. Ailigandi, 2/85 (JA).

Published Works

Aiban Wagwa: see Victoriano Smith

Adas, Michael
1979 *Prophets of Rebellion: Millenarian Protest Movements against the European Colonial Order.* Chapel Hill: University of North Carolina Press.
1989 *Machines as the Measure of Men: Science, Technology, and Ideologies of Western Dominance.* Ithaca, N.Y.: Cornell University Press.
1992 "From Avoidance to Confrontation: Peasant Protest in Precolonial and Colonial Southeast Asia." In *Colonialism and Culture,* edited by Nicholas Dirks. Ann Arbor: University of Michigan Press, pp. 89–126.

Alcedo y Herrera, Dionisio de
1972 [1743] "Diario y derrota de Don Dionisio de Alcedo y Herrera Gobernador y Comandante General del Reino de Tierra Firme. . . ." *Hombre y Cultura* 2:141–161.

Allen, Grace
1926 "Reactions of Eight San Blas Indians to Performance Tests." *American Journal of Physical Anthropology* 9:81–85.

Andagoya, Pascual de
1865 "Narrative of the Proceedings of Pedrarias Davila. Edited and translated by Clements Markham. London: *Publications of the Hakluyt Society* 34.

Andreve, Guillermo
1926 *Directório General de la Ciudad de Panamá.* 2d ed. Panamá: Andreve y Compañia.

Anonymous
1916 *Excursión á la costa de San Blas en Panamá.* Madrid: Publicaciones del Boletín de la Real Sociedad Geográfica.
1924 "The White Indians of Darien." *Science* 60:xii.
1940 [1739] *Anonymous Spanish Manuscript from 1739 on the Province Darien: A Contribution to the Colonial History and Ethnography of Panama and Colombia.* Edited by S. Henry Wassén. Göteborg: Etnologiska Studier 10.
1960 [1740s–1750s] "Descripción y derrotero de la Provincia de Santo Domingo del Darién. . . ." *Lotería* 61:58–64.
1961 "Nele Kantule (1868–1944)." *Lotería* 65:1101.
1974 [c. 1741] "Noticia de la Provincia del Darién: Copia que se sacó de unos papeles antiguos que envió al Sr. Virrey en el año de 1789 el Conde del real Agrado." *Hombre y Cultura* 2(5):143–157.

Antorveza, Adolfo (editor)
1980 *Legislación indígena nacional: leyes, decretos, resoluciones, jurisprudencia, y doctrina.* Bogotá: Editorial América Latina.

Arias, Miñoso
1996 "Revolución Kuna y la educación." *Onmaked* 2:10.

Araúz, Celestino
1988 "Belisario Porras y las relaciones de Panamá con los Estados Unidos." *Cuadernos Universitarios* 3. Panamá: Imprenta Universitaria.

Araúz, Celestino, and Patricia Pizzurno
1991 "Las incursiones extranjeras y el sistema defensivo de Panamá." Panama: *La Prensa* Fascículo Mensual.
1993 *El Panamá colombiano.* Panamá: Primer Banco de Ahorros y Diario la Prensa de Panamá.

Ariza S., Alberto E.
1964 *Los Domínicos en Panamá.* Bogotá: Convento-Seminario de Santo Domingo.

Ariza, Andrés de

1971 [1774] "Comentos de la rica y fertilisma Provincia del Darién Año de 1774." *Hombre y Cultura* 2:107-115.

Arnold, David

1993 *Colonizing the Body: State Medicine and Epidemic Disease in Nineteenth Century India.* Berkeley: University of California Press.

Arosemena, Gustavo

1980 "Metabolismo de la tirosina en albinos cunas." *Revista Médica de Panamá* 5:61-67.

Arosemena de Arosemena, Marcia

1972 "La estrategia Española de la colonización del Darién en el siglo XVIII." *Actas del III Simposium Nacional de Antropología, Arqueología, y Etnohistoria de Panamá.* Panamá: INAC.

Assembly of Jamaica

1747 *Journals of the Assembly of Jamaica,* vol. 3, for 5/04-7/13/1731. Jamaica: Alexander Aikman.

Atz, James

1986 "C. M. Breder, Jr." *Copeia* 3:853-856.

Axtell, James

1985. *The Invasion Within: The Contest of Cultures in Colonial North America.* Oxford University Press.

Ayarza Pérez, Virgilio

1981 *Genesis del movimiento revolucionário del pueblo kuna de 1925.* Thesis, Universidad de Panamá.

Bakhtin, Mikhail

1984 *Rabelais and His World.* Translated by Hélène Iswolsky. Bloomington: Indiana University Press.

Bancroft, Hubert Howe

1990 [1883] *History of Mexico.* Irvine, Calif.: Reprint Services.

Beach, Rex

1917 "The San Blas People." *Cosmopolitan,* January 1917, 143-145.

Beidelman, T. O.

1974 "Social Theory and the Study of Christian Missionaries in Africa." *Africa* 44:235-249.

1982 *Colonial Evangelism: A Sociohistorical Study of an East African Mission at the Grassroots.* Bloomington: Indiana University Press.

Berkhofer, Robert

1978 *The White Man's Indian: Images of the American Indian from Columbus to the Present.* New York: Random House.

1988 "White Conceptions of Indians." In *History of Indian-White Relations,* edited by Wilcomb E. Washburn, pp. 522-547. Handbook of North American Indians, vol. 4, William C. Sturtevant, general editor. Smithsonian Institution, Washington, D.C.

Bhabha, Homi

1985 "Signs Taken for Wonders: Questions of Ambivalence and Authority under a Tree outside Delhi, May 1817." In *"Race," Writing, and Difference,* edited by Henry Louis Gates, pp. 163-184. Chicago: University of Chicago Press.

Biesanz, John, and Mavis Biesanz

1955 *The People of Panama.* New York: Columbia University Press.

Blocker, Jack S.

1976 *Retreat from Reform: The Prohibition Movement in the United States, 1890-1913.* Westport Conn.: Greenwood Press.

1989 *American Temperance Movements: Cycles of Reform.* Boston: Twayne.

Boas, Franz

1911a *The Mind of Primitive Man.* New York: Macmillan.

1911b "Changes in the Bodily Form of Descendants of Immigrants." *Reports of the Immigration Commission,* 61st Cong., 2d sess., SDoc. 208. Washington, D.C.: Government Printing Office.

1928 *Anthropology and Modern Life.* New York: Norton.

Brandes, Joseph

1962 *Herbert Hoover and Economic Diplomacy: Department of Commerce Policy, 1921-1928.* Pittsburgh, Pa.: University of Pittsburgh Press.

1981 "Product Diplomacy: Herbert Hoover's Anti-Monopoly Campaign at Home and Abroad." In *Herbert Hoover as Secretary of Commerce: Studies in New Era Thought and Practice.* Iowa City: University of Iowa Press.

Brandon, William

1986 *New Worlds for Old: Reports from the New World and their Effect on the Development of Social Thought in Europe, 1500-1800.* Athens: Ohio University Press.

Breder, Charles

1925 "In Darien Jungles: Experiences of a Student of Reptile and Amphibian Life in a Little-Known Part of Panama." *Natural History* 25:324-337.

1927 *The Fishes of the Rio Chucunaque River Drainage, Eastern Panama.* Bulletin of the American Museum of National History 57.

1946 *Amphibians and Reptiles of the Rio Chucunaque Drainage, Darien, Panama, with Notes on Their Life Histories and Habits.* Bulletin of the American Museum of Natural History 86.

Breslin, Patrick, and Mac Chapin

1984 "Ecología estilo kuna." *Desarrollo de Base* 8:26-35.

Breuer, Kimberly Henke

1993 *Colonies of Happenstance: The English Settlements in Central America, 1525-1787.* Ph.D. dissertation, University of Texas at Arlington.

Brinton, Crane

1938 *The Anatomy of Revolution.* New York: W. W. Norton.

Brown, Judith K.

1970 "Sex Division of Labor among the San Blas Cuna." *Anthropological Quarterly* 43:57-63.

Brown, Michael

1996 "On Resisting Resistance." *American Anthropologist* 98:729-735.

Browne, Janet

1995 *Charles Darwin: Voyaging.* Princeton, N.J.: Princeton University Press.

Burkhardt, Louise

1989 *The Slippery Earth: Nahua-Christian Moral Dialogue in Sixteenth-Century Mexico.* Tucson: University of Arizona Press.

Burner, David

1979 *Herbert Hoover, A Public Life.* New York: Knopf.

Burns, Bradford

1980 *The Poverty of Progress: Latin America in the Nineteenth Century.* Berkeley: University of California Press.

Bushnell, David

1993 *The Making of Modern Colombia: A Nation in Spite of Itself.* Berkeley: University of California Press.

Bushnell, David, and Neil Macaulay

1988 *The Emergence of Latin America in the Nineteenth Century.* Oxford: Oxford University Press.

Callahan, William

1984 *Church, Politics, and Society in Spain, 1750-1874.* Cambridge, Mass.: Harvard University Press.

Canduela, H. Macario

1909 "Ministerios apostólicos entre los karibes: Carta del H. Macario Canduela al P. Socio. Panamá, 1o de Agosto de 1908." *Cartas Edificantes de la Asistencia de España,* Año 1908, pp. 198-202. Burgos.

Castillero Calvo, Alfredo

1984 "La ruta transístmica y las comunicaciones marítimas Hispanas, Siglos XVI a XIX." Panamá: n.p.

1991 "Subsistencias y economía en la sociedad colonial: El caso del istmo de Panamá." *Hombre y Cultura* 1(2):3-93.

1995 *Conquista, evangelisación, y resistencia: ¿Triunfo o fracaso de la política indigenista?* Panamá: INAC.

Castillero R., Ernesto

1946 "Historia de la extraña república de Tule. *Biblioteca Selecta* 1(10):17-36.

Castillo, Angelica, and Micaela Méndez

1962 *La Revolución de Tule, 1925.* Master's thesis, Universidad de Panamá.

Castro Vega, Oscar

1996 *Pedrarias Dávila: La ira de dios.* Costa Rica: Litografía e Imprenta LIL.

Castillo, Bernal

1995 "Una visión histórica de los Kunas en el periodo colonial de los siglos XVI-XVII." *Onmaked* 1:5-6.

1996 "Intendencia: su orígen." *Onmaked* 2:4-5.

Chalk, Robert

1970 *The United States and the International Struggle for Rubber, 1914-1941.* Ph.D. dissertation, University of Wisconsin, Madison.

Chapin, Mac

1970 *Pab igala: Historias de la tradición kuna.* Panamá: Centro de Investigaciones Antropológicas. Reprinted 1989. Quito: Ediciones Abya Yala. Colección 500 Años.

1983 *Curing among the San Blas Kuna of Panama.* Ph.D. dissertation, University of Arizona.

1991 "Losing the Way of Great Father." *New Scientist* 10(August):40-44.

1992 "The Final Journey of Padre Jesús: A Narrative for the Quincentenary." *Encounters* 10(Fall):31-37, 48.

Chardkoff, Richard

1970 "The Cuna Revolt" *Américas* 22:14-21.

Chase, Allan

1977 *The Legacy of Malthus: The Social Costs of the New Scientific Racism.* New York: Knopf.

Cheville, Lila, and Richard Cheville

1977 *Festivals and Dances of Panama.* Panama: n.p.

Chomsky, Noam

1979 *Language and Responsibility.* Based on conversations with Mitsou Ronat. Translated by John Viertel. New York: Pantheon.

Coates, Austin

1987 *The Commerce in Rubber: The First 250 Years.* Singapore: Oxford University Press.

Coatesworth, John

1988 "Patterns of Rural Rebellion in Latin America: Mexico in Comparative Perspective." In *Riot, Rebellion, and Revolution: Rural Social Conflict in Mexico,* edited by Friedrich Katz, pp. 21-62. Princeton, N.J.: Princeton University Press.

Cohn, Norman

1970 *The Pursuit of the Millennium: Revolutionary Messianism in Medieval and Reformation Europe and Its Bearing on Modern Totalitarian Movements.* New York: Harper.

Comaroff, Jean

1985 *Body of Power, Spirit of Resistance: the Culture and History of a South African People.* Chicago: University of Chicago Press.

Comaroff, Jean, and John Comaroff

1991 *Of Revelation and Revolution: Christianity, Colonialism, and Consciousness in South Africa.* Vol. 1. Chicago: University of Chicago Press.

Congreso General Kuna de la Cultura

1994 "¡Noticias de sangre de nuestro pueblo!: Nuestros padres nos lo relatan así." Pamphlet. Translated and synthesized by Aiban Wagua. San José: Ediciones COOPA.

Conniff, Michael

1985 *Black Labor on a White Canal, 1904-1981.* Pittsburgh, Pa.: University of Pittsburgh Press.

1988 "Panama since 1903." In *The Cambridge History of Latin America,* vol. 7, edited by Leslie Bethell, pp. 603-642. New York: Cambridge University Press.

1992 *Panama and the United States: The Forced Alliance.* Athens: University of Georgia Press.

Conrad, Joseph

1973 [1902] *The Heart of Darkness.* London: Penguin Books.

Cooke, Richard

1984 Review of: Mary Helms, *Ancient Panama: Chiefs in Search of Power. Ethnohistory* 31: 115-116.

Coope, Anna

1917 *Anna Coope: Sky Pilot of the San Blas Indians.* New York: American Tract Society (2d ed., 1931).

Cravens, Hamilton

1978 *The Triumph of Evolution: American Scientists and the Heredity-Environment Controversy 1900-1941.* Philadelphia: University of Pennsylvania Press.

Cuervo, Antonio (editor)

1891 *Colección de documentos ineditos sobre la geografía y la historia de Colombia.* Bogotá: Zalamea Hermanos.

Cullen, Edward

1853 *Isthmus of Darién Ship Canal.* London: Effingham Wilson.

Dampier, William

1927 [1697] *A New Voyage Round the World.* London: Argonaut Press.

Davenport, Charles

1911 *Heredity in Relation to Eugenics,* New York: Holt.

Davis, Nathaniel

1934 [1704] "'The Expedition of a Body of Englishmen to the Gold Mines of Spanish America. . . .'" In *A New Voyage and Description of the Isthmus of America,* edited by L. E. Elliott Joyce, pp. 152-165. Oxford: Hakluyt Society.

Deas, Malcom

1985 "Venezuela, Colombia, and Eduador: The First Half-Century of Independence. In *The Cambridge History of Latin America,* vol. 3, edited by Leslie Bethell, pp. 507-538. Cambridge: Cambridge University Press.

Degler, Carl

1991 *In Search of Human Nature: The Decline and Revival of Darwinism in American Social Thought.* Oxford: Oxford University Press.

DeLeón Madariaga, Edgardo

1980 *Presencia y symbolismo del traje nacional de Panamá, la pollera.* Panamá: n.p.

Densmore, Frances

1926 *Music of the Tule Indians of Panama.* Smithsonian Institution Miscellaneous Collections 77. Washington, D.C.

Department of the Navy, Naval History Division
　　1963 *Dictionary of American Fighting Ships.* Washington, D.C.: Government Printing Office.
de Puydt, Lucien
　　1868 "Account of Scientific Expeditions in the Isthmus of Darien in the Years 1861 and 1865." *Journal of Royal Geographic Society* 38:69-110.
Dietrick, Jackie
　　1925 "For Twelve Years a Saver of San Blas Souls." *Panama Times* (May 9, 16, 23, and 30).
Dirks, Nicholas
　　1992 "Introduction: Colonialism and Culture." In *Colonialism and Culture,* edited by Nicholas Dirks. Ann Arbor: University of Michigan Press, pp. 1-25.
Drolet, Patricia
　　1980 *The Congo Ritual of Northeastern Panama: An Afro-American Expressive Structure of Cultural Adaptation.* Ph.D. dissertation, University of Illinois.
Dunham, Jacob
　　1850 *Journal of Voyages.* New York: Hucstis and Cozans.
Earle, Peter
　　1981 *The Sack of Panama: Sir Henry Morgan's Adventures on the Spanish Main.* New York: Viking.
Erice, Jesús
　　1949 [Biography of Nele Kantule] *Juventud Sanblaseña.* Cited in Holloman, ms. "Nele Kantule. . . ."
　　1951 "El trágico episodio de Río Azúzar." *Juventud Sanblaseña* 31, n.p. (16pp.).
　　1961 "Primer etapa de la civilización de San Blas." *Lotería* 65:67-68.
　　1975 "Historia de la revolución de los indios kunas de San Blas." *Estudios Centroamericanos* 319-320:283-304; 321:362-388; also *Hombre y Cultura* 3:135-167, 1975.
Esquemeling, John [or Alexandre]
　　1924 *The Buccaneers of America.* New York: E. P. Dutton.
Fábrega, Ramón, and Mario Boyd Galindo
　　1981 *Constituciones de la República de Panamá, 1972, 1946, 1941, 1904.* Panamá: n.p.
Fairchild, H. L.
　　1924 "White Indians of Darien." *Science* 60:235-237.
Falla, Ricardo
　　n.d. [mid-1970s] *Historia kuna, historia rebelde: la articulación del archipielago kuna a la nación panameña.* Panamá: Ediciones Centro de Capacitación Social.
Faron, Louis
　　1961 "A Re-interpretation of Chocó Society." *Southwestern Journal of Anthropology* 17:94-102.
　　1962 "Marriage, Residence, and Domestic Group among the Panamanian Chocó." *Ethnology* 1:13-38.
Fernández, Jesús Maria
　　1911. "Panamá, Noticias de la misión de los caribes: Carta del P. Jesús Ma. Fernández al P. Juan Ma. Restrepo; Colón, 11 de Septiembre de 1910." *Cartas Edificantes de la Asistencia de España,* Año 1910, pp. 285-289. Burgos. Reprinted in *Lotería* (Panamá) II, 66(1961):97-100.
Figueroa Navarro, Alfredo
　　1978 *Dominio y sociedad en el Panamá colombiano (1821-1903).* Panamá: Impresora Panamá.
　　1987 *Los grupos populares de la ciudad de Panamá a fines del siglo diecinueve.* Panamá: Impretex.
Fock, Niels
　　1963 *Wai-wai: Religion and Society of an Amazonian Tribe.* Copenhagen: National Museum.
Foster, George
　　1960 *Culture and Conquest: America's Spanish Heritage.* Viking Fund Publications in Anthropology 27. New York.

Foucault, Michel
1979 *Discipline and Punish: The Birth of the Prison.* Translated by Alan Sheridan. New York: Vantage.

Franck, Harry
1913 *Zone Policeman 88: A Close Range Study of the Panama Canal and Its Workers.* New York: Century.

Galvin, Peter R.
1991 *The Pirates' Wake: A Geography of Piracy and Pirates as Geographers in Colonial Spanish America, 1536-1718.* Ph.D. dissertation, Louisiana State University.

Garay, Narciso
1982 [1930] *Tradiciones y cantares de Panamá: ensayo folklórico.* Panamá: n.p.

Gassó, Leonardo
1908a *Doctrina y catecismo popular en castellano y karibe-kuna.* Barcelona: Tipografía Católica.

1908b *Gramática karibe-kuna.* Barcelona: Tipografía Católica.

1909a "Ministerios apostólicos entre los karibes: Carta del Padre Leonardo Gassó al P. Cesáreo Ibero; Panama, 7 de Noviembre de 1908." *Cartas Edificantes de la Asistencia de España,* Año 1908, pp. 204-211. Burgos.

1909b "The Establishment of the Mission among the Caribs: Letter of Father Leonardo Gassó to Father Alós; Panama, November 7th, 1908." *Woodstock Letters* 38:228-240. Baltimore, Md.: Woodstock College.

1910a "Fundación de un pueblo cristiano entre los caribes: Carta del P. Leonardo Gassó al R. P. Antonio Iñesta; Panama, 28 de Mayo de 1909." *Cartas Edificantes de la Asistencia de España,* Año 1909, 1, pp. 319-338. Burgos. Reprinted in *Lotería* (Panamá) II, 63(1961):79-95.

1910b "Informe sobre la catequización de los indios karibes de la Costa de San Blas y del Río Bayano, en la República de Panamá." *Las Misiones Católicas* 18:152-153, 163-165. Barcelona.

1910c "Panama—The Mission among the Caribs, From a Letter of Father Leonardo Gassó, S.J., to Father Juan Bautista Ferreres, Panama, March 1909." *Woodstock Letters* 39:180-184. Baltimore, Md.: Woodstock College.

1911a "Viaje á la isla de San José, y entrevista con los caribes de la isla del sagrado corazón: Carta del P. Gassó al P. Alós; Panamá, 3 de Enero de 1910." *Cartas Edificantes de la Asistencia de España,* Año 1910, 1, pp. 282-290. Burgos. Reprinted in *Lotería* (Panamá) II, 65(1961):75-82.

1911b "Funciones religiosas y bautizo de catecúmenos entre los caribes; conversaciones á la hora de la muerte: Carta del P. Gassó al P. Cesáreo Ibero; Panamá, 14 de Septiembre de 1910." *Cartas Edificantes de la Asistencia de España,* Año 1910, 2:289-296. Burgos.

1911-1914 *La Misión de San José de Nargana entre los Karibes (República de Panamá), Las Misiones Católicas* 19-22, Barcelona. [Intermittent serial publication.]

1913 "Cartas del P. Leonardo Gassó, misionero entre los caribes [to P. Alós] Panamá, 27 de octubre de 1911." [to P. Nonell, n.d.]. *Cartas Edificantes de la provincia de Aragón,* Año 1912, 1:345-356. Barcelona.

Gates, Henry Louis
1991 "'Authenticity' of the Lesson of Little Tree (Effect of the Ethnic Identity of the Author on the Interpretation of the Work)." *New York Times* Book Review, November 1991.

Gil y Lemos, Francisco, et al.
1977 [1789] "Acuerdo de no agresión firmado entre los dirigentes cunas y las autoridades españolas . . . firmada el 25 de Oct. de 1789." *Hombre y Cultura* 3(2):155-162.

Gisborne, Lionel
1854 *The Isthmus of Darién in 1852.* London: Saunders and Stanford.

Gould, Jeffry
1996 "Gender, politics, and the Triumph of Mestizaje in Early 20th Century Nicaragua." *Journal of Latin American Anthropology* 2:4-33.

Gramsci, Antonio

1971 *Selections from the Prison Notebooks.* Edited and translated by Q. Hoare and G. N. Smith. London: Lawrence and Wishart.

Grant, Madison

1916 *The Passing of the Great Race, or the Racial Basis of European History.* New York: Scribner's.

Griffin, Walt

1988 *George W. Goethals and the Panama Canal.* Ph.D. dissertation, University of Cincinnati.

Guha, Ranajit

1983 *Elementary Aspects of Peasant Insurgency in Colonial India.* New Delhi: Oxford University Press.

1984 "The Prose of Counter-Insurgency." In *Subaltern Studies II,* edited by Ranajit Guha. New Delhi: Oxford University Press.

Guionneau-Sinclair, Francoise

1991 *Legislacion amerindia de Panamá.* Panamá: Imprenta Universitaria.

Gurruchaga, Leonardo

1909. "Ministerios apostólicos entre los karibes: Carta del H. Coadjutor, Leonardo Gurruchaga, al H. Portero del Colegio de Belén; Panamá; 30 de Octubre de 1908." *Cartas Edificantes de la Asistencia de España,* Año 1908, pp. 202-204. Burgos.

Gutiérrez, Ramón

1991. *When Jesus Came, the Corn Mothers Went Away.* Stanford, Calif.: Stanford University Press.

Hale, Charles

1996 "Mestizaje, Hybridity, and the Cultural Politics of Difference in Post-Revolutionary Central America." *Journal of Latin American Anthropology* 2:34-61.

Harlan, Harry

1932 "Early References to the White Indians of Panama." *Journal of Heredity* 8:319-322.

Harp, William

1994 "Ecology and Cosmology: Rain Forest Exploitation among the Emberá-Chocó. *Nature and Resources* 30:23-27.

Harris, Reginald

1922 "Eugenics in South America." *Eugenical News* 7(3):17-42.

1925a "The White Indians of the San Blas and Darien" *Science* 61:460-461.

1925b "The Scientific Importance of the White Indians." *World's Work,* June, pp. 211-217.

1926a "The San Blas Indians." *American Journal of Physical Anthropology* 9:17-63.

1926b "Los Indios Tule de San Blas." Pamphlet. Panamá: Imprenta Nacional.

Hayans, Guillermo

1938 "The Life of Nele de Kantule," In *Original Documents from the Cuna Indians of San Blas, Panama,* edited by S. Henry Wassén, pp. 31-44. Etnologiska Studier 26. Göteborg: Etnografiska Museum.

Healy, David

1988, *Drive to Hegemony: The United States in the Caribbean, 1898-1917.* Madison: University of Wisconsin Press.

Hellman, Geoffry

1968 *Bankers, Bones, and Beetles: The First Century of the American Museum of Natural History.* Garden City, N.Y.: Natural History Press.

Hendricks, Janet

1991 "Symbolic Counterhegemony among the Ecuadorian Shuar." In *Nation-States and Indians in Latin America,* edited by Greg Urban and Joel Sherzer, pp. 53-71. Austin: University of Texas Press.

Helms, Mary

1976 "Domestic Organization in Eastern Central America: The San Blas Cuna, Miskito, and Black Carib Compared." *Western Canadian Journal of Anthropology* 6:133-163.

1979 *Ancient Panama: Chiefs in Search of Power.* Austin: University of Texas Press.

1988 *Ulysses' Sail: An Ethnographic Odyssey of Power, Knowledge, and Geographical Distance.* Princeton: Princeton University Press.

Herbert, Wally

1989 *The Noose of Laurels: Robert E. Peary and the Race for the North Pole.* New York: Anchor Books.

Herlihy, Peter

1985 "Settlement and Subsistence Change among the Chocó Indians of the Darién Province, Eastern Panama: An Overview." *Conference of Latin Americanist Geographers Yearbook* 11:11-16.

1986 *A Cultural Geography of the Emberá and Wounan (Chocó) Indians of Darien, Panama, with Emphasis on Recent Village Formation and Economic Diversification.* Ph.D. dissertation, Louisiana State University.

1987 "Cambios en el paisaje cultural de los indios Emberá y Wounán (Chocóes) del Darién, Panamá." *Lotería* 5:131-143.

Hernández, Artinelio

1996 "Pos-revolución de 1925; (etapa de desculturización)." *Onmaked* 2:3-4.

Herrera, Francisco

1984. *La revolución de Tule: antecedentes y nuevos aportes.* Thesis, Universidad de Panamá.

1987 "La rebelión de Tule y el papel de la Legación Norteamericana." *Revista Panameña de Antropología* 3:40-56.

1989 *Indian-State Relations in Panama, 1903-1983.* Master's thesis, University of Florida, Gainesville.

Higham, John

1966 *Strangers in the Land: Patterns of American Nativism, 1860-1925.* New York, Atheneum.

Hirschfeld, Lawrence

1977 "Art in Cunaland: Ideology and Cultural Adaptation." *Man* n.s. 12:104-123.

Hobsbawm, Eric

1975 *The Age of Capital.* New York: Scribner.

1983 "Mass-Producing Traditions: Europe, 1870-1914." In *The Invention of Tradition,* edited by Eric Hobsbawn and Terence Ranger. New York: Cambridge University Press.

1987 *The Age of Empire, 1875-1914.* New York: Pantheon.

Hoffman, Paul E.

1980 *The Spanish Crown and the Defense of the Caribbean, 1535-1585.* Baton Rouge: Louisiana State University Press.

Holloman, Regina

1969 *Developmental Change in San Blas.* Ph.D. dissertation, Northwestern University.

1976 "Cuna Household Types and the Domestic Cycle." In *Frontier Adaptations in Lower Central America,* pp. 133-149. Philadelphia, Pa.: Institute for the Study of Human Issues.

Horton, Mark

n.d. [1980 or 1981] "Archaeological Project." *Operation Drake: Panama Report.* Pt. II, sec. 1, pp. 26-53.

Howe, James

1974 *Village Political Organization among the San Blas Cuna.* Ph.D. dissertation, University of Pennsylvania.

1976a "Communal Land Tenure and the Origin of Descent Groups among the San Blas Cuna." In *Frontier Adaptations in Lower Central America,* edited by Mary Helms and Franklin Loveland, pp. 151-163. Philadelphia, Pa.: Institute for the Study of Human Issues.

1976b "Smoking out the Spirits: A Cuna Exorcism." In *Ritual and Symbol in Native Central America,* edited by Philip Young and James Howe, pp. 67-76. University of Oregon Anthropological Papers 9. Eugene.

1977a "Algunos problemas no resueltos de la etnohistoria del Este de Panamá." *Revista Panameña de Antropología* 2:30-47.

1977b "Carrying the Village: Cuna Political Metaphors." In *The Social use of Metaphor,* edited by David Sapir and Christopher Crocker, pp. 132-163. Philadelphia: University of Pennsylvania Press.

1985 "Marriage and Domestic Organization among the San Blas Kuna." In *The Botany and Natural History of Panama,* edited by William Darcy and Mireya Correa, pp. 317-331. St. Louis: Missouri Botanical Garden.

1986 *The Kuna Gathering: Contemporary Village Politics in Panama.* Austin: University of Texas Press.

1990 "Mission Rivalry and Conflict in San Blas, Panama." In *Class, Politics, and Popular Religion in Mexico and Central America,* edited by Lynn Stephen and James Dow, pp. 143-166. Society for Latin American Anthropology Publication Series 10.

1991 "An Ideological Triangle: The Struggle over San Blas Kuna Culture, 1915-1925." In *Nation-States and Indians in Latin America,* edited by Greg Urban and Joel Sherzer, pp. 19-52. Austin: University of Texas Press.

1992 "Protestants, Catholics, and 'Gentiles': The Articulation of Missionary and Indigenous Culture on the San Blas Coast of Panama." *Journal of the Anthropological Society of Oxford* 23:139-155.

1994 With the assistance of Jesús Alemancia and Cebaldo de León, based on oral texts by Carlos López, Samuel Morris, and Jimmy Solís. "Sounds Heard in the Distance: Poetry and Metaphor in the Kuna Struggle for Autonomy." *Latin American Indian Literatures Journal* 10:1-21.

1995 "La lucha por la tierra en la costa de San Blas (Panamá), 1900-1930. *Mesoamerica* 29:57-76.

Howe, James, Joel Sherzer, and Mac Chapin

1980 *Cantos y oraciones del congreso cuna.* Panamá: Editorial Universitaria.

Hrdlička, Aleš

1926 "The Indians of Panama and Their Physical Relation to the Mayas." *American Journal of Physical Anthropology* 9:1-15.

Hyatt, Marshall

1990 *Franz Boas, Social Activist: The Dynamics of Ethnicity.* New York: Greenwood Press.

Iglesias, David

1992 "A Kuna Homecoming." *Native Peoples* 5:20-25.

1993 "Drawing the Line." *Native Peoples* 6:10-18.

Iglesias, Marvel, and Marjorie Vandervelde

1977 *Beauty Is a Ring in My Nose?* N.p.

Iguaniginape Kungiler

1994 "Ologindibipilele, Caminante y Guerrero de 1925." Panama: Colectivo de Editores Kunas, Instituto Cooperativo Interamericano.

Inakeliginia [Carlos López]

1997 *Así lo vi y así me lo contaron.* Recopilado, sintizado, y traducido por Aiban Wagwa. Kuna Yala, Panamá: Congreso General de la Cultura Kuna.

Isaza Calderón, Baltasar

1982 *Carlos Mendoza y su generación: historia de Panamá, 1821-1916.* Panamá: Academia Panameña de la Historia.

Jaén Suarez, Omar

1978 *La población del istmo de Panamá, del siglo XVI al siglo XX.* Panama: n.p.

JanMohamed, Abdul
1985 "The Economy of Manichean Allegory: The Function of Racial Difference in Colonialist Literature." In *"Race," Writing, and Difference*, edited by Henry Louis Gates, pp. 78-106. Chicago: University of Chicago Press.

Johnson, Harold
1925 "Crossing the Isthmus via Panama's Longest River: With the 1924 Scientific Expedition up the Rio Chucunaque." *Panama Times*, October 31, pp. 30, 32, 34, 36, 37.
1958 *Heads and Tails*. New York: Vantage Press.

Jones, Oakah
1986 "Cuna Rebellion and Panamanian Power, 1925." In *Proceedings of the Pacific Coast Council on Latin American Studies, 1982*. San Diego: San Diego State University Press.

Joyce, L. E. Elliott
1934 Introduction, Appendices, and Notes to Lionel Wafer. In *A New Voyage and Description of the Isthmus of America*, edited by L. E. Elliott Joyce, pp. xi-lxvii, 166-201. Oxford: Hakluyt Society 73, series 2.

Kane, Stephanie
1994 *The Phantom Gringo Boat*. Washington, D.C.: Smithsonian Institution Press.

Kantule, Rubén Pérez
1938 "Una resumen de la vida de Nele de Ustup." In *An Historical and Ethnological Survey of the Cuna Indians*, edited by Eland Nordenskiöld et al., pp. 89-91. Göteborg: Etnografiska Museum.

Keeler, Clyde
1953 "The Caribe Cuna Moon-Child and Its Heredity." *Journal of Heredity* 44:162-171.
1956 *Land of the Moon Children*. Athens, Ga.: University of Georgia Press.
1964 "Pigment Gene Pleiotropy in the Cuna Indian Moon-Child." *Mind over Matter* 9:30-41.
1964 "The Incidence of Cuna Moon-Child Albinos." *Journal of Heredity* 55:115-120.
1966 "Cuna Moon-Child Albinism." *Dermatology Digest*, February, pp. 41-49.
1968 "Note on Sweating and Odor of Cuna Albinos." *Dermatologia Internationalis* 7:78-80.

Keeler, Clyde, Irville MacKinnon, et al.
1963 "The Albino Moon-Child Research Project." *MSH Bulletin of Current Research* 2:3-27. Milledgeville (Ga.) State Hospital.

Keesing, Roger
1992 *Custom and Confrontation: The Kwaio Struggle for Cultural Autonomy*. Chicago: University of Chicago Press.

Kemp, Peter, and Christopher Lloyd
1960 *The Brethren of the Coast*. London: Heinemann.

Kevles, Daniel
1985 *In the Name of Eugenics: Genetics and the Uses of Human Diversity*. Berkeley: University of California.

Krieger, Herbert
1926 *Material Culture of the People of Southeastern Panama, Based on Specimens in the United States National Museum*. U.S. National Museum Bulletin 134. Washington, D.C.: Smithsonian Institution.

Kuhl, Stefan
1994 *The Nazi Connection: Eugenics, American Racism, and German National Socialism*. Oxford: Oxford University Press.

Laird, Carobeth

   1975 *Encounter with an Angry God: Recollections of My Life with John Peabody Harrington.* Banning, Calif.: Malki Museum Press.

Lane, Sherry Dixon

   1983 "The Influence of Missionary Activity among the San Blas Kuna, Panama." Master's thesis, Department of Geography and Anthropology, Louisiana State University.

Langebaek, Carl

   1991 "Cuna Long Distance Journeys: The Result of Colonial Interaction." *Ethnology* 30:371–380.

Lannon, Frances

   1987 *Privilege, Persecution, and Prophecy: The Catholic Church in Spain, 1875–1975.* Oxford: Clarendon Press.

Las Casas, Bartolomé

   1992 [1552] *The Devastation of the Indies: A Brief Account.* Translated by Herma Briffault. Baltimore, Md.: Johns Hopkins Press.

Lawrence, Peter

   1964 *Road Belong Cargo.* Manchester: Manchester University Press.

Leis, Raúl

   1992 *Machi: Un Kuna en la ciudad.* Panamá: CEASPA.

Lemaitre, Eduardo

   1971 *Panamá y su separación de Colombia.* Bogotá: Editorial Pluma.

Little, Daniel

   1989 *Understanding Peasant China: Case Studies in the Philosophy of Science.* New Haven, Conn.: Yale University Press.

López, Carlos [see Inakeliginia]

Lowen, Jacob

   1972 "El cambio cultural entre los Chocó de Panamá." *América Indígena* 32:159–168.

Luengo Muñoz, Manuel

   1959 "El Darién en la política internacional del siglo XVIII." *Estudios Americanos* 18(96-97):139–156.

   1961 "Génesis de las expediciones militares al Darién en 1785-6." *Anuario de Estudios Americanos* 18:335–416.

McCain, William

   1937 *The United States and the Republic of Panama.* Durham, N.C.: Duke University Press.

McCullough, David

   1977 *The Path between the Seas: The Creation of the Panama Canal, 1870-1914.* New York: Simon and Schuster.

McGrane, Bernard

   1989 *Beyond Anthropology: Society and the Other.* New York: Columbia University Press.

Major, John

   1993 *Prize Possession: The United States and the Panama Canal, 1903-1979.* Cambridge University Press.

Marsh, Richard

   1925 "Blond Indians of the Darien Jungle." *The World's Work,* March, pp. 483–497.

   1934 *White Indians of Darien.* New York: Putnam.

Martínez, Atilio

   1996 "Acta de la revolución Kuna de 1925." *Onmaked* 2:6–9.

Mega, Pedro

   1958 *Compendio biográfico de los iltmos. y excmos. monseñores, obispos, y arzobispos de Panamá.* Panama: Ministerio de Educación.

Mejicanos, Luis

   1914 "Hechos edificantes del H. Domingo González: Carta del H. Luis Mejicanos al P. Benito

Pérez; Panamá, 20 de Septiembre de 1913." *Cartas Edificantes de la Provincia de Castilla* 2(1):392-396. Oña.

Mellander, G. A.
1971. *The United States in Panamanian Politics: The Intriguing Formative Years.* Danville, Ill.: Interstate.

Mena Garcia, Maria del Carmen
1984 *La sociedad de Panamá en el siglo XVI.* Seville: Publicaciones del Excma. Diputación Provincial de Sevilla.

Méndez, Teodoro
1979 *El Darién: Imágen y Proyecciones.* Panamá: Instituto Nacional de Cultura.

Mendizabal, Rufo
1972 *Catalogus defunctorum in renata Societate Iesu ab a. 1814 a. 1917.* Rome: aped Curiam P. Gen.

Misioneros Hijos del Corazón de Maria
1939 *Memoria del Vicariato Apostólico del Darién, Panamá.* Panama: Imprenta Acción Católica.

Mitchell, Timothy
1988 *Colonizing Egypt.* Cambridge: Cambridge University Press.

Mitchell Hedges, F. A.
1923 *Battles with Giant Fish.* London: Duckworth.

Moore, Alexander
1981 Basilicas and Kingposts: A Proxemic and Symbolic Event Analysis of Competing Public Architecture among the San Blas Cuna. *American Ethnologist* 8:259-277.
1983 Lore and Life: Cuna Indian Pageants, Exorcism, and Diplomacy in the Twentieth Century. *Ethnohistory* 30:93-106.

Moore, Evelyn R.
1982 "Character of Western Illinois River Town Preserved in Warsaw Historic District." *Historic Illinois* 1982:8-10.

Morgan, Christine
1958 *I Married a San Blas Indian: The Story of Marvel Elya Iglesias.* New York: Vantage Press.

Nida, Eugene
1966 "Principles of Translation as Exemplified by Bible Translating." In *On Translation,* edited by Rueben Brower, pp. 11-31. New York: Oxford University Press.

Nordenskiöld, Erland, with Rubén Pérez Kantule; S. Henry Wassén (editor)
1938 *An Historical and Ethnological Survey of the Cuna Indians.* Göteborg: Etnografiska Museum.

Norgress, Rachel
1947 "The History of the Cypress Lumber Industry in Louisiana." *Louisiana Historical Quarterly* 30:3-83.

Obeyesekere, Gananath
1992 *The Apotheosis of Captain Cook: European Myth-making in the Pacific.* Princeton, N.J.: Princeton University Press.

Ocampo, Manuel
1966 *Historia de la misión de la Tarahumara (1900-1965).* México: Editorial Jus.

Olien, Michael
1988 "After the Indian Slave Trade: Cross-Cultural Trade in Western Caribbean Rimland, 1816-1820." *Journal of Anthropological Research* 44:41-66.

Olivardía Rangel, Aida
1963 *Esquema histórico de las rebeliones indígenas en el Istmo de Panamá.* Thesis, Universidad de Panamá.

Ortega, Joaquín
1965 *Gobernantes de la República de Panamá, 1903-1968.* Panamá: IRHE.

Oviedo y Valdés, Gonzalo Fernandez de
1944 *Historia general y natural de las Indias.* Asunción: Editorial Guaraní.
1950 *Sumario de la natural historia de las Indias.* México: Biblioteca Americana.
Paez, Gumersinda
1941 *Indios de San Blas y la rebelión indígena del año 1925.* Thesis, Universidad de Panamá.
Pares, Richard
1936 *War and Trade in the West Indies, 1739-1763.* Oxford: Clarendon Press.
Parker, Ann, and Avon Neal
1977 *Molas: Folk Art of the Kuna Indians.* Barre, Mass.: Barre Publishing.
Parry, Benita
1987 "Problems in Current Theories of Colonial Discourse." *Oxford Literary Review* 9:27-58.
Paul, Diane
1984 "Eugenics and the Left." *Journal of the History of Ideas.*
Perrett, Geoffry
1982 *America in the Twenties: A History.* New York: Simon and Schuster.
Piedrahita, Lucas Fernández
1971 [1684] "El Obispo de Panamá informa a V.M. sobre el estado que tiene la Provincia del Darién y la entrada de los corsarios por ella." *Patrimonio Histórico* 1(1):117-121.
Pike, Frederick
1992 *The United States and Latin America: Myths and Stereotypes of Civilization and Nature.* Austin: University of Texas Press.
Pistilli S., Vicente
1978 *Vikingos en el Paraguay,* Asunción: Ediciones "Comuneros" R. Rolón.
Pizzurno Gelos, Patricia
1990 *Antecedentes, hechos, y consecuencias de la Guerra de los Mil Días en el Istmo de Panama.* Panamá: Universidad de Panamá, Ediciones Fomato 16.
Porras, Belisario
1931 *Trozos de vida.* San José: Imprenta Alsina.
1973 *Memorias de las campañas del istmo, 1900.* Panamá: Patrimonio Histórico, Instituto Nacional de la Cultura.
Prebble, John
1968 *The Darien Disaster.* London: Secker and Warburg.
Prestán, Arnulfo
1975 *El uso de la chicha y la sociedad kuna.* México: Instituto Indigenista Interamericano. Ediciones Especiales 72.
Puig, Manuel Maria
1948 *Los indios cunas de San Blas: su origen, tradición, costumbres, organización social, cultura, y religión.* Panama: n.p.
Quinan, Clarence
1924 "White Indians of Darien." *Science* 15:476-477.
Rafael, Vicente
1988 *Contracting Colonialism: Translation and Christian Conversion in Tagalog Society under Early Spanish Rule.* Ithaca, N.Y.: Cornell University Press.
Réclus, Armand
1881 *Panama et Darien: Voyages d'Exploration.* Paris: Librairie Hachette.

Rediker, Marcus
1987 *Between the Devil and the Deep Blue Sea: Merchant Seamen, Pirates, and the Anglo-American Maritime World, 1700-1750.* Cambridge: Cambridge University Press.

Remón, Miguel
1985 [1754] "El Informe de Don Miguel Remón, Gobernador de la Provincia de Santo Domingo del Darién dado a S.M.C. el Rey de España, 10 de Abril de 1754." In *Geografía de Panamá,* edited by Omar Jaén Suarez, pp. 130-139. Panamá: Universidad de Panamá, Biblioteca de la Cultura Panameña.

República de Panamá, Ministerio de Gobierno y Justicia
1942 *Homenaje al Dr. Belisario Porras.* Panamá: Imprenta Nacional.

Requejo Salcedo, Juan
1908 [1640] "Relación histórica y geográfica de la Provincia de Panamá." *Colección de Libros y documentos referentes a la historia de América,* vol. 8, pp. 85-136. Madrid.

Restrepo, Vicente
1888a *Estudio sobre las Minas de oro y plata de Colombia.* 2d ed. Bogotá: Silvestre y Compañía.
1888b Prologue, Introduction, Notes, and Appendices to *Viajes de Lionel Wafer al Istmo del Darién (cuatro meses entre los indios).* Translated and edited by Vicente Restrepo, pp. v-xi, 55-129. Bogotá: Silvestre y Compañia.

Richmond, H. W.
1920 *The Navy in the War of 1739-48.* Vol. 1. Cambridge: Cambridge University Press.

Richmond Brown, Lady Lilian Mabel
1925 *Unknown Tribes, Uncharted Seas.* New York: Appleton.

Ricord, Humberto
1989 *Panamá en la Guerra de los Mil Días.* Panamá: n.p.

Riffenburgh, Beau
1994 *The Myth of the Explorer: The Press, Sensationalism, and Geographical Discovery.* Oxford: Oxford University Press.

Rivière, Peter
1971 "The Political Structure of the Trio Indians as Manifested in a System of Ceremonial Dialogue." In *The Translation of Culture,* edited by T. O. Beidelman. London: Tavistock. pp. 293-311.

Roberts, Orlando
1965 *Narrative of Voyages and Excursions on the East Coast and in the Interior of Central America.* Gainesville: U. of Florida Press. Facsimile edition of the 1827 original.

Rodriguez, Frederick Mars
1979 *Cimarrón Revolts and Pacification in New Spain, The Isthmus of Panama and Colonial Colombia, 1503-1800.* Ph.D. dissertation, Loyola University, Chicago.

Rojas y Arrieta, Guillermo
1929 *History of the Bishops of Panama.* Translated by T. J. McDonald. Panama: Imprenta de la Academia.

Romoli, Kathleen
1953 *Balboa of Darién.* Garden City: Doubleday.
1987 *Los de la lengua cueva: Las tribus del istmo oriental al tiempo de la conquista española.* Bogotá: ICAN.

Romero, Fernando
1975 "El 'Rey Bayano' y los negros panameños en los mediados del siglo XVI." *Hombre y Cultura* 3(1):7-39.

Rosenberg, Charles

1961 *No Other Gods: On Science and American Social Thought.* Baltimore, Md.: Johns Hopkins.

Rotberg, Robert (editor)

1970 *Africa and Its Explorers: Motives, Methods, and Impact.* Cambridge, Mass.: Harvard University Press.

Rydell, Robert

1984 *All the World's a Fair: Visions of Empire at America's International Expositions, 1876-1916.* Chicago: University of Chicago Press.

1993 *World of Fairs: The Century-of-Progress Expositions.* Chicago: University of Chicago Press.

Said, Edward

1978 *Orientalism.* London: Routledge.

Salvador, Mari Lyn

1978 *Yer Dailege! Kuna Women's Art.* Albuquerque, N.M.: Maxwell Museum of Anthropology.

Sands, William F., with Joseph M. Lalley

1944 *Our Jungle Diplomacy.* Chapel Hill: University of North Carolina Press.

Sauer, Carl O.

1966 *The Early Spanish Main.* Berkeley: University of California Press.

Science Service

1924a "'White Indians.'" *Science,* July, p. viii.

1924b "White Indians." *Science,* October, pp. x-xii.

1924c "Investigation of the White Indians." *Science,* October, pp. xiii-xiv.

Scoullar, William

1916-17 *El "Libro Azul" de Panamá / The "Blue Book" of Panama.* Latin American Publicity Bureau, Panama.

Scott, James

1985 *Weapons of the Weak: Everyday Forms of Peasant Resistance.* New Haven, Conn.: Yale University Press.

1990 *Domination and Resistance: Hidden Transcripts.* New Haven, Conn.: Yale University Press.

Selfridge, Oliver

1874 *Reports of Explorations and Surveys to Ascertain the Practicability of a Ship Canal between the Atlantic and Pacific Oceans.* Washington, D.C.: Government Printing Office.

Severi, Carlo

1981 "Image d'étranger." *Res* 1:88-94.

1988 'L'Etranger, l'envers de soi et l'echec du symbolisme: deux représentations du Blanc dans la tradition chamanique cuna. *L'Homme* 28: 174-183.

Severino de Santa Teresa, Padre

1956 *Historia documentada de la Iglesia en Urabá y el Darién, IV, Segunda Parte, América Española, 1550-1810.* Bogotá: Editorial Kelly.

Sherzer, Dina, and Joel Sherzer

1976 "Mormaknamaloe: The Cuna mola." In *Ritual and Symbol in Native Central America,* edited by Philip Young and James Howe, pp. 21-42. University of Oregon Anthropological Papers 9.

Sherzer, Joel

1983 *Kuna Ways of Speaking.* Austin: University of Texas Press.

1990 *Verbal Art in San Blas: Kuna Culture through its Discourse.* Cambridge: Cambridge University Press.

Shrubsall, F. C., A. C. Haddon, and L. H. D. Buxton

1924 "The "White Indians" of Panama." *Man* 119-121, 162-164.

Sisnett, Manuel Octavio

1956 *Belisario Porras, o la vocación de la nacionalidad.* Panamá: Imprenta Universitária.

Skocpol, Theda

1979 *States and Social Revolutions.* Cambridge: Cambridge University Press.

Smith, Carol

1996 Myths, Intellectuals, and Race-Class-Gender Distinctions in the Formation of Latin American Nations." *Journal of Latin American Anthropology* 2:148-169.

Smith, Victoriano [same as Aiban Wagwa]

1981 *Los Kuna entre dos sistemas educativas.* Ph.D. dissertation, Universidad Pontificia Salesiana, Rome.

Speck, Frank

1926 Review of Lady Richmond Brown, 1925, *Unknown Tribes, Uncharted Seas.* Annals of American Academy of Political and Social Science 124: 231-232.

Spencer, Frank

1979 *Aleš Hrdlička M.D., 1869-1943: A Chronicle of the Life and Work of an American Physical Anthropologist.* Ph.D. dissertation, University of Michigan.

Spivak, Gayatri Chakravorty

1988 "Can the Subaltern Speak?" In *Marxism and the Interpretation of Culture*, edited by Cary Nelson and Lawrence Grossberg, pp. 271-313. London: Macmillan.

Spurr, David

1993 *The Rhetoric of Empire: Colonial Discourse in Journalism, Travel Writing, and Imperial Administration.* Durham, N.C.: Duke University Press.

Stern, Steve

1987a "New Approaches to the Study of Peasant Rebellion and Consciousness: Implications of the Andean Experience." In *Resistance, Rebellion, and Consciousness in the Andean Peasant World, 18th to 20th Centuries*, edited by Steve Stern, pp. 3-25. Madison: University of Wisconsin Press.

1987b "The Age of Andean Insurrection, 1742-1782: A Reappraisal." In *Resistance, Rebellion, and Consciousness in the Andean Peasant World, 18th to 20th Centuries*, edited by Steve Stern, pp. 34-93. Madison: University of Wisconsin Press.

Stier, Frances

1979 *The Effect of Demographic Change on Agriculture in San Blas.* Ph.D. dissertation, University of Arizona.

Stirling, Matthew

1963 "John Peabody Harrington, 1884-1961." *American Anthropologist* 65:370-381.

Stocking, George

1968 "The Scientific Reaction against Cultural Anthropology." In *Race, Culture and Evolution: Essays in the History of Anthropology*, pp. 270-307. New York: Free Press.

Stoler, Laura Ann

1985 "Perceptions of Protest: Defining the Dangerous in Colonial Sumatra." *American Ethnologist* 12:642-658.

1989 "Making Empire Respectable: The Politics of Race and Sexual Morality in 20th-century Colonial Cultures." *American Ethnologist* 16:634-660.

1992 "Sexual Affronts and Racial Frontiers: European Identities and the Cultural Politics of Exclusion in Colonial Southeast Asia." *Comparative Studies in Society and History* 34:514-551.

1995 *Race and the Education of Desire: Foucault's "History of Sexuality" and the Colonial Order of Things.* Durham, N.C.: Duke University Press.

Stoler, Ann Laura, and Frederick Cooper

1997 Between Metropole and Colony: Rethinking a Research Agenda." Introduction to *Tensions of*

Empire: Colonial Cultures in a Bourgeois World, edited by Frederick Cooper and Ann Laura Stoler, pp. 1-56. Berkeley: University of California Press.

Stout, David

1947 *San Blas Cuna Acculturation: An Introduction.* New York: Viking Fund Publications in Anthropology.

Suleri, Sara

1992 *The Rhetoric of English India.* Chicago: University of Chicago Press.

Sullivan, Paul

1989 *Unfinished Conversations: Mayas and Foreigners between Two Wars.* Berkeley: University of California Press.

Swain, Margaret

1977 "Cuna Women and Ethnic Tourism: A Way to Persist and an Avenue of Change." In *Hosts and Guests: The Anthropology of Tourism,* edited by Valene Smith, pp. 71-81. Philadelphia: University of Pennsylvania Press.

Sweet, David

1995 "The Ibero-American Frontier Mission in Native American History." In *The New Latin American Mission History,* edited by Erick Langer and Robert Jackson. Lincoln: University of Nebraska Press.

Taussig, Michael

1980 *The Devil and Commodity Fetishism in South America.* Chapel Hill: University of North Carolina Press.

1993 *Mimesis and Alterity: A Particular History of the Senses.* New York: Routledge.

Taylor, William

1979 *Drinking, Homicide, and Rebellion in Colonial Mexican Villages.* Stanford, Calif.: Stanford University Press.

Thomas, Nicolas

1991 *Entangled Objects: Exchange, Material Culture, and Colonialism in the Pacific.* Cambridge, Mass.: Harvard University Press.

1994 *Colonialism's Culture: Anthropology, Travel, and Government.* Princeton, N.J.: Princeton University Press.

Tice, Karen

1995 *Kuna Crafts, Gender, and the Global Economy.* Austin: University of Texas Press.

Tilley, Charles

1978 *From Mobilization to Revolution.* New York: Random House.

Todorov, Tzvetan

1984 *The Conquest of America: The Question of the Other.* New York: Harper and Row.

Torres de Araúz, Reina [or Torres de Ianello]

1958 "La organización política Cuna." *Lotería* 30:81-96.

1961 "El valor ethnographic de las Cartas del Misionero Jesuit Rev. Padre L. Gassó." *Lotería* 65:69-74.

1973 "La leyenda de los indios blancs del Darién y su influence en la historia política nacional." *Hombre y Cultura* II.

1974 "Etnohistoria Cuna." Pamphlet. Panamá: Instituto Nacional de Cultura.

1975 *Darién: Etnoecología de Una region histórica.* Panamá: Instituto Nacional de Cultura.

1977 "Introducción y transcripción del Tomo X del documento sobre caciques e indios." *Hombre y Cultura* 3:155-162.

1980. *Panamá Indígena.* Panamá: Instituto Nacional de Cultura.

Treadwell, John, C. Reed Hill, and H. H. Bennett

1926 *Possibilities for Para Rubber Production in Northern Tropical America*. Department of Commerce, Bureau of Foreign and Domestic Commerce, Trade Promotion Series 40. Washington, D.C.: Government Printing Office.

Turpana, Arysteides

1985 "Power Ejecutivo de la Unión, Decreta." In: "Y nos recortaron la patria," *Niskua Ginid*. Panama.

Tutino, John

1986 *From Insurrection to Revolution in Mexico: Social Bases of Agrarian Violence, 1750-1940*. Princeton, N.J.: Princeton University Press.

Urban, Greg

1986 "Ceremonial Dialogues in South America." *American Anthropologist* 88:371-386.

Urban, Greg, and Joel Sherzer

1991 "Introduction: Indians, Nation-States, and Culture." In *Nation-States and Indians in Latin America*, edited by Greg Urban and Joel Sherzer, pp. 1-18. Austin: University of Texas Press.

Valenzuela, Mario

1912 "La residence, el seminario, y la misión de los caribes: Carta del P. Mario Valenzuela al P. González Pintado; Panamá, February 16 de 1912." *Cartas Edificantes de la Provincia de Castilla* 1(1):257-259. Oña.

Vander Laan, Joseph

1927 *Production of Gutta-Percha, Balata, Chicle, and Allied Gums*. Department of Commerce, Bureau of Foreign and Domestic Commerce, Trade Promotion Series 41. Washington, D.C.: Government Printing Office.

Vandervelde, Marjorie, and Marvel Iglesias

1983 *Nacido Primitivo*. Emmetsburg, Iowa: Velde Press.

Vargas S., Patricia

1993 *Los Emberá y los Cuna: Impact y reacción ante la ocupación española, Siglos XVI y XVII*. Bogotá: CEREC.

Vasconcelos, José

1948 *La raza cósmica*. México: Espasa-Calpe Mexicana.

Ventocilla, Jorge, Heraclio Herrera, and Valerio Nuñez (editors)

1995 *Plants and Animals in the Life of the Kuna*. Translated by Elizabeth King. Austin: University of Texas Press.

Ventocilla, Jorge, Valerio Nuñez, Francisco Herrera, Heraclio Herrera, and Mac Chapin

1995 "Los indígenas kunas y la conservación ambiental." *Mesoamerica* 29:95-124.

Vernon, Admiral Edward

1744 *Original Papers Relating to the Expedition to Panama*. London: M. Cooper.

1757 *Original Letters to an Honest Sailor*. London: R. Thomas.

Verrill, A. Hyatt

1921 *Panama, Past and Present*. New York: Dodd, Mead.

1924 "Hunting the White Indians." *McClure's Magazine*, July.

Viola, Herman

1981 *Diplomats in Buckskins: A History of Indian Delegations in Washington City*. Washington D.C.: Smithsonian Institution Press.

Wafer, Lionel

1970 [1699] *A New Voyage and Description of the Isthmus of America*. Edited by George Parker Winship. New York: Burt Franklin. [1934 edition, edited by L. E. Elliott Joyce. Oxford: Hakluyt Society.]

Wali, Alaka

1989 *Kilowatts and Crisis: Hydroelectric Power and Social Dislocation in Eastern Panama.* Boulder, Colo.: Westview Press.

1995 "La política de desarollo y las relaciones entre region y estado: el caso del oriente de Panamá, 1972-1990." *Mesoamerica* 29:125-158.

Wallace, Anthony F. C.

1969 *The Death and Rebirth of the Seneca.* New York: Random House.

Wallace, Lew

1873 *The Fair God, or, the Last of the 'Tzins: A Tale of the Conquest of Mexico.* Boston: J. R. Osgood.

Ward, Christopher

1993 *Imperial Panama: Commerce and Conflict in Isthmian America, 1550-1800.* Albuquerque: University of New Mexico Press.

Wassén, S. Henry

1938 *Original Documents from the Cuna Indians of San Blas, Panama.* Etnologiska Studier 6. Göteborg: Etnografiska Museum.

1949 *Contributions to Kuna Ethnography: Results of an Expedition to Panama and Colombia in 1947.* Etnologiska Studier 16. Göteborg: Etnografiska Museum.

Westerman, George

1956 *Carlos Antonio Mendoza, Father Of Panama's Independence Act.* Panamá: Departamento de Bellas Artes and Departamento de Educación.

Williamson, Joel

1984 *The Crucible of Race: Black-White Relations in the American South since Emancipation.* New York: Oxford University Press.

Wilson, Carter

1972 *A Green Tree and a Dry tree.* New York: Macmillan.

Wissler, Clark

1924 "'White Indians' of Darien." *Science,* July 18.

Zarate, Manuel

1962 *Tambor y socavón.* Panamá: n.p.

Index